Baedeker's
ITALY

The Principal Places of Tourist Interest at a Glance

The places listed above are merely a selection of the principal sights – places of interest in themselves or for attractions in the surrounding area. There are of course innumerable other sights throughout Italy, to which attention is drawn by one or more stars.

Preface

This guide to Italy is one of the new generation of Baedeker guides.

These guides, illustrated throughout in colour, are designed to meet the needs of the modern traveller. They are quick and easy to consult, with the principal places of interest described in alphabetical order, and the information is presented in a format that is both attractive and easy to follow.

The present guide covers the whole of Italy, including the large Mediterranean islands of Sardinia and Sicily and the smaller Italian islands and archipelagoes. The guide is in three parts. The first part gives a general account of the country, its geography, climate, flora and fauna, population, government and society, economy, history, famous people, art and culture. The second part describes the places and features of tourist interest – cities and towns, the different regions and islands. The third part contains a variety of practical information. Both the sights and the practical information are listed in alphabetical order.

The new Baedeker guides are noted for their concentration on essentials and their convenience of use. They contain numerous specially drawn plans and colour illustrations; and at the end of the book is a large map making it easy to locate the various places described in the "A to Z" section of the guide with the help of the co-ordinates given at the head of each entry.

Facts and Figures

Italy has been called the "paradise of travellers", and its endless charms continue to draw visitors from far and wide, as they have down the centuries. Few countries offer such a diversity of scenery, from the Alpine peaks with their perpetual covering of snow to the sun-kissed coasts of Sicily; few others possess such a wealth of historical remains, left by a world empire which extended from Britain to Africa and, in later centuries, by the powerful city states of the Middle Ages; and few have such a range of magnificent museums and galleries displaying archaeological remains, art treasures from all the great periods of history, and painting and sculpture which are of central importance in the history of European art. And in addition to all this there are the many beautiful resorts which, year after year, attract countless thousands of visitors to Italy's coasts and lakes.

General

Italy lies in southern Europe – a long peninsula in the shape of a high-heeled boot extending south-eastwards into the Mediterranean. In addition to its mainland territory it includes a number of islands and archipelagoes. The two largest islands, Sardinia and Sicily, lie on the south-west side of the Tyrrhenian Sea, the section of the Mediterranean which separates them from the mainland. Between Italy's east coast and Yugoslavia is the Adriatic Sea. Among the smaller islands and island groups are the Tuscan islands (Elba), the Pontine Islands, Ischia, Capri and the Lipari Islands in the Tyrrhenian, the Tremiti Islands in the Adriatic, and the Isole Egadi, Pantelleria and the Isole Pelagie in the Sicilian Channel.

Italy has a total area of 301,252 sq. km/116,314 sq. miles.

Situation and territory

The Republic of Italy is divided into 20 regions *(regioni)* and 95 provinces *(province)*. The autonomous regions of Trentino–Alto Adige, Valle d'Aosta, Friuli–Venezia Giulia, Sardinia and Sicily have a special status (statuto speciale). These are predominantly regions inhabited by other ethnic groups with their own language as well as by Italians (Alto Adige, Valle d'Aosta), or by Italians with their own local dialect (Friuli–Venezia Giulia, Sardinia).

Political divisions (see map, p. 10)

In northern Central Italy is the tiny independent republic of San Marino, an enclave within Italian territory, which has a treaty of friendship with Italy.

San Marino

Regions and Provinces

Lombardia (Lombardy)
Bergamo (BG), Brescia (BS), Como (CO), Cremona (CR), Milano (Milan; MI), Mantova (Mantua; MA), Pavia (PV), Sondrio (SO), Varese (VA)

Trentino–Alto Adige
Bolzano (BZ), Trento (TN)

◀ *On Lake Garda*

**Italy
Repubblica
Italiana**

(I)

Boundaries
of regions

Capitals
of regions

Veneto (Venezia Euganea)
Belluno (BL), Padova (Padua; PD), Rovigo (RO), Treviso (TV), Venezia
(Venice; VE), Verona (VR), Vicenza (VI)

Friuli–Venezia Giulia
Gorizia (GO), Pordenone (PN), Trieste (TS), Udine (UD)

Piemonte (Piedmont)
Alessandria (AL), Asti (AT), Cuneo (CU), Novara (NO), Torino (Turin;
TO), Vercelli (VC)

Valle d'Aosta/Val d'Aoste
Aosta (AO)

Liguria
Genova (Genoa; GE), Imperia (IM), La Spezia (SP), Savona (SV)

Emilia–Romagna
Bologna (BO), Ferrara (FE), Forlì (FO), Modena (MO), Parma (PR), Piacenza (PC), Ravenna (RA), Reggio nell'Emilia (RE)

Toscana (Tuscany)
Arezzo (AR), Firenze (Florence; FI), Grosseto (GR), Livorno (LI), Lucca (LU), Massa-Carrara (MS), Pisa (PI), Pistoia (PT), Siena (SI)

Marche (Marches)
Ancona (AN), Ascoli Piceno (AP), Macerata (MC), Pesaro e Urbino (PS)

Umbria
Perugia (PG), Terni (TR)

Lazio (Latium)
Frosinone (FR), Latina (LT), Rieti (RI), Roma (Rome; ROMA), Viterbo (VT)

Abruzzo (Abruzzi)
Chieti (CH), L'Aquila (AQ), Pescara (PE), Teramo (TE)

Molise
Campobasso (CB), Isernia (IS)

Campania
Avellino (AV), Benevento (BN), Caserta (CE), Napoli (Naples; NA), Salerno (SA)

Puglia (Apulia)
Bari (BA), Brindisi (BR), Foggia (FG), Lecce (LE), Taranto (TA)

Basilicata
Matera (MT), Potenza (PZ)

Calabria
Catanzaro (CZ), Cosenza (CS), Reggio di Calabria (RC)

Sicilia (Sicily)
Agrigento (AG), Caltanissetta (CL), Catania (CT), Enna (EN), Messina (ME), Palermo (PA), Ragusa (RG), Siracusa (Syracuse; SR), Trapani (TR)

Sardegna (Sardinia)
Cagliari (CA), Nuoro (NU), Oristano (OR), Sassari (SS)

Note: Since 1992 there have been changes in administrative divisions; some provinces have been added.

Since the national referendum of 2 June 1946, which put an end to the monarchy (the House of Savoy), Italy has been a democratic and parliamentary republic, the Repubblica Italiana. The Italian Parliament (Parlamento) consists of two chambers, the House of Representatives (Camera dei Deputati) and the Senate (Senato). The 630 members of the House of Representatives are elected in a general election held every five years; the 320 members of the Senate are elected on a regional basis, also for five years. The Parliament is a legislative body which is also responsible for controlling the executive.

The President of the Republic, whose functions are mainly of a representative nature, is elected for a seven-year term by both houses of Parliament together with three additional delegates from each region. The government consists of the Prime Minister (Presidente del Consiglio) and other ministers, who together form the Cabinet (Consiglio

State and government

dei Ministri). There is a Constitutional Court (Corte Costituzionale) responsible for ensuring that the requirements of the constitution are observed.

Capital

The capital of Italy is Rome, situated in Central Italy some 20 km/ 12 miles inland from the coast of the Tyrrhenian Sea. It is the seat of the President (in the Palazzo del Quirinale), the government and both houses of Parliament (the Senate in the Palazzo Madama, the House of Representatives in the Palazzo di Montecitorio).

Vatican City

Within the territory of Rome is the tiny state of Vatican City (Stato della Città del Vaticano), of which the Pope is sovereign.

International commitments

Italy is a member of the United Nations (UN) and its subsidiary organisations, a founder member of the European Community (EC) and a member of the Council of Europe, Western European Union (WEU), the Organisation of Economic Cooperation and Development (OECD), the North Atlantic Treaty Organisation (NATO) and many other international organisations. It has a military assistance agreement with Malta.

Population

Population and population density

Italy has a population of 57 million and a population density of around 190 inhabitants to the sq. km (492 to the sq. mile). Densities, apart from the concentrations of population round Rome and the Bay of Naples, are higher in the north than in the south, as is the proportion of population living in towns.

Social structure

The level of social and economic development falls from north to south, while the birth rate is significantly higher in the south (reaching a maximum in Naples) than in the north. Northern Italy, too, is much better supplied with educational institutions, including well known universities and colleges, and this makes it more difficult to train the skilled workers urgently required in the Mezzogiorno.

Religion

Almost all Italians belong to the Roman Catholic church, and the (sometimes naïve) religious faith of the population is reflected in the social structure. The family bond is generally stronger in Italy than in other European countries, though the position of women is now increasingly in process of radical change (divorce having been possible since 1970).

Language groups

In addition to Italians in the narrower sense the population includes many people belonging to other ethnic groups. They are found mainly in border regions or on islands, and they speak the language of the neighbouring country or a local dialect as well as Italian. The largest group is the 1.5 million Sardinians, who speak Sard; and Sardinia also has numbers of Catalan-speakers, particularly in and around the town of Alghero (L'Alguer in Catalan). Another minority is the Rhaeto-Romanic group (550,000), to which the Friulians and Ladins belong; Friulian, a Rhaeto-Romanic dialect, is spoken in the Friuli–Venezia Giulia region. There are 280,000 German-speakers in the Alto Adige (in German called Südtirol, Southern Tirol), where German is now recognised as an official language, after many years of repression. The Alto Adige also has a number of Ladins, speaking their own dialect. In the Aosta valley, which has changed its political allegiance several times in the course of its history, and in Piedmont there are between 100,000 and 200,000 Franco-Provençals, who speak French or a Franco-Provençal dialect. In the Valle d'Aosta region, by law, French has equal status with Italian. In Trieste, near the Italian–Yugoslav frontier, there are over 50,000 Slovenes. There are an Albanian minority in Calabria and a Greek minority in Apulia.

The inhabitants of areas in which another language as well as Italian is spoken have long been concerned to secure the right of self-government, and a number of regions have been granted a special status giving them autonomy in domestic affairs.

Economy

In the later Middle Ages Italy enjoyed great economic prosperity. Its port towns, in particular Venice and Genoa, achieved economic predominance in the Mediterranean through their commercial participation in the Crusades, and Italian merchants established trading companies *(commendie)* to carry on their extensive foreign business. Double-entry book-keeping was an Italian invention, and many financial terms come from Italian. Italy retained its leading place in commerce and finance into the 16th century.

After the Second World War Italy enjoyed a sharp economic upswing, developing from an agricultural into an industrial state. This development was promoted by various forms of government assistance, particularly in the field of heavy industry.

Developments since Second World War

Italy is now one of the world's leading industrial nations. Only about 10% of the working population is engaged in agriculture, producing less than 10% of the gross domestic product, while around a third is employed in industry, contributing fully 40% of the gross domestic product. A similar proportion is engaged in commerce and the service industries.

Although income per head has more than doubled since 1950 it is still below that of other countries in the European Community. The unemployment rate is around 10%.

The so-called "shadow economy" plays a much greater part in the country than in most industrial states, and is a major cause of the budget deficit.

History

Prehistory and Early Historical Times
(c. 600,000 to 400 B.C.)

The name of Italia (from Latin *vituli* = bull-calves, sons of the bull god) was first applied by the Greeks to the south-western tip of the peninsula; it was extended only in Roman Imperial times to mean the whole territory as far as the Alps. The names of the original inhabitants have sometimes been preserved in modern place-names. Italy was already occupied by man in the Palaeolithic period.

1800–1600 — Early Metal Age in northern Italy: Remedello culture (copper daggers), named after the find-spot near Brescia.

1600–1200 — Bronze Age: Terramare culture (Italian *terramara* = "earth mound") in northern Italy, with fortified villages of pile dwellings.

from 1200 — Migrations of Indo-European peoples coming from the north. The Italic peoples break up into the Latin group, to which the Romans belong, and the Umbro-Sabellian group, to the main branch of which, the Oscans, the Samnites of Campania belong. Other Oscan tribes later move into southern Italy and Sicily.

from 1000 — An Illyrian people, the Veneti, move into the Veneto.

1000–500 — The Iron Age Villanovan culture, developed by an Indo-European people (named after the type site near Bologna).

900–500 — The Etruscans, apparently coming from Asia Minor, move into Etruria (Tuscia, Tuscany), Campania and the Po plain. Confederation of twelve cities on the Ionian model; active trade, centred on Felsina (Bologna), with central and northern Europe; highly developed cult of the dead (cemeteries). The Etruscans bring to Italy the culture and art of Greece and Asia Minor, technology and administrative skills.

from 800 — Establishment of naval bases in western Sicily and Sardinia by the Phoenicians in order to protect their sea trading routes in the western Mediterranean.

750–550 — The Greeks establish colonies in southern Italy and Sicily (Magna Graecia): Kyme (Cumae), Neapolis (Naples), Kroton (Crotone), Taras (Taranto), Akragas (Agrigento), Rhegion (Reggio di Calabria), Syracuse and many more. Conflicting commercial interests lead to wars with the Carthaginians and Etruscans.
Development of the Latin alphabet from the Greek alphabet.

600–400 — Building of temples in Magna Graecia (remains at Segesta, Selinunte, Agrigento, Paestum, etc.).

485–467 — Tyranny (absolute rule) of Gelo and Hiero I in Syracuse, now the dominant power in the western Greek territories. Aeschylus and Pindar at Hiero's court.

Italy under Roman Rule
(753 B.C.–A.D. 476)

Rome, at first merely a city state, wins control, in spite of the resistance of the Italic peoples, of the whole of the Italian mainland, then of the islands, and finally of western Europe and the East. Under Roman generals and later under the Emperors, ruling with absolute power, the Roman Empire is held together and defended for centuries against attacks by neighbouring peoples. The spread of Christianity and urban life provide the basis for the cultural development of western Europe.

Legendary foundation of Rome (probably from Etruscan *Rumlua)* by Romulus, a descendant of the Trojan Aeneas. (Settlement on Palatine as early as *c.* 900).	753
Rome is ruled by the Etruscan Tarquins until the establishment of the Republic in 510.	600–510
The Celts invade northern Italy. The Romans are defeated in the battle of the River Allia (387/386).	*c.* 400
Rome conquers central Italy and ensures control of its territory by the building of military roads and the foundation of military colonies. Latinisation of the Italic peoples.	396–280
Rebuilding of Rome after its destruction by the Gauls and erection of walls round the seven hills.	*c.* 378
Construction of the Via Appia, a military road to Capua, later extended to Brundisium (Brindisi).	312
Extension of Roman rule to northern Italy, southern Italy and Sicily. In the three Punic Wars Carthage is defeated and its dominant role in the western Mediterranean is taken over by Rome.	*c.* 300–146
By conquering Macedonia, Greece and Asia Minor Rome gains control of the eastern Mediterranean. Exploitation of the provinces, use of slave labour, development of a monetary economy, increased Hellenistic influence (assimilation of Greek and Oriental culture), increasing luxury.	229–64
Construction of the Via Flaminia to Rimini; extended in 187 to Placentia (Piacenza).	220
Civil wars, caused by increasing impoverishment of the peasants, and slave risings reveal grave shortcomings in the state.	133–30
Wars with Cimbri and Teutons.	113–101
Caesar conquers Gaul.	58–51
Caesar becomes sole ruler (murdered March 14th 44); end of Republic.	45 B.C.
Augustus establishes the Empire (Principate) and maintains peace both internally and externally (the Pax Augusta). Cultural flowering (Virgil, Horace, Ovid) and much building activity in Rome. The Empire is romanised.	30 B.C.–A.D. 14
The Roman Empire reaches its greatest extent.	A.D. 14–195
Burning of Rome. Nero initiates the first persecution of Christians.	64
Pompeii and Herculaneum are destroyed in a great eruption of Vesuvius.	79
Arabs, Germans, Persians and others attack the frontiers of the Empire.	from 220

303	Last and greatest persecution of Christians in the reign of Diocletian.
313	Constantine the Great grants freedom of worship to Christians (Edict of Milan).
330	Constantine makes Byzantium capital of the Roman Empire under the name of Constantinople.
c. 375	The Huns thrust into Europe: beginning of the great migrations.
391	Theodosius makes Christianity the state religion.
395	Division of the Empire by Theodosius into the Western Empire (capital Ravenna) and the Eastern Empire.
410	The Visigoths, led by Alaric, take Rome.
452	Devastation by the Huns in the Po plain.
455	Sack of Rome by the Vandals, led by Gaiseric.
476	Romulus Augustulus, the last Western Roman Emperor, is deposed by the Germanic general Odoacer.

Italy in the Early Middle Ages and under the German Emperors
(493–1268)

	The great migrations of the Germanic peoples have a profound effect on the development of western and southern Europe. In spite of the Great Schism (1045) Byzantium remains in contact with the West, on which it exerts a strong influence, through its possessions in southern Italy. The attempts by German kings and emperors to re-establish the unity of Italy founder mainly on the resistance of the Papacy: the Investiture conflict.
493–526	Theodoric the Great, with the authority of the Eastern Roman Emperor, founds an Ostrogothic kingdom in Italy, with Ravenna, Pavia and Verona as capitals.
535–553	Justinian makes Italy a province (exarchate) of the Eastern Roman Empire.
568–774	Lombard kingdom in northern Italy (Lombardy: capital Pavia). Tuscia, Spoleto and Benevento become Lombard duchies.
754–756	The Carolingian King Pepin defeats the Lombards and compels them to recognise Frankish suzerainty. The Exarchate of Ravenna and the Pentapolis (Ancona, Rimini, Pesaro, Fano and Senigallia) are handed over to the Pope.
773–774	Charlemagne conquers the Lombard kingdom and unites it with his Frankish kingdom; the duchies, with the exception of Benevento, become Frankish marquisates.
800	Charlemagne is crowned Emperor in Rome.
827	The Magyars move into the Po plain for the first time.
827–901	The Saracens, coming from Tunisia, conquer Sicily, which becomes an independent emirate in 948 and enjoys a great cultural flowering (capital Palermo).

Fighting between native and Frankish nobles for the Lombard crown.	887–1013
The Magyars plunder northern Italy.	899
The German Emperor, Otto the Great, is appealed to for help by Adelheid, widow of the Lombard king, and gains control of northern Italy. Beginning of German intervention in Italian affairs.	951
Otto I is crowned Emperor in Rome.	962
Italy ruled by the German Emperors. Perpetual conflicts with the Popes, native rulers and the towns. Formation of two parties – the Ghibellines, who support the Emperor, and the Guelfs, who support the Pope.	951–1268
The Arabs inflict an annihilating defeat on Otto II at Cotrone.	982
Southern Italy and Sicily are united by the Normans in a new kingdom. Although this puts an end to Byzantine and Arab rule their cultural influence continues.	1000–1200
The Pope invests the Norman Duke Robert Guiscard with southern Italy and Sicily (not yet conquered).	1059
In the Investiture conflict, the decisive confrontation between the Empire and the Papacy, the Pope breaks free of the influence of the Emperor and turns to the rising Latin states.	1076–1122
The excommunicated Emperor Henry IV travels to Canossa as a penitent and humbles himself before the Pope.	1077
Foundation of a medical school at Salerno.	c. 1110
Foundation of the first university in Europe at Bologna.	1119
After the union of southern Italy and Sicily Roger II is crowned king in Palermo. Heyday of the Norman/Saracen culture.	1130
Frederick I Barbarossa tries to secure recognition of his suzerainty from the Lombard towns, but after a defeat at Legnano in 1176 is compelled to recognise their privileges. He becomes reconciled with Pope Alexander III in 1177.	1154–1177
Henry VI marries Constance, heiress of the Norman kingdom. The struggle between the Emperor and the Pope is exacerbated by the encirclement of the Papal possessions by the Hohenstaufens.	1186
Southern Italy and Sicily under Hohenstaufen rule.	1194–1268
Frederick II, crowned Emperor in Rome in 1220, makes the Norman kingdom a rigidly organised absolutist state and a base of imperial power; conflicts with the Papal and Lombard party. Art and learning are fostered.	1212–1250
Foundation of Padua University, followed by Naples University in 1224.	1222

From the Rise of the City States to the Congress of Vienna
(1250–1815)

In a politically fragmented country city states are established, and later also princely states, which rise to great intellectual, cultural and economic importance in Europe and come into conflict with the neighbouring great powers.

History

from 1250	Rise of independent states in Italy. The republican constitutions of the towns give place, following internal party strife, to rule by *signorie*. Through the conquest of neighbouring towns a number of larger units are formed: In Milan the Viscontis come to power, and Giangaleazzo Visconti purchases the ducal title. From 1450 the city is ruled by the Sforzas. Verona is ruled by the Della Scala (Scaliger) family. Dante Alighieri, after his banishment from Florence, lives at their court. In 1387 the Scaligers lose the whole territory to the Viscontis of Milan. Mantua is ruled by the Gonzaga family. Venice achieves naval superiority over Genoa and a commanding position in the Levantine trade. In the 13th century it establishes trading posts in the Peloponnese, Crete, Cyprus and elsewhere, and in 1339 begins to expand on to the Italian mainland. Venice has a strictly aristocratic constitution; the Doge is elected for life. From 1050 Piedmont is ruled by the Counts (from 1416 Dukes) of Savoy. The aristocratic republic of Genoa develops into an important commercial city, and in 1284 gains possession of Sardinia, Corsica and Elba. From 1264 Ferrara is ruled by the Este family. Florence, an important commercial city and the home of large banking houses, gains a democratic constitution in 1282. Around 1400 the Medici rise to prominence and, as ruling princes, to great political influence.
c. 1250–1600	Humanism and the Renaissance. Italian humanists (Dante, Petrarch, Boccaccio, etc.) rediscover ancient literature, which becomes a stimulus to literature and learning. The Renaissance, concerned with this world rather than the next, finds its principal expression in painting and architecture, but also in science and learning. Increasing wealth of the cities and princely rulers; luxurious and often unprincipled life of both lay and ecclesiastical rulers; patronage of the arts (Florence, Rome). From the end of the 16th century the Renaissance spreads to all the courts and great commercial cities of Europe (painters, sculptors and architects, among them Giotto, Raphael, Michelangelo and Leonardo da Vinci).
1268–1442	Naples is ruled by the House of Anjou.
1282	The "Sicilian Vespers": murder or expulsion of all the French in Palermo, and later in the whole of Sicily. The kingdom of Charles of Anjou (1265–1285) is reduced to Naples.
1282–1442	Sicily is ruled by the House of Aragon.
1310–1452	Last campaigns of the German Emperors in Sicily.
1347	Unsuccessful attempt by Cola di Rienzo to re-establish the Roman Republic.
c. 1350	Milan becomes the most powerful state in northern Italy.
1378–1381	War of Chioggia, a naval war between Genoa and Venice for supremacy in the Mediterranean. Venice is victorious, and further extends its influence in the East. Genoa turns towards the West.
1442–1504	The Aragonese rulers of Sicily succeed in reuniting it with the kingdom of Naples.
1494	In Florence, after the temporary expulsion of the Medici, the Dominican prior Savonarola establishes a republic. In 1498 he is burned at the stake as a heretic.

The French attempt, without success, to assert their supremacy in Italy.	1494–1556
Sicily is ruled by the Spanish Habsburgs. A number of risings are repressed by the Spanish viceroys.	1504–1713
Francis I of France takes Milan.	1515
The Emperor Charles V fights four wars with Francis I, who is taken prisoner at Pavia in 1515.	1521–1544
Rome is plundered by Charles V's troops (the "Sacco di Roma").	1527
Charles V gives his son Philip II the duchy of Milan, which remains a possession of the Spanish crown until 1700 and together with the kingdom of Naples and Sicily maintains Spanish influence in Italy.	1540
Cosimo de' Medici, Duke of Florence, becomes Grand Duke of Tuscany.	1569
Galileo is compelled by the Roman Inquisition to retract his acceptance of the Copernican picture of the universe.	1633
Mantua (1703), Lombardy (1714) and Tuscany (1737) fall into the hands of the Austrian Habsburgs.	1703–1737
After the Turkish War (1714–1718) Venice loses its possessions in the Levant and with them its leading position in trade with the East.	1718
Victor Amadeus II, Duke of Savoy, receives Sardinia, and with it the title of king.	1718–1720
Herculaneum, buried by the eruption of Vesuvius in A.D. 79, is rediscovered. Excavations at Herculaneum in 1737, at Pompeii in 1748.	1719
The Bourbons in Naples and Sicily. From 1735 Charles of Bourbon carries through reforms based on the principles of the Enlightenment.	1735–1806
A new national consciousness comes into being in Italy, preparing the way for the liberation and unification movement of the 19th century.	c. 1750
Genoa sells Corsica to France.	1768
Severe earthquake in Messina.	1783
Bonaparte's Italian campaign.	1796
Establishment of the Cisalpine Republic (Milan, Modena, Ferrara, Bologna, Romagna) and the Ligurian Republic (Genoa).	1797
Tiberine Republic (Rome).	1798
Napoleon defeats the Austrians at Marengo.	1800
Napoleon King of Italy; the Ligurian Republic is incorporated in France.	1805
Napoleon's brother Joseph becomes King of Naples, followed in 1808 by his brother-in-law Murat.	1806
Congress of Vienna, presided over by Prince Metternich (Austria). The former petty states are re-established.	1814–1815

From the Risorgimento to the End of the First World War
(1815–1919)

The Napoleonic era had strengthened the newly awakened national consciousness, but it is left to Cavour to bring the idea of an independent national state within sight of realisation. After achieving reunification Italy, like other national states, seeks to promote its imperialistic interests.

History

1816	Ferdinand IV unites Naples and Sicily in the Kingdom of the Two Sicilies and henceforth styles himself Ferdinand I.
1820–1832	Austrian troops suppress several risings against reactionary governments. The secret society of the Carbonari ("Charcoal-Burners") and the underground republican movement of Giovine Italia (Young Italy) founded by Mazzini in Marseilles lead the fight for unification and liberation.
1847	The newspaper which gives its name to the whole unification movement, "Il Risorgimento", appears in Turin.
1848–1849	Revolution in Italy and Sicily, of which King Charles Albert of Sardinia puts himself at the head. After the victory of the Austrian Field-Marshal Radetzky at Custozza and Novara he abdicates in favour of his son Victor Emmanuel II.
1859–1860	The process of reunification begins with a rapprochement with France initiated by Count Cavour.
1859	The allied army of Sardinia and France defeats Austrian forces at Magenta and Solferino. Austria loses Lombardy to Napoleon III, who cedes it to Sardinia in exchange for Nice and Savoy.
1860	Expulsion of the ruling princes from the states of central and northern Italy. Garibaldi and his irregular forces defeat the Bourbons and occupy the States of the Church. Plebiscites all over the country declare for union with Sardinia.
1861	Victor Emmanuel II becomes king. The first capital of the Kingdom of Italy is Florence.
1866	War with Austria. In spite of defeats at Custozza and Lissa Italy acquires Venice by negotiation. Mazzini puts forward Italian claims to Istria, Friuli and South Tirol ("Italia irredenta", "unrecovered Italy").
1870	Rome is occupied by Italian troops and becomes capital of Italy. The Pope retains sovereignty over Vatican City.
1878–1900	Under Umberto I Italy develops into a great power.
1882	Italy forms the Triple Alliance with Germany and Austria–Hungary.
1882–1883	Foundation of the Italian Socialist Party.
1887–1889	War with Abyssinia. Italy gains the colonies of Eritrea and Italian Somaliland.
1900	Treaty defining Italian and French spheres of influence in Morocco and Tripoli.
1911–1912	War with Turkey. Italy annexes Cyrenaica, Tripoli and the Dodecanese, including Rhodes.
1912	Introduction of universal suffrage.
1914	On the outbreak of the First World War Italy declares its neutrality (Aug. 3rd).
1915–1918	Italy in the First World War.

Secret treaty of London: Italy's colonial and irredentist claims are guaranteed by Britain and France (Apr. 26th). Italy declares war on Austria–Hungary (May 23rd) and Germany (Aug. 28th 1916). — 1915

Austrian and German troops hold the Isonzo line in eleven battles, and in the twelfth battle of the Isonzo (Oct.–Dec. 1917) break through at Caporetto and reach the Piave. — 1915–1917

Italian counter-offensive: collapse of the Austro-Hungarian front at Vittorio Veneto. — 1918

Treaty of St-Germain-en-Laye (Sept. 10th): Italy receives South Tirol as far as the Brenner, Istria (apart from Fiume) and a number of Dalmatian islands. — 1919

From the End of the First World War to the Present Day
(from 1919)

After the First World War Italy seeks to acquire further territory by an expansionist policy and to overcome the "crisis of democracy" by a new ideology, Fascism. Although during the Second World War it fights on the side of the Allies from 1943 onwards, it has to bear the consequences of the power politics of the Fascist period. After the war the new Republic of Italy is rent by ideological conflict and faced with grave social and economic problems. Internal political developments are influenced by the numerous separate parties with their changing relationships and alliances.

Mussolini forms "fighting groups" *(fasci di combattimento)*; growing influence of the Fascists; attacks on Communists, with open violence. — 1919–1921

The "March on Rome": Mussolini is granted dictatorial powers by Parliament; the Fascists gradually take over the government. — 1922

Beginning of a rigorous policy of assimilation in Alto Adige (South Tirol). — 1923

Fiume becomes Italian. — 1924

British–Italian agreement on Abyssinia, which is divided into economic spheres of interest. Treaty of Friendship with Spain. — 1926

Measures of state control to deal with the economic crisis. — 1931

Treaty of Friendship with the Soviet Union. — 1933

"Economic Protocol of Rome" between Italy, Austria and Hungary. First meeting between Mussolini and Hitler in Venice. — 1934

Invasion and annexation of Abyssinia. — 1935–1936

Establishment of the "Rome–Berlin Axis" in a treaty with Germany. Italian troops support Franco in the Spanish civil war. — 1936

Italy leaves the League of Nations (of which it had been a founder member). — 1937

Occupation of Albania (April). Military alliance with Germany. — 1939

Second World War. Mussolini attempts to mediate, without success. Italy at first remains neutral. — 1939–1945

History

1940	Italy declares war on France and Britain (June 10th). Italian–French armistice signed in Rome (June 24th). Three-power pact with Germany and Japan (Sept. 27th).
1941	Military failures in North Africa; Abyssinia is lost.
1943	Surrender of Italian forces in North Africa (May 13th). Allied landings in Sicily (July 10th). Fall of the Fascist regime; Mussolini is arrested (July 24th). Formation of a new government under Badoglio, who signs an armistice with the Allies (Sept. 3rd) and declares war on Germany (Oct. 13th). Rival government established by Mussolini (freed by a German commando group), who continues the war against the Allies.
1945	Surrender of German forces in Italy (Apr. 28th). Mussolini is shot by partisans. The Christian Democrat party (Democrazia Cristiana, DC) forms a government, led by de Gasperi (until 1953).
1946	King Victor Emmanuel III abdicates. Plebiscite in favour of a Republic (June 18th).
1947	Treaty of Paris: Italy cedes the Dodecanese to Greece and Istria to Yugoslavia; Trieste becomes a free state. Italy renounces its colonies.
1948	A new democratic constitution comes into force. Economic and social disparities between the well developed North of Italy and the under-developed South. After the economic difficulties of the immediate post-war period (Marshall Aid) there is an economic resurgence. Italy joins the Western powers, becoming a founder member of NATO (1949), the European Coal and Steel Community (1951), the European Economic Community (1957), etc.
1950	Partial expropriation of large landowners, with compensation, under the Sila Law.
1953	The Christian Democrats lose their absolute parliamentary majority; thereafter frequent changes of government.
1954	The free state of Trieste is divided between Italy and Yugoslavia.
from 1957	Rapid increase in emigration from southern Italy to the industrial North and to other countries.
1960	Summer Olympic Games in Rome.
1963	Moro (DC) forms the first Centre–Left government. The latent governmental crisis remains unresolved.
1966	Catastrophic floods in northern and central Italy.
1969	Self-government for the Alto Adige (recognition by Austria of the package in June 1992).
from 1970	Increased contacts with East European and Balkan states.
1972	Government of the Centre.
1973	Centre–Left government. Domestic political crisis: balance of payments deficit, inflation, economic crisis.
from 1974	The world-wide energy crisis and the economic recession hit Italy particularly hard: increasing unemployment, high inflation, foreign

debts, etc. New economic programme, frustrated by increasingly acute domestic political crisis, party strife, numerous strikes and acts of terrorism, corruption scandals and kidnappings accompanied by ransom demands.

Final settlement of the Trieste problem.   1975
Great gains by the Communist party (PCI) in regional, provincial and municipal elections.

Severe earthquake in the provinces of Udine and Pordenone (Friuli;   1976
May 6th).
Minority DC government, dependent on Communist support (June).
Escape of poisonous gas at Seveso, near Milan (July 10th).

Heavy destruction in street fighting with demonstrating students (Mar.   1977
13th).
Parliament approves a programme of economic reform, stepping-up of internal security, educational and press policy and regionalisation (July 16th).
Violent political reactions after a former SS officer named Kappler escapes from the military prison in Rome (Aug. 15th).

Moro, chairman of the Christian Democrats and a former prime minis-   1978
ter, is kidnapped on Mar. 13th by members of the "Red Brigades" and found murdered 54 days later. Tightening-up of the laws against terrorism (March).
Political crisis following the resignation of President Leone (June 15th); the 81-year-old Socialist Pertini is elected to succeed him (July 8th).

Parliamentary elections in June confirm the DC as the strongest party,   1979
while the Communists suffer losses. Cossiga forms a new cabinet (minority government of Christian Democrats, Liberals and other parties), the fortieth since the Second World War. The Communists go into opposition. Large increases in the cost of energy.

Death of the Socialist leader Nenni (Jan. 1st).   1980
Renewed terrorist attacks on judges, politicians and the police.
A new fiscal regulation requires hotels and restaurants to give all customers receipted bills.
Since the Socialists and Republicans are no longer willing to support the government by abstaining from voting, Cossiga resigns (Mar. 19th), but at the beginning of April forms a new government composed of Christian Democrats, Socialists and Republicans.
Economic summit of the leading western industrial nations in Venice (June 22nd–23rd).
Bomb attack in Bologna railway station kills over 80 people (Aug. 2nd).
After a vote of no confidence in Parliament Cossiga finally resigns (Sept. 27th).
The Christian Democrat Arnoldo Forlani forms a new government (Oct. 18th) of Christian Democrats, Socialists, Social Democrats and Republicans, and introduces a programme of economies.
Severe earthquake in southern Italy, with almost 3000 dead (Nov. 23rd).

The Forlani government wins a vote of confidence.   1981
The Italian Parliament ratifies a treaty of neutrality with Malta (Apr.).
Pope John Paul II is dangerously wounded in an attempt on his life in front of St Peter's (May 13th).
The most important result of referendums on domestic political questions is the retention of the liberal laws on abortion, the anti-terrorist laws and the sentence of life imprisonment (May 17th–18th).

The affair of the P2 freemasonry lodge, whose members are accused of currency frauds and of forming secret quasi-military organisations, leads to the resignation of the Forlani government (May 27th).

The Republican Giovanni Spadolini forms a coalition government of Christian Democrats, Socialists, Republicans, Social Democrats and Liberals (June 28th).

The Italian government give the United States bases for their cruise missiles.

Kidnapping of the American General J. L. Dozier, deputy head of NATO forces in southern Europe, by the Red Brigades (Dec. 17th).

1982

General Dozier is freed by the anti-terrorist police (Jan. 28th).

After two firms terminate a 1975 agreement on the index-linking of wages (the *scala mobile*) there are numerous strikes.

A government decree introduces measures for bringing the budget under control (end July).

Tensions between Socialists and Christian Democrats lead to the resignation of the Spadolini government (Aug. 7th).

Spadolini forms a new government (end August).

Resignation of the new Spadolini government (mid November).

Amintore Fanfani (CD) forms Italy's 43rd post-war government, a coalition of Christian Democrats, Socialists, Social Democrats and Liberals (Dec. 1st).

1983

Signature of a "Social Pact" to combat the recession (partial reform of the *scala mobile;* end Jan.).

The Socialists' withdrawal from the government leads to prime minister Fanfani's resignation (Apr. 29th). President Pertini dissolves Parliament (May 4th).

Socialist gains in parliamentary elections (June 26th–27th). A new government of Socialists, Christian Democrats, Social Democrats, Republicans and Liberals, with the Socialist Bettino Craxi as prime minister, is sworn in (Aug. 4th).

1984

On the basis of a new concordat between the Italian government and the Vatican Catholicism ceases to be the state religion of Italy, and Rome ceases to be the "holy city" (Feb. 18th).

1985

Francesco Cossiga (DC) is elected President in succession to Sandro Pertini (June 24th).

Resignation of the Cossiga government following the "Achille Lauro" affair (hijacking of the cruise liner "Achille Lauro" by Palestinians, leading to disagreement with the United States); the five-party coalition government continues in office with Bettino Craxi as prime minister (Oct.).

1986

Italy signs the anti-terrorism convention of the Council of Europe in Strasbourg (spring).

Following a government defeat in a vote on municipal budgets Craxi resigns (June 27th).

The hijackers of the "Achille Lauro" are sentenced to long terms of imprisonment.

Agreement is reached on the continuation of the five-party government under Bettino Craxi (July 29th).

1987

Resignation of Craxi (Mar. 3rd); formation of an interim government (Apr.). In parliamentary elections in June the Christian Democrats gain and the Communists lose votes. Giovanni Goria (DC) becomes prime minister, leading a five-party coalition of Christian Democrats, Socialists, Social Democrats, Republicans and Liberals (July 19th).

Goria resigns (Mar. 11th) and is succeeded by Ciriaco De Mita (DC);   1988
continuation of the five-party coalition.
The government promulgates regulations on autonomy for the Alto
Adige (South Tirol), including provision for the use of German in court
proceedings (May 13th).

At the beginning of the holiday season large stretches of the Adriatic   1989
coast suffer from a plague of algae.
Resignation of the Christian Democrat prime minister, De Mita, since
the Socialists have announced that they have joined the five-party
coalition (May). On July 23rd Guilio Andreotti forms a new government
to which the five parties of the previous coalition belong.
In north Italy the protest movement "Lega Lomboarda" (Lombardian
League) demands a solution from the central government; at the same
time the aim of joining Europe beyond the Alps is declared.

In September Italy joins the Schengen agreement, an association of   1990
several West European countries, with the aim of removing all frontier
controls within Europe.

In late February large numbers of Albanian refugees flee by ship and   1991
arrive at the Italian ports of Brindisi and Otranto; subsequently several
thousand are forced to return to their own country.
Resignation of Andreotti's government for politico-financial reasons
(end of March). In mid April Andreotti forms a new cabinet to which the
Republicans do not belong (four-party coalition).
In April an oil-tanker explodes and sinks off the Ligurian coast; in a
second disaster two ships collide off the Tuscan coast and over 140
people lose their lives.

In parliamentary elections at the beginning of April the ruling coalition   1992
(Christian Democrats, Socialists, Social Democrats and Liberals) gain
majorities in both the House of Representatives and the Senate. The
"Liga Nord" (an amalgamation of the political movements of the north
Italian regions of Lombary, Liguria, Piedmont, Friuli-Giulia, Venetia)
gain almost 10% of the votes cast; the Christian Democrats, however,
lose heavily. At the end of April President Cossiga regirns.
On May 25th, at the 16th ballot, Oscar Luigi Scalfaro (DC), a politician
from Piedmont, is elected as the new president of Italy. Giuliano Amato
(PS) becomes prime minister (end of July); he forms a four-party
coalition government of Christian Democrats (DC), Socialists (PSI),
Social Democrats (PSDI) and Liberals (PLI).

Art and Culture

Art

The Italian peninsula, like the rest of the Mediterranean world, has been occupied by man since the remotest times, and over this long period Italy has accumulated an almost incalculable wealth of art treasures. In spite of serious difficulties the Italian authorities have considerable achievements to their credit in the preservation, study and presentation of these treasures.

Prehistory and the Early Historical Period

Stone Age

Remains of the Stone Age are to be found particularly in Sicily and northern Italy, and the museums of Florence, Bologna, Turin, Milan and many smaller towns have much valuable material dating from this period, including domestic utensils, weapons and articles buried in graves from the settlements of pile-dwellings on the North Italian lakes. Remains of buildings, chambered tombs and standing stones belonging to the Megalithic culture can be seen at Taranto and on the islands of Lampedusa and Pantelleria. On Sardinia there are the curious round towers known as *nuraghi,* and on both Sardinia and Sicily there are remains of the Iberian Beaker culture.

Bronze Age

During the Bronze Age Italy appears to have had links with the Creto-Mycenaean culture, as is shown, for example, by finds from Ascoli Piceno. The Terramare culture which came to Italy from Illyria can be ascribed with reasonable certainty to the original Italic population (urn burials).

Iron Age

The Villanovan culture (Umbrians, Latins), an Iron Age culture which developed out of the Terramare culture in the Po plain and Central Italy (900–400 B.C.), produced the characteristic situla, a kind of bucket with rich figured decoration which attained its finest form about 500 B.C.. The best place to study the cultures of the prehistoric and early historical periods is the Museo Preistorico Etnografico Luigi Pigorini in Rome.

Transitional Period

Central and
northern Italy:
the Etruscans

From the 8th to the 5th century B.C. the Etruscans (Latin Tusci or Etrusci) occupied a dominant position in central and northern Italy. In addition to numerous local centres there was a confederation of twelve cities to which Velathri (Volterra), Arretium (Arezzo), Curtuns (Cortona), Perusia (Perugia), Camars/Clevsin/Clusium (Chiusi), Rusellae (Roselle), Vatluna (Vetulonia), Volsinii (Orvieto), Vulci, Tarchuna/Tarquinii (Tarquinia), Caere (Cerveteri) and Veii (Veio) belonged. The Etruscans appear to have been a non-Indo-European people of advanced culture who came to Italy from the East. The magnificent works of art they produced are mostly known to us from their tombs (sarcophagi with life-size recumbent terracotta figures from the Banditaccia cemetery, Cerveteri; wall paintings, in a realistic style showing Greek influence, in chamber tombs at Tarquinia and elsewhere). The famous She-Wolf in the Capitoline Museum in Rome is also Etruscan work. In architecture the Etruscans had mastered the structure of the true arch and the technique

Etruscans and Greeks in Italy

● Etruscan Centres

1 Arretium (Arezzo)
2 Velathri (Volterra)
3 Curtuns (Cortona)
4 Perusia (Perugia)
5 Camars/Clevsin/Clusium (Chiusi)
6 Rusellae (Roselle)
7 Vatluna (Vetulonia)
8 Velsna/Volsinii (Orvieto)
9 Velch/Vulci (Vulci)
10 Tarchuna/Tarquinii (Tarquinia)
11 Cisra/Caere (Cerveteri)
12 Veii (Veio)

● Greek Foundations

13 Neapolis (Naples)
14 Poseidonia (Paestum)
15 Metapontion (Metaponto)
16 Taras (Taranto)
17 Kroton (Crotone)
18 Rhegion (Reggio di Calabria)
19 Zankle (Messina)
20 Tauromenion (Taormina)
21 Katana (Catania)
22 Syrakousai (Syracuse)
23 Akragas (Agrigento)
24 Selinus (Selinunte)
25 Segesta

27

An Etruscan ash-chest

Tomba della Pietrera, Vetulonia

of the barrel vault. Their arts and crafts are represented by an abundance of objects of high quality to be seen in the Archaeological Museum in Florence, the Villa Giulia in Rome and museums in Cerveteri, Chiusi, Tarquinia, Veii, Volterra and many other towns.

Southern Italy and Sicily: the Greek period

Between the 8th and 5th centuries B.C. more than forty Greek colonies were founded in Sicily and southern Italy (Greek Megale Hellas, Latin Magna Graecia, "Greater Greece"), including Neapolis (Naples), Poseidonia (Paestum), Metapontion (Metaponto), Taras (Taranto), Kroton (Crotone), Rhegion (Reggio di Calabria), Zankle (Messina), Tauromenion (Taormina), Katana (Catania), Syrakousai (Syracuse), Akragas (Agrigento), Selinus (Selinunte) and Segesta. Unlike the Etruscans, who used wood and terracotta, the Greeks constructed their monumental buildings in marble. The most impressive demonstration of their skill is provided by the temple precinct of Paestum. The Paestum temples, magnificent examples of Doric architecture (metopes from the Temple of Hera in the Paestum Museum), together with the temples of Selinunte and Segesta and the theatres of Syracuse, Catania, Segesta and above all Taormina, give a powerful impression of the beauty, power and nobility of ancient Greek architecture.

Only a few examples of Greek sculpture from southern Italy have been preserved, among them the metopes from Selinunte (in the National Museum, Palermo), a bronze statue of Apollo from Pompeii (in the National Archaeological Museum, Naples), a Medusa head (in the Museo delle Terme, Rome) and the famous Laocoön group (in the Museo Pio-Clementino in the Vatican). Examples of Greek sculpture can also be seen in the National Museum in Reggio di Calabria. Terracotta sculpture is better represented, with numerous examples in various museums in southern Italy.

Greek Theatre, Syracuse

Greek painting is known only from the work of the vase-painters (particularly the black-figure type) and the Hellenistic wall paintings of Pompeii in a later period.

The Roman Period

Between 400 and 200 B.C. the Romans became masters of Italy. Originally a people of farmers and warriors, they assimilated the art and culture of the territories they conquered – first of the Etruscans, later of the Greeks and finally of the East.

The remains of Roman buildings are to be found all over Europe, in western Asia and North Africa. A vivid impression of Roman life is provided by the remains, excavated from the 18th century onwards, of the towns of Pompeii and Herculaneum, which were buried under layers of lava, ash and cinders by an eruption of Vesuvius in A.D. 79. Imposing examples of Roman architecture can also be seen in Rome itself (Forum Romanum, etc.), in spite of later destruction and new buildings. Perhaps the main Roman contribution to Western architecture was the development of the method of vaulted construction which the Romans took over from the Etruscans. Roman industrial and commercial buildings can be seen in the excavations of Ostia, the port of ancient Rome.

Buildings

The centre of any Roman town was the forum, which served as a market square, a meeting-place and a political arena. In and around the forum were the principal public buildings.

Forum

The Roman temple, which like its Etruscan counterpart is built on a platform, differs from the Greek temple in having only a single

Temple

29

Arch of Constantine, Rome

entrance; the cella is usually preceded by an open hall (as in the temple of Fortuna Virilis in Rome).

Basilica

Another important feature of a Roman town was the basilica (law-court), a long pillared hall with the entrance on one of the side walls: a structure which developed into the early Christian churches of basilican type.

Baths

Roman baths *(thermae)* had cold, warm and hot rooms and were often large and extravagantly luxurious. The church of Santa Maria degli Angeli in Rome, built by Michelangelo, incorporates the tepidarium (warm bath) of the Baths of Diocletian.

Palaces

The palaces of the Roman Emperors were large architectural complexes with barrel vaulting and domes, richly decorated with frescoes, mosaics and festoons and articulated by columns.

Theatres

The Roman theatre developed out of its Greek forerunner. The auditorium was semicircular, and the stage wall became an elaborate architectural structure. Alongside the theatre there developed the amphitheatre, oval in plan, with seating for many thousands of spectators (Colosseum, Rome; Arena, Verona).

Triumphal arches

The triumphal arch was originally a gateway erected for the ceremonial entrance of victorious troops, but developed into an elaborate structure, richly decorated with sculpture, commemorating the victories of Roman emperors (Arches of Constantine, Septimius Severus and Titus in Rome; illustration, above). Triumphal columns served a similar purpose (Trajan's Column, Rome).

Aqueducts

Roman aqueducts were masterpieces of engineering which carried water into the towns from many miles away, often on a long series of towering arches. The roads and bridges are also impressive demonstrations of Roman technical skill.

The houses of wealthy Romans were built around an open inner courtyard, the *atrium*, and entered through a hall or *vestibulum*. Along the sides of the houses were private apartments, and to the rear were a pillared courtyard, a dining room and a garden. The interior was richly decorated with frescoes, mosaics and sculpture (often copies of Greek originals); good examples can be seen in Pompeii.

Houses

Roman sculpture was largely based on Greek models, but in the portrait sculpture of the Republican period achieved a remarkable degree of realism. Under the Empire the most imposing form of portrait sculpture, the equestrian statue, came to the fore; the only surviving example is the figure of Marcus Aurelius (A.D. 179) on the Capitol in Rome. Sculptured reliefs were also used to depict great historical events (Trajan's Column and the Ara Pacis in Rome).

Sculpture

Roman painting shows Hellenistic influence. The fine wall paintings of which numerous examples can be seen in Pompeii show great diversity of style; realistic and almost impressionistic grotesques alternate with *trompe-l'oeil* architecture, classical Greek themes, gay bucolic scenes and heroic legends. Mosaics were also used for the decoration of walls and floors (pavement mosaics of "Alexander's Battle" in Pompeii, A.D. 50).

Painting

Early Christian Period

In the early Christian period the basilican church developed out of the Roman law-court *(basilica)*. The nave, which probably had a flat roof, was usually divided into three or five aisles, the central aisle being as a rule higher than the others; the west end faced on to the street, and there was a semi-circular apse at the east end. Externally the basilicas were plain brick buildings, but the interiors were usually sumptuously decorated, showing Byzantine influence. From the 7th century onwards there was usually a separate bell-tower. A small circular baptistery served for adult baptism.
In the reign of Justinian (527–565) churches began to be built also on a circular plan, the model for this new type being the Great Church (Hagia Sophia) in Constantinople. The central feature was the space under the dome, with four barrel-vaulted wings opening off it in the form of a cross. These might also be domed, as in St Mark's in Venice (begun in 830).

Churches

Ravenna now became an important political and religious centre, and it still preserves magnificent examples of early Christian and Byzantine art, such as the basilicas of Sant'Apollinare in Classe and Sant'Apollinare Nuovo, the Mausoleum of Galla Placidia and the Baptistery of the Orthodox (both on a centralised plan), and the church of San Vitale, an octagonal structure with a central dome supported on piers. The rows of columns are now spanned by arcades in the Byzantine fashion.

Ravenna

The great achievement of this period in the artistic field was the mosaic decoration of the churches. Byzantine art, subject to strict hierarchical rules, evolved a series of formal prototypes, with no sense of space or perspective, which were set on a golden ground, the symbol of heaven (San Vitale, Sant'Apollinare Nuovo, Mausoleum of Galla Placidia, all in Ravenna).

Mosaics

Mention should also be made of the Roman catacombs; underground burial places constructed on several levels with an extensive system of

Catacombs

Mosaics in the church of San Vitale, Ravenna

corridors and passages and frequently decorated with painting on Christian themes.

Sculpture

Christian sculpture began by following pagan models – sarcophagi with carved decoration, figures of Christ depicted as a young man (e.g. the "Good Shepherd", a marble statuette of the 3rd century A.D. in the Vatican Museum, Rome).

Tomb of Theodoric

The great migrations from 400 A.D. onwards brought a succession of Germanic peoples into Italy – Goths, Vandals, Lombards. The tomb of the Ostrogothic King Theodoric the Great (c.456–526) in Ravenna, a circular structure roofed with a single massive slab of stone, is one of the few surviving examples of Germanic architecture in stone, though it was undoubtedly based on Roman and Eastern models.

Romanesque

Romanesque architecture developed out of early Christian architecture in the 11th century, with variations in style in different regions. At first Rome remained backward in this field, while the cities of Tuscany vied with one another in building churches in the new style. An early example is San Frediano in Lucca (1112–1147), a basilica of rather old-fashioned stamp. About 1050 a new type of façade, with inlaid marble decoration, came into vogue (San Miniato, Florence; pillared arcades of Pisa and Lucca cathedrals). Pisa Cathedral (begun 1063), with its massive transepts, is the most imposing building of this period.

Churches

The Lombard churches of northern Italy show German and Burgundian influence. They are mostly basilicas, with groined vaulting and richly

Interior of Pisa's Romanesque cathedral

articulated façades (Sant'Ambrogio, Milan; San Zeno, Perugia; cathedrals of Piacenza, Modena, Parma and Ferrara).

In Apulia many fine churches (Barletta and Trani cathedrals; pilgrimage church of San Nicola and Cathedral, Bari; Bitonto Cathedral) were built in Apulian Romanesque, which shows a mingling of Byzantine, Lombard, Norman and even Saracen influences.

In Sicily the Norman influence was less strongly felt than in Apulia, but there are a number of notable buildings of this period in Palermo – the church of San Giovanni degli Eremiti, a building of rather Oriental aspect with its five tall red domes; the Martorana, a beautiful church with fine Byzantine mosaics; San Cataldo, a domed Byzantine church of 1161; and the Cappella Palatina, built by Roger II in 1132–1140, with superb mosaic decoration which makes it surely one of the finest of all royal chapels. Monreale Cathedral (c. 1180) is the largest Norman building in Sicily, with a magnificent choir; adjoining it is the largest and most beautiful cloister in the Italian Romanesque style.

The secular architecture of this period also has some fine buildings to its credit. In northern Italy, for example, the castles in the Dora Baltea valley and at Canossa, Cannero and Prato, and the defensive towers built by noble families in the towns (e.g. in Bologna). The thirteen towers of San Gimignano and its picturesque town walls are particularly impressive. In central and southern Italy there are also elegant palaces (Palazzo dei Normanni, Palermo; the Cuba and Zisa, showing Saracen influence) and town halls (Orvieto). — Secular buildings

Romanesque sculpture long remained under strong Byzantine influence. From the end of the 11th century the casting of bronze doors with — Sculpture relief decoration reached a consummate degree of skill (San Zeno, Verona; door by Barisanus, Trani Cathedral; doors of Amalfi, Atrani and Salerno cathedrals; door by Bonanus, Pisa Cathedral, 1180).

Sculpture in stone enjoyed a great flowering along with architecture, and Lombard sculptors in particular produced work of the highest quality. The first to undertake large figures was Wiligelmus, who carved the scenes from Genesis on the façade of Modena Cathedral about 1100. Around 1135 Master Niccolò was working on the doorways of Ferrara and Verona cathedrals.

The leading sculptor of the High Romanesque period in northern Italy was Benedetto Antelami, among whose principal works are the "Descent from the Cross" in Parma Cathedral, the bishop's throne in the choir and the outer walls and doorway of the baptistery. French and above all Provençal influences can be detected in his work.

There were also notable sculptors in Tuscany, like Guidetto and Guido Begarelli of Como (font in Baptistery, Pisa). In Rome the group known as the Cosmati (from the name Cosmas borne by some of its members), worked on the decoration of churches and religious houses, evolving the distinctive style known as Cosmatesque.

In southern Italy the busts from the Volturno Gate of Capua (now in the Campanian Provincial Museum, Capua) are particularly notable. The Apulian churches also have rich sculptural decoration (episcopal thrones at Canossa and Bari; pulpit, Bitonto).

Romanesque sculpture reached its final culmination in the work of Nicola Pisano (1225–1278), the first artistic personality of the Middle Ages with whom we have any real acquaintance, who bases himself on ancient models (marble pulpits in the Baptistery, Pisa, 1260, and in Siena Cathedral, 1268; fountain outside Perugia Cathedral).

Painting

The painting of the Romanesque period is dominated by Byzantine influence (the *maniera greca);* and the mosaics of Venice and those produced in Sicily in the 12th century are still wholly within the Byzantine tradition. The leading master of Romanesque painting, who towards the end of the 13th century sought to break away from the old rigid tradition and thus prepared the way for Giotto, was Giovanni Cimabue (mentioned in 1272 and 1301–1302; "Madonna Enthroned with Angels", Uffizi, Florence).

Duecento, etc.

Italian art first begins to show distinctive national characteristics in the age of Dante, at the end of the 13th century. Thereafter the centuries are known by the following names:
Duecento = 13th century
Trecento = 14th century
Quattrocento = 15th century
Cinquecento = 16th century
Seicento = 17th century
Settecento = 18th century
Ottocento = 19th century
Novecento = 20th century

Gothic

Italy now entered the Gothic period, at a time when French Gothic had already passed its peak. But the older traditions were never entirely

"Gate of Paradise", Baptistery, Florence

forgotten; reflected in countless buildings which still survive, the inheritance from the East *(maniera greca* or *maniera bizantina)* made its way into Europe by way of Italy. Alongside all these various influences, however, there now began to emerge new and distinctively Italian creative forces which were to extend their influence over the whole of Europe.

The art of the late Middle Ages (Trecento, 14th century), the *stile gotico,* was introduced into Italy mainly by the mendicant orders; but the Italian sense of form soon displaced the Burgundian influence (Santa Croce, Florence, begun by Arnolfo di Cambio in 1295, still without vaulting). Particularly notable are the double church in Assisi (upper church completed 1253, the earliest Gothic church in Italy), Sant'Anastasia in Verona and, in Venice, the Dominican church of Santi Giovanni e Paolo (1330–1390) and the Franciscan church of Santa Maria Gloriosa dei Frari (1330–1470). Italian taste, however, was against the excessive reduction of the wall surfaces; the horizontals were still stressed, as they had been in Romanesque architecture, and the façades of cathedrals were lavishly encrusted with decoration.

Trecento
(14th century)

The cathedrals built at municipal expense became steadily more sumptuous as each town sought to outdo the other (Siena, Florence, Bologna). The Duomo in Florence, a three-aisled church with a triple-apsed choir which was probably begun by Arnolfo di Cambio in 1296, the dome being added later by Brunelleschi, is the most impressive of these cathedrals, exceeded in size and massiveness only by Milan Cathedral, a cruciform church begun in 1386. The radiant exterior, with its 135 pinnacles and 2300 marble statues *(giganti),* is in striking contrast to the rather dark interior with its 52 massive piers and its huge windows.

Cathedrals

Art

Secular buildings

Gothic secular architecture continues the tradition of Romanesque with a strict sense of form. Huge Gothic public buildings and palaces were now built in towns (Palazzo Vecchio, Florence; Palazzo Pubblico, Siena; Scaliger castles in Verona and Sirmione; Gonzaga palace, Mantua; Este palace, Ferrara; Doges' Palace and Ca' d'Oro, Venice), and the houses of patrician families steadily increased in comfort and luxury.

Hohenstaufen castles

Romanesque and Gothic features are combined in the Hohenstaufen castles in Apulia. Castel del Monte, near Foggia (built about 1240), a polygonal structure crowning an isolated hill, is particularly impressive; it is said to have been designed by the Emperor Frederick II himself, who paid frequent visits to the region for relaxation or for hunting. Other important Hohenstaufen buildings are the castles of Gioia del Colle and Lagopesole and Frederick II's castle at Lucera, of which only fragments survive, though sufficient to show the monumental character of the original palace.

Sculpture

Gothic sculpture established itself only towards the end of the 13th century. Its greatest master was Giovanni Pisano, son of Nicola (pulpits in Sant'Andrea, Pistoia, and Pisa Cathedral; Madonna in Scrovegni Chapel, Padua). Andrea Pisano continued Giovanni's rhythmically flowing style (oldest of the three bronze doors of the Baptistery, Florence). Other sculptors of the period were Andrea di Cione, known as Orcagna (d. about 1368 in Florence), who was also active as an architect and a painter (tabernacle in Or San Michele, Florence, 1348–1359), and Tino di Camaino (Gothic tombs of the Anjou family in Santa Chiara, Naples).

Funerary monuments

In the 14th century the practice of erecting huge monuments to the dead came into vogue (equestrian figures of Paolo Savelli, 1305, in the Frari church, Venice; Scaliger tombs in San Francesco cemetery, Verona).

Painting Giotto

In the field of Gothic painting the work of Giotto (Giotto di Bondone, c. 1266–1337) marked a great advance. Although influenced by Cimabue and Duccio di Buoninsegna ("Maestà", the Madonna enthroned with angels, 1308–1311; now in Cathedral Museum, Siena), in whom reminiscences of the *maniera greca* can still be detected, Giotto took the decisive step which provided the basis for the whole of modern painting. Painting now acquired, as sculpture had done at an earlier stage, the ability to depict spiritual events; and Giotto, breaking away from the constraints of Byzantine iconography, was able to give his Biblical subjects a new form and a new content. His principal works are the overwhelming cycle of scenes in the Scrovegni Chapel in Padua, freed only a few years ago from later overpaintings, and the frescoes in the two choir chapels in Santa Croce, Florence (unfortunately much repainted). In Florence the school of Giotto remained active throughout the whole of the 14th century (series of frescoes in Santa Croce, Santa Maria Novella and the Cappella degli Spagnoli by Andrea da Firenze; frescoes in Campo Santo, Pisa).

A distinctive school also developed at the Visconti court in Milan around 1500 (Zavattari and Giovannino de' Grassi, Casa Borromeo, Milan; representations of the Months in the Torre dell'Aquila, Castello, Trento).

Renaissance

In this period the separate discussion of painting, sculpture and architecture is no longer appropriate, since many Renaissance artists worked in more than one of these fields.

The Renaissance (Italian *Rinascimento)* was literally a rebirth of the spirit of antiquity. While the Middle Ages had seen the purpose of life in overcoming the terrestrial world and preparing for the world beyond, men now began, in a return to the attitudes of antiquity, to discover themselves and the world as independent entities in their own right and to seek their tasks in the world here below. The metaphysical orientation of Gothic, concerned only with the world to come, was no longer adequate: the new conception of the beauty of the world, the joys of life and the freedom of the spirit demanded quite new forms of expression. There was no smooth transition as there had been between Romanesque and Gothic, but a sudden break. The master craftsman of the past now became an artist, who was no longer content to take second place to his work. He was now an individual artistic personality putting his work before a critical public, not a devout community of believers.

Origin and meaning of the term

The architects of the Quattrocento (15th century) were the first to adopt the new style modelled on the architectural forms of antiquity. Filippo Brunelleschi (1377–1446) was the pioneer of the early Renaissance, using new techniques in building the dome of Florence Cathedral, the churches of San Lorenzo and the Santo Spirito, and the Pazzi Chapel.

Quattrocento (15th century) Filippo Brunelleschi

Leon Battista Alberti (1404–1472), an artistic personality of universal scope and author of an interesting treatise on architecture, began the church of Sant'Andrea in Mantua in the last year of his life: forward-looking in its conception of space, it ranks with the church of San Francesco in Rimini as his finest achievement.

Leon Battista Alberti

The indebtedness of the new period to classical art is particularly evident in the field of sculpture. The range of subject matter was now extended to take in secular themes, and mythology and contemporary history alike supplied subjects for artistic treatment. The study of anatomy enabled artists to depict the human body in a new way. Portrait sculpture now also developed, producing realistic representations of the sitters who commissioned them. Medieval symbolism gave place to delineations of actual people, the world of spiritual forces to visible down-to-earth reality.

Lorenzo Ghiberti (1378–1455), painter and sculptor, created the second and the famous third door (the Porta del Paradiso) of the Baptistery in Florence. Other major works by Alberti are the reliefs on the font in San Giovanni, Siena, and the bronze figures of Or San Michele, Florence.

Lorenzo Ghiberti

Donatello (Donato de' Bardi, 1368–1466) is generally regarded as the leading figure of the early Renaissance. A pupil of Ghiberti, he produced both marble sculpture (Duomo, Florence) and bronze statues ("David", *c.* 1430; in the Bargello, Florence). One of his most powerful works is the equestrian statue of the condottiere Gattamelata in Padua; other major works are "Judith and Holofernes" (in front of the Palazzo Vecchio in Florence), the first free-standing sculptured group of modern times, and "St George", also in Florence.

Donatello

Andrea del Verrocchio (1436–1488) worked mainly for the Medici in Florence ("David", 1465; bronze group, "Christ and Thomas", Or San Michele), but also created the equestrian statue of the condottiere Bartolommeo Colleoni in Venice – less massive than Donatello's Gattamelata but livelier and tauter.

Andrea del Verrocchio

Luca della Robbia (1399–1482) was the third of the great masters of the early Renaissance in Florence. He applied the techniques of faience to

Luca della Robbia

"Adoration" (school of Della Robbia)   *Piero della Francesca: "Duke of Urbino"*

larger works of sculpture and produced a whole series of works in majolica (Madonna figures).

Early Renaissance painting began with the work of Masaccio (Tommaso di Giovanni di Simone Guidi), who died young (1401–1428). He painted the frescoes in the Brancacci Chapel of Santa Maria del Carmine and the "Virgin with St Anne" in the Uffizi.

Andrea Mantegna

Andrea Mantegna (1431–1506) was the leading North Italian painter of the Quattrocento. His pictures, works of high seriousness and rigour, depict plastic bodily forms with almost exaggerated clarity, achieving a very characteristic effect of depth by the use of perspective, with drastic foreshortening (altarpiece, San Zeno, Verona; "St Sebastian", Museo Nazionale, Florence; Camera degli Sposi in the Castello, Mantua, with the first group portrait and the first *trompe-l'oeil* ceiling painting in the history of art; "Madonna della Vittoria", Louvre, Paris).

Fra Angelico

Fra Angelico (Fra Giovanni da Fiesole, 1387–1455) created works of an exclusively religious character, deeply devout and peopled with graceful angel figures (frescoes in the monastery of San Marco, Florence).

Piero della Francesca

Piero della Francesca (c. 1420–1492) was the Quattrocento's great master and teacher of perspective. Among his principal works are the votive picture of Sigismondo Malatesta (in San Francesco, Rimini), the portrait of Federigo da Montefeltro (Uffizi, Florence), the "Resurrection" in Urbino and the "Adoration of the Child" in the National Gallery, London.

Sandro Botticelli

Sandro Botticelli (1444–1510), a Florentine, worked during the most brilliant period of the Medici. A kind of dreamy melancholy hangs over his graceful youths and maidens, and there is a touch of the same feeling even in his pagan mythological pictures ("Spring" and "Birth of Venus", both in the Uffizi, Florence).

Fra Filippo Lippi (1406–1469), a Carmelite friar working in Florence, painted pictures transfiguring Biblical scenes by the depiction of secular and terrestrial beauty. His work radiates fresh sincerity and love of nature ("Coronation of the Virgin", Uffizi; "Annunciation", San Lorenzo, Florence; frescoes in Spoleto Cathedral).

Fra Filippo Lippi

Domenico Veneziano (*c.* 1400–1461) worked in Venice, where painting was concerned primarily with brilliance of colour and delicacy of sentiment. In his "Sacra Conversazione" the Virgin is surrounded by a group of saints.

Domenico Veneziano

The High Renaissance falls into the first half of the Cinquecento (16th century). One of its great masters was Donato Bramante (1444–1514), the clarity and harmonious beauty of whose buildings is best seen in his plan for the new St Peter's in Rome, a centralised structure in the form of a Greek cross. He did not live to complete the building, which was continued by Michelangelo and crowned with a mighty dome.

Cinquecento (16th century) Donato Bramante

Michelangelo Buonarroti (1475–1564), a universal genius and one of the greatest artistic personalities in a period rich in geniuses, was the leading master of the High Renaissance. A pupil of Ghirlandaio, he worked as an architect, painter and sculptor, and in addition made a name for himself as a poet with his sonnets. Among the works he produced in Florence were his "David" (Accademia), the Medici mausoleum in San Lorenzo (Sagrestia Nuova) and the staircase of the Biblioteca Laurenziana. Summoned to Rome by Pope Julius II, he

Michelangelo

Filippo Lippi: "Madonna and Child"

Titian: "Portrait of a Nobleman"

Art

worked on Julius's tomb (figure of Moses, "Fettered Slave" and "Dying Slave"), which remained unfinished, completed the building of St Peter's and painted the magnificent frescoes in the Sistine Chapel. With the "harmony" and "power" (Michelangelo's watchwords) of his work he moved beyond the High Renaissance and prepared the way for the Baroque.

Leonardo da Vinci

The second universal genius *("uomo universale")* of the High Renaissance was Leonardo da Vinci (1452–1519), sculptor, architect, painter, scientist and engineer. Working at the Sforza court in Milan, in Florence, in Rome and finally for Francis I in France, he was the richest incarnation of the universal man of the Renaissance. In him art and science were fused into a unity, and his achievements in the field of natural science alone would entitle him to a leading place in the history of human intellectual development. Among his greatest works are the "Virgin of the Rocks", the "Virgin and Child with St Anne and the Infant St John" and "Mona Lisa" ("La Gioconda"), all in the Louvre, and his "Last Supper", a mural (unfortunately much damaged) in the monastery of Santa Maria delle Grazie in Milan. A unique insight into his methods of working is given by his drawings and studies, in a great variety of techniques.

Raphael

The name of Raphael (Raffaello Santi, 1483–1520) calls up the image of a serene artist, beloved of gods and men, the painter of charming Madonnas ("Madonna della Sedia", Madonna Tempi, Sistine Madonna). In Rome he decorated the Stanze di Raffaello in the Vatican with wall and ceiling paintings, worked as an architect and directed excavations of ancient Rome.

Giovanni Bellini

Another important painter of the High Renaisance was Giovanni Bellini (1430–1516), who sought to achieve simplicity, clarity and grandeur. His paintings of Madonnas are built up symmetrically, in the form of a pyramid *(figura piramidale)*. One of his principal works is an altarpiece, "Madonna Enthroned with Saints", in San Zaccaria in Venice. Among his pupils were Giorgio, Palma Vecchio and Titian.

Vittore Carpaccio

Vittore Carpaccio (*c.* 1460–*c.* 1526) was a master of the narrative picture and a vivid portrayer of the Venice of his day ("Miracle of the Cross"; scenes from the life of St Ursula, Accademia, Venice).

Giorgione

In Venice Giorgione (Giorgio da Castelfranco, 1478–1510) continued the tradition of Bellini and became the founder of the Venetian school of High Renaissance painting ("Three Philosophers", "Tempesta", "Sleeping Venus").

Andrea Palladio

The neo-classical architecture of the Late Renaissance, exemplified by the work of Andrea Palladio (1508–1580), provided models for the whole of Europe. Palladio was both a practical architect and an architectural theorist, author of "Quattro libri dell'architettura", and his return to the styles of ancient Rome was of major importance to the development of architecture. His principal works were the Basilica and the Palazzo Chiericati in Vicenza and the churches of San Giorgio Maggiore and the Redentore in Venice. A new type of building now developed in Italy, the *palazzo*, successor to the old castles built in towns in the Middle Ages (Palazzo Pitti and Palazzo Rucellai, Florence; Cancelleria and Palazzo dei Conservatori, Rome).

Titian

The great master of Venetian painting, already belonging to the Late Renaissance, is Titian (Tiziano Vecellio, 1477–1576), whose work in many ways looks forward to the Baroque ("Assunta" in the Frari

Filippo Brunelleschi   Sandro Botticelli   Tintoretto

church, Venice; "Worship of Venus" and "Bacchanal", both in the Prado, Madrid; portraits of the Emperor Charles V, seated and on horseback; "Danaë", "Nymph and Shepherd", "Jacopo da Strada").

Palma Vecchio (1480–1528) also worked in Venice. His favourite theme was the "Sacra Conversazione" (altarpiece in Santa Maria Formosa, Venice).

Palma Vecchio

Tintoretto (Jacopo Robusti, 1518–1594), all of whose work was done in Venice, stood at the point of transition to the Mannerist and Baroque style (wall and ceiling paintings in Scuola di San Rocco, Venice; "Paradise", Sala del Maggior Consiglio, Doges' Palace, Venice).

Tintoretto

Mannerism, the style which flourished in the second half of the 16th century, between the late Renaissance and the early Baroque period, was characterised by its delight in the unusual and bizarre: it loved allegory and metaphor and the extravagantly complex, corkscrew-like movement of the *figura serpentina*.
Leading representatives of this period were the painters Parmigianino (Francesco Mazzola, 1503–1540) and Giuseppe Arcimboldo (1527–1593), who worked in Prague as court painter to Rudolf II, and Giovanni Bologna (Giambologna, 1529–1608), the most notable sculptor of the late Mannerist period.
Mannerism achieved some of its most remarkable effects in the field of landscape gardening, in which natural scenery, architecture and grotesque sculpture in classical style combined to produce startling results (e.g. in the Parco dei Mostri at Bomarzo, between Terni and Viterbo).

Mannerism

Baroque

The age of Baroque was marked in architecture by the emergence of a new type of church. The rectangular nave now increasingly gave place to a centralised plan, crowned by a dome.
An intermediate position is occupied by the Jesuit church of the Gesù in Rome, built by Giacomo Vignola (1507–1573). Carlo Maderna (1556–1629) lengthened St Peter's by the addition of a basilican nave (c. 1610).

Architecture

In the Seicento (17th century) the most influential Baroque architect and sculptor was Giovanni Lorenzo Bernini (1598–1680), who was responsible for the semicircular colonnades in St Peter's Square in

Seicento
Giovanni Lorenzo Bernini

41

Rome and the magnificent fountains in the Piazza Barberini (Triton Fountain) and Piazza Navona (Four Rivers Fountain). Among his other works of sculpture are his "Apollo and Daphne" (Villa Borghese, Rome), the tomb of Pope Urban VIII in St Peter's and "Santa Teresa" (Santa Maria della Vittoria, Milan).

Francesco Borromini

Contemporary with Bernini was Francesco Borromini (1599–1667), a master of the flowing lines and curves characteristic of the High Baroque, whose work at first encountered violent opposition (San Carlo alle Quattro Fontane, Rome).

Guarino Guarini

Guarino Guarini (1624–1683) worked in a similar style, mainly in Turin. Baldassare Longhena (1604–1682) worked in Venice (Palazzo Pesaro, Palazzo Rezzonico).

Painting
Paolo Veronese

An early representative of Baroque painting was Paolo Veronese (P. Caliari, 1528–1588), a master of illusionist painting who marshals large numbers of figures in lively attitudes of rather theatrical effect.

Caravaggio

Michelangelo da Caravaggio (M. Meristi, 1573–1610) was the initiator of the realistic chiaroscuro painting which was to be so influential in the whole of European painting; his concern was to achieve a plastic modelling of his figures in a setting which was often merely hinted at.

Annibale Carracci

Annibale Carracci (1560–1609) painted frescoes on themes from ancient mythology in the Palazzo Farnese in Rome, and was also a considerable landscape painter (ideal landscapes, often with mythological figures). Domenichino (Domenico Zampieri, 1581–1641) and Guido Reni (1575–1642) were two of Carracci's principal pupils. Other painters of this period were Guercino (Giovanni Francesco Barbieri, 1591–1666) and Pietro da Cortona (1596–1669), the great master of illusionist ceiling painting (Palazzo Barberini and Palazzo Pamphili, Rome; Palazzo Pitti, Florence). Two later exponents of this art were Andrea del Pozzo (ceiling paintings in Sant'Ignazio, Rome, 1685) and Giovanni Battista Tiepolo (1696–1770), both of whom also worked outside Italy.

Two artists of the period who worked in Naples were the Spanish painter Jusepe de Ribera, known as Lo Spagnoletto (1599–1652), and Salvatore Rosa (1615–1673), a painter of very distinctive style who specialised in wild and rugged landscapes and battle scenes teeming with life and activity.

Rococo

Settecento
(18th century)

In the Settecento the leading place in Italian painting was taken by Venice. The principal masters of the Rococo period, in addition to Tiepolo (frescoes in the Villa Vilmarana, Vicenza; numerous altars and frescoes in Venice) and Giovanni Battista Piazzetta (1682–1754), were the two Canalettos, Antonio Canale (1697–1768) and Bernardo Bellotto (1720–1780), who painted views *(vedute)* of great architectural exactness (Canale of Venice, Bellotto of Vienna, Warsaw and Dresden). Francesco Guardi (1712–1793) depicted Venetian life and festivals in lively scenes with numerous figures. The woman painter Rosalba Carriera (1675–1757) specialised in charming pastel portraits and miniatures.

In parallel with the characteristic painting of the Rococo period there was a neo-classical school of artists who devoted themselves to depicting the excavated sites of Pompeii and Herculaneum (which began to be revealed in the first half of the 18th century) and to romantically idealised pictures of the ruins of ancient Rome. The leading member of this group was Giovanni Battista Piranesi (1720–1778), an architect and engraver working in Rome, who also produced eerie and grotesque architectural fantasies ("Prisons", 1745).

In this period the architect Filippo Juvara (1678–1736) built some notable palaces and churches in Piedmont.

Neo-Classicism

The 18th century also saw the emergence in Italy of Neo-Classicism, the principal exponent of which was Antonio Canova (1757–1822). His tomb of Pope Clement XIV in Rome (1783–1787) was a work of epoch-making significance, but perhaps his best known work is the statue of Pauline Borghese (1807; Villa Borghese, Rome).

Historicism

In the 19th century Italian architecture lived on the traditions of a great past, with various brands of Historicism (a return to the styles of the past). Giuseppe Piermarini (1734–1808) was a typical representative of the neo-classical school of architecture, which looked to antiquity for its models. Among the buildings he designed was Milan's great opera-house, La Scala. A master of neo-classical town planning was Giuseppe Valadier, who laid out the Piazza del Popolo in Rome. These trends appealed to the Fascist regime which came to power after the Second World War, and it was only with the formation in 1927 of the group of architects known as Gruppo 7 that Italian architecture began to break out of this eclectic fossilisation.

Ottocento
(19th century)

The painting of the 19th century was of purely local importance; and, as in the rest of Europe, it was committed to the ideas of Historicism. Only Giovanni Segantini (1858–1899) achieved international reputation as a Neo-Impressionist and Symbolist. The graphic artist Alberto Martini (1876–1954) also merits mention.

Modern Art

In the early years of the 20th century the Futurists (a movement which came into being in 1909) called for a break with tradition. Leading members of this school were Carlo Carrà (1881–1966), Umberto Boccioni (1882–1916), Gino Severini (1883–1966) and Luigi Russolo (1885–1947).

Novecento
(20th century)
Futurism

Giorgio de Chirico (1880–1978), regarded by many as the leading painter of his day, founded the school of *pittura metafisica,* which came to an end about 1920. Thereafter its objectives were pursued by the Surrealists.

Giorgio Morandi (1890–1964) came under the influence of Cubism at an early stage, and was then associated with de Chirico for a time before evolving a very individual style of great clarity and purity. Mario Sironi (1885–1961) sought to find common ground between *pittura metafisica* and Cubism/Futurism. The painter and sculptor Amedeo Modigliani (1884–1920) worked principally in Paris, where he came under the influence of Cézanne and the Cubists.

Renato Guttuso (1912–1987), a painter with socialist leanings, was aware of modern artistic trends but for the most part followed the

Art

realist line prescribed by the party. In his pictures he gave expression to his sympathy with the suffering and the oppressed.

Architecture

After the Second World War there was a great industrial building boom (Olivetti building, Ivrea, 1948–1950), and the Neo-Liberty architectural style, using Art Nouveau detailing, came into vogue (R. Gabetti, A. d'Isola). Leading industrial firms like Olivetti, Pirelli and Fiat promoted the development of architecture and industrial design (Pirelli building, 1955–1958, and Torre Velasca, 1957, in Milan; car design, office machinery, furniture, lamps, etc.).

Pier Luigi Nervi (1891–1979), one of the leading architects of the 20th century, was a representative of "rationalist" architecture and has had great influence on whole generations of artists. He was one of the first architects to use reinforced concrete. He built exhibition halls (Turin, 1950 and 1961), sports stadia (stadium, Florence, 1930–1932; large and small sports palaces and stadium for the Summer Olympics in Rome, 1956–1959), airport terminals and office blocks (UNESCO, Paris, 1953–1957).

Sculpture

In our own day Italian sculpture has at last produced successors to Canova in the persons of Marino Marini (1901–1980), famed for his horses and riders, and Giacomo Manzù (1908–1991), who returned to an older genre with his bronze doors decorated in relief (door of Salzburg Cathedral, 1959; Porta della Morte, St Peter's, Rome, 1964).

Abstract painting and sculpture

After 1945 abstract painting and sculpture came to the fore in Italy as in other Western countries, in a great range of variations (Tachism, Montage, "Lyrical Abstraction"). Leading exponents of non-representational painting are Giuseppe Santomaso (b. 1907), Afro Basaldella (1912–1976) and Emilio Vedova (b. 1919).
In the field of sculpture there are a variety of trends, represented by Fausto Melotti (1901–1986), Carmelo Cappello (b. 1912), Pietro Consagra (b. 1920) and the brothers Arnoldo Pomodore (b. 1926) and Giò Pomodore (b. 1930). The ingenious Piero Manzoni (1934–1963) finally declared the whole earth to be a work of art and set himself up on a pedestal to become a forerunner of Concept Art (1962).

A central figure, at the intersection of the most varied artistic trends, was the painter and sculptor Lucio Fontana (1899–1968), who developed the theory of "Spatialism". Antonio Corpora (b. 1909) and other Italian artists became associated with the Ecole de Paris. Among painters of the younger generation are Enrico Castellani (b. 1930), Lucio del Pezzo (b. 1933), Michelangelo Pistoletto (b. 1933), Agostino Bonalumi (b. 1935), Gino Marotta (b. 1935), Giuseppe Spagnulo (b. 1936), Mario Ceroli (b. 1938), Ugo La Pietra (b. 1938), Giulio Paolini (b. 1940) and Gianni Piacentino (b. 1945).

As "objective artists" of the Arte Povera school Mario Merz (b. 1925), Giovanni Anselmo (b. 1934), Alighiero Boetti (b. 1940), Piero Gilardi (b. 1942) and Gilberto Zorio (b. 1944) have made a name for themselves.

Photo-Realism

Finally mention should be made of the Italian school of Photo-Realism, represented by Gianni Bertini (b. 1922), Vincenzo Agnetti (b. 1926), Carlo Massimo Asnaghi (b. 1927), Luca Patella (b. 1934), Mario Schifano (b. 1934), Antonio Paradiso (b. 1926), Mirko Tagliaferro (b. 1936), Franco Vaccari (b. 1936), Bruno di Bello (b. 1938), Ketty La Rocca (b. 1938), Luigi Ontani (b. 1943), Elio Mariani (b. 1943) and Claudio Parmiggiani (b. 1943).

Music

Early Christian period

Among all the countries of the West the Italian peninsula has the richest heritage of vocal music from the early Christian period, with much early liturgical music (Milan, Rome, Benevento). The medieval neums (an early form of musical notation) have not yet been satisfactorily deciphered, but nevertheless reflect, in their short-paced melodic structure, a national characteristic, and probably also the influence of the folk music of southern Italy. This early music was supported by the theoretical writings of St Augustine ("De musica", 387–389) and Boethius ("De institutione musicae", c. 500). The father of Western church singing was St Ambrose, Bishop of Milan in the 4th century, who introduced the Ambrosian Liturgy still used in parts of northern Italy. This was the foundation on which Pope Gregory the Great developed Gregorian chant at the end of the 6th century.

11th–13th centuries

In the 11th century Guido of Arezzo (992–1050) devised a new form of musical notation, the origin of the system still used today.
The origins of unison liturgical singing (plainsong) are closely bound up with folk music, Greco-Roman and Jewish traditions. The folk music, which was for long repressed by the Church, enjoyed a revival between the 11th and 13th centuries in the form of *laudi* and *ballati*.

Renaissance (14th–16th c.)

At the beginning of the 14th century the stylistically more refined art of the Renaissance developed in Italy, facilitated by the increasing importance of Italian as a literary language (Dante, Petrarch, Boccaccio). Forms like the *caccia*, the ballade and the madrigal sought to give expression to the new spirit, the most notable figures in this field being Jacopo da Bologna (14th c.), Batilinus of Padua (c. 1400) and above all the poet and organist Francesco Landino (1325–1397), the leading representative of the Florentine "Ars Nova".

Dutch and Flemish composers, among them Johannes Ciconia (1335–1411), Guillaume Dufay (c. 1400–1474) and Heinrich Isaac (1450–1517), dominated musical life at the Italian princely courts in the 15th and early 16th centuries. In addition to the madrigal, the main form of secular music, and the motet and mass in sacred music, a number of forms derived from folk music also came into vogue – the *frottola,* the villanelle, the *villota,* the laud and, from the end of the 15th century, the *canti carnascialeschi*.

In the 16th century differences began to arise between the musical centres of Venice and Naples on the one hand and Rome on the other. In the Papal chapel in Rome there grew up a Roman school, the most celebrated representative of which was Giovanni Pierluigi Palestrina (1525–1594). In his contrapuntally perfect masses, motets and other works he brought *a cappella* polyphony to a pitch of perfection which marked one of the peaks of the Roman Catholic church music of the Renaissance. In Venice Andrea Gabriele (1515–1586) and his nephew Giovanni Gabrieli (1557–1612) wrote music for several choirs *(canzoni,* sonatas) which provided a basis for the development of independent orchestral and chamber music.

A group of poets (among them O. Rinuccini, 1562–1621), musicians (E. di Cavalieri, 1550–1662, Jacopo Peri, 1561–1633, and others) and humanist scholars who met in the houses of Counts Bardi and Corsi in Florence (the "Camerata fiorentina") were concerned to renew ancient tragedy with their music and to achieve a harmonious relationship between words and music. This gave rise in the 16th century to solo singing with a basso continuo accompaniment.

Music

The first operas were now composed by Jacopo Peri ("Dafne", 1594) and Giulio Caccini ("Euridice", 1600).

Baroque (17th–18th c.)

With the Baroque began a period which was of the greatest importance for the development of music throughout Europe right down to the 20th century. In the work of Claudio Monteverdi (1567–1643) the opera had its first flowering ("Orfeo", "L'Incoronazione di Poppea"). He made opera available to a wider public, a change reflected in the opening of Italy's first opera-house in Venice in 1637. Among Venetian operatic composers were Francesco Vacalli (1602–1676) and Marc'Antonio Cesti (1623–1669). Opera-houses were now also opened in Rome and Naples. Recitative and the *da capo* aria now evolved. The work of the leading representatives of *opera seria,* including Alessandro Scarlatti (1660–1725), Leonardo Vinci (1690–1730) and Leonardo Leo (1694–1744), influenced foreign operatic composers like Handel, Gluck and Mozart. *Opera seria,* however, soon degenerated into sterility, since it increasingly developed into virtuoso concert opera, in which the voices of the castrati and the ingenious stage machinery were more important than the content and the musical and dramatic expression.

From Naples and Rome *opera buffa* set out on its victorious progress through Europe. The works of Giovanni Pergolesi (1710–1736; "La Serva Padrona"), Giovanni Paisiello (1740–1816; "The Barber of Seville") and Domenico Cimarosa (1749–1801; "The Secret Marriage") are still performed today.

Along with opera the oratorio and the cantata also developed (G. Carissimi, 1605–1674; A. Stradella, 1641–1682).

The instrumental music of the 17th century also evolved an expressive virtuoso style and a variety of new forms (sonata, concerto grosso, overture, suite, concerto with soloist). For long the keyboard instruments (organ, harpsichord) took pride of place, and Girolamo Frescobaldi (1583–1643) wrote numerous compositions for these instruments *(canzoni,* partitas, toccatas, etc.). From about 1650, however, the Italian tradition of violin-playing was established, beginning with Arcangelo Corelli (1653–1713) and fostered by the violin-making skill of the Amati, Stradivari and Guarneri families. The works of Antonio Vivaldi (c. 1678–1741), Domenico Scarlatti (1685–1757), Giuseppe Tartini (1692–1770), Luigi Boccherini (1743–1805) and Muzio Clementi (1752–1843), which gave a prominent place to stringed instruments, promoted the development of instrumental music as an independent form. Niccoló Paganini (1782–1840) carried virtuoso violin-playing to a peak of perfection.

19th century

In 19th century Italian music opera played a central part. The best known operatic composers in the first half of the century were Caetano Donizetti (1797–1848; "L'Elisir d'amore", "Lucia di Lammermoor", "Don Pasquale"), Vincenzo Bellini (1801–1835; "Norma", "La Sonnambula") and Gioacchino Rossini (1792–1868; "The Barber of Seville", "William Tell", "The Thieving Magpie").

Giuseppe Verdi

Giuseppe Verdi (1813–1901), whose early works (particularly "Nabucco") were very much in tune with the aspirations of the Risorgimento, was the outstanding Italian musical personality in the second half of the 19th century. The operas he composed between 1851 and 1853 ("Rigoletto", "Il Trovatore" and "La Traviata") made him famous in Italy, but it was only with his late works ("Don Carlos", 1867; "Aida", 1871; "Otello", 1887; "Falstaff", 1893) that he achieved international recognition and became accepted as one of the world's great operatic composers.

Other composers who worked in Verdi's shadow were Arrigo Boito (1842–1918; "Mefistofele"), Umberto Giordano (1867–1948; "Andrea Chénier") and Amilcare Ponchielli (1834–1896; "La Gioconda").

Antonio Vivadi   *Giuseppe Verdi*   *Giacomo Puccini*

The opera "Cavalleria Rusticana" by Pietro Mascagni (1863–1945) was seen as the first work in the style known as Verismo (musical naturalism), another representative of which was Ruggiero Leoncavallo (1858–1919; "Pagliacci").

Verismo

The works of Giacomo Puccini (1858–1924; "La Bohème", "Tosca", "Madame Butterfly", "Gianni Schicchi", "Turandot") formed the last great high point of Italian opera.
Ermanno Wolf-Ferrari (1876–1948; "I Quattro Rusteghi") returned to the tradition of *opera buffa*.

Giacomo Puccini

In the 20th century instrumental music once again came into its own. The compositions of Ottorino Respighi (1879–1936) are notable for their rich musical colour. Ildebrando Pizzetti (1880–1968), Gian Francesco Malipiero (1882–1973) and Alfredo Casella (1883–1947) sought to achieve a synthesis between traditional and modern music.
Goffredo Petrassi (b. 1904), Luigi Dallapiccola (1904–1975), Mario Peragallo (b. 1910), Bruno Maderna (1921–1973), who was the first composer to combine tape-recorded and instrumental music, and Luigi Nono (1924–1990) largely follow the compositional principles of the modern Western European school (dodecaphony, serialism, punctualism).
The problem of Italy's Fascist past is reflected in the opera "La Speranza" (1970) by Franco Mannino (b. 1924).

20th century

Folk Traditions

Although Italy has assimilated much of American and Northern European culture, old traditions have been preserved in many parts of the country, folk music and traditional costumes are still cherished, and in spite of all external influences the old popular festivals have for the most part retained their original character. A distinction must be made between secular festivals (often of pagan origin) and religious festivals. Some traditional festivals commemorating events in the history of a town which had fallen into oblivion have been revived in recent years, no doubt with the tourist trade in mind; but the local people have shown themselves very ready to return to their ancient traditions and enjoy the festivals for their own sake. In addition to well known events like the Palio in Siena and the Giostra del Saracino in Arezzo there are numerous local festivals all over Italy – village festivals, fishermen's

Popular festivals

Folk Traditions

festivals, vintage and harvest festivals – which give visitors an interesting opportunity of observing the customs and way of life of ordinary people.

Church festivals

An important part is played in Italian life by the various church festivals, which are usually celebrated with much more spontaneity than in northern Europe and often take on the character of folk celebrations. Particularly notable are the numerous processions on the occasion of Corpus Christi, the Assumption and Holy Week. On Good Friday the richly decked Santo Sepolcro (Holy Sepulchre) which is displayed in all churches attracts large numbers of worshippers. In northern Italy the Christmas tree is increasingly becoming a regular feature of the Christmas celebrations, but in the south the *presepio* ("crib", Nativity group) retains its almost exclusive role as the symbol of Christmas. Children usually receive their presents at Epiphany (Epifania, January 6th). The Carnival is now celebrated only in a few places (e.g. at Viareggio and San Remo); but some traditional features still survive from earlier times, like the *mamutones* (fools, jesters) in Sardinia, witches in Alto Adige and the "burning of Winter" in northern Italy.

Costumes

The old traditional costumes are still often worn at the various festivals celebrated throughout the year, particularly in country areas. At any time of year, therefore, it is possible to see people wearing the old traditional dress in the Abruzzi, Sardinia and many parts of Calabria and Piedmont. The local costumes of Italy show remarkable variety. In the Valle d'Aosta the peasants wear dark-coloured and rather severe costumes reminiscent of French models, while in the Alto Adige with its German-speaking population the traditional dress shows Austrian and Bavarian features, including leather trousers and the typical Tirolean hat. In central and southern Italy the variety and vivid colours of the costumes are often almost overwhelming, and a diversity of influences – Yugoslav, Greek and even Oriental – can be detected. The women's costumes on Sardinia frequently include a veil.

Music in
everyday life

On festive occasions visitors may have an opportunity of hearing some of the old traditional tunes which in everyday life now tend to be crowded out by the hit tunes of the day. Music is an essential element in Italian life, and this is particularly true of singing. A passer-by will frequently hear the voice of some amateur singer from the courtyard of a house, through an open window or on a canal in Venice; and the cliché of the baker singing as he makes his pizzas has some foundation in reality. It is no accident that Italy is known as the land of *bel canto* and the home of opera. Although the famous Neapolitan *canzoni* ("O sole mio", "Torna a Surriento", "Tu ca' nun chiange", "Na sera e maggio", etc.) can hardly be called folk songs in the proper sense of the term, they do represent a curious and typically Italian combination of folk music, pop song and musical composition. Genuine Neapolitan folk music is performed to high standards of musicianship by such groups as the Nuova Compagnia di Canto Popolare; and a great body of Italian folk music has been collected and recorded by the Ricordi firm of music publishers in Milan, the Italian Radio Corporation (RAI) and the Accademia di Santa Cecilia (the National Academy of Music) in Rome.

Folk music

Italian folk music uses a number of characteristic instruments, often centuries old. Among wind instruments, in addition to the reed pipe and the fife *(piffero)*, there are the triple-piped *launedda* and various kinds of Pan pipes. Different types of bagpipes, like the *zampogna*, are played by shepherds in the Abruzzi and Sardinia. Guitars and mandolines are also popular, as is the concertina, particularly in the country, where it often accompanies the *ballo liscio*.

In earlier times dancing, often of ritual or religious significance, played an important part in Italian life. Although many of the old dances have not survived the centuries, a few, like the *ballo tondo* – a round dance, popular particularly in Sardinia, with some similarity to the Catalan *sardana* – have been preserved. The martial *danze delle spade* (sword dances) have also survived, and are danced with particular verve and vigour by the *spadonari* of Venaltio (May 17th), Giaglione (April 5th) and San Giorgio Canavese. The most popular Italian folk dances, however, are undoubtedly the Neapolitan *tarantella* and the *saltarello,* which both have love as their theme and are usually danced to a lively rhythm.

Dances

Sights from A to Z

Some of the important museums in the larger towns and cities are open only in the morning (on weekdays from 9 a.m.–2 p.m. and on Sun. from 9 a.m.–1 p.m.); most of them are closed on Mon. Please note that the opening times can change at short notice.

Tip

A visitor who has only one day to spend in a town or city is advised to check in advance the days and times on which the museum he wishes to visit is open.

Advice

Abruzzi

K/L7

Region: Abruzzi/Abruzzo
Province: L'Aquila (AQ), Chieti (CH), Pescara (PE) and Teramo (TE)
Area: 10,794 sq. km/4152 sq. miles
Population: 1,224,400

The Abruzzi, the wildest and highest part of the Apennines in the east of Central Italy extend from the watershed of the Central Apennines to the Adriatic and take in the four provinces of L'Aquila, Pescara, Chieti and Teramo. On the north they are bounded by the Marche, on the west by Latium and on the south-east by Molise, with which they have been combined since 1963 to form the administrative unit of Abruzzi e Molise.

Situation

The heart of the Abruzzi is formed by three mighty mountain chains, the most easterly and highest of which contains the highest peaks in the peninsula, in the Gran Sasso d'Italia group (Corno Grande 2912 m/9610 ft). Between these mountain chains lie the central uplands of the Abruzzi, in which the longitudinal valley of the Aterno, the high valleys of L'Aquila and Sulmona and the wide and fertile Fucino basin form substantial indentations. The north-eastern part, beyond the Gran Sasso massif, which is occupied by an upland region traversed by numerous rivers, slopes down gradually towards the Adriatic. Along the coast are many fine seaside resorts.

Scenery

*Gran Sasso
d'Italia

The population is concentrated in the towns of the region – L'Aquila, Chieti, Lanciano, Vasto, Teramo, Pescara, Sulmona and Avezzano. The rest is only thinly populated.

Population

With the exception of few areas, especially in the south and in the lower regions, the largest part of the Abruzzi is sparsely wooded, has partly karstic areas, a harsh climate, an abundance of snow and an infertile soil. Arable farming is possible only in the valleys and depressions, particularly in the Fucino basin; the mountain regions are good only for grazing land.

Agriculture

Supplementary to agriculture the development of tourism is of great importance. Particularly in the Gran Sasso, which has been equipped with facilities for winter sports (cableway to Campo Imperatore; 2130 m/7029 ft).

Winter sports

◀ *Siena: Palazzo Pubblico und Torre della Mangia*

51

Abruzzi National Park

The southernmost part of the Abruzzi is occupied by the Abruzzi National Park (Parco Nazionale d'Abruzzo) with its beautiful beech forests. It covers an area of some 400 sq. km/154 sq. miles in the valley of the upper Sangro and its numerous side valleys. With its network of footpaths and its mountain huts it is ideally suited for tourists; another 200 sq. km/77 sq. miles belong to the nature reserve. The park was established in 1921 as a nature reserve to protect the landscape, flora and fauna of the Abruzzi; among the mountain animals which can still be seen here are the Abruzzi brown bear (Ursus arctos marsicanus), the Abruzzi chamois (Rupicapra rupicapra ornata), the Apennine wolf (Canis lupus italicus) and the golden eagle.

Pescasseroli

The central point of the park is the village of Pescasseroli (1167 m/3851 ft) in the Sangro valley – visited both by tourists who enjoy a summer vacation and winter sports enthusiasts – with its enclosures in which animals can live in natural surroundings; botanic garden and museum on the natural history of the park. The philosopher Benedetto Croce (1866–1955) was born here.

About 5 km/3 miles south-east is the village of Opi, starting point for the rewarding climb of Monte Marsicano (2242 m/7398 ft).

Teramo

In the northern Abruzzi lies Teramo (265 m/875 ft; pop. 51,500), the capital of the province of the same name (a road tunnel runs from Teramo to L'Aquila). In the centre of the town is the Piazza Orsini with the Town Hall, the Bishop's Palace and the cathedral (12th c.), which was restored in 1932. The cathedral has a Gothic doorway of 1332. Its interior is furnished in both Roman and Gothic style; worth seeing are a silver altar frontal by Nicola da Guardiagrele (1433–1448) and a great polyptychon (1450) by Jacobello del Fiori. South-east of the cathedral are the remains of a Roman amphitheatre.

The west front of the cathedral faces on to the Piazza dei Martiri della Libertà, from which the Corso San Giorgio, the town's main street, runs to the municipal park (small local museum).

Avezzano

In the north-west corner of the Fucino basin (Conca del Fucino; 655–670 m/2261–2211 ft), once Italy's largest lake, which was drained in 1875, is Avezzano (698 m/2303 ft; pop. 35,000). The town was almost completely destroyed by an earthquake in 1915 in which 30,000 people lost their lives.

Albe

An interesting excursion can be made to Albe (7 km/4 miles north), with the remains of the strongly fortified ancient town of Alba Fucens, which once belonged to the Aequi (massive town walls, baths, an amphitheatre, a basilica); an 11th c. Romanesque church, built into a temple of Apollo, can be found here.

Chieti

Above the Pescara valley, in a situation affording extensive views, is Chieti (330 m/1089 ft; pop. 55,000), capital of the province of the same name and the see of an archbishop. In Piazza Vittorio Emanuele are the Town Hall (collection of pictures) and the Gothic cathedral of San

Avezzano in the Fucino basin

Giustino, with a Baroque interior. From the rear of the Town Hall the town's principal street, Corso Marrucino, runs south-west, passing near a group of three temples (to the right, 1st c.), to the municipal park and the Villa Comunale (views!). In the Villa Comunale is the National Museum of Antiquities (Museo Nazionale di Antichità), containing a remarkable collection of prehistoric and Roman material.

Just below Strada Marrucina, which flanks the east side of the town hill, is a large rock-cut Roman cistern, with the remains of the baths which it supplied.

Pescara

On the Adriatic coast, astride the River Pescara which reaches the sea here, is the provincial capital of Pescara (6 m/20 ft; pop. 132,000). The town was badly damaged during the Second World War but has been rebuilt on an impressive scale. In Piazza Italia, on the left bank of the river, is the imposing Palazzo del Governo. On the other side of the river, stands the Tempio della Conciliazione, built 1935–1938 to commemorate the Lateran treaties. On the Corso Manthonè is the house where the poet Gabriele D'Annunzio (1863–1938) was born; inside (open to visitors) there are many relics. In the Museo Ittico (Via Paolucci), close to the Porto Canale, can be seen the skeleton of a sperm whale.

Resorts on the Adriatic coast

Along the Adriatic coast is a whole series of resorts, some of them with beautiful beaches. From north to south: Martinsicuro, Alba Adriatica,

Agrigrento

Tortoreto Lido (5 km/3 miles west, the medieval town of Tortoreto Alto), Giulianova, Roseto degli Abruzzi (formerly Rosburgo), Pineto (11 km/7 miles west, the little town of Atri, with a Romanesque-Gothic cathedral dating from the end of the 13th c., contains fine frescoes), Silvi Marina, Montesilvano Marina, Francavilla al Mare, Ortona (ruins of a castle, fine views), San Vito Chietino (12 km/7½ miles south-west, the walled town of Lanciano with the Gothic church of S. Maria Maggiori which was rebuilt in the 18th c., with a campanile dating from the 12th c.), Fossacesia Marina (near which is the Romanesque basilica of San Giovanni in Venere, 8th–13th c.) and Vasto, with several interesting churches and, in the cathedral square, the Palazzo d'Avalos (18th c.).

Agrigrento K12

Region: Sicily/Sicilia
Province: Agrigento (AG)
Altitude: 230 m/759 ft
Population: 54,000

Situation

Agrigento, capital of the province of the same name, lies half way along the south coast of Sicily – some 100 km/62 miles south-east of Marsala. With its magnificent ruined temples it is one of the most beautifully situated towns in Sicily. However, the skyline of the town itself has been drastically changed by the blocks of new housing developments, particularly on the south side of the old town.

History

Agrigento was founded in 581 B.C., under the name of Akragas by settlers from the Greek colony of Gela (80 km/50 miles south-east). Magnificently situated on a ridge between the rivers Akragas (San Biagio) and Hypsas (Santa Anna), it was celebrated by Pindar as "the most beautiful city of mortal men". On the north side of the hill, now occupied by the modern town, was the acropolis; to the south, on the land, sloping gradually towards the sea, lay the ancient city with extensive remains of its walls and temples. The town was mostly ruled by tyrants, one of whom, Phalaris (c. 549 B.C.), was notorious for his cruelty: he is said to have crucified his enemies to Zeus Atabyrios (the Moloch of Mount Tabor) by roasting them in a brazen bull. The town rose to wealth and power by trade with Carthage, and some of its citizens lived in princely state. Akragas reached its peak of prosperity as a free state under the leadership of Empedocles (who died c. 424 B.C.), but soon afterwards (406 B.C.) succumbed to the Carthaginians. The town was plundered and the temples were set on fire. Akragas had a new peak under the leadership of Timoleone, who defeated the Carthaginians in 340 B.C. The Roman Agrigentum (from 210 B.C.) was a place of no importance. In A.D. 827 it was taken by the Saracens and grew to rival Palermo. In 1086 the Norman ruler Roger I established a bishopric here which developed during the Middle Ages into the richest in Sicily. Until 1927 the town was known by its Saracenic name of Girgenti. Agrigento was the birthplace of the writer Luigi Pirandello (1867–1936).

Old town

Cathedral

At the north-west corner of the old town, a huddle of narrow winding streets, stands the cathedral, built on the foundation of a temple of Jupiter of the 6th *c.* B.C. It was begun in the 11th c., enlarged in the 13th–14th *c.* and largely remodelled in the 16th–17th *c.* A landslip in 1966 caused considerable damage but now it is mostly restored. At the

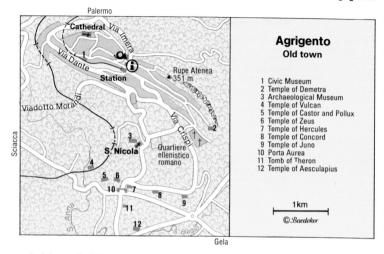

Palermo

Agrigento
Old town

Cathedral Via Imera
Via Dante
Station
Rupe Atenea
▲ 351 m
Viadotto Mora
Sciacca
S. Nicola
Quartiere
ellenistico
romano
Via Crispi
S. Anna
S. Biagio

1 Civic Museum
2 Temple of Demetra
3 Archaeological Museum
4 Temple of Vulcan
5 Temple of Castor and Pollux
6 Temple of Zeus
7 Temple of Hercules
8 Temple of Concord
9 Temple of Juno
10 Porta Aurea
11 Tomb of Theron
12 Temple of Aesculapius

1 km

© *Baedeker*

Gela

end of the north aisle is the chapel of De Marinis, with the tomb of Gaspare de Marinis (1493). To the right of the choir is a fine silver reliquary (1639) with the remains of San Gerlando, first bishop of Agrigento.

By the steps – west of the cathedral – is the Museo Diocesano. | Museo Diocesano

To the south of the old town, in Piazza Pirandello, is the Museo Civico, containing medieval and modern art as well as paintings by Sicilian artists. | Museo Civico

The principal street of the town is the busy Via Atenea. It runs east to the Piazzale Aldo Moro, east of the old town. 1.5 km/1 mile farther east in a private garden is the Rock of Atenea (Rupe Atenea; 351 m/1158 ft), from which there are extensive views. | Rupe Atenea

North of the Via Atenea the church of Santo Spirito (13th c.) is worth visiting. It is decorated with fine stucco by Giacomo Serpotta. | Santo Spirito

Passeggiata Archeologica (Archaeological Tour)

The temple area is reached via the Piazzale Aldo Moro, immediately south of the Piazza Marconi with its railway station. The tour is sign-posted "Passeggiata Archeologica" and runs south-east along Via Crispi.

In 1 km/¾ mile a road goes off on the left to the cemetery. At its south-east corner are remains of the Greek town walls. | Cemetery

From here it is only 500 m/550 yd east on the stony ancient road to the Temple of Demeter (Tempio di Demetra) which stands on high ground. Originally built c. 470 B.C., it was converted by the Normans into the little church of San Biagio. To the east below the terrace is a cave sanctuary of Demeter (c. 650 B.C.). | Tempio di Demetra

Soon afterwards another road on the right branches off the Via Crispi. After 500 m/550 yd a recently excavated section of the Greco-Roman

Agrigrento

city (4th *c.* B.C. to 5th *c.* A.D.) is reached; with fine wall paintings and mosaic pavements.

* Museo Archeologico Regionale

Close to the site is the Museo Archeologico Regionale with prehistoric finds, ancient sarcophagi, vases, coins and architectural fragments; particularly precious is a marble statue of an ephebe (*c.* 490 B.C.).

San Nicola

Immediately south of the museum is the little Gothic church of San Nicola (13th *c.*) with a fine doorway. Inside is a marble sarcophagus carved with scenes from the story of Phaedra and Hippolytus (2nd–3rd *c.* A.D.). Close to the church, to the west, is the so-called Oratory of Phalaris and an almost square cella, the tomb of a Roman matron (1st *c.* B.C.).

Temple Area

Tempio di Ercole

1 km/¾ mile beyond San Nicola the road reaches the entrance to the enclosed Temple Area (freely open at all times). To the right is the Temple of Zeus; immediately to the left of the road, near the south wall of the ancient city, the so-called Temple of Hercules (Tempio di Ercole; 6th *c.* B.C.), with eight columns – out of the original 38 – which were re-erected on the south side in 1923.

** Tempio di Concordia

From the Temple of Hercules a new road runs east past the Villa Aurea (offices of the Temple Area administration; temporary exhibitions) to the Doric Temple of Concord (Tempio di Concordia) which was built in the 5th *c.* B.C. and converted into a church in the Middle Ages. With all its 34 columns still standing, it ranks with the Theseion in Athens as the best preserved ancient temple.

** Tempio di Giunone

About 700 m/770 yd farther east, magnificently situated above a steep escarpment at the south-east corner of the ancient city, near the road

Agrigento: Temple of Castor and Pollux . . .   . . . and stumps of columns

Temple of Concordia

from Agrigento to Gela, is the so-called Temple of Iuno Lacinia (Tempio di Giunone; 5th c. B.C.), a classic example of the Doric style. The temple, actually dedicated to Hera, has 25 complete columns standing and nine others partly re-erected. 15 m/17 yd east is the sacrificial altar.

Between the temples of Hercules and Zeus is the harbour gate, the so-called Porta Aurea, through which passes the road to Porto Empedocle (10 km/6 miles south-west) and the ancient port, which lies due south at the mouth of the Fiume San Biagio.

Porta Aurea

Outside the Porta Aurea is the so-called Tomb of Theron (Tomba di Terone), the remains of a tower-like Roman mausoleum (1st c. B.C.).

Tomba di Terone

Further to the south is the small Temple of Aesculapius (Tempio de Esculapio; 5th c. B.C.), from which there are extensive views.

Tempio di Esculapio

North-west of the Porta Aurea are the ruins of the unfinished Temple of Zeus (Tempio di Giove Olimpico; 5th c. B.C.). With its length of 113 m/124 yd it is the largest temple of Greek antiquity (Temple G at Selinunt 111 m/121 yd; Artemision at Ephesus 109 m/119 yd; Parthenon at Athens 70 m/77 yd). The entablature was probably supported by the huge male and female Telamones or Atlas figures; one of them was restored ("il Gigante", 7.75 m/25½ ft, lying on the ground). One of the Telamones can be seen in the Archaeological Museum.

Tempio di Giove Olimpico

West of the Temple of Zeus is the so-called Temple of Castor and Pollux (Tempio di Castor e Polluce) or Temple of the Dioscuri, of which four columns have been re-erected. A little way north is the Sanctuary of the Chthonic Divinities (Santuario delle Divinità Ctonie; 6th c. B.C.), a unique cult place dedicated to the divinities of the underworld, probably Demeter and Persephone. The remains of twelve altars and eight small temples in the form of treasuries have been excavated.

Tempio di Castor e Polluce

Tempio di Vulcano   Farther to the north-west, beyond the railway, are the remains of the so-called Temple of Vulcan (Tempio di Vulcano, built *c.* 470 B.C.). From here there is a view of the range of temples.

Naro

Situation
35 km/22 miles east

East of Agrigento, on a hill, lies the picturesque little town of Naro with fine remains of medieval buildings, among which parts of the town walls and the Castello dei Chiaramonte.

Alto Adige (South Tirol)   G/H3

Region: Trentino-Alto Adige
Province: Bolzano (BZ)
Area: 7400 sq. km/2857 sq. miles
Population: 422,000

Situation

The Alto Adige (Upper Adige) lies in the extreme north of Italy on the southern fringe of the Alps. The area extends north-south from the Brenner to the Saluner Klause, on the west it is bounded by the Resia (Rentschen) pass and the Stilfser Joch, and on the east by the Pusteria valley (Pustertal) and the Kreuzbergpass. The situation of the Alto Adige gives it a varied range of topography from the eternal snow of the great glaciated peaks of the Central Alps and the Ortles group (3902 m/12,877 ft) to the Mediterranean climate and the vineyards of the Bolzano (265 m/875 ft) and Merano area.

Geology

The geological structure is determined by the girdle of ancient Alpine rocks (gneisses, granites, schists and quartz phyllites) in the north and west, the considerable area of dolomitic limestone crags in the east and the great spread of porphyries around Bolzano in the south, extending far into the neighbouring Trentino.

** Scenery

Extending south from the Réesia (Reschen) pass is the upper Adige (Etsch) valley, which from here to Merano is known as the Val Venosta (Vintschgau), with the most massive peaks (*c.* 3000 m/10,000 ft) of the Eastern Alps, from which the Val Passiria (Passeiertal) branches off and runs north to the Passo di Monte Giovo (Jaufenpass, 2094 m/6910 ft). Beyond this is Vipiteno (Sterzing) in the Isarco (Eisack) valley, which farther south is joined by the Pusteria (Puster) valley.

Ortles group

Between the Valtellina, the Val Venosta and the upper Noce valley (Val di Sole and Val di Non) extends the Ortles (Ortler) group, a range of mainly crystalline rocks but with its highest peaks, Ortles (Ortler, 3902 m/12,877 ft) and the majestic Gran Zebrù (Königsspitze, 3859 m/12,735 ft), built up from Triassic limestones. On the north side of the range are the Solda (Sulden), Martello (Martell) and Ultimo (Ulten) valleys, on the west the Valfurva and on the south the Péio and Rabbi valleys, all much glaciated in the upper reaches.

Adamello-Presanella group

To the south of the Passo Di Tonale (1893 m/6214 ft), bounded on the west by the Oglio valley (Val Camónica) and on the east by the Sarco valley, is the Adamello-Presanella group (Cima Presanella, 3556 m/11,735 ft; Monte Adamello, 3554 m/11,728 ft), consisting mainly of tornalites, through which runs the wild Val de Génova with its water-falls.

Along the east side of the Ortles and Adamella-Presanella groups runs the Valli Giudicarie (the middle valley of the Sarca and upper valley of the Chiesa or Chiem), one of the most striking fault lines in the Alps. To the east of this line the land has sunk 2000 m/6660 ft in places, so that here, in contrast to the crystalline Central Alps, the substance of the Etschbuchtgebirge which belongs to the Southern Alps and owes its name to its geological situation rather than to its geographical setting, is made up of Triassic and Jurassic dolomites and limestones. The best-known range is the dolomitic Brenta group (Cima Tosa, 3173 m/10,471 ft), which in spite of its geographical separation from the main Dolomites east of the Adige ranks equal with them in the magnificence of its mountain scenery.

Brenta group

The parallel chain to the east, the Etschgebirge, the northern part of which is called Nonsberger Alps, with the Monte Roén (Mendelgebirge, 2116 m/6983 ft) being part of this, falls down in sheer limestone walls to the morainic uplands on the upper Adige in the north and the wide Adige valley, covered with later fluvial deposits.

Adige valley

South of the Pusteria valley and to a lesser extent in the north-eastern Sarentine Alps (Sarntaler Alpen) is a zone of quartz phyllites, mainly dark coloured. In Rasciesa (Raschötz, 2283 m/7534 ft) and the southern Sarentine Alps this is overlaid by the Bolzano porphyries, hard reddish volcanic rocks of the Permian period.

Sarentine Alps
Bolzano porphyries

This porphyry zone, extending south as far as the Trento region and reaching its highest point in the Lagorai chain (Cima de Cece, 2772 m/9148 ft) near Predazzo, is cut by deep valleys, notably the Val d'Ega (Eggental) at Bolzano and the Tires valley (Tierser Tal). The infertile porphyry has been covered, particularly on the Renón (Ritten) by old moraines, which have been eroded by heavy rain, leaving the famous "earth pillars" capped by their protective boulders.

Lagorai chain
Renón

The porphyries combine with melaphyres and sandstones of the late Permian, soft schists, clays and variegated marls of the Lower Triassic and intrusions of dark-coloured lavas and volcanic tuffs to form the undulating basement formation, covered with beautiful Alpine meadows and coniferous forests, of the Dolomites.

Dolomites

Climate and vegetation

The climate of the region reflects its geographical diversity, ranging from the Alpine conditions of the mountain valleys with their abundance of snow through the normal European climate of the intermediate areas to the Mediterranean type, with mild winters and sometimes very hot summers, of the wide valleys of the Adige and the Isarco with their southern exposure and their sheltered situation, protected from the north winds by the mountains. The Val Venosta in the west of the region has the reputation of being the driest valley in the Eastern Alps; in the north it has an Alpine climate, but in the southern part it approximates to the climatic pattern of Merano.

Climate

The flora varies according to the climate. Differences in the Alpine flora reflect differences in the subsoil – ancient rocks or dolomitic limestones – and the Alpe de Siusi (Seiser Alm) offers a famous example of this diversity.

Flora

The Alto Adige has several national parks and all alpine species of plants and shrubs are statutorily protected. The picking of any plants of the following is strictly prohibited: yellow Alpine anemone, lady's slipper, common mezereon, garland flower, striated mezereon, fire lily,

Conservation

The Rosengarten range in the Alto Adige

martagon lily, spring snowflake, poet's narcissus, white water-lily, yellow water-lily, bulrush, lesser bulrush, dwarf bulrush, burning bush, peony, auricula, devil's claw and edelweiss.

The flora of the south of the Alto Adige is charterised by the zone of downy oaks, interspersed with some evergreen species, which reaches up from Lake Garda and by the famous parks and gardens of Bressanone, Bolzano and Merano, in which olives, holm-oaks and winter jasmine flourish as well as various exotic species.
These climatic islands were used for vine-growing at a very early period, in pre-Roman times, and the vine now extends as far north as Bressanone and Silandro (Schlanders) and to an altitude of around 800 m/2640 ft. No less famous than the wines of the Alto Adige is the fruit grown in the valleys, and the blossoming orchards are one of the great sights of the region at Easter.

Population

The population of the Alto Adige is mixed, consisting of Germans, Italians, and Ladins, the descendants of the original Rhaeto-Romanic inhabitants; and, lying as it does on one of the great European transit routes from north to south, it has suffered many vicissitudes in the course of its history, from the time of the great migrations to the present day.

The German-speaking population of 280,000 have German schools; they can develop their cultural life freely, and their language has equal status with that of the 124,000 Italians who live chiefly in the towns. The culture and language of the Ladins, some 18,000 in number, are also protected. Nearly the entire population (98%) is Roman Catholic, no matter which ethnic group they belong to. Each linguistic group is entitled to a proportionate share of posts in the government service.

History

This begins with the finds of Neolithic material in the south of the region and Bronze Age material in the Alpine territory. The indigenous

population, known to the Romans as Rhaetians but subject also to Celto-Illyrian, Ligurian and Etruscan influences, were incorporated in the Roman Empire by Augustus in 15 B.C. and over the course of half a millennium were Romanised, at least in language. During the period of the great migrations this relatively thinly settled region, occupied by peoples who were now known as Raeto-Romanic, saw the passage of the invading Gothics and Lombards, but the first invaders to settle here were the Bajuwari, who had occupied the whole of the region by the end of the 6th c., making it a purely German-speaking area, along the fringes of which (the Dolomite valleys, the Val Venosta) the Rhaeto-Romanic population have contrived to survive down to modern times, perserving at least in part their language and their way of life as in the Val Gádera (Gadertal and Val Gardena (Gröden).

The Alto Adige then became a part of the Frankish kingdom, and at the beginning of the 11th c. passed into the hands of the prince-bishops of Trento and Bressanone, whose lay governors, principally the Counts of Tirol, sought to unite their territories. These territories, lying on both sides of the Brenner, fell into the hands of the Habsburgs in 1363 and remained Austrian until 1918, with a short interruption during the Napoleonic period (Andreas Hofer's successful rising and subsequent defeat). Thereafter South Tirol became Italian against its will and was subjected to a process of denationalisation under Fascist rule. After the Second World War, under the Treaty of Paris, the region was granted a substantial measure of self-government.

Art

The vicissitudes of history are reflected in the art and architecture of the region, with examples of Romanesque (Val Venosta, San Cándido Cathedral), a rich range of Gothic (frescoes, altars with side panels) and major works of Renaissance and Baroque architecture. The Alto Adige is also notable for its numerous fortified castles.

A short survey of art and architecture can properly begin in the Val Venosta, which has mainly work in Romanesque style but also monuments dating back to the early days of Christianity, such as the crypt of Monte Maria (Marienberg) abbey, the Carolingian church of San Benedetto in Malles (Mals), numerous other churches in the valley which

Survey of art
Romanesque style

61

now stand empty, and above all San Prócolo at Naturno (Naturns), with the oldest surviving wall paintings in German-speaking territory. Other fine examples of Romanesque architecture which must be seen are the doorways in Castel Tirolo (Schloss Tirol) with their carved bestiary and the completely preserved cathedral at San Cándido (Innichen) in the Val Pusteria.

Gothic style

Bolzano (Bozen) offers fine examples of Gothic, in particular its late Gothic cathedral and the altar by Michael Pacher (Coronation of the Virgin) in the old parish church of Gries. There are some fine exhibits to be seen in Bolzano Museum and the Diocesan Museum in Bressanone (Brixen). Both of these museums also contain Baroque pictures, while some of the finest painting to be found in the Alpine countries can be seen in the famous cloisters of the Franciscan and Dominican monasteries in Bolzano and in those of Novacella (Neustift) and above all Bressanone.

Baroque style

The Alto Adige is poor in major buildings of the Baroque period, apart from the beautiful church at Dobbiaco (Toblach) in the Val Pusteria. The finest Baroque palace in the region, Castello Mareta (Wolfsthurn), lies in the Val Ridanna, a remote side valley near Vipiteno.

Folk art and traditions

Folk art and traditions have always been important to the inhabitants of the Alto Adige. In Teodone (Dietenheim), near Brunico (Bruneck), the regional folk museum has an interesting collection and an open air department. Fine examples of the craftmanship of the Alto Adige can also be seen in the Folk Museum in Innsbruck (Austria). Old traditions are well maintained by the many local bands with their smart costumes. The beautiful old peasant costumes are still worn in the Val Sarentina, during the ordinary working week and not merely on special occasions. The pre-Christmas period is celebrated here with an old tradition, the so-called "Klöckeln", an ancient fertility cult combined with later Christian elements. The Corpus Christi procession of Castelrotto (Kastelruth) is famous, and many towns and villages, particularly in the mountain valleys, still have impressive processions which show a charateristic combination of genuine piety with attachment to traditional practices.

Economy

The road and rail route over the Brenner and through the Isarco and Adige valleys is the most important north-south link in the Eastern Alps. The wide stretch of the Adige valley between Merano and the Salorno defile is also of great economic importance as the main area of production of the region's high-quality fruit (particularly apples and pears) and its renowned wines.

Wines of the Alto Adige

The wine-producing region extends from the Isarco valley in the north to the Salorno defile in the southern Adige valley, taking in part of the Val Venosta to the west and part of the Rienza valley to the east. It is divided into six main areas – the Isarco valley, the Val Venosta, the area round Merano, the Bolzano basin, the Upper Adige and the Adige valley. The total area under vines is over 14,826 acres, which produce some 70,000,000 litres of wine annually (85% red, 15% white). About four-fifths of the output is exported, mainly to Switzerland, Germany and Austria.

Well known quality wines are Santa Maddalena (ruby-red, full-bodied, velvety), grown on the hillsides of the Bolzano basin; Merano (ruby-red, strong, well-rounded); and Lago di Caldaro (light red to ruby-red, light, harmonious).

A characteristic feature of vine-growing in the Alto Adige is the use of "pergolas" – wooden frames on which the vines grow, enabling large quantities of grapes to be produced in a relatively small area.

The wine is pressed with an ancient type of wine-press known as the "torkel". At the time of the vintage (September-October) the local people like to visit the wine-cellars and wine-shops to taste the new wine, accompanying it with walnuts, roast chestnuts and home-made bread.

The "Alto Adige wine route" (Südtiroler Weinstrasse), 30 km/19 miles long, runs down the west side of the Adige valley from Castle Firmiano (Sigmundskron), west of Bolzano, to Frangarto, Cornaiano (Girlan), Appiano (Eppan: with San Michele/St Michael, San Paolo/St Pauls and Missiano/Missian), Caldaro (Kaltern), San Giuseppe (St Josef), Termeno (Tramin), Cortaccia (Kurtatsch), Magré (Margreid), Cortina all'Adige (Kurtinig: possible continuation via Rovere della Luna to Mezzocorona) and Salorno (Salurn). | Alto Adige wine route

The Bolzano area has the greatest concentration of commerce and industry (Bolzano Trade Fair; metal-working, particularly iron, aluminium and magnesium; engineering, vehicle manufacture; chemicals; textiles, leather goods, woodworking, canning). Merano has chemical plants (artificial fertilisers, etc.). There are numerous smaller industrial and craft establishments in the Isarco valley (Bressanone), Val Pusteria (Brunico) and the Val Venosta. | Industry

The economy of the region still depends mainly on the vigour and energy of its farming population. Corn-growing is steadily declining in favour of fodder crops (maize) and seed potatoes. In this region forestry is an important activity, while the extensive Alpine meadows provide pasture for cattle (particularly dairy cows); Haflinger horses are prized both as working and as riding animals. | Agriculture

One of the main pillars of the economy is now tourism, promoted by the incomparable beauty of the scenery, the excellent snow conditions in the high valleys in winter and the favourable climate. The region is well equipped for the tourist trade, with numerous funiculars, ski-lifts and other recreational facilities, a dense system of way-marked footpaths and routes for climbers, as well as ample accommodation for visitors, ranging from modestly priced rooms in private houses to first-class hotels offering every amenity. | Tourism

L9

Amalfi

Region: Campania
Province: Salerno (SA)
Altitude: 0–11 m/0–36 ft
Population: 6000

The seaside resort of Amalfi lies on the south coast of the Sorrento peninsula at the northern edge of the Gulf of Salerno – at the mouth of a deep gorge. Amalfi is one of the most popular holiday resorts in Italy, particularly favoured by the people of Naples. | Situation

Amalfi

According to legend Amalfi was founded by Constantine the Great. During the Middle Ages it was an independent state with a population of some 50,000, ruled by self-appointed dukes who later became hereditary. In 1077 the town was incorporated by Robert Guiscard in the Norman kingdom; through its active trade with the Orient it rose to influence and wealth. As a sea power Amalfi came into conflict with Pisa and Genoa. Amalfi's code of maritime law (Tabulae Amalfitanae) prevailed throughout the whole of the Italian Mediterranean from the 13th to the 16th c. The invention of the ship's compass is attributed to Flavio Gioia (1302), a citizen of Amalfi.

* Sights

Harbour

Along the coast runs a promenade and a beach. From the harbour, the Marina Grande, there are boat services to Naples, Capri and Salerno in the summer.

The houses cling to the bay. From the harbour it is a short distance by way of Piazza Flavio Gioia to the Town Hall; the façade is decorated with modern mosaic. The municipal museum (Museo Civico) is housed in the Town Hall; its major attraction is the so-called "Tavole amalfitane", a medieval document with the maritime law of ancient times. To the north lies the little Piazza del Duomo, from which a flight of 62 steps leads up to the cathedral.

Cathedral

The Cathedral of Sant'Andrea, originally built in the 9th c., was remodelled in Sicilian Lombard-Normanesque style in 1203; the campanile dates from 1180 to 1276. The magnificent portico, with pointed arches, was completely rebuilt in 1865. The front which was restored in

Amalfi

Atrani

1890 is decorated with modern mosaic; the fine bronze door was cast in Constantinople in 1066. Inside there are ancient columns of Paestum, supporting the choir. The crypt contains the remains of the Apostle St Andrew, brought here in the 13th c.

To the left, in the portico, is the entrance to the cloister (Chiostro del Paradiso, 1266–1268), which contains ancient sarcophagi, marble and mosaics.

About 500 m/550 yd west of the cathedral, high above Amalfi (also reached by lift from the coast road), is the former Capuchin monastery (now a hotel) with a beautiful cloister and affording fine views.

Capuchin monastery

*Grotta di Amalfi

There is an attractive trip by motorboat (15 minutes) to a stalactitic cave, the Grotta di Amalfi, also known as the Grotta dello Smeraldo or Grotta Verde, west of the Capo Conca (fee).

Situation
1 km/¾ mile west

Atrani

On the coast road, beyond the Capo di Amalfi, at the mouth of a gorge of the Dragone, is the little town of Atrani (12 m/40 ft). In the Piazza is the church of San Salvatore de' Bireto (10th c.), the church where the doges of Amalfi were crowned. Its Byzantine bronze doors were cast in Constantinople in 1087.

Situation
1 km/¾ mile east

Ravello

From the east side of Atrani a winding road with two sharp bends ascends through orange-groves to Ravello (350 m/1155 ft), an old town in a superb situation above the Amalfi coast. The town founded during the Norman period, had its heyday under the Anjou dynasty in the 13th c. when it had a population of 36,000; it possessed many churches, monastic houses and palaces.

Situation
6 km/4 miles north

In the centre of the town is the Romanesque cathedral of San Pantaleone (begun in 1086, remodelled in Baroque style) with fine bronze doors (covered externally with wooden doors) by Barisanus of Trani (1179). Inside there is a marble pulpit with a mosaic ground by Niccolo di Bartolomeo (1272). In the choir stands the bishop's throne, to the left the Capella di San Pantaleone in which some of the saint's blood is preserved.

South-east of the cathedral is the Villa Rufolo, in Saracenic style (11th c.), with a little pillared courtyard in the centre. The garden with its lookout terrace (340 m/1122 ft) provided Wagner with the model for Klingsor's enchanted garden.

A walk (about eight minutes) from the cathedral, first south through an arcade, then up through the portico of the church of San Francesco (cloister in Romanesque style) and past the church of Santa Chiara leads to the Villa Cimbrone. An avenue runs through the beautiful park to the Belvedere Cimbrone, from which there are incomparable views of the Amalfi coast.

About 200 m/220 yd north-east of the cathedral is the church of San Giovanni del Toro (12th c.; remodelled in Baroque style and modernised). Inside there is a mosaic pulpit adorned with Persian majolica (c. 1175); on the pulpit steps and in the crypt are frescoes of scenes from the life of Christ.

Region: Marche
Province: Ancona (AN)
Altitude: 16 m/53 ft
Population: 106,000

Situation

Ancona, capital of the Marche region and the province of the same name, is picturesquely situated between foothills and the bay on the Italian Adriatic coast.

Importance

At present Ancona is an important traffic junction (railway; airport 13 km/8 miles west at Falconara) and a developing port: ferry services to Yugoslavia and Greece and the growing fishing industry mean a considerable economic upswing in recent years. The making of musical instruments contributes to this.
During the Second World War Ancona suffered heavy damage and the part of the old town around the harbour was completely destroyed. Since the war new districts have been developed to the east of the town. An earthquake damaged these buildings in 1972; restoration and rebuilding are continuing.

History

Ancona was founded by refugees from Syracuse about 390 B.C. under the name of Dorica Ancon (from the Greek word ankón = bend or curve, after the shape of the promontory on which the town was built). In the 3rd c. B.C. it became a Roman colony, and in the reigns of Caesar and Trajan it was fortified and developed into a naval base. Although the town was presented to the Pope by Charlemagne in 774 and at the end of the 16th c. was formally incorportated in the Papal States, it contrived in practice to maintain its independence throughout the Middle Ages.
Ancona has been the seat of a bishop since 462.

Harbour

Piazza della
Repubblica

The hub of the town's traffic is the Piazza della Repubblica. On its west side is the harbour, an oval basin 800-900 m/875–985 yd in diameter, the northern part of which is of Roman origin. At the north end of the

Arco di Traiano

breakwater is the Roman triumphal arch Arco di Traiano with an inscription recording that it was erected in A.D. 115 in honour of the Emperor Trajan and his wife and sister; to the west is the Arco Clementino (18th c.).

Porta Pia

At the south end of the harbour stands the former hospital, built on a pentagonal bastion; adjoining is the Porta Pia (1789). The modern port installations are situated to the north-west.

Town Centre

Palazzo de Governo

From the Piazza della Repubblica a street on the right leads past the theatre (1826) into the elongated Piazza del Plebiscito. In this square stands the Palazzo de Governo (15th c.) with the prefecture and, approached by a flight of steps, is the Baroque church of Santa Domenico (18th c.); inside can be seen a painting of the crucification of Christ by Titian (1558).

Loggia dei Mercanti

To the west is the Loggia dei Mercanti (exchange), a late Gothic building with a façade by Giorgio Orsini (1451–1459). Adjoining stands the beautiful Palazzo Benincasa (15th c.).

Santa Maria di Portonova, near Ancona

From the exchange a street on the right leads to the church of Santa Maria della Piazza (10th c.) which was erected in the 13th c. It has an over-decorated façade (1210).

Santa Maria della Piazza

Farther north, in the Piazza San Francesco, is the church of San Francesco alle Scale with a Gothic doorway by Giorgio Orsini (1454).

San Francesco alle Scale

Museums

From the Piazza San Francesco the Via Pizzecolli runs north to the church of del Gesù (18th c.) and the Palazzo Bosdari (1550), which houses the Pinacoteca Comunale (municipal picture collection). It contains work by Titian, Lotto, Crivelli and other masterpieces. In the modern art section are works by present-day Italian painters.

Pinacoteca Comunale

A little way north stands the Palazzo Ferretti (16th c.), which houses the Museo Nazionale delle Marche (state-run museum of the Marche region) with prehistoric and Roman material of the Marche region, particularly finds of tombs, such as vases, etc.

Museo Nazionale delle Marche

** Cathedral

From the museum a walk up a flight of steps or a drive up a winding panoramic road, built after the destruction of the harbour district, leads to the top of Monte Guasco, on which stands the cathedral, built on the site of a temple of Venus. The domed cruciform church in Byzantine-Romanesque style (12th c.) is dedicated to San Ciriaco. The façade has a Gothic doorway, which is decorated with reliefs. In the crypt are the remains of an early Christian church (6th c.) and a temple (3rd c. B.C.). The diocesan museum is housed in a building to the left of the cathedral. Notable is the early Christian sarcophagus with carved decoration belonging to Flavius Gorgonius, a praetorian prefect (4th c.).

Museo Diocesano

Numana

Situation
15 km/9½ miles

A drive southwards on the coast road leads to the church of Santa Maria di Portonovo (11th c.) and to Monte Conero (572 m/1888 ft) from which there are extensive views. From there the road continues to the picturesque village of Sirolo and the little seaside resort of Numana.

Aosta   D4

Region: Autonomous region of Valle d'Aosta (AO)
Province: Aosta (AO)
Altitude: 583 m/1924 ft
Population: 37,500

Situation

Aosta (French Aoste), capital of the autonomous region of Valle d'Aosta, lies some 100 km/62 miles east of Turin, in a fertile valley at the confluence of the Buthier and the Dora Baltea, ringed by an imposing circle of mountains, with Grand Combin to the north rising to 4317 m/ 14,246 ft.

Importance

The town, which has been a place of importance from time immemorial as the gateway to the Great and Little St Bernard passes, was originally built as the Roman fort of Augusta Praetoria Salassorum soon after 25 B.C., and its plan still reflects the regular layout of the Roman station. It preserves numerous monuments dating from the Roman and medieval periods. It is still an important traffic junction at the meeting of the access roads to the Mont Blanc tunnel and the Great St Bernard pass.

Sights

Porta Pretoria

The old town is still surrounded by well-preserved Roman town walls, forming a rectangle 724 by 572 m/792 by 626 yd, with twenty towers. The east gate or Porta Praetoria, originally three-arched, lies some 2.5 m/8¼ ft below the present street-level, with a spacious courtyard at the rear. Close by is the square tower of a medieval castle which belonged to the Lords of Quart.

Teatro Romano
Anfiteatro Romano

From here it is only a few yards north-west to the stage wall, 22 m/73 ft high, of the Roman theatre, actually four storeys high. In the neighbouring garden of a monastery there are some arches of the amphitheatre.

Arco di Augusto

About 400 m/440 yd east of the Porta Praetoria stands the Arch of Augustus (Arco di Augusto) with ten Corinthian pilasters.

Saint Ours

A little way north-west is the former collegiate church of Saint Ours (Collegiata di S Orso), originally built in the 10th c., remodelled in Late Gothic style at the end of the 15th c. with fine 11th c. frescoes and beautifully carved choir stalls (16th c.). In front of the church is a fine campanile, partly built of Roman hewn stones (c. 1150); on the south side is a Romanesque cloister (1133) with fine carved capitals.

Museo Archeologico
Regionale

Near the church – in Via S. Orso – can be found the Archaeological Museum (Museo Archeologico Regionale) containing Roman finds and objects.

Cathedral

In the centre of the town, at the point where the main roads of the Roman fort crossed, is the Piazza Chanoux with the Town Hall. A little

Aosta: Roman theatre

Saint-Pierre Castle in the Aosta valley

way north-west stands the cathedral, erected in the 11th and 12th c; the present church originates from the 15th–16th c. It has a Renaissance façade (*c.* 1526) with a classical porch, added in 1837. The treasury (admission fee) houses the ivory diptych of the Emperor Honorius (406).

On the west side of the cathedral are remains of the Roman forum.

Lac de Chamolé

South of Aosta is Les Fleurs (1360 m/4488 ft), which can be reached by cableway or by road (11 km/7 miles). From here there is a cabin cableway to the Conca di Pila (1800 m/5940 ft), then a chair-lift to the Lac du Chamolé (2312 m/7630 ft).

Situation
south of Aosta

Great St Bernard

There is a very fine excursion north-west from Aosta on the S.S. 27, with sharp turns and hairpin bends to the Vallée du Grand-St-Bernard up the Great St Bernard pass (2649 m/8148 ft). There is also a road tunnel 5828 m/6376 yds long, between St-Rhémy and Bourg-St-Bernard on the Swiss side). The pass, which lies between the Mont Blanc massif and the Valais Alps (small lake),marks the Italian-Swiss frontier. In Swiss territory is the hospice (dog breeding), founded by St Bernard (d. 1081).

Situation
34 km/21 miles
north-west

Aosta Valley/Valle d'Aosta/Val d'Aosta   C/D4

Region: Valle d'Aosta/Val d'Aosta
Area: 3262 sq. km/1259 sq. miles
Population: 113,600

Situation

The autonomous region of the Aosta valley lies in the north-west of Italy – in the deeply eroded valley of the Dora Baltea and its beautiful side valleys. Set amid magnificent mountain scenery at the foot of the Mont Blanc massif and surrounded by the highest summits of the Alps, the Aosta valley ranks high among the regions of Italy for scenic beauty and grandeur.

Importance

The valley, important since ancient times as the access route to the principal Alpine passes, the Little and Great St Bernard, was guarded throughout its entire length by numerous castles and other fortified buildings, often very picturesquely situated.

History and population

The Aosta valley, strongly fortified by the Romans, became in 1191 part of Savoy, and together they passed temporarily to France in the early 19th c. and later to Piedmont. When it was incorporated in Italy in 1861, the French-speaking population resisted the threat of Italianisation in language and culture. The growth of separatist feeling finally led in 1948 to the recognition of the special status of the Aosta valley as an autonomous region.

Language

The inhabitants of the Aosta valley speak a Franco-Provençal dialect; the use of pure French is declining. However, French has equal status with Italian as an offical language and also in the cultural field.

Economy

The beautiful scenery and the excellent snow to be found at the higher altitudes even in summer have promoted the development of a flourishing tourist trade. Other important sources of revenue are vine-growing at the lower levels, pasturing and some industry.

Up the Aosta valley

Pont-Saint-Martin

The route goes from Pont-Saint-Martin to Entrèves (94 km/58 miles). The road from Turin, S.S. 26 (also the A5 motorway), enters the autonomous region of the Aosta valley at Pont-Saint-Martin (345 m/1139 ft; Roman bridge from the 1st c. B.C.), where the River Lys, coming from the north, flows into the Dora Baltea.

Gressoney-La-Trinité

Excursion:
From Pont-Saint-Martin an attractive detour (34 km/21 miles) can be made up the Valle di Gressoney, following the deeply indented and regularly dammed course of the Lys, via the village of Issime (14 km/9 miles; 960 m/3168 ft), which was founded by German-speaking settlers from the Valais in the 13th c., and the little holiday resort of Gressoney St-Jean (14 km/9 miles; 1385 m/4571 ft) to Gressoney-La-Trinité (1635 m/5396 ft); from which a chair-lift leads to Punta Jolanda (2333 m/7699 ft; upper station 2247 m/7415 ft) and also a cabin cableway to Lago Gabiet (2367 m/7811 ft; upper station 2342 m/7729 ft).

* Monte Rosa

Gressoney-La-Trinité is known as a base for many interesting climbing excursions in the Monte Rosa range, particularly for the ascent (6–7 hours, guide required) of the Pointe Dufour (4634 m/15,292 ft), the highest peak in the Monte Rosa group. A chair-lift goes from Staval up to the Colle Bettaforca.

The Aosta valley road continues from Pont-Saint-Martin up the valley, which becomes steadily narrower. Beyond Donnaz (322 m/1063 ft) the massive Fort Bard (391 m/1290 ft; 11th c.) stands on a hill on the right.

10 km/6 miles: Arnad (412 m/1360 ft) with a ruined castle high above it (634 m/2092 ft); beyond this, on the right bank of the Dora, is the castle of Issogne, built in 1480, with an interesting interior.

*Castle of Issogne

4 km/2½ miles: Verrès (391 m/1290 ft) with an old castle, the Rocca (1390), picturesquely situated on a rocky hill.

Verrès

Excursion:
From Verrès there is a rewarding excursion (27 km/17 miles north) up the valley of the River Evançon, the Valle di Challand. The route goes via the summer holiday resort of Brusson (16 km/10 miles; 1338 m/4415 ft) in the lower part of the valley to Champoluc (11 km/7 miles; 1570 m/5181 ft), the principal place in the upper part of the valley, known as the Val d'Ayas. This is also a popular summer and winter holiday resort with views of the twin mountains Castor (4230 m/13,950 ft) and Pollux (4094 m/13,510 ft) and the Breithorn (4171 m/13,764 ft), all of them south of the Matterhorn. A cabin cableway leads up to the Crest (1974 m/6514 ft), then a chair-lift continues to 2500 m/8250 ft.

Brusson Champoluc

Beyond Verrès the Aosta valley road passes the castle of Montjovet, then runs through the picturesque Montjovet defile, beyond which there is a first glimpse of Mont Blanc.

12 km/7 ½ miles: Saint-Vincent (575 m/1898 ft), is a popular summer holiday resort with a casino and mineral springs (recommended for liver and stomach disorders). Beyond this, perched on the left, is the castle of Ussel (c. 1350).

Saint Vincent

3 km/2 miles: Châtillon (549 m/1812 ft; population 4700), is a charming village with a fine castle.

Châtillon

Excursion:
From Châtillon there is a rewarding drive (27 km/17 miles north) up the Valtournenche, through which the River Matmoire (in Italian Marmore) flows down from the Matterhorn. The road runs through Antey St André (7 km/4 miles; 1074 m/3544 ft), beyond which the Matterhorn comes into sight, and Buisson (4 km/2½ miles; 1128 m/3722 ft; cableway east to the Chamois, 1815 m/5997 ft: from there a chair-lift to Lago di Lod; 2015 m/6650 ft) and comes to Valtournenche (7 km/4 miles; 1528 m/5042 ft), which is popular both with summer visitors and winter sports enthusiasts (chair-lift east to the Alpe Chanlève; 1850 m/6105 ft; cableway to Monte Molar, 2484 m/8197 ft-2244 m/7405 ft).

Valtournenche

The road then continues through a gorge, just before which a footpath (10 minutes' walk) goes off to the Gouffre des Busserailles (waterfall; admission fee), 104 m/114 yd long and 35 m/116 ft deep, and reaches Breuil or Cervinia (2006 m/6620 ft), a winter sports resort which is also popular in summer (bobsleigh run 1540 m/5082 ft long to the Lac Bleu) with fantastic scenery: to the north the mighty peak of the Matterhorn (Monte Cervino; 4478 m/14,777 ft; the climb with guide takes 12 hours), to the west the rock wall of the Grandes Murailles (3872 m/12,778 ft). From Breuil there is a cableway east to the Plan Maison (2557 m/8438 ft) and from there north-east to the Furggen ridge (3488 m/11,510 ft) or alternatively east, either directly or via Cime Bianche (2823 m/9316 ft), to the Plateau Rosà (3480 m/11,484 ft). 1 km/¾ mile north of the Plateau Rosà is the Theodul pass (3322 m/10,963 ft), from which there are fine views, extending also into the Zermatt valley.

Breuil (Cervinia)
**Matterhorn

Beyond Châtillon the Aosta valley road affords open views of the fertile valley and the mountains around Aosta, with the three-peaked Rutor in the background. Farther on, above the mouth of the Val de Clavalité or Val de Fénis, in which the snowy peak of the Tersiva can be seen, stands the mighty castle of Fénis on the left (1330, with later additions) with a beautiful courtyard (15th c.) and wall paintings; inside there are 15th c. frescoes.

*Castle of Fénis

12 km/7½ miles: Nus (529 m/1746 ft), a village at the mouth of the Vallée de St Barthélemy, with a ruined castle. On the slope above, to the left, the village of St Marcel (631 m/2082 ft), at the mouth of the valley of the same name, comes into sight.
12 km/7½ miles: —see Aosta.

Sarre
Val de Cogne

6 km/4 miles: Sarre (631 m/2082 ft), is a village with a castle of 1710. This is a good base for a pleasant detour (28 km/17 miles south), up the Val de Cogne, past the castle of Aymavilles with its four towers (16th–17th c.; restored) and up the monotonous valley high above the ravine of the roaring Grand'Eyvie. Far below can be seen the Pont d'El, with a Roman aqueduct of the Augustan period, 120 m/396 ft above the stream. The road then continues to Cogne (1534 m/5062 ft), the chief town in the valley which is popular both as a summer and a winter holiday resort (iron mine; tunnel 6 km/3½ miles long on a mine railway to Aosta). From here there is a beautiful view to the south of Gran Paradiso (4061 m/13,401 ft; the climb by way of Valsavarenche takes 17 hours with guide) and to the north-west of Mont Blanc. Lift to Mont Cuc (2075 m/6848 ft).

Cogne
*Gran Paradiso
National Park

Cogne is a good base for climbing expeditions, particularly in the fascinating Gran Paradiso National Park (Parco Nazionale de Gran Paradiso; 600 sq. km/231 sq. miles; perimeter 180 km/112 miles; many ibexes and other animals), which occupies the northern part of the Graian Alps.

Saint Pierre

Beyond Sarre the road continues past the castles of Saint-Pierre (17th c.; inside is the Scientific Museum with records of animals and plants, found in the Aosta valley), Sarriod de La Tour (14th c.) and the Tour

Autumn in the Gran Paradiso National Park

Colin (13th c.). It then passes the junctions of the Val de Rhêmes and the Val Grisanche which run south to the French frontier, and enters the wild defile of Pierre Taillée (waterfalls); beyond this, on the hillside to the right, is the village of La Salle (1001 m/3303 ft), with the castle of Châtelard (1171 m/3864 ft; 13th c.); ahead the towering mass of Mont Blanc can be seen.

22 km/13 miles: Morgex (920 m/3036 ft).

4 km/2 ½ miles: Pré-Saint-Didier (1004 m/3313 ft), a picturesquely situated village, has an arsenical chalybeate spring (36 °C) at the point where the Thuile forces its way through precipitous cliffs into the Dora valley.

Pré-Saint-Didier

Excursion:
At Pré-Saint-Didier S.S. 26 leaves the Aosta valley and runs south-west to La Thuile (1441 m/4755 ft), the starting point for climbing the glaciated Rutor (3486 m/11,504 ft; 7–8 hours, with guide), passing the Rutor Falls (1934 m/6382 ft). From Gollette (1496 m/4937 ft) there is a cableway south-west to Les Suches (2180 m/7194 ft; mountain hut) and then a chair-lift to Mont Chaz Dura (2581 m/8517 ft).

La Thuile
Rutor

The road then continues for another 13 km/8 miles, with many bends and magnificent retrospective views to reach the Italian-French frontier at the little Lac Verney and the Little St Bernard Pass (2188 m/7220 ft). Until 1947 the frontier was 2 km/1 mile farther south.
Beyond Pré-Saint-Didier the Aosta valley road passes below the village of Verrand (1263 m/4168 ft), with fine panoramic views.

Little St Bernard

5 km/3 miles: Courmayeur (1224 m/4039 ft), a major tourist centre (particularly for winter sports enthusiasts), with mineral springs (chalybeate; spa establishments) lies at the foot of the Mont Blanc massif (Alpine Museum). A chain of cableways leads from here first up to the Plan Chécrouit (1704 m/5623 ft), from there to the Lago Chécrouit (2256 m/7445 ft), then to the Cresta de Youla (2624 m/8659 ft) and finally to the Cresta d'Arp (2755 m/9092 ft); there is also a cableway to the Pré de Pascal (1912 m/6310 ft) and a cabin cableway to the Val Vény.

Courmayeur

4 km/2½ miles beyond Courmayeur is Entrèves (1306 m/4310 ft), a magnificently situated village with open views of Mont Blanc to the north-west and the Dent du Géant (4014 m/13,246 ft) and the Grandes Jorasses (4206 m/13,880 ft) to the north-east; there is an even finer prospect 2 km/1 mile west from the pilgrimage church of Notre-Dame de la Guérison (1486 m/4901 ft; striking close view of the Brenva glacier). From La Palud (1 km/⅔ mile north-east) there is a very attractive drive (15 km/9 miles) with three cableways (1½ hours) by way of the Pavillon du Mont Fréty (2130 m/7029 ft) and the Rifugio Torino (3322 m/10,963 ft; view!), below the Col du Géant (3354 m/11,068 ft), then by the Punta Helbronner (3462 m/11,425 ft; passport control) to the Gros Rognon (3448 m/11,378 ft) and to the Aiguille du Midi (3842 m/12,679 ft; view!) and so on to Chamonix.

Entrèves

Mont Blanc (in Italian: Monte Bianco, 4810 m/15,873 ft), the highest peak in the Alps, over which the Italian-French frontier runs was first climbed in 1786 by Jacques Balmat of Chamonix and the village doctor, Michel Paccard; then in 1787 again by the Geneva scientist Horace-Bénédict de Saussure, accompanied by Balmat and 16 porters. The best starting point for the climb (10-12 hours, with guide) is Les Houches, a village 10 km/6 miles south-west of Chamonix.

**Mont Blanc

The construction of the Mont Blanc Tunnel (Galleria del Monte Bianco; boring completed 1962; opened to traffic 16 July 1965) is very important, particularly for tourist traffic. The tunnel begins at Entrèves

*Mont Blanc
Tunnel

(altitude 1381 m/4557 ft) above sea-level, and ends 11.6 km/7¼ miles farther on at an altitude of 1274 m/4204 ft above the hamlet of Les Pèlerins, a suburb of Chamonix. The tunnel (toll), which is open throughout the year, shortens the journey from Italy to western Switzerland and central and northern France by several hundred kilometres during the period from October to June when the high Alpine passes are closed.

Apennines/Appennino   F-N5–12

Situation

The Apennines (from the Celtic word "pen" = mountain) are the mountain range 1400 km/868 miles long and 30–150 km/19–93 miles wide, which extends in a long arc down the whole length of the Italian peninsula from the Alps at the Ligurian Gulf to the south-west tip of Calabria and continues into Sicily.

History and landscape

As a result of late folding during the early Tertiary period the outer side of the range facing the Po plain and the Adriatic has a more gradual slope, composed of sedimentary rocks, while the inner side, in consequence of later collapses, slopes down in a steeper scarp to the sea and the basins of Tuscany, Umbria and eastern Latinum. The northern Apennines, reaching their highest point in Monte Cimone (2163 m/7138 ft), and the Central Apennines have more regular slopes and continuous summit ridges, which are crossed by several traffic routes at heights of between 650 and 1300 m/2145 and 4290 ft. The rocks are mainly of Cretaceous and Tertiary date. There are large expanses of sandstones and schists, clays and marls, with rounded summits and gentle slopes with only little variation, though when soaked with rain they are very vulnerable to landslides ("frane"). Sharper contours are produced by the dolomites and limestones, which have developed into rugged and contorted karstic land-forms, particularly in the Monti Sibillini (2478 m/8177 ft) and the wild Abruzzi, which reach their highest point in the Gran Sasso d'Italia (2914 m/9616 ft). The lower Neapolitan Apennines, abutting at its southern end of the Abruzzi and the Lucanian Apennines run slowly into the Calabrian Apennines, in which the landscape pattern from the Crati valley onwards is formed by ancient rocks such as granites, gneisses and micaceous schists; the Sila range (1929 m/6366 ft) and the Aspromonte (1956 m/6455 ft) with their beautiful forests of deciduous and coniferous trees are reminiscent of the upland regions of central Europe.

Climate

The climate of the Apennines is relatively harsh at higher altitudes. Rainfall in the northern Apennines is very high, while in the lower areas the aridity of the Mediterranean climate predominates. At the foot of the hills there are numerous mineral springs. The water-level of the rivers is irregular.

Flora and fauna

At the foot of the Apennines the flora is of Mediterranean type, with edible chestnuts and fruit-trees. Above this is a zone of open forests, with beeches predominantly at the lower levels and conifers higher up. Long human occupation, however, has destroyed many of the original forests, which have been replaced over large areas by an evergreen macchia. In consequence there is an almost total absence of the larger fauna; the wolf is a protected species here. At heights above 1800 m/5940 ft the slopes are covered with carpets of stones.

Population

Within the mountaineous area settlement is confined to the basins and valleys. The principal occupations are stock-farming (goats and sheep), some modest arable farming and forestry.

Apulia/Puglia

Region: Puglia
Provinces: Bari (BA), Brindisi (BR), Foggia (FG), Lecce (LE) and
Taranto (TA)
Area: 19,347 sq. km/7468 sq. miles
Population: 3,978,100

The region of Apulia (in Italian Puglia or Puglie) consists of the pro-   Situation
vinces of Bari, Brindisi, Foggia, Lecce and Taranto; it lies east of the
Apennines, in the south-east of Italy, and extends as far as the spur (the
Gargano hills) and the heel of the Italian boot, the Salentine peninsula.

The northern part of the region is occupied by the plain round Foggia,   Scenery
the Tavoliere di Puglia, at the east end of which are the limestone hills
of the Gargano promontory (Monte Calvo; 1055 m/3482 ft). In the
centre is the karstic limestone plateau, with numerous caves and swal-
low-holes, of the Murge (altitude up to 680 m/2244 ft), which merges in
the south into the varied terrain, partly flat and partly hilly, of the
Salentine peninsula (up to 200 m/660 ft).

Apulia is a purely agricultural region, its main crops being wheat on the   Economy
Tavoliere, tobacco around Lecce, vegetables on the coast; other important agricultural products are grapes (wine and eating), almonds, figs
and olives. The itinerant grazing economy which once played an important part is now confined to a few karstic hill regions. Large-scale water
supply schemes (the 3600 km/2232 miles long "Aquedotto Pugliese"
through the Apennines, partly in a tunnel) have promoted considerable
development of agriculture in this very dry but fertile region. There is
fishing on the coast (around Bari); in recent years modest industries,
particularly petro-chemicals, have been established here.

In ancient times the name of Apulia was confined to the Gargano hills.   History
The region was conquered by the Romans in 272 B.C. and together with
Calabria became Regio II, which played an important part in Roman
trade with the East. After the fall of the Roman Empire Apulia passed
into the hands of the Ostrogoths and later the Byzantines, and in 568
part of it was occupied by the Lombards. Robert Guiscard conquered it
for the Normans from 1141 onwards and was granted it as a fief by
Pope Nicholas II. Under Roger II it was united with the kingdom of
Naples and Sicily and enjoyed a period of high prosperity under the
Staufen dynasty. Foggia was a favourite residence of Frederick II, also
known as "Child of Pulli", who left behind him fine buildings and objets
d'art, foremost among them the Castel del Monte. Apulia was united
with Italy in the 19th c.

** Zona dei Trulli

Every tourist should visit the Trulli country (Zona dei Trulli), an area of
some 1000 sq. km/386 sq. miles in the Murge region dominated by
thousands of the curious dwellings called "trulli", which are small
round stone-built houses, often linked together in groups, with conical
roofs of overlapping courses of stone (cf. the nuraghi of Sardinia).

The area takes in several towns: Alberobello (428 m/1412 ft; pop.   Alberobello
10,000), a picturesque little town with more than 1000 trulli in the Zona
Monumentale, including the church of Sant'Antonio, a modern building built in trullo style, and the two-storey Trullo Sovrano in the north of
the town, the largest in Alberobello.

75

Apulia/Puglia

Locorotondo	The little town of Locorotondo (410 m/1353 ft; pop.13,000) is circular in plan.
Martina Franca	Martina Franca (431 m/1422 ft; pop. 44,000) is a town with charming Baroque buildings, for example the Palazzo Ducale (1669) and the collegiate church of San Martino (18th c.).
Cisternino Fasano	Two other towns in the Zona dei Trulli are Cisternino (394 m/1302 ft; pop. 12,000) and Fasano (118 m/389 ft; pop. 37,000). Also worth visiting is the park outside Fasano (1 km/³⁄₄ mile) which occupies an area of 80,000 sq. m. More than 600 animals (including lions) can be seen here. Close to Egnazia, 9 km/5 miles north of Fasano, is one of the most important Apulian sites.
*Valle d'Itria	Between Locorotondo and Martina Franca is the Valle d'Itria, also with numerous trulli.
Ostuni	At the southern end of the Zona dei Trulli close to the sea is Ostuni (218 m/719 ft; pop. 32,000), a picturesque little town with white, rustic houses; on a hill stands the late Gothic cathedral (15th c.).

**Grotte di Castellana

Monopoli	To the north of the Zona dei Trulli, 15 km/9 miles south-west of the port of Monopoli (9 m/30 ft; pop. 45,000), which has an 18th c. cathedral, are the caves of Castellana (tours); they rank with the Postojna caves in Yugoslavia as the finest stalactitic caves in Europe. The caves have a total length of approximately 1.2 km/³⁄₄ mile – much more if the various ramifications are included (two lifts). The finest cave is the Grotta Bianca (special conducted tours), unsurpassed in Europe for its perfect condition and its profusion of stalagmites and stalactites. Above the cave is an lookout tower (28 m/92 ft high, 170 steps); nearby a cave museum.

Valle d'Itria

Castel del Monte (Apulia)

See Barletta

L'Aquila

Region: Abruzzi. Province: L'Aquila (AQ)
Altitude: 615–721 m/2093–2379 ft
Population: 65,000

L'Aquila, capital of the Central Italian region of the Abruzzi and of the province of l'Aquila, lies beyond the Aterno valley, surrounded by the mighty limestone heights of the Abruzzi. It is the see of an archbishop.
Situation

L'Aquila was founded about 1240 by the Hohenstaufen emperor Frederick II as a protection against the rebellious tribes of the Abruzzi. Charles I of Anjou surrounded the town with walls which are partly preserved.
History

Piazza del Duomo

In the centre of the town is the spacious Piazza del Duomo, on the west side of which is the cathedral of San Massimo, (originally built in the 13th c.; several times destroyed by earthquakes and rebuilt). It contains (to the right of the entrance) a monumental effigy of Cardinal Agnifili (1480).
Cathedral

To the north is the little church of San Giuseppe, with the tomb of the Camponeschi family (1432) by Gualterius di Alemania (Walter of Germany).
San Giuseppe

L'Aquila: Castello

Façade of Church of San Bernadino

Rose window Santa Maria di Collemaggio

Palace of Margaret of Parma

Also north of the cathedral, in Piazza del Palazzo, is the former Palace of Margaret of Parma (1573; campanile), now occupied by the Court of Appeal.

Churches east of the town

*San Bernardino

South-east of Piazza del Palazzo is the porticoed street intersection known as the Quattro Cantoni, in the Corso Vittorio Emanuele II, the town's principal street. From here Via San Bernardino leads to the church of San Bernardino (originally 1454), with a fine façade of 1527. It contains the tomb of Bernardino di Siena who died in l'Aquila in 1440.

*Santa Maria di Collemaggio

From San Bernardino we descend to the piazza, follow Via Fortebraccio straight ahead and continue through the Porta Bazzano to the magnificent church, formerly belonging to the Celestine order, of Santa Maria di Collemaggio, founded about 1280 by Pietro da Morrone, who was crowned here as Pope Celestine V in 1294. The church has a Baroque interior, with the Pope's Renaissance tomb (1517) and wall paintings by Ruter, a pupil of Rubens, depicting his life and deeds.

Parco del Castello

Museum Nazionale d'Abruzzo

In the north-east of the town is the Parco del Castello with the beautiful Fontana Monumentale. From here there are far-ranging views of the Aterno valley and the Gran Sasso and Maiella range. On the east side of the park is the Castello, built by the Spaniards in 1534, which now houses the Museo Nazionale d'Abruzzo (National Museum of the Abruzzi; entrance on the east side), with medieval and modern art as well as arts and crafts. Particularly notable is its collection of Abruzzi majolica (17th–18th c.) from Castelli.

*Fontana delle 99 Cannelle

At the foot of the hill on the west side of the town, near the station and the Porta Rivera, is the Fontana delle 99 Cannelle (Fountain of the 99 Pipes; 1272), with sides of red and white marble, from which the water spouts through 99 different masks (male and female heads).

Amiternum

North of L'Aquila are the remains of the ancient city of Amiternum, which was first occupied by the Sabines and later by the Romans, with remains of a theatre, an amphitheatre and baths.

Situation
10 km/6 miles north

*Gran Sasso d'Italia

The route to the Gran Sasso d'Italia first passes the cemetery, with the convent church of Santa Maria del Soccorso, and then continues via the village of Assergi (church of Santa Maria Assunta, with a fine Gothic rose window), on the south-west slopes of the Gran Sasso group, to Fonte Cerreto (1105 m/3547 ft), starting point of the cableway to the Gran Sasso d'Italia (3240 m/3545 yds long; 16 minutes). A panoramic road (27 km/17 miles) leads to the upper station of the cableway (2130 m/7029 ft), on the western edge of the Campo Imperatore (1600–2200 m/5280–7260 ft; Albergo Campo Imperatore), a high valley 20 km/12 miles long and up to 5 km/3 miles wide which is an excellent walking and climbing centre and a popular winter sports area. Near the cableway station are the modern chapel of the Madonna della Neve and an observatory. 45 minutes' climb above the hotel, on the Portelle ridge, is the Rifugio Duca degli Abruzzi (2301 m/7587 ft; views) from which it is another 3½–4 hours climb to the Corno Grande or Monte Corno (2912 m/9610 ft), the highest peak in the Gran Sasso d'Italia, the most elevated mountain range in the Italian peninsula, with sheer rock walls like those of the Calcareous Alps (road tunnel). From the summit there are views extending over the whole of Central Italy to the Adriatic in the east and over the Sabine hills, and on clear days as far as the Tyrrhenian Sea in the west.

Situation
48 km/30 miles
north-east

Avezzano

Another worth-while trip is from L'Aquila to Avezzano. The road winds up the north-east slopes of Monte d'Orce (2206 m/7280 ft), with many bends and fine retrospective views, and continues through the wide high valley between Monte Velino on the right and Monte Sirente on the left, with a number of villages which are popular summer and winter resorts. It then winds its way downhill, with attractive views of the little town of Celano (800 m/2640 ft), with the ruins of an old church and a castle (Castello Piccolomini), and the wide Fucino basin. Avezzano lies in the western part of the Fucino basin (see Abruzzi).

Situation
62 km/38 miles south

From Celano an excursion can be made to a wild gorge, the Gole di Celano by taking the Sulmona road south for 1.5 km/1 mile or to the Abruzzi National Park (see Abruzzi), then by a footpath on the left (15 minutes).

Aquileia

K4

Region: Friuli-Venezia Giulia. Province: Udine (UD)
Altitude: 5 m/17 ft. Population: 3400

Aquileia

Situation

Aquileia lies in central Italy – west of the place where the River Isonzo, flowing down from the Alps, flows into the Adriatic.

History

Founded by the Romans in 181 B.C. as a defensive post against the Celts, Aquileia became one of the great cities of ancient Italy, a major trading centre in the Gulf of Trieste and from the 6th c. the seat of a Patriarch. Later it lost its importance.

Sights

**Cathedral

The most important monument of this great past is the cathedral, built at the beginning of the 11th c. on the site of an earlier church and remodelled in Gothic style at the end of the 14th c. It has a fine interior with a mosaic pavement (depicting humans, animals and plants) from the original church (4th c.). There are also a fine Renaissance pulpit and remains of 11th c. frescoes in the apse. At the main entrance is an Easter Sepulchre (11th c.) and close by the entrance to the Cripta degli Scavi can be seen 3rd c. mosaics.

From the 73 m/241 ft high belltower (11th and 14th c.) there are far-ranging views.

Museo
Paleocristiano

From the military cemetery behind the chancel of the cathedral the Via Sacra, lined by cypresses, runs 700 m/765 yds north to the recent excavations of the Roman river harbour. A little way north-east is the Museo Paleocristiano with funeral urns, etc.; to the west the Forum (partly reconstructed).

To the west of the cathedral are the meagre remains of an amphitheatre, the Roman street of tombs, a Roman mausoleum (reconstructed) and a number of partly excavated oratories with well-preserved mosaic pavements.

Aquileia: Roman forum

South-west of the cathedral is the Museo Archeologico, containing
Roman material recovered by excavations, among which are precious
stones, amber and glass (in the courtyard are many pyramidal
ash-urns).

Grado

South of Aquileia, on the spit of land south of the lagoon, the popular
seaside resort of Grado (2 m/7 ft; pop. 9650) can be found. Half way
along the spit of land is the little fishing port, to the north lies the
harbour canal, to the east, along the beautiful sandy beach (3 km/2
miles long; hot sand baths), is the hotel and villa quarter. Grado came
into being as the resort of Roman Aquileia when the Patriarch fled here
in 568 to escape the Lombards. The cathedral of Sant' Eufemia was
built during this period with a mosaic pavement, a Romanesque pulpit
and a silver frontal (Venetian; 1372). To the left of the cathedral stands
the Baptistery (5th c.), and beyond this the church of Santa Maria delle
Grazie, with a mosaic pavement.

Situation

Palmanova

The little town of Palmanova (26 m/86 ft; pop. 5600) is interesting
because of its urban development. In 1593 it was built as a fort to a
star-shaped nine-sided plan. The town can only be entered through one
of the three gates. The Venetians built Palmanova as a bastion to
protect them from the Habsburgs and the Turks. However, it was
impossible to persuade more than 2000 people to live in this artificial
creation. An informative exhibition of the town's history can be seen in
the Museo Civico Storico (Borgo Udine 4c).

Situation
15 km/9 miles north

Arezzo

H6

Region: Toscana
Province: Arezzo (AR)
Altitude: 296 m/977 ft
Population: 92,000

Arezzo, capital of the province of the same name, lies in north-eastern
Tuscany some 80 km/50 miles south-east of Florence and near the left
bank of the Arno.

Situation

Umbrians and the Etruscans settled on the hill which rises above the
surrounding fertile countryside. The Roman military post was founded
here by Gaius Maecenas (c. 70 B.C.–8 B.C.); he was a friend of Augustus
and used his influence to promote the poets who came to visit the
Emperor's palace.
Arezzo was the birthplace of Guido Monaco (Guido of Arezzo, c. 990–
1050), who invented our system of musical notation, Francesco
Petrarca (1304–1374), the great poet and father of humanism and the
satirical poet Pietro Aretino (1492–1556).

History and art

San Francesco

In the centre of the town is the Gothic church of San Francesco
(13th–14th c.), dedicated to St Francis. The main feature of the church is

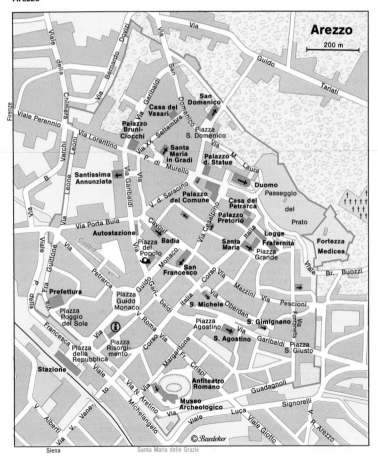

Siena   Santa Maria delle Grazie

the choir chapel with frescoes by Piero della Frances, painted during the period 1453–1464, which depict scenes from the legend of the Cross.

*Pieve di Santa Maria

From San Francesco we go south-east along Via Cavour and then turn left up the Corso Italia to reach the Romanesque church of Pieve di Santa Maria (12th–14th c.) with a late Romanesque façade and a tower (59 m/165 ft) completed in 1332. The principal feature is the polyptychon "Madonna and Saint", a masterpiece by P. Lorenzetti (1320).

*Piazza Grande   Behind the church is the picturesque Piazza Grande, scene of the Giastro del Saracino, the medieval joust performed on the first Sunday in

September. At the west side of the square stands the beautiful Palazzo della Faternità dei Laici (1375–1460), on the north side the Palazzo delle Logge, built in 1573 and named after the loggias which face the piazza. Opposite the west end of the Palazzo delle Logge, in the Corso Italia stands the Palazzo Pretorio (1322); it is decorated with the coats of arms of the former "podestá" (mayors).

Palazzo Pretorio

From the Palazzo Pretorio it is only a short way, skirting a beautiful park, the Passeggio del Prato, to the Via dell' Orto, with Petrarch's birthplace (Casa del Petrarca), on the left.

Casa del Petrarca

From the Casa del Petrarca it is only a few steps to the Palazzo del Comune (Town Hall, 1333, decorated with coats of arms) and from there to the cathedral.

Palazzo del Comune

*Cathedral

The cathedral, a Gothic building begun in 1277, has a modern façade. Inside, behind the high altar, can be seen the Arca di San Donato, a marble tomb of St Donatus, the martyr bishop of Arezzo. The tomb of Guido Tarlati, a warlike bishop of Arezzo (d. 1327), at the east end of the north aisle, is decorated with 16 bas-reliefs. Close to the tomb is a fine fresco by Piero della Francesco, dedicated to St Magdalene.

North of the cathedral stands the Gothic church of San Domenico (13th–14th c.) with a fine campanile; on the high altar is a painted crucifix by Cimabue (1250–1265).

San Domenico

Some 500 m/550 yd north-west of the cathedral, in the Via Garibaldi, is the Palazzo Bruni-Ciocchi, containing the collections of the Galleria e Museo Medioevale e Moderno (Gallery and Museum of Medieval and

Museum of Art

Arezzo: Via della Torre Rossa   *Church of Santa Maria della Pieve*

83

Modern Art) with ceramics, majolicas and paintings (altarpiece by Luca Signorelli, 1520).

*Archaeological Museum

In the south of the town near the remains of the Roman amphitheatre is the Archaeological Museum; it contains a collection of the famous "vasi aretini" (fragments of red clay urns with fine reliefs) and Etruscan reliefs on terracotta, urns, sarcophagi, amphoras and Roman mosaics.

Santa Maria delle Grazie

Some 500 m/550 yd south of the museum, stands the church of Santa Maria delle Grazie (15th c.), dedicated to the Madonna; the colonnaded portico is an Early Renaissance masterpiece.

Ascoli Piceno   K7

Region: Marche
Province: Ascoli Piceno (AP)
Altitude: 154 m/508 ft
Population: 54,000

Situation

Ascoli Piceno, capital of the province of the same name, lies in the southern part of the coastal region of the Marches, in Central Italy, at the confluence of the rivers Castellano and Tronto. The town is some 30 km/19 miles from the Adriatic.

The painter and architect Cola Filotesia dell'Amatrice worked here between 1519 and 1542.

Piazza del Popolo

The centre of the town is the picturesque Piazza del Popolo, in which the "Torneo cavalleresco della Quintana", a medieval joust preceded by a parade with musical accompaniment, is held on the first Sunday in August. In the Piazza is the Palazzo dei Capitani del Popolo (13th c., remodelled in 16th c.).

*San Francesco

On the north side of the Piazza del Popolo, here traversed by the Corso Mazzini, the long principal street of the town, stands the Gothic hall-church of San Francesco (1258–1371) with a doorway in Venetian Gothic style, and linked to it the crenellated Loggia dei Mercanti (covered market; 1513). On the north side are two beautiful cloisters.

Some 300 m/330 yd north-west of the Piazza del Popolo are the Romanesque church of Santi Vincenzo e Anastasio (11th c.) with a façade of 64 square compartments, and the church of San Pietro Martire.

Ponte Romano Augustea

Farther north-west Via di Solestà leads to the Ponte Romano Augustea, a Roman bridge over the Tronto. A little way south-west stands the Palazzetto Longobardo (10th c.?) and adjoining it the Torre Ercolani, a tower 40 m/132 ft high.

Porta Gémina

At the west end of the Corso Mazzini, in the Piazza di Cecco, is the Porta Gémina (1st c. B.C.), a double gate through which in Roman times the Via Salaria entered the town; nearby can be seen the remains of a Roman amphitheatre.

Piazza dell'Arringo

Palazzo Comunale (Museum)

A little way south-east of the Piazza del Popolo is the Piazza dell'Arringo with the massive Palazzo Comunale (Town Hall; 1683-1745), which houses a Museum of Art containing paintings by Cola dell'Amatrice, Crivelli and Titian, etc. and a very valuable cope (worn by Catholic priests during the ritual duties) which was presented to the cathedral of Ascoli Piceno by Pope Nicholas IV in 1288.

On the east side of the square is the Cathedral of Sant'Emidio, originally an Early Romanesque building, which has been altered several times. The façade is attributed to Cola dell'Amatrice. In the large chapel in the south aisle is an altarpiece by Crivelli (1473).

Cathedral

To the left, adjoining the cathedral, is the Early Romanesque baptistery, an octagonal building.

*Baptistery

From the Piazza dell'Arringo the Corso Vittorio Emanuele runs east past the municipal park to the medieval bridge over the Castellano, the Ponte Maggiore. From here there is a fine view to the left of the Monte dell'Ascensione (1103 m/3640 ft) and to the right of the Ponte di Cecco, a two-arched Roman bridge (restored after destruction in the Second World War).

Bridges

Close by the Ponte di Cecco is the picturesque Forte Malatesta (1348).

Forte Malatesta

Sights in the south-west

Above the town to the south-west rises the monastic church of the Santissima Annunziata (views). There are even more extensive views from the castle "Fortezza Pia" (16th c.), farther to the west.

Monte Piselli

A road runs south from Ascoli Piceno and winds its way up to the Colle San Marco (694 m/2290 ft). 5 km/3 miles farther south, beyond the Rigugio Paci (905 m/2987 ft) is the starting point of the cableway up the Monte Piselli (1676 m/5531 ft). From the summit there are magnificent views, on a clear day as far as the Dalmatian coast of Yugoslavia.

Situation
20 km/12 miles

Assisi

Region: Umbria
Province: Perugia (PG)
Altitude: 403–500 m/1330–1815 ft
Population: 25,000

Assisi lies some 14 km/9 miles south-east of Perugia in the medieval region of Umbria. The town, the ancient Umbrian city of Asisium, is situated on artificial terraces on a westerly outlier of the Monte Subasio.

Situation and
importance

The town, one of the most important places of pilgrimage in Italy, owes its fame to St Francis, born here in 1182, the son of a wealthy merchant, who after spending his early years in a life of dissipation devoted himself to the service of the poor and the sick, founded the Franciscan order and died in 1226 in poverty and abstinence. His life, around which are many legends, has inspired major works from famous artists (including Giotto).

With its well-preserved medieval streets and houses and its treasures of art Assisi is one of Italy's great tourist sights.

St Francis of Assisi

Franciscan convent

North-west of the town on the edge of the hill rises the Franciscan convent with its massive substructures. Building began soon after the

Assisi

Panorama of Assisi

Assisi: Basilica of San Francesco

saint's death. The courtyard and the external passage, from which there are magnificent views, were renewed by Pope Sixtus IV (1471–1484).

Part of the convent is the impressive two-storeyed church, the Basilica di San Francesco, built over St Francis's tomb. The dark lower church has squat Late Romanesque vaulting (1228–1253) and a vestibule added in 1488, the upper church, completed in 1253, is Italy's earliest Gothic church.

**Basilica di San Francesco

Both churches are decorated with beautiful frescoes (13th–14th c.). In the first chapel of the lower church remarkable scenes from the life of St Francis by Giotto and Simone Martini can be seen. In the choir of the upper church and in the transepts there are frescoes by Cimabue, in the nave 28 scenes from the life of St Francis by Giotto and his pupils. In the crypt, added in 1818 and enlarged in 1925–1932 can be seen a stone sarcophagus, containing the saint's remains. In the large cloister is the treasury.

*Frescoes

South of the convent, beyond the Porta San Francesco, stands the church of San Pietro, with a fine doorway.

San Pietro

*Piazza del Comune

Leaving the lower church we go uphill to the left into the Via San Francesco and its continuation which lead to the Piazza del Comune, the town's main square, built on the site of the Roman forum.

On the left is the portico of the Temple of Minerva, perhaps dating from the Augustan period, which was converted into the church of Santa Maria della Minerva.

*Temple of Minerva

Near the temple stands the Palazzo del Capitano del Popolo (13th c.) with a tower.

At the end of the square, on the right, is the Palazzo Comunale or Palazzo dei Priori (Town Hall; 14th c.) with the municipal picture gallery (Pinacoteca).

Palazzo Comunale (Pinacoteca)

A little way south, on a lower level, is the Chiesa Nuova (1615), a small church on a centralised plan, erected, it is said, on the site of St Francis's birthplace.

Chiesa Nuovo

San Rufino

From the Piazza del Comune the Via di San Rufino leads east to the cathedral of San Rufino (12th–13th c.), with a beautiful façade.

South of the cathedral, in the Piazza Santa Chiara, stands the Gothic church of Santa Chiara (1257). Under the high altar is the open tomb of St Clare (d. 1253), the enthusiastic disciple of St Francis who founded the order of Clarissines or Poor Clares.

*Santa Chiara

Rocca Maggiore

From the Piazza di San Rufino the old Via Santa Maria delle Rose ascends to the Rocca Maggiore, a castle high above the town, (re-built by Cardinal Albornoz in 1365) in which the Emperor Frederick II sometimes stayed during his youth. From here there are panoramic views.

Convento di San Damiano

South-east of the town centre is the little convent of San Damiano (305 m/1007 ft), founded by St Francis, of which St Clare was the first abbess. On the small terrace, gay with flowers, in front of the

Situation
2 km/1½ miles
south-east

convent, St Francis is said to have composed his famous "Canticle of the Sun".

Santa Maria degli Angeli

Situation
6 km/4 miles south
** Church

South of Assisi on the S.S. 75, is the small village of Santa Maria degli Angeli (218 m/719 ft). The church of the same name, a massive domed structure in Renaissance style, built between 1569–1630 over St Francis' oratory (Porziúncola) and the cell in which he died. The nave and choir were re-erected after the earthquake in 1832 and the church was provided with a new façade in 1925–1928.

To the east of the sacristy is a small garden, in which it is said the roses have been thornless since an act of penance by the saint. Adjacent is the Cappella delle Rose with fine frescoes by Tiberio d'Assisi (1518), depicting scenes from the saint's life.

Le Carceri near Assisi

Situation
4 km/2½ miles east
of Assisi

East of Assisi, charmingly situated in a small wood of holm-oaks above a ravine between the bare rock faces of Monte Subasio, is the hermitage of Le Carceri (791 m/2610 ft), to which St Francis retired for his devotional exercises. The convent dates from the 14th c.; visitors are also shown the saint's rock-bed.

From the convent it is an hour and a half's climb to the broad ridge of Monte Subasio (1290 m/4257 ft; panoramic views).

Asti   E5

Region: Piemonte
Province: Asti (AT)
Altitude: 123 m/406 m
Population: 76,500

Situation

Asti, the Roman Asta, lies in the valley of the Tarano, some 55 km/34 miles from Turin.
The town, seat of a bishop and one of the most powerful city-republics of northern Italy in the Middle Ages, lies in the very fertile wine-producing area of the Montferrato, which is particularly known for its sparkling wine, Asti Spumante.

Sights

* Baptistery of San
Pietro

At the east end of the Corso Vittorio Alfieri, the principal street of the town, are the Romanesque baptistery of San Pietro (12th c.) and the former church of San Pietro in Consavia (1467), decorated with beautiful terracotta. The cloister and other parts of the church house the Archaeological and Paleontological Museum.
Near the Town Hall stands the Romanesque-Gothic church of Chiesa de San Secondo (13th–15th c.) with a notable crypt (7th c.).

Palazzo Alfieri

In the western part of the main street can be found the Palazzo Alfieri (museum); inside is the room in which the dramatist Vittorio Alfieri (1749–1803) was born.

Near the Palazzo Alfieri is the Romanesque-Gothic cathedral, built 1309–1348 on the site of an earlier church. It has a brick façade, and the south doorway is decorated with statues. The spacious interior contains Baroque paintings. The Romanesque campanile originates from 1266. On the north side of the cathedral is the Baroque church of San Giovanni with a 9th c. crypt.

Cathedral

In Asti there are a number of tower-houses belonging to noble families, among them the Torre Troiana and the Torre dei Comentini, both in the west of the town.

Bari

Region: Puglia
Province: Bari (BA)
Altitude: 4 m/13 ft
Population: 368,000

Bari, capital of the region of Apulia and the province of the same name, lies in southern Italy – on the Adriatic coast. It is the largest city in Apulia and the second largest in southern Italy after Naples.
The port of Bari, a leading commercial and industrial centre (petro-chemicals and shipbuilding), is particularly important by virtue of its trade with the eastern Mediterranean. It is also the see of an archbishop and possesses a university and a naval college.

Situation and importance

The picturesque old town, with its narrow winding streets, frequently spanned by arches, lies to the north, on a promontory between the old and new harbours. To the south is the spacious and regularly planned new town, which has developed considerably since 1930, when the Levant Fair was first held here.

The ancient Barium was a place of little importance. Until it was captured by Robert Guiscard in 1071 it was used by the Byzantines as their main base in southern Italy. From 1324 it was an almost independent fief which finally passed to the kingdom of Naples in 1558.

History

New town

The centre of the new town is the palm-shaded Piazza Umberto I. On its west side is the imposing building of the university, with a well-stocked library (160,000 volumes), and the interesting Museo Archeologico Nazionale.

Museo Archeologico Nazionale

From the north side of the square the new town's principal traffic artery, Via Sparano, coming from the station, runs north past the modern church of San Ferdinando into the busy Corso Vittorio Emanuele II, which separates the new town from the old. 100 m/110 yds along the Corso Vittorio Emanuele II to the left is the Piazza della Libertà, the traffic centre of the town. On the right is the prefecture, on the left the Town Hall, which also houses the Teatro Piccinni.
From the east end of the Corso Vittorio Emanuele II the Corso Cavour, lined with fine buildings, leads towards the station.

Town Hall

The east end of the Corso Vittorio Emanuele II is also the starting point of the Lungomare Nazario Sauro, a magnificent seafront promenade which runs along the old harbour.

*Lungomare Nazario Sauro

Bari

Pinacoteca
Provinciale

1 km/¾ mile southwards along the Lungomare Nazario Sauro is the palace of the provincial administration in which is the picture gallery (Pinacoteca Provinciale). Most of the pictures are older scenes of Bari and the surrounding area, together with works by Moretto da Brescia, A. Vaccaro, C. Maratta, Giovanni Bellini, Vivarini, Paolo Veronese, Tintoretto, etc.

Old town

*San Sabino

In the centre of the old town rises the cathedral of San Sabino (originally 1170–1178), with important remains of Norman ornaments. In the crypt is an elaborately adorned painting of the Madonna; the archives include two parts of a large exsultet roll (the Catholic Easter liturgy; 11th c.).

**San Nicola

A little way north of the cathedral is the church of San Nicola, a large pilgrimage church begun in 1087 but not completed until the 13th c., which is one of the finest achievements of Romanesque architecture in Apulia.

Inside, above the high altar, is a tabernacle (12th c.) and to the right of the altar is a "Madonna with Saints" by Vivarini (1476). In the apse is the tomb (1593) of Bona Sforza, wife of King Sigismund II of Poland and last duchess of Bari (d. 1558) and a marble bishop's throne. The crypt with 26 different columns contains a silver altar (1684) underneath which is a vault containing the remains of the popular Saint Nicholas of Bari (c. 350), patron of seamen, prisoners, pupils and children (principal feast 8 May). It was brought here from Myra in Lycia (Asia Minor). The church has also a remarkable treasury.

San Gregorio

Beside San Nicola stands the little church of San Gregorio (11th c.) with richly decorated windows.

San Nicola

To the west of the old town is the Castello, originally a Byzantine-Romanesque building, reconstructed by Frederick II in 1233. Bona Sforza converted it into a palace in the 16th c.; later it was used as a prison and signal station. The building now houses an interesting museum with copies of Apulo-Norman sculptures (temporary art exhibitions).

Castello (Museum)

From the Castello the wide Corso Vittorio Veneto runs west past the Great Harbour (Gran Porto or New Harbour) to the grounds of the Levant Fair (Fiera de Levante), 2.5 km/1½ miles away on the seafront.

Great Harbour

From Bari to Gravina di Puglia (55 km/34 miles)

About 15 km/9 miles south-west of Bari is the little town of Bitetto (139 m/459 ft; pop. 9000) with the cathedral of San Michele (14th c), a building in late Apulo Romanesque style.

Bitetto

From here it is another 29 km/18 miles south-west over the Murge plateau to Altamura (478 m/1577 ft; pop. 53,000), a town still partly surrounded by its old walls. There is an imposing cathedral, built by Frederick II in 1231 and renewed in the 14th and 16th c. It has a richly decorated doorway (1312) on the main façade. Inside are a pulpit, a bishop's throne (16th c.) and beautifully carved choir-stalls (1543).

Altamura

About 11 km/7 miles west of Altamura is Gravina di Puglia (338 m/1115 ft; pop. 37,000), picturesquely situated above a deep gorge (gravina) with an interesting cathedral (15th c. choir-stalls), the church of Santa Sofia (tomb of a duchess of Gravina; 1518) and a municipal museum. Outside the town, in a gorge, is the rock-hewn church of San Michele with remains of Byzantine paintings; another rock-hewn church is beyond the viaduct. On a hill north of the town are the ruins of a Hohenstaufen castle, which was built by Frederick II in 1231.

Gravina di Puglia

Bitonto

West of Bari lies Bitonto (118 m/389 ft; pop. 51,000), with well-preserved town walls. In the centre of the old town is the cathedral (c. 1200), perhaps the finest example of Apulian Romanesque architecture. Particularly beautiful are the richly decorated main doorway and the delicately pillared gallery on the south side. Inside there are two fine pulpits. Beneath the church is a crypt supported by 24 columns. East of the cathedral stands the Palazzo Vulpano Sylos (Renaissance court-yard; 1500).

Situation
17 km/10½ miles
west of Bari

Barletta

Region: Puglia
Province: Bari (BA)
Altitude: 15 m/50 ft
Population: 85,000

The busy port of Barletta, one of the principal towns of Apulia, lies on the Adriatic coast between Foggia and Bari.

Situation

Sights

At the junction of Corso Vittorio Emanuele and Corso Garibaldi, Barletta's busiest traffic intersection, stands the church of San Sepolcro

San Sepolcro

Barletta: Emperor Valentinian I (?)   *and Emperor Frederick II (?)*

(end 13th c.), an early Gothic building on the Burgundian model with a rich treasury.

*Bronze statue

In front of the church is a bronze statue, over 5 m/16 ft high, of a Byzantine emperor (perhaps Valentinian I; d. 375), the finest piece of colossal sculpture in bronze from ancient times. The Venetians brought it back from Constantinople to Italy in the 13th c. and left it after a shipwreck on the beach of Barletta.

Museo Comunale

North-east of the church is the Municipal Museum (Museo Comunale) with a picture gallery.

*Santa Maria Maggiore

A little way to the north-east, at the end of the narrow Via del Duorno, the continuation of the Corso Garibaldi, is the cathedral of Santa Maria Maggiore. The façade and the campanile (13th c.) are built in Romanesque style, while the other parts of the building, including the choir, were added in the 14th–15th c. The church contains a tomb of the count of Barby and Mühlingen (d. 1566), with an inscription in German and a fine pulpit and tabernacle (both 13th c.).

Castello

Beyond the cathedral is the massive Castello, originally built by the Hohenstaufens in the 13th c., with four bastions added in 1537.

Sant'Andrea

North-west of the cathedral stands the church of Sant'Andrea with a Romanesque doorway (13th c.).

Porta Marina

On the promontory north of the town is the Porta Marina (1751); to the east of this is the harbour and to the west the bathing beach.

Excursion from Barletta via Castel del Monte (approximately 90 km/56 miles)

Andria

There is an attractive drive south to Castel del Monte. The road comes first in 12 km/7 miles, to Andria, once the favourite residence of the

Castel del Monte

Emperor Frederick II; the crypt of the cathedral contains the tombs of Iolante of Jerusalem (d. 1228) and Isabella of England (d. 1241 at Foggia), the second and third wives of the emperor. The church of Sant'Agostino has a richly decorated doorway (14th c.).

From Andria it is another 18 km/11 miles to the Castel del Monte or Casteldelmonte (540 m/1782 ft), the most imposing Hohenstaufen castle in Italy, built about 1240 as a hunting lodge for Frederick II, probably to his own design. The massive limestone structure, in Early Gothic style, is an exact octagon, with a beautiful courtyard and eight towers; on each floor there are eight rooms of the same size, which originally had rich marble decoration. The rooms on the upper floor, with particularly fine windows, are believed to have been the emperor's apartments. Later the castle served as the prison of his grandsons, the sons of Manfred. From the roof there are panoramic views extending as far as Monte Gargano.

**Castel del Monte

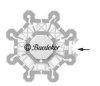

There is another attractive drive west of Castel del Monte (21 km/13 miles) to Minervino Murge (429 m/1416 ft; pop. 14,000), splendidly situated on the highest part of the Murge. Because of the extensive views from here it is also called "Balcony of Apulia". The town has a castle and a small cathedral. In a park outside the town is a large war memorial, the Faro votivo ai Caduti. From the north side of the park there are fine views of the town and surroundings.

Minervino Murge

16 km/10 miles north of Minervino Murge is Canosa di Puglia (105 m/347 ft; pop. 31,000), built on the site of the important Roman town of Canusium. There are remains of Roman walls, a town gate (to the west, outside the modern town) and the ruins of an amphitheatre of some size (near the station). The principal church, San Sabino, contains eighteen ancient columns; in the choir is a marble bishop's throne

Canosa di Puglia

supported by elephants (1078–1089, by Romualdus) and in the nave a marble pulpit (c. 1120). In the court to the south (entered from the south aisle) is the chapel, with a massive bronze door by Rogerius of Melfi, where Prince Boemond of Taranto (d. 1111, ruler of the Latin principality of Antioch) is buried.

Cannae

From Canosa di Puglia it is 22 km/14 miles north-east back to Barletta. About half-way there, off the road to the left, is the cemetery of the ancient town of Cannae, the place where Hannibal defeated the Romans in 216 B.C. (museum; medieval cemetery of the 91th–11th c.).

Basilicata/Lucania   M/N8/10

Region: Basilicata
Province: Potenza (PZ) and Matera (MT)
Area: 9992 sq. km/3858 sq. miles
Population: 617,300

Situation

The region of Basilicata or Lucania, consisting of the provinces of Potenza and Matera, lies in southern Italy. Most of it is occupied by the southern Neapolitan Apennines, with many rivers, mountain chains and table-land. The region is bounded in the north by Apulia, in the south by Calabria and in the west by Campania; it is open to the Tyrrhenian Sea in the Gulf of Policastro and to the Ionian Sea in the Gulf of Taranto.

In spite of the relatively fertile soil, which yields wheat, maize, vines, olives and edible chestnuts, many of the inhabitants of the region still live in poverty.

History

Despite the establishment of Greek colonies and Hellenistic settlements on the coast of the Ionian Sea in the 8th–7th c. B.C. and the fact that the area was later romanised, becoming Regio III of the Roman Empire, Basilicata remained throughout its history an area of only little consequence.

The region suffered severe damage in an earthquake in November 1980.

Potenza

Potenza (819 m/2703 ft), capital of the more westerly province and of the region of Basilicata, lies above the River Basento on a ridge between two valleys. It was severely damaged in an earthquake in 1857 and again during the Second World War, but has since largely been rebuilt. In the centre of the old town (1980 further earthquake damage), on the main street, Via Pretoria, is the Piazza Matteotti; a little way to the north-east stands the 18th c. cathedral. Just off the west end of the Via Pretoria rises the Romanesque church of San Michele (11th c.). To the north of the town the Museo Archeologico Provinciale, with finds from tombs, architectural fragments from the temple of Apollo Lyceus at Metaponto, is worth visiting.

Excursion from Potenza

Rionero in Vulture

There is a rewarding trip along the road which runs N via Castel Lagopesole (756 m/2495 ft) with a well-preserved castle in Gothic style, built by Frederick II about 1242 on an eminence (829 m/2736 ft) west of the former Lake Lagopesole to Rionero in Vulture (656 m/2165 ft; pop. 12,500).

From here it is 6 km/4 miles north-west to Monte Vulture (1330 m/ 4389 ft), an extinct volcano visible from all over Apulia.

10 km/6 miles west of Rionero are the two small lakes of Monticchio (in the double crater of an extinct volcano; 650 m/2145 ft; 35–38 m/116– 125 ft deep); on the smaller lake are the former Capuchin monastery of San Michele and a hydro-electric station. Between the two lakes are the ruins of the abbey of San Ippolito (12th c.). 7 km/4½ miles away, on the western slopes of the Monte Valtura, is the little spa of Monticchio Bagni (540 m/1782 ft).

From Rionero the road continues north 9 km/5½ miles to Rapolla (438 m/1445 ft), a spa (recommended for rheumatism) with a beautiful Gothic cathedral.

From Rapolla a detour (20 km/12 miles east) can be made to Venosa (415 m/1370 ft; pop. 12,000), an ancient Samnite town, from 291 B.C. the Roman colony of Venusia and the birthplace of the poet Horace.

Excavations have brought to light considerable remains of the town dating from the Roman Imperial period. Square stone blocks from the amphitheatre were used in the 12th c. in the construction of the convent of the Santissima Trinità, founded in 1046, which is situated to the north-east of the town. The original church was intended by the Nor- man duke Robert Guiscard (d. 1085) as a family burial place but remained unfinished. It contains 11th c. frescoes, the tomb of Robert Guiscard's wife, Roman inscriptions and fragments of sculpture.

To the north, on the road to the station, are Jewish catacombs (4th–5th c.) with inscriptions in Hebrew, Latin and Greek. In the centre of the town stands a 15th c. castle.

About 6 km/4 miles north-west of Rapolla, on a much-eroded lateral crater of Monte Vulture, is the little town of Melfi (531 m/1752 ft; pop. 16,000), the market town of an extensive wine-producing and olive- growing area. It has a fine 12th c. cathedral, modernised in 1851; adjoining it is the former Archbishop's Palace. The Norman castle above the town houses the Museo Nazionale Archeologica, which contains a magnificent Roman sarcophagus from Rapolla, made in Asia Minor of a Roman lady (A.D. 165–170).

*Monte Vulture

Rapolla

*Venosa

Melfi

Matera

Matera, the chief town of the more easterly province of Basilicata (399 m/1317 ft; see of an archbishop), is picturesquely situated above a rocky gorge. In November 1980 there was severe earthquake damage. Most of the houses in the old town are hewn from the rock and built in tiers on the hillside; they are known as "sassi" but at present most of them are unoccupied. However, it is intended to restore them and use them for public purposes and all kinds of events. On the highest point of the old town stands the 13th c. cathedral with a chapel decorated with sculpture, and containing a 15th c. crib (Nativity group). To the south of the cathedral is the church of San Francesco, with paintings by Vivarine in the apse. North-west of San Francesco, past the old church of San Domenico, is the Romanesque church of San Giovanni Battista (13th c.).

South of San Francesco, in Via Ridola, is the Museo Ridola (prehistoric material from the surrounding area).

The Strada Panoramica runs along the top of the gorge past the church of San Pietro Caveoso to the church of Santa Maria de Idris (Byzantine frescoes), on the rocky hill of Montorrone.

Tavole Palatine, near Metaponto

Metaponto

Near the north-west coast of the Gulf of Taranto is Metaponto, with the remains of the famous Greek city of Metapontion, the Roman Metapontum. The town, probably founded by Archaean settlers at the beginning of the 7th c., became in the 6th c. a centre of Pythagorean teaching, the home of the great mathematician and philosopher Pythagoras, who is said to have died here in 497 B.C. at the age of 90. To the north of the town are the Tavole Palatine, the remains of a Doric temple, with fifteen of the original 32 columns still standing. The Antiquarium can display at any one time only a selection of the rich store of finds recovered in the excavations of recent years. Most of the material comes from the sacred precinct containing the remains of four large temples, which probably collapsed when they were undermined by rising ground-water in the 3rd c. B.C.

A remarkable feature of the area is the carefully planned layout of the fertile plain, with regular field boundaries, roads and water channels and more than 300 Greek farmsteads, eleven of which have been excavated. The theatre (3rd c. B.C.), the walls of which were pulled down and the stones removed at an early period, had a semicircular cavea and Doric columns, anticipating some of the main features of the Roman theatre.

Benevento

L8

Region: Campania
Province: Benevento (BN)
Altitude: 135 m/446 ft
Population: 60,000

Benevento, chief town of its province, lies in Campania, some 50 km/ 31 miles north-east of Naples. The town, beautifully situated on a flat-topped hill between the rivers Savato and Calore, is the economic and communications centre of the fertile Benevento basin.

Situation

The town was originally called Maleventum, but after the "Pyrrhic victory" of King Pyrrhus of Epirus over the Romans in 275 B.C. and the establishment of a Roman military colony in 268 B.C. it was given the more auspicious name of Beneventum. Situated at the junction of the Via Appia with four other Roman roads, it developed into one of the most important towns in southern Italy, and from the 6th to the 11th c. it was the seat of powerful Lombard dukes. Thereafter the town belonged to the Papal State (with a short interruption under Napoleon) until it became part of Italy in 1860.
It has been the see of an archbishop since 969.

History

Sights

The town's principal street, running from north-west to south-east, is the Corso Garibaldi, in which stands the cathedral (founded c. 1200), which was completely destroyed in 1943 apart from the façade and the campanile but has since been rebuilt.

Cathedral

South-west of the cathedral are the remains of a Roman theatre (2nd c. A.D.); operatic performances now take place here.

Teatro Romano

Another 500 m/550 yd south-west is the Ponte Leproso, still incorporating part of the Roman bridge which carried the Via Appia over the Sabato.

Ponte Leproso

East of the cathedral along Corso Garibaldi is the Town Hall, beyond which (to the left, along Via dell'Arco di Traiano) rises the Arch of Trajan (Arco di Traiano), the so-called Porta Aurea, dedicated by the senate and people of Beneventum to the "best of princes" in A.D. 114 in anticipation of his return from the Parthian wars. The arch, built of Greek marble, stands 15.5 m/51 ft high and is excellently preserved. One of the finest of its kind, it is decorated with reliefs glorifying the emperor.

**Arco di Traiano

Farther east along Corso Garibaldi is the Piazza Santa Sofia (officially Piazza Matteotti), where stands the church of Santa Sofia, a circular structure of the Lombard period (760; 12th c. doorway).

Santa Sofia

Adjoining the church is the beautiful cloister of a former convent of Benedictine nuns, now housing the interesting Museo de Sannio, which contains a very fine prehistoric and early historical department, including Samnitic and Greco-Roman finds and Egyptian sculpture, as well as a rich coin collection and medieval and modern pictures.

*Museo del Sannio

Still farther east, in Piazza IV Novembre, is a 14th c. castle, the Rocca dei Rettori, which contains the historical section of the museum. There are fine views from the municipal park.

Rocca dei Rettori

Bergamo   F4

Region: Lombardia
Province: Bergamo (BG)
Altitude: 249–365 m/822–1205 ft
Population: 120,000

The provincial capital of Bergamo lies north-east of Milan at the foot of the Bergamo Alps.

Situation

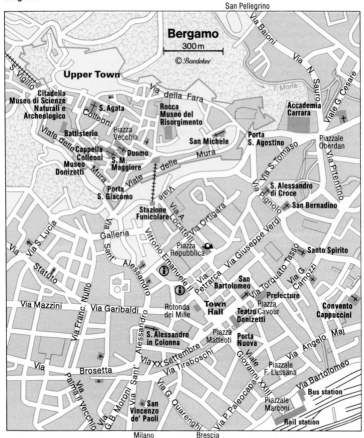

It consists of an old town of narrow winding streets on a hill, defended by bastions erected in the 16th c., and a lower town extending out on to the Po plain with modern buildings and busy industries (textiles, cement, printing).

History

Originally a Gallic settlement and recorded in 200 B.C. as the Roman Municipium Bergomum, the town achieved no great importance until the Lombard period. In 1167 it became a member of the Lombard league of towns; then in 1264 it passed under the control of Milan and from 1427 it belonged to Venice. In 1859 it finally passed to the kingdom of Sardinia.

Lower Town

Piazza Matteotti

The centre of the Lower Town (Città Bassa; 249 m/822 ft) is the Piazza Matteotti, with beautiful gardens, parks and monuments, adjoining

which on the north-west is the imposing Piazza Vittoria Veneto, with the
Torre dei Caduti, a war memorial.

On the south-east side of Piazza Matteotti are the twin neo-classical
gatehouses of the Porta Nuova (view of the upper town), from which
the wide Viale Papa Giovanni XXIII runs south to the station. This street
and the Viale Vittoria Emanuele II, which leads from the Piazza Vittorio
Veneto to the upper town, form Bergamo's principal traffic artery.

Porta Nuova

East of Piazza Matteotti, in the busy avenue called the Sentierone,
stands the Teatro Donizetti and in the east side of the Piazza Cavour is a
monument to the Bergamo-born composer Gaetano Donizetti
(1797–1848).

Teatro Donizetti

At the north-east end of the Sentierone is the church of San Bartolomeo
(17th c.; façade 1901). Inside there are fine choir-stalls and behind the
high altar Lorenzo Lotto's "Madonna with Child and Saints", one of his
chief works.

San Bartolomeo

From San Bartolomeo Via Torquato Tasso runs to the church of the
Santo Spirito, which has another "Madonna" by Lotto (1521) and a
painting by Previtali which depicts John the Baptist and other saints.

Santo Spirito

A short distance north, in the steep Via Pignolo, is the little church of
San Bernardino in Pignolo, with a "Madonna Enthroned" by Lotto
(1521) in the choir. Higher up are a number of palaces with beautiful
Early Renaissance courtyards.

San Bernardino in Pignolo

Accademia Carrara

In Via San Tommaso, which goes off Via Pignolo on the right, is a
palace, housing the Accademia Carrara, with a picture gallery with fine
works by Lorenzo Lotto, Palma il Vecchio, Giovanni Battista Moroni,
Vittore Carpaccio, Jacopo and Giovanni Bellini, Andrea Mantegna,
Girolamo Romani Romanino, Giovanni Battista Tiepolo, Titian, Paolo
Veronese, Raffael Santi, Sandro Botticelli, Luca Signorelli and Carlo
Crivelli as well as works by Albrecht Dürer and Anton van Dyck.
From here a stepped lane leads up to the Porta Sant'Agostino.

Picture Gallery

Upper Town

From Piazza Vittorio Veneto the Viale Vittorio Emanuele II runs past the
lower station of the funicular and through the Porta Sant'Agostino into
the Upper Town (Città Alta, 325–365 m/1073–1205 ft).

Porta Sant'Agostino

From the gate we keep straight ahead, past the church of Sant'Agostino
on the right, and then bear left and continue steeply uphill on the Via di
Porta Dipinta, past the beautiful churches of San Michele al Pozzo
Bianco and Sant'Andrea (inside the latter is a "Madonna Enthroned
with Saints" by Moretto), to the Piazza Mercato delle Scarpe, with the
upper station of the funicular on the left.

Piazza Mercato delle Scarpe

From here Via alla Rocca, to the right, ascends to the Rocca (14th c.), an
old bastion, with the Museo del Risorgimento e della Resistenza (documents of Italy's recent history). From the castle keep and the adjoining
Parco della Rimembranza there are very fine views.

Rocca Museum

From the Piazza Mercato delle Scarpe the narrow Via Gombito, in which
is a patrician tower-house, the Torre di Gombito (c. 1100), leads to the
Piazza Vecchia, which together with the neighbouring Piazza del
Duomo (cathedral square) forms the architecturally impressive centre
of the upper town. Between the two squares is the Palazzo della
Ragione (late 12th c.; largely rebuilt 1538–1554), with an open colonnade. Adjoining is the tall Torre del Comune (lift).

Piazza Vecchia
Palazzo della Ragione

Cathedral doorway and Cappella Colleoni   *Santa Maria Maggiore*

On the north side of the Piazza Vecchia is the Palazzo Nuovo (Municipal Library), a Late Renaissance building.

*Santa Maria Maggiore

In the Piazza del Duomo the church of Santa Maria Maggiore, begun in 1137 as a Romanesque basilica, has a stepped-back tower over the crossing and a picturesque choir. On the south and north sides are doorways guarded by lions, with beautiful Gothic canopies (1353 and 1360). Inside there are fine choir-stalls in Renaissance style.

*Capella Colleoni

Adjoining the church is the Capella Colleoni in early Lombard Renaissance style, with a lavishly decorated marble façade, built 1470–1476 to house the tomb of the condottiere Bartolomeo Colleoni. Inside are the tombs of Colleoni and his daughter Medea (d. 1470), both by Amadeo; ceiling paintings by Tiepolo (1732).

Baptistery

To the right of the Capella Colleoni is the Baptistery (1340), an octagonal building, originally in Santa Maria Maggiore, which was re-erected here in 1898.

Cathedral

Opposite is the cathedral of Sant'Alessandro (1459; choir 1560; dome and façade modern), with fine pictures by Tiepolo, Previtali and Moroni.

Archaeological Museum

From the Piazza Vecchia the narrow Via Colleoni runs north-west to the Citadel, which houses a museum of natural science and archaeology (Museo di Scienze Naturali e Museo Archeologico).

Viale delle Mura

Beyond it is the Porta Sant'Alessandro, from which Viale delle Mura (nearby, on the left, is the Donizetti Museum) leads round the walls (fine views) to the Porta San Giacomo, the most handsome of the town gates, and so back to the Porta Sant'Agostino, the starting point for the walk through the upper town.

San Pellegrino Terme

In the Bergamo Alps is the spa of San Pellegrino Terme (358 m/1181 ft), which also atttracts visitors because of its beautiful situation in the wooded Brembo valley and its equable climate. Its widely renowned alkaline mineral water (recommended for gout and stomach, liver and urinary disorders) comes from three springs (26 °C/79 °F) on the right bank of the Brembo (pump room, Kursaal, casino, theatre). From the Kursaal a funicular runs up in 10 minutes to San Pellegrino Vetta (653 m/2155 ft; restaurant).

Situation
24 km/15 miles north
of Bergamo

Bologna   H5

Region: Emilia-Romagna
Province: Bologna (BO)
Altitude: 55 m/165 ft
Population: 442,000

Bologna, capital of the region Emilia-Romagna and the province Bologna, lies in the fertile Upper Italian plain under the northern end of the Apennines.
The town is the see of an archbishop and has a famous university. It has a character all its own, with its long arcaded streets, its brick-built palaces, its numerous old churches, its curious leaning towers and the remains of its 8 km/5 mile circuit of 13th and 14th c. walls.

Situation

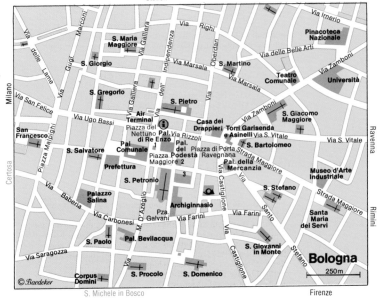

1 Neptune Fountain   2 Palazzo dei Banchi   3 Museo Civico Archeologico

101

Bologna

Economy

Bologna's principal industries are the manufacture of pasta and sausages (particularly mortadella), shoe manufacture, chemicals, engineering, precision instruments and publishing.

The town is also famous for its culinary specialities, chief among them is the meat sauce "à la bolognese".

History

The town, known to the Etruscans as Felsina, became a Roman colony in 189 B.C.; the city centre still shows the regular layout of a Roman camp. It was declared a free city by the Emperor Henry V in 1116, and thereafter became a member of the Lombard League and took an active part in the struggle against the Hohenstaufens. The Imperial School of Bologna, which is said to have been in existence as early as the 5th c., became a university in the 13th c. – the oldest in Europe – and attracted students from many lands; in the 14th c. it pioneered the teaching of human anatomy.

The noble families of the town, who were in constant conflict with the Papacy, managed to assert their authority in the 14th c., but in 1506 Pope Julius II was able to incorporate the town in the Papal State. In 1530 Charles V was crowned Emperor here – the last imperial coronation on Italian soil. In 1796 the town was incorporated in Napoleon's Cisalpine Republic. In 1816 it reverted to Papal rule, and in 1860 finally became part of a united Italy. During the last war there was heavy fighting near Bologna.

Art

The characteristic feature of the architecture of Bologna is the use of brick. The first buildings of any consequence date from the Gothic period (church of San Petronio). The Renaissance and Baroque are abundantly represented, outstanding among local architects being Fioravante Fioravantini (d. after 1430) and his son Rodolfo, known as Aristotele (d. 1486), Pellegrino Tibaldi (d. 1597) and Sebastiano Serlio (1475–1522), one of the great architectural theorists of the late Renaissance. Serlio's school of theatre architects and painters achieved an international reputation in the 17th and 18th c. through the work of the Bibiena family of Tuscany, laying the foundations of modern stagecraft.

Sculpture was practised mainly by artists from other parts of Italy. Michelangelo worked in San Domenico in 1494.

In painting, the first artist to attain more than local fame was Francesco Francia (1450–1517). Later the academy founded by Lodovico Carracci (1555–1619) and carried on by Annibale and Agostino Carracci fostered the school known as Eclecticism, whose leading representatives were Guido Reni (1575–1642), Domenichino (1581–1668) and Guercino (1581–1666).

*Piazza Maggiore and Piazza del Nettuno

*Neptune Fountain

The life of the town centres around two adjoining squares (both pedestrian precincts), the Piazza Maggiore and the Piazza del Nettuno. In the Piazza del Nettuno is the Neptune Fountain by Giambologna (1563–1567), one of the finest fountains of the 16th c.

San Pietro

From the Piazza del Nettuno the busy shopping street Via dell'Indipendenza leads to the station. In this street, on the right, is the cathedral of San Pietro (the Metropolitana), founded in 910, with a choir by Pellegrino Tibaldi (1575) and a nave, remodelled in Baroque style (17th c.). Beyond the choir is the Archbishop's Palace.

Parallel to the Via dell'Indipendenza to the west is Via Galleria, with many old aristocratic mansions.

Palazzo Comunale
Art Gallery

The west side of the Piazza del Nettuno and Piazza Maggiore is occupied by the Palazzo Comunale (Town Hall), an extensive Gothic build-

Palazzo di Re Enzo

Bologna: silhouette of the city

ing begun in 1290 and largely rebuilt in 1425–1430. Above the main entrance (1555) is a bronze statue (1580) of Pope Gregory XIII, a native of Bologna. On the second floor is the Municipal Art Gallery (Collezione Comunale d'Arte).

Palazzo di Re Enzo   Nearby the Town Hall is the Gothic Palazzo di Re Enzo (restored in 1905), in which Enzo, the poet son of Frederick II, was kept prisoner from 1249 to 1272.

Palazzo del Podestà   On the north side of the Piazza Maggiore is the former Palazzo del Podestà (1201; rebuilt from 1484 onwards in Early Renaissance style), with a tower, Torre dell'Arengo dating from 1212.

**San Petronio

The south side of the Piazza Maggiore is dominated by San Petronio, the largest church in Bologna, which is dedicated to the town's patron saint. Begun in 1390 in emulation of other large Gothic churches of the day, it was not completed according to the original plan, work being suspended about 1650 after the construction of the nave (117 m/128 yd long, 48 m/52 yd wide, 40.4 m/133 ft 4 in high). The sculpture on the main doorway of the unfinished façade is by Jacopo della Quercia (1425–1438). The interior ranks as the supreme achievement of Gothic architecture in Italy. An unusual feature is the meridian line set into the pavement. To the left of the choir is the Museo di San Petronio.

*Museo Civico Archeologico

To the south of San Petronio, in Via dell'Archiginnasio (No. 2), is the Archaeological Museum (Museo Civico Archeologico), with a collection of prehistoric and Etruscan material from the surrounding area, and other antiquities; the museum has the finest Egyptian department after those of Turin and Venice (Rooms III-V). The Greek department (Room VI) contains a head of Athena Lemnia (copy of a work by Phidias, 5th c. B.C.).

Palazzo Galvani   From the museum the Via dell'Archiginnasio, with the Portico del Pavaglione and its numerous shops, runs south to the Piazza Galvani, where stands a marble statue of the Bologna-born physiologist Luigi Galvani (1737–1798), discoverer of the "Galvanic discharges" (though he himself interpreted them wrongly). On the left is the Archiginnasio (1562–63), until 1803 occupied by the university (with the old anatomy lecture-room, the Teatro Anatomico) and now housing the Municipal Library (600,000 volumes).

*Palazzo Bevilacqua   To the south-west, in Via d'Azeglio, is the Palazzo Bevilacqua, built in 1474–1482 in the Early Renaissance style of the Florentine palaces, with a fine courtyard.

Piazza San Domenico

Via d'Azeglio runs by way of Via Marsili to the Piazza San Domenico, in which are two columns bearing statues of Saint Dominic and the Virgin, and the Gothic tombs of two learned lawyers Rolandino de'Passeggeri (d. 1300) and Egidio Foscherari.

*San Domenico   On the south side of the square is the church of San Domenico (begun c. 1221; façade unfinished), with an interior remodelled in Baroque style, containing the tomb of St Dominic (d. in Bologna 1221), a marble sarcophagus with carving by Nicola Pisano, Arnolfo di Cambio and Fra Guglielmo (1267); cover by Niccolò dall'Arca (d. 1494); the angel on the right, the figure of St Petronius on the cover and the youthful St Proculus (to rear) are early works by Michelangelo (1494). Fine intarsia (mosaic woodwork) choir-stalls (1541–1551).

To the left of the choir, between the first and second chapels is a wall monument to King Enzo ("Hencius Rex", d. 1272; restored 1731).
In the sacristy is the Museo San Domenico.

Piazza di Porta Ravegnana

From the Piazza del Nettuno Via Rizzoli runs east to the Piazza di Porta Ravegnana, on the south side of which is the beautiful Gothic Palazzo della Mercanzia (1384), home of the Chamber of Commerce.

Palazzo della Mercanzia

In the middle of the square are the Leaning Towers, two plain brick towers (Torre degli Asinelli and Torre Garisenda) originally built for defensive purposes, which have become a landmark and an emblem of the city. The Torre degli Asinelli (1119; 498 steps), 97.6 m/322 ft high, leans 1.23 m/4 ft from the vertical; the Torre Garisenda (begun end of 11th c.), 48 m/158 ft high, is 3.22 m/10¾ ft aslant.

Leaning Towers

From the Piazza di Porta Ravegnana five streets radiate to the gates on the east side of the town – Via Castiglione, Via Santo Stefano, Strada Maggiore, Via San Vitale and Via Zamboni.

In Via Santo Stefano is the basilica of Santo Stefano, a complex of eight buildings of which three have frontages on the street – the Chiesa del Crocifisso, now the principal church, originally Romanesque but rebuilt in 1637, with an external pulpit (12th c.) and a crypt (1019); the church of Santo Sepolcro, an octagonal building on a centralised plan containing the tomb of St Petronius, bishop of Bologna in the 5th c.; and the Romanesque church of Santi Vitale e Agricola (founded 5th c.; present building 1019; façade 1885), with the 13th c. Chiesa della Trinità. Behind San Sepolcro is the Cortile di Pilato, a pillared courtyard of 1142 (marble basin, 741), adjoining which is a two-storey cloister.
The museum contains pictures of the 13th–17th centuries.

Via Santo Stefano
Santo Stefano

In Strada Maggiore, immediately left, is the church of San Bartolomeo (1530; interior 17th c.). Farther along, on the right (No. 19), is Casa Isolani, a 13th c. aristocrat's mansion with a projecting upper storey supported on oak beams. Opposite (No. 24) is the Palazzo Sampieri, with admirable frescoes from the story of Hercules by Carracci and Guercino. Next door (No. 26) is the house of the composer Gioacchino Rossini, who lived mostly in Bologna between 1825 and 1848 (commemorative tablet).

Strada Maggiore
Casa Isolani

In Strada Maggiore (No. 44) is the Palazzo Davia-Bargellini (1638–1658), with a Picture Gallery and Museum of Industrial Art.

Almost opposite is the church of Santa Maria dei Servi (begun 1346), with a beautiful portico; inside is a "Madonna Enthroned" by Cimabue. Some 500 m/550 yd south-east of the church, in Piazza Carducci, is the house which belonged to Giosuè Carducci (1835-1907), the most popular Italian poet of the 19th c.; to the right, on the town walls, is a momument to the poet (1928).

Picture Gallery and Museum of Industrial Art
Santa Maria dei Servi
Piazza Carducci
Casa Carducci

In the Via Zamboni (No. 13) is the Palazzo Malvezzi-De'Medici (1560), now the headquarters of the provincial administration. Farther along, on the right, is the church of San Giacomo Maggiore (originally 1267; rebuilt c. 1500), which contains the tomb of the jurist Antonio Bentivoglia (d. 1435), by Jacopo della Quercia. To the left of this, is the Capella del Bentivoglio, containing a "Virgin Enthroned" by Francesco Francia. The Oratory of Santa Cecilia behind the apse of the church, has

Via Zamboni
San Giacomo Maggiore

beautiful frescoes by Lorenzo Costa, Francesco Francia and their pupils (1504–06). Farther along Via Zamboni, on the left, stands the Teatro Comunale (1756–63), an opera-house.

University

Opposite the Teatro Comunale is the former Palazzo Poggi, with a façade and ceiling paintings by Pellegrino Tibaldi (1569), which has been occupied since 1803 by the University (with some 40,000 students). Farther north-east is the finely planned "University City".

Pinacoteca Nazionale

*Picture Gallery

To the north of the university, in Via delle Belle Arti (No. 56), is a former Jesuit college which now houses the National Picture Gallery (Pinacoteca Nazionale), with some of the best works of Bolognese painters of the 14th–18th c., the 17th c. being particularly well represented. Outstanding among other works are a "Madonna with Saints" by the Ferrarese artist Francesco del Cossa, one of his finest works, and a masterpiece by Raphael, "St Cecilia"; there are also works by Guido Reni, Guercino, Perugino, Vasari and Carracci, as well as pictures by Venetian masters, including Tintoretto, Palma il Giovane, Cima da Congliano and Vivarini.

San Martino

At the west end of the Via delle Belle Arti stands the Carmelite church of San Martino (Gothic, 13th–16th c.); in the first chapel on the left can be seen a "Madonna with Saints" by Francesco Francia.

*San Francesco

In Piazza Malpighi, to the west of the town centre, is the Gothic church of San Francesco, built 1236–1263 on the model of French churches, with a tower erected 1397–1402. It contains a large Gothic marble altar (1388).

Textile Museum

500 m/550 yd south-east, in the Palazzo Salina (Via Barberia 13), we find the Textile Museum.

Museum of Modern Art

Exhibition grounds

Outside the town to the north lie the exhibition grounds with the Museum of Modern Art.

San Michele in Bosco

Situation
1 km/¾ mile south

From the south town gate Porta San Mamolo a road leads to Via Cadivilla, at the end of which stands the former convent of San Michele in Bosco (124 m/409 ft), now an orthopaedic hospital. From the convent there are fine views.

Certosa

Situation
1.5 km/1 mile west of
Bologna

West of Porta Sant'Isaia, on the site of an Etruscan cemetery, is the Certosa (founded 1333; used as a cemetery since 1801), with old and new cloisters and magnificent colonnades.
Also to the west of the Porta Sant'Isaia is the Stadio Comunale, which can accommodate 50,000 spectators.

Basilica Madonna di San Luca

500 m/550 yd west of the Porta Saragozza, the south-west town gate, begins a colonnade (built 1674–1739) of 666 arches, 3.5 km/2 miles long, which extends by way of Meloncello (where a branch goes off to the Certosa) to the Monte della Guardia (reached also by a motor road), with the pilgrimage church of Madonna di San Luca. From here there are beautiful views as far as the Adriatic Sea and the Apennines, and in clear weather the Alps.

Situation
4 km/2½ miles
south-west of
Bologna

Bolzano/Bozen

H3

Region: Trentino-Alto Adige
Province: Bolzano (BZ)
Altitude: 165 m/545 ft
Population: 98,000

Bolzano (in German Bozen), capital of the autonomous province of the same name, lies in a fertile basin at the junction of the River Isarco (Eisack), coming from the Brenner, with the Talvera (Talfer), coming from Val Sarentina. The Isarco, thus reinforced, flows into the Adige (Etsch) to the south of the town.
The background to the east is formed by the magnificent Catinaccio group, with the Torri del Vaiolet, typical Dolomite peaks.

Situation and
importance

Situated at the intersection of important through routes and at the starting point of popular mountain roads, Bolzano has a busy transit traffic, but its convenient situation and beautiful surroundings also make it an excellent base from which to explore the region.

Bolzano is the chief commercial, industrial and tourist centre of the mainly German-speaking region of Alto Adige (South Tirol).

The old town, lying within the confluence of the Talvera and the Isarco, is with its handsome Renaissance and Baroque buildings, its pictur-esque oriel windows, inner courts and staircases, a typical Germanic town. To the west of the Talvera, nearby Gries and Quirain, are typical Italian residential districts. South of the Isarco is Bolzano's industrial zone.

Bolzano was the Roman Bauzanum. In 680 it was taken by the Lombards and in 740 by the Franks, and later became the seat of Bavarian lords of the marches. For a time it belonged to the bishopric of Trient, which was compelled to cede it to the count of Tirol in the 13th c. It came under Habsburg rule in 1363, and thereafter shared the destinies of Tirol until 1919, when it passed to Italy. In 1948 the provinces of Bolzano and Trento were formed into the autonomous region of Trentino-Alto Adige, and German was granted the status of a second offical language in the province of Bolzano.
Since 1964 Bolzano has been the headquarters of the bishopric of Bolzano and Bressanone, in which the communes in Bolzano province previously belonging to the diocese of Trento were also incorporated.

History

Piazza Walther

The central feature of the town is the Piazza Walther (Waltherplatz), named after the German minnesinger Walther von der Vogelweide

Parish church

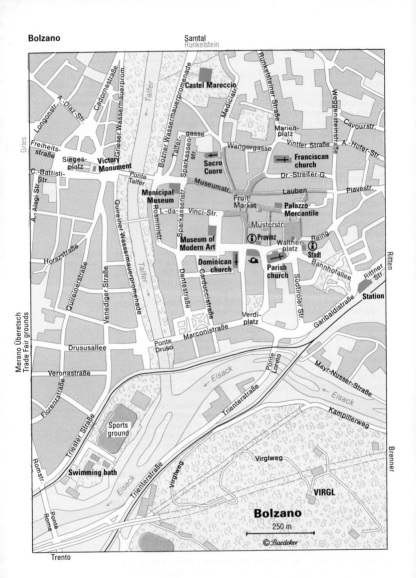

Bolzano

(*c.* 1170–1230), with a monument to the poet (1889; Heinrich Natter). At the south-west corner of the square is the Gothic parish church (14th–15th c.), which, like its counterpart in Bressanone, has the status of a cathedral. It has an elegant tower 65 m/215 ft high (1504–1519) and a Lombard doorway; fine interior with a Late Gothic pulpit (1513–1514) decorated with carved reliefs and frescoes of the 14th–15th c.

To the west of the Piazza Walther is the Gothic Dominican church (13th c.; remodelled in 1498 as a hall-church with three naves), with fine late 14th c. frescoes.

In the adjoining St John's Chapel are frescoes of the school of Giotto (1330–1350), including a fine "Triumph of Death".

The cloister of the former Dominican monastery (now the Conservatoire) has frescoes by Friedrich Pakker and other artists.

Via dei Portici

To the north of Piazza Walther is the arcaded Via dei Portici (Laubengasse) the town's principal shopping and commercial street (pedestrian precinct with textile shops, perfumeries and boutiques), with fine 17th c. town houses. The fine Palazzo Mercantile (1708–1727; now the Chamber of Commerce) on the south side of the street, is the only example of an Italian palazzo in Bolzano (fine hall for conferences, etc.).

At the east end of Via dei Portici in a small square stands the Town Hall, a building in Baroque style erected in 1907; at the west end of the street is the fruit market, with a Neptune Fountain (1777).

A little way north of the fruit market stands the Franciscan monastery. Its church (originally 13th–15th c.), has 20th c. stained-glass windows; concerts are held in the adjoining late Romanesque cloisters (14th c.). In the Lady Chapel is a fine Late Gothic altar of carved wood by Hans Klocker (c. 1500).

Farther east stands the Late Gothic church of the Teutonic Order (Deutschhauskirche).

Museums

The east end of the pedestrian precinct leads into the Via Sernesi; here can be found the Museum of Modern Art, with contemporary sculptures in the courtyard (temporary exhibitions).

From the fruit market the Via del Museo runs west to the Municipal Museum, with archaeological material, peasant house interiors, traditional costumes, folk art and works by local artists.

Castles

From the Lungotalvera Bolzano, which begins at the Municipal Museum and follows the east bank of the Talvera for 1300 m/¾ mile, there are fine views of Monte Sciliar and the Catinaccio group. A little way along this promenade, on the right, is Castel Mareccio (Schloss Maretsch, 13th–16th c.), with five towers, now a Congress Centre. At the north end of the promenade is the 17th c. Castel Sant'Antonio (Schloss Klebenstein).

North-east above Castel Sant'Antonio on a precipitous porphyry crag stands the 13th c. Castel Roncolo (361 m/1191 ft), with frescoes of the 14th–15th c. Since 1893 the castle has belonged to the community of Bolzano.

Suburban district west of the Talvera

To the west of the Talvera extends the predominantly Italian new town. Just west of the Talvera Bridge is a large triumphal arch, the Victory Monument (Monumento della Vittoria, 1928).

Bolzano: Castel Mareccio

Bolzano Trade Fair

To the left is the Viale Venezia, which runs south to the Lido (open-air and indoor swimming pools and other sports facilities), 1 km/¾ mile away. A little way west of this are the grounds of the Bolzano Trade Fair, with the Palazzo della Fiera (at present an ice-rink).

From here the Corso Italia runs north past the massive Law Courts to the Piazza Mazzini, where it meets the Corso Libertà, a street which runs west, lined by tall arches, from the Victory Monument and continues to the main square of Gries.

Gries

The suburban district of Gries (273 m/901 ft), lies at the foot of the hill of Guncinà (Guntschna-Berg) and was formerly a popular winter resort noted for its mild climate. The old central area is surrounded by numerous villas set in trim gardens.

Benedictine
monastery
Old Parish Church

On the east side of the main square of Gries is a Benedictine monastery, originally built as a castle, with a beautiful church in late Rococo style (1769–1778; ceiling paintings and altarpiece by Martin Knoller). Not far to the north-west stands the old Parish Church of Gries (15th–16th c.). The chief feature of the interior and at the same time one of the most important Gothic works of art in the Alto Adige is the beautifully carved

**Pacher Altar

altarpiece by Michael Pacher with a representation of the Coronation of the Virgin, now to be seen in the Erasmus Chapel. Also of interest is a 12th c. Romanesque-Byzantine crucifix.

*Passeggiata del Guncinà

To the north of the Old Parish Church in Gries is the beginning of the Passeggiata del Guncinà, an attractive path which winds its way up the hill and ends at the Reichrieglerhof hotel (45 minutes). The hotel can also be reached by road (3.5 km/2 miles) from the Victory Monument by way of Via Cadorna and Via Miramonti.

*Passeggiata Sant'Osvaldo

Beyond the St Anton Bridge are Castel Sant'Antonio and the beginning of the Passeggiata Sant'Osvaldo, which climbs through the vineyards, affording fine views, to a height of 400 m/1320 ft and then runs down past the picturesque wine village of Santa Maddalena to the suburban district of Rencio (Rentsch) on the road to the Brenner (1¼ hours).

San Genesio Atesino

A little way north of the St Anton Bridge over the Talvera a cableway and a well engineered panoramic road lead up to San Genesio Atesino (Jenesien; 1087 m/3587 ft; also reached on a narrow road), a village which is a popular health resort with magnificent views of the Schlern and the Dolomites.

From Bolzano to Collalbo (17 km/11 miles)

North-east of Bolzano is the Renón (Ritten), an extensive porphyry plateau lying between the Talvera and the Isarco, reached by an excellent road (17 km/11 miles) from Bolzano. *Renón

12 km/7 miles: Auna di Sotto (Unterinn, 908 m/2996 ft, where a narrow road (5 km/3 miles) branches off, past the little Lago di Castro, to Soprabolzano (Oberbozen, 1220 m/4026 ft), which can also be reached by cableway from Bolzano. Auna di Sotto

5 km/3 miles: Collalbo (Klobenstein, 1190 m/3927 ft), which, like Soprabolzano, is a popular summer resort, with superb views of the Dolomites. To the north, in the Fosco gorge beyond Longomoso (Lengmoos), are interesting earth pyramids which are reached in ½ hour. Collalbo

From Bolzano over the Passo di Pennes to Vipiteno (67 km/42 miles)

A beautiful run on an excellent engineered road. Leave Bolzano by way of Via Castel Roncolo and Via Beato Arrigo; then past Castel Sant'Antonio (on left: road to San Genesio cableway), and below Castel Roncolo (on right) over the Talvera to join the road which comes in from Gries on the left.

Continue north on this road, passing on the right a covered wooden bridge carrying an old road over the river, and beyond this, in the valley, the old moated Castel Novale (Schloss Ried); then up the Val Sarantina (Sarntal), which narrows in places into a gorge between sheer walls of porphyry, with 24 tunnels. The road passes the extensive ruins of Castel Sarentino (Schloss Rafenstein; 16th c.; 692 m/2284 ft) on the left and Castel Vanga (Schloss Wangen) on the right. Soon afterwards Monte San Giovanni, a massive porphyry crag 230 m/759 ft high, with the old church of San Giovanni, can be seen ahead.

10 km/6 miles: Locanda alla Posta (Gasthaus zur Post Halbweg). The road continues up the valley, which here widens out.

5 km/3 miles: Ponticino (Bundschen-Dick; 923 m/3046 ft) with houses built for workers in the hydro-electric power station.

1 km/¾ mile farther on, on the right, is the Pino inn (Gasthaus Fichte), and soon afterwards lower down on the left the little spa of Bagni di Serga (Bad Schörgau: chalybeate water).

Bolzano

Bolzano and the Rosengarten group

Sarantino

4 km/2½ miles: Sarantino (Sarnthein; 981 m/3237 ft), the chief place in the valley, a beautifully situated little town which is a favourite summer holiday resort. Two castles stand here: Regino (Reineck, 13th c.) and Kränzelstein. The little church of San Cipriano contains over-painted 16th c. frescoes. Picturesque local costumes are worn on Sundays.

The road continues from Sarantino up the Val Sarentina to the Passo di Pennes.

Campolasta

3 km/2 miles: Campolasta (Astfeld; 1023 m/3376 ft), a pretty village at the junction of two valleys – to the right the Valdurna (Durnholzer Tal), with the village of the same name, situated on the beautiful Lago di Valdurna (Durnholzer See; 12 km/7 miles; 1568 m/5174 ft); to the left the pretty Val di Pennes (Penser Tal). Going up the Val di Pennes, the road climbs gradually, coming in 9 km/6 miles to the Alpenrose inn (on left). It then continues past a reservoir and the modest Edelweiss inn, running along the slope of the hillside.

Pennes

18 km/11 miles: Pennes (Pens; 1459 m/4815 ft), a straggling village, which is the chief settlement of the valley.

The road then climbs more steeply up the bare hillside, with three sharp bends: to the left is the Corno Bianco (Weisshorn; 2705 m/8927 ft).

*Passo di Pennes

10 km/6 miles: Passo di Pennes (Penser Joch; 2211 m/7296 ft), with magnificent views, particularly of the peaks in the Ötz and Stubai valleys (Zuckerhütl; 3507 m/11,573 ft).

Dosso

Beyond the pass the road descends (gradient of 10%), at first high up on the bare slopes above the Val di Dosso (Eggertal). In 8 km/5 miles, below the Schönblick inn, it comes to the hamlet of Dosso (Egg), with a chapel. It then runs down through forest country, with picturesque glimpses of the Isarco valley (Vipiteno, Burg Sprechenstein).

Then a steep descent (13%) into the Isarco valley, joining the road from the Passo di Monte Giovo shortly before reaching the parish church of Vipiteno.

17 km/11 miles: Vipiteno (Sterzing; 948 m/3128 ft), an old village popular as a summer and winter sports resort. In the Multscher Museum there are painted panels and carvings by the Master of Ulm.

Vipiteno

Bordighera

D6

Region: Liguria
Province: Imperia (IM)
Altitude: 5 m/17 ft
Population: 12,000

The little town of Bordighera lies on the Riviera di Ponente near the French frontier, some 30 km/19 miles east of Nice and 10 km/6 miles west of San Remo.
The town has long been a popular health resort and has become equally popular as a seaside resort.

Situation and importance

Bordighera is famed for the date-palms (Phoenix dactylifera) which grow here because of the mild climate, though the dates seldom ripen sufficiently to be edible. Large quantities of branches are supplied to Roman Catholic churches in spring for Palm Sunday and to Jewish communities in autumn for the Feast of Tabernacles.
Flower-growing is also an important local industry.
This part of the Riviera is also called "Riviera dei Fiori" (the Riviera of Flowers).

*Sights

Bordighera consists of the picturesque old town (Città Vecchia), high above Capo Sant'Ampelia, and the newer districts west of the cape.

The main traffic artery of Bordighera is Via Vittorio Emanuele, in which are the theatre and the Chiesa di Terrasanta. From this street various side streets climb up to the Via Romana. In one of these side streets, in Via Regina Margherita, is the Museo Bicknell, which houses the Istituto Internazionale di Studi Liguri. From the Via Romana there are charming views of beautiful palm-gardens. It ends in the west at the Rio Borghetto, in the east at the Spianata del Capo, on top of the promontory, from which there are magnificent views: of the Ospedaletti bay to the north-east and Ventimiglia, the Côte d'Azur and the peaks of the Maritime Alps, usually snow-capped, to the west. At the foot of the cliff-fringed promontory is a seafront promenade, the Lungomare Argentina.

Just north of the Spianata del Capo is the old town, a huddle of narrow winding streets, still with the old town gates. From here the Via dei Colli runs west above the little town, affording superb views.

Old town

In the outlying district of Arziglia, to the east, near the mouth of the Sasso valley and the Kursaal, are the Vallone Gardens (private property, visiting possible on special request), laid out by a German gardener named Ludwig Winter (d. 1912), where palms are cultivated for their leaves.

Arziglia

About 1.5 km/1 mile east, on the road to Ospedaletti, is the Madonna Garden, also laid out by Winter (and also private property).

Sasso

From the Via dei Colli a road runs north above the Sasso valley to the fortress-like village of Sasso, situated on the summit of a hill.

Situation
3 km/2 miles north

113

Bordighera: the yacht harbour

Seborga · Some 8 km/5 miles farther on is the little village of Seborga, which commands extensive views.

Bormio G3

Region: Lombardia
Province: Sondrio (SO)
Altitude: 1225 m/4430 ft
Population: 4000

Situation · Bormio (formerly Worms) lies in the Veltlin (Italian Veltellina) at the north-west foot of the Ortles group and at the western end of the pass across the Stilfser Joch, close to the Italian-Swiss frontier.

Townscape · The little town popular as a health resort, tourist centre and winter sports resort, has a fine old centre. In its surroundings are several mineral springs which can be used for therapeutic purposes.

Sights

Parish church · In the Piazza Cavour, east of the centre of the village, is the Baroque parish church, the Chiesa Collegiata SS. Gervasio e Protasio; (17th c.); to the left stands the loggia of the Kuèerc, the former court of justice, behind which is the Torre Civica (town tower).

Museo Civico · North-west of the parish church, in Via Buon Consiglio, is the Palazzo De Simoni, which houses the municipal museum, the Museo Civico, with a historic collection.

At the extreme northern end of Bormio, in Via Monte Ortigara, is a mineralogical museum (Museo Mineralogico Naturalistico Valli di Bormio).

Near the museum, in Via Sertorelli, can be found the Botanical Garden.

Museo Mineralogico

A short way to the south of the river is Combo with the Santuario del Crocifisso (or Sant'Antonio Abbate; 14th c.); the interior is decorated with 15th and 16th c. frescoes.

Santuario del Crocifisso

Outside the village, to the west, are the sports stadium and ice rink, built to a pentagonal plan.

Sports stadium and ice rink

Bagni di Bormio

Bagni di Bormio (1318 m/4349 ft), the popular spa district of Bormio, consists of the Bagni Vecchie (old baths) and the Bagni Nuovi (new baths).

Situation
3 km/2 miles north

The seven springs of the Bagni Vecchi, mentioned by Pliny, in the Dolomites beyond the deep gorge of the Adda. Interesting are the so-called "piscine", bathing basins, rock-hewn by the Romans.

Bagni Vecchi

The Bagni Nuovi are situated on a mountain terrace. Their radioactive water, containing traces of gypsium, issues at temperatures between 38 and 41 °C/94 and 99 °F and is recommended for rheumatism, asthma and arteriosclerosis.

Bagni Nuovi

Bormio 2000 / Bormio 3000

At the south edge of Bormio is the lower station of the cableway which goes up to Bormio 2000 near the tree line. The second section leads to Bormio 3000, immediately at the foot of the Cima Bianca (3012 m/ 9940 ft). The surrounding area offers superb winter sports facilities, including an artificial snow-making installation.

From Bormio 3000 a 45-minute climb can be made up to the Vallecetta.

Also in this area is a cableway to the Ciuk (1620 m/5346 ft), from where a chairlift continues to La Rocca (2126 m/7016 ft).

Brescia

G4

Region: Lombardia
Province: Brescia (BS)
Altitude: 149 m/492 ft
Population: 205,000

Brescia, capital of the province of the same name, second in importance only to Milan among the towns of Lombardy, lies below two foothills of the Brescian Alps, some 25 km/15 miles west of Lake Garda. The picturesque old town, surrounded by gardens, has Roman remains dating from the early Empire and fine Renaissance buildings. Following heavy damage during the Second World War some parts of the town have been rebuilt with wider streets and larger squares.

Situation

The town's industries include textiles and hardware, and it is also an important market centre for the agricultural products of the fertile surrounding area.

Brescia

The ancient Brixia became a Roman colony in the time of Augustus under the name of Colonia Augusta Civica and rose to prosperity as a result of its situation on the road which ran from Bologna through the Alps by way of the Splügen pass. During the Middle Ages it was an active member of the Lombard league of towns. From 1428 to 1797 it belonged to Venice.

Brescia produced two notable painters – Alessandro Bonvicino, known as Il Moretto (1498–1554), whose colouring vies with that one of the Venetians, and Girolama da Romano, known as Il Romanino (c. 1485–after 1562). Their works are well represented in the town's churches and in the Pinacoteca.

Piazza del Duomo

Duomo Nuovo

In the Piazza del Duomo is the 17th c. cathedral, the Duomo Nuovo, with a central dome of 1825.

*Rotonda

On its south side is the Rotonda or Duomo Vecchio, a massive circular structure crowned by a dome (11th–12th c.) containing works by Moretto and Romanino. Beneath the transept lies the Cripta di San Filastrio; the columns have capitals of the former Basilica di S Maria Maggiore (6th and 9th c.).

Broletto

To the north of the Duomo Nuovo is the Broletto (1187–1230), the old Town Hall, now housing the prefecture, with the Torre del Popolo.

Piazza della Vittoria

*Loggia

To the west of the Piazza del Duomo is the Piazza della Vittoria, the town's central square (rebuilt 1932). Behind the Post Office lies the

Piazza del Duomo

Piazza della Loggia, one of the most picturesque squares in northern Italy. On its west side is the superb Loggia (Town Hall), begun in Early Renaissance style (1492–1508) and completed between 1526 and 1674 (windows by Palladio). Opposite on the east side can be seen a façade with a 16th c. clock-tower.

On the south side is the Monte di Pietà (pawnshop), with a beautiful Early Renaissance loggia (15th c.).

The life of the town centres on the Corso Zanardelli, on the south side of the Piazza del Duomo. On its north side, behind some houses, is the Teatro Grande (18th c.), with a handsome auditorium and foyer.

Teatro Grande

Castello

From the Broletto steps lead up to the Castello, an old stronghold of the Visconti family, surrounded by a park (zoo, observatory); the Castello houses the Risorgimento Museum. A tunnel, the Galleria Tito Speri, under the castle hill leads to the developing district of Borgo Trento.

Via dei Musei

From the Broletto the Via dei Musei, once the Via Aemilia, the main street of the Roman town, runs east to the Tempio Capitolino, a Corinthian temple built in A.D. 73, in the reign of Vespasian, and dedicated to Jupiter, Juno and Minerva, with a pronaos of eight columns and three cellas. The three cellas contain a collection of Roman inscriptions.

*Tempio Capitolino

Behind it is the Museo Romano, with Roman material from Brescia and the surrounding area, including a bronze statue, almost 2 m/7 ft high, of a winged Victory, dating from the period of construction of the temple, and six Roman bronze busts (2nd–3rd c.).

Museo Romano

Farther east, in Via Piamarta, is the Museo dell'Età Cristiana (Museum of Christian Antiquities), in the former church of Santa Giulia, with religious art, including carved ivories of the 3rd–5th c. and a gold cross which belonged to the Lombard king Desiderius (8th c.).

Museo dell'Età Cristiana

Immediately east of this is the 9th c. church of San Salvatore, which has a beautiful crypt (42 columns).

In the western cloister of the former convent of Santa Giulia is the Galleria d'Arte Moderna, with works of the 19th c. Adjoining stands the remarkable Romanesque church of S Maria in Solario (12th c.).

Galleria d'Arte Moderna

Sights in the west of Brescia

In the Corso Martiri della Libertà, to the south-west of the town, is the little church of Santa Maria dei Miracoli (restored), with an elegant Early Renaissance vestibule (1487–1508) and an impressive interior.

Santa Maria dei Miracoli

A little way south-west stands the church of Santi Nazaro e Celso (1780), with altarpieces by Moretto and a "Resurrection" by Titian behind the high altar.

Santi Nazaro e Celso

To the north is the Gothic church of San Francesco (1254–1265) with fine pictures by Romanino and a beautiful Gothic cloister (1393).

San Francesco

North-west of the Piazza della Vittoria is the church of San Giovanni Evangelista, with paintings by Moretto and Romanino.

San Giovanni Evangelista

Farther west stands the former convent church of Santa Maria delle Grazie, with a sumptuous interior and a beautiful cloister.

Madonna delle Grazie

*Pinacoteca Tosio Martinengo

About 500 m/550 yd south-east of the Teatro Grande, in Piazza Moretto, is the Pinacoteca Tosio Matinengo, with masterpieces by Brescian artists, including pictures by Moretto and Romanino and paintings by Lotto, Foppa and Raffael.

Monte Maddalena

Situation
13 km/8 miles east

From Brescia a road with many bends leads to Monte Maddalena (875 m/2888 ft), from which there is a panoramic prospect extending as far as Monte Rosa.

Lake Iseo

See Lombardy

Bressanone   H3

Region: Trentino – Alto Adige
Province: Bolzano (BZ)
Altitude: 562 m/1855 ft
Population: 16,000

Situation

Bressanone (German Brixen), the third largest town of the Alto Adige, lies in a broad part of the Isarco valley on the Brenner motorway. It is here that the River Rienza, coming from the Pusteria valley, flows into the Isarco.

History

Bressanone was founded in 901 on the remains of an old settlement. In 970 Bishop Albuin transferred the seat of the bishopric to Bressanone; the first Ottonian cathedral was built c. 990. In 1091 the town became the centre of the Bressanone diocese; the town wall was erected in the 12th c. and farther north the Neustift convent was founded. In 1179 Frederick I granted the Bishop the right to mint coins, to conduct markets and to levy taxes, as well as full legal jurisdiction. In 1348 the town was afflicted by the plague; in 1444 many buildings were destroyed in a fire. The famous humanist and theologist Cusanus (Nikolaus van Kues) was from 1450 to 1451 bishop of Bressanone.
Building of the Baroque cathedral was begun in 1745, but is was not consecrated until 1758. From 1797 onwards during the Napoleonic Wars the town was occupied by the French; however, after the defeat of the French army in the battle of Spinges the occupying forces withdrew.

The German deputation order of 1803 put an end to ecclesiastical sovereignty in Bressanone; from 1806 to 1814 the town was under Bavarian rule and then it became part of Tyrol.

The 19th and 20th c. brought large scale development in the technical field (road construction, railways). In 1962 the academy, housed in the building of the seminary, was opened and named after Cusanus.

The refoundation of the diocese of Bolzano-Bressanone took place in 1964; at the same time the seat of the bishop was transferred to the provincial capital (see Bolzano).

*Cathedral

The eastern edge of the Old Town is dominated by the Baroque Cathedral of the Assumption. Its plain, flat façade reveals a Lombard influence; the Neo-Classical portico supported on pillars and columns was not added until 1785. The lower sections of the two west towers are relics of its Romanesque predecessor.

The single-naved interior with its vaulted roof is flanked on each side by altar-chapels separated by marble-clad columns. The ceiling of the nave has a giant fresco by Paul Troger (1750); he was also responsible for the painted ceiling in the choir.

From the right of the portico a corridor leads to the cloisters, which were originally built in the Romanesque period (around 1200). Special mention should be made of the magnificent and partly restored frescoes on the vaulted ceiling, dating from the Gothic period (1390–1510) and portraying scenes from the Old and New Testaments.
On the east side of the cloisters a passage leads to the cathedral treasury (closed on Sun.).

**Cloisters

On the southern edge of the cathedral and cloister complex stands the church of St John, a Romanesque building from the period after 1200, with a Gothic vaulted ceiling and 13th–15th c. frescoes. The church is not open to visitors at the present time.

Church of St John

Parish Church

To the north of the cathedral on its left will be found the original Parish Church of St Michael dating from c. 1500. In 1757–1758 the interior was renovated in the Baroque style and the ceilings painted by Josef Hauzinger. In the churchyard, in a niche in the outside wall of the cathedral, is a figure in memory of the poet Oswald von Wolkenstein.

Opposite the northern façade of the nave stands the 16th c. home for foundlings, with its metal-barred windows.

Home for foundlings

The northern side of the cathedral courtyard is bounded by the Town Hall. Exhibitions are held in its gallery.

Town Hall

**Court Palace (Hofburg)

South-west of the cathedral stands the former royal episcopal palace, now restored. There was a castle here from 1260, which gave place in 1595 to a new Renaissance palace, which was not finally completed until 1710; the latter stages of construction show Baroque influence.

In the typical inner courtyard with its three-storeyed loggias stand terracotta figures (1600) by the master sculptor from Schongau, Hans Reichle.

In 1909 the column commemorating the millennium was erected in the wide courtyard in front of the palace.

Millennium Monument

The collection in the Bressanone Museum in the palace includes medieval and modern works of art, paintings and porcelain and a world-famous collection of cribs.

Diocesan Museum

Seminary

South-east of the cathedral precincts stands the block of buildings housing the seminary. It was founded in 1607 and the buildings are

Baroque. In 1764 the church of the Crucifixion was built on to the existing main façade. The interior contains frescoes by Franz Anton Zeiller.

Cusanus Academy

Adjoining the priests' seminary are the buildings of the Cusanus Academy which was officially opened in 1962.

New Cathedral Chapter/Novacella

Location
3 km/2 miles north

The Augustinian New Canonical Cathedral Chapter was founded in 1124 and completely renewed only fifty years later. There are several blocks of buildings enclosing two courtyards. At the entrance to the monastic precinct stands the Romanesque Chapel of St Michael ("Engelsburg" or Castle of the Angels), a unique Romanesque round building with battlements. There is space to park in the courtyard at the back; guided tours start from here at 10 a.m., 11 a.m., 2 p.m., 3 p.m. and 4 p.m., closed on Sun. An arched gateway leads into the monastery courtyard proper where stands a pretty octagonal Renaissance fountain with its canopy decorated with frescoes.

Monastery Church

The triple-naved Basilica to Our Lady dates from the time when the monastery was first built in the late 12th c.; it underwent considerable changes during the Baroque period, however, especially between 1734–1737. The ceiling frescoes are by Matthias Günther.
The monastery's Late Baroque library with its multicoloured parquet floor, rocaille ornamentation and delicate gallery deserves special attention; the Gothic cloisters with their frescoes and the panelled pinacoteca are also worth seeing.

Brindisi   O8

Region: Puglia
Province: Brindisi (BR)
Altitude: 15 m/50 ft
Population: 90,000

Situation

The port of Brindisi, the Roman Brundisium, lies at the head of a wide inlet on the east coast of Apulia near the Adriatic – some 55 km/34 miles north-east of Taranto or 100 km/62 miles south-east of Bari. The town, capital of the province of the same name and see of an archbishop, has been since ancient times an important centre of trade with the Eastern Mediterranean.
The poet Virgil died here in 19 B.C. on his way back from Greece.

Harbour

The sheltered Inner Harbour consists of two arms – to the west the Seno di Ponente, 600 m/198 ft long, with extensive quays and a bathing beach, and to the east the Seno di Levante, 450 m/1485 ft long, in which very large vessels can berth. A channel 525 m/1733 ft long connects both arms with the Outer Harbour, the entrance to which is divided into two by the islet of Sant'Andrea, with a 15th c. fort.

Sights

Piazza del Popolo

The life of the town centres on the Piazza del Popolo. A little way south stands the church of Santa Lucia, with a Byzantine crypt and catacombs.

Marine Station

From the Piazza del Popolo the Via Garibaldi runs north-east to the Piazza Vittorio Emanuele, which overlooks the Seno di Levante. On the

Brindisi: end of the Via Appia

right is the Marine Station (Stazione Marittima; ferry services to Greece). The Viale Regina Margherita, to the left, leads to a marble column, 19 m/63 ft high, marking the end of the Via Appia (constructed from 312 B.C. onwards), the "Queen of Roads", which ran from Rome via Taranto to Brindisi. Of a second column, which was partly destroyed in 1528, only the lower part is left.

A little way south-west of the column is the cathedral, with a 12th c. mosaic pavement which was remodelled in Baroque style. Adjoining it on the left stands the Archaeological Museum (Museo Archeologico Provinciale), with medieval sculpture, Roman portrait statues, etc. Facing the museum, to the west, is the 13th c. Palazzetto Balsamo, with a richly decorated balcony.

Cathedral and Museum

Farther south-west is the former baptistery of San Giovanni al Sepolcro (11th c.), and beyond this the Norman church of San Benedetto (c. 1100), with a Romanesque side doorway and a cloister (fine relief carving).

Baptistery

About 500 m/550 yd west of the cathedral, above the western harbour gate, is the Castello Svevo (not open to the public), built by Frederick II in 1227, with massive round towers (15th c.).

Castello

Monumento al Marinaio d'Italia

There is a boat trip from Viale Regina Margherita across the Seno di Ponente to the Monumento al Marinaio d'Italia, a naval war memorial (brick tower; 1933), in the form of a ship's rudder, 53 m/175 ft high (lift; fine views from the top).

121

*Santa Maria del Casale

Situation
3 km/2 miles north-
west of Brindisi

North-west of Brindisi is the former convent church of Santa Maria del Casale (end 13th c./beginning 14th c.), with a beautiful doorway and fine frescoes.

Cagliari

F10

Region: Sardegna
Province: Cagliari (CA)
Altitude: 10 m/33 ft
Population: 225,000

Situation

Cagliari (in Sardinian Casteddu), capital of the autonomous region of Sardinia and the province of Cagliari, lies on the south coast of the island – in the wide Gulf of Cagliari.

**Plan of
Inner City**

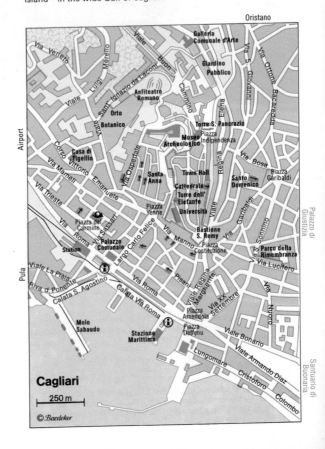

The oldest part of the town, which was founded by the Phoenicians and became the Roman "Carales", is known as the Castello (Sardinian Castedd'e susu). It clings picturesquely to the slopes of a precipitous hill, around the foot of which are the newer districts and suburbs of the town. To west and east are two large lagoons, the Stagno di Santa Gilla and the Stagno di Molentargius (salt-pans).
During roadworks, remains of a medieval town were discovered.

Centre

The tree-shaded Via Roma runs along the busy harbour quay, with the railway station and the modern Town Hall (two towers; in the interior murals by F. Filgari) at its north-west end. From the Town Hall the wide Largo Carlo Felice goes north-east, gently uphill, to Piazza Yenne, from which the busy Corso Vittorio Emanuele runs north-west. In Via Tigello, a side street off the Corso Vittorio Emanuele, are the remains of three Roman houses.

Town Hall

Via G. Manno, a shopping and commercial street popularly known as the Costa, descends south-east from Piazza Yenne to the Piazza della Costituzione. A little way off the Via Garibaldi, which begins here, is the church of San Domenico, with a beautiful cloister.

Piazza della Costituzione

From the Piazza della Costituzione, the beautiful Viale Regina Elena, affording fine views, runs north below the sheer east side of the old bastion to the Giardino Pubblico.

*Viale Regina Elena

A flight of marble steps, the Passeggiata Coperta, climbs to the Bastione San Remy, a magnificent terrace (fine views), laid out on the medieval bastions, which are preserved in part. Higher up, to the north, is the Bastione Santa Caterina, which also commands extensive views. From the Bastione Santa Caterina Via dell'Università leads north-west to the university (founded 1956; fine library) and the massive Torre dell'Elefante (1307), a fine building in medieval Sardinian style.

*Bastione San Remy

Torre dell'Elefante

From the Bastione San Remy we pass through the gate of the old Torre dell'Aquila into the narrow Via Lamarmora, the main street of the old town, which runs north along the steep hillside, linked with parallel streets to right and left by steep lanes or dark archways and flights of steps. Half-way along is the terraced Piazza del Palazzo, above the east side of which is the cathedral of Santa Cecilia, built by the Pisans in 1312, with beautiful old doorways in the transepts. Inside, on either side of the entrance, are the two halves of a pulpit from Pisa Cathedral, a masterpiece of 12th c. Pisan sculpture by Guillelmus, which was presented to Cagliari in 1312.

Old town
Cathedral

*Museo Archeologico Nazionale

At the north end of Via Lamarmora is the Piazza dell'Indipendenza, in which are the Torre San Pancrazio (erected in 1305 to defend the old bastion; view) and the Museo Archeologico Nazionale, with Punic, Greek and Roman material as well as the largest collection of Sardinian antiquities. Of particular interest in Room I are the bronze statues found in the nuraghi (dolmens). On the upper floor are pictures of the 14th to 18th centuries.

Adjoining the museum is the 16th c. Chiesa della Purissima, built in Gothic-Aragonian style.

Chiesa della Purissima

From the museum, Viale Buon Cammino runs north through the outer courtyard of the Citadel and along the ridge of the hill. In 500 m/550 yd a

*Amphitheatre

Cagliari: view of the Old Town

road leads down on the left to the Roman amphitheatre (88.5 by 73 m/292 by 241 ft; arena 50 by 34 m/165 by 112 ft), constructed in a natural depression in the rock, which is now used as an open-air theatre. To the south-west lies the Botanic Garden.

Cittadella dei Musei

North-west of the Piazza dell'Indipendenza is the new Cittadella dei Musei (Museum), built on the remains of older buildings, with a fine collection of Eastern Art.

Municipal Art Gallery

Nearby the museum is the Municipal Art Gallery, which contains modern masterpieces of the most important Sardinian artists. Adjoining is a Sardinian ethnographical museum.

Sights to the east

San Saturno

East of the centre, in Piazza San Cosimo, is the church of San Saturno, also called Santi Cosma e Damiano. The church (founded in the 6th c.; enlarged in the 11th–12th c.), is dedicated to St Saturnus.

Santuario di Bonario

Farther south stands the Santuario di Bonario, where the famous painting "Madonna of Bonario" can be seen; adjoining the sacristy is a small museum (votive pictures).

Dolianova

Situation
20 km/12 miles
north-east

At Dolianova (212 m/700 ft) stands the Romanesque-Gothic Basilica S Pantaleone (12th–13th c.), with a notable façade; some of the decoration has Arabic features.

Uta

The village of Uta, situated on the road to Iglesias, is worth visiting for its Romanesque church of Santa Maria (12th c.), the finest country church in Sardinia.

Situation
22.5 km/14 miles
west

Capo Carbonara

There is an attractive trip (7 km/4½ miles south-east), passing close to Monte San Elia (139 m/459 ft) and the extensive Molentargius salt-pans to the Spiaggia di Poetto, Cagliari's popular bathing beach, which extends for 10 km/6 miles along the Golfo di Quartu.

Situation
50 km/31 miles
south-east

From here the road traverses an extensive agricultural development area, then beyond the hamlet of Flumini a beautiful stretch of road keeps close to the indented coast, passing many old watch-towers and nuraghi (dolmens), to Capo Carbonara, the extreme south-easterly point of Sardinia (views), with the Torre Santa Caterina (115 m/378 ft). Nearby is the Fortezza Vecchia (17th c.).

Tour of the Iglesiente (about 200 km/124 miles)

Another rewarding excursion is a tour of the Iglesiente, the hilly region in the south-west of the island. Leave Cagliari on S.S. 195, which runs south-west along the spit of land between the Stagno di Santa Gilla and the sea and past the large Santa Gilla salt-pans.

Sante Gilla

At the village of Sarroch (20 km/12½ miles) is a very characteristic nuraghi. 7 km/4½ miles farther on is Pula, from which a road leads south (4 km/2½ miles) to the remains of the Phoenician and later Roman

*Nora

Roman excavation of Nora, near Cagliari

town of Nora, on a narrow peninsula (forum, amphitheatre, baths, temples, foundations of villas, well-preserved mosaic pavements).

Teulada

After some time the road leaves the coast. 38 km/23 miles from Pula it crosses a pass (301 m/993 ft), with the Nurag de Mesu, and comes in another 14 km/9 miles to the attractively situated little town of Teulada, chief place of the southern part of the Iglesiente, known as Sulcis. About 36 km/22 miles from Teulada S.S. 195 joins S.S. 126 at San Giovanni Suergiu.

Sant'Antioco

From San Giovanni Suergiu there is an interesting excursion (11 km/7 miles south-west) to the volcanic island of Sant'Antioco (109 sq. km/42 sq. miles) with the popular little seaside resort of the same name (15 m/50 ft; pop. 13,000). On either side of the castle is a well-preserved Phoenician cemetery (5th–3rd c. B.C.; museum). North-west of Sant'Antioco is Calasetta (29 m/96 ft), a little place of rather Oriental appearance, the inhabitants of which managed, like those from Carloforte on the neighbouring island of San Pietro, to preserve the language and costumes of Genoa.

Carbonia

Beyond San Giovanni Suergiu the tour of the Iglesiente continues north on S.S. 126, which comes in 6 km/4 miles to Carbonia (pop. 33,000), a new town founded in 1938 in the middle of the Sardinian coalfield. In another 11 km/7 miles a road branches off on the left to the little ports of Portoscuso (tuna fishing) and Portovesme, from which there are boats to Carloforte (10 m/33 ft; pop. 6000).

Iglesias

13 km/8 miles beyond the turning for Portoscuso and Portovesme is Iglesias (176 m/581 ft; pop. 30,000), an old episcopal town in the centre of the Iglesiente which still preserves remains of its medieval walls and has a Mining Academy (museum). In the Piazza del Municipio stands the cathedral built by the Pisans in 1288, and to the south of the square is the medieval church of San Francesco. Above the town to the east rises the Castello Salvaterra (14th c.).

From Iglesias it is 56 km/35 miles east on S.S. 130 to Cagliari.

Calabria

Region: Calabria
Provinces: Catanzaro (CZ), Cosenza (CS) and Reggio di Calabria (RC)
Area: 15,080 sq. km/5281 sq. miles
Population: 2,116,700

Situation

The region of Calabria occupies the south-west of the peninsula, the toe of the Italian boot, between the Ionian and Tyrrhenian seas.

Landscape and vegetation

The region is traversed by the Calabrian Apennines – three massive ranges of granite and gneiss belonging to an ancient mountain rump. In the north is the Sila (Botte Donato, 1930 m/6369 ft) and in the south the Aspromonte range (Montalto, 1956 m/6455 ft), separated by an expanse of low-lying land, once marshy and malaria-ridden, which is caught between the Golfo di Squillace and the Golfo di Santa Eufemia. Along the west coast of northern Calabria, separated from the Sila by the fertile Crati valley, extends the Calabrian Coastal Chain (Catena Costiera), falling down to the sea in precipitous cliffs.

The lower uplands are covered with dense mixed forests of beeches and pines (representing about 40% of the total area of Calabria) and give the landscape an almost Central European character. There are few beaches along the coasts, which are much indented by bays and coves. The region has been frequently devastated by violent earthquakes, particularly along the Strait of Messina.

Population and economy

Economically Calabria is one of the most under-developed parts of Italy. The overwhelming majority of the population live by agriculture.

In the fertile low-lying land a mixed agriculture of Mediterranean type predominates, producing wheat, olives, citrus fruit, wine and figs; at the higher levels only pasturing is possible. The only minerals of any consequence are rock salt (at Lungro) and sulphur (at Strongoli). A number of dams in the Sila range supply electric power for the industrial area around Crotone.

In ancient times the name of Calabria was given to the Salentine peninsula, the "heel" of Italy between the Gulf of Taranto and the Adriatic, which was occupied by the Iapyges and conquered by Rome in 272 B.C. Present-day Calabria was then the land of the bruttii, and formed part of magna graecia from the 8th c. B.C. until occupied by Rome during the second Punic War. After the fall of the Ostrogothic kingdom it passed to Byzantium and was given the name of Calabria after the loss of the Salentine peninsula. In the 9th and 10th c. Calabria suffered repeated Saracen raids. It was conquered by the Normans in 1060, and later became part of the kingdom of Naples until its union with Italy in 1860.

History

Catanzaro

The capital of the region is Catanzaro (320 m/1056 ft; pop. 100,000), well-known as industrial centre and the see of an archbishop, beautifully situated on a plateau which falls away to the south, east and west. In the centre of the town are the cathedral and the church of San Domenico or Chiesa del Rosario, (richly decorated with good pictures and sculpture). There are very fine views from Via Bellavista, on the south side of the town, and the municipal gardens to the east.

13 km/8 miles south of Catanzaro, on the coast of the Ionian Sea between the mouths of the rivers Corace and Fiumarella, is the port and seaside resort of Catanzaro Marina (5 m/17 ft).
On the Gulf of Squillace is the Robinson Club Calabria.

Catanzaro Marina

About 17 km/11 miles west of Catanzaro, in a delightful setting, is the little town of Tiriolo (690 m/2277 ft; pop. 5000), renowned for the beautiful costumes of its women and for its embroidery and lace. Above the town to the north-east (½ hour's climb) is Monte di Tiriolo (838 m/2765 ft), with a ruined castle. From here there are fine views.

Tiriolo

34 km/21 miles north-west of Catanzaro, in a gorge near the coast and on the hillside above, is the little town of Paola (94 m/310 ft; pop. 17,000).
1.5 km/1 mile north-west of Paola is the convent of San Francesco di Paola (1416–1507, founder of the mendicant order of the Minims), built in the 15th c. across a gorge and enlarged in the 17th c.
There is also an attractive drive from Paola (17 km/11 miles) to the Passo Crocetta (979 m/3231 ft; view).

Paola

About 70 km/43 miles south-west of Catanzaro is the little town of Tropea (61 m/201 ft; pop. 7000), an elegant seaside resort on the Tyrrhenian Coast, with a fine cathedral.

Tropea

Cosenza

In the fertile Crati valley in north-west Calabria lies Cosenza (240 m/792 ft; population 107,000), once capital of the Bruttii (Cosentia), now a provincial capital and the see of an archbishop. The Visigothic leader

Alaric died in Cosentia in A.D. 410 and was buried with his treasure in the bed of the River Busento. To the north-west – on the slopes of the castle hill – lies the handsome new town; the old town with its narrow winding streets is built on the tongue of land within the confluence of the Crati and the Busento. In the winding main street, Corso Telesio, is the early Gothic cathedral (consecrated 1222), in which the unhappy Hohenstaufen king Henry VII was buried in 1242; in the north transept is the tomb of Isabella, wife of Philip III of France, who died in Cosenza in 1271.

From the municipal gardens on the south side of the old town the road climbs north-west to the Castello (385 m/1271 ft; view), with walls 3 m/10 ft thick which nevertheless were not strong enough to withstand the frequent earthquakes (particularly severe in 1783 and 1905).

*Sila range

A very rewarding trip can be made into the Sila range. La Sila consists of three parts – the main range, Sila Grande, the Sila Piccola to the south, and along the northern edge of the range the Sila Greca, named after the Albanians of the Greek Orthodox faith who have been settled here since the 15th c. The Sila is a plateau-like massif of ancient rocks with a total area of 3300 sq. km/1274 sq. miles and an average height of 1300–1400 m/3900-4620 ft, rising to 1930 m/6370 ft in Botte Donato, which presents a precipitous face to the Crati valley, but falls away gradually towards the Gulf of Taranto. Its extensive forests of chestnuts, beeches, oaks, black spruces and pines are still inhabited by wolves as well as by numerous black squirrels. Since 1927 the rivers have been harnessed to provide electricity by the construction of dams which form large artificial lakes; the most attractive of these are Lago Arvo (1280 m/4224 ft) and Lago Ampollino.

On the high plateaux, with their extensive areas of grazing, the trim houses of the new settlers who have been established here under the government's land reform form a striking contrast to the wretched cottages of the past.

Rossano

In the north of the Sila Greca, picturesquely situated on a hillside a few kilometres from the sea, is Rossano (275 m/908 ft; pop. 33,000), once capital of Calabria and still the see of an archbishop. On a crag to the south-east of the town is the church of San Marco, a church of Byzantine type on a centralised plan, with five domes, dating from the Norman period. The Museo Diocesano contains a valuable 6th c. Gospel manuscript. From the terrace half-way along Via Garibaldi there is a very fine view of Monte Pollino and the Apulian plain.

Sybaris

About 32 km/20 miles north-west of Rossano, in the lower course of the Crati, not far from sea, are the remains of the ancient city of Sybaris, founded in 709 B.C. by Achaeans, which became proverbial for its luxury but was destroyed in 510 B.C. by the people of Croton. Systematic excavations have been carried out here since 1960 by Milan Technical College and Pennsylvania University.

San Giovanni in Fiore

To the south of the Sila range, near Lago Ampollino, lies San Giovanni in Fiore (1049 m/3462 ft; pop. 20,000), the centre of the Sila region and a summer resort, renowned for its beautiful costumes and craft work.

Crotone

On the east coast of northern Calabria is the port and industrial town of Crotone (43 m/142 ft; pop. 60,000), in antiquity the famous Achaean colony of Croton, founded in the 8th c. B.C., which was ruled in the 6th c. B.C. by Pythagoras and his disciples. Noteworthy is the cathedral with a Byzantine Madonna and treasury. Near the Castello is the Museo Archeologico Statale (Via Risorgimento), with prehistoric and classical material.

From Crotone an interesting excursion can be made (11 km/7 miles) to Capo Colonna which has the remains of a temple of Hera Lacinia. The rounding of this cape by the Romans in 282 B.C. led to the outbreak of the Pyrrhic War. In 203 B.C. Hannibal sailed from here, leaving a record of his deeds in the temple.

Capo Colonna

Reggio di Calabria

See entry

24 km/15 miles north, in a charming situation, is the little town of Scilla (73 m/241 ft; pop. 6000), with a picturesque castle rearing above it. This was the ancient Scylla. The town was destroyed by an earthquake in 1908 but subsequently rebuilt.
The rock of Scylla, represented by Homer in the "Odyssey" as a roaring and devouring marine monster (the upper part a beautiful virgin and the lower a monster with a wolf's body and a dolphin's tail), is depicted by ancient writers as combining with Charybdis on the opposite shore to form a hazardous passage for all shipping – no doubt reflecting the dangerous eddies produced by the action of wind and tide in these straits.

Scilla

9 km/5½ miles south-west of Scilla is the little town of Villa San Gio-vanni (38 m/125 ft; population 12,000), from which there are ferries across the Strait of Messina (here 4 km/2½ miles wide) to Sicily. There are plans to build a bridge.

Villa San Giovanni

Verbicaro and the Catena Cositiera

Scilla: The Castello

Locri

Excavation site

On the east coast of southern Calabria, 3 km/2 miles south of the resort of Locri (5 m/17 ft; pop. 13,000), are the remains of the ancient Greek city of Lokroi Epizephyrioi (signposted "Scavi di Locri"), famous for the code of laws compiled by Zaleucus (c. 650 B.C.). Near the coast road are the foundations of a temple rebuilt in Ionic style in the 5th c. B.C., and on the hill of Mannella, to the north of the excavation site, are remains of the town walls. There are also a notable theatre, a Doric temple and a pre-Greek and Greek cemetery.

Campania   K–M8/9

Region: Campania
Provinces: Avellino (AV), Benevento (BN), Caserta (CE), Napoli (NA) and Salerno (SA)
Area: 13,595 sq. km/5249 sq. miles
Population: 5,607,700

Situation

The region of Campania covers an area, extending from the Neapolitan Apennines (Monte Cervati, 1898 m/6263 ft) to the coast of the Tyrrhenian Sea, here much indented (gulfs of Gaeta, Naples, Salerno and Policastro). It is a fertile low-lying region, well watered by the rivers Garigliano, Volturno and Sele.
Violent volcanic activity (Vesuvius) has left its marks on the area. The region suffered a severe earthquake in November 1980.

Scenery

The extraordinary fertility of the soil, the mild climate and the availability of water earned the region the name of "Campania Felix" in

Campania: View over Naples to Vesuvius

ancient times. It has long been one of the most densely populated parts of Italy and is intensively cultivated (wheat, fruit, vines, vegetables, tobacco).

The original inhabitants were an Italic people, the Osci. In the 8th c. the Greek colonies of Kyme, Dikaiarchia and Neapolis (Magna Graecia) were established on the coast. At the end of the 6th c. Campania was occupied by the Etruscans; in 430 B.C. it was captured by the Samnites, and in 338 B.C. by the Romans. Under the Empire it was much favoured by noble Romans as a place of residence, and the wealth and ostentation of this period has been preserved in the ruins of Herculaneum and Pompeii. In the early medieval period Campania was divided into Lombard and Byzantine spheres of influence, but was reunited by the Normans in the 12th c. and thereafter passed to the kingdom of Sicily and the kingdom of Naples.

History

Naples and Salerno

The most important towns in Campania are Naples and Salerno (see entries).

Cava de' Tirreni

Near Salerno, surrounded by hills, is the attractively situated little town of Cava de' Tirreni (180 m/594 ft; pop. 50,000), a popular holiday resort. On the hills around the town are slender round towers, many of which are still used to trap wild pigeons in October, the birds being attracted by small white stones thrown from the towers and are then caught in nets.

2.5 km/1½ miles south-east of Cava is Alessia (270 m/891 ft), from which it is a 45 minutes' walk up Monte San Liberatore (466 m/1538 ft), perhaps the finest viewpoint in the Gulf of Salerno.

*Monte San Liberatore

3.5 km/2 miles south-west of Cava, on Corpo di Cava, is the Benedictine abbey of La Trinità della Cava, founded in 1011. The present buildings date from the late 18th c. The church contains marble and mosaic altars, tombs of the earliest abbots and a 12th c. marble pulpit. Other notable features are the chapter-house (16th c.), the Romanesque cloister (small museum), the crypt, a picture gallery and the archives.

*La Trinità della Cava

Velia

In addition to Pompeii, Herculaneum and Paestum (see entries) there is the interesting Roman site of Velia (south of Salerno and Paestum), once a popular resort of the Roman aristocracy, which has the remains of a number of villas and town gates. 5 m/17 ft beneath the Roman city were found remains of the Greek town of Elea including some fine pieces of statuary and the notable Porta Rosa (4th c. B.C.), a masterpiece of Greek architecture. The Greek town was founded in 536 B.C. by Phocaeans who had been driven out of their original settlement at Alalia on Corsica. Between about 540 and 460 B.C. this was the home of the famous Eleatic school of philosophy led by Xenophanes, Parmenides and Zeno, and the town also had a noted school of medicine. At that time Elea probably had a population of 40,000, and its walls had a total length of 6 km/3½ miles, later extended to 7 km/4½ miles. The excavation of the ancient city (under which earlier remains dating from

Elea

131

the 8th c. were found) is still in progress (museums exhibits in various buildings).

On a hill to the north of the site excavations have brought to light the foundations of a temple of the 5th c. B.C., which was destroyed during the construction of the medieval castle, together with remains of a square tower of the 4th c. B.C., three smaller temples, a sacrificial altar, several dwelling-houses (2nd c. B.C.) and the road from the acropolis to the harbour.

Cales

In northern Campania, about 8 km/5 miles south-east of Teano, are considerable remains of the ancient city of Cales, which was captured from the Greeks in 335 B.C. during the Romans' victorious campaign in southern Italy and later developed into an important trading centre. Excavations have so far revealed remains of baths (1st c. B.C.), parts of the forum, remains of dwelling-houses of the 8th c. B.C., a theatre and an amphitheatre, a temple, a Christian cemetery and a 5th c. church. The town was destroyed by the Saracens in A.D. 879.

Avellino

About 30 km/19 miles north of Salerno is Avellino (348 m/1148 ft; pop. 57,000), capital of the province of the same name and the see of an archbishop. The town has food and textile industries and is a trade centre for agricultural produce.

Palinuro in Campania

Campania has numerous seaside resorts, some of them very elegant and fashionable, particularly in the bays of Naples and Salerno. Farther south is the resort of Palinuro, with excellent facilities for all kinds of water sports (diving centre). To the west of the town is the Grotta Azzurra, which is accessible only by boat.

Capo Palinuro

2.5 km/1½ miles south-west is Capo Palinuro (203 m/670 ft; lighthouse), the south side of which falls sheer down to the sea. Here too are several caves accessible only from sea.

*Grotta di Pertosa

From the Salerno-Messina motorway (A3) an attractive detour can be made by way of the little town of Auletta (280 m/924 ft), below the north side of the Monti Alburni (1742 m/5749 ft), to the stalactitic Grotta di Pertosa, a cave system 2250 m/7425 ft long. The caves have been occupied since the end of the neolithic period.

*Certosa di San Lorenzo

Another detour can be made off the A3 motorway in southern Campania. Just outside Padula (699 m/2307 ft; pop. 6000), is the Certosa di San Lorenzo, founded in 1308, a massive building, mostly dating from the 17th and 18th c., with three beautiful arcaded courtyards and a large external staircase by Vanvitelli.

Capri/Isola di Capri

Region: Campania
Province: Napoli (NA)
Area: 10.5 sq. km/4 sq. miles
Population: 12,500

Regular service several times daily from Naples (taking car not worth while; use prohibited in summer); also hydrofoil service. Also services from Sorrento, Positano, Amalfi and Ischia.

Boat services

The island of Capri, one of the most beautiful and most visited of the islands in the Tyrrhenian Sea, is in fact an extension of the peninsula of Sorrento, and lies at the southern end of the Gulf of Naples.
In Roman times, when it was known as Caprae, it was a favourite resort of the emperors Augustus and Tiberius.

*Situation

**A holiday destination rich in tradition

The island, about 6 km/4 miles long and between 1 and 2.5 km/½ and 1½ miles wide, has rugged limestone crags rising to a height of 589 m/1944 ft above the sea. The only places of any size are the picturesque little towns of Capri and Anacapri.
The island has a rich flora, including the acanthus, whose leaves form the characteristic ornament of Corinthian capitals.

Capri, the town

The regular boats land their passengers in the picturesque port of Marina Grande, on the north coast of the island. From here a funicular (5 minutes), a stepped footpath (½ hour) and a road (3 km/2 miles) leads up to the town of Capri (124 m/409 ft; pop. 8000), the island's capital, situated on a saddle between the hills of Il Capo to the east, Monte Solaro to the west, San Michele to the north-east and Castiglione to the south-west.

*Marina Grande

The central feature of the town is the little Piazza Umberto I ("the Piazza" for short), at the top of the funicular from Marina Grande. From here it is a short walk past the steps leading up to the church of Santo Stefano (1683) and along the main shopping street to the Certosa di San Giacomo (founded 1371, restored 1933), a former Carthusian

Certosa di San Giacomo

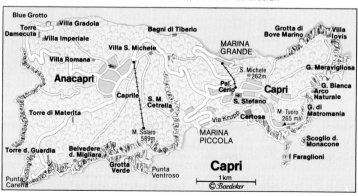

Capri: Marina Grande

house, which houses the Museo Diefenbach, with late Romanesque pictures by Diefenbach (1851–1915). The adjoining church of San Giacomo has a Gothic doorway, 17th c. frescoes and two cloisters (access to the Belvedere).

*Punta Tragara

From the Hotel Quisisana it is a 15 minutes' walk to the terrace on Punta Tragara, the south-east promontory of the island, which commands a picturesque view of the south coast and the three stacks known as the Faraglioni.

Via Tiberio

From Capri a very attractive footpath, the "Via Tiberio" (¾ hour), runs north-east to the promontory of Il Capo. Immediately beyond a gateway is the rock known as the Salto di Tiberio (297 m/980 ft) from which legend has it that the tyrannical Emperor Tiberius had his victims thrown into the sea (view). To the right are the substructures of an ancient lighthouse.

*Villa di Tiberio

In the extreme north-east of the island are the remains of the Villa de Tiberio or Villa Iovis, rising in terraces to the top of the hill, in which Tiberius is said to have lived from A.D. 27 until his death in 37.

Santa Maria del Soccorso

On the adjoining promontory is the chapel of Santa Maria del Soccorso, with a conspicuous figure of the Virgin; magnificent views from the top.

*Arco Naturale

From the Villa di Tiberio a footpath to the right leads in 15 minutes to the Arco Naturale, a natural archway in the rock (view), from which steps run down to the Grotta di Matromania, perhaps a sanctuary of the nymphs. From the cave a footpath (¾ hour) runs along above the sea, with views of the Monacone, a rocky islet, and the Faraglioni, and so back to Punta Tragara.

South-west of Capri is the little harbour of Marina Piccola, reached by a wide footpath, the Via Krupp. The path begins west of the Certosa and runs below the beautiful Parco Augusto (terrace with fine views) and round the steep-sided Castiglione to join (15 minutes) the road from Capri, on which it is another 10 minutes' walk to the harbour of Marina Piccola on the south coast of the island.

Marina Piccola
*Via Krupp

Trip to Anacapri

Anacapri, in the west of the island, is reached either by a beautiful road (3.5 km/2 miles; bus service) which winds its way up the rocky slope from the town of Capri or from Marina Grande on an ancient flight of over 500 steps, the so-called Scala Fenicia (not all usable) to the view-point of Capodimonte, 10 minutes' walk east of the town. Above the viewpoint is the Castello di Barbarossa, the ruins of a castle destroyed by the pirate Khaireddin Barbarossa in 1535.

*Capodimonte

On the slopes of Capodimonte is the conspicuous Villa San Michele, home of the Swedish doctor and author Axel Munthe (1857-1949).

San Michele

Anacapri (275 m/908 ft), a little town of almost Oriental aspect, straggles over the plateau, surrounded by vineyards. The church of San Michele has a fine majolica pavement (1751). In the Piazza is the town's principal church, Santa Sofia.

**Anacapri

Half an hour's walk south-west of the town is the viewpoint of Belvedere di Migliara, about 300 m/990 ft above the sea.

Belvedere di Migliara

From Anacapri a chair-lift (12 minutes) and a footpath (1 hour) lead up to the top of Monte Solaro (598 m/1973 ft; restaurant), to the south-east, the highest point on the island, from which on clear days there are magnificent views extending as far as the Abruzzi.

Monte Solara

"I Faraglioni" rocks

135

**Blue Grotto

About 3 km/2 miles north-west of Anacapri is one of Capri's great tourist attractions, the Blue Grotto (Grotta Azzurra), which can be reached either by boat from Marina Grande or by the Via Pagliaro (3 km/2 miles) from Anacapri. This, the most famous of Capri's caves, was carved out of the rock in prehistoric times by the constant battering of the sea, and as a result of the sinking of the land is now half-filled with water. The entrance, only about 1 m/39 in high, can be negotiated only by small boats when the sea is calm. The cave is 54 m/178 ft long, 30 m/99 ft wide and 15 m/50 ft high, with 14 to 22 m/46 to 66 ft depth of water. When the sun is shining it is filled with an extraordinary blue light (at its best from 11 a.m. to 1 p.m.).

Boat trip round the island

Another very attractive excursion is a boat trip round the island (1½–2 hours by motorboat, 3–4 hours by rowing-boat), which allows visitors to see the other caves around the coasts of Capri. The finest are the Grotta Bianca and the Grotta Meravigliosa above it (on the east coast near the Arco Naturale), the Grotta Verde at the foot of Monte Solara and the Grotta Rossa.
A boat trip to the Faraglioni is also worthwhile.

Carrara   G5

Region: Toscana
Province: Massa-Carrara (MS)
Altitude: 100 m/330 ft
Population: 70,000

Situation
The town of Carrara lies in a valley in the Apuan Alps only a few kilometres from the Ligurian Sea.

*Marble quarries
Carrara is famous for the 400 marble quarries around the town which provide employment for most of its population. The stonemasons' workshops are of great interest.

Sights

Cathedral
In the north of the town is the Cathedral of Sant'Andrea (11th–14th c.), with a fine Romanesque and Gothic façade, the lower part of which consists of half-columns and pointed arches; the centre part of the doorway is richly decorated.

Academy of Fine Art
To the south, in Via Roma, the town's principal street, is the Accademia di Belle Arti, with pictures and marble sculptures. 500 m/550 yd west of the cathedral is the Church of the Madonna delle Grazie, with sumptuous marble decoration.

Museo Civico del Marmo (Marble Museum)

Viale XX Settembre
South-west of the town's centre is the Museo Civico del Marmo (Municipal Marble Museum) with five departments, demonstrating the history of marble, from antiquity to its present-day artistic and technical uses.

Marble quarry near Carrara

*Marble quarries in the surroundings of Carrara

Every tourist should visit the marble quarries in the three valleys which meet at Carrara, the Colonnata, Fantiscritti and Ravaccione valleys. They can be reached on reasonably good roads. The quarries were already being worked in Roman times, but achieved their widest fame through Michelangelo, who greatly prized the marble of Carrara. Particularly impressive are the quarries at Piastre (4 km/2½ miles east), which yield the fine marmo statuario.

The marble is shipped from the nearby Mediterranean ports (Marina di Carrara, e.g.) to places all over the world.

Massa

South-east of Carrara is Massa (65 m/215 ft; pop. 66,000), chief town of the province of Massa-Carrara, which also has large marble quarries. Notable are the former Palazzo Ducale (now a prefecture), a fine Baroque building of 1701, the cathedral and, north-east of the town (15 minutes), the massive 15th–16th c. castle, from which there are fine views. 5 km/3 miles south-west is the seaside resort of Marina di Massa, with a long beach.

Situation
7 km/4½ miles
south-east

Pietrasanta   G6

Farther south-east of Carrara is the town of Pietrasanta (14 m/46 ft; pop. 26,000), beautifully situated among hills.

It is the principal resort of the Versilia region, the district between

Situation
18 km/11 miles
south-east of Carrara

137

Massa and Viareggio. The campanile of the 13th–14th c. cathedral of San Martino is unfinished. Adjoining the cathedral is the baptistery with a fine font (1509). In the cathedral square is the Archaeological Museum (Museo Archeologico Versiliese).

There are numerous good hotels at Marina Pietrasanta (4 km/2½ miles south-west).

Caserta L8

Region: Campania
Province: Caserta (CE)
Altitude: 68 m/224 ft
Population: 66,000

Situation

The provincial capital of Caserta, the "Versailles" of the Bourbon rulers of Naples, lies at the foot of the Monti Tifatini in the northern part of the Campanian plain – some 30 km/19 miles north of Naples.

Sights

*Palazzo Reale

Opposite the station is the former Royal Palace (247 m/925 ft long, 41 m/135 ft wide; 1200 rooms and 1790 windows), a magnificent residence in the manner of Versailles built by Luigi Vanvitelli for King Charles III of Naples and Sicily from 1752 onwards. During the Second World War it was the headquarters of the Allied Mediterranean Command, and the document of surrender of the German forces in Italy was signed here on 29 April 1945. The interior, with its well-preserved decoration and furnishings, forms a museum of the Bourbon dynasty which ruled the kingdom of the Two Sicilies (1734–1860). Particularly fine are the Grand Staircase (116 steps), the Cappella Reale, the Royal Apartments and the Theatre.

Behind the palace is the park, with magnificent fountains adorned with statues, and the magnificent "Grand Cascade". From the terrace beyond the beautiful English Garden (45 minutes' walk north of the palace) there are very fine views.

Caserta Vecchia

About 10 km/6 miles north-east of Caserta is the dilapidated village of Caserta Vecchia (401 m/1323 ft), originally founded by the Lombards, which has retained its medieval character. It boasts a castle of the counts of Caserta and a cathedral (12th-13th c.), built in Normano-Sicilian style, with a fine campanile (1234).

Santa Maria Capua Vetere

Situation
7 km/4 miles west

From Caserta there is an interesting trip (7 km/4 miles west) to the developing town of Santa Maria di Capua Vetere (36 m/119 ft; pop. 32,000), on the site of the ancient capital of Campania, Capua, which was originally founded by the Etruscans. As the centre of this fertile region Capua became a wealthy and powerful city renowned for its luxury, but after its destruction by the Saracens in the 9th c. the town was moved to its present-day site. In the north-west of the town is the Amphitheatre, built in the reign of Augustus (1st c. A.D.) and restored by Hadrian, which was the largest in Italy until the building of the Colos-

Caserta: fountains and statuary of the Palazzo Reale

seum in Rome (170 m/561 ft long, 140 m/462 ft across). Under the arena (76 m/251 ft long, 46 m/152 ft across) are well-preserved substructures (passages, cages for wild beasts). Near the amphitheatre are the remains of a fine triumphal arch (three arches), dedicated to the Emperor Hadrian (2nd c. A.D.).

About 500 m/550 yd south, in an underground passage, is a mithraeum (2nd c. A.D.), a shrine of the Persian god of light, Mithras, richly decorated with paintings.   *Mitraeum

About 500 m/550 yd south-east is the cathedral of Santa Maria Maggiore, with columns from the amphitheatre.   Cathedral

5 km/3 miles north-west of the ancient city of Capua Vetere, in a bend of the River Volturno, is the modern town of Capua (25 m/83 ft; pop. 19,000), the see of an archbishop, built on the site of the ancient Capua after its destruction in the 9th c. and held for many years by Norman rulers. In the centre of the town, near the Volturno, is the cathedral, rebuilt after its destruction during the Second World War, the only parts which survived unscathed being the campanile and the 11th c. forecourt, with its ancient columns (3rd c.). Nearby is the Campanian Provincial Museum, the most important archaeological museum in Campania after the National Museum in Naples.   Capua

5 km/3 miles east, on the western slopes of Monte Tifata (604 m/1993 ft), lies the village of Sant'Angelo in Formis, with a Romanesque basilica built in 1058 on the site of a temple of Diana Tifatina. The beautiful portico has Oriental pointed arches. The church contains ancient marble columns and fine frescoes of the school of Montecassino (11th c.).   Sant'Angelo in Formis

Catania

Region: Sicilia
Province: Catania (CT)
Altitude: 10 m/33 ft
Population: 378,000

Situation and importance

Catania, capital of the province of the same name, lies half-way along the flat eastern coast of Sicily to the south-east of Mount Etna. It is Sicily's second largest town after Palermo and one of the most important ports in Italy, shipping the produce of the wide and fertile Piana di Catania, the principal grain-growing region in Sicily.
Catania possesses a university and is the see of an archbishop.

Catania is a town of imposing modern aspect, having been almost completely rebuilt, with long straight streets, after a devastating earthquake in 1693. The wealth of the city is demonstrated by its fine Baroque churches and large aristocratic mansions, frequently rebuilt after earthquake damage.

History

Katana was founded about 729 B.C. by Greek settlers from Naxos, and was one of the first places on the island to be taken by the Romans (263 B.C.). Under Roman rule it grew into one of the largest towns on Sicily, but during the early medieval period it declined into insignificance, recovering its prosperity only in the 14th c. under Aragonese rule. The 1693 earthquake, which affected the whole of Sicily, was particularly destructive in Catania.

Cathedral

The central feature of the town is the beautiful Piazza de Duomo, in the centre of which is a fountan with an ancient elephant, carved from lava, and bearing a granite Egyptian obelisk. On the east side of the square rises the 18th c. cathedral (choir apses and east wall of transept 13th c.).

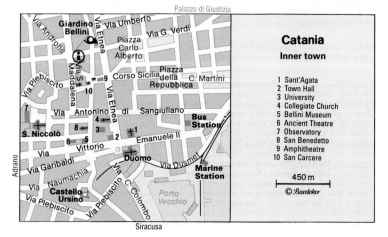

Catania

Inner town

1 Sant'Agata
2 Town Hall
3 University
4 Collegiate Church
5 Bellini Museum
6 Ancient Theatre
7 Observatory
8 San Benedetto
9 Amphitheatre
10 San Carcere

450 m

© Baedeker

In the interior (by the second pillar on the right) lies the tomb of the composer Vincenzo Bellini (1801–1835), a native of Catania. To the right, in front of the choir (beautiful choir-stalls), is the chapel of St Agatha, with the tomb of the Spanish viceroy Acuña (d. 1494).

Across the street from the cathedral, to the north, stands the abbey of Sant'Agata.   Sant'Agata

A little way south-east of the Piazza del Duomo, beyond the railway viaduct, lies the harbour.   Harbour

Castello Ursino

About 500 m/550 yd south-west of the Piazza del Duomo, in Piazza Federico di Svevia, is the Castello Ursino, lying close to the sea, which was built for Frederick II about 1240 and later, in the 14th c., became the residence of the kings of Aragon. Thereafter it served as a prison and as barracks, and since 1934 has housed the Museo Civico, with a fine collection including Greek sculptures of the 5th–4th c. B.C.   Museo Civico

From the south-west corner of the Piazza del Duomo the busy Via Garibaldi runs past the Piazza Mazzini, to the Porta Garibaldi (1768).   Via Garibaldi

Piazza San Francesco

To the north, in Via Vittorio Emanuele, a wide street 3 km/2 miles long, is the Piazza San Francesco, with the Bellini Museum, the house in which the composer was born.

Catania: Piazza del Duomo

141

Catania

Teatro Romano Immediately to the west (entrance from the Via Teatro Greco) stands the Ancient Theatre (Teatro Romano), on Greek foundations, most of it now underground. On its west side is the Odeon, a small and well-preserved Roman theatre for rehearsals and musical competitions.

San Nicola

In Via Crociferi, which runs north from the Piazza San Francesco, are two churches with Baroque façades, San Benedetto and Chiesa dei Gesuiti (both on the left). On the right stands the church of San Guiliano.

About 500 m/550 yd west, in Piazza Dante, is the former Benedictine monastery of San Nicola (founded 1518, rebuilt 1735), used from 1866 as a barracks and a school.

*Monastery church The monastery church, with an unfinished façade, is a massive Baroque structure. From the lantern of the dome (internal height 62 m/205 ft) there are extensive views. There are also fine views from the observatory which adjoins the church on the north-west.

Via Etnea

Town Hall From the Piazza del Duomo Via Etnea, the town's wide principal street, runs north for 3 km/2 miles, interrupted by a series of spacious squares, with a prospect of Etna in the background. Immediately on the left stands the Town Hall.

University Nearby the Piazza dell'Università on the left, is the University, founded in 1444, in a fine building erected in 1818. Farther on is the Collegiate Church, with a fine Baroque façade (1768). The next square is the palm-shaded Piazza Stesicoro, with a monument to Bellini.

Anfiteatro On the left side of the square are the remains of a Roman amphitheatre (perhaps 2nd c. A.D.), partly demolished during the reign of Theodoric in order to provide material for building the town walls; only the north end is visible. The amphitheatre originally measured 126 × 106 m/416 × 350 ft; its unusually large arena (70 × 50 m/231 × 165 ft) was second only to the Colosseum in Rome (86 × 54 m/284 × 178 ft).

A little way to the west is the church of San Carcere (13th c. doorway).

Giardino Bellini Farther along Via Etnea, on the left, a few steps beyond Piazza Stericoro, is the main entrance to the Giardino Bellini, an attractive public garden (pleasant views from the terrace).

Northern part of the city

Along the north side of the Villa Bellini runs the tree-lined Viale Regina Margherita, which with its eastward continuation the Viale XX Settembre and the wide Corso Italia, beginning at the beautiful Piazza Verga (with the modern Law Courts), forms the main traffic artery, 6 km/4 miles long, of the northern part of the city.

*Coast road At its eastern end is the Piazza Europa, which looks down on to the sea and from which a magnificent coast road (lookout terraces) leads north to the suburban district of Ognina, with the little Porto d'Ulisse in a sheltered bay.

**Etna

The most rewarding excursion from Catania is the ascent of Etna or the subsidiary craters of Monti Rossi, or alternatively the trip round the volcano.

Cefalù

Region: Sicilia
Province: Palermo (PA)
Altitude: 16 m/33 ft
Population: 13,000

The little port of Cefalù, picturesquely situated under a bare limestone crag which falls sheer down to the sea, lies on the northern coast of Sicily, some 50 km/30 miles from Palermo (west) and 100 km/62 miles from Messina (east). It has preserved much of its character and charm. Cefalù is the seat of a bishop.

Situation

Sights

On the east side of the town's principal street, the Corso Ruggero, which runs north towards the sea, is the spacious Piazza del Duomo, with the Town Hall and the cathedral, one of the finest buildings of the Norman Period, which was begun by King Roger in 1131–1132.
The interior (74 m/244 ft long, 29 m/96 ft wide) has fifteen granite columns and one of cipollino, with beautiful capitals. The apse contains magnificent mosaics, including one of the Saviour (1148), as well as the "Virgin with Four Archangels", and the "Twelve Apostles". In the south aisle is a fine 12th c. font. The cloister (beautiful capitals) is entered from the north aisle.

**Cathedral

A short way west of the Piazza del Duomo is the little Museo Mandralisca, with antiquities from the Lipari Islands and fine pictures, including the "Picture of an Unknown Person" by Antonello da Messina (1470).

Museo Mandralisca

View of Cefalù

143

La Rocca

At the north end of the Corso Ruggero is the starting point of the climb (¾-1 hour) of the crag known as the Rocca (269 m/888 ft), which is composed almost entirely of fossils; remains of a medieval castle and of an ancient polygonal structure known as the Tempio di Diana (9th c. B.C.). From the highest point, on which are remains of a Norman castle, there are magnificent views.

Santuario di Gibilmanna

Situation
15 km/9 miles south

South of Cefalù is the Santuario di Gibilmanna (17th–18th c.), a place of pilgrimage and above it an observatory (1005 m/3317 ft; views).

Cerveteri   18

Region: Lazio
Province: Roma (ROMA)
Altitude: 81 m/267 ft
Population: 14,000

Situation

The little country town of Cerveteri, now a place of no particular importance, occupies the site of the ancient Caere, once one of the leading Etruscan cities, on a tufa ridge 45 km/28 miles north-west of Rome.

Sights

In the Piazza Santa Maria is the medieval Rocca, a castle which is partly built on Etruscan walls of the 4th c. B.C.

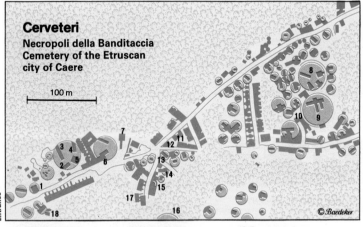

Cerveteri
Necropoli della Banditaccia
Cemetery of the Etruscan city of Caere

100 m

© Baedeker

Entrance

1 Tomba dei Capitelli	7 Tomba dei Rilievi	13 Tumulo della Quercia
2 Tomba dei Letti e Sarcofagi	8 Tumulo del Colonello	14 Tumulo dei 2 Ingressi
3 Tomba della Capanna	9 Tumulo Mengarelli	15 Tumulo della Cornice
4 Tomba dei Dolii	10 Tumulo Maroi	16 Grande Tumulo della Tegola Dipinta
5 Tomba dei Vasi Greci	11 Tomba di Marce Ursus	17 Tomba dei 6 Loculi
6 Tomba dei 13 Cadaveri	12 Tomba della Casetta	18 Tombe della Spianata

Opposite stands the 16th c. Palazzo Ruspoli, which houses the Museo Nazionale Cerite, containing material from the Etruscan cemeteries round the town; the most important items, however, are in Rome (Etruscan Museum in the Vatican, Villa Giulia Museum).

Museo Nazionale Cerite

*Etruscan cemetery

To the north of the town, extending along the edge of the tufa hill known as the Banditaccia, is a large Etruscan cemetery (7th–1st c. B.C.); a city of the dead which bears impressive witness, in the scale of the necropolis and the richness of the buried goods, to the importance attached by the Etruscans to the cult of the dead. On either side of a "main street" some 2 km/1½ miles long, with a number of side streets, lie hundreds of tombs, including huge tumuli up to 30 m/99 ft in diameter and many tomb chambers hewn from the rock in the form of dwelling-houses, often with several rooms. Many tombs have holes showing the point of entry of early tomb-robbers (a torch should be taken).

*Tumuli

Particularly fine is the Tomba dei Rilievi, with painted bas-relief representations of everyday objects.

*Tomba dei Rilievi

Cinqueterre   F5

Region: Liguria
Province: La Spezia (SP)
Population: 7000

The very picturesque coastal region known as the Cinqueterre, fringed by tall and precipitous cliffs, lies between La Spezia and Levante on the Gulf of Genoa, the so-called Riviera di Levante, with the five villages ("cinque terre") of Monterosso al Mare, Vernazza, Corniglia, Manarola and Riomaggiore, of which Monterosso al Mare, a medieval fishing village, is the largest.

Situation

Landscape of the Cinqueterre

These picturesque villages, linked with one another only by a narrow winding country road but accessible individually by road, railway or boat, have in consequence of their remoteness preserved their old-world aspect. With their beautiful setting and their pleasant climate they have a charm and a character all their own.
The inhabitants live by agriculture (vines, olives) and fishing.

This charming coastal stretch, with its steeply sloping vineyards, should be explored on foot. Numerous footpaths link Monterosso al Mare with the other villages of the Cinqueterre.

Walks

Città di Castello   I6

Region: Umbria
Province: Perugia (PG)
Altitude: 288 m/950 ft
Population: 38,000

Città di Castello lies on the Tiber in northern Umbria – some 50 km/30 miles north of Perugia.

Situation

Cinqueterre: Monterosso al Mare

History   Città di Castello occupies the site of a Roman town, Tifernum Tiberi-
                 num, which was destroyed by the Ostrogothic king Totila. During the
                 Renaissance period it was ruled by the Vitelli family, and later belonged
                 to the Papal State.

Sights

                 The central feature of the town, which is still partly surrounded by its
                 old walls, is the Piazza Matteotti, enclosed by fine old palaces, among
                 which the Palazzo Vitelli (16th c.).
Cathedral   To the west of the Piazza Matteotti is the Piazza Gabriotti, in which
                 stands the fine rusticated Palazzo Comunale (Town Hall). Beyond this,
                 on the west, is the Cathedral of Santi Florido e Amanzio, originally
                 11th c. but remodelled in Renaissance style in the 15th and 16th c. The
                 treasury contains an embossed silver antepedium with designs in
                 silver-gilt (*c.* 1150).
                 On the west side of the square is the little Giardino Pubblico.

San Domenico   South-east of the cathedral is the Gothic church of San Domenico
                 (1424), with old frescoes and a pretty monastic courtyard.
*Pinacoteca   Near the church by the town wall stands the fine Palazzo Vitelli della
Comunale   Cannoniera, which contains the municipal picture collection, with nu-
                 merous altarpieces (13th–15th c.), a maestà by the master of Città di
                 Castello (13th c.), early work by Raffael and the "Martyrdom of St
                 Sebastian" by Luca Signorelli.

San Francesco   North of Piazza Matteotti stands the church of San Francesco, with a
                 Vitelli Chapel built by Vasari.

Cividale del Friuli K3

Region: Friuli-Venezia Giulia
Province: Udine (UD)
Altitude: 138 m/455 ft
Population: 11,000

Cividale del Friuli, formerly capital of Friuli, lies a little way east of   Situation
Udine, on the River Natisone below the Julian Alps, which have
belonged to Yugoslavia since 1947.
With its early medieval buildings, it has much of interest to offer the
visitor. The town suffered some damage in an earthquake in May 1976.

Cividale, the Roman Forum Iulii – which gave its name to the region of   History
Friuli – was from 569 to 774 the seat of Lombard dukes, and from 730
the residence of the Patriarch of Aquileia. After his conquest of the
Lombard kingdom in 774 Charlemagne made it the seat, under the
name of Civitas Austriae, of a line of Frankish margraves, the most
important of whom, Berengarius I, ruled Italy as king from 888 to 924,
with Cividale as his capital.
Even after the seat of the Patriarchate was transferred to Udine in 1238
Cividale remained for centuries the most important place in Friuli by
virtue of its command of major Alpine passes. In 1419 the town was
occupied by the Venetians, who in 1439 compelled the Patriarch to
renounce his secular authority. Thereafter the town fell into a steady
decline. In 1752 the Patriarchate was replaced by the archbishopric of
Gorizia and Udine.

Cividale del Friuli: Devil's Bridge and Cathedral

Sights

Cathedral	In the Piazza del Duomo, in the centre of the town, stands the cathedral (originally 8th c.; remodelled in Early Renaissance style by Pietro and Tullio Lombardi from 1502 onwards). It contains the remains of an octagonal baptistery (8th c.), the altar of Duke Ratchis (8th c.) and a Romanesque silver-gilt antependium (*c.* 1200). Notable are the crypt and the treasury. Also in the Piazza del Duomo are the Palazzo del Comune (Town Hall) and the Palazzo Pretorio (formerly Palazzo del Provveditore), built by Palladio.
*Museo Archeologico Nazionale	Opposite the cathedral is the Museo Archeologico Nazionale, with valuable Lombard antiquities (fine gold ornaments) and prehistoric, Roman and medieval material (including two psalters which belonged to St Elizabeth of Thuringia, d. 1231).
*Tempietto	At Porta Brossana is the former Benedictine convent of Santa Maria in Valle, picturesquely situated on the banks of the Natisone, with the Tempietto, the front part of a Lombard church destroyed by a spate of the river (stucco reliefs of the 8th–9th c.; Byzantine frescoes of the 8th c.; 14th c. choir-stalls). Lower down, on the river bank, is the church of Santi Pietro e Biagio, with the remains of ancient frescoes.

Santiuario di Castelmonte

Situation 10 km/6 miles east	There is a rewarding excursion through steep and narrow roads to the Santuario di Castelmonte (618 m/2039 ft), the most famous pilgrimage centre in Friuli.

Como   F4

	Region: Lombardia Province: Como (CO) Altitude: 202 m/667 ft Population: 95,000
Situation	Como, capital of the province of the same name, some 50 km/31 miles north of Milan, lies at the southern end of Lake Como, surrounded by rocky hills, which are partly forest-covered. The walled old town, with a rectangular layout derived from that of a Roman camp, is fringed by attractive suburbs. Como is an important centre of the silk industry.
History	Como was founded by the Romans in 195 B.C., on the site of an earlier settlement, as the frontier fortress of Comum, directed against the Rhaetians. During the Middle Ages the town – which in 1058 had the status of an episcopal see independent of Milan – was the key to Lombardy and an important base of the German emperors. In 1451 it passed to the control of Milan. In recent years considerable subsidence has been noted.

Sights

The town's life centres on the Piazza Cavour, by the harbour, from which the short Via Plinio runs south-east to the Piazza del Duomo. On

Como: Cathedral façade   *Tempio Voltiano*

the east side of this square is the Broletto (1215), formerly a lawcourt,
now a banqueting hall.

Adjoining it to the south-east is the cathedral, built entirely of marble   *Cathedral
(originally erected 1396, remodelled in Renaissance style 1426–1596;
dome over crossing 1730–1770). On either side of the principal doorway, which has fine sculptured decorations, are statues (1498) of Pliny
the Elder and Younger, natives of Como. South-east of the cathedral in
Via Vittorio Emanuele II, Como's principal street, is the Romanesque
church of San Fedele (12th c.). Opposite it is the Town Hall.

Farther south, in the Palazzo Giovio, are the Musei Civici, with archae-   Museums
ological finds and documents on local history.

Via Vittorio Emanuele II runs south to end at the town walls, which
enclose Como on three sides. On the south-east side of the old town are
three well-preserved 12th c. towers.

About 500 m/550 yd from the south-west corner of the town walls is the   Sant'Abbondio
twin-towered church of Sant'Abbondio, a basilica in Lombard Romanesque style (11th c.; modernised in 1587). The choir contains 14th c.
frescoes.

A little way south-west of Piazza Cavour is Piazza Volta, with a statue of
the physicist Alessandro Volta (1745–1827), a native of Como who was
born in No. 50 Via Volta.

At the north-east corner of the Giardino Pubblico, on the shores of the   Tempio Voltiano
lake, stands the neo-classical Tempio Voltiano, with the Volta Museum,   (Museum)
the exhibits in which include the first voltaic pile.

Brunate

From the Piazza Vittoria it is 5 km/3 miles by road (also funicular) to
the villa suburb of Brunata (716 m/2363 ft), on a terrace on the hillside,

with beautiful views of Como, the plain extending as far as Milan, the Pre-Alps and the mountains from Monte Rosa to Monviso.

San Maurizio

There are even more extensive views from San Maurizio (871 m/2874 ft), 2.5 km/2 miles above Brunate.

Monte Boletto

From Brunate there is a footpath (2 hours) to the top of Monte Boletto (1234 m/472 ft; views).

Lake Como/Lago di Como/Lario   F3/4

Region: Lombardia
Province: Como (CO)
Altitude: 198 m/653 ft

Situation

Lake Como (Lago di Como or Lario), the Roman Lacus Larius, lies 50 km/31 miles north of Milan between the Lugano and the Bergamo Alps. Narrow and fjord-like, the lake fills the glaciated valley of the Adda, which flows through it from end to end. From its northern end to its southern tip at Como the lake is 50 km/31 miles long; at its half-way point, between Menaggio and Varenna, it is 4 km/2½ miles wide; it has an area of 146 sq. km/56 sq. miles; and its greatest depth is 410 m/1353 ft, making it the deepest of the lakes of northern Italy.

*Scenery

On the south-west arm, the Lago di Como, are numerous villas surrounded by beautiful gardens and vineyards. The rather more austere south-east arm, the Lago di Lecco, with the outflow of the Adda, is less crowded with visitors. On the steep hillsides bordering the lake, rising to 2610 m/8613 ft in Monte Legnone, are plantations of chestnuts and walnuts, the green of their foliage contrasting strongly with the greyish tints of the olives. The inhabitants live by fishing, the production of wine and oil, and by industry (ironworking, marble-quarrying, textiles).

Boat services

Boat services (from Bellano throughout the year): Between Colico and Como, with varying ports of call on both sides of the lake; between Bellano and Como; between Varenna and Lecco. In summer there are also hydrofoil services.

*Round the lake (248 km/154 miles)

*Villa Olmo

Leave Como on the Lugano road, going north-west and in 2 km/1¼ miles turn into S.S. 340, which runs up the west side of the lake. On the right of the road is the neo-classical Villa Olmo (1782–1797; damaged by fire 1983); now used for exhibitions, concerts and congresses; fine views from the park.

Cernobbio

3 km/2 miles: Cernobbio (201 m/663 ft; pop. 7500), with many villas set in beautiful gardens and the palatial Villa d'Este (1568; now a hotel). From here a narrow road winds its way up (16 km/10 miles) to Monte Bisbino (1325 m/4373 ft; views), on which there is a pilgrimage church.

Lenno

22 km/14 miles: Lenno, the most southerly place in the district of Tremezzina, over which towers Monte Crocione (1641 m/5415 ft). From here an attractive visit can be made to the Punta di Balbianello or Punta d'Avedo, a long promontory projecting into the lake, with the Villa Arconati (late 16th c.; access only by boat), from the terrace of which there are beautiful views.

Tremezzo

3 km/2 miles: Tremezzo, a popular resort in a warm and sheltered situation on the lake, surrounded by beautiful gardens.

*Villa Carlotta

500 m/550 yd: Villa Carlotta (formerly Sommariva, named after Charlotte, Duchess of Meiningen, mother of an earlier owner; now the property of the State). The palace built in 1747 contains Thorwaldsen's

famous marble frieze of Alexander the Great's triumphal entry into Babylon, and sculptures by Canova. The gardens are a riot of southern vegetation (azaleas in bloom in May).

550 m/550 yd: Cadenabbia (201 m/663 ft), with a Romanesque church, many villas and a beautiful lakeside promenade.

Cadenabbia

4 km/2½ miles: Menaggio (203 m/670 ft; pop. 3000), one of the most popular resorts on Lake Como. The road then passes the rocky walls of the Sasso Rancio.

Menaggio

12 km/7 miles: Dongo (208 m/686 ft), outside which Mussolini and his mistress Clara Petacci were caught by partisans in 1945 while fleeing to Switzerland. They were shot on the following day at Mezzagra, near Lenno.

Dongo

4 km/2½ miles: Gravedona (201 m/663 ft) with the Romanesque-Lombard church of Santa Maria del Tiglio (12th c.).

Gravedona

10 km/6 miles: Gera Lario (208 m/686 ft), the most northerly place on Lake Como.

Gera Lario

4 km/2½ miles beyond Gera Lario the road joins S.S. 36, coming from Chiavenna, which runs down the east side of the lake to Milan.

8 km/5 miles: Colico (209 m/690 ft), dominated by the mighty Monte Legnone.

Colico

7 km/4½ miles: The abbey of Piona, an old Cluniac monastery, with a fine 11th c. church (restored), contains Byzantine frescoes and an interesting Romanesque-Gothic cloister (1257).

Abbey of Piona

4 km/2½ miles: Dervio (202 m/667 ft), from which a detour can be made to Monte Legnone (2610 m/8613 ft: 18 km/11 miles by road, then 4 hours' climb).

Dervio

8 km/5 miles: Varenna (220 m/726 ft), situated on an promontory at the mouth of the Valle d'Esino, with beautiful gardens and quarries of black marble; magnificent views of Bellagio on a promontory and of the three arms of the lake. The Villa Monastero (park) is occupied by the Italian Institute of Hydrobiology.

Varenna

11 km/7 miles: Mandello del Lario (214 m/706 ft), on a delta running far out into the lake at the foot of the jagged Grigna Meridionale, with one of the largest motorcycle factories in Italy (Moto Guzzi).

Mandello del Lario

10 km/6 miles: Lecco (214 m/706 ft), an industrial town magnificently situated at the south-east tip of Lake Como, at the outflow of the River Adda. In the Largo Manzoni is a monument to the novelist Alessandro Manzoni (1785–1873), author of "I Promessi Sposi", the scene of which is partly set in Lecco.

Lecco

East of Lecco are the Piani d'Erna (1329 m/4386 ft), reached by cableway or by road. To the north is the Piano dei Resinelli (1272 m/4198 ft), from which the Grigna Meridionale (2184 m/7207 ft) can be climbed (2½ hours).

At the south-west end of Lecco we leave S.S. 36 and turn right into a road which runs below the precipitous slopes of Monte Moregallo (1276 m/4211 ft), passing through a number of tunnels.

16 km/10 miles: Bellagio (229 m/756 ft), a very popular spa on the west side of the Punta di Bellagio, one of the great beauty spots of the north Italian lakes. On the promontory is the Villa Serbelloni, with a park (conducted tour) from which there are views of the three arms of Lake Como. Farther along the road are the park of the Villa Melzi and the gardens of the Villa Trotti.

Bellagio

14 km/9 miles: Nesso (275 m/908 ft), a picturesque village at the mouth of the Val di Nesso, with a waterfall 20 m/66 ft high.

Nesso

8 km/ 5 miles: Below the road on the right, in Molina bay, is the Villa Pliniana (1570), named after a spring mentioned by Pliny the Younger which daily changes its level.

Villa Pliniana

Torno

4 km/2½ miles: Torno (225 m/743 ft), a finely situated village on a rocky promontory, surrounded by villas. Near the picturesque harbour is the church of Santa Tecla, with 15th c. frescoes.
7 km/4½ miles: Como.

Cortina d'Ampezzo   I3

Region: Veneto
Province: Belluno (BL)
Altitude: 1224 m/4039 ft
Population: 8000

Situation

The internationally renowned tourist centre of Cortina d'Ampezzo, Italy's most popular winter sports resort, lies at the eastern end of the Strada delle Dolomiti in a wide valley enclosed by the high peaks of the Dolomites.
The Winter Olympics 1956 took place in Cortina d'Ampezzo.

Sights

* Parish church

In the Corso Italia, the lively main street of Cortina (pedestrian precinct), is the fine parish church (18th c.), with ceiling paintings and wall paintings in the choir by Franz Anton Zeiller (1774) and an altar dedicated to the Virgin by Andrea Brustolon (1724).

Casa de Ra Regoles (Museums)

A short distance south-east, in the Casa de Ra Regoles, are the Mario Rimoldi Collection (contemporary art) and the Museum (fossils; material of folk interest), with works by De Chirico, De Pisis, Guttuso, Morandi.
Farther south-east, by the cemetery, is the beautiful Baroque church of the Madonna della Difesa.

Sport stadiums

Ice Stadium

To the north of Cortina is the Olympic Ice Stadium (Stadio Olimpico del Ghiaccio) with a memorial to the French geologist Dieudonné Dolomieu (1750–1801), after whom the Dolomites are named.

Olympic ski-jump

To the south of the town, on the road to Pieve di Cadore, a little way off, to the right, is the Olympic ski-jump (Trampolino Olimpico di Salto "Italia").

Cableways west of the valley

Tofana

A cableway (Freccia del Cielo) runs from the Ice Stadium to the Col Drusciè (1770 m/5841 ft) and Ra Valles (2470 m/8151 ft); from here there is a double chair-lift to Bus Tofana 2823 m/9316 ft) with a connection to the Tofana di Mezzo (3244 m/10,705 ft; upper station 15 minutes below the peak).

Forcella Pomedes

There is a chair-lift from Campo Corono (1220 m/4026 ft) via Colfiere (1462 m/4825 ft) to the Col Drusciè; two parallel lifts from Rumerlo (1678 m/5537 ft) via the Rifugio Duca d'Aosta (2098 m/6923 ft) to the Forcella Pomedes (2282 m/7531 ft; mountain hut).

Pocol-Belvedere

From the Piazza Roma (near the parish church), a cableway leads to Pocol-Belvedere (Belvedere on the Crepa; 1539 m/5079 ft); the hotel complex of Pocol rises above the valley of Cortina d'Ampezzo.

Cortina d'Ampezzo in winter

Cableways east of the valley

A chair-lift from Guargnè (1304 m/4303 ft) goes via the Col Tondo (1437 m/4742 ft) to the Rifugio Mietres (1710 m/5643 ft).

Rifugio Mietres

From the bus station a cableway leads via Mandres (1480 m/4884 ft) to the Rifugio Faloria (2123 m/7006 ft) and from there to the Capanna Tondi di Faloria (2327 m/7679 ft).

Capanna Tondi di Faloria

Strada delle Dolomiti

See Dolomites

Cortona

H/I6

Region: Toscana
Province: Arezzo (AR)
Altitude: 500–650 m/1650–2145 ft

The town of Cortona lies close to the eastern border of Tuscany, north of the Lake Trasimene in Umbria, and 30 km/19 miles south of Arezzo.

Situation

Cortona is one of the oldest towns in Italy. It was one of the twelve cities of the Etruscan League, and later became a Roman colony. During the Middle Ages it passed through various vicissitudes before coming under the control of Florence in 1411. The painter Luca Signorelli (d. 1523) was born in Cortono in 1441 or 1450.

History

153

Piazza della Repubblica

Palazzo Comunale

The central feature of the walled old town is the Piazza della Repubblica, on the west side of which stands the Palazzo Comunale (Town Hall; 13th c., with later rebuilding), with a broad flight of steps.

Palazzo Pretorio
(Museum)

To the north-west of the Town Hall is the Piazza Signorelli, with the Palazzo Pretorio, the façade of which bears the coats of arms of former podestàs; it now houses the Accademia Etrusca (founded 1726) and the Museum of Etruscan Antiquities (Etruscan bronze candelabrum; 5th c. B.C.).

Cathedral

North-west of the Piazza Signoreli, in the Piazza del Duomo (extensive views), stands the cathedral (originally Romanesque, remodelled in Renaissance style by Giuliano da Sangallo, 1456-1502).

*Museo Diocesano

Opposite the cathedral, in the former Baptistery (or Chiesa del Gesù), is the Museo Diocesano, which contains some fine pictures, including works by Fra Angelico, Luca Signorelli, Pietro Lorenzetti and other artists, and a Roman sarcophagus of the 2nd c. A.D.

Town walls

To the east of the cathedral, from the Porta Colonia, there is an impressive view of the town walls (2600 m/8580 ft long; lower parts Etruscan).

Santa Maria Nuova

1 km/¾ mile north-east, below the Porta Colonia, is the church of Santa Maria Nuova (16th c.), a Renaissance building with a quadrangular plan (high dome).

San Francesco

The church of San Francesco is to the east of the town (begun in 1245 in Gothic style and remodelled in the 17th c.) has a remarkable reliquary of the Holy Cross on the high altar and a Byzantine ivory picture of the 10th c.

Piazza Garibaldi

*San Domenico

From the Piazza della Repubblica the Via Nazionale runs south-east to the Piazza Garibaldi, outside the town walls. To the east of this square, on the north side of the Giardino Pubblico (public park), stands the 15th c. church of San Domenico, originally part of a Dominican convent, with pictures by Signorelli and a winged altar by Lorenzo Ghiberti (14th–15th c.).

Luca Signorelli: "Scourging" in the Cortona Diocesan Museum

From the Piazza Garibaldi a twisting road with four sharp bends descends for 3 km/2 miles to the southern slope of the town hill, on which stands the church of Santa Maria del Calcinaio, a beautiful domed building on a cruciform plan by Francesco di Giorgio of Siena. The church was dedicated to a miraculous Madonna (originally on the wall of a lime pit = calcinaio).

*Madonna del Calcinaio

Fortezza Medicea

High above the town rises the Fortezza Medicea (fortress of the Medici family), the north-eastern corner pillar of the town wall. From here there are magnificent views.
A little way below the fortress, clinging to the hill, are the buildings of the Santuario di Santa Margherita (pilgrimage church), with the tomb of St Margaret of Cortona (dates from 1362; her silver reliquary is on the high altar).

Santuario di Santa Margherita

Castiglion Fiorentino

The village of Castiglion Fiorentino is picturesquely situated on a hill, surrounded by medieval town walls (14th and 15th c. towers).

Situation
12 km/7½ miles
north-west of
Cortona

Cremona

G4

Region: Lombardia
Province: Cremona (CR)
Altitude: 79 m/261 ft
Population: 85,000

The provincial capital of Cremona lies in the fertile North Italian plain just north of the Po, near the mouth of the River Adda, some 70 km/43 miles south-east of Milan, the capital of Lombardy.
The town is world-famed for the violin-makers who worked here, particularly in the 16th–18th c. The violins made by Niccolò Amati, Antonio Stradivari, Guarneri de Gesù and other violin-makers are famous for their sound.

Situation

Violin-makers

The Gallic settlement on this site became a Roman colony in 218 B.C., and in later centuries suffered destruction on many occasions – by Vespasian's army (in A.D. 70), by the Goths and the Lombards, and during the struggle between Guelfs and Ghibelines. The town was an important base of the emperor Frederick II. In 1334 it passed to Milan. Cremona was the birthplace of the composer Claudio Monteverdi (1567–1643).

History

*Piazza del Comune

In the Piazza del Comune, in the centre of the picturesque old town, stands the town's principal landmark, the imposing Torrazzo (1267), an octagonal tower 111 m/366 ft high, from which there are extensive views.
East of the Torrazzo, linked with it by a Renaissance loggia (begun 1497, completed in the 18th c.), is the cathedral, in Lombard Gothic style

*Torrazzo

*Cathedral

(1107–1190), which has a richly sculptured façade embellished with columns. It contains frescoes (1506–1573) by Pordenone, Boccaccino and others.

Baptistery
Adjoining the cathedral are the octagonal Baptistery (1167), with a font by L. Trotti (16th c.) and the subterranean Campo Santo.

*Palazzo Comunale
On the west side of the square is the Gothic Palazzo Comunale (Town Hall, 1206–1245), which contains four violins by the famous Cremonese violin-makers. To the left of the Town Hall is the Gothic Loggia dei Militi (1292).

Museum of Natural History
Worth visiting is the Museum of Natural History, situated some 500 m/550 yd south-west of the cathedral, in Piazza Marconi.

San Pietro al Po
About 250 m/275 yd west, stands the church of San Pietro al Po (1563–1568), the interior of which contains rich stucco ornament and ceiling paintings by Antonio Campi (d. 1591).

Ponchielli Theatre
Nearby the church is the Ponchielli Theatre (concerts, operas and other events).

Piazza Roma

A little way north of the cathedral is the Piazza Roma, laid out with gardens, on which the life of the town is centred (memorial stone to Stradivarius). From here the Corso Mazzini (pedestrian precinct) leads to the Palazzo Fodri (15th–16th c.; formerly a pawnshop), a fine Renaissance mansion with a notable loggia-courtyard. North-west of the Piazza Roma, in Via Ugolani Dati, we find the imposing Palazzo Affaitati (1561), a massive Late Renaissance building with a Baroque courtyard and staircase, which now houses the Museo Civico, with numerous works by the Cremona school of painters (15th–18th c.) founded by Boccaccio Boccaccino (c. 1467–1525), as well as archaeological finds, ceramics, and Cremona terracotta work. The old town has fine churches and palaces, many of them with terracotta decoration. The Palazzo Affaitati (corner Via Ugolani Dati/Via Palestro) houses the Stradivarius Museum, with more than 700 examples by the famous violin-maker of Cremona, together with drawings and models. Antonio Stradivarius, called Stradivari (1644–1737), a pupil of Niccolò Amati, was the most famous violin-maker of Cremona. He had the ability to appreciate the acoustic quality of various types of wood. Stradivarius acquired great wealth, and the Italians still use the expression "as rich as Stradivari".

Palazzo Fodri

Museo Civico

Stradivarius Museum

San Sigismondo

Situation
2 km/1¼ miles east
East of Cremona is the church of San Sigismondo, a superb Early Renaissance building by Bartolomeo Gadia (1463), with frescoes and pictures by Camillo Boccaccio, the younger Campi and others.

Dolomites   H/I3

Regions: Trentino-Alto Adige and Veneto
Provinces: Bolzano (BZ), Trento (TN) and Belluno (BL)

Situation and importance
The Dolomites are a range of mountains in the eastern part of the Alps, situated in northern Italy, actually in the Alto Adige – east of Bolzano and Trento.

The magnificent range of mountains called the Dolomites after the French geologist Dieudonné (or Déodat) Dolomieu (1750–1801) is one of the most beautiful and most visited parts of the Alps. Taken in its widest sense, the range is bounded by the rivers Isarco, Adige, Brenta, Piave and Rienza. Scattered among the mountains are beautiful little lakes, including the Lago di Braies, Lago di Carezza, Lago di Misurina, Lago di Landria and Lago d'Álleghe.

The famous Alpine glow, bathing the Alps in the flaming red of the setting sun, is particularly beautiful in the Dolomites. The real Alpine glow, when the rock faces and snowfields are clad in brilliant hues of yellow, purple and red, occurs only very rarely, and then only for five to ten minutes after sunset, when there is a light haze in the west and dusk has already fallen in the valleys. `Alpine glow`

The natural flora of the Dolomites is of Alpine character. The valley floors and gentler slopes are mostly covered with arable land and pasture, while the steeper slopes, up to 2200 m/7260 ft, are wooded – mostly with conifers but in the southern Dolomites also deciduous trees. Above the tree level are great expanses of upland meadows spangled with Alpine flowers. `Flora`

Population

The Isarco valley and its side valleys and the Val Pusteria were settled from the 6th c. onwards by German-speaking Bajuwari (Bavarians), while at the same time Italians advanced into the region from the south. The Rhaetians, speaking a Romance language and now known as Ladins, withdrew into the inner valleys of the Dolomites, and are now mainly found in the Val Gardena and Val Gadera. There are newspapers and magazines in the Ladin language which is derived from Latin. The Ladins are noted for their fine wood-carving, particularly in the Val Gardena.

Legends of giants and dwarfs, witches and ghosts, princes and heroes have grown up in the Dolomite area, most of them originating from the the Ladin region. `Legends`

Tourism

The main source of income of the population, apart from stock-farming and forestry, is alpine tourism, particularly winter sports.
The Dolomites are remarkably easy of access, thanks to the valleys which cut deeply into the mountains and to an excellent network of roads (for example the Strada delle Dolomiti). In addition to large and widely famed winter sports and health resorts, such as Cortina d'Ampezzo, Corvara and San Martino di Castrozza, there are numerous small and middle-sized resorts and a host of remote mountain hotels and inns.
The military roads of the First World War, many of them still in good condition, make it possible even for non-climbers to reach the heights and enjoy the extensive views they offer. The summits are being brought within easier reach by the steadily increasing numbers of cableways and lifts of various kinds.
The area between the Isarco valley, the Val Pustera and the Val di Fiemme forms the greatest skiing area in the Alps, the so-called "Dolomiti Superski", a "Mecca" for skiers. Some 500 lifts give access to 1000 kilometres/620 miles of pistes, descents through deep snow and `**Dolomiti Superski`

Three pinnacles in the Dolomites

cross-country skiing and all can be used with a single ski pass. The cableways cover a difference in altitude of some 100,000 m/330,000 ft.

**Dolomite Road

The 110 km/68 mile-long Great Dolomite Road runs from Bolzano to Cortina d'Ampezzo (see entries).

Eggen Valley
Karneld

Not far from Bolzano (see entry) we cross the Brenner motorway and climb the gorge in the Eggen valley through which flows the Karneld stream. On a steep rocky height on the left stands Karneld Castle (13th c., restored about 1880; chapel and frescoes) above the village of the same name. In Kardaun is the Eisack power station, beyond which a road bridge crosses the Eggen valley waterfall.

Then the valley broadens out; near Birchabruck (Ponte Nova; 877 m/2728 ft) there is a fine view of the Laternar (on the right) and the Rosengarten (on the left). Beyond Birchabruck the Dolomite Road leaves the Eggen valley and ascends the Welschofen valley.

Welschofen/Nova
Levante

The village of Welschofen, picturesquely situated on the hillside, is popular both as a summer and as a winter sports resort. From the Hainzer sawmill a chair-lift goes up to the Frommer Alm (1730 m/5678 ft) and continues to the Kölner Hütte, (2337 m/7679 ft). From the Cologne Path (Kölner Weg) it is about 1¼ hours to the Paolina Hut (2127 m/6981 ft) above the Karer Pass (see below).

*Carezza Lake

After almost 6 km/4 miles we reach the little hotel settlement of Karersee (Carezza al Lago; 1609 m/5281 ft) not far above the Carezza Lake (Lago di Carezza; 1530 m/5121 ft; nature reserve), in which are reflected the rough rocky walls of the Laternar (2794 m/8611 ft) which rises in the south. In the north-east towers the Rotwand (2806 m/9209 ft).

The Dolomite Road now continues downhill above meadows to the Passo di Costalunga (1753 m/5753 ft) on the German/Ladin language frontier between the Laternar and the Rotwand.
High above the top of the pass stands a monument to the Dolomite pioneer Theodor Cristomanos.

Passo di Costalunga

On the far side of the summit of the pass is Vigo di Fassa (1382 m/4536 ft), a popular holiday and winter sports resort on the slopes above the Fassa valley. In the 15th c. parish church in the community of San Giovanni can be seen frescoes dating from the 16th c. Above the village is a military cemetery.

Vigo di Fassa

Further up the Fassa valley in which flows the River Avisio lies the resort of Pozza di Fassa (1290 m/4234 ft), with a chair-lift to the Buffaure slope (2020 m/6629 ft; ski-lifts).

Pozza di Fassa

Campitello di Fassa, dominated by the jagged peaks of the Langkofel, is much visited both in summer and in winter. A chair-lift goes up to the Col Rodella (2387 m/7834 ft); it takes about 15 minutes to climb to the Rodella (2485 m/8156 ft; TV transmission aerial; refuge hut).

Campitello di Fassa

*Rodella

At the end of the Val Lastie lies Canazei a very popular touring base and winter sports resort of the upper Fassa Valley.

Canazei

A cableway leads to Pecol on the road over the Pordoi ridge where there is an extensive skiing area. A chair-lift ascends to the Belvedere (2389 m/7841 ft; refuge hut). From the Pordoi ridge the Viel dal Pan track leads in 2½ hours via the Viel dal Pan Refugio (2346 m/7746 ft; refuge hut) to the Refugio Marmolada/Castiglioni on the artificially dammed Fadaia Lake (2046 m/6715 ft).

Pecol

On the road leading south from Canazei to the Fadaia Pass is the village of Alba (cableway to Ciampac, 2136 m/7010 ft; skiing area). The road to the pass reaches the picturesque mountain village of Penia (1556 m/5107 ft) and, above Pian Trevisam (1717 m/5635 ft; Refugio Villetta Maria), continues to the Fedaia Lake (see above).

Alba
Road to the Fadaia Pass

On a two-hour mountain tour over the Baita Robinson (1828 m/5999 ft) we reach the Refugio Contrin (2016 m/6617 ft). The path continues in 4½ hours above the 2704 m/8875 ft-high Ombretta Pass, then below the mighty south wall of the Marmolada along to the Refugio O. Falier (2080 m/6827 ft) and on to the hotel settlement of Malga Ciapela (1446 m/4746 ft) on the east side of the Marmolada.

Malga Ciapela

This stretch via Pecol (see above) continues uphill with numerous bends to the 2239 m/7348 ft-high Pordoi Col, the highest point on the Great Dolomite Road. It offers a magnificent view; in the east are the Ampezzo Dolomites with Tofana. From the Pordoi Col there is a cableway to the 2950 m/9682 ft-high Sasso Pordoi. From here it is another 1½ hours via the Refugio Forcella Pordoi (2850 m/9354 ft) to Piz Boè (3151 m/10,342 ft), the highest peak of the Sella group.

*Sasso Pordoi

The Dolomite Road winds its way down from the Pordoi ridge and in 10 km/6 miles reaches Arabba (1602 m/5258 ft), primarily a winter sports resort at the foot of the Sella group.

Arabba

A cableway (with a chair-lift in winter running parallel to it) leads to Porta Vescovo (2510 m/8238 ft; mountain hut), a depression between

Porta Vescovo

the Belvedere (2650 m/8697 ft) and the Mesola (2739 m/8989 ft), from which there is an impressive view over the Fedaia Lake (see above) on the north flank of the Marmolada.

Livinallongo/ Buchenstein

The Dolomite Road now follows the Livinallongo Valley watered by the Cordevole river, first along the floor of the valley and later high on the northern slope and over a gorge. Then we reach Pieve di Livinallongo, the administrative centre of the extensive district of Livinallongo del Col di Lana.

South-east below Pieve is the Sacrario di Pian di Salesi, an Italian military cemetery. The road to it continues south to Caprile and Alleghe on the lake of the same name.

*Col di Lana

To the north above Pieve di Livinallongo towers the 2462 m/8080 ft-high Col di Lana which can be reached on foot in three hours via the Refugio Gaetani (1835 m/6022 ft). The summit was the scene of intense fighting in 1915 to 1918; Italian alpine troops drove a tunnel under the positions of the Austrian Imperial infantry on the summit and on April 17th/18th 1916 blew it up. Near the summit stands a memorial chapel and remains of the military positions; from the top there is an exceptional panorama.

Falzarego Pass/ Passo di Falzarego

Beyond Pieve di Livinallongo the Dolomite Road turns north and climbs the 2177 m/7145 ft-high Falzarego Pass, a broad depression which is overlooked on the west by the Sasso di Stria ("witches' rock"; 2477 m/8130 ft), on the east by the curiously named Cinque Torri ("five towers"; 2362 m/7752 ft) and on the south by Nuvolauo (2575 m/8451 ft). North of the pass a cableway goes up to the Piccolo Lagazuoi (2728 m/8953 ft).

Valparola ridge

From the Falzarego Pass a road leads north-west along the beautiful Lago di Valparola to the 2192 m/7194 ft-high Valparola ridge, over-

In the Ampezzo Dolomites

looked on the north-east by the Lagazuoi (2803 m/9199 ft), then winds downhill to Armentarola (1640 m/5382 ft); from here we continue through the charmingly situated village of San Cassiano (1537 m/5044 ft) to the villaɡɔ of La Villa (Stern; 1483 m/4867 ft), high in the valley of the Gader.
The Dolomite Road continues in curves and S-bends steadily downhill; on the left is the mighty rock wall of Tofana (see Cortina d'Ampezzo, mountain railways).

A good 5 km/3 miles beyond the summit of the pass a road branches off to the Refugio Cinque Torri (2131 m/6994 ft); from here there are climbs on the rocks of the Cinque Torri ("five towers"; main summit 2362 m/7752 ft). About 15 minutes west of the hut is the Refugio Scoiattoli (2230 m/7319 ft; ski-lift), from where a chair-lift descends to the Refugio Bai de Dones (1900 m/6236 ft) on the Dolomite Road.

Cinque Torri

About 7 km/4½ miles beyond the summit of the Falzarego Pass a 6 km/4 mile-long military road branches off to the Refugio Cantore (2545 m/8353 ft), the starting point for climbing the 3244 m/10,647 ft-high Tofana (see Cortina d'Ampezzo, mountain railways).
Via Pocol we reach in 9 km/5½ miles the winter sports resort of Cortina d'Ampezzo (see entry).

**Tofana

Elba/Isola d'Elba

Region: Toscana
Province: Livorno (LI)
Area: 223 sq. km/86 sq. miles

Regular services (including car ferries) run several times daily from Piombino to Portoferraio and between Livorno and Portoferraio. In summer there are also hydrofoil services from Piombino and Livorno to Portoferraio.

Boat services

The island of Elba, the largest of the islands off Tuscany, lies in the Ligurian Sea 10 km/6 miles south of the mainland port of Piombino.
Elba, 27 km/17 miles long, up to 18.5 km/11 miles wide, consists mainly of granite and porphyry, and has considerable deposits of high-quality iron ore, particularly in the eastern part of the island, with a metal content of 40–80%.

Situation

The possession of the iron-mines of Elba enabled the Etruscans to assert their dominance in Italy, and the mines were later worked by the Romans. Together with the tuna and anchovy fisheries and agriculture (fruit, vines) the working of iron is still one of the island's main sources of income.
Elba's mild and equable climate, its great scenic beauty and the excellent conditions for scuba diving off its cliff-fringed coast have drawn increasing numbers of visitors to the island in recent years.

Population and economy

*Holiday resort

Elba belonged to Pisa from the 11th c. onwards; then in 1284 it passed to Genoa, later to Lucca and in 1736 to Spain. After Napoleon's defeat in 1814 he was granted full sovereign rights over the island, and lived there from 3 May 1814 to 26 February 1815. Elba was returned to the Grand Duchy of Tuscany by the Congress of Vienna.

History

Portoferraio

The chief place of the island, Portoferraio (10 m/33 ft; pop. 11,500), lies on a promontory on the west side of the entrance to a wide bay on the

Elba: the beach at Secchetto

north coast. In the main street, Via Garibaldi, stands the Town Hall and a little way north-east, in Via Napoleone, the Misericordia church, in which a mass is said for Napoleon's soul on 5 May every year; it contains a reproduction of his coffin and a bronze cast of his death-mask. On the highest point in the town is the Piazza Napoleone, from which there are fine views. To the west rises Forte Falcone (79 m/261 ft), to the east, above the lighthouse, Forte Stella (48 m/158 ft), both originally built in 1548 and later completed by Napoleon. On the seaward side of the square is the simple Villa dei Molini, Napoleon's official residence, which contains his library.

Villa Napoleone   About 6 km/4 miles south-west of Portoferraio, set amid luxuriant vegetation on the slopes of the wooded Monte San Martino (370 m/1221 ft), is situated the Villa Napoleone, the emperor's summer residence (fine views from terrace).

Pinacoteca Foresiana   Near the summer residence is a building which houses the Pinacoteca Foresiana, with works by Antonio Canova ("Galatea"), Guido Reni and Salvatore Rosa.

Drive through the island of Elba

Procchio
Marciana Marina   A road runs west from Portoferraio to the seaside resort of Procchio, in the bay of the same name, and the village of Marciana Marina (18 km/11 miles), another popular resort.

Poggio
Marciana   About 4 km/2½ miles inland is the fort of Poggio (359 m/1185 ft), and 4 km/2½ miles west of this the village of Marciana (375 m/1238 ft; ruined castle), a summer resort surrounded by fine chestnut woods.

From here there is a cableway up Monte Capanne (1019 m/3363 ft), the island's highest peak (views).

Monte Capanne

From Poggio there is an attractive walk up Monte Perone (630 m/2079 ft), to the south-east (1 hour).

Monte Perone

On the east coast is Rio Marina (pop. 2500) with large open-cast iron workings.

Rio Marina

Picturesquely situated in a long inlet lies the little fishing port of Porto Azzurro (pop. 3000), which was fortified by the Spaniards in the 17th c.

Porto Azzurro

Worth visiting is the charming mining and wine producing village of Capoliveri, situated on a promontory in the south-east of the island.

Capoliveri

On the lonely south coast is the popular seaside resort of Marina di Campo, finely situated in the Golfo di Campo.

Marina di Campo

Emilia Romagna

Region: Emilia-Romagna
Provinces: Bologna (BO), Ferrara (FE), Forli (FO), Modena (MO), Parma (PR), Piacenza (PC), Ravenna (RA) and Reggio nell'Emilia (RE)
Area: 22,124 sq. km/8542 sq. miles
Population: 3,947,100

Emilia-Romagna, the south-eastern part of the north Italian plain occupies the area extending from the River Po to the Apennines and then eastward to the Adriatic coast.
It comprises the provinces of Bologna, Ferrara, Forli, Modena, Parma, Piacenza, Ravenna and Reggio nell'Emilia.

Situation

The high fertility of the soil and the advantages of its situation in an area of passage traversed by ancient traffic and trade routes between the Adriatic, northern Italy and the Gulf of Genoa enabled this region, and particularly the larger towns, to attain considerable prosperity from an early period.
Emilia-Romagna is still one of Italy's most highly developed regions. The main elements in its agriculture are meat and dairy farming, tomatoes and fruit, wine, sugar-beet, maize and rice. Its industries have an international reputation – petro-chemicals, based on the recently developed resources of oil and natural gas in the Po plain, engineering, car manufacture, textiles, boots and shoes. On the Adriatic coast fisheries and the tourist trade also make important contributions to the economy of the region.

Population and economy

Emilia, the western part of the region, derives its name from the Roman Via Aemilia (now Via Emilia), a military road running from Rimini along the south edge of the north Italian plain via Bologna, Parma and Piacenza to Tortona which was built by the consul Marcus Aemilius Lepidus in 187 b.c. to protect the Roman provinces north of the Apennines. After the Lombard conquest of northern Italy the south-east part of the region, including Forli and Ravenna, remained in Byzantine hands under the name of Romagna.

History

The modern Via Emilia is an attractive route, passing through a series of important towns with much of interest to offer, such as Piacenza – Parma – Reggio nell'Emilia – Modena – Bologna – and Forli (see entries).

Tip

Fidenza

*Cathedral

Between Piacenza and Parma is Fidenza (72 m/236 ft; pop. 25,000), the ancient Fidentia Iulia, which was known between 387 and 1927 as Borgo San Donnino. The fine cathedral is in Lombard Romanesque style (12th c.), with lion doorways and statues of prophets on the unfinished façade. Inside, to right of the entrance, there is a Romanesque holy-water stoup.

Salsomaggiore Terme

About 10 km/6 miles south-west of Fidenza is Salsomaggiore Terme (165 m/541 ft; pop. 18,000), a spa attracting many visitors between March and November, with springs (high iodine, bromine and salt content) which are effective in the treatment of disorders of the joints, muscles, heart and nerves.

Cesena in Emilia

Within the triangle formed by Ravenna, Forli and Rimini, also on the Via Emilia, is the walled town of Cesena (40 m/131 ft; pop. 90,000), with the famous Biblioteca Malatestiana (1452), a Gothic cathedral and the Rocca Malatestiana (built 14th c., completely remodelled 15th c.), a bastion standing on a hill.

*Abbazia Santa Maria di Pomposa

Between Choggia and Ravenna, near the Adriatic coast, is the Benedictine abbey of Santa Maria di Pomposa (founded in the 7th c.), of importance during the Middle Ages, but abandoned in the 17th c. because of the prevalent malaria. It has a church, built in the 8th–9th c. and enlarged in the 10th–11th c., with an interesting atrium and a campanile 48 m/158 ft high; in the interior there are a fine mosaic pavement and mid 14th c. frescoes. Other remains of the abbey are the chapter-house with well-preserved frescoes, the refectory (c. 1320) and the Palazzo della Ragione (now a college of agriculture).

Enna

Region: Sicilia
Province: Catania (CT)
Altitude: 931 m/3072 ft
Population: 30,000

Situation

The town of Enna, previously known as Castrogiovanni, reverted to its classical name in 1926. It is picturesquely situated on a horseshoe-shaped plateau in the Monti Erei, in the centre of Sicily, and has been aptly called the "belvedere" or the "navel" of the island.

Sights

The main square, the Piazza Vittorio Emanuele, lies on the north side of the town, with the church and convent of San Francesco (15th c. campanile) and a terrace commanding fine views. From the smaller Piazza Crispi, to the west, there is a superb view of the little town of Calascibetta, 3 km/2 miles north-west.

Enna: Piazza Armerina

From the Piazza Vittorio Emanuele the south-east section of the town's main shopping street, Via Roma, passes the Theatre and the Town Hall and reaches the Piazza Mazzini.

On the north side of the Piazza Mazzini stands the cathedral or Chiesa Madre (begun in 1307) which has a picturesque interior (14th c.), with four half-columns and eight full columns on bizarrely carved bases. Beyond the cathedral is the Museo Alessi, which houses the cathedral treasury containing Greco-Roman material and medieval paintings.

Cathedral

The Via Roma ends at the Castello di Lombardia, a huge pile, with three courtyards, which still preserves six of its original twenty towers. From the platform of the Torre Pisana there are magnificent views, particularly at sunset: to the east the towering mass of Etna, to the north the Monti Nebrodi and the Madonie range, to the south the Lago di Pergusa and, on clear days, the distant Mediterranean.

Castello di
Lombardia

The south-east section of the Via Roma runs from the Piazza Vittorio Emanuele past the churches of San Cataldo and San Tommaso to the Giardino Pubblico, in the centre of which, on a hill, is the octagonal tower of a castle built by Frederick II of Aragon (*c.* 1300; fine views).

Outside the gates of the town is a great wall painting by Fausto De Marinis.

From Enna via Piazza Armerina to Caltagirone (*c.* 70 km/43 miles)

A fascinating excursion from Enna is via the Lago di Pergusa to Piazza Armerina (35 km/22 miles; pop. 25,000), a town also known as Chiazza

Piazza Armerina

to the Sicilians, with a handsome cathedral and the Norman church of Sant'Andrea (1096; fine 12th–15th c. frescoes), 1 km/¾ mile north.

**Villa Romana del Casale

6 km/4 miles south of the Piazza Armerina is the site of the Villa Romana del Casale, a magnificent example of a Roman country house of the late Empire (3rd–4th c. A.D.; occupied until about 1200), with baths, a peristyle and a basilica. The villa is notable for its splendid series of mosaics, particularly in the Triclinium (dining-room), covering more than 3000 sq. m/3588 sq. yd, which are among the largest and best of their kind.

*Morgantina

In the vicinity of the Piazza Armerina are other excavations of the ancient city of Morgantina, with a Greek theatre, extensive Agora and remains of a shrine and of the town walls, 10 km/6 miles long.

Caltagirone

From Piazza Armerina it is well worth continuing south-west (32 km/20 miles) to visit Caltagirone (568 m/1874 ft; pop. 62,000), which is famous for its majolica and terracotta work. It has an interesting Museum of Ceramics.

Caltanisetta

Situation
34 km/21 miles
south-west

South-west of Enna is Caltanisetta (588 m/1940 ft; pop. 65,000), a provincial capital and the most important town in the interior of Sicily (sulphur mines). The main square of the town is the Piazza Garibaldi, in which are the cathedral (consecrated 1622; frescoes by Borremans, 1720; splendid Maundy Thursday procession) and the Town Hall (Museo Civico). Beyond the Town Hall are the Law Courts, in Baroque style. From the Piazza Garibaldi the Corso Umberto I runs south into the Viale Regina Margherita, in which are the Palazzo del Governo and the Villa Amadeo gardens. In the east of the town are the disused church of Santa Maria degli Angeli (13th–14th c.) and the ruins of the Aragonese castle of Pietrarossa (727 m/2399 ft; view), to the north of the town, stands a statue of Christ 18 m/59 ft high.

Etna   L/M12

Region: Sicilia
Province: Catania (CT)

Situation

Etna (3343 m/11,032 ft), also called "Mongibello" (from the Italian "monte" and the Arabic "giabal" = mountain) lies in the east of the island of Sicily – close to the coast and north-west of Catania. It is Europe's largest active volcano and after the Alpine peaks the highest mountain in Italy. The area has been designated as a National Park.

**Etna

Etna is one of the youngest geological features in Sicily and rises in the form of a truncated cone probably where an arm of the sea existed in Tertiary times. The almost circular base is 40 km/25 miles in diameter and 165 km/102 miles in circumference.

Altitude of the
Vegetation zones

The upper slopes have only a meagre cover of vegetation; the porous rock allows water to sink down rapidly to lower levels, where it meets an impervious bed of rocks and emerges in many places as springs.

Oranges and lemons are grown up to about 500 m/1650 ft, olives and vines to 1300 m/4290 ft. Above this are forest trees and macchia up to 2100 m/6930 ft, sometimes with recent lava flows cutting through them. The summit region up to the snow line is a dull black wasteland glistening in the sun.

There are more than one hundred known eruptions of Etna. The volcanic vents, more than 260 in number, are mostly on the flanks of the mountain. Major activity occurs at intervals of four to twelve years (the most recent eruption was in 1992). | Eruptions

On the south slope of Etna, where the sun shines for 3000 hours in a year, stands the solar power-station "Eurhelios" (surface 6000 sq. m/7176 sq. yd). | Solar power-station

Ascent of Etna

The little town of Nicolosi (698 m/2303 ft; pop. 3850) on the south side of Etna, is the starting point for the ascent to the subsidiary craters of the Monti Rossi (948 m/3128 ft; the climb takes 45 minutes to 1 hour; view). The walls of the crater show clear volcanic stratification; to the north-west, at the foot of the Monti Rossi, is the Grotta delle Palombe (lava cave).

From Nicolosi the road runs first north-west and then north between lava flows and comes in 17 km/11 miles to the turning (1 km/¾ mile, left) to the Grande Albergo Etna and in another 1 km/¾ mile to the Casa Cantoniera (roadman's house) which now houses the vulcanological and meteorological station of Catania University; nearby is the restau-

Etna the volcanic landmark of Sicily

rant and Rifugio-Albergo G. Sapienza. Opposite the rifugio is the lower station of a cableway which is once again threatened by outbreaks of lava, and which only goes up to a little over 2600 m/8580 ft (at present not in operation; ascent by cross-country vehicle). The observatory (2943 m/9712 ft) was destroyed in 1971.

Crater

The crater of Etna, which is filled with gases, is always changing its shape by eruptions. It is impossible to get very close to the crater. As Etna is never really inactive the area is declared dangerous to visitors; the climb leads through a rugged moonlike landscape.

Valle del Bove

South-east of the former observatory is the beginning of the Valle del Bove (Valley of the Ox), a black and desolate chasm (5 km/3 miles wide) surrounded on three sides by rock walls 600–1200 m/1980–3960 ft high. Experienced climbers can go down (with guide) through the Valle del Bove to Zafferanda Etnea (600 m/1980 ft).

Round Etna

A drive round Etna, starting from Catania (144 km/89 miles, also possible by rail), is very rewarding. The road runs via Misterbianco (213 m/703 ft; pop. 15,000), Paternò (225 m/743 ft; pop. 46,500) with a castle built by Roger I in 1073 (rebuilt in the 14th c.; well-preserved interior), towering above the town, to Adrano (588 m/1940 ft; pop. 34,000), beautifully situated on a lava plateau, with a Norman castle containing an Archaeological Museum and the convent of Santa Lucia, 15th–17th c.

About 9 km/5½ miles south-west of Adrano, picturesquely situated on a steep hill above the Simeto valley, with a magnificent view of Etna, is the little town of Centuripe (730 m/2409 ft; pop. 6750), formerly Centorbi, with the so-called Castello di Corradino (1st c. B.C.). The Archaeological Museum contains finds from the ancient Siculan town of Centuripae which rose to importance in the late Hellenistic-Roman period and was destroyed by Frederick II in 1233 (interesting the Hellenistic-Roman house "Contrada panneria", with paintings of the 2nd–1st c. B.C.).

From Adrano the road continues via Bronte (760 m/2508 ft; pop. 20,000), Maletto (960 m/3168 ft; old castle), Randazzo and Linguaglossa (600 m/1980 ft; pop. 4500) to Fiumefreddo (62 m/205 ft). Then back to Catania on the motorway A18 or S.S.114.

Faenza   H5

Region: Emilia-Romagna
Province: Ravenna (RA)
Altitude: 35 m/116 ft
Population: 55,000

Situation and importance

Faenza lies in the Po plain between Bologna and Rimini – about 45 km/28 miles north-west of Bologna and 55 km/34 miles south-east of Rimini.

Faenza is famous for the faience (majolica) which is named after the town. The great age of this ware was in the 15th and 16th c., and it is only in recent years that the craft has again been practised and deliberately promoted.

Sights

The town, still surrounded by its old town walls, suffered severe war damage, but this has been almost completely made good. The main street is the Corso Giuseppe Mazzini, at the east end of which are two elongated squares joining one another at right angles – the Piazza della Libertà to the north and the Piazza del Popolo to the south. In the Piazza della Libertà are the Torre dell'Orologio (Clock-Tower) and a beautiful fountain of 1621.

Notable is the cathedral (1474–1513) in Early Renaissance style, with the tomb of St Savinus (by Benedetto da Maiano; 1476) to the left of the high altar.
In the Piazza del Popolo are the Town Hall (left) and the Palazzo del Podestà (right; 1256), both with high arcades.

Cathedral

In a palace in Via Santa Maria dell'Angelo are the Pinacoteca, with paintings by old masters of Emilia and Romagna (wooden statue of St Hieronymus by Donatello and his pupils) and the Museo Civico. A building in Corso Matteotti (No. 2) houses the modern department of the Museo Civico (Fattori, Signorini, Rodin, De Pisis, Morandi and others).

Pinacoteca
Museo Civico

In Viale Baccarini we find the richly stocked Ceramic Museum (Museo delle Ceramiche), with majolica of the area and ceramics from all over the world.

*Museo delle
Ceramiche

Fano

K6

Region: Marche
Province: Pesaro e Urbino (PS)
Altitude: 14 m/46 ft
Population: 53,000

Fano, the ancient Fanum Fortunae, built on the site of a temple of Fortuna, and now a popular seaside resort, lies on the Adriatic, south-east of Pesaro.

Situation

Sights

The central feature of the town, which is still surrounded by its medieval walls and a deep moat, is the Piazza XX Settembre, in which are the Palazzo della Ragione (built in 1299 and used since 1862 as a theatre) and the Torre Civica. On the south side of the square is the beautiful Fontana della Fortuna (1593).
The Palazzo Malatesta, at the north end of the square, contains a lapidarium and a small collection of pictures.

Piazza XX Settembre
*Palazzo della
Ragione

North-west of the Piazza XX Settembre is the Piazza Mercato, from which Via dell'Arco d'Augusto leads to the Romanesque cathedral of San Fortunato; inside are frescoes by Domenicchino (1623).

Cathedral

Near the cathedral the triumphal triple Arch of Augustus (Arco di Augusto; 2nd c.; remodelled in the 9th c.) spans the street. The original form of the arch can be seen on the façade of the adjoining church of San Michele (Renaissance doorway).

*Arco di Augusto

To the south of the Piazza XX Settembre stands the church of Santa Maria Nuova, which contains a "Madonna Enthroned with Six Saints" by Perugino and a "Visitation" by Giovanni Santi.

Santa Maria Nuova

Ferrara   H5

Region: Emilia-Romagna
Province: Ferrara (FE)
Altitude: 9 m/30 ft
Population: 148,000

Situation

Ferrara, capital of the province of the same name, lies 5 km/3 miles
south of the River Po in the fertile north Italian plain. The distance from
Ferrara to the Adriatic coast is about 50 km/31 miles.
Ferrara, see of an archbishop, and with a small university, was once the
splendid capital of the dukes of Este and an important trading centre. Its
wide streets, forbidding castle and sumptuous Renaissance palaces
still bear witness to the great days of its past.

History

The town first appears in the records at the time of the great migration.
In 1332 it fell into the hands of the Este family, one of the oldest noble
houses in Italy (961–1598), which reached its period of greatest splendour in the 16th c. Ariosto (1474–1533), the greatest Italian poet of the
day, and the poet Torquato Tasso (1544–1595) lived at the brilliant
Renaissance court. Girolamo Savonarola was born in Ferrara in 1452.
In 1598 the town was incorporated in the Papal State and in 1860 it was
united with the Kingdom of Italy.

* Castello Estense

In the centre of the town is the picturesque Castello Estense, the four-
towered moated castle of the Este family, begun in 1385 and partly
rebuilt after 1554. The castle contains frescoes by pupils of Dosso Dossi
(1489/90–1542).

Piazza Savonarola

South of the Castello is the Piazza Savonarola, with a monument to
Savonarola, the great preacher and reformer. Here, too, we find the
Palazzo Comunale, once the palace of the dukes of Este (originally built
in 1243, rebuilt in the 14/15th c.), with a façade of 1924.

* Cathedral

A little way south-east of the Castello rises the cathedral, with a magnificent façade in Lombard Romanesque style (12th–14th c.); it contains
pictures by artists of the Ferrara school; near the altar are two 15th c.
bronze statues (St Maurelius and St Georg).

Cathedral Museum

Over the narthex is the Cathedral Museum, with pictures and sculptures, among which are the "Madonna del Melograno" by Jacopo della
Quercia, as well as a Dutch tapestry by G. and C. Filippi.

Campanile

At the south-east corner of the cathedral is the unfinished campanile
(15th–16th c.).

Facing the cathedral, to the south, was the Palazzo della Ragione, which
was destroyed in 1945 and replaced by a new building in 1957.

San Francesco

About 500 m/550 yd south-east of the cathedral stands the church of
San Francesco, a brick-built Early Renaissance building (15th c.) roofed
with a series of domes. Immediately east is the University (founded
1391).

Municipal Museum

Farther south-east, in Via Scandiana, is the Palazzo Schifanoia (late
14th c.; remodelled in 1466–93), an Este summer residence, now incorporating the Municipal Museum (Museo Civico), with miniatures,

Castello Estense

medals and fine frescoes by Francesco del Cossa and his pupils (*c.* 1470).

About 500 m/550 yd south of the Palazzo Schifanoia is the Palazzo di Ludovico il Moro (16th c.; unfinished), with a beautiful courtyard and fine frescoes, early examples of trompe-l'oeil painting (*c.* 1500). It now houses the Archaeological Museum (Museo Civico d'Arte Antica), which has a splendid collection of vases and other finds from the Greek-Etruscan necropolis of Spina, near Comacchio (see p. 170).

Archaeological Museum

South-west of San Francesco, in Via delle Scienze (No. 17), is the Palazzo del Paradiso, occupied from 1586 to 1962 by the university and now by the Biblioteca Comunale Ariostea, with Ariosto's tomb and some of his manuscripts.

Biblioteca Comunale Ariostea

Sights in the north

In the north of the town, at the intersection of Corso Ercole I d'Este with Corso Rosetti/Corso di Porta Mare, are two fine palaces. On the north-west corner is the Palazzo Sacrati or Prosperi (*c.* 1500), with a fine doorway.

Palaces

Opposite, to the south, is the Palazzo dei Diamanti, a superb example of Early Renaissance architecture (1492–1567) which takes its name from the faceted stones of its façade. It now contains the National Gallery, with works by 15th–16th c. painters of the Ferrara school.

National Gallery

About 500 m/550 yd north-west, at Via Ariosto 65, is the house in which Ariosto lived; on the first floor is the room where the poet died.

Ariosto's house

Farther north-east is the Certosa, a former Carthusian house founded in 1452 and dissolved in 1796, now a cemetery; here also is a fine 15th–16th c. church.

Ferrara: Palazzo Comunale

Boldini Museum

From the Certosa it is only a few steps to the building complex of the Palazzo Massari-Palazzina Cavalieri di Malta, which houses the Boldini Museum (Museo Boldini e dell'Ottocento Ferrarese) and works by other painters of Ferrara. Boldini (1842–1931) painted portraits and scenes of the Parisian street-life.

Art Collection

The Palazzo Massari contains the Municipal Collection of Contemporary Art (Civica Galleria d'Arte Moderna).

Comacchio I5

Situation
57 km/35 miles
south-east

Comacchio (pop. 21,500), a picturesquely situated town, is the centre of the Valli di Comacchio, which consists of thirteen islands connected by canals. Near Comacchio is the site of two cemeteries of the Greek-Roman port of Spina (4th-3rd c. B.C).

Abbazia Santa Maria di Pomposa

See Emilia-Romagna

Florence/Firenze H6

Region: Toscana. Province: Firenze (FI)
Altitude: 50 m/165 ft. Population: 436,000

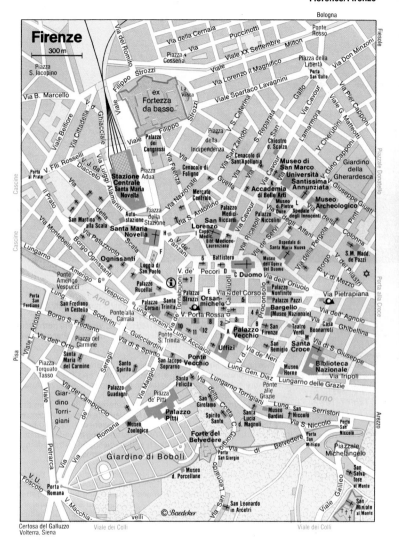

Florence/Firenze

A Piazza della Signoria
B Piazza San Firenze
C Piazza del Duomo
D Piazza San Giovanni
E Piazza della Repubblica
F Piazza Santa Maria Novella
G Piazza Ognissanti

H Piazza dell' Unità Italiana
I Piazza Madonna degli Aldobrandini
K Piazza San Marco
L Piazza della Santissima Annunziata
M Piazza Santa Croce

1 Loggia dei Lanzi
2 Palazzo Fenzi
3 Palazzo Uguccione
4 Badia Fiorentina
5 Casa di Dante
6 Santa Maria Maggiore

7 San Gaetano
8 Mercato Nuovo
9 Palazzo Davanzati
10 Palazzo Spini-Ferroni
11 Santi Apostoll
12 Palazzo di Parte Guelfa

173

Florence: Panorama of the city from the south-west

Tip

The description of Florence in this guide to Italy is purposefully brief, as there is a Baedeker guide devoted entirely to the city.

Much of the centre of Florence is barred to cars. Visitors are permitted to drive to their hotel and unload their luggage, but must then remove their vehicle from the prohibited zone.

Situation and importance

Florence (in Italian Firenze), the old capital of Tuscany, called "la Bella", and now a provincial capital, a university town and the see of an archbishop, is picturesquely situated on both sides of the River Arno, surrounded by foothills of the Apennines.

While in ancient times the life of Italy was centred on Rome, from the Middle Ages to our own day Florence has been its intellectual centre. Here the Italian language and Italian literature were created, and here

**Art treasures

Italian art attained its finest form. With its astonishing abundance of art treasures, its historical associations and its beautiful surroundings, Florence is one of the world's greatest tourist centres.

History

The Etruscan and Roman town of Florentina played no great part in history. At the beginning of the 13th c. the fortunes of war and the industry of its people (wool, silk) made it the leading town in Central Italy, but the ruling noble families were weakened by continual internecine strife between Guelfs (followers of the Pope) and Ghibelines (followers of the Hohenstaufens). The town's craft guilds grew steadily in strength and in 1282 their leaders, the priori (convenors) gained control of the city's government.

In 1434 power fell into the hands of the wealthy merchant family of the Medici, whose leading members Cosimo (1434–64), the "father of his country" (pater patriae), and Lorenzo the Magnificent (1469–1492), brought the republic to its greatest prosperity and made it a brilliant centre of art and learning. In 1494 the Medici were driven out, and four

years later, in 1498, the great preacher and reformer Girolamo Savonarola was burned at the stake in the Piazza della Signoria. In 1512 the Medici returned to Florence under the protection of Spanish troops, but in 1527 they were again expelled. Only three years later, however, after the capture of the town by Charles V (1530), Alessandro de'Medici was installed as hereditary duke. After his murder in 1537 he was succeeded by Cosimo I, who became Grand Duke of Tuscany in 1569.

After the house of Medici became extinct in 1737 the Grand Duchy passed to the house of Lorraine, which held it, with an interruption during the Napoleonic period (1810–14), until 1860. Tuscany then became part of the kingdom of Italy, and Florence enjoyed a fresh period of prosperity as temporary capital of the new kingdom (1865–1870).
The city did not suffer much during the Second World War, except for the destruction of the bridges across the River Arno, which were blown up by the Germans, but the most beautiful one, the Ponte Vecchio, was not damaged and the other bridges have been rebuilt in their original style. In November 1966 flooding of the River Arno caused severe damage to many historic buildings and the flood cost many lives.

In literature Florence is associated with Dante Alighieri (1266–1321), author of the "Divine Comedy" and creator of the Italian literary language; Giovanni Boccaccio (1313–1375), whose "Decameron" provided the model for Italian prose; and Francesco Petrarca (Petrarch), who played a major part in preparing the way for humanism.

Literature

From the end of the 13th c. Florence played a leading part in the development of art. Arnolfo di Cambio (d. 1302), the great forerunner of the architects of the Renaissance, worked on Santa Croce and the cathedral, and Giotto (1266–1337), father of modern painting, began

Art

175

his career here. Among his principal pupils were Taddeo Gaddi (d. 1366) and Orcagna (d. 1368), also noted as a sculptor.

The year 1402 can be regarded as marking the beginning of the Renaissance (competition for the north door of the Baptistery), although in architecture the new spirit did not find full expression until 20 years later. Filippo Brunelleschi (1377–1446) applied his knowledge of ancient architecture to meet new requirements, and was followed by Leon Battista Albert (1404–72).

The sculptors of the Florentine Renaissance included Lorenzo Ghiberti (1378–1455), Luca della Robbia (1400–82), noted for his glazed terracotta reliefs, and above all Donatello (1386–1466), the greatest master of the century. After Donatello's death the leading sculptor was Andrea Verrocchio (1436–88), also noted as painter.

The pioneers of Renaissance painting were Masaccio (1401–28), Andrea del Castagno (1423–65) and Paolo Uccello (1397–1475). Outstanding in fervour of religious feeling was Fra Angelico da Fiesole (1387–1455), who influenced Fra Filippo Lippi (1406–69) and Benozzo Gozzoli (1420–97). The zenith of the Florentine Early Renaissance was reached in the work of Andrea Verrocchio, the brothers Antonio and Piero del Pollaiuolo (1429–98, 1443–c. 1495), Sandro Botticelli (1444–1510), Fra Filippo's son Filippino Lippi (c. 1459–1504) and Domenico Ghirlandaio (1449–94). Of the three great masters of Italian art the Tuscans Leonardo da Vinci and Michelangelo received their training in Florence, and here too Raphael shook off the trammels of his earlier years; from 1506 all three were working in Florence. About the same time Lorenzo di Credi (1459–1537), Piero di Cosimo (1462–1521), Fra Bartolomeo (1472–1517) and the talented colourist Andrea del Sarto (1486–1531) were also working in Florence, as were Franciabigio and Pontormo. Among painters of a slightly later period were Agnolo Bronzino (1503–72), Alessandro Allori (1535–1607) and Giorgio Vasari (1511–74), noted for his "Lives of the Artists". Leading sculptors of this period were Benvenuto Cellini (1500–71), also famous as a goldsmith, and Giovanni Bologne (c. 1524–1608; actually Jean Boulogne of Douai).

** Piazza della Signoria

The old centre of Florentine life is the Piazza della Signoria, the former forum of the Republic which has had its present form since 1386. The Palazzo Vecchio and the Loggia dei Lanzi are the dominating buildings on the south side of the square.

** Palazzo Vecchio   The Palazzo Vecchio (old palace), the Town Hall, a castle-like building with a tower 94 m/310 ft high, was built for the Signoria between 1298 and 1314 as Palazzo dei Priori – probably in accordance with a plan by Arnolfo di Cambio – and extended to the rear in the 16th c.

To the left of the entrance can be seen a modern copy of Michelangelo's "David" (original in Galleria dell'Accademia); in the outer courtyard (remodelled 1454) is a copy (original on second floor) of the "Boy with a Fish" by Andrea del Verrocchio.

On the first floor the Salone dei Cinquecento (1495) houses Michelangelo's marble group "Triumph of Virtue over Vice" (c. 1520). The state apartments (Quartieri Monumentali) are on the first and second floors.

* Views from the tower   From the wall-walk and the tower there are extensive views.

Fontana del Nettuno   At the north-west corner of the palazzo in front of the Neptune Fountain (Fontana del Nettuno; 1563–75) is a stone slab marking the spot where Savonarola was burned at the stake.

Loggia dei Lanzi

Adjoining the Palazzo Vecchio is the Loggia dei Lanzi (originally Loggia dei Signori; 1376–1382), an open hall designed for addressing the people, named after Cosimo I's German pikemen. In the loggia are a number of sculptures, including Giovanni da Bologna's marble group "Rape of the Sabine Women" (1583) and Benvenuto Cellini's bronze "Perseus with the Medusa's Head" (1553).

*Loggia dei Lanzi

On the east side of Piazza della Signoria is the former chamber of commerce (Mercanzia; 1359); to the north the 16th c. Palazzo Uguccioni; at the west side of the square the Palazzo Fenzi (1871), an imitation of the early Florentine palaces.

Palazzi

From the Piazza della Signoria the busy Via del Calzaiuoli ("Street of the Hosiers") runs north to the Piazza del Duomo.
At the junction of the Via de'Lamberti, on the left, stands the mighty three-storeyed church of Orsanmichele (Or San Michele), built in 1284–91 as a corn exchange, and rebuilt 1337–1404. The exterior is decorated with important pictures by Verrocchio, Ghiberti, Donatello and others.

*Orsanmichele

A little way north-east of the Piazza della Signoria, in Piazza San Firenze, stands the fortress-like Palazzo del Podestà commonly known as the Bargello, which was the headquarters of the chief of police (bargello) and a prison. Since 1865 the building has housed the Museo Nazionale del Bargello, devoted to the history of Italian culture and modern times, with an excellent collection of Florentine Renaissance sculpture. The courtyard with its pillared hall, a fine flight of steps and walls decorated with coats of arms, is a fine example of a medieval castle courtyard.

**Museo Nazionale del Bargello

Opposite the Bargello, to the west, is the Badia Florentina, an old Benedictine abbey, founded in 978, with a delicate pointed campanile.

Badia Florentina

Florence/Firenze

San Firenze

At the south-east side of the Piazza Firenze stands the Baroque building complex of San Firenze; the church was rebuilt in 1633–48.

Casa di Dante
(Dante Museum)

Via Dante Alighieri, to the north of the Bargello, leads to the so-called houses of Alighieri (Case degli Alighieri); it is assumed that Dante was born in one of them. The house No. 4 is called Casa di Dante and contains a Dante Museum.

**Uffizi (Palazzo and Galeria degli Uffizi)

Palazzo

South of the Palazzo Vecchio and the Loggia dei Lanzi, extending towards the Arno, stands the Palazzo degli Uffizi, built in 1560–74 by Vasari.

**Galleria

Today it houses the Galleria degli Uffizi (Uffizi for short), the world-famed art collection, founded by the Medici, the former rulers of Florence and the Grand Dukes of Tuscany. Gradually it became the most important art collection in Italy and one of the greatest in the world, with some 4500 pictures. They provide an almost complete survey of Florentine painting and also include major works by north Italian, particularly Venetian, painters, as well as outstanding pictures by

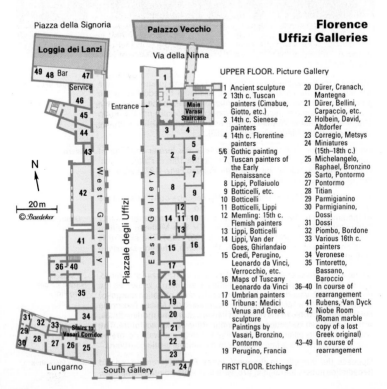

Piazza della Signoria

Palazzo Vecchio

**Florence
Uffizi Galleries**

Loggia dei Lanzi

Via della Ninna

49 48 Bar 47
Service
46
45
44
43
N
42
20 m
© Baedeker
41
36–40
35
34
31 32 33
29
30 28 27 26 25
Lungarno   South Gallery

Main Vasari Staircase
Entrance

UPPER FLOOR. Picture Gallery

1 Ancient sculpture
2 13th c. Tuscan painters (Cimabue, Giotto, etc.)
3 14th c. Sienese painters
4 14th c. Florentine painters
5/6 Gothic painting
7 Tuscan painters of the Early Renaissance
8 Lippi, Pollaiuolo
9 Botticelli, etc.
10 Botticelli
11 Botticelli, Lippi
12 Memling: 15th c. Flemish painters
13 Lippi, Botticelli
14 Lippi, Van der Goes, Ghirlandaio
15 Credi, Perugino, Leonardo da Vinci, Verrocchio, etc.
16 Maps of Tuscany Leonardo da Vinci
17 Umbrian painters
18 Tribuna: Medici Venus and Greek sculpture Paintings by Vasari, Bronzino, Pontormo
19 Perugino, Francia

20 Dürer, Cranach, Mantegna
21 Dürer, Bellini, Carpaccio, etc.
22 Holbein, David, Altdorfer
23 Correggio, Metsys
24 Miniatures (15th–18th c.)
25 Michelangelo, Raphael, Bronzino
26 Sarto, Pontormo
27 Pontormo
28 Titian
29 Parmigianino
30 Parmigianino, Dossi
31 Dossi
32 Piombo, Bordone
33 Various 16th c. painters
34 Veronese
35 Tintoretto, Bassano, Baroccio
36–40 In course of rearrangement
41 Rubens, Van Dyck
42 Niobe Room (Roman marble copy of a lost Greek original)
43–49 In course of rearrangement

FIRST FLOOR. Etchings

Dutch and old German masters including ancient paintings. There are also valuable sculptures, as well as tapestries, drawings, jewellery, weapons, scientific instruments and archaeological finds.

From the Uffizi the Vasari corridor (Corridoio del Vasari or Vasariano) about 400 m/440 yd long, with an interesting gallery of self-portraits, leads across the Ponte Vecchio to the Palazzo Pitti (see page 185).

Corridoio del Vasari

** Piazza del Duomo/Piazza San Giovanni

The Via de' Calzaiuoli runs from the north end of the Piazza della Signoria to the Piazza del Duomo (on the right) with the cathedral and the campanile; to the left is the Piazza San Giovanni with the Baptistery. Immediately on the right, at the corner of the cathedral square, is the Oratory of the Misericordia, a charitable fraternity which succoured the poor and the sick and buried the dead.

Squares

Misericordia

To the left, at the corner of Piazza di San Giovanni, we find the Gothic Loggia del Bigallo, which was built in 1352–58.

Loggia del Bigallo

In the centre of the Piazza San Giovanni is the Baptistery (Battisterio San Giovanni), an octagonal structure which was probably founded on the remains of a Roman building and was rebuilt in the 11th–13th c., when it was clad externally and internally with variegated marble.

**Baptistery

It is famous for the three gilded bronze doors with relief decoration (the original gilding was uncovered in 1948): the south door by Andrea Pisano (1330–36), the north door (1403–24) and the principal door facing the cathedral (1425–52), the Porta del Paradiso ("Gate of Paradise") by Lorenzo Ghiberti.

**Bronze doors

In the interior are superb mosaics (diameter 25.6 m/84 ft) by several Florentine artists of the 13th c.

The Florentine Cathedral (Cattedrale di Santa Maria del Fiore, so called after the lily which is the emblem of Florence), a mighty Gothic building, was begun by Arnolfo di Cambio in 1296, continued by Francesco Talenti from 1357 onwards and consecrated in 1436. The octagonal dome (1420–34) is Filippo Brunelleschi's master-work. The building, clad externally with variegated marble, is 169 m/554 ft long, the width of the crossed wings is 104 m/341 ft, the height of the dome is 91 m/300 ft; to the top of the lantern (finished 1461) it is 107 m/353 ft. The façade dates only from 1875 to 1887.

**Cathedral

The spacious interior is dominated by the strict Gothic forms and impresses with its bareness.

Steps lead down to the old cathedral of Santa Reparata (4th-5th c.), which has been excavated since 1965.

Santa Reparata

It is well worth the trouble of climbing up to the dome as the view is even more magnificent than from the campanile.

*Dome

The quadrangular campanile (82 m/271 ft high; begun in 1334 by Giotto and finished in 1387), faced with coloured marble, is one of the finest in Italy. There is sculpture by Donatello and his assistant Rosso (1420) and by Andrea Pisano and Luca della Robbia (1437).

**Campanile

The entrance to the Cathedral Museum (Museo dell'Opera del Duomo) is opposite the choir of the cathedral, in the courtyard of the house No. 9 (on the right). It contains art from the cathedral and the baptistery, among which the choir gallery with the famous relief of children by Lucca del Robbia and Donatello.

*Cathedral Museum

A little way south-east of the cathedral square, in Via del Proconsolo are two fine palaces, No. 2 the imposing Palazzo Nonfinito ("unfinished palace"; 1592) which since 1869 has housed the Museum of Ethnology

Palazzo Nonfinito
Museum of Ethnology

(Museo Nazionale di Antropologia ed Etnologia), and No. 10 the Palazzo dei Pazzi dating from 1470, a building with interesting architectural detail.

Town centre

The area south-west of the cathedral, the so-called Centro (centre) was modernised at the end of the 19th c.

Centro

The town's traffic centre, the scene of lively activity, particularly in the evening, is the Piazza della Repubblica.

Piazza della Repubblica

From the south-east corner of the square Via Calimara runs south to the Mercanto Nuovo (new market), a loggia-like building dating from 1547–51, at present a craft market (hand embroidery, etc.).

Mercanto Nuovo

In the Piazza Davanzati stands the mighty 14th c. Palazzo Davanzati with the Museo della Casa Florentina Antica (Museum of the Florentine House), which provides a good impression of Florentine everyday life in the Middle Ages.

Museo della Casa Fiorentina Antica

At the west side of the Centro is the busy Via de' Tornabuoni with its fine palaces and elegant shops.

Via de' Tornabuoni

Particularly interesting is the Palazzo Strozzi, a magnificent example of Florentine palace architecture, built in 1489–1536, with an interesting courtyard by Cronaca. On the façade there are fine wrought-iron lanterns, torch holders and rings. In the palace temporary art exhibitions are held.

*Palazzo Strozzi

In Via de' Tornabuoni to the south stands the church of Santa Trinità, originally one of the oldest Gothic churches in Italy, rebuilt in the 13th–15th c. with a façade of 1593.

Santa Trinità

Opposite the church to the south-west, on the banks of the River Arno, stands the Palazzo Spini-Ferroni, built in 1289 and restored in 1874, the largest medieval palace in Florence.

Palazzo Spini-Ferroni

North-west behind the church of Santa Trinità, between Via del Parioni and the River Arno (Lungarno Corsini), stands the 17th c. Palazzo Corsini, with a privately owned art collection.

Palazzo Corsini

From Palazzo Strozzi Via della Vigna Nuova runs west to the Palazzo Rucellai (erected in 1446–51), one of the finest Florentine Renaissance palaces.

Palazzo Rucellai

Near the Palazzo Rucellai is the old church of San Pancrazio which houses a museum, with work of the painter and sculptor Marino Marini (1901–80; 176 pictures, sculptures and other work). Marini's fame is based on his horse and rider compositions.

Marini Museum

*Piazza di Santa Maria Novella

To the north-west of the town centre is the spacious Piazza di Santa Maria Novella with the Loggia Di San Paolo (1489–1496) and two obelisks, which served in the past as the finishing-post in chariot races.

On the north side of the square stands the Dominican church of Santa Maria Novella, a Gothic building (1278–1350) with an inlaid marble façade and a Renaissance doorway. In the choir are frescoes which rank as Domenico Ghirlandaio's finest work.

*Santa Maria Novella

To the left of the church is the entrance to the cloisters (Chiostri monumentali di Santa Maria Novella); on the north side of the "Green Cloister" we find the former chapter-house, known as the Cappellone degli Spagnoli (Spanish chapel; c. 1355).

Cloisters

◀ Façade of the Cathedral of Santa Maria del Fiore

Florence/Firenze

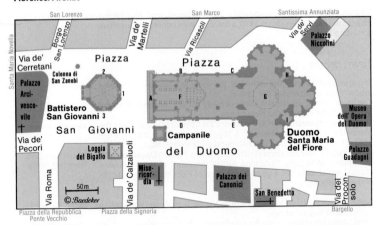

Florence
Piazza del Duomo

BAPTISTERY
1 East door
   (Porta del Paradiso)
2 North Door
3 South Door (entrance)

CATHEDRAL
A Portale Maggiore
B Porta della Balla
C Porta della Mandorla
D Porta del Campanile

E Porta dei Canonici
F Santa Reparata (crypt)
G Dome by Brunelleschi
H New Sacristy
I Old Sacristy

Baptistery: Details of sculpture on the South Doorway . . .   . . . and on the East Doorway

North-west of Santa Maria Novella is the Piazza della Stazione (station square) with the Stazione Centrale di Santa Maria Novella (1935), Florence's central station.

South-west of Santa Maria Novella in Piazza Ognissanti which leads to the Arno, stands the church of Ognissanti, one of the first Baroque churches in the town (originally 13th c.; rebuilt in the 16th and 17th c.); inside there are fine frescoes by Botticelli (St Augustinus) and Ghirlandaio (St Hieronymus).

*San Lorenzo

From the Piazza dell'Unità Italiana, on the east side of Santa Maria Novella, the short Via del Melarancio leads east to the church of San Lorenzo, originally consecrated by St Ambrose in 393 as Florence's first cathedral (rebuilt in Romanesque style in the 11th c.). The present building, in the form of an early Christian basilica with columns, was re-erected in 1421 by Brunelleschi and his successors. The inside wall of the façade is by Michelangelo.

In the north transept is the Old Sacristy (by Brunelleschi, 1421–28), an early work of Renaissance architecture, with sculpture by Donatello.

Adjoining the church to the left is an idyllic cloister with a double-columned hall.

North-west from the cloister a staircase leads up to the Biblioteca Mediceo Laurenziana (in a 16th c. building), which was founded in 1444 by Cosimo the Elder, with several thousand manuscripts of Greek and Latin classical authors collected by the Medici.

Behind the church of San Lorenzo, in the Piazza Madonna degli Aldobrandini, is the entrance to the Medici Chapels (Capelle Medicee). From the crypt a staircase leads up to the Chapel of the Princes (Capella dei Principi), decorated with fine stone mosaics, which was built in 1604–10 to house the sarcophagi of the Grand Dukes of Tuscany.

On the left a passage leads to the New Sacristy (Sagrestia Nuova), a square, domed edifice, built by Michelangelo (1520–24) as the mausoleum of the Medici family. It contains the tombs of a son and grandson of Lorenzo the Magnificent.

At the north-east corner of the Piazza San Lorenzo rises the massive Palazzo Medici-Riccardi, which was built for Cosimo the Elder in 1444–52 and extended in the 17th and 18th c.

In the courtyard is the entrance to the chapel, with fine frescoes by Benozzo Gozzoli (c. 1460), and to the Medici Museum (Museo Medaceo) with relics of the Medici family who occupied the palace until 1537.

*San Marco

From the east side of the Medici Palace Via Cavour runs north-east to the Piazza San Marco, in which are the church of San Marco and the monastery of San Marco, now the Museo di San Marco, rebuilt in the 15th c. for the Dominicans, with notable frescoes by Fra Angelico da Fiesole.

South of San Marco, at Via Ricasoli 52, is the Accademia di Belle Arti (Art Academy), with the Galleria dell'Accademia, a study collection which supplements the Uffizi and the Galleria Pitti (13th–16th c. Tuscan painting). Its most notable feature is the famous David ("il Gigante"), carved from a single block of stone by the youthful Michelangelo (1501–03; copies in the Piazza della Signoria and the Piazzale Michelangelo).

*Santissima Annunziata

From the Piazza San Marco the Via Cesare Battisti runs past the former university to the magnificent church of the Santissima Annunziata (originally 1250, remodelled 1444–60; entrance replaced 1601). The forecourt contains frescoes by Andrea de Sarto (1505–14) which rank among the finest achievement of the Florentine High Renaissance.
The interior of the church is partly Baroque. Beyond the door, leading from the north transept into the cloister (Chiostro dei Morti) is a fresco by Andrea del Sarto ("Madonna del Sacco", 1525), one of his late masterpieces.

Foundling hospital

To the east, opposite the church, is the foundling hospital of Spedale degli Innocenti, an early example of Renaissance architecture, begun in 1419 by Brunelleschi. Between the arches are coloured medallions with infants in swaddling clothes by Andrea della Robbia (c. 1463).

Archaeological Museum

South-east of the Santissima Annunziata stands the Palazzo della Crocetta (1620) which houses the Museo Archeologico Centrale dell'Etruria (entrance Via della Colonna No. 38), the Archaeological Museum founded in 1870, with a fine collection of Etruscan and Greco-Roman material and a notable Egyptian collection.

*Santa Croce

On the south-east side of the old town, near the Arno, we find the church of Santa Croce, a Franciscan church begun in 1295 but not completed until 1442, with a façade of 1857–63. The spacious interior contains the tombs of many famous Italians, including Michelangelo, Alfieri, Macchiavelli, Rossini, Cherubini and Galileo. Notable are the remains of the frescoes in the choir chapels by Giotto and his pupils and the magnificent marble pulpit by Benedetto da Maiano (1472–1476).

*Pazzi Chapel
Cloisters

On the far side of the first cloister is the Pazzi Chapel (Cappella de' Pazzi; by Brunelleschi, 1430), an early work of the Renaissance; to the left on the façade are Arno high-water level marks (4 November 1966: 4.9 m/16 ft 2 in). The second cloister (Secondo Chiostro) is one of the finest examples of the Early Renaissance.

Church Museum

Adjoining the first cloister, to the south, is the former refectory, which houses the rich Church Museum (Museo dell' Opera di Santa Croce).

Central Library

Adjoining the church of Santa Croce to the south, is the building complex of the National Library (Biblioteca Nazionale Centrale, 1911–35). It is one of the largest and most important libraries in Italy, with more than four million volumes, among which are precious manuscripts, incunabula, musical compositions, atlasses and geographical maps.

Casa Buonarotti
(Michelangelo Museum)

A little way north of Santa Croce, in Via Ghibellina 70, is the Casa Buonarotti which Michelangelo bought for his nephew Leonardo di Buonarotti, whose son furnished it and turned it into a memorial to Michelangelo in 1620. The museum contains early work by the master as well as copies of his work, also drawings, manuscripts, pictures and other relics.

Museo Horne

About 200 m/220 yd west of the Central Library, at the end of Corso de' Tintori (Via de Benci 6), is the Museo della Fondazione Horne. This museum is based on the gift of the British art critic Herbert Percy Horne (1864–1916) and contains a valuable collection of pictures, drawings, sculpture and furniture, as well as ornaments and utensils of the 14th–16h centuries.

Only a few steps south of the Museo Horne the Ponte alle Grazie (fine views) leads to the northern bank of the Arno.

Ponte alle Grazie

**Ponte Vecchio

Some 200 m/220 yd south-west of the Piazza della Signoria the narrowest part of the Arno is spanned by the Ponte Vecchio (old bridge), the oldest of the bridges, leading to the southern bank. The bridge was so wide that arcades were built on both sides; soon apartments and shops appeared (butchers were able to throw their waste into the river). By the end of the 16th c. Grand Duke Ferdinand I decreed that only goldsmiths shops were to be allowed on the bridge, a regulation which is still in force today.

**Palazzo Pitti

South-west of the Ponte Vecchio, at the foot of the Boboli hill, stands the imposing square building of the Palazzo Pitti, begun by Luca Pitti c. 1458 and extended in the 16th–18th c.

In the left-hand half of the first floor the famous Pitti Gallery (Galleria Palatina), founded by the Medici in the 16th and 17th c., now contains hundreds of pictures, including masterpieces by Raphael, Fra Bartolommeo, Andrea del Sarto and Titian. Adjoining the gallery are ten of the former Royal Apartments (Appartamenti Reali; 18th–19th c.).

**Galleria Palatina

On the ground floor is the Silver Chamber, with silver and gold work as well as other precious objects which belonged to the Medici. There is

Silver Chamber

Ponte Vecchio, the "Old Bridge" across the Arno

185

Carriage Museum	also a Carriage Museum (Museo delle Carrozza), with carriages of the Duca di Modena, Francescos II and King Ferdinand of Naples.
Gallery of Modern Art	On the second floor the Gallery of Modern Art (Galleria d'Arte Moderna) contains 19th and 20th c. works, mostly by Tuscan artists, and also present-day sculpture.
Costume Gallery	The Palazzina della Meridiana contains an interesting costume gallery.
* Boboli Gardens	To the south of the Palazzo Pitti extend the Boboli Gardens (Giardino di Boboli; 45,000 sq. m/53,820 sq. yd). The beautiful park, decorated with fountains and statues extends up a slope and from the terraces there are attractive views of Florence.
Porcelain Museum	The Casino del Cavaliere houses a fine Porcelain Museum.
Forte del Belvedere	Above the gardens to the south-east rises the Forte del Belvedere (Forte di San Giorgio), which was built by Bernardo Buontalenti in 1590–95.
Santo Spirito	North-east of the Palazzo Pitti stands the church of the Santo Spirito (begun in 1436 to a plan by Brunelleschi and completed in 1487), with a campanile of 1543. Notable features are the sacristy (1489–92), numerous altarpieces and two 16th c. cloisters.
Santa Maria del Carmine	Farther west is the former Carmelite monastic church of Santa Maria del Carmine, almost completely rebuilt in 1782 after a fire. The Brancacci Chapel contains famous frescoes on the lives of the Apostles (by Masolino and Masaccio 1424–27) which marked the beginning of Renaissance painting.

* Viale dei Colli

	The Viale dei Colli, laid out from 1868 onwards, which runs along the south side of the town from the Porta Romana to the Piazza Francesco Ferrucci, with a total length of almost 6 km/3¾ miles, is one of Italy's finest promenades.
* * Piazzale Michelangelo	The road winds its way up through magnificent scenery to the Piazzale Michelangelo, with a spacious terrace from which there is a famous view of the town and the Arno valley.
San Miniato al Monte	Above the square to the south is the monastic church of San Miniato al Monte, conspicuous from afar with its inlaid marble façade, one of the finest examples of Tuscan Romanesque architecture of the 11th–12th c. In the apse is a fine mosaic (1297); the crypt contains frescoes by Taddeo Gaddi.
	To the right of the church rises a fortress built by Michelangelo in 1529 (now an Olivetan monastery), the walls of which surround a cemetery. From the terrace there are fine views.

Cascine in Florence

Almost 2 km/1¼ miles west of the Ponte Vecchio, at the Piazza Vittorio Veneto, is the beginning of the municipal park called le Cascine (originally the estates of the Medici and the Lorena), which extends along the northern bank of the Arno (swimming pool, cycle circuit and horse race course).

* Fiesole

Situation 8 km/5 miles north-east of Florence	The little town of Fiesole which was originally an Etruscan town and later the Roman Faesulae, still preserves parts of its massive walls. In the centre of the town is the cathedral (11th and 13th c.), in Tuscan Romanesque style, and behind it are the remains of a Roman theatre and an Etrusco-Roman temple (museum of antiquities). From the ter-

race of the church of Sant'Alessandro, a little way west of the cathedral in the municipal park, there is a very fine view of the low-lying country around Florence.

Foggia

Region: Puglia
Province: Foggia (FG)
Altitude: 74 m/244 ft
Population: 158,000

Foggia, chief town of the province of the same name, which was also known as "Capitanata", is situated in the northern part of the Adriatic coastal region of Apulia, south of the Monte Gargano promontory. Once a favourite residence of the Emperor Frederick II, it is both the geographical and the economic centre of the extensive Apulian plains, the Tavoliere di Puglia.

Situation

Almost all the town's medieval buildings were destroyed in an earthquake in 1731. With its wide tree-lined streets and its many new buildings, including those erected after the Second World War to make good the severe destruction which the town had suffered, Foggia is now a town of very modern appearance.

Sights

The hub of the town's traffic is the Piazza Cavour, to the east of the centre. Adjoining the east side of the square, beyond a colonnade, is the municipal park, extending eastwards. From the Piazza Cavour Viale XXIV Maggio, lined by fine buildings, runs north-east to the station. To the west of the Piazza Cavour is the Piazza Umberto Giordano, from the far end of which the busy Corso Vittorio Emanuele, Foggia's principal street, leads into the old town centre. 300 m/990 ft west it is crossed by another busy street, the Corso Garibaldi, along which, to the south-west, are the Prefecture and the Town Hall.

A little way north of the Prefecture is the cathedral, built about 1172 in Romanesque style but rebuilt in Baroque style after the 1731 earthquake.

Cathedral

Farther north, in Piazza Nigri, is the Municipal Museum (Musei Civici) which contains archaeological and folklore material as well as a collection of modern pictures.

*Around the Monte Gargano promontory (some 230 km/143 miles)

There is a very attractive trip around the Monte Gargano promontory (1056 m/3485 ft), the "spur" of the Italian boot, a hilly tongue of land which extends 65 km/40 miles into the Adriatic and, geologically, already belongs to the Dalmatian limestone formations.

Leave Foggia on S.S. 89 (the "Gargánica"), which runs north-east through the extensive and well-cultivated Apulian plain. In 27 km/17 miles, on the right, is San Leonardo, formerly a lodge of the Teutonic Order but now a farmhouse (Masseria), with a square Romanesque church (richly sculptured 12th c. doorway). Soon afterwards the road reaches the coast at Lido di Siponto (5 m/17 ft), the Roman Sipontum, which was abandoned in the 13th c. Among the remains is the cathedral of Santa Maria Maggiore (consecrated 1117), on a square ground plan, with an interesting crypt.

Lido di Siponto

Foggia

Manfredonia

43 km/27 miles from Foggia the road comes to Manfredonia (5 m/17 ft; pop. 54,000), a port founded in the 13th c. by King Manfred, son of Frederick II, in place of the abandoned town of Sipontum, and now the see of an archbishop. After its destruction by the Turks in 1620 it was rebuilt on a regular plan with streets intersecting at right angles. Interesting features are the cathedral, the 13th c. church of San Domenico, a 13th c. castle and the Museo Archeologico Nazionale del Gargano. There are boat sevices several times weekly to the Tremiti Islands (4–5 hours).

About 7 km/4½ miles beyond Manfredonia the road forks: to the left is the shorter road through the hills, to the right the longer but scenically more attractive coast road.

Monte Sant'Angelo

Road through the hills:

9 km/5½ miles from the fork the hill road reaches Monte Sant'Angelo (796 m/2627 ft; pop. 17,000), the centre of the Gargano area. This little town is charmingly situated with a fine ruined castle (1494) and the pilgrimage church of San Michele Arcangelo which is visited by something like a million pilgrims every year. The church occupies a cave in the centre of the town which according to legend was chosen as a shrine by the Archangel Michael himself when he appeared to St Lawrence, archbishop of Sipontum, in 493. From the vestibule beside the campanile (1273) 86 steps lead down to the church, which has Biblical scenes on bronze doors and an inscription recording that they were cast in Constantinople. The church contains a fine 12th c. bishop's throne. Near the church is the so-called "tomb of Rothari" (a Lombard king), a curious domed building (c. 1200) which was probably a baptistery. Nearby is the church of Santa Maria Maggiore (begun 1170), with a beautiful doorway (1198).

San Giovanni Rotondo

About 5 km/3 miles beyond Monte Sant'Angelo a road goes off on the left to San Giovanni Rotondo (566 m/1868 ft; pop. 23,000), situated below Monte Calvo (1056 m/3485 ft), the highest summit in the range. On the west side of the town is the modern church of Santa Maria delle Grazie, to the left of which is a Capuchin monastery famous as the home of Padre Pio da Pietrelcina (d. 1968), who bore the stigmata from 1918 until his death. The monastery is visted by large numbers of pilgrims seeking a cure for their ailments, and there is a modern hospital adjoining.

*Foresta Umbra

Beyond the turning for San Giovanni Rotondo the main road winds its way uphill and then crosses the karstic plateau of Monte Gargano and down through the magnificent beech forest of Foresta Umbra to the coast, joining the coastal road from Manfredonia 43 km/27 miles beyond San Giovanni.

Vieste

Coast road:

The much more attractive coast road (19 km/12 miles longer), running partly inland and partly above the coast, through magnificent scenery, comes in 49 km/30 miles to the picturesque little port of Vieste (43 m/142 ft; pop. 13,000). From the castle, built by Frederick II, there is a fine view of the coast.

Some 13.5 km/8½ miles beyond Vieste a road on the right leads to the hotel and villa colony of Manacore.

Peschici

5 km/3 miles farther on is the old-world little town of Peschici, picturesquely situated on a crag rising sheer from the sea.

Bellariva

The road then continues, with many bends, to Bellariva, where it is joined by the road from Monte Sant'Angelo.

San Menaio

18 km/11 miles beyond Bellariva is San Menaio (10 m/33 ft), a seaside resort, with villas set amid pine-woods.

About 7 km/4½ miles farther on is the port of Rodi Garganico (42 m/ 139 ft; pop. 4000). From here there are boat services (approximately 1½ hours) to the beautiful Tremiti Islands, 22 sea miles north-west.

Soon afterwards the road skirts a coastal lagoon, the Lago di Varano (12 km/7½ miles long, 8 km/5 miles across), which is separated from the sea by a long spit of sand – dunes known as the "Isola", and passes either to the south or to the north along the dunes. It then continues through barren hill country to join the motorway to Foggia either at Poggio Imperiale (45 km/28 miles), at the west end of the Lago di Lesina, or at San Severo (65 km/40 miles).

Lucera

West of Foggia, on a plateau above the wide Apulian plain, is Lucera (219 m/723 ft; pop. 34,000), the ancient Luceria. The town was developed into an important stronghold, the key to Apulia, by the Emperor Frederick II, and populated by 20,000 Saracens brought in from Sicily between 1233 and 1245. Most of the population was killed by Charles II of Anjou around 1300.

Notable are the Gothic cathedral, built by Charles II of Anjou after 1300 on the site of the old Saracen mosque (inside a wooden 14th c. crucifix) and the Museo Civico Giuseppe Fiorelli, with coins, inscriptions, numerous terracottas, a beautiful statue of Venus of the 1st c. A.D. and other treasures.

About 1 km/¾ mile west of the town, beyond the beautiful Giardino Pubblico, is a castle (251 m/828 ft) built by Frederick II in 1233 and rebuilt by Charles I of Anjou, a well-preserved example of medieval

The coast of Monte Gargano, near Foggia   *The Hohenzollen Castle of Lucera*

military architecture, from the top of which there are far-ranging views. East of Lucera, at the foot of a hill, is a Roman amphitheatre of the time of Augustus.

Troia

17 km/11 miles south of Lucera is the little town of Troia (439 m/1449 ft; pop. 8000), with an interesting cathedral (begun 1092) showing Toscanian Pisan influence. The two bronze doors are by Oderisius of Benevento, 1119 and 1127. Also in Troia can be seen the remains of the old town walls.

Foligno

Region: Umbria
Province: Perugia (PG)
Altitude: 234 m/772 ft
Population: 53,000

Situation

The industrial town of Foligno lies on the left bank of the River Topino, in the fertile Umbrian plain – some 35 km/22 miles south-east of Perugia and 25 km/16 miles north of Spoleto.

The earliest printed book in Italy was published here (in Italian) in 1472 – the first edition of Dante's "Divine Comedy".

Sights

Cathedral

In the centre of the town is the spacious Piazza della Repubblica, on the east side of which is the cathedral of San Feliciano (1133), with a beautiful façade and a neo-classical interior (1770). The transept contains a picture of St Francesco by the painter Tizzoni of Foligno.
Facing the cathedral, to the south-west, stands the 17th c. Town Hall.

Palazzo Trinci
(museums)

On the north side of the square is the Palazzo Trinci (14th–15th c.), in which are the Archaeological Museum, a library and an interesting collection of pictures.

From here Via A. Gramsci runs past the fine Palazzo Deli (1510; on the right) to the former 13th c. church of San Domenico and the old church of Santa Maria Infraportas; inside three representations of the crucifixion.
A little way north is the Scuola d'Arti e Mestieri (School of Arts and Crafts), in the courtyard of which are casts of monuments of Umbrian art. Adjoining the school the church of San Niccolò houses some fine paintings.

In a narrow lane to the south-east of the cathedral is the former Oratorio della Nunziatella (15th c.), with a fine fresco of the Baptism of Christ by Perugino.

Abbey of Sassovivo

Situation
6 km/3¾ miles east

The abbey of Sassovivo (Abbazia di Sassovivo), standing in splendid isolation, was founded by Benedictine monks in the 11th c. Particularly remarkable is the Romanesque cloister.

Bevagna

Situation 10 km/
6 miles south-west

South-west of Foligno, in the valley of the Clitunno, lies the little town of Bevagna (210 m/693 ft; pop. 4500). In the picturesque main square are the churches of San Silvestro and San Michele, with early medieval façades.

From Bevagna it is 11 km/7 miles up a winding road, with sharp bends, to the little walled hill-town of Montefalco (473 m/1561 ft; pop. 5500), with churches which contain fine examples of Umbrian painting: outside the town gate the monastic church of Santa Chiara, inside the gate the church of Sant'Agostino and in the town the former church of San Francesco (now a museum), with frescoes by Benozzo Gozzoli (1452). There are also frescoes by Gozzoli in the church of San Fortunato, 1.5 km/1 mile south of the town.

Montefalco

Spello

16/7

North-west of Foligno, picturesquely situated on the lower slopes of Monte Subasio, is Spello (280 m/924 ft; pop. 8000), the ancient Hispellum, which still preserves part of its walls and gates, among which the Porta Venere of the Augustan period. From the Porta Consolare, with three portrait-statues, a street leads up to the church of Santa Maria Maggiore (12th–13th c.), with a number of notable works of art – in the Cappella Baglioni frescoes by Pinturicchio (1501), as well as majolica flooring from Deruta (1566); on the high altar a magnificent marble tabernacle by Rocco da Vicenza (1515); in the sacristy a Madonna by Pinturicchio. Above Santa Maria rises the church of Sant'Andrea (13th c.), which has a Madonna by Pinturicchio and Eusebio da San Giorgio (1508).

Situation
5 km/3 miles
north-west of
Foligno

Trevi

South of Foligno, off S.S. 3 to the east, is Trevi (412 m/1360 ft; pop. 7000), the Roman Trebiae, magnificently situated on the slopes of a steep hill. Below the town, standing by itself, is the church of the Madonna delle Lacrime (1487), with a beautiful doorway and fine pictures of the Umbrian school, including work by Perugino. The Town Hall, in Piazza Mazzine, contains a small picture gallery. The nearby church of Sant'Emiliano (12th c.) has a richly decorated altar by Rocco da Vicenza (16th c.).

Outside the town stands the church of San Martino, with fine frescoes; in the outer chapel is a Madonna by Spagna.

Situation
11 km/7 miles south
of Foligno

Forlì

15

Region Emilia-Romagna
Province: Forlì (FO)
Altitude: 34 m/112 ft
Population: 110,000

Forlì, capital of the upper Italian province of the same name, lies on the Via Emilia between Bologna and Rimini – some 55 km/34 miles southeast of Bologna and 45 km/28 miles from Rimini.

The town, the Roman city of Forum Livii and in the late medieval period an independent republic.

Situation

Sights

In the centre of the town the large Piazza Saffi is surrounded by fine palaces. On the west side of the square stands the Town Hall, beside it is the Gothic Palazzo del Podestà (1460).

Frascati

San Mercuriale	At the east corner of the square stands the Romanesque church of San Mercuriale (12th–13th c.), with a fine campanile. To the right of the church is the cloister of the old Benedictine abbey (16th c.). From Piazza Saffi the Corso Garibaldi runs north-west to the cathedral of Santa Croce (rebuilt 1841).
Museums	From Piazza Saffi the Corso della Repubblica leads south-west to the municipal Pinacoteca and the museums, in a palace dating from 1172. In the Pinacoteca works by Guercino (c. 1590 to 1666), Melozzo da Forlì (1438 to 1494) and Beato Angelico can be seen. On the second floor are the Romagna Folk Museum and the little Museo del Risorgimento; on the ground floor the Museo Archeologico can be found.
Piazzale della Vittoria	At the end of the Corso della Repubblica is the spacious Piazzale della Vittoria, with a war memorial (1932) in the form of a tall marble column.
Citadel	In the south-west of the town is the citadel, the Rocca di Ravaldino (1361).

Region: Latium/Lazio
Province: Roma (ROMA)
Altitude: 322 m/1063 ft
Population: 20,000

Situation	The little town of Frascati lies some 20 km/12 miles south-east of Rome on the north-west slopes of the Alban Hills. Frascati, the most important of the so-called "Castelli Romani", is a town famous for its healthy climate, which makes it a favourite summer resort with the people of Rome.

It is notable also for the many fine villas, belonging to old noble families, mostly dating from the 16th and 17th c., set in magnificent parks and gardens.

Piazza Marconi

Villa Torlonia	The focal point of the town is the Piazza Roma, with the adjoining Piazza Marconi. To the south is the beautiful park of the Villa Torlonia (destroyed in the Second World War).
*Villa Aldobrandini	Above the south-east side of the Piazza Marconi stands the Villa Aldobrandini or Belvedere (1598–1604), in a magnificent park (terrace with extensive views; grottoes, fountains, cascade).

Piazza San Pietro

A little way north of the Piazza Roma is the Piazza San Pietro, the main square of the old town, with a beautiful fountain and the cathedral of San Pietro (16th–17th c.).

Villas around the town

Villa Falconieri	About 1 km/¾ mile east of Frascati we find the entrance to the picturesque park of the Villa Falconieri, built by Borromini in 1545–48 (frescoes).
Villa Mondragone	2 km/1¼ miles east of Frascati stands the Villa Mondragone (1573–1575), since 1865 a Jesuit seminary, with magnificent cypresses.

Frascati: Villa Aldobrandini

Outside the town, to the south-east, is the splendid Villa Rufinella or Tuscolana, built by cardinal Rufini in accordance with a plan by Luigi Vanvitelli. The villa and park are neglected and are not open to the public.

Villa Rufinella

Tusculum

From Frascati a recently constructed panoramic road winds its way uphill through beautiful scenery and areas of forest to the remains of ancient Tusculum, 5 km/3 miles south-east. This was the birthplace of Cato the Elder and a favourite resort of Cicero. Held during the early Middle Ages by warlike counts, it was destroyed by Rome in 1191. There are remains, much overgrown, of an amphitheatre, a theatre, the forum, a well-house and a stretch of the old town walls.

Situation
5 km/3 miles
south-east

It is a 15-minute walk up the hill above the site to a ruined castle (670 m/2211 ft), which commands extensive views.

Rocca di Papa

There is a very attractive trip from Frascati to the little town of Rocca di Papa, with numerous summer residences (620–720 m/2046–2376 ft; pop. 9000), picturesquely perched on a rock on the outer margin of a large extinct crater known as the Campo di Annibale, and surrounded by beautiful woods.

Situation
8 km/5 miles south
of Frascati

From Campo di Annibale it is possible either to walk (45 minutes) or drive (6.5 km/4 miles) to the summit of Monte Cavo (949 m/3132 ft;

Monte Cavo

television transmitter), the second highest of the Alban Hills, from which there are far-reaching views (particularly clear after rain) of most of Latium. Here there stood in antiquity a temple of Jupiter, the shrine of the Latin League.

Friuli

Regions: Friuli–Venezia Giulia
Provinces: Pordenone (PN) and Udine (UD)

Situation and general information

The north Italian region of Friuli, in the basins of the Tagliamento and the lower Isonzo, extends from the Carnic and Julian Alps to the Adriatic.

Together with the eastern part of the old province of Veneto (provinces of Trieste en Gorizia) it now forms the region of Friuli–Venezia Giulia, which occupies 7846 sq. m/3029 sq. miles (pop. 1,224,000).

History

The region, originally occupied by an Illyrian tribe, the Carni, was conquered by Rome around 150 B.C.. Its name comes from the Roman town of Forum Iulii (Cividale del Friuli). Later a Lombard duchy, in the time of Charlemagne it was held by a Frankish margrave, in 952 it passed to Bavaria, in 976 to Carinthia, and in 1077 was a gift to the Patriarchate of Aquileia. In the 15th c. the western (and larger) part was conquered by Venice, while the smaller eastern part was granted to the counts of Gorizia as a fief and in 1500 passed to Austria, which in 1797 also acquired the territory held by Venice. Italy secured the Venetian territory in 1866 and the county of Gorizia in 1918, but in 1947 was compelled to cede the eastern part, predominantly inhabited by Slovenes, to Yugoslavia.

Landscape in the Friuli region

Much of the region was ravaged by a series of earthquakes in 1976 in which more than 1000 people lost their lives, and many valuable works of art and architecture as well as complete villages were destroyed. In many places many houses, streets, castles and palaces have since been rebuilt or restored.

Earthquake damages

Of the 1.2 million inhabitans of the region of Friuli–Venezia Giulia some 520,000 are Friulians (in Italian "Friulani", in Friulian "Furlani"), the descendants of Rhaetians who were Romanised at an early date. They speak Friulian, a Rhaeto-Romanic dialect. The economy is traditionally based on agriculture (including viticulture), but many Friulians now find employment in other parts of Italy in building or other trades.

Population and economy

In the mountains the opening up of new skiing areas has made tourism an increasingly important element in the economy of the region. The favourite winter sports resorts are Piancavallo, Forni di Sopra, Ravas-cletto, Sella Nevea and the area around Tarvisio. In Sella Nevea there is a summer ski-school.

Tourism

On the Adriatic coast there are a great number of popular seaside resorts, including Grado, nearby which bird's nesting areas (lagoon) and small fishing islands (see Aquileia) can be found, and Lignano Sabbiardoro, with a wide beach.

Interesting to visit are the towns of Aquileia, Cividale del Friuli and Udine.

Lake Garda/Lago di Garda

G4

Regions: Lombardia, Veneto and Trentino–Alto Adige
Provinces: Brescia (BS), Verona (VR) and Trento (TN)
Altitude: 65 m/215 ft

With an expanse of 370 sq. km/143 sq. miles of deep blue water, Lake Garda (Lago di Garda), the Roman Lacus Benacus, is the largest of the north Italian lakes (52 km/32 miles long, 5– 16.5 km/3–10 miles wide, up to 346 m/1142 ft deep), lying in a deeply eroded valley between Venetia and Lombardy. Its main feeder in the north is the River Sarca, and its outlet at the south end is the Mincio, which flows into the Po.

Situation

The northern part of the lake is narrow and fjord-like; towards the south end the shores slope down gradually to the extensive morainic cirque left by the old Garda glacier. The east side of the lake is separated from the Adige valley by the 80 km/50 miles long limestone ridge of Monte Baldo (2200 m/7260 ft). The west side, hemmed in towards its northern end by sheer rock faces, opens out between Gargnano and Salò to form the beautiful and fertile coastal strip known as the Riviera Bresciana. Until 1918 the northern tip of Lake Garda, with Riva and Torbole, belonged to Austria.

General information

The climate in the area of Lake Garda is extraordinarily mild, and snow is rare. The lake is seldom entirely calm, and in a storm coming from the north can be quite rough. In fine weather a very cold wind known as the ora blows around midday in winter and spring.
Sailing and surfing is popular on the lake.

Climate

The vegetation is luxuriant on the more sheltered stretches of the lakeside, in places almost Mediterranean. Olives grow up to 300 m/ 1000 ft, and palms, cedars, magnolias and agaves flourish in the gardens.
The lake fish are excellent.

Flora and fauna

**Round Lake Garda (approximately 135 km/84 miles)

Gardesana
Occidentale

Gardesana Orientale

The lake is surrounded by fine modern roads. Along the west side runs the famous "Gardesana Occidentale", a masterpiece of modern road engineering, with numerous galleries and tunnels hewn from rock, and also a route of great scenic beauty, while on the east side there is the "Gardesana Orientale".

Riva del Garda

The tour of the lake begins at the little town of Riva del Garda (70 m/231 ft; pop. 13,000), a summer and winter resort and congress centre at the north-west tip of the lake. To the west of the town is the precipitous Rocchetta (1527 m/5039 ft), with a Venetian watch-tower.

The town's busiest traffic intersection is the square by the harbour, with arcades and a massive old clock-tower. To the east, by the lakeside, is the little Piazza Carducci. Nearby stands the old moated castle of the Scaliger family, the Rocca (12th–15th c.). On the road to Arco is the church of the Inviolata, with a Baroque interior (1603).

On the south side of the town is the Ponale hydro-electric power station (88,000 kW), fed by water brought from the Lago di Ledro, 585 m/1930 ft above Riva, in a pipeline 6 km/3¾ miles long.

Gargnano
* Riviera Bresciana

29 km/18 miles from Riva on the road which follows the west side of Lake Garda, on the lower slopes of a precipitous hill, is the attractive village of Gargnano (98 m/323 ft), where the Riviera Bresciana begins. The Villa Feltrinelli, a little way north of the lakeside promenade, was occupied by Mussolini from September 1943 to April 1945 (it is now a department of the university of Milan).

Bogliaco

2 km/1¼ miles: Bogliaco, with the large country house of Count Bettoni (park).

Road along the shore of Lake Garda

6 km/3¾ miles: Toscolano-Maderno (70 m/231 ft). In Maderno are the Romanesque church of Sant'Andrea (12th c.) and the Palazzo Gonzaga (17th c.). Beautiful views from the lakeside promenade. — Toscolana-Maderno

4 km/2½ miles: Gardone Riviera (70 m/231 ft), which attracts many visitors with its mild climate and luxuriant southern vegetation; magnificent Hruska Botanic Garden; bar serving whisky specialities. — Gardone Riviera

About 1 km/¾ mile north surrounded by beautiful gardens is Gardone di Sopra (130 m/429 ft). Near the church (view from the terrace) is the Villa Vittoriale degli Italiani, the last home of Gabriele d'Annunzio (1863–1938), with mementoes of the poet.

3 km/2 miles: Salò (75 m/248 ft; pop. 10,000), charmingly situated in a long narrow bay under Monte San Bartolomeo (568 m/1874 ft). This was the birthplace of Gasparo da Salò (1542–1609), inventor of the violin, and from 8 September 1943 the seat of the Fascist government of Italy ("Republic of Salò"). The Gothic parish church of Santa Maria Annunziata (1453) is worth seeing. — Salò

21 km/13 miles: Desenzano del Garda (67 m/221 ft; pop. 20,000) at the south-west tip of Lake Garda, has an old castle and remains of a Roman villa of the 4th c. A.D. (mosaics). — Desenzano del Garda

From Desenzano S.S. 11 runs along the south end of the lake.

Excursion:

In 4.5 km/3 miles a road on the right leads to the village of San Martino della Battaglia (110 m/363 ft), 5 km/3 miles south-east, where a Piedmontese army, allied with the French, defeated the Austrians on 24 June 1859 (commemorative tower, war museum). — San Martino della Battaglia

About 11 km/7 miles south is the village of Solferino (132 m/436 ft); here a French army led by Napoleon III defeated the Austrians on the same day (museum, ossuary). From the Rocca, above the village, there are extensive views. The sufferings of the wounded in the battle of Solferino gave Henri Dunant the idea of founding the Red Cross. — Solferino

2.5 km/1½ miles beyond Desenzano on S.S. 11 a road goes off on the left (3.5 km/2 miles) to the picturesque little town of Sirmione, on a long promontory reaching out into the lake. The Roman poet Catullus (84–54 B.C.) had a villa here. The town which is also visited for its sulphur springs has a large and picturesque castle of the Scaligers (13th c. restored); fine view from the tower. — *Sirmione

About 1 km/¾ mile north is the Punta di Sirmione, with a terrace from which there are fine views, built on late Roman substructures ("Grotte di Catullo").

7 km/4½ miles: Peschiera del Garda (68 m/224 ft; pop. 9000), is a strongly fortified little town at the south-east corner of Lake Garda, at the outflow of the River Mincio. — Peschiera del Garda

From Peschiera the road continues up the east side of the lake.

In 9 km/5½ miles it reaches Lazise (76 m/251 ft; pop. 5000), with medieval town walls and a Scaliger castle (14th c.). — Lazise

5 km/3 miles: Bardolino (68 m/224 ft), famous for its wine. To the left of the road is the little Romanesque church of San Severo (8th and 12th c.), with frescoes (12th and 13th c.). — Bardolino

4 km/2½ miles: Garda (69 m/228 ft; pop. 3500), a small old town. A footpath leads up in 45 minutes to the Rocca (294 m/970 ft), on the site of an earlier castle which gave its name to the lake. — Garda

About 3 km/2 miles beyond Garda is the promontory of San Vigilio (fine views), set amid cypresses (1540; no admission). — *Promontory San Vigilio

5 km/3 miles: Torri del Benaco (68 m/224 ft), with the medieval Castello Scaligero (1383). — Torri del Benaco

197

Sirmione: Castle of the Scaligers

Bathing beach at the San Viglio promontory

Excursion:
From Torri del Benaco an attractive excursion can be made to the summer holiday resort of San Zeno di Montagna, 9 km/5½ miles northeast (583 m/1924 ft), situated high above the lake (views) on the southwest slopes of the Monte Baldo range.

San Zeno di
Montagna

11 km/7 miles: Malcesine (90 m/297 ft), in a fine situation below the rugged cliffs of Monte Baldo (2200 m/7260 ft). At the north end of the town, almost sheer above the lake, is a Scaliger castle (13th–14th c.). A cableway leads to the Bocca Tratto Spin (1720 m/5676).

Malcesine

14 km/8½ miles: Torbole (85 m/281 ft), a picturesque little fishing village lying under bare crags at the north-east corner of Lake Garda.
4 km/2½ miles: Riva

Torbole

A trip on Lake Garda is an attractive way of seeing both sides of the lake. There are boats from Riva to Desenzano which call at various places on the east and west sides of the lake, and also from Toscolona-Maderno via Garda to Peschiera del Garda or Desenzano. Hydrofoils operate from Riva to Desenzano.

Boat trip

Lago di Ledro

From Riva there is a very rewarding trip up the Ponale Road to the Lago di Ledro, 10 km/6 miles west. The road winds its way up above the west side of Lake Garda, with several sharp bends and magnificent views, skirts the cliffs of the Rocchetta and passes through a number of tunnels. At Pieve di Ledro (660 m/2178 ft), at the west end of the lake, are the remains of a Bronze Age settlement.

Situation
10 km/6 miles west

*Lago di Molveno   G3

A road runs north from Riva through magnificent scenery fo the hamlet of Foci del Varone, near which is the Cascata del Varone, a waterfall in a gloomy gorge, and Ponte delle Arche (26 km/16 miles; alt. 401 m/1323 ft), an old road intersection where S.S. 237 runs east through the magnificent Sarca gorge to Trento and west through the wild Gola della Scaletta to Tione. 20 km/12 miles farther north from Ponte delle Arche is the beautiful blue Lago di Molveno (alt. 821 m/2709 ft; 4 km/2½ miles long, up to 119 m/393 ft deep), below Monte Gazza (1990 m/6567 ft) to the east and the precipitous crags of the Brenta group to the west. At the north end of the lake is Molveno, a summer holiday resort, with a chair-lift to Pradel (1342 m/4429 ft) and the Palòn di Torre (1530 m/5049 ft), to the north.

Situation
46 km/29 miles north
Ponte delle Arche

About 4 km/2½ miles north of Molveno is the holiday and winter sports resort of Andalo (1042 m/3439 ft), with views of the Brenta group. From here there is a cableway to Malga Terlago (1772 m/5848 ft) and Pian del Dosson) and from there a chair-lift to the Paganella (2126 m/7016 ft).

Andalo

Arco

North-east of Riva, on the right bank of the Sarca, is the old town of Arco, a resort set in luxuriant southern vegetation, which attracts many visitors in winter as well as summer by reason of its mild climate. In the Kurpark, south of the church, is a bronze monument to the painter Giovanni Segantini (1858–1899), who was born in Arco. To the west are two beautiful promenades, one planted with magnolias and the other

Situation
6 km/3¾ miles
north-east of Riva
del Garda

with palms; the Kurcasino is between the two promenades. On a
cypress-clad rock (284 m/937 ft) are the ruins of a castle (view).

Genoa/Genóva   E5

Region: Liguria
Province: Genova (GE)
Altitude: 25 m/83 ft
Population: 738,000

Situation and importance

Genoa (in Italian Genóva), capital of the region of Liguria, lies in the
Gulf of Genoa (Golfo di Genova), the northern bay of the Ligurian Sea.
Genoa is a conurbation (Greater Genoa) extending from Nervi to Voltri
for a distance of 35 km/22 miles along the coast. It is Italy's leading port
and centre of maritime trade, ranking with Marseilles as one of the two
principal Mediterranean ports. It is also a university town and the see of
an archbishop.

Genoa, known as "la Superba" on account of its splendid marble
palaces, has a magnificent situation, particularly when seen from the
sea, rising in a wide arc on the lower slopes of the Ligurian Apennines.
The various parts of the town are linked by five road tunnels and high
bridges, and two huge tower blocks form striking landmarks in the
town centre.

The old town is a maze of narrow streets, many of them steep, which
are filled with the colourful and noisy activity of a Mediterranean town.
The new parts of the town with their tall modern buildings, gardens and
villas lie in the plain at the mouth of the River Bisagno and on the higher
ground to the north and west. On the landward side Genoa has been
protected since the 12th c. by a rampart 15 km/9 miles long extending
from the tall lighthouse on the west side of the town to the Forte
Sperone (516 m/1703 ft) and then descending past Forte Castellaccio
(489 m/1614 ft) into the Bisagno valley to the south-east.

The districts of Sanpierdarena and Cornigliano (with the Italsider
works) are the main centre of Italian heavy industry. Other major
industries are chemicals, foodstuffs, papermaking, textiles and
transport.

History

Genoa first appears in history in 218 B.C. as capital of the Ligurians. In
the 10th c. A.D. it was an independent republic, which in 1284, after
almost 200 years of war, finally defeated its most dangerous com-
petitor, Pisa, in the naval battle of Meloria. In the 14th c. the Genoese
fought with Venice for control of the trade with the East, but were
decisively defeated at Chioggia in 1381. During this period the town
was torn by internal disputes and fell into the hands of foreign masters.
The independence of the republic was restored by Admiral Andrea
Doria (1466–1560) in 1528, but Genoa's power was now in decline. In
1684 the town was bombarded by a French fleet, and in 1746 it was
occupied for some months by Austrian troops. In 1805 the "Ligurian
Republic" was incorporated in the Napoleonic Empire, and ten years
later (1815) became part of the Kingdom of Sardinia and Piedmont.

1 Accademia Linguistica
  di Belle Arti
2 Exchange (Borsa)
3 Grattacielo
4 Porta Soprana
5 Casa di Colombo
6 Sant'Ambrogio

7 Doge's Palace (Pallazzo Ducale; Art Centre)
8 San Matteo
9 Cathedral
10 Palazzo Rosso
11 Palazzo Bianco
12 Palazzo Spinola
13 Casa di Mazzini

14 San Filippo Neri
15 Palazzo Balbi
16 Santissima Annunziata
17 San Carlo
18 Museo Chiossone
19 Prefecture
20 San Donato

Genova

Torre Lanterna
Riviera di Ponente, Palazzo Doria-Pamphili

Castello
d'Albertis

Corso

Righi

Corso

Firenze

Albergo
dei
Poveri

Via Pertinace

Porta Principe
Station

Dogali

Corso Carbonara

Via Firenze

S. Maria
della Sanità

Via Balbi

17

Università

Corso Carbonara

V. Brignole De Ferrari

N. S. delle
Grazie

Corso

Via Balbi

Via Pré

Palazzo
Reale

16

Piazza d.
Nunziata

Funicolare per il Righi

Corso

Paganini

Museo
Americanistico

Via Antonio Gramsci

15

Galleria Garibaldi

Spianata
Castelletto

Corso

Via Caffaro

Corso

Solferino

Campo Santo

Porto
Vecchio

14

13

Funicolare Santa Anna

Via Santa Anna

Cappuccini

Via Palestro

S. Maria
Immacolata

San Siro

11

Town Hall

Via Magenta

12

Via Garibaldi

10

Piazza del
Portello

Villetta
di Negro

Gan N. Bixio

Via Assarotti

Molo Vecchio

S. Maria
d. Vigne

Piazza
Fontane
Marose

18

Piazza
Corvetto

19

Via SS. Giac.
e Filippo

Via Serra

Piazza
Caricamento

Via Luccoli

V. 25 Aprile

Salita S.
Caterina

Stazione Brignole

Palazzo
San Giorgio

Via

Via Roma

PICCAPIETRA

Porto
Nuovo

Via S. Lorenzo

Via Turati

9

8

Piazza
De Ferrari

1

Acquasola

Arco dei Caduti

7

2

© Baedeker

20

6

V. Dante

5

4

Piazza
Dante

S. Stefano

S. Maria
di Castello

S. Agostino
(Museo)

3

Via XX Settembre

Ponte
Monumentale

Via XX Settembre

Piazza
Sarzano

Via Fieschi

Galleria
C. Colombo

Corso Podestà

Via Ipp. d'Aste

Via Madre di Dio

Corso Maurizio Quadrio

Via Alessi

Museo di
Storia Naturale

S. Maria di
Assunta
Carignano

Via Corsica

Via A. Volta

Yacht Harbour

Sacro
Cuore

Avamporto

Via Aurelio

Corso

Saffi

Mura di Cappuccine

Molo Umberto Cagni

Palazzo
dei Congressi

Corso

Saffi

Viale di Brigate Partigiane

Fiera Internazionale

Corso

Aurelio

Lido d'Albaro

300 m

© Baedeker

Palazzo
dello Sport

Riviera di Levante

Famous natives of Genoa include the Italian freedom fighter and revo-
lutionary Giuseppe Mazzini (1805–72), the national hero Giuseppe
Garibaldi (1807–82), son of a Genoese from Nice, Christopher Columbus (Christoforo Colombo, 1451–1506), discoverer of America, and the
great virtuoso of the violin Niccolò Paganini (1782–1840).

Art

The old palaces of the nobility, more numerous and more splendid in
Genoa than in any other Italian town, give some impression of the
magnificent life-style of the 16th and 17th c. The pattern of the Genoese
palace, with its grandiose distribution of architectural masses and its
skilful use of rising ground, was set by the Perugian architect Galeazzo
Alessi (1512–72) and his successors.

The churches of Genoa, many of them of very ancient origin, were
mostly rebuilt during the Gothic period and adorned with Pisan and
Lombard sculpture.

Outstanding Genoese painters were Luca Cambiaso (1527–85) and
Bernardo Strozzi, called "Il Prete Genovese" (1581–1644).

Piazza De Ferrari

The hub of the city is the Piazza De Ferrari, surrounded by public
buildings, banks and the offices of the big shipping lines, and with the
busiest streets in Genoa radiating from it in all directions.

Opera

On the north-east side of the square is the neo-classical Teatro Carlo
Felice (1828), one of the largest opera-houses in Italy (burned down
during the Second World War and re-opened in 1991).

Picture Gallery

To the right of the theatre stands the Accademia Lingustica di Belle Arti
(picture gallery), with a museum, containing works of art, particularly
sculptures from Genoa and Liguria.

Exchange

On the east side of the Piazza De Ferrari is the Exchange (Borsa), an
imposing neo-Baroque building (19th c.). From here the city's principal
street, Via XX Settembre, runs south-east, lined by fine modern buildings and arcades containing numerous shops.

Piazza Dante

From the right-hand side of the Exchange a short street, Via Dante,
leads south to Piazza Dante, surrounded by modern tower blocks.

Porta Soprana

On the west side of Piazza Dante is the Gothic Porta Soprana or Porta di
Sant'Andrea, the south-east town gate (1155). The little house in front
of it to the right is known as the Casa di Colombo (Columbus's House),
in which Columbus spent his childhood.

Piazza Matteotti

Santi Ambrogio e
Andrea

A short distance south-west of the Piazza De Ferrari is Piazza Matteotti,
in which stands the fine Jesuit church of Santi Ambrogio e Andrea
(1589–1606) which contains pictures by Rubens and Reni.

Doge's Palace

On the north side of the square is the former Doge's Palace (Palacio
Ducale), a group of buildings dating from the 13th c. It has been
converted into an exhibition and function centre and opened in 1992.
The frescoes by Carlone and Tiepolo have been restored.

San Matteo

From here Via Tommaso Reggio (left of the palace) and the Salita
all'Arcivescovado lead to the little Gothic church of San Matteo (1278),
with many relics of the noble Doria family (on the façade inscriptions in
their honour, in the crypt the tomb of Andrea Doria). To the left of the
church is a beautiful early Gothic cloister (1308–1310).

Palaces

In the square in front of the church are several palaces of the Doria
family, some of them faced with black and yellow marble; and in the

narrow surrounding streets, once the most aristocratic part of the town, are numerous other noble mansions.

From Piazza Matteotti the busy Via San Lorenzo runs north-west to the harbour. Immediately on the right is the Cathedral of San Lorenzo, originally a Romanesque pillared basilica (consecrated 1118), remodelled in Gothic style in 1307–12 and crowned with a Renaissance dome by Galeazzo Alessi in 1567. It contains fine pictures and sculpture. In the north aisle is the large Cappella San Giovanni Battista (1450–65), the earliest example of Renaissance architecture in Genoa. In the south aisle can be seen an unexploded shell 1.40 m/4½ ft high which burst through the façade of the cathedral during a naval bombardment on 9 February 1941 without causing serious damage. Under the cathedral lies the Treasury.

**San Lorenzo

Villetta di Negro

From the Opera-House the busy Via Roma, in which are various entrances to the Galleria Mazzini, a shopping arcade, runs east to the Piazza Corvetto. From here the Via XXV Aprile runs north to the Piazza Fontane Marose. On higher ground to the north-west of this square is the Villetta di Negro park (view), with the Museo Edoardo Chissone which contains a collection of Oriental art (3rd c. B.C. to 19th c.).

Museo Chiossone

Piccapietra

To the east of Via Roma, between the Piazza De Ferrari, the Piazza Corvetto and the Acquasola Park, is the Piccapietra district, which suffered heavy bomb damage during the Second World War and was rebuilt in magnificent style from 1954 onwards, with modern office buildings and flats, including many tower blocks.

From Via Garibaldi-Via Cairoli-Via Balbi to Piazza Acquaverde

From the west side of Piazza Fontane Marose a major traffic artery formed by Via Garibaldi, Via Cairoli and Via Balbi runs north-west to Piazza Acquaverde and the station. Laid out in the 16th and 17th c., this area contains a number of churches and Genoa's finest palaces, approached by magnificent flights of steps which are one of the particular sights of Genoa.

In the narrow Via Garibaldi, designed by Galeazzo Alessi, are a succession of palaces, with fine collections of pictures. On the right (No. 9) is the former Palazzo Doria Tursi, now the Palazzo Municipale (Town Hall), begun in 1564. It contains Niccolò Paganini's violin and manuscripts by Christopher Columbus. On the left (No. 18) is the Palazzo Rosso, a splendid 17th c. mansion which belonged to the Brignole-Sale family (17th c.), containing a picture gallery on the first and second floors; notable particularly for its fine family portraits (works by Van Dyck, Paris Bordone, Bernardo Strozzi, Veronese, Moretto, Titian, Tintoretto, Caravaggio, etc.). Almost opposite (No. 11) is the Palazzo Bianco, a Brignole palace (originally 1548, altered after 1712), which also houses a notable picture gallery, with works by Italian, Dutch and Flemish masters.

*Via Garibaldi
Palaces

Crossing the Piazza della Meridiana, we enter the wide Via Cairoli. Off this street, to the left, is the old cathedral (San Siero: remodelled in Baroque style 1586), the interior of which is richly decorated with frescoes.

Via Cairoli
San Siero

Galleria Nazionale | South-west of the church, in the Palazzo Spinola, is the National Gallery (Galleria Nazionale), with works by Antonello da Messina, Anthonis van Dyck, etc. as well as valuable sculpture and a triptych by Joos van Cleve (1485).

Largo della Zecca | Via Cairoli meets the Largo della Zecca, from which a road tunnel, the Galleria Giuseppe Garibaldi, runs to the Piazza Corvetto; the same tunnel continues on the other side of Piazza Portello as Galleria Nino Bixio. On the right-hand side of the Largo della Zecca is the lower station of the funicular to the Righi (302 m/997 ft).

Palazzo Balbi | On the south side of the Largo della Zecca stands the Palazzo Balbi, with an unusual and distinctive staircase (1750).

Casa di Mazzini | Beyond the Balbi Palace is Via Lomellini, which runs south past the Baroque church of San Filippo Neri (completed 1712) to the Casa di Mazzini, the birthplace of Giuseppe Mazzini, the founder of "Young Italy", with the Museo del Risorgimento containing relics of the freedom fighter of the Risorgimento.

Santissima Annunziata | The Largo della Zecca joins the Piazza della Annunziata, in which is the magnificent church of the Santissima Annunziata, originally belonging to the Capuchins (built 1522–1620; neo-classical colonnade of 1843).

*Via Balbi Palaces | West of the church is the beginning of Via Balbi, laid out by Bartolomeo Bianco in the early 17th c. and lined with splendid palaces. Immediately on the right (No. 1) is the Palazzo Durazzo-Pallavicini (c. 1620), with a Rococo entrance hall and a fine staircase of 1780. On the left (No. 4) stands the Palazzo Balbi-Senarega (1620 onwards) with a fine courtyard, from which there is a view of the orangery. No. 5 (on right) is the Palazzo dell'Università, begun in 1634–40 as a Jesuit college, with the finest courtyard and gardens in Genoa. To the left of the university stands the church of San Carlo (sculpture of 1650). Opposite is the Palazzo Reale (begun 1650), with fine staircases, large balconies and a richly decorated interior (pictures).

Main Station

Palazzo Dora-Pamphili | Via Balbi leads north-west to the Piazza Acquaverde, the large square in front of the main station, the Stazione Porta Principe, with an impressive monument to Columbus (1846–62). To the west is the Piazza del Principe, in which is the Palazzo Doria-Pamphili or Palazzo del Principe, built in 1522–1529 as a country house for Doge Andrea Doria, with frescoes by Perin del Vaga, a pupil of Raphael (1528–1533).

Harbour area

Marine Station | To the south of Piazza del Principe, beyond Via Adua and the railway line, is the Stazione Marittima (Marine Station).

Porto Vecchio
Porto Nuovo | The Harbour (22 km/14 miles wharves, 128 km/79 miles of railway lines; annual turnover 50 million tonnes) consists of the inner harbour or Porto Vecchio, constructed about 1250, the Porto Nuovo (1877 onwards), the naval harbour (Darsena) and the outer harbour, or Avamporto, together with the more recently constructed Bacino della Lanterna and Bacino di San Pier d'Arena. On the north edge of Porto Vecchio rises the tower "Lanterna" (1543; 76 m/251 ft), the symbol of the city.

The eastern part of the harbour, along Corso Maurizio Quadrio, is occupied by the little Porticciolo Duca degli Abruzzi, used by yachts and sailing boats. The whole harbour is enclosed by two breakwaters, the Diga Foranea (over 5 km/3 miles long) and the Molo Duca di Galliera. There are very attractive boat trips around the harbour (about two hours).

Genoa: View of the town from the harbour

At the west end of the harbour is the international Cristoforo Colombo   Airport
Airport.

From Piazza del Principe Via A. Gramsci runs alongside the high-level   Palazzo San Giorgio
motorway which skirts the inner harbour to Piazza Caricamento, in
which is the Gothic Palazzo di San Giorgio (*c.* 1260), occupied from 1408
to 1797 by the Banca di San Giorgio, an influential bank which financed
the Genoese republic (beautiful courtyard).

Circonvallazione a Mare

From the former bank Via F. Turati runs south past the warehouses of
the free port to the Piazza Cavour, the starting point of the Circonvallazione a Mare, a seafront highway (now flanked by the high-level motorway) laid out in 1893–95 in the place of the outer walls. Under the
names of Corso Maurizio Quadrio and Corso Aurelio Saffi the highway
passes the grounds of the International Trade Fair, on land recently
reclaimed from the sea, to the Piazza della Vittoria.

A little way south-east of Piazza Cavour is the Romanesque church of   Churches
Santa Maria di Castello. In the adjoining Dominican monastery is the
small Museo di Santa Maria di Castello (good pictures). Farther east are
the Romanesque church of San Donato and the early Gothic church of
Sant'Agostino, both with fine campaniles. From here Via Eugenio
Ravasco and a viaduct 30 m/99 ft high lead south to the conspicuous
domed church of Santa Maria Assunta di Carignano, begun in 1552 to
the design of Galeazzo Alessi and completed about 1600, a smaller
edition of the plan adopted by Bramante and Michelangelo for St
Peter's in Rome. Under the dome are four large Baroque statues. From
the dome there are magnificent views of the city and the harbour.

In the Palazzo Reale

* Passegiata a Mare

Lido d'Albaro

From Piazza della Vittoria the Viale delle Brigate Partigiane, built over the bed of the Bisagno and lined by tall modern blocks, leads south to join the Passeggiata a Mare, a fine promenade which runs along the seafront under the names of Corso G. Marconi and Corso Italia. 2 km/1½ miles along this road, near its east end, is the Lido d'Albaro, a beautifully situated recreation park.

Circonvallazione a Monte

From the Piazza Corvetto the Via Assarotti runs east up to Piazza Manin, the starting point of the beautiful Circonvallazione a Monte.

Museum of America

In the Corso Solferino is the Museum of America (Museo Americanistico), with a fine collection of pre-Columbian art.

Castello d'Albertis

The road runs west along the slopes of the hill to the Spianata del Castelletto (79 m/261 ft; two lifts down to the town), from which there are fine views, and then above the imposing buildings of the 17th c. Albergo dei Poveri (poorhouse) to the Corso Ugo Bassi, near which stands the fortress-like Villa Castello d'Albertis (Museum of Archaeology and Ethnology).

Campo Santo

Situation
3 km/2 miles north

North of the Piazza della Vittoria, up the Bisagno valley, is the beautifully situated Campo Santo or Cimitero di Staglieno, one of the most famous cemeteries in Italy. In the lower arcades are numerous monuments, richly decorated and often overloaded with ornament. Steps lead to the upper arcades, the central feature of which is a domed rotunda. Above this, in the Boschetto dei Mille, is the tomb of Giuseppe Mazzini.

Madonna della Guardia

North of Genoa, on a prominent conical hill, stands the 19th c. pilgrimage church of the Madonna della Guardia (804 m/2653 ft).

Situation
10 km/6 miles north

Gorizia

K4

Region: Friuli–Venezia Giulia
Province: Gorizia (GO)
Altitude: 86 m/284 ft
Population: 42,000

The provincial capital of Gorizia lies just on the Yugoslav frontier at the west end of the karstic limestone country, where the fertile valley of the Isonzo emerges into the plain of Friuli.
Gorizia is the see of an archbishop.
The old town lies around the castle on its hill (148 m/488 ft); the newer districts adjoin the station.

Situation

The fruit and wine trade, as well as some industry (cotton, silk, paper, furniture) and tourism are important features of the economy.

Economy

From 1500 until 1918 the country of Gorizia belonged to Austria. During the First World War, lying as it did on the important road to Austria, it was almost continuously in the front line and was largely destroyed. In 1947 the eastern suburbs of the town, with the Montesanto station, were transferred to Yugoslavia.

History

Sights

At the foot of the north-west side of the castle hill is the triangular Piazza della Vittoria, in which are the Prefecture and the Jesuit church of Sant' Ignazio (17th c.). From here Via Rastello runs south to the cathedral (originally 14th c.; completely rebuilt 1927), with a treasury containing gold and silver objects of the 12th–14th c. (no admission).

Cathedral

From the Piazza del Duomo a road climbs east to the Castello, once the seat of the counts of Gorizia. Nearby is the Museo di Storia e Arte, which houses exhibits of local history, archaeology and applied art.
About 500 m/550 yd north of the Piazza della Vittoria are the Musei Provinciali, the Museo della Guerra (patriotic relics of the First World War) and a small collection of pictures, with works of artists of Gorizia and its surroundings.

Castello

Museums

Battlefields of the Isonzo

From Gorizia the battlefields of the Isonzo, where twelve battles were fought in 1915–17, can be visited (though some of the battle area now lies within Yugoslavia).

Gubbio

Military cemetery of Oslavia	3.5 km/2¼ miles north, on a hill (175 m/578 ft) beyond the Isonzo, is the military cemetery of Oslavia, laid out in 1938, with an ossuary containing the remains of 60,000 Italians who fell in the First World War.
Monte San Michele	11 km/7 miles from Gorizia on the Trieste road a minor road branches off to San Martino del Carso (163 m/538 ft) and Monte San Michele (277 m/914 ft; far-ranging views), with old military positions and a small war museum.

Gubbio

Region: Umbria
Province: Perugia (PG)
Altitude: 478–529 m/1577–1746 ft
Population: 32,000

Situation

The Umbrian town of Gubbio, the Roman Iguvium, lies some 40 km/ 25 miles north of Perugia, at the mouth of a gorge on the north-east edge of a fertile basin, under Monte Calvo (983 m/3244 ft) and Monte Ingino (906 m/2990 ft).
In 1984 the region suffered severe damage in an earthquake.

Palazzo dei Consoli

Museums

The central feature of the town is the Piazza della Signoria, laid out on the slope of the hill. On the north-west side of the square is the Palazzo dei Consoli, a massive Gothic battlemented structure of dressed stone

Gubbio: Palazzo dei Consoli

(1332–1337; fine Renaissance courtyard) which houses a Museum of Archaeology and the Municipal Picture Gallery. In the museum are the "Iguvine Tablets", found on the site of the ancient theatre in 1444 – seven (out of an original nine) bronze tablets with inscriptions partly in the Old Umbrian language and alphabet (2nd c. B.C.) and partly in Neo-Umbrian and the Latin alphabet, dating from a somewhat later period, which are the most important documentary evidence on the Umbrian language.

Opposite the Palazzo dei Consoli is the 14th c. Palazzo Pretorio (Town Hall).   Town Hall

Cathedral

To the north, above the Piazza Grande, stands the Gothic Palazzo Ducale, rebuilt 1476–80 on the model of the Ducal Palace in Urbino. Opposite, partly built into the hillside, is the 13th c. cathedral, with a fine Gothic façade. Inside there are frescoes by Dono Doni.

Santa Maria Nuova

The 14th c. church of Santa Maria Nuova, with the "Madonna del Belvedere" (1403), one of the principal works of the Gubbio-born painter Ottaviano Nelli, is situated in the south-east of the town, near the Porta Romana.

Farther south-east, outside the town gate, is the 13th c. church of Sant'Agostino (modern façade) with frescoes by Ottaviano Nelli in the choir.

Sights in the west

North-west of the Piazza Grande, in the medieval Via dei Consoli, are a number of old houses (see particularly No. 34) with "doors of the dead" set some distance above street level, said to have been used for the removal of the dead, but probably in fact serving as entrances to the upper floors of houses, the ground floors of which were occupied by shops and storage places.   Houses with "doors of the dead"

Also in Via dei Consoli stands the 13th c. Gothic Palazzo del Bargello and at the end of the street the church of San Domenico (14th c.), with 15th c. frescoes.

In the lower south-west part of the town is the Gothic church of San Francesco (12th, 13th and 15th c. frescoes); to the west of the church are the remains of an ancient theatre (1st c. A.D.).
About 500 m/550 yd south, is the so-called Mausoleum of Pomponius Graecinus.   San Francesco

Sant' Ubaldo

From the cathedral a steep road ascends to the monastery of Sant' Ubaldo (820 m/2706 ft), on the slopes of Monte Ingino (906 m/2990 ft; chair-lift).
From the peak (20 minutes' walk) there are magnificent views.   Situation
2 km/1¼ miles east

Herculaneum/Ercolano L9

Region: Campania
Province: Napoli (NA)
Altitude: 44 m/145 ft
Population: 60,000

Situation

The remains of Roman Herculaneum lie within the area of modern Ercolano (until 1969 known as Resina), 8 km/5 miles south-east of Naples, near the Gulf of Naples in a bay of the Tyrrhenian Sea.
Although much of Herculaneum is still buried under the modern town, it offers a vivid impression of the aspect of an ancient city, comparable with the remains of Pompeii and Ostia.

History

Probably founded by Greek settlers under the name of Herakleion and later occupied by Oscans, Etruscans and Samnites, Herculaneum fell into Roman hands in 89 B.C.. In A.D. 63 it suffered severe damage in an earthquake, and in A.D. 79 it was buried under ashes and pumice during an eruption of Vesuvius. At that time the town, a favourite summer resort of the Romans, had a population of perhaps 6000. Subsequent eruptions increased the depth of ashes and lava to between 12 and 30 m/40 and 100 ft. The hardness of this covering, in contrast to the situation at Pompeii, hindered the activity of plunderers in antiquity.

Excavations

From 1719 onwards shafts were sunk into the site at random, yielding some splendid finds which now rank among the principal treasures of the National Museum in Naples, including papyrus rolls and bronze statues. Systematic excavations carried on since 1927 have brought to light the sumptuous villas of wealthy merchants, the furnishings of which have so far as possible been left in situ.

Herculaneum: Excavations and modern building

In contrast to the mostly single-storeyed buildings of Pompeii, the houses of Herculaneum are mostly of two or three storeys, with much use of wood in half-timbered construction, doors and staircases. Extensive excavations are still in progress.

Severe damage took place during an earthquake in November 1980.

Scavi d'Ercolano (excavation site)

From the main entrance (general view) at the north-east corner of the excavation site, the Scavi d'Ercolano, a road 400 m/438 yd long leads to the south end of Cardo III, which runs through an area excavated in the 19th c. On the left is the House of Aristides, a sumptuous country villa, and beyond it the House of Argus, with wall paintings and a pillared garden.

Opposite, on the right-hand side of Cardo III, the Large Inn, a patrician house converted into an inn, has a terrace overlooking the sea. Farther along, on the right, is the House of the Skeleton (wall paintings, mosaics), and on the left the House of the Genius, a fine patrician mansion with a garden enclosed by colonnades.

Half-way along its length Cardo III is crossed by the Decumanus Inferior, along which are the recent excavations. Beyond the crossing, on the left of Cardo III, is the House of Galba, another fine patrician mansion, with a cruciform water-basin.

* * Recent excavations

At the north end of Cardo III, on right, the Sacello degli Augustali, a square shrine lit by an opening in the roof, was originally dedicated to Hercules, patron of Herculaneum, but later consecrated to the Imperial cult (fine frescoes).

* Sacello degli Augustali

Along the Decumanus Inferior to the right is the Cloth-Merchant's Shop, with a wooden hand-press (restored). To the left are the Baths,

* Baths

Mosaic in Herculaneum

211

	much of the structure well preserved, with separate sections for men and women.
Samnite House	At the corner of the Decumanus Inferior and Cardo IV is the Samnite House, one of the oldest patrician mansions in the town, with regular paving and rich stucco and fresco decoration.
	Adjoining is the House with the Large Doorway.
House of the Wooden Partition	On Cardo IV, immediately on the right, is the House of the Wooden Partition, a patrician house of Samnite type (without a peristyle or colonnaded court). The bedrooms still contain bedsteads and a wooden chest. The adjoining Casa a Graticcio, was a more modest house with interior walls of wattle. Immediately to the south is the House of the Bronze Herm, named after a bronze herm (head of Hermes) which is probably a portrait of the owner of the house.
House of the Mosaic Atrium	In the southern section of the street, on left, is the House of the Mosaic Atrium, a spacious and sumptuously furnished mansion.
*House of the Deer	Adjoining it on the east is the House of the Deer.
	In the northern part of the street, on the right, is the House of the Charred Furniture, and beyond it the House of the Mosaic of Neptune and Amphitrite. Nearby are the House with the Fine Courtyard, and opposite a building called the Salon of Nero.
*Suburban Baths	To the south-east, on the far side of Cardo V, the House of the Gem is beautifully painted in reddish-brown tones, and adjoining it on the south-east are the Suburban Baths (Terme Suburbane).
House of the Relief of Telephus	To the north-east of the House of the Gem, towards the sea, is the House of the Relief of Telephus, one of the most elegant mansions in the town, with a spacious colonnaded atrium containing a marble basin and a colonnade leading into the park.
*Palaestra	On the east side of the town is the extensive complex of the Palaestra.
*House of the Bicentenary	On the Decumanus Maximus (only partly excavated), parallel to the Decumanus Inferior on the north, the House of the Bicentenary contains on the first floor the oldest known Christian cross.

Ischia/Isola d'Ischia   K9

	Region: Campania Province: Napoli (NA) Area: 46 sq. km/18 sq. miles Population: 45,000
Boat services	Several times daily (including car ferries) to and from Naples, Capri, Procida and Pozzuoli. Hydrofoil services.
Situation	The volcanic island of Ischia, lying at the entrance to the Bay of Naples, is the largest island in the vicinity of Naples. It was known to the Greeks as Pithekousa, to the Romans as Aenaria and from the 9th c. as Iscla.
*Scenery	An island of luxuriant vegetation (vineyards, fruit orchards, pine-woods), Ischia is of great scenic beauty, particularly on the north side.
Hot springs	Its strongly radioactive hot springs attract many visitors seeking a cure for gout or rheumatism.

Sights in the north of Ischia

Town of Ischia *Ischia Ponte	Ischia (pop. 17,000), the chief place on the island, is picturesquely situated on the north-east coast; it consists of the two districts of Ischia

Ischia Ponte: Castello Aragonese

Ponte and Ischia Porto. In Ischia Ponte a mighty Castello stands on a
91 m/300 ft-high rocky crag accessible by a stone causeway.
About 2 km/1¼ miles west is the busier spa and seaside resort of Ischia   Ischia Porto
Porto with the island's oldest harbour, a former crater lake.

4 km/2½ miles west of Ischia Porto, half-way along the north coast of   Casamicciola Terme
the island, Casamicciola Terme (3 m/10 ft), surrounded by gardens and
vineyards, is situated on the lower slopes of Monte Epomeo, with hot
springs (65 °C/149 °F) and a good bathing beach.

Farther on from Casamicciola Terme is the resort of Lacco Ameno (7   Lacco Ameno
m/23 ft; pop. 4000) where, near Graeco-Roman excavations there are
hot radioactive mineral springs (55 °C/131 °F). From here it is 6 km/3¾
miles south-west to Forio on the west coast (18 m/59 ft; pop. 10,000),
also with thermal springs and an impressive 15th c. round tower.

Southern part of the island

From Forio a beautiful road (20 km/12 miles) leads through the south-   Gardens of Poseidon
ern part of the island. It passes above the Gardens of Poseidon (magnificent bathing facilities, with thermal springs) and continues via Panza
(155 m/512 ft).

At Panza a road goes off to the village of Sant'Angelo (hot springs),   ⁕Sant'Angelo
picturesquely situated on the slopes of a promontory.

The road continues to Serrara (366 m/1208 ft), Fontana (452 m/1492 ft)   Barano d'Ischia
and Barano d'Ischia (212 m/700 ft; large beach with hot springs), past a
16th c. aqueduct and so back to Ischia Ponte.

*Monte Epomeo   From Fontana there is a rewarding climb (1 hour) up Monte Epomeo
(789 m/2604 ft), a massive volcano (extinct since 1302), with an almost
vertical north face, in the centre of the island (panoramic views).

Latium/Lazio

Region: Latium/Lazio
Provinces: Roma (ROMA), Frosinone (FR), Latina (LT), Rieti (R) and
Viterbo (VB)
Area: 17,203 sq. km/6640 sq. miles
Population: 5,080,100

Situation   The historic area and the present-day region of Latium occupies the
west side of the Central Apennines, extending south-west from the
Monti Sabini to the coast of the Tyrrhenian Sea between the mouths of
the River Chiarone in the north and the Garigliano in the south. The
centre of Latium is the densely populated city of Rome.

Montains and lakes   Most of the region is occupied by four volcanic massifs of the Qua-
ternary era, in the craters of which four large lakes and a number of
smaller ones have been formed. To the north-west are the Monte
Volsini (639 m/2109 ft), with the Lago di Bolsena; farther south-east the
Monti Cimini (1053 m/3475 ft), with the Lago di Vico, and the Monti
Sabatini (612 m/2020 ft), with the Lago di Bracciano; and south-east of
Rome the Monti Albani or Alban Hills (948 m/3128 ft), with the Lago
Albano.

Tiber
Maremma   Through the fertile volcanic soil of the region the Tiber has carved out
its wide bed. Along the coast extends the Maremma, a broad strip of
alluvial soil, once marshy and malaria-ridden, which has been drained
and brought under intensive cultivation. This varied geological and
geographical pattern has made Latium a region of great scenic
diversity.

Agriculture and
fishing   The main elements in the economy are still arable and sheep-farming.
The lower-lying areas produce corn, vegetables and sugar-beet, while
the volcanic soils of the uplands yield citrus fruits, olives and good
quality grapes.
Along the coast (e.g. at Civitavecchia) fishing is of some economic
importance.

Industry   In recent years there has been a rapid development of modern industry,
particularly around Rome, in the Sacco and Liri valleys and in the
catchment area of the Autostrada del Sole – chemicals and pharmaceuticals, metal-working, textiles, building materials, etc. There are
thermo-electric power stations at Civitavecchia and Borgo Sabatino. A
considerable contribution is also made to the economy by tourism,
particularly in and around Rome.

History   Present-day Latium was occupied in early antiquity by Etruscans and,
around the mouth of the Tiber, by the Latin peoples, who formed a
league of 30 republics under the leadership of the city of Alba Longa.
During the 6th and 5th c. b.c. the rising city of Rome became a member
of the Latin League and steadily increased in influence until, after the
transfer of the federal sanctuary to the Temple of Diana on the Aventine, it became de facto the leading city of the League. The Latin towns
sought to counter the predominance of Rome by force of arms (Latin

War, 340–338 B.C., but were defeated. Thereupon the League was dissolved and the various towns became subject to Rome, on varying terms, and thereafter shared the destinies of Rome.

Rome

The main centre of attraction in Latium is Rome (see entry).

Segni

On the road from Rome to Frosinone and on to Naples there are numerous places of interest. 19 km/12 miles south-east of Rome on S.S. 6 (the Via Casilina), which runs parallel to the motorway, a minor road leads south via Collefero (225 m/743 ft; pop. 18,000), with a castle on a hill, to the little town of Segni (668 m/1841 ft; pop. 8000), situated on an outlier of the Monti Lepini, with extensive views. This was the very ancient city of Signia, and preserves most of its 2 km/1¼ mile circuit of town walls dating from the 6th c. B.C., with the remarkable Porta Saracinesca to the north-west. On the acropolis stands the 13th c. church of San Pietro, built on the central cella of an ancient temple.

Anagni

11 km/7 miles farther along S.S. 6 a road goes off to Anagni (424 m/1399 ft; pop. 18,000), on a hill 6 km/3¾ miles north-east, still surrounded by Roman walls. This was the ancient Anagnia, capital of the Hernici, and in the Middle Ages was frequently the residence of the Pope. The cathedral of Santa Maria (11th c., rebuilt in the 13th c.) contains a mosaic pavement by Magister Cosmas (1226), an Easter candlestick and a bishop's throne by Vassalletto (1263); in the crypt are old frescoes and an altar by Cosmas and his sons; to the right of the choir is the Diocesan Museum. Also of interest is the 13th c. Town Hall.

Ferentino

Farther along the main road is the old town of Ferentino (393 m/1297 ft; pop. 18,000), with almost completely preserved town walls (5th–2nd c. B.C.); on the south side the Porta Sanguinaria and on the east side the Porta Maggiore or Porta di Casamira. On the highest point in the town, the old acropolis, are the Bishop's Palace and the cathedral, which has a mosaic pavement by Magister Paulus (c. 1116). To the north-east, near the Porta Sanguinaria, stands the church of Santa Maria Maggiore (12th–13th c.; fine doorway).

Frosinone

12 km/7½ miles beyond Ferentino we reach the provincial capital, Frosinone (291 m/960 ft; pop. 46,000), picturesquely situated on a hillside above the Cosa valley, with remains of ancient buildings.
16 km/10 miles east is the Cistercian abbey of Santi Giovanni e Paolo di Casamari (1203–17), which ranks with Fossanova as one of the finest achievements of early Burgundian Gothic in Italy.

*Santi Giovanni e Paolo di Casamari

Aquino

42 km/26 miles beyond Frosinone on S.S. 6 a side road branches off to the village of Aquino (106 m/350 ft), the ancient Aquinum, home of the

215

satirist Juvenal (c. A.D. 60–140) and of the scholastic philosopher Thomas Aquinas (1226–74), known as the "Doctor Angelicus" or "Doctor Ecclesiae", who was born in the castle of Roccasecca (10 km/6 miles north) and trained in Montecassino abbey. On the Via Latina, which passed here, are remains of the Roman city. Near the river is the 12th c. church of Santa Maria della Libera, a Lombard foundation built on the ruins of a temple of Hercules, with a fine doorway (friezes, mosaics, frescoes).

12 km/7½ miles farther along is the little town of Cassino (see Montecassino).

Palestrina

On S.S. 155 (Via Prenistina), which also leads from Rome to Frosinone north of S.S. 6, we reach in 40 km/25 miles Palestrina (450 m/1485 ft; pop. 14,000), the ancient Praeneste and one of the oldest towns in Italy, birthplace of the greatest Italian composer of church music, Giovanni Pierluigi da Palestrina (1525–94; tomb in St Peter's, Rome). In 1630 the town fell into the hands of the noble Barberini family. Almost the whole area of the present-day town was occupied by the massive temple of Fortuna Primigenia, the seat of a frequently consulted oracle, which was built on four terraces on the slope on the hill, and of which there are considerable remains. On the second terrace, by the cathedral, are the well-preserved remains of the Antro delle Sorti ("Cave of Destiny") and the Aula dell'Oracolo, home of the oracle. On the fourth terrace, above the massive arches of the third, stands the Palazzo Barberini (15th and 17th c.; Archaeological Museum), on the site of the shrine of Fortuna, with magnificent views extending as far as Rome.

Castel San Pietro Romano

From here a road (3 km/2 miles) winds its way up to the village of Castel San Pietro Romano (752 m/2482 ft), linked with Palestrina by ancient walls, with the massive ramparts of its acropolis and a ruined 15th c. castle. From the Spianata delle Torricelle there are panoramic views.

Fiuggi

39 km/24 miles from Palestrina on S.S. 115, situated among beautiful forests of chestnut-trees, is Fiuggi (621–747 m/2049-2465 ft; pop. 8000), the most popular spa in southern Italy, with radioactive thermal springs (120 °C/248 °F). 3.5 km/2 miles north is the medieval part of the town, Fiuggi Città (747 m/2465 ft).

Alatri

7 km/4½ miles beyond Fuggi on the main road is Alatri (502 m/1657 ft; pop. 23,000), the ancient Aletrium, which has the finest surviving circuit of ancient walls. Especially well preserved are the walls (4th c. B.C.) of the acropolis, built of huge polygonal blocks: note in particular the south-west gate, the Porta dell'Areopago, with a lintel slab 5 m/5½ yd long and 1.60 m/1¾ yd thick. On the castle hill are the cathedral and the church of Santa Maria Maggiore.

12 km/7½ miles beyond Alatri is Frosinone.

Cisterna di Latina

In the southern part of Latium is the little town of Cisterna di Latina (81 m/267 ft; pop. 17,000).

Castle tower in the ruined town of Ninfa

From here, 10 km/6 miles north-east, on an outlier of the Monti Lepini, is the little town of Cori (384 m/1267 ft; pop. 10,000), the ancient Cora. The town, which claims to have been founded by the Trojan Dardanus, preserves considerable remains of its ancient polygonal walls (5th c. B.C.). In the upper town stands the church of Sant'Oliva, built on ancient foundations, with a two-storey cloister, ancient columns and unusual ceiling paintings (16th c.). Higher up, by the church of San Pietro, is the antechamber of the so-called Temple of Hercules (1st c. B.C.), probably in fact dedicated to the three Capitoline deities, Jupiter, Juno and Minerva. From here there are beautiful views over the town to the sea, the plain and Monte Circeo. Below the temple (½ hour's walk) are the remains of another temple dedicated to Castor and Pollux.

Cori

12 km/7½ miles east of Cisterna di Latina is Ninfa, a ruined town still partly surrounded by its walls. The town, mostly dating from the 12th and 13th c. (castle of the Caetani family with an imposing tower, monastery, two small churches) was abandoned in the 17th c. on account of malaria. The enclosed area, with a garden of botanic interest, is open only from April to October on the first Saturday in the month; it is private property.

*Ninfa

8 km/5 miles north of Ninfa, at Norba (417 m/1376 ft; pop. 4000), are the remains (15 minutes' walk on a hill track) of the old Volscian city of Norba, which became a Latin colony in 492 B.C. and was destroyed by supporters of Sulla during the Roman civil wars. The site, surrounded by a polygonal wall 2.5 km/1½ miles long (4th c. B.C.), contains the remains of four temples (museum).

Norba

8 km/5 miles north-east of Ninfa is the little medieval town of Sermoneta (257 m/848 ft; pop. 6500), dominated by a castle which belonged to

Sermoneta

217

the Caetani family from 1297 onwards, but which was taken over by Pope Alexander VI (Borgia) in 1500–03 for his daughter Lucrezia and was fortified by Cesare Borgia (14th–15th c. frescoes). The cathedral contains a Madonna ascribed to Benozzo Gozzoli.

Gaeta

In the extreme south of Latium, charmingly situated on a rocky promontory in the gulf of the same name, the port of Gaeta (10 m/33 ft; pop. 25,000), was until 1861 the principal strong point of the kingdom of Naples and Sicily. The cathedral of Sant' Erasmo has a campanile in Sicilian Romanesque style (1279). Inside, behind the high altar, is a banner presented by Pope Pius V to Don John of Austria, the victor of Lepanto and opposite the principal doorway an Easter candlestick with Late Romanesque reliefs (c. 1200), is borne on four lions. A short distance west of the Piazza stands the large church of San Francesco. The church of the Santissima Annunziata to the north was originally built in 1320 (Baroque façade); to the south is the Citadel, with the Angevine Tower.

On the highest point of the promontory (171 m/564 ft) rises the Mausoleo di Lucio Munazio Planco, the imposing tomb of Lucius Munatius Plancus (d. after 22 B.C.), who worked successively for Caesar, Antony and Augustus.

At the south-west tip of the promontory (2 km/1¼ miles; extensive views) is the Montagna Spaccata, with a cleft in the rock which according to tradition was caused by the earthquake at the death of Christ. From the new pilgrimage church steps lead down to the beautiful Grotta del Turco (admission fee), on the sea.

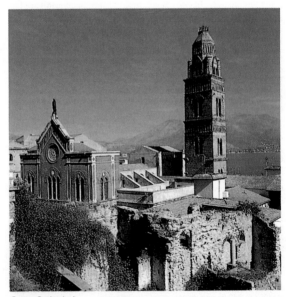

Gaeta Cathedral

On the west side of the promontory is an excellent bathing beach, the Spiaggia di Serapo.

In the surroundings of Gaeta are many places with remains of Roman Villas.

About 20 km/12 miles south of Gaeta is the resort of Baia Domizia.

Formia

About 6 km/3¾ miles north of Gaeta, the pretty little town of Formia is charmingly situated on the Golfo di Gaeta; it is a resort much frequented by Italians in summer. At the west end of the town, near the sea, is the Villa Rubino or Villa di Cicerone, which once belonged to the kings of Naples.

Sperlonga

On a promontory 15 km/9 miles west of Gaeta lies the picturesque fishing village of Sperlonga, still partly surrounded by walls, with a good bathing beach.

Outside the town, in an olive-grove, the very interesting Museo Archeologico Nazionale di Sperlonga houses an excellent collection of original Greek sculpture in marble. Most of the items, found in the Grotta di Tiberio, are now reduced to the condition of huge torsos. The finest piece is the "Ship of Odysseus", by the sculptor responsible for the famous Laocoön group now in Rome, which depicts Odysseus and his companions struggling with the marine monster Scylla. Between the museum and the sea are remains of the Emperor Tiberius's villa and of ancient basins hewn from the rock, which were used for the rearing of fish (aquationes). Close by is the entrance to the Grotta di Tiberio, in which the Emperor Tiberius is supposed to have caroused with his friends. Since 1957 some 7000 fragments of Greek statues have been discovered here.

*Museo Archeologico Nazionale

Itri

15 km/9 miles north of Gaeta is the little town of Itri (170 m/561 ft; pop. 8000), formerly notorious as a centre of brigandage and birthplace of the bandit Fra Diavolo, the hero of Auber's opera. Some of the houses in the town are built into the substructures of the Via Appia; above it towers a massive ruined castle.

In the vineyards between Itri and Formia is a round tower known as the Tomb of Cicero, who was murdered at the age of 64 in this area, near his country estate at Formia, in the year 43 B.C.

Tomb of Cicero

Fondi

14 km/9 miles north-west of Itri is Fondi (8 m/26 ft; pop. 20,000), still partly surrounded by ancient walls. In the Corso Appio Claudio, the main street which runs through the whole length of the town on the line of the old Via Appia, are the church of Santa Maria Assunta, with an early Renaissance doorway, and the Gothic church of San Pietro, with a pulpit and bishop's throne of the 13th c. On the south-east side of the town is the Palazzo del Principe (15th c.), with the crenellated 13th c. Castello opposite.

Rieti

80 km/50 miles north-east of Rome is the provincial capital of Rieti (402 m/1327 ft; pop. 44,000), situated on a fertile plateau, fringed by hills, on

Castle ruins in Itri

the right bank of the River Velino. Along the north side of the town stretch defensive walls and towers. In the central Piazza Vittorio Emanuele is the Palazzo Comunale with the Museo Civico. To the southwest stands the cathedral (completed 1458, almost completely altered in the 17th c.), with a 13th c. campanile. Inside, in the fourth chapel on the north side, is a statue of St Barbara by Bernini. From the Piazza del Duomo there are fine views. Behind the cathedral lies the Bishop's Palace, with the beautiful Loggia Papale (13th c.).

Terminillo

From Rieti attractive trips can be made into the Monti Reatine, particularly to Terminillo (21 km/13 miles north-east: cableway, chair-lift, ski-lifts), a popular summer resort and winter sports centre, much favoured by the people of Rome (the "montagna di Roma"). From Monte Terminillo (2216 m/7313 ft), the highest peak in the Monti Reatini, there are panoramic views extending to the Gran Sasso and Maiella, and on clear days as far as the Adriatic and the Tyrrhenian Sea.

Civita Castellana

In northern Latium, situated at the west end of a tufa plateau surrounded by deep gorges, is the ancient town of Civita Castellana (145 m/479 ft; pop. 15,000), capital of the Faliscan territory lying between Etruria and Latium. In 241 b.c. the Faliscan town, known to the Romans as Falerii Veteres, was destroyed by Roman forces and the inhabitants transferred to a new settlement at Falerii Novi, from which they later returned. The noteworthy 12th c. cathedral of Santa Maria has a beautiful porch of 1210 and some ancient columns in the crypt. In a commanding situation to the west of the town stands the Citadel, built by Pope Alexander VI in 1494–1500 to the design of Antonio da Sangallo the Elder; in the large arcaded courtyard are decorative paintings by the Zuccaro brothers (16th c.). The Citadel houses the Archaeological Museum of the Faliscan Territory.

6 km/3¾ miles west are the remains of Falerii Novi, founded in 240 B.C. to rehouse the inhabitants of the older town of Falerii Veteres, which has preserved its complete circuit of walls (2108 m/2315 yd long, with nine gates and 50 towers). Within the walls, near the Porta di Giove on the west side, the ruined abbey of Santa Maria di Falleri has ancient columns in the nave. Near the Porta del Bove, to the south-east are the remains of a theatre, the forum and a swimming pool.

Falerii Novi

*Lago di Bolsena

Another attractive place in northern Latium is the Lago di Bolsena (alt. 305 m/1007 ft; area 114 sq. km/44 sq. miles; up to 151 m/496 ft deep), known to the Romans as Lacus Vulsiniensis. The lake occupies the crater of a collapsed Tertiary volcano. In the southern half of the lake are two little rocky islets, Bisentina (361 m/1191 ft) and Martana (377 m/1244 ft). On the island of Martana the Gothic queen Amalasuntha, only daughter of Theodoric the Great, was strangled in her bath in the year 535 on the orders of her co-Regent Theodahad.

At the north-east corner of the lake the picturesquely situated little town of Bolsena (348 m/1148 ft; pop. 4000) lies below the site of Etruscan Volsinium, political centre of the league of twelve Etruscan cities (remains of a wall of dressed stone), and the Roman Volsinium Novum, built in 263 B.C. An ancient road paved with basalt blocks leads up (½ hour) to the scanty remains. Features of interest in Bolsena itself are the

Bolsena

Distant view of the Lago di Bolsena

221

13th c. Castello and the church of Santa Cristina (13th c.) to the south of the town. The church has a fine Renaissance façade (c. 1500) with two terracotta reliefs by Andrea della Robbia above the doors. In the interior is the Grotta di Santa Cristiana, with the saint's tomb, and, under the high altar, the stone with which she was drowned in the year 278. The altar is known as the Altare del Miracolo, following the "miracle of Bolsena" in 1263, when a Bohemian priest who had doubted the doctrine of transubstantiation (i.e. the transformation of bread and wine into the body and blood of Christ in the mass) was convinced of his error by the appearance of drops of blood on the consecrated Host. To commemorate the event Pope Urban IV made the feast of Corpus Christi (which had recently been initiated in Belgium) a universal festival of the Church (1264) and caused the splendid cathedral of Orvieto to be built.

Montefiascone

South-east of Bolsena, on a subsidiary crater just inland from the lake, is Montefiascone (590 m/1947 ft; pop. 12,000), noted for the famous sweet white wine "Est Est Est". The cathedral of Santa Margherita (by Sanmicheli, 1519) has an octagonal dome. From the gardens around the castle above the town there are extensive views. To the north-east, below the town on the Orvieto road, is the double church of San Flaviano (12th c.), with 14th c. frescoes.

Lago di Bracciano

Also in northern Latium is the beautiful Lago di Bracciano (alt. 279 m/921 ft; area 57.5 sq. km/22 sq. miles; up to 165 m/541 ft deep, the ancient Lacus Sabatinus, which, like Lake Bolsena, was created by the explosion and subsequent collapse of a volcanic cone.

Bracciano

Above the lake to the south-west is the little town of Bracciano (279 m/921 ft; pop. 11,000), with the massive five-towered Castello Orsini-Odescalchi (built 1470, in the possession of the princely Odescalchi family since 1696), a fine example of a fortified medieval castle. Notable interior and pillared courtyard; from the wall-walk there are magnificent views of the lake.

Cerveteri

See entry.

Lecce   P9

Region: Puglia
Province: Lecce (LE)
Altitude: 49 m/162 ft
Population: 94,000

Situation

The provincial capital of Lecce lies mid-way along the Salentine peninsula, the heel of the Italian boot, in the southernmost part of Italy – some 30 km/19 miles south-east of Brindisi.
Lecce is one of the most interesting towns in southern Italy, notable for its magnificent Baroque buildings erected by local architects using the beautiful and easily worked yellow limestone of the area.

Piazza Sant' Oronzo

In the centre of the town is the Piazza Sant' Oronzo, with an ancient column bearing a statue of the saint, and marking the end of the Via Appia. To the west of the column is the Palazzo del Sedile, a loggia built in 1592, and adjoining it the doorway of the little church of San Marco (founded 1543). On the south side of the square are the excavated remains of a Roman amphitheatre (2nd c. A.D.).

South-east of the Piazza Sant' Oronzo is the Castello, built by Charles V in 1539–1548, on a trapezoid ground-plan.   Castello

South of the town centre in the Piazza Vittorio Emanuele stands the 18th c. church of Santa Chiara and farther south the church of San Matteo (built c. 1700), with a bizarrely curved façade.

*Piazza del Duomo

From the Piazza Sant' Oronzo the Corso Vittorio Emanuele II runs west,   Cathedral
past the Theatine church of Sant' Irene (1639), into the Piazza del Duomo, with the cathedral of Sant' Oronzo (1658–70; tower 70 m/231 ft high), the Bishop's Palace and the Seminary, which has a richly decorated façade and a courtyard containing a fountain.

500 m/550 yd south of the Piazza del Duomo is the large Dominican church of Santa Maria del Rosario (1691–1728).

To the south of the town, in Piazza Argento, is the Palazzo Argento,   Museo Provinciale
which houses the Provincial Museum (ancient vases, terracottas, statues and pictures).

Churches of Santí Nicolò e Cataldo . . .   *. . . and Santa Croce*

223

Lecce

* Santa Croce

North of Piazza Sant' Oronzo in the Piazza della Prefettura the magnificent Baroque church of Santa Croce has an elaborately decorated façade (begun 1548, completed 1697 onwards) and a fine interior. Adjoining it on the north is the extensive and richly ornamented façade of the Celestine convent (13th c.) which belonged to the church; now Palazzo del Governo.

Behind this is the beautiful Giardino Pubblico.

** Santi Nicolò e Cataldo

From the Palazzo del Governo we go north along Via Umberto I and in 100 m/110 yd turn left into Via Principe di Savoia to reach the Porta di Napoli, on the west end of the old town, a triumphal arch erected in 1548, and a memorial to Charles V. North-west of this is the Campo Santo, with the church of Santi Nicolò e Cataldo, founded by the Norman Count Tancred in 1180, with a superb Romanesque doorway in the centre of the Baroque façade of 1716 showing Arabian influence. The harmonious interior, with strong influence of French Gothic, has beautiful capitals.

Gallipoli   O9

Situation
38 km/24 miles
south-west

There is an attractive drive over the Apulian plain, passing through the little country town of Galatone (59 m/195 ft; pop. 14,000), with a cathedral and the Baroque church of the Crocifisso, to Gallipoli (14 m/46 ft; pop. 22,000), a little port beautifully situated on a rocky island in the Golfo di Taranto and linked by a bridge with its modern suburb on the mainland. At the east end of the bridge is a fountain of 1560, with ancient reliefs. Beyond the bridge, to the left, is the Castello (16th c.), from which the main street, Via Antonietta de Pace, runs across the town. In this street, on the left, stands the cathedral (1629–96), with fine choir-stalls, and, on the right, the Municipal Museum.

Santa Maria al
Bagno

A pleasant trip from Gallipoli is on a road, partly hewn from the rock, along the "Riviera Neretina" to the little resort of Santa Maria al Bagno, which lies 12 km/7½ miles north. In another 2 km/1¼ miles the road comes to the hamlet of Santa Caterina Riviera.

From Lecce to Capo Santa Maria di Leuca (about 65 or 100 km/40 or 62 miles)

Otranto

Another attractive trip is from Lecce to Capo Santa Maria di Leuca, either on the direct road (65 km/40 miles) via Maglie (81 m/267 ft) or on the longer but scenically superior coast road (about 100 km/62 miles). The coast road traverses the seaside resort of San Cataldo which has a good beach and a lighthouse, and comes to Otranto (15 km/9 miles; pop. 5000), a little fishing town beautifully situated in a bay. Under the name of Hydrus or Hydruntum, often referred to in the ancient sources as a port of embarkation for Apollonia in Epirus, Otranto was destroyed by the Turks in 1480. From the Castello, built in 1495–98, there is a view across the Straits of Otranto (75 km/47 miles wide) to the mountains of Albania. The cathedral of the Santissima Annunziata (begun 1080) contains ancient columns with 12th c. capitals, a unique mosaic pavement, completely preserved, with representations of the months and of heroic subjects (1163–66) and a five-aisled crypt. In a side street in the

Santa Catarina, near Gallipoli

upper part of the town is the little church of San Pietro (10th–11th c.), with a Byzantine dome and frescoes, depiciting the saints and scenes of the life of Christ.

From Otranto the road continues, running inland for part of the way and then winding its way along the coast, to Santa Cesarea Terme (56 m/185 ft), a popular resort, charmingly situated above the sea. It has four springs of sulphureous water (36 °C/97 °F) in large caves in the cliffs.

Santa Cesarea Terme

From here there is an interesting boat trip (4–5 km/2½–3 miles south), along the rocky coast with its numerous coves to two stalactitic caves which were inhabited in prehistoric times, the Grotta Romanelli and the Grotta Zinzulusa.

Stalactitic caves

Beyond Santa Cesarea Terme the road continues along the rocky coast to the little fishing port of Castro Marino, below the fortified village of Castro, and Capo Santa Maria di Leuca (59 m/195 ft), the south-eastern tip of Italy, named after its white limestone cliffs (Greek ákra leuká). On the cape is the church of Santa Maria de Finibus Terrae ("St Mary of the Ends of the Earth"), with an altar constructed of stone from the temple of Minerva which stood here, and an image of the Virgin which is revered as miraculous. From the lighthouse there are magnificent views, extending in clear weather as far as Albania.

Capo Santa Maria di Leuca

West of the cape is the little seaside resort of Leuca and to the south-west Punta Ristole.

There are attractive boat trips along the magnificent rocky coast with its numerous caves.

Leghorn (Livorno)   G6

Region: Toscana
Province: Livorno (LI)
Altitude: 3 m/10 ft
Population: 176,000

Situation

Leghorn (in Italian Livorno), capital of its province and the most important harbour in Tuscany, is situated on the low-lying coast of the Tyrrhenian Sea, some 20 km/12 miles south of Pisa.

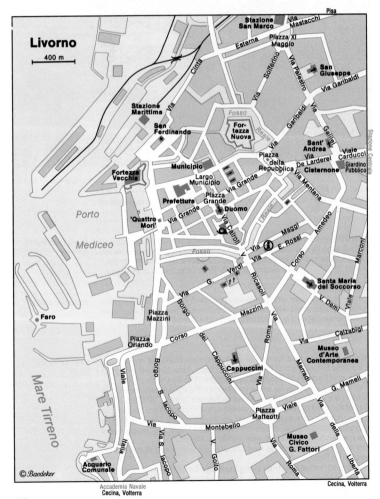

© Baedeker

Accademia Navale
Cecina, Volterra

Leghorn owed its rise to the Medici, who during the 16th and 17th c.
offered asylum to refugees from many lands.
The city is of modern aspect, and the heavy destruction of the Second
World War has left it with no great monuments of the past. Leghorn was
the birthplace of the painter Amedeo Modigliani (1884–1920).

Piazza Grande

The central feature of the old town is the long Piazza Grande, now
surrounded by modern buildings. At its southern end stands the
cathedral, rebuilt in accordance with the original plan; in the centre of
the square is the Palazzo Grande (1951) and at the north-east corner the
Town Hall. From here Via Cairoli runs south to the Piazza Cavour, the
new centre of the city's traffic, which is partly laid out over a canal,
the Fosso Reale.

Via Grande

Leghorn's main street, the Via Grande, cuts across the Piazza Grande;   Fortezza Nuova
at its east end is the Piazza della Repubblica, with statues of Ferdinand
III (d. 1824) and Leopold II (d. 1870), the last Grand Dukes of Tuscany.
Immediately north of the square is the Fortezza Nuova (bastion; 1590),
surrounded by canals.

Harbour

The harbour, at the west end of the old town, is one of the most
important ports of the Mediterranean. The old part of the harbour is
called Porto Mediceo in honour of its founders. On the north side of the
Piazza Michele, flanking the docks, stands a statue of Grand Duke   Statue of Grand
Ferdinand I (1587–1609) by Giovanni Bandini, which, because of the   Duke Ferdinand I
bronze figures on the plinth (by Pietro Tacca, 1624), is also called
"Monumento dei Quattro Mori" (monument of the four moors).

At the northern end of the harbour and its docks is the Fortezza Vecchia   Fortezza Vecchia
(old bastion; 1534), with a massive tower.

Viale Italia in Livorno

The southern boundary of the docks is the starting point of the beautiful   Aquarium
Viale Italia which runs south, along the coast, past parks and beaches.
In the Terrazza Mascagni is the Aquarium (Aquarino Comunale);
adjoining it is a marine research institute.

Museo d'Arte Contemporanea

South-east of the old town, set amid a park, is the Museo d'Arte
Contemporanea (Museum of Contemporary Art), with works by mainly
Italian artists (temporary exhibitions).

Museo Civico

The Museo Civico, in the park of the Villa Fabbricotti to the south of the
new town, contains works by the Macchiaioli, a group of painters

Leghorn (Livorno): Fosso Reale and Fortezza Vecchia

formed in the mid-19th c., whose principal aim was to overcome academic restrictions. Modern art is also on display including paintings by Modigliani.

Liguria

E–F5/6

Region: Liguria
Provinces: Genova (GE), Imperia (IM), La Spezia (SP) and Savona (SV)
Area: 5416 sq. km/2090 sq. miles
Population: 1,778,000

Situation

The region of Liguria, with Genoa as capital, lies on the southern slopes of the arc of mountains which extends around the Gulf of Genoa (Ligurian Sea) from the Ligurian Alps in the west to the Ligurian Apennines in the east.

History

The region, originally occupied by Ligurians, was Romanised in the 2nd c. B.C. Fragmented during the early medieval period into numerous Lombard and Frankish principalities, it fell from the 12th c. onwards under the control of Genoa, then growing in strength as a sea power. In 1805 Liguria was annexed by Napoleon, and in 1814 it was assigned by the Congress of Vienna to Piedmont, becoming part of the new united Italy.

Scenery

The mountains which here fall steeply down to the sea provide almost complete protection against unfavourable weather from the north, and the region's southern exposure gives it a mild and sunny climate, particularly along the coastal strip known as the Riviera, which has long been a favourite winter resort.

The population of the region is mainly concentrated in the industrial areas around the ports of Genoa, La Spezia (see entry) and Savona. In the country regions, with only moderately productive soil, vegetables and fruit are grown, as well as the flowers (also used in the manufacture of perfume) for which the region is renowned.

Population

Tourism is of great economic importance along the whole of the Riviera (see entry).

Tourism

Lipari Islands/Aeolian Islands

L/M11

Region: Sicilia
Province: Messina (ME)
Area: 117 sq. km/45 sq. miles
Population: 1,778,000

Regular services from Milazzo and Messina as well as from Palermo and Naples to Lipari, Vulcano, Salina and Panarea, with connections several times weekly to Filicudi and Alicudi. Car ferries from Milazzo, Messina and Naples.

Boat services

The Lipari Islands (Isole Lipari), also known as the Aeolian Islands (Isole Eólie) after the Greek wind god Aeolus, lie between 30 and 80 km/19 and 50 miles off the north coast of Sicily in the Tyrrhenian Sea.
They form an archipelago of seven larger islands and ten uninhabited islets, the tips of mountains of volcanic origin rising from the sea-bed far below.

Situation

The islands were long used as penal colonies and places of banishment. In more recent times their mild climate and unusual scenery have

General information
*Holiday resort

View from Lipari towards Vulcano

attracted increasing numbers of visitors. They offer excellent scuba diving.

Island of Lipari

The largest and most fertile of the islands is Lipari (area 38 sq. km/14 sq. miles, pop. 11,000). In the more southerly bay on the east coast lies the

Lipari town

little town of Lipari (5 m/17 ft; pop. 4500), the chief place of the island. To the south of the harbour, on a rocky promontory, is the Castello, within which are the cathedral (1654) and three other churches. Adjoining the cathedral, in the former Bishop's Palace, is the Museo Eoliano containing rich finds of the prehistoric period and historical times from recent excavations on the island (painted Greek vases, a statuette of Isis, tombs, etc.). To the west of the cathedral, on an excavation site in front of the Immacolata Church, can be seen a series of building levels ranging in date from the Early Bronze Age (17th c. B.C.) through the Iron Age (11th–9th c. B.C.) and the Hellenistic period to Roman times (2nd c. A.D.). North of the Castello is the fishermen's quarter; to the south the warehouses in which the island's exports, including pumice-stone, currants, Malvasia wine, capers and figs, are stored to await shipment.

Canneto

3 km/2 miles north of Lipari, beyond Monte Rosa (239 m/789 ft), the village of Canneto (10 m/33 ft) is the centre for the extraction, processing and export of pumice-stone. The pumice quarries in the valley of the Fossa Bianca, north-west of the village (45 minutes) are an interesting sight.

Monte Sant'Angelo

West of Canneto (1½ hours), beyond the massive lava flows at Forgia Vecchia, rises Monte Sant'Angelo (594 m/1960 ft). From its summit, roughly in the centre of the archipelago, there is the best panoramic view of the Lipari Islands.

The town of Lipari

In the middle of the lake lies the steep sided Monte Isola (559 m/1845 ft), an island 3 km/2 miles long, covered with dense chestnut forests. On its highest point is the pilgrimage church of the Madonna della Ceriola (views). At the south-eastern extremity of the island is the fishing village of Peschiera Maraglio, at its north-western end the village of Siviano, at its south-western tip Sensole.

Monte Isola

On the south side of the lake the little port of Iseo (198 m/653 ft) has a parish church and an old Scaliger castle.

Iseo

At the northern end of the lake, prettily situated on a sloping hillside, the little industrial town of Lovere (208 m/686 ft; pop. 7000) boasts the fine Renaissance church of Santa Maria in Valvendra (15th c.; Baroque interior; pictures) and the Accademia Tadini, a picture gallery containing works by Bellini. From the lakeside promenade there are beautiful views.

Lovere

13 km/8 miles north-east of Lovere, in the Val Camonica, is the spa of Darfo Boario Terme (225 m/743 ft), with chalybeate springs.

Darfo Boario Terme

From here there is an attractive excursion to the north-west, through the 10 km/6 mile long Dezzo gorge, known as the "Via Mala Lombarda", to Dezzo.

*Dezzo gorge

Breno (343 m/1132 ft; pop. 6000) is situated 13 km/8 miles north-east of Darfo Boario Terme. It is the chief town of the Val Camonica, with a ruined castle and two interesting churches, San Salvatore and Sant'Antonio. To the north rises a fine dolomitic peak, the Corna di Concarena (2549 m/8412 ft), to the north-east the Pizzo Badile (2435 m/8036 ft), the "Matterhorn of the Val Camonica".

Breno

At Capo di Ponte, in the Val Camonica, is the Parco Nazionale delle Incisioni Rupestri (National Park of the Rock Paintings); in the area of which are numerous rock paintings made by the former inhabitants, the Camuni (a total of 876 scenes from the Late Bronze and Iron Age). From Breno a beautiful road, narrow and sometimes steep, runs southeast (49 km/30 miles) via Campolaro (1442 m/4759 ft) to the Passo di Croce Domini (1895 m/6254 ft) and then continues through the Valle Sanguinara and the Valle Cafforo to the picturesquely situated mountain village of Bagolino (778 m/2567 ft) and beyond this to the church of Sant'Antonio on the beautiful Lago d'Idro (alt. 368 m/1214 ft; 10 km/6 miles long, 1½–2 km/1–1¼ miles wide, up to 122 m/400 ft deep), known to the Romans as Lacus Eridius.

Capo di Ponte
*Rock paintings

Loreto

Region: Marche
Province: Ancona (AN)
Altitude: 127 m/419 ft
Population: 11,000

The little town of Loreto lies on a hill near the Adriatic Sea, some 20 km/13 miles south of Ancona.

Situation

Since the 14th c. it has been Italy's second most important place of pilgrimage after Rome.

According to legend the Virgin's house in Nazareth, the Santa Casa, was transported by angels to Trsat near Rijeka (Fiume) in Yugoslavia in 1291, then in 1294 to a "laurel wood" (lauretium) at Recanati and in 1295 to its present site in Loreto.

General information

In 1586 Pope Sixtus V gave the town a municipal charter and the right to build walls. Since 1920 the Madonna of Loreto has been the patroness of airmen.

The pilgrimage town of Loreto

*Santuario della Santa Casa in Loreto

In the Piazza della Madonna, with a beautiful 17th c. fountain, stands the Santuario della Santa Casa, a Gothic hall-church with a fortress-like exterior begun in 1468 under Pope Paul II and continued in 1479–86 by the Florentine Giuliano da Maiano; the dome dates from 1500. The handsome façade, showing influence of Late Renaissance, was added in 1583–87. The three bronze doors are decorated with figures and bas reliefs. A bronze statue of Pope Sixtus V stands on the left in front of the façade.

The interior of the church was altered from 1526 onwards. To the left of the entrance is a beautiful font (1607). Adjoining the south transept are the two sacristies, with celebrated wall paintings: on the right frescoes by Melozzo da Forli (1438–94), on the left much restored frescoes by Luca Signorelli and an assistant together with a marble fountain by Maiano. In the choir apse ("Capella dei Tedeschi") are paintings by Ludwig Seitz (1893–1908).

Santa Casa

In the centre of the church, under the dome, is the Santa Casa, a simple brick building (4.2 m/13¾ ft high, 8.8 m/9½ yd long, 3.9 m/4¼ yd wide) surrounded by a high marble screen designed by Bramante (16th c.). On the walls are scenes of the life of the Madonna and of the transportation of the Santa Casa to Loreto.

Museum

Opposite the Santuario, in Piazza della Madonna is the Palazzo Apostolico, with a picture collection, tapestries (from designs by Raphael) and majolica from Urbino.

Lucca

Region: Toscana
Province: Lucca (LU)
Altitude: 17 m/56 ft
Population: 90,000

The provincial capital of Lucca, the see of an archbishop, lies in the north-west of Tuscany, on the left bank of the River Sergio, almost 25 km/16 miles inland from Viareggio. The Alpi Apuane are to the north of the town, the Monti Pisani to the south.

Situation

Lucca was the home of the sculptor Matteo Civitali (1436–1501) and the composer Giacomo Puccini (1858–1924), whose birthplace is now a museum and open to the public.

The ancient Lucca, which became a Roman colony in 177 B.C., belonged after the fall of the Roman Empire to the Ostrogoths, the Lombards and the Franks in turn. It later became capital of the marquisate of Tuscia, and subsequently fell into the hands of the Scaligers and Florence. In 1369 the town purchased its freedom from Charles IV for 100,000 gold florins, and thereafter it remained independent until the French invasion in 1799. In 1805 Napoleon gave Lucca together with Massa-Carrara as a principality to his sister Elisa Bacciocchi. In 1817 it passed to the house of Bourbon-Parma as a duchy, and in 1847 was ceded to Tuscany.

History

Lucca played a prominent part in the history of architecture from the Lombard period onwards; but its early medieval churches, partly built with ancient material, were altered and restored in the 12th c.

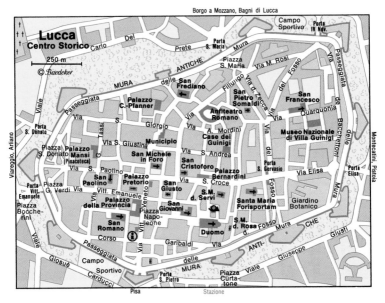

Piazza Napoleone

Palazzo della
Provincia

The central feature of the town is the Piazza Napoleone, the largest square in Lucca, laid out under Elisa Bacciocchi. On the west side of the Piazza Napoleone stands the Palazzo della Provincia, the old ducal palace (begun in 1578, continued in 1728), the courtyard of which is unfinished.

*Cathedral

From Piazza Napoleone Via Duomo runs south-east to the Piazza San Martino, in which stands the cathedral of San Martino, founded in the 6th c. and mainly dating in its present form from the 12th c. (nave remodelled in Gothic style in 14th c.). On the richly decorated Romanesque façade (1204), to the right of the principal arch, is St Martin with the beggar (copy; the original is inside the church). In the vestibule are reliefs, probably early works by Nicola Pisano. The cathedral has pictures and fine sculpture, including work by Jacopo della Quercia and Matteo Civitali. The Tempietto, a small octagonal chapel (by Civitali, 1482–84) in the north aisle contains an ancient crucifix (11th–12th c.) from the Holy Land known as the Volto Santo, displayed only on certain feast days in May and September.

Beyond the cathedral is the Archbishop's Palace, rebuilt in the 18th c., with a fine library. Behind it is the graceful Gothic chapel of Santa Maria della Rosa (1309).

San Giovanni

A little way west of the cathedral is the 12th c. church of San Giovanni with a fine relief of the Madonna (1187) above the doorway. The interior is divided by rows of columns into three naves; notable is the old baptistery at the end of the north transept.

San Michele in Foro

Piazza San Michele

From the Piazza Napoleone the busy Via Vittorio runs north to the
Piazza San Michele, on the site of the ancient forum. On the right-hand
side of this street is the Palazzo Pretorio (begun 1492), in Early Renaissance style. On the north side of the square the church of San Michele
(12th c.) has a high Pisan-style façade; on top of the ground floor,
separated by arches with half-columns, are four arcaded galleries. The
gable is crowned with a statue of the Archangel Gabriel, flanked by two
angels.

*San Michele in
Foro

Opposite San Michele in Via di Poggio is the birthplace of Giacomo
Puccini (Casa Natale di Giacomo Puccini).

House of Puccini

A short distance west of the House of Puccini stands the 17th c. Palazzo
Mansi which houses the notable Pinacoteca Nazionale (National Pic-
ture Gallery), with pictures by Veronese, Tintoretto, Bergognone, G.
Reni and other painters of the school of Tuscany.

Pinacoteca
Nazionale

East of Piazza San Michele in Via Fillungo stands the Romanesque
church of San Cristoforo (11th–12th c.). To the north is the Chiesa San
Salvatore or Chiesa della Misericordia, also 11th–12th c.

Churches

* San Frediano

Via Fillungo leads north past a number of old towers, belonging to
noble families, to the Piazza San Frediano, on the west side of which is
the church of San Frediano, said to have been founded in the 6th c. by
an Irish saint, Frigidianus. It was rebuilt in Romanesque style from 1112
onwards. On the façade is a 12th c. mosaic of Christ enthroned with
Apostles. The church contains a 12th c. font with fine reliefs by Rober-
tus and a marble altar by Jacopo della Quercia (1422); adjoining the
church is an impressive campanile with open arcades.

Anfiteatro Romano

A short distance south-east of Piazza San Frediano is the Piazza del
Mercato, originally the arena (80 by 53.5 m/88 by 58½ yd) of the Roman
amphitheatre, on the foundations of which the houses around the
square have been built. Two series of 54 arches can still be seen on the
north-east side.

To the east of the amphitheatre stands the church of San Pietro
Somaldi, a pillared basilica of the late 12th c. (façade 13th c.). Farther
east is the church of San Francesco (1228).

Churches

South of the amphitheatre in Via Guinigi is a mighty tower, the top of
which is overgrown. It is part of the building complex called the Case
del Guinigi, which comprised town houses of the noble families who
ruled Lucca in the beginning of the 15th c., a period of peace and
prosperity.

Case dei Guinigi

A little way south-east of the building complex is the 13th c. church of
Santa Maria Forisportam. The church owes its name to the fact that it
was built outside the port ("forisportam"). Inside there is an Early
Christian sarcophagus, now used as a font.

Santa Maria
Forisportam

To the east of the church, at the end of Via Santa Croce, is the old Porta
San Gervasio, a remnant of the town's second circuit of walls (13th c.),
with two massive round towers.

Porta San Gervasio

*Museo Nazionale di Villa Guinigi

To the east of the town in Via della Quarquonia is the 15th c. villa built
for Paola Guinigi which now houses the Museo Nazionale (National

Lucca: Market place on the site of the old Roman theatre

Museum), with a large art collection. Of interest are the Etruscan and Roman sculptures, sculptures from the medieval churches of Lucca and paintings by several Italian masters.

Ramparts

The present ramparts (4.2 km/2½ miles long), now shaded by fine old trees, were built between 1504 and 1645. There is an attractive walk around the whole circuit ("Passeggio delle Mura Urbane"), affording charming views of the town with its numerous towers and of the beautiful surrounding hills.

San Guiliano Terme

Situation
13 km/8 miles
south-west

South-west, prettily situated under the west side of the Monti Pisani, is the spa of San Giuliano Terme (10 m/33 ft; pop. 27,000), with radio-active sulphur springs.

Bagni di Lucca   G5

Situation
25 km/16 miles north

North of Lucca, Bagni di Lucca (150 m/495 ft; pop. 9000), comprises a number of separate villages, known as early as the 10th c. as the "Baths of Corsena", with springs containing salt and sulphur (37–54 °C/99–129 °F: season May–September). The principal village is Villa, once a residence of the dukes of Lucca, with its own thermal spring. The village of Bagni Caldi is the most important spa, with a warm spring, the "Doccione" (54 °C/129 °F), in a cave.

Lake Maggiore

Regions: Lombardia and Piedmonte
Provinces: Varese (VA) and Novara (NO)
Altitude: 194 m/640 ft

Lake Maggiore (Lago Maggiore), known to the Romans as Lacus Verba-   Situation
nus, lies in north Italy; the northern part of the lake, with the town of
Locarno, is in Switzerland. The distance between the southern tip of the
lake and the town of Novara is about 30 km/19 miles.

Lake Maggiore, with an area of 212 sq. km/82 sq. miles (length 65 km/40   General information
miles, breadth 3–5 km/2–3 miles, greatest depth 372 m/1228 ft), is the
second largest of the north Italian lakes. Less intricately patterned than   * Scenery
Lake Como and without the sheer rock faces of the northern part of Lake
Garda, it nevertheless offers scenery of southern splendour which may
lack the grandeur of the other lakes but is perhaps even more appeal-
ing. The east side belongs to Lombardy and the west side to Piedmont.
The lake's principal tributaries are the Ticino and the Maggia to the
north and the Toce on the west side. The river which flows out of the
southern end is the Ticino.
The northern part of the lake is enclosed by mountains, for the most
part wooded, while towards the south the shores slope down to the
plain of Lombardy. In clear weather the water in the northern part of the
lake is green, in the southern part deep blue.

The climate is mild. From midnight until morning the tramontana   Climate
blows, usually coming from the north; from midday until evening the
inverna blows from the south. The trees of Lake Maggiore, like that of   Vegetation
lakes Garda and Como, include numerous subtropical species: figs,
olives and pomegranates flourish in the mild climate, and in August the
myrtle blooms. On the Borromean Islands lemons, oranges, cork-oaks,
sago-palms and carob-trees grow.

The most popular tourist areas are around Locarno and on the western   Tourism
arm of the lake between Pallanza and Stresa, where the magnificent
Borromean Islands with their subtropical parks are the main attraction.

Near the east side of the lake, at Ispra, is the first Italian atomic research   Ispra
centre, now a Euratom research centre, with an atomic reactor (1959)
and a tower 120 m/396 ft high belonging to a meteorological station.

There is an attractive drive around the lake on an excellent road.   Drive around lake

Another very worth-while excursion is a boat trip on the lake (services   Boat services
throughout the year). The boats ply between Locarno and Arona (also
hydrofoil services), calling alternately at places on the west and east
sides; between Cannobio and Stresa, and between Verbania and
Stresa. There are also car ferry services.

Verbania

On the west side of Lake Maggiore, beautifully situated near the Borromean Islands, lies Verbania (205 m/677 ft; pop. 32,000), a town formed
by the amalgamation of Pallanza and Intra together with other adjoining villages. It attracts large numbers of visitors with its mild climate
and beautiful scenery.

The district of Pallanza lies on both sides of the Punta della Castagnola   Pallanza
(magnificent view from the park of the former Eden Palace Hotel).

Just offshore, to the west, is the little island of San Giovanni.

On the lakeside road is the Kursaal with its park (fine views). Beyond this, by the lake, is the mausoleum of General Cadorna (1850–1928), commander-in-chief of the Italian army during the First World War. To the north stands the parish church of San Leonardo (16th c. restored). Farther west are the Palazzo di Città (Town Hall) and the landing-stage, from which there are good views of the Borromean Islands (with Isola Madre in the foreground) and Monte Mottarone.

Madonna di Campagna

About 1.5 km/1 mile north, at the foot of Monte Rosso (693 m/2287 ft), the domed church of the Madonna di Campagna, contains frescoes by Lanino and the Procaccini.

**Park of the Villa Taranto

On a hill 1 km/⅗ mile north of the Punta della Castagnola is the park of the Villa San Remigio (no admission) and nearby is the little Roma-nesque church of San Remigio (11th c.). Immediately north is the magnificent park of the Villa Taranto, laid out after the Second World War, (open April–October, good guide book, with plan; boat landing-stage), with botanical research laboratories and numerous rare and exotic plants.

Intra

North-east of Pallanza, between the Torrente San Bernardino and the Torrente San Giovanni, is the industrial district of Intra, with the fine church of San Vittore. From here there is a car ferry across the lake to Laveno.

Premeno

From Intra a panoramic road runs 13 km/8 miles north to the village of Premeno (840 m/2772 ft), a summer holiday resort.

*Monte Zeda

North of Intra rises Monte Zeda (2157 m/7118 ft; extensive views), which can be climbed in seven hours.

Cannero Riviera

About 13 km/8 miles north-east of Intra Cannero Riviera (226 m/746 ft) is beautifully situated on the shores of the lake amid vineyards, orchards and olive-groves. The climate here is the mildest on the lake, and lemon and orange trees can survive the winter in the open. There is also a beautiful beach.

*Castelli di Cannero

Farther north, on rocky islets in the lake, are the ruins of the two Castelli di Cannero, built by Lodovico Borromeo in 1519 in place of earlier castles which had been held by brigands.

Cannobio

7 km/4½ miles north of Cannero – also on the west bank of Lake Maggiore – on a plateau at the mouth of the wide, cool Valle Canno-bina, the old town of Cannobio (214 m/706 ft) has picturesque narrow streets. Notable are the Palazzo della Ragione (1291) and near the landing-stage the Santuario della Pietà, a Renaissance church in the manner of Bramante (on the high altar "Christ bearing the Cross" by Gaudenzio Ferrari, c. 1525).

Stresa

Also on the west side of Lake Maggiore, south of its western arm, the little town of Stresa (210 m/693 ft; pop. 5000) looks on to the Borromean Islands. Stresa is the largest resort on Lake Maggiore after Locarno. Cooler and windier than other places on the lake, it is busiest during the warmer part of the year. The long lakeside road affords beautiful views of the lake and the Borromean Islands.

Lake Maggiore: View over Stresa towards the Borromean Islands

A garden on the Isola Bella

The life of Stresa centres on its lakeside promenade (fine views), on which are the parish church and most of the large hotels.

*Park of the Villa Pallavicino

About 1 km/¾ mile south, above the landing-place, is the Collegio Rosmini (267 m/881 ft), an educational institution run by the Rosminians; in the church is the tomb of the priest and philosopher A. Rosmini (1797–1855). 500 m/550 yd farther on is the beautiful park of the Villa Pallavicino (closed in winter), with luxuriant vegetation and an interesting menagerie.

*Monte Mottarone

From Stresa a toll road, the Borromea (about 30 km/19 miles; also a cableway), runs up via Gignese (707 m/2333 ft), with an unusual Umbrella Museum, to the summit of Monte Mottarone (1491 m/4920 ft), from which the view embraces the chain of the Alps from Monte Viso to Ortles, with Monte Rosa to the west (particularly fine in the morning).

Giardino Alpinia

Half-way up, at the hamlet of Alpino (768 m/2534 ft), a road branches off to the Giardino Alpinia (807 m/2663 ft), 500 m/550 yd north, with some 2000 species of plants (magnificent views).

**Borromean Islands

*Isola Bella

From Stresa there is a very attractive boat trip to the Borromean Islands. The boat calls first at Isola Bella which owes its present appearance to Count Vitaliano Borromeo, who between 1650 and 1671 transformed what had been a barren rock, with a parish church and a few houses, by building up terraces of fertile soil and creating a splendid summer residence. The palace, left unfinished, contains magnificent state apartments, numerous pictures (including some good Lombard works of the 16th and 17th c.) and a gallery of 17th c. Flemish tapestries. The Italian-style garden (beautiful views), rises in ten terraces to a height of 32 m/106 ft and is covered with luxuriant southern vegetation – lemon and orange trees, cherry-laurels, cedars, magnolias, cork-oaks, sago-palms, carob-trees, camellias, oleanders, etc.

Isola dei Pescatori

About 500 m/550 yd north-west of Isola Bella is the Isola dei Pescatori or Isola Superiore, with a picturesque fishing village.

*Isola Madre

Between the Isola dei Pescatori and Pallanza lies Isola Madre, which, like Isola Bella, belongs to the Borromeo family. It has beautiful English-style grounds surpassing even Isola Bella in the variety and luxuriance of their vegetation. On the highest point is an uninhabited palace (view).

Baveno

About 4 km/2½ miles north-west of Stresa is Baveno (205 m/677 ft), a popular resort, with a fine parish church. From the lakeside promenade there is a picturesque view of the lake with the Borromean Islands. At the southern end of the town stands the large Villa Branca, which belongs to the manufacturer of the well-known vermouth Fernet Branca, with a beautiful park (no admission).

Meina

San Carlone

About 13 km/8 miles south of Stresa is Meina (214 m/706 ft), with the splendid Villa Farragiana (museum). An eminence south of the village – between Meina and Arona – is crowned by the "San Carlone", a 23 m/76 ft high statue of St Charles Borromeo (1538–84), Cardinal-Archbishop of Milan, who played an important part in the moral revival of Catholicism.

On the east side of the lake, opposite the statue, is Angera, with an old Visconti castle (view).

Domodossola

From Stresa or Verbania there is an attractive drive (42 or 45 km/26 or 28 miles) first along the Lago di Mergozzo, a former arm of Lake Maggiore which was cut off by soil deposited by the River Toce, then continuing up the valley of the Toce to Domodossola (272 m/898 ft; pop. 20,000), a little hill town, with a pretty market-place and a notable collegiate church with three naves portal with 15th c. frescoes).

Half-way to Domodossola a road goes off, passes through Piedimulera and continues up the Anzasca valley (gold-mines), the upper part of which has been occupied since the 13th c. by German-speaking settlers from the Valais, to Macugnaga (1327 m/4379 ft), a holiday resort in a magnificent situation below the east face of Monte Rosa.

Mantua/Mantova

Region: Lombardia
Province: Mantova (MN)
Altitude: 19 m/63 ft
Population: 60,000

The provincial capital Mantua, former residence of the Gonzaga family, lies south of Lake Garda in the Po plain on the lower course of the

View of the towers of Mantua

Mincino, which here forms a marshy lake divided into three parts: Lago Superiore, Lago di Mezzo and Lago Inferiore.
The town is still surrounded by a ring of walls and bastions.

History and art

Originally founded by the Etruscans, the town was noted in antiquity only as the home of the poet Virgil (70–19 B.C.). It rose to some importance in the 12th and 13th c. under the Hohenstaufen Emperors.
From 1328 the town was ruled by the Guelf house of Gonzaga, who acquired the title of marquis in 1433 and of duke in 1530 and made Mantua one of the most refined and cultivated of princely capitals, a great centre of art and learning. Marquis Lodovico (1444–78) summoned the Florentine architect Leon Battista Alberti to Mantua, and in 1463 enrolled Andrea Mantegna, leader of the Padua school of painters, in his service; the beautiful and accomplished Isabella d'Este (1490–1539), wife of Giovanni Francesco II, carried on a lively correspondence with the great men of the day; and Raphael's outstanding pupil, Giulio Romano (1492–1546), came to Mantua in 1524 and was active as an architect and painter.
After the Gonzaga line died out (1707) the town passed to Austria, as one corner of the defensive "quadrilateral" of Peschiera–Verona–Legnago–Mantua and held it until 1866 (except for a brief interlude during the Napoleonic period. The Austrian patriot Andreas Hofer was shot in Mantua in 1810 on Napoleon's orders (memorial tablet, outside the town, to the north).

Piazza Mantegna

** Sant'Andrea

In Piazza Mantegna, in the centre of the town, stands the church of Sant'Andrea, a masterpiece of Early Renaissance architecture built by Leon Battista Alberti in 1472–94, with a transept and choir of 1600, and a dome of 1782. The white marble façade, in the style of a classical temple, has beside it the earlier Gothic tower of red brick (1413). The interior, with its massive barrel vault, is of imposing effect. In the first chapel on the left is the tomb of Mantegna, with a bronze bust; in the last chapel on the right are frescoes by Giulio Romano.

From Piazza Mantegna the arcaded Corso Umberto I, the town's principal shopping and business street, leads west to Piazza Cavallotti, from which the Corso della Libertà, a wide street built over an old canal, runs to Piazza Martiri di Belfiori.

Palazzo della Ragione

Adjoining Piazza Mantegna on the east in the Piazza delle Erbe, are the Torre dell'Orologio (clock-tower), the Palazzo della Ragione (13th c., with much later alteration) and the little Romanesque church of San Lorenzo (11th c.) on a circular plan.

Piazza Sordello

Palaces

To the north, in the medieval Piazza Sordello, are two crenellated Gothic palaces, the Palazzo Guervieri (12th–13th c.), with the 55 m/182 ft high Torre della Gabbia, and the 13th c. Palazzo Bonacolsi or Palazzo Castiglioni.

Bishop's Palace

Adjoining is the Baroque Bishop's Palace (18th c.).

Cathedral

On the north-east side of Piazza Sordello stands the cathedral of San Pietro, originally built in Romanesque style as the burial church of the marquises of Canossa and the Gonzaga family, remodelled in Gothic style between 1393 and 1401 and reconstructed internally to the design of Giulio Romano after a fire in 1545; it has fine Baroque façade (1756). Behind the church stands a Romanesque campanile.

**Palazzo Ducale

Opposite the cathedral the massive Palazzo Ducale, the sumptuous residence of the Gonzagas and one of the most splendid palaces in Italy, now houses a number of important museums and collections – the Municipal Collection of Antiquities (Greek and Roman sculpture); the Museo Medievale e Moderno (mainly medieval and Renaissance sculpture); and the Galleria, a valuable collection of pictures displayed in a series of rooms richly decorated with frescoes and ceiling paintings. Outstanding among these rooms are the Appartamento degli Arazzi, with nine tapestries made in Brussels about 1528 (scenes from the life of SS Peter and Paul) after cartoons by Raphael; the Gallery of Mirrors; the Appartamento del Paradiso, from which there are beautiful views of the lakes. On the ground floor are the rooms occupied by Isabella d'Este, the Gabinetti Isabelliani, with richly sculptured ceilings.

Museums

At the north-east corner of the Palazzo Ducale stands the palace church, Santa Barbara, in High Renaissance style (1565) and the older castle, the massive Castello San Giorgio (1395–1406). On the first floor the Camera degli Sposi contains magnificent frescoes by Mantegna (1474), depicting the brilliant life of the court of Lodovico and his wife Barbara of Hohenzollern. On the ceiling are fine trompe-l'oeil paintings.

Castello San Giorgio

North-west of Piazza Sordello is the Piazza Virgiliana, with a monument to the poet Virgil (1927).

Monument to Virgil

Sights in the south

In the south of the town, at Via Carlo Poma 11, is the Palazzo di Giustizia (16th c.), with colossal hermae (heads of the god Hermes) on the façade.

Mantua: Castello San Giorgio

San Sebastiano	South of the Palazzo di Giustizia the church of San Sebastiano was the first Renaissance church built on a Greek cross plan (1460–1529); the crypt serves as a war memorial chapel.
* Palazzo Te Museum	Farther south still is the single-storey Palazzo Te, built 1525–35 by Giulio Romano as a country house for the Gonzagas and decorated with frescoes and stucco work under his direction. The palazzo houses the Museo Civico di Palazzo Te, with a department of modern art and an Egyptian collection.

Santa Maria degli Angeli

Situation 3 km/2 miles west	On the Cremona road, lying off the road on the right, on the Lago Superiore, the church of Santa Maria degli Angeli (1429) is in Lombard Gothic style, with a beautiful altarpiece by Mantegna.

Santa Maria delle Grazie

Situation 7 km/4½ miles west	A short distance farther on, near the west end of the Lago Superiore, stands the Gothic pilgrimage church of Santa Maria delle Grazie (1399). The over-furnished interior contains 44 figures in wood and wax of notable visitors to the shrine (including Charles V) and a fine altarpiece ("St Sebastian") by F. Bonsignori.

San Benedetto Po

Situation 20 km/12 miles south-east	There is a rewarding trip to the little town of San Benedetto Po (18 m/59 ft; pop. 8000), with a former Benedictine monastery (Abbazia di Polirone) founded in 1007 by Marquis Tedaldo of Canossa and dissolved in 1789. The church, originally built in Gothic style was remodelled by Giulio Romano as a splendid Renaissance building with an octagonal dome over the crossing and a fine portico; in front of the presbytery are floor mosaics (12th c.).

Marches/Marche L/K6/7

	Region: Marche Provinces: Ancona (AN), Ascoli Piceno (AP), Macerata (MC), Pesaro e Urbino (PS) Area: 9693 sq. km/3741 sq. miles Population: 1,424,400
Situation	The region of Marche (the Marches) in Central Italy covers mountainous country, consisting partly of inhospitable terrain (Monte Vettore, 2476 m/8171 ft) but mostly of very fertile uplands, which extends between the rivers Foglia and Tronto down the eastern slopes of the Appennino Umbro-Marchigiano to the Adriatic coast. The capital of the region is Ancona.
General information	The people earn their living from agriculture and horticulture (wheat, barley, maize, fruit, vegetables, vine) and from stock raising (cattle and pigs). Along the coast fishing and shipbuilding are of some importance. The production of majolica is a traditional industry, particularly at Pesara and Urbino and new industries are being developed including both light and heavy engineering.

Mountain village in the Marches

Tourism makes a major contribution to the economy in the seaside resorts along the Atlantic coast.
While in the past a small number of towns in the region, particularly Urbino and Ancona, gained prosperity and influence, the entire region of the Marches which already first in the records in the 10th c., was without any notable importance.

Macerata

Apart from the towns along the Adriatic coast and Ascoli Piceno it is well worth visiting the provincial capital of Macerata (314 m/1036 ft; pop. 44,000), which occupies a commanding situation on high ground between the rivers Chienti and Potenza. The central feature of the town is the Piazza della Libertà, in which are the Palazzo Comunale (statues of toga-clad figures and inscriptions from Helvia Ricina in courtyard), the Prefecture (in a 16th c. Gonzaga palace), the beautiful Loggia dei Mercanti (16th c.) and the Theatre. From the Piazza della Libertà the Corso della Repubblica leads to the Piazza Vittorio Veneto, with the Biblioteca Comunale, which contains the municipal collection of pictures (including works by the local painter Paganini, Carlo Crivelli, Allegretto Nuzi da Fabriano and Lanfranco). Also of interest are the cathedral and the Sferisterio Festival Theatre (theatrical and operatic productions). There is also a small university.

Fermo

South of Macerata is the town of Fermo (319 m/1053 ft; pop. 35,000), the see of an archbishop, with churches containing a number of fine pictures. At Porta San Francesco are remains of the town's ancient cyclopean walls. In the Piazza del Popolo, reached by steep lanes running up from the Porta San Francesco, are the Town Hall and the Palazzo degli Studi (library, museum, picture gallery). On the commanding Rocca is the 13th c. cathedral, in the porch of which is the Gothic tomb of Giovanni Visconti (d. 1366) by Bonaventura da Imola. Nearby are remains of the ancient theatre. Under the church of San Domenico, below the Piazza del Popolo, is an ancient cistern (1st c. A.D.).

Iesi

In the north of the region, 30 km/19 miles south-west of Ancona, is Iesi (96 m/317 ft; pop. 42,000), birthplace of the German Emperor Frederick II of Hohenstaufen (1194–1250) and Giovanni Battista Pergolesi (1710–36), composer of the "Stabat Mater". The main features in the town, which is still surrounded by medieval walls, are the fine Palazzo della Signoria, in Early Renaissance style (1487–1498; fine pillared courtyard), and the Pinacoteca, which contains pictures by Lorenzo Lotto.

Marsala | I12

Region: Sicilia
Province: Trapani (TP)
Altitude: 12 m/40 ft
Population: 80,000

Situation

The port and commercial town of Marsala, situated at the western tip of Sicily, is best known for its rich golden-yellow dessert wine.
The principal wine-making establishments (stabilimenti or bagli: visitors admitted) lie along the shore to the south of the town. The Woodhouse establishment near the station was named after its English founder, who introduced wine-making to Marsala about 1773. 500 m/550 yd farther south is Florio, the town's most famous wine-making establishment, and another 500 m/550 yd beyond this Ingham-Whitaker. Other leading firms are Rallo and Pellegrino.

Sights

Cathedral

The hub of the town's traffic is the Piazza della Repubblica, with the beautiful 18th c. Old Town Hall, built in the form of a loggia, and the cathedral of San Tomaso, dedicated to St Thomas of Canterbury, which contains fine sculpture by Antonello Gagini and eight magnificent 16th c. Flemish tapestries, displayed only on certain feast days.
From the Piazza della Repubblica the town's main street, Via XI Maggio, runs north-west past the monastery and church of San Pietro (16th c.) to the Porta Nuova. On a house on the left is a plaque commemorating the second visit in 1862 by Garibaldi, whose victorious campaign against the Bourbons had begun two years earlier, on 11 May 1860, with his landing in Marsala harbour. Beyond the Porta Nuova, to the right, are the Villa Cavallotti gardens, at the north end of which is a belvedere affording wide views.

Insula Romana

Below the belvedere and along the Viale Vittorio Veneto, which continues the line of Via XI Maggio, are remains of the ancient Lilybaeum, including fragments of the town walls. Off the road to the right are the ruins of the Insula Romana, living quarters of the 3rd c. A.D., with a fine animal mosaic in the associated baths. From the end of the avenue there is a beautiful view of the sea and the coast; and from Capo Boeo or Capo Lilibeo, a little way south-west, there are more extensive views north-east over the old harbour to Monte Erice and north-west of the Isole Égadi.

A museum in Capo Lilibeo contains the remains of a Punic ship which was found in 1969 near the island of Langa dello Stagnone.

Museum

Half-way between the cape and the Porta Nuova, off the road to the right, is the church of San Giovanni Battista, from which steps lead down to the "Grotta della Sibilla" (Roman mosaic).

Grotta della Sibilla

Mozia

On the island of San Pantaleo are the remains of the Punic city of Mozia, founded in the 8th c. B.C. and destroyed in 397 B.C. Preserved are the crenellated town walls and towers, a shrine with an altar and a cemetery.

Situation
about 10 km/6 miles
north

Merano

H3

Region: Trentino–Alto Adige
Province: Bolzano (BZ)
Altitude: 324 m/1069 ft
Population: 35,000

Merano is situated at the outflow of the River Passirio into the broad valley of the Adige which emerges from the Val Venosta.

Situation

View of Merano

Merano

General information

Merano in the Alto Adige is the largest health resort on the south side of the Eastern Alps, with its main season in spring and autumn for the grape cure and with radioactive thermal springs.

History

Merano came into the hands of the counts of Tirol in 1233, and in 1310, together with the Passirio and Ultimo valleys, was formed into a separate burgraviate. From 1317 to 1420 it was capital of Tirol. From the middle of the 19th c., thanks to its sheltered situation under the south side of Monte Benedetto and the low humidity of the air, Merano developed into a health resort.

Old town

Piazza del Teatro

At the south-west corner of the old town, near the right bank of the Passirio, is the Piazza del Teatro, Merano's busiest square, with the Municipal Theatre (by Martin Dülfer, 1899–1900).

From here the Corso della Libertà runs west to the station and east, past the Kursaal, to the Piazza della Rena. The busy Via delle Corso, which bounds the old town on the west, runs north from the Piazza del Teatro to the Piazza del Grano and beyond this to the Porto Venosta.

Via dei Portici

From the Piazza del Grano the old-world Via dei Portici (Laubengasse), a busy shopping street, runs east through the old town, lined with arcades (the Portici di sinistra or Berglauben to the left and the Portici di destra or Wasserlauben to the right). Half-way along the Portici di sinistra is the Town Hall (1928–32).

Castello Principesco

Behind the Town Hall stands the Castello Principesco (1480), still with its original furnishings and a collection of musical instruments.

Municipal Museum

A little way north-west of the castle, at Via Galilei 5, is the rich Municipal Museum, with prehistoric material, local history, medieval sculpture and modern pictures.

San Nicolò

At the east end of the Via dei Portici is the Piazza del Duomo, with the Gothic parish church of San Nicolò (14th–15th c.), whose characteristic campanile dominates the town.

From here the old Porta Bolzano leads into the Piazza della Rena.

Maia Bassa and Maia Alta

Maia Bassa
Salvar Baths

On the left bank of the Passirio the district of Maia Bassa (Untermais) is reached from the Piazza della Rena by way of the Ponte Nazionale. Immediately beyond the bridge is the Late Gothic church of the Santo Spirito (15th c.). A little way west are the Salvar Baths (1971), with an indoor bath (radioactive water, 30–35 °C/86–91 °C), an outdoor pool, sauna facilities, a treatment centre, a restaurant and a Congress Centre.

Maia Alta

From the Santo Spirito church Via Cavour climbs east to the select villa suburb of Maia Alta (Obermais), in which are many old aristocratic residences such as Castello di Nova (Trautmannsdorf), Castello Rametz (vine-growing estate), Castello Labers (hotel), Castello Rundegg (hotel), Castello Planta (pension) and Castello Gaiano (Schloss Goyen).

Promenades

Passeggiata Lungo
Passirio

Along the broad embankment on the right bank of the Passirio runs the Passeggiata Lungo Passirio, in the centre of which is the Kursaal (1907).

Farther west is the Protestant Church of Christ (1885). The Passeggiata
Lungo Passirio is continued eastward by the sheltered Passeggiata
d'Inverno.

From the Ponte Nazionale the Passeggiata d'Estate follows the left bank
of the Passirio and is linked by a bridge with the Passeggiata d'Inverno
on the right bank. The two promenades run upstream to the Ponte
Romano (1616), from which the Passeggiata Gilf continues along the
right bank to the gorge under Castello San Zeno.

Passeggiate d'Estate

From the Ponte Romano and the Passeggiata Gilf we can continue on
the Passeggiata Tappeiner, a beautiful high-level promenade which
begins at the medieval Torre della Polvere and runs for 4 km/2½ miles at
a height of some 150 m/495 ft above Merano (magnificent views,
particularly from the Torre del Polvere) along the slopes of Monte
Benedetto (Küchelberg, 531 m/1752 ft). There is a chair-lift up the hill
from near the Castello Principesco, and it makes an attractive trip to
take the lift up and walk down. From Monte Benedetto there is a
footpath (½ hour) to the village of Tirolo.

*Passeggiata
Tappeiner

*Castel Tirolo

From the Porta Passiria a good road (4 km/2½ miles) runs north-east
alongside the Passeggiata Gilf and past Castello San Zeno (12th and
13th c.), and then turns north-west up the slopes of Monte Benedetto to
the village of Tirolo (1596 m/5267 ft; cableway up La Mutta, 1350 m/
4455 ft).
From here it is a 25 minutes' walk, passing above Castel Fontana and
through a narrow gorge 52 m/172 ft long, to the 12th c. Castel Tirolo
(Schloss Tirol, 647 m/2135 ft), the residence in the 12th and 13th c. of the
counts of Tirol (who died out in 1253), which has given its name to the
whole region of Tirol. The castle now houses the Regional Museum
with an archaeological department.

West of Castel Tirolo (30 minutes) is Castello Torre (Schloss Thurnstein
(551 m/1818 ft; with a beautiful view). Lower down is Castello Fontana
(Brunnenburg; restored in 1904).

Castello Torre

From Plars di Mezzo (Mittelplars), 5 km/3 miles west of the town centre,
there is a chair-lift to Velloi (908 m/2996 ft), and from there a basket-lift
to the Leiter-Alm (1528 m/5042 ft). At the half-way stage of the chair-lift
there is an inviting footpath which ends at the Castello Torre.

Castello di Scena

3.5 km/2 miles north of Maia Alta, above the village of Scena, at the
mouth of the Passirio valley, the Castello di Scena (Schloss Schenna,
14th–16th c.; 596 m/1967 ft) commands magnificent views. The castle
(admission charge) contains a collection of arms and armour, Renaissance furniture, portraits of members of princely families and Andreas
Hofer's cradle).
At the village of Scena (587 m/1937 ft) are the castle-like parish church
(1914–1931; adjoining it the old Gothic church) and next to it the small
neo-Gothic parish church of St John (1869), with the tomb of Archduke
John of Austria (1782–1859) and his wife Anna. The building is known
as one of the best examples of neo-Gothic architecture in Alto Adige.

*Castello

Parish church
St John's
(mausoleum)

2 km/1¼ miles north-east of Scena is a cableway up Monte Scena
(Taser; 1460 m/7082 ft).

Monte Scena

Scena: Church and Mausoleum

Avelengo

From Maia Alta a road runs south-east to the village of Avelengo (Hafling; 1298 m/4283 ft), famous for the horses which are bred here.

* Merano 2000

North-east of Avelengo, now easily accessible by various cableways and lifts, is the extensive skiing area of Merano 2000. From the outlying district of Falzeben (1610 m/5313 ft), to the north-east, reached by a road (6 km/3¾ miles) from Avelengo or the upper station of the cableway, a chair-lift (lower station at Rosa Alpina inn) runs up to the Malga Pivigna (Pifinger Köpfl, 1905 m/6287 ft), which can also be reached by a cableway from the Val di Nova (Naiftal: lower station 4 km/2½ miles east of Merano). From here there is a cableway to Sant' Osvaldo (Kirchsteiger Alm, 1938 m/6395 ft), from which there are chair-lifts north-east to the Kesselwand-Joch (2265 m/7475 ft: ski-lift in winter) and south-east to Monte Catino (Mittager, 2234 m/7372 ft).

From Merano to the Giogo di San Vigilio

Marlengo

The road runs west from Maia Bassa past the sports ground, crosses the Adige and continues south along the west side of the broad Adige valley. On the hillside to the right is the prettily situated village of Marlengo (Marling, 370 m/1221 ft), from which a footpath, the "Waal-weg", following the line of an irrigation canal half-way up the slope, runs north to Tel (Töll) or south below Castello Monteleone (open Sat.–Thurs.) to Lana di Sopra.

Lana

In another 8 km/5 miles the road reaches Lana di Sopra (Oberlana), the most northerly part of the large village of Lana (pop. 7000), at the mouth of the Val d'Último (Ultental), which attracts visitors who want a quiet holiday either in summer or in winter (reservoirs).

From Lana di Sopra a cableway runs up in 7 minutes to the Hotel Monte San Vigilio (Vigiljoch, 1486 m/4904 ft), from where there are magnificent views of the Adige valley and the Dolomites.

From the upper station of the cableway there are two possibilities – either by chair-lift (15 minutes) to the Dosso dei Lárici (Larchbühel, 1824 m/6019 ft) or on an easy winding footpath to the Albergo al Giogo. From here it is only a few minutes' climb to the old chapel of San Vigilio on the Giogo di San Vigilio (Vigiljoch, 1795 m/5924 ft), from where there are fine views of the Val Venosta, the Ötztal and the Texel group.

2 km/1¼ miles south of Lana di Sopra by way of Lana di Mezzo (Mitterlana) is Lana di Sotto (Niederlana), the parish church of which has a richly gilded Gothic altar of carved wood, the largest in Tirol, by the Merano sculptor Hans Schnatterpeck (1503–11; conducted visits from 10 a.m. onwards). The Romanesque church of Santa Margherita is also of interest.

Lana di Sotto

Messina   M11

Region: Sicilia
Province: Messina (ME)
Altitude: 5 m/17 ft
Population: 266,000

The port of Messina, capital of the province of the same name and the see of an archbishop, lies near the north-east tip of Sicily on the busy

Situation

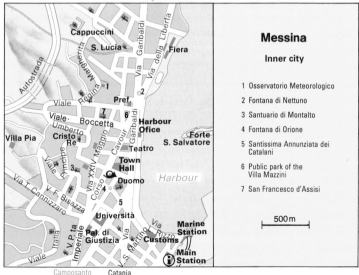

Regional Museum

Messina

Inner city

1 Osservatorio Meteorologico

2 Fontana di Nettuno

3 Santuario di Montalto

4 Fontana di Orione

5 Santissima Annunziata dei Catalani

6 Public park of the Villa Mazzini

7 San Francesco d'Assisi

500 m

Messina

View across the Strait of Messina

Strait of Messina, with its western districts extending along the foot-hills of the Monti Peloritani.

After the great earthquake in 1908 which killed some 60,000 people and destroyed 91% of its houses Messina was rebuilt with wide streets.

History

Messina was founded by Greek settlers about 730 B.C. on the site of an earlier Siculan settlement and named Zankle ("sickle") after the shape of the harbour.

It was renamed Messana about 493 B.C., when is was occupied by Greek refugees.

It was destroyed by the Carthaginians in 396 B.C. and subsequently rebuilt, and became a Roman town in 264 B.C. It was captured by the Saracens in A.D. 843 and by the Normans in 1061. Under the Normans the town enjoyed a long period of prosperity, which continued into the 17th c. under Spanish rule.

Thereafter Messina suffered a rapid decline, due partly to internal conflicts but mainly to the town's bitter rivalry with Palermo, the process being hastened by a plague in 1740 and severe earthquakes, particularly in 1783. Its subsequent recovery was promoted by its favourable situation on one of the most important traffic routes in the Mediterranean.

Viale San Martino

Marine Station

From the Marine Station on the south side of the harbour it is a short distance west to the north end of the town's main street, Viale San Martino, which cuts through the southern part of the city. In 400 m/440 yd it crosses the tree-shaded Piazza Cairoli, Messina's busiest traffic intersection, and in another 1.5 km/1 mile it joins the spacious Piazza Dante.

On the west side of the square is the Camposanto (or Cimitero), one of Italy's most beautiful cemeteries. On top of the hill is an Ionic colonnade, the Pantheon of the town's leading citizens, from which there are fine views of the city and the strait.

Cathedral

From Piazza Cairoli the broad Corso Garibaldi runs north. 1.5 km/1 mile along this street Via I Settembre leads left into the large Piazza del Duomo, the centre of the old town, with the richly decorated Orion Fountain (1547–51) by Giovanni Angelo Montorsoli, a pupil of Michelangelo. On the east side of the square, dominating the town, is the cathedral, originally built by Roger II in the 12th c., destroyed in 1908 and rebuilt in its original form in 1919–29, incorporating architectural fragments from the ruins, and again rebuilt after being damaged by fire in 1943. The interior is 93 m/102 yd long. In the apse is a beautiful mosaic, a reproduction of the 13th c. original which was destroyed in 1943. Adjoining the church rises the 60 m/198 ft high campanile (1933), on the main front of which is an elaborate astronomical clock, with numerous moving figures. The lion, above, roars at 12 noon; the cock, below, crows. The clock was the work of the Strasbourg clock-maker Ungerer.

A short distance south-east of the cathedral, in Corso Garibaldi, a beautiful Norman church, the Santissima Annunziata dei Catalani (12th c.) is to be found. Beside the church is a bronze statue of Don John of Austria, son of the Emperor Charles V and hero of the battle of Lepanto (1571), under whose leadership the Spaniards and Venetians defeated the Turks.

North-west of the cathedral is the circular Piazza Antonello, with the Palazzo Municipale, the Town Hall and the Head Post Office.

From Piazza Antonello Corso Cavour runs north, passing the Teatro Vittorio Emanuele, to the Villa Mazzini public gardens (with an aquarium), on the north side of which stands the Palazzo del Governo (prefecture). West of the gardens is the church of San Francesco d'Assisi (1254; rebuilt).

*Museo Regionale

From the north-east corner of the gardens the Viale della Libertà runs north past the buildings of the Fiera di Messina (fair) and along the seafront to the Museo Regionale, which contains material salvaged from the Municipal Museum after the 1908 earthquake, together with sculpture and pictures from the hundred or so churches which were also devastated at the same time. Particularly notable items in room IV are a "triptych of St Gregory" by Antonello da Messina (1479; badly damaged in 1908), the central panel of which depicts a Madonna enthroned, and two sculptures by G. Montorsoli, depicting Neptune, and Scylla, the sea monster which is said to have devoured shipwrecked sailors.

At present the museum is being remodelled and the archaeological department is stored in a pavilion.

Circonvallazione a monte

There is a pleasant drive around Messina on the Circonvallazione a monte, which, under various names, describes a circuit above the west side of the town, passing the Santuario di Montalto, a pilgrimage centre, and the modern church of Cristo Re.

Torre di Faro

Situation 15 km/9 miles north-east	There is also a very attractive trip (15 km/9 miles) along the coast road, which runs north-east, between villas and gardens, passes two salt-water lagoons, the Pantani, also known as the Laghi de Ganzirri, and comes to the village of Torre di Faro, on the Punta del Faro, Sicily's north-eastern tip, with fine views from the lighthouse.
Tour	From Torre di Faro the coast road continues around the most northerly cape in Sicily; then the return to Messina is over the Colle San Rizzo (465 m/1535 ft).

Milan/Milano   F4

Region: Lombardia
Province: Milano (MI)
Altitude: 122 m/403 ft
Population: 1,480,000

Situation	Milan (Milano), capital of Lombardy and Italy's second largest city, lies in the north-west of the Po plain at the junction of several important traffic routes from the Alps.
Importance	Milan is Italy's principal industrial centre, its most important railway junction and its leading banking and commercial city. It was one of the largest silk markets in Europe and also a State and a Catholic university; it is the see of an archbishop.
	The main industries are textiles, the manufacture of cars, machinery and rolling-stock, chemicals (the Montecatini group) and papermaking.
City	Milan is a city of predominantly modern aspect. Even the old town centre around the Piazza del Duomo, though it still has many narrow old streets, is traversed by wide arteries radiating in all directions. Between the old town and the outer ring of bastioni, on the line of the Spanish ramparts built in 1549, is a zone of more modern streets, and farther out are the city's steadily expanding suburbs. Since the Second World War large modern buildings, including tower blocks of 30 storeys and more, have been erected in every part of the city.
	Nevertheless Milan is still full of art treasures and fine old buildings which have survived war damage, which was particularly severe in the town centre, or have been rebuilt in the original style.
History	Milan, founded by Celts about 400 B.C., was conquered by Rome in 222 B.C. and thereafter, as Mediolanum, became the second most important town in northern Italy (after Verona). Later it became one of the capitals of the Lombard and Frankish kingdoms. As capital of the Lombard League it led the opposition to the Hohenstaufens. In consequence it was destroyed by Frederick Barbarossa in 1162, but was rebuilt five years later. Internal feuds between the nobility and the people led to the dominance of the Visconti family, who won control of much of northern Italy; and in 1395 Gian Galeazzo (d. 1402) gained the ducal title. In 1450 the Vicontis were succeeded by the dynasty founded by the mercenary leader Francesco Sforza, but the Sforza line died out in 1535, and the duchy then passed to Spain under Charles V. In 1714, after the War of the Spanish Succession, it was assigned to Austria, which apart from an interlude of French occupation in Napoleonic

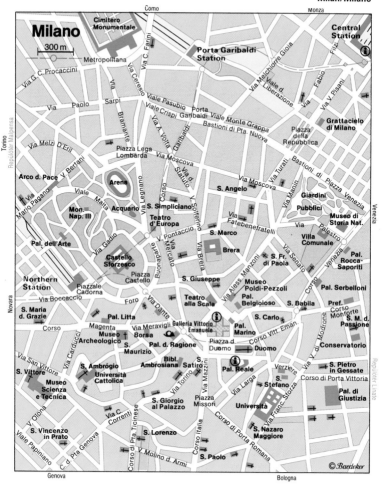

Milan/Milano

Como   Monza

Milano

300 m

Metropolitana

Via G. C. Procaccini

Via Paolo Sarpi

Via Melzi D'Eril

Torino   Repubblica Malpensa

Via Melzi D'Eril

Via Mario Pagano

Arco d. Pace

V. Bertani

Viale

Pal. dell'Arte

Castello Sforzesco

Northern Station   Piazzale Cadorna

Via Boccaccio

Novara

S. Maria d. Grazie

Corso

Magenta

Via Carducci

Via San Vittore

S. Vittore

Museo Scienza e Tecnica

Via C. Olona

S. Vincenzo in Prato

Viale Papiniano

Genova

Cimitero Monumentale

Via C. Farini

Via Ceresio

Porta Garibaldi Station

Viale Pasubio

Viale Crispi   Porta Garibaldi

Via A. Volta   Viale Monte Grappa

Bastioni di Pta. Nuova

Piazza Lega Lombarda

Via Moscova

Piazza della Repubblica

Via Melchiorre Gioia

Viale d. Liberazione

Via

Fabio

Via V. Pisani

Central Station

Grattacielo di Milano

Via Turati   Bastioni di   Piazza Venezia

Via Moscova

S. Angelo

Via Manin

Giardini Pubblici

Venezia

Arena

Mon. Nap. III

Acquario

S. Simpliciano

Teatro d'Europa

Via Gadio

Via Legnano

Corso

V. d. Statuto

V. Soferino

Via Fatebenefratelli

S. Marco

V. Pontaccio

V. Mercato

Brera

Via Brera

Via Aless. Manzoni

S. Fr. di Paola

Via Senato

Museo di Storia Nat.

Villa Comunale

Palestro

Pal. Rocca-Saporiti

Piazza Castello

Foro

S. Giuseppe

Via Dante

Teatro alla Scala

Museo Poldi-Pezzoli

Pal. Belgioioso

S. Babila

Pal. Serbelloni

Pref.

Pal. Litta

Magenta   Via Meravigli   Galleria Vittorio Emanuele

Museo Archeologico   Borsa

S. Maurizio

Pal. d. Ragione

Bibl. Ambrosiana

Satiro

Piazza d. Duomo

Pal. Marino

S. Carlo

Duomo

Corso Vitt. Eman.

Pal. Reale

Verziere

Corso Monforte

S. M. d. Passione

Conservatorio

S. Pietro in Gessate

Pal. di Giustizia

Università Cattolica

S. Ambrogio

Via Torino

Via Mazzini

S. Giorgio al Palazzo

Piazza Missori

S. Stefano

Via Larga

Università

Via Franc. Sforza

Corso di Porta Vittoria

Repubblica Linate

S. Lorenzo

Via C Correnti

Corso di Pta. Ticinese

Piazza Italia

V. Molino d. Armi

Corso di Porta Romana

S. Nazaro Maggiore

C. d Pta Genova   S. Paolo

Corso Italia

Bologna

© Baedeker

---

times (1796–1814) held on to it until 1859, in spite of repeated popular risings. In 1919 Mussolini founded the Fascist party in Milan; and in April 1945 the body of the fallen dictator was put on show in Piazzale Loreto.

Remains of early Christian architecture have been preserved in one or two churches, notably San Lorenzo and Sant'Ambrogio. 13th c. buildings are to be found mainly in the Piazza dei Mercanti. The Gothic period is represented almost exclusively by the cathedral.
Around 1450 the Florentines Filarete and Michelozzo brought the Tuscan Early Renaissance to Milan (Ospedale Maggiore). The heyday of

Art

Milan: Panorama of the city at sunset

Milanese art began with the coming of Bramante and Leonardo da Vinci, who produced his major works here between 1485 and 1500; and these two masters influenced the work of subsequent generations of painters, including Andrea Solario, Bramantino, Luini, Sodoma and Gaudenzio Ferrari. The present aspect of central Milan is due to the architects of the Late Renaissance and Baroque periods, particularly Galeazzo Alessi and Pellegrino Tibaldi, the neo-classical architect Giuseppe Piermarini and two practitioners of the Empire style, Luigi Canonica and Luigi Cagnola. A competent neo-classical painter was Andrea Appiani.

Piazza del Duomo

The life of Milan centres on the Piazza del Duomo, flanked on the north and south sides by palatial buildings, designed by Mengoni and erected from 1876 onwards. Near the west end is an equestrian statue of Victor Emanuel II (1896). Under the square are the foundations of the Basilica di Santa Tecla (4th–5th and 7th c.; "winter church") and the 4th c. baptistery (Battisterio di San Giovanni alle Fonti), which were discovered during the construction of the Metropolitana (access from the cathedral).

Adjoining the Piazza del Duomo to the north-west is the Piazza dei Mercanti, beyond which is the Piazza Cordusio. From the cathedral to the Piazza Cordusio extends an underground passage, with numerous shops.

* Galleria Vittorio Emanuele II

On the north side of the Piazza del Duomo, giving access to the Piazza della Scala, is the Galleria Vittorio Emanuele II, designed by Giuseppe

Mengoni and built in 1865–77. It was then the largest shopping arcade in Europe (195 m/215 yd long, dome 48 m/158 ft high; restored in 1988–89).

**Cathedral

The cathedral, a cruciform basilica faced with white marble, is one of the world's largest and most magnificent churches. With a length of 157 m/172 yd and a façade 61.5 m/67 yd wide, it covers an area of 11,700 sq. m/13,993 sq. yd and can accommodate a congregation of 40,000. The dome rises to 68 m/224 ft, and its total height including the statue of the Virgin known as the "Madonnina" is 108.5 m/358 ft. The roof is adorned with 135 pinnacles, the exterior with 2245 marble statues. Building, in Gothic style, began in 1386 but made slow progress (dome completed c. 1500, spire 1765–69, façade under Napoleon 1805–13). The imposing bronze doors are modern: the one to the left dates from 1840 and the large central door from 1908; the reliefs on two other doors were carried out between 1948–51, and the last one in 1965.

The rather dark interior, in striking contrast to the brilliant and richly patterned exterior, nevertheless makes a powerful impression with its 52 gigantic pillars. The stained-glass windows in the nave (mostly 15th–16th c.) are the largest in the world; the eight windows in the dome date from 1968.

In the north transept is a fine seven-branched bronze candelabrum by Nicholas of Verdun (c. 1200), and on the east wall of the south transept is a statue, by Marco Agrate (1562), of St Bartholomew, flayed.

In the crypt is the Scurolo di San Carlo with the reliquary of San Carlo Borromeo, richly adorned with gold and jewels.

Milan Cathedral and Piazza del Duomo

Treasury

In the south sacristy is the valuable treasury, with gold and silver work (4th–17th c.).

A walk on the roof of the cathedral is an impressive experience, offering magnificent views, which extend on clear days to the mountains flanking the west side of the Po plain. (Access outside the cathedral, on the west side of the north transept: 158 steps, or lifts on east side of transept; then 73 steps to the platform of the dome.)

Palazzo Reale

Museo del Duomo

On the south side of the cathedral is the Palazzo Reale, the former Royal Palace, built in 1788 on the site of an earlier palace which had belonged to the Visconti and Sforza families. On the ground floor is the Museo del Duomo (Cathedral Museum).

Museo d'Arte Contemporanea

The rooms on the second floor house the Civico Museo d'Arte Contemporanea, the City's Art Museum, with works by modern Italian painters. To the rear of the palace stands the old palace church, San Gottardo in Corte (c. 1330), with a fine tower (campanile). To the east the Archbishop's Palace (remodelled by Pellegrino Tibaldi, 1570 onwards) has a fine colonnaded courtyard.

Palazzo del Turismo

Adjoining the Palazzo Reale on the west is the Palazzo del Turismo, to the south of which is the Piazza Diaz, surrounded by modern buildings, including a 16-storey office block.

*Ospedale Maggiore

South-east of Piazza Diaz, in an area rebuilt since the Second World War (with the Torre Velasca, a 99 m/327 ft high office block erected in 1958), is the old Ospedale Maggiore, a brick building 285 m/312 yd long, the town's first hospital, begun in 1456 by Antonio Filarete and continued from 1465 onwards in Gothic and Renaissance style. It now houses the Rector's Office and two faculties of the State university.

Palazzo di Giustizia (Law Courts)

500 m/550 yd east of the Ospedale Maggiore, between the broad Corso di Porta Vittoria and Via San Barnaba, rises the massive Palazzo di Giustizia (Law Courts), completed in 1940.

Teatro alla Scala

Museo Teatrale

In Piazza della Scala is a monument to Leonardo da Vinci (1872). On the north-west side of the square stands the Teatro alla Scala (1775–78), one of the largest and most important opera-houses in the world. To the left of the main building is the Museo Teatrale, with material on the history of the theatre; it incorporates a Verdi Museum with numerous mementoes of the composer (d. in Milan 1901).

Palazzo Marino

On the south-east side of the square, opposite the Scala, the Palazzo Marino (by Galeazzo Alessi, 1558–60) is now the headquarters of the municipal administration.

San Fedele

Behind the Palazzo Marino, in Piazza San Fedele, stands the fine Jesuit church of San Fedele, begun by Pellegrini in 1569 under San Carlo Borromeo.

Palazzo Belgioioso

Beyond San Fedele, in the beautiful Piazza Belgioioso, is the fine Palazzo Belgioioso, built by Piermarini in 1781.

Manzoni's House

At the corner of Via Morone (No. 1) is Manzoni's House, with the room in which the novelist Alessandro Manzoni (1785–1873) worked and in which he died (recently closed).

*Museo Poldi Pezzoli

Almost opposite (Via Manzoni 12), in an elegant old patrician house, the Museo Poldi-Pezzoli contains pictures by Botticelli, Mantegna,

La Scala opera house in Milan

Piero della Francesca, Guardi and other artists; there are also Flemish and Persian carpets, tapestries, jewellery, silver, bronzes and weapons.

Corso Vittorio Emanuele and Corso Venezia

From Piazza Belgioioso the Corso Matteotti, with fine modern buildings, runs east to the Piazza San Babila, which has been considerably enlarged since the Second World War, with large modern blocks and the little Romanesque church of San Babila. From the south-west corner of the square the Corso Vittoria Emanuele (pedestrian precinct), lined with elegant shops, leads towards the cathedral.

Piazza San Babila

Immediately on the right-hand side of the Corso is the church of San Carlo al Corso, a circular building modelled on the Pantheon (by Carlo Amati, 1836–47).

San Carlo al Corso

From Piazza San Babila the line of Corso Vittorio Emanuele is continued north-east by the broad Corso Venezia.

On the right-hand side, at the corner of Via San Damiano, are the Palazzo Serbelloni (1793) and the Palazzo Rocca-Saporiti (1812), both in neo-classical style.

Palaces

Almost opposite the Palazzo Rocca-Saporiti is the Museo Civico di Storia Naturale (Museum of Natural History), notable in particular for its large collection of birds (25,000 specimens). Behind the museum extend the Giardini Pubblici, with an interesting planetarium.

Museo Civico di Storia Naturale

The Corso Venezia joins the Piazzale Oberdan, in which are two little gatehouses of the Porta Venezia. From here the busy Corso Buenos Aires continues the line of Corso Venezia north-east to the circular Piazzale Loreto.

Porta Venezia

265

Milan/Milano
Central Station

	1 km/¾ mile north-west, at the end of the broad Via Andrea Doria, is the Central Station, an imposing building richly clad in marble (by Ulisse Stacchini, 1925–31), and one of the largest stations in Europe.
Museo delle Cere	In the station is the Museo delle Cere (Wax Museum), with wax figures of famous Italians.
Pirelli Building	Facing the station, to the south-west, is the 32-storey Pirelli Building (1955–59), 127 m/419 ft high (conducted tours).
Piazza della Repubblica	From the station Via Pisani runs south-west to the spacious Piazza della Repubblica, laid out from 1931 onwards on the site of the old railway station and now surrounded by huge modern buildings, including the 31-storey "Grattacielo di Milano", 114 m/376 ft high, built in 1955. From the north-west corner of the square the wide Viale della Liberazione leads to the Porta Garibaldi Station, 1 km/¾ mile away, which relieves pressure on the Central Station. The area west of the Piazza della Repubblica is being rebuilt as the administrative quarter ("Centro Direzionale") of Milan.

Piazza Cavour

Giardini Pubblici	From the Piazza della Repubblica the Via Turati runs south to the Piazza Cavour, a busy traffic intersection at the south-west corner of the beautiful Giardini Pubblici, the Municipal Gardens laid out in 1783–86. On the south-east side of Piazza Cavour are three tower blocks, including the 22-storey Centro Svizzero (completed 1952).
Galleria d'Arte Moderna	A little way east of the Piazza Cavour, to the west of the Natural History Museum, stands the neo-classical Villa Comunale (or Villa Reale; 1790), which houses the Galleria d'Arte Moderna, a museum of modern art (19th and 20th c. painting and sculpture). Adjoining the villa is the Padiglione d'Arte Contemporanea (1954), a pavilion with work of modern Italian artists, including works by Boccioni, Carrà, De Chirico, Modigliani, Morandi, etc.
	From Piazza Cavour the Via Alessandro Manzoni runs south to the Piazza della Scala.

Palazzo di Brera

West of Piazza Cavour and north-west of Piazza della Scala, in Via Brera, is the Renaissance Palazzo di Brera (1651–1773), originally a Jesuit college, which has been occupied since 1776 by the Accademia di Belle Arti. In the courtyard can be seen a monument to Napoleon I by Canova (1809).

The palace contains a library (800,000 volumes) founded in 1770 and an observatory.

**Pinacoteca di Brera

On the first floor is the Pinacoteca di Brera, one of Italy's finest picture galleries, which contains among many other exhibits futuristic paintings of the 20th c. The picture collection was founded as a didactic collection of the Art Academy and its principal exhibits were formed by pictures from churches and acquisition from Rome. Only some of the rooms of the Pinacoteca are open to the public.

The chief strength of the Pinacoteca di Brera lies in the works by the north Italian masters. Notable among 15th c. pictures are works by

Mantegna ("Madonna in a Ring of Angels' Heads" and "Lamentation"). The Venetian masters are represented by Carlo Crivelli (including "Enthroned Madonna della Candeletta"), Gentile ("Preaching of St Mark in Alexandria"), Giovanni Bellini ("Lamentation" and two Madonnas) and Cima da Conegliano.

Pictures from later periods include works by Paolo Veronese, Titian ("Count Antonio Porcia" and "St Jerome") and Tintoretto ("Finding of St Mark's Body" and "Descent from the Cross", and portraits by Lorenzo Lotto and Giovanni Battista Moroni.

The Lombard masters, disciples of Leonardo da Vinci, are well represented, with works by Bramantino, Sodoma, De Predis, Boltraffio and Andrea Solario.

Outstanding among the frescoes by Bernardino Luini is the "Burial of St Catherine", among his easel paintings the "Madonna of the Rose-Garden".

Artists of the Ferrarese school include Ercole de' Roberti ("Madonna with Saints") and Dosso Dossi.

Coreggio of Parma is represented by a "Nativity" and an "Adoration of the Kings".

There is an excellent representation of the Umbrian school, including works by Gentile da Fabriano ("Coronation of the Virgin with Saints"), Piero della Francesca ("Madonna with Saints and Duke Federico da Montefeltro") and Bramante (eight frescoes "Christ of the Column").

The most famous picture in the gallery is Raphael's "Marriage of the Virgin" ("Lo Sposalizio"), the finest work of his first period.

There are also important works by 17th and 18th c. artists.

Outstanding among foreign masters are Rembrandt (portraits of women, including "The Artist's Sister"), Van Dyck ("Princess Amalie of Solms"), Rubens ("Last Supper") and El Greco ("St Francis").

Piazza Mercanti

From the Piazza della Scala the Via Santa Margherita runs south-west into the Piazza dei Mercanti, centre of the old town of Milan. In the centre of the square is the single-storey Palazzo della Ragione (1228–33), originally a law court, with an equestrian statue of the builder on the south side. The Palazzo dei Giureconsulti (1564), on the north side of the square, has a tower dating from 1272. On the south side is the Gothic Loggia degli Osii (1316).

Palazzo della Ragione

Piazza Cordusio

North-west of the Piazza Mercanti the oval Piazza Cordusio is the meeting-place of important streets. To the south-east the Via Orefici, lined with shops, leads to the Piazza del Duomo; to the west the Via Meravigli goes past the Exchange to the church of Santa Maria delle Grazie; to the north-west the Via Dante leads to the Castello and from here an underground shopping arcade extends to the Piazza del Duomo.

South of Piazza Cordusio is the Palazzo dell'Ambrosiana (1603–09), with a famous library (700,000 printed volumes, 35,000 manuscripts, 2000 incunabula) and an important picture gallery founded in 1618 by Cardinal-Archbishop Federico Borromeo (works by Leonardo da Vinci, including the "Codex Atlanticus", and by Botticelli, Ambrogia de Predis, Raphael, Titian, Tiepolo and Caravaggio).

Palazzo dell'Ambrosiana Library and Picture Gallery

South-east of the Palazzo dell'Ambrosiana is the little church of San Satiro (by Bramante; 1478 onwards), with a campanile dating from the

San Satiro

end of the 10th c. and a modern façade. The interior has a choir seen in perspective. The baptistery in the south aisle is a gem of Lombard Early Renaissance architecture by Bramante (1480–88). At the end of the north transept is the curious little domed Capella della Pietà (9th c.).

Largo Cairoli

The Largo Cairoli at the north-western end of Via Dante is crossed by the broad Foro Buonaparte, which has a bronze equestrian statue of Garibaldi. From there the short Via Beltrami continues into the beautiful Piazza Castello.

*Castello

Musei del Castello Sforzesco

The Castello Sforzesco, held successively by the Viscontis and the Sforzas, was built in 1368, demolished by the people of Milan in 1447 and rebuilt from 1450 onwards. The Torre de Filarete, on the nearside (70 m/231 ft high), is a reproduction (1905) of the original gate-tower. The Castello houses the Musei del Castello Sforzesco, with a collection of sculpture which consists mainly of medieval and modern works together with some Early Christian material and graves. Its greatest treasure is the "Pietà Rondanini", Michelangelo's last masterpiece, brought here in 1953 from the Palazzo Rondanini in Rome. Other important items are the unfinished tomb of Gaston de Foix of Bambaia and the large tomb, with an equestrian statue, of Bernabò Visconti (d. 1385) by Bonino da Campione. There is also a collection of decorative art, as well as pictures by old masters (including Bellini, Correggio, Mantegna, Bergognone, Foppa, Lotto, Tintoretto and Antonello da Messina), prehistoric and Egyptian antiquities, a collection on musical history and an armoury.

Park

Between the two rear courtyards of the Castello is a passage leading to the park, laid out in 1893–97, once the pleasure garden of the dukes of

Pirelli Building (on right)

Castello Sforzesco

Milan and later a military training ground. In the north-east of the park is the Arena, an amphitheatre constructed in 1807 for sporting and other events. To the south-east is an interesting Aquarium.

On the west side of the park stands the Palazzo dell'Arte, used for exhibitions of modern art. A lookout tower to the north of this, 109 m/ 360 ft high, was built in 1932. On the north-west side of the park is the Arco della Pace, a triumphal arch of white marble (1806–38). About 1 km/³⁄₄ mile west of the Arco della Pace are the grounds of the Milan Trade Fair.

Palazzo dell'Arte

Arco della Pace

*Santa Maria delle Grazie

South-west of the Castello, past the Northern Station and along Via Boccaccio and Via Caradosso, can be found the church of Santa Maria delle Grazie, in the Corso Magenta. This is a brick-built Gothic structure (begun about 1465), with a choir and a massive six-sided dome in the finest Early Renaissance style designed by Bramante (1492 onwards). During the repair of war damage in the dome old sgraffito paintings were brought to light. At the end of the north aisle is the Baroque chapel of the Madonna delle Grazie, with an altarpiece of the Madonna.

In the refectory of the former Dominican monastery is Leonardo da Vinci's "Last Supper" (the Cenacolo Vinciano), his most famous work, painted on the wall in tempera between 1495 and 1497: a dramatic presentation of the scene which was quite novel and marked an important new stage in the development of art. The painting is much damaged from the flaking off of the paint and during the last decades has been restored several times.

**"Last Supper" by Leonardo da Vinci

To the south of Santa Maria delle Grazie, in Via San Vittore, stands the beautiful church of San Vittore al Corpo, an early Christian foundation,

"The Last Supper" by Leonardo da Vinci

269

which was remodelled by Galeazzo Alessi in Late Renaissance style (1530 onwards), with a sumptuous Baroque interior.

**Museo Nazionale della Scienza e della Tecnica

Adjoining it on the east is the Leonarda da Vinci National Museum of Science and Technology, housed in a former Olivetan monastery. The museum, opened in 1953, illustrates the history of science and technology down to modern times. Of particular interest are the Leonardo da Vinci Gallery; the department of physics, with apparatus used by Galileo, Newton and Volta and the departments of optics, acoustics, telegraphy, transport, shipping, railways, flying, metallurgy, motor vehicles, clocks and watches, and timber. There is also a library and reading room (film presentations).

** Sant'Ambrogio

The church of Sant'Ambrogio east of the National Museum was founded in 386 by St Ambrose. The present church is a masterpiece of Romanesque architecture (12th c.; choir 9th c.). Notable features of the interior are the pulpit, restored about 1200, with late Romanesque carving, and the casing (paliotto) of the high altar, a masterpiece of Carolingian art (made in 835 at either Milan or Rheims).

Museum

On the north-west side of the church are the Museo di Sant'Ambrogio and a monumental war memorial (1930).

The Catholic University of the Sacred Heart (del Sacro Cuore), adjoining the church on the south-east, was founded in 1921 and has two cloisters by Bramante.

Sights in the south-west

San Lorenzo Maggiore

South-east of Sant'Ambrogio, in the Corso di Porta Ticines, San Lorenzo, a fine building on a centralised plan, dates from the Early Christian period; it has a Renaissance dome (1574) and the chapel of St Aquilinus (4th c. mosaics). In front of the church a portico of sixteen Corinthian columns, the largest surviving monument of Roman Mediolanum, has been re-erected.

* Sant'Eustorgio

500 m/550 yd farther south the church of Sant'Eustorgio, a Romanesque basilica (12th–13th c.) has a fine campanile (1297–1309) and a façade which was added in 1863. Beyond the choir is the Cappella Portinari (by Michelozzo, 1462–68), the earliest example of Renaissance architecture, with frescoes by Vincenzo Foppa. In the chapel is the marble tomb (1339) of St Peter Martyr, a Dominican monk murdered in 1252.

San Giorgio al Palazzo

Just north of the church of San Lorenzo the Corso di Porta Ticinese runs into the Piazza Carrobbio. In Via Torino, which runs north-east from this square to the Piazzo del Duomo, stands the church of San Giorgio al Palazzo, with paintings by Bernardino Luini.

*Cimitero Monumentale

In north-western Milan, at the Porta Volta, lies the Cimitero Monumentale (opened 1866), Italy's most splendid cemetery, with numerous highly elaborate marble tombs.

Chiaravalle Milanese

**Situation
7 km/4½ miles
south-east**

South-east of Milan is Chiaravalle Milanese, noted for its Cistercian abbey church, a fine brick edifice with a tall tower; it was founded by St Bernard of Clairvaux in 1135 and remodelled between 1170 and 1221 and has magnificent Baroque choir-stalls of 1640, an elegant little cloister and a cemetery.

Metanopoli

South-east of Milan, in the commune of San Donato Milanese, is Meta-
nopoli (188 m/620 ft), also called "Captital of Methane" or "Oil City", a
satellite town which has grown up since 1940 with the headquarters or
branch establishments of the leading Italian oil companies, such as ENI
(Ente Nazionale Idrocarburi), SNAM (Società Nazionale Metanodotti),
AGIP (Azienda Generale Italiana Petroli, with departments of mining
and atomic research) and ANIC (Azienda Nazionale Idrocarburi).

Situation
8 km/5 miles
south-east

Monza

North-east of Milan, on the River Lambro, is the industrial town of
Monza (162 m/535 ft; pop. 124,000), which together with Pavia was the
place of coronation of the Lombard kings from the 11th c. In the Piazza
Roma stands the old Town Hall ("Arengario") of 1293, and close by the
cathedral, founded in 590 and rebuilt in the 13th and 14th c. in Lombard
Gothic style, with a beautiful façade and a harmonious interior. In the
Cappella di Teodolinda are frescoes and the famous "Iron Crown", said
to be the royal crown of the Lombards, with which the German emperors were crowned as kings of Italy. Under the little cloister on the left
side of the cathedral the Museo Serpero contains the rich Cathedral
Treasury.

To the north of Monza stands the Villa Reale, built 1777–80 in Classical
style by G. Piermarini (formerly a royal castle; small picture gallery).
Nearby is the main entrance to the Parco Reale, through which flows
the River Lambro. In the extensive park are the Mirabello racecourse
and the well-known motor-racing circuit.

Situation
15 km/9 miles
north-east

Modena

G5

Region: Emilia-Romagna
Province: Modena (MO)
Altitude: 34 m/112 ft
Population: 178,000

The provincial capital of Modena, lies between the rivers Secchia and
Panaro near the southern edge of the north Italian plain on the Via
Emilia. It is the see of an archbishop.

Situation

The town centre has wide arcaded streets and large squares, and the
old fortifications have given place to beautiful avenues and gardens.

Originally a Celtic settlement of the Boii, the town, lying astride the
ancient Via Aemilia, became a Roman colony in 183 B.C. under the
name of Mutina. In 1288 it came into the hands of the house of Este,
who held it for some 500 years, acquiring the ducal title in 1452. In 1814
the territory passed into the possession of Archduke Francis of Austria
and his son Francis V. After several attempted risings against the
Austrians' reactionary rule, which were ruthlessly repressed, Modena
at last broke free in 1859 and was united with the new Italian kingdom in
1860.

History

The private possessions of the Este family and their name were inherited by the heir to the Austrian throne, Francis Ferdinand, who was
assassinated in 1914.

In the history of art Modena is noted for its fine 14th c. school of painters
and for its terracottas – dramatic groups conceived for pictorial rather

Art

271

than plastic effect, a genre developed by the strongly realistic Guido Mazzoni (1450–1518) and perfected by Antonio Begarelli (*c.* 1498–1565).

*Cathedral

The main traffic artery of the town is the Via Emilia, on the line of the old Roman road. Just off the south side of this street, in the central Piazza Grande, stands the imposing Cathedral, a basilica begun in 1099 in Romanesque style, consecrated in 1184 and completed in the 13th c., with beautiful sculpture on the exterior walls and in the interior. On the façade are scenes from the Creation by Wiligelmus (*c.* 1100), and over the fine central doorway is a large window rose. The interior is notable for some good pictures and for sculptures of the Passion (12th c.) on the choir screen and the pulpit. In the crypt, its roof supported by 30 slender columns, is a realistic group representing the "Adoration of the Infant Christ" by Guido Mazzoni (after 1480).

*Torre Ghirlandina
On the north side of the cathedral, in the Piazza del Torre, rises the 88 m/290 ft high Torre Ghirlandina (slightly off the perpendicular), one of the finest campaniles in northern Italy and a distinctive city landmark.

Museo Lapidario del Duomo
Also on the north side of the cathedral stands the Museo Lapidario del Duomo, which has Romanesque metopes from the cathedral roof.

San Giovanni Battista
North-west of the cathedral is the Piazza Matteotti, a large square on the west side of which, at the corner of Via Emilia, stands the church of San Giovanni Battista, a plain domed building (1730) containing, to the left of the high altar, a beautifully painted terracotta of the "Lamentation" by Mazzoni (1477–80).

Palazzo dei Musei

Museums
The Palazzo dei Musei, farther west along Via Emilia, houses the municipal collections.

In the courtyard is the Museo Lapidario with Roman finds including sarcophagi.

On the ground floor the Museo Civico del Risorgimento contains mementoes of the fight for freedom in the 19th c.

On the first floor can be found the Biblioteca Estense, with more than 380,000 volumes, 1640 incunabula and a valuable collection of manuscripts. Particularly notable is a 15th c. Bible which belonged to Borso d'Este, with more than a thousand pages illustrated by French artists, and the "Sphaera", a masterpiece of Lombardian miniature painting. The second floor contains several collections: the Museo Civico (archaeology and ethnology), the Museo Estense, with medallions, terracotta sculpture, statuettes, porcelain, musical instruments, etc. and the Galleria Estense.

*Este Picture Gallery
The Este Picture Gallery is famous for its large collection of early Emilian and Tuscan art, including 15th c. pictures of the Po plain, as well as Modena art of the 15th c., with works by Correggio, Dosso Dossi, Titian, Tintoretto, Guercino, Veronese, Velázques, Giovanni di Paolo, Bassano, Domenichino, Strozzi, Rosa, Guardi and other artists.

Sant'Agostino
Adjacent to the museum is the 17th c. church of Sant'Agostino (remodelled), the "Pantheon" of the house of Este, "one of the most imaginative flat-roofed creations of the Baroque" (Burkhardt). To the right of the entrance is a "Lamentation", an early work by Antonio Begarelli.

Other terracottas by Begarelli can be seen in the church of San Fran-

cesco, near the south-west corner of the old town, and in the church of
San Pietro (1476), in the south-east of the old town.

Palazzo Ducale

In the north of the old town in Piazza Roma, about 500 m/550 yd
north-east of the cathedral, rises the massive Palazzo Ducale, begun in
1634 in accordance with a plan by Bartolomeo Avanzini, an excellent
example of secular architecture of the 17th c. The balustrade is decorated with numerous figures, depicting the virtues and figures of mythology; the doorway is flanked by massive figures of Hercule and
Aemilius Lepidus. The Palazzo Ducale is now a military academy.

North-east of the Palazzo are the palace gardens, today a public park
(Giardini Pubblici), with a botanic garden. Notable is a 17th c. villa, built
to a plan by the famous architect Gaspare Vigarini for the dukes of Este.
The villa, a long building, the central part of which is crowned by an
octagonal domed tower has been used for exhibitions for many years.

Giardini Pubblici

Carpi

North of Modena is the interesting town of Carpi (28 m/92 ft; pop.
60,000). In the centre of the town is the large Piazza dei Martiri, in which
stand the New Cathedral (begun 1514; façade 1667), the Loggia, the
15th c. Colonnades (52 arches) and the old Castello (now partly occupied by a museum) of the Pio family, who ruled here from 1327 to 1525;
in the second courtyard is a memorial to the victims of the Second
World War. Behind the Castello is the Old Cathedral, founded in 751, La
Sagra (Romanesque interior, with a 12th c. pulpit), adjoining which is a
campanile of 1221. Near the Loggia is the Franciscan church of San
Nicolò (1493–1522), the dome of which was painted by Giovanni del
Sega (16th c.).

Situation
18 km/11 miles from
Modena

*Abbazia di Nonantola

At Nonantola (24 m/79 ft; pop. 11,000) stands the well-known Abbazia
di Nonantola, founded in the 8th c. and dedicated to St Silvester. It was
destroyed several times by fire and rebuilt, the latest building in Romanesque style dating from the 12th c. The abbey was restored in the
20th c., in particular the crypt, the vault of which is supported by 64
small columns decorated with capitals. The south aisle of the abbey
church is decorated with 15th c. wall paintings by a master of Modena.
The church treasury includes manuscripts with miniatures and gold
work. Notable is the relief on the doorway with scenes from the Gos-
pels and episodes from the history of the abbey.

Situation
10 km/6 miles
north-east of
Modena

Molise

Region: Molise
Provinces: Campobasso (CB) and Isernia (IS)
Area: 4438 sq. km/1713 sq. miles
Population: 332,700

The region of Molise, one of the poorest and remotest in Italy, lies in the
Neapolitan Apennines (Appennino Napolitano) in eastern Central Italy.

Situation

General information   Bounded on the north by the region of Abruzzi, with which it is linked by historical and cultural tradition and with which it was combined until 1963 to form the region of Abruzzi e Molise. Molise extends from the karstic hills of the Monti del Matese (Monte Miletto, 2050 m/6765 ft) in the south-west to the edge of the wide Apulian plain in the east and the Adriatic to the north-east. The inhabitants gain a modest subsistence from arable and pastoral farming.

Campobasso

The principal town in the region is Campobasso (701 m/2313 ft; pop. 50,000), capital of the province of the same name and the see of an archbishop. Above the town are the ruins of the Castello di Montforte (16th c.; view). Also of interest is the Romanesque church of San Bartolomeo.

Sepino   South of Campobasso, near the border with Apulia, is the village of Sepino (698 m/2303 ft).

Saepinum   About 3 km/2 miles north of Sepino are the remains of the old Roman town of Saepinum. Excavations have brought to light a theatre, a basilica, the forum, the baths and the town walls with four towers.

Isernia

The capital of Molise's other province is Isernia (423 m/1396 ft; pop. 21,000), also the see of a bishop.

Excavations   Near the town are the excavated remains (uncovered in 1979) of a Palaeolithic settlement over a million years old. Excavations are still in progress and it is planned to make the area into an archaeological site with a museum, accessible to the public.

Abbazia di San Vincenzo   About 20 km/13 miles north-west of Isernia in the Volturno valley are the ruins of the Abbazia di San Vincenzo, founded about 700 and destroyed by the Saracens in 880. The crypt, with fine frescoes (9th c.), has been preserved.

Pietrabbondante   30 km/19 miles north-east of Isernia, at Pietrabbondante, are the excavated remains of a Samnite town (theatre, temple, etc.).

Montecassino/Cassino   K8

Region: Latium/Lazio
Province: Frosinone (FR)
Altitude: 45 m/149 ft
Population: 40,000

Situation   The town of Cassino lies between Rome (110 km/68 miles north-west) and Naples (about 80 km/50 miles south-east), in southern Latium. The town is noted chiefly for the great abbey of Montecassino which towers above it on a hill. During the Second World War there was bitter fighting around Cassino, and the town was completely destroyed and rebuilt on a new site slightly farther south.

*Abbey of Montecassino

The road to the abbey of Montecassino (9 km/5½ miles) winds steeply up the hill in hairpin bends from the west side of the town. Just outside

In the Monastery of Montecassino

the town, on the left of the road, are the remains of the Roman Casinum, including the massive ruins of an amphitheatre, a mausoleum and a theatre. At the next bend, on the right, are the ruins of the Rocca Ianula (193 m/637 ft), built 949–86.

Just before the monastery, on the right, is a road leading to the Polish military cemetery, with over 1000 graves. Beyond this are pre-Roman polygonal walls (4th–3rd c. B.C.).

On the summit of the hill (519 m/1713 ft) is the abbey of Montecassino, founded by St Benedict in 529, and acknowledged as the cradle of the Benedictine order, which became a great centre of learning and art. During the Second World War the hill of Montecassino was a corner-stone of the German defensive line from October 1943 to May 1944, and on February 15th 1944 the abbey was almost completely destroyed by an Allied air attack, although the Germans had declared that it was clear of troops. The abbey has since been rebuilt in its original form, the only surviving features of the old buildings being the crypt, with paintings from the school of Beuron (1898–1913), and the tombs of St Benedict and his twin sister St Scholastica (both c. 480–543). The contents of the valuable library (80,000 volumes), the abbey's archives and many pictures were removed to safety in the Vatican during the fighting.

Above the abbey is Monte Calvario (593 m/1557 ft), crowned by a Polish war memorial, from which there are magnificent views.

Montecatini Terme G6

Region: Toscana. Province: Pistola (PT)
Altitude: 27 m/89 ft. Population: 22,000

Montecatani Terme: the Stabilimento del Tettuccio

Situation and importance	The famous spa of Montecatini Terme lies in the north-west of Tuscany, some 30 km/19 miles east of Lucca, in the fertile but in summer very hot Nievole valley (Val die Nievole).

Montecatini Terme is Italy's leading spa, attracting large numbers of visitors, mainly Italians, throughout the whole year (high season July–August). The baths and mineral springs (temperature 19–25 °C/66–77 °F; water containing sulphur and sodium carbonate) have been used for treatment since the 14th c.

*Spa area

Piazza del Popolo	The central feature of the town is the Piazza del Popolo with the neo-classical church of Santa Maria Assunta; a little way north-west is the Kursaal.

The wide Viale Verdi runs north-east from the Piazza del Popolo to the spa centre. At the edge of the large spa park are several thermal baths – to the left the Stabilimento Excelsior, built in 1915 and enlarged in 1968, the Terme Leopoldine (1775; rebuilt 1927) and the Stabilimento Tamerici; at the end of the street is the Stabilimento Tettucio (1927), a large building with fine colonnades. In Viale A. Diaz, opposite the Stabilimento Regina, is the Accademia d'Arte, with a small museum. North-west of the Stabilimento Tettucio are the smaller houses, the Torrettas and the Rinfresco. At the north-east corner of the spa park is the lower station of the cableway up to Montecatini Alto (see below). South-west of the town are the sports stadium and the horse-racing course.

Montecatini Alto (Montecatini Val di Nievole)

About 260 m/285 yd above the thermal bath, on the top of a hill, is the old-world village of Montecatini Val di Nievole (usually called Montecatini Alto), which can be reached either by funicular from Montecatini Terme or by road.

Situation
5 km/3 miles
north-east

On the access road from the thermal bath is the entrance to the Grotta Maona, a dripstone cave discovered in the 19th c.

Grotta Maona

Only ruins remain of the Castello Montecatini Alto.

Castello

*Parco di Pinocchio

North-west of Montecatini Terme, near the village of Collodi, is the Parco di Pinocchio. Between a fairytale park and playgrounds can be found a monument to Pinocchio. The adventures of the famous character, created by the Florence-born writer Carlo Collodi (originally Carlo Lorenzini) who grew up in Collodi, are known all over the world.

* Parco di Pinocchio
Situation
14 km/9 miles
north-west

Montepulciano   H6

Region: Toscana. Province: Siena (SI)
Altitude: 605 m/1997 ft. Population: 14,000

The little town of Montepulciano lies on a hill in eastern Tuscany, about 70 km/43 miles south-east of Siena and 20 km/12 miles west of Lake Trasimene (Lago Trasimeno) in the region of Umbria.
Montepulciano is one of the most attractive little towns in Central Italy, with its walls and its beautiful Gothic and Renaissance buildings.
Montepulciano was the birthplace of the poet A. Ambrogini (1454-94), who took the name Poliziano (Politian) after his native town, and of Cardinal Roberto Bellarmino (1542–1621), a protagonist of the Counter-Reformation.

Situation

Piazza Grande

The life of the town centres on the Piazza Grande, on the south side of which is the cathedral, begun in 1570 by Bartolomeo Ammannati and completed by Ippolito Scalza, with the exception of the façade, in 1630. Inside to the left of the main doorway, is a recumbent figure of Bartolomeo Aragazzi (the secretary of Pope Martin V; 15th c.) from the magnificent tomb by Michelozzo di Bartolomeo (1427–36) which was taken down, parts of it being dispersed about the cathedral and some parts being lost. Behind the main altar is a fine triptych by Taddeo di Bartolo ("Assumption of the Virgin Mary"; 1401).

Cathedral

To the right of the cathedral stands the Palazzo Comunale (Town Hall; 14th c.), a massive building, with fine views from the tower.

Palazzo Comunale

To the left of the cathedral is the Palazzo Contucci, begun in 1519 by Antonio da Sangallo the Elder and completed by Peruzzi. Inside can be seen fine frescoes by Andrea Pozzo (1642–1709).
Opposite the cathedral is the Palazzo Tarugi, the town's finest Renaissance palace, and to the left of it a fountain of 1520.

Palaces

North of the Piazza Grande, in Via Ricci (on right), is the Palazzo Neri-Orselli (14th c.), with the Museo Civico (municipal museum), with fine medieval and Renaissance pictures, also some terracotta work by Andrea della Robbia.

Museo Civico

277

Montepulciano
Old town

1 Palazzo Avignonesi
2 Palazzo Cocconi
3 Palazzo Venturi
4 Palazzo Cervini
5 Palazzo Ricci
6 Palazzo Neri Orselli
  (Museo Civico)
7 Palazzo della Pretura
  (Formerly Palazzo del
  Capitano del Popolo)
8 Palazzo Tarugi
9 Palazzo Comunale
10 Palazzo Contucci
11 Casa del Poliziano
12 Sant' Agnese
13 San Bernardo
14 Santa Lucia
15 San Francesco
16 Church of Gesù
17 Santa Maria dei Servi

200 m

© Baedeker

Via dell' Opio and Via di Voltaia

To the east of Piazza Grande Via dell' Opio with its northward continuation, Via di Voltaia, forms the main street of the town which is lined with fine palaces and churches.

Palazzo Cervini
At the north end of Via di Voltaia, on the right, is the Palazzo Cervini, by Antonio da Sangallo the Elder. The palace was commissioned by Cardinal Marcello Cervini, later Pope Marcellus II, but remained uncompleted.

Sant'Agostino
The church of Sant'Agostino is reached by way of Via di Gracciano, north of the Palazzo Cervini. It has a Renaissance façade by Michelozzo di Bartolomeo and inside there are a notable wooden crucifix (15th c.) and a number of pictures, particularly of the 16th–17th c.

*San Biagio

The church of San Biagio, about 2 km/1¼ miles south-west of the town, at the end of a long avenue lined with cypresses, is a centralised structure which was built in 1518–45 by Antonio da Sangallo the Elder, but it still shows the influence of Bramante. The church is built of

San Biagio, near Montepulciano

gold-coloured travertine, and is considered one of the finest buildings of the Renaissance.

Pienza

West of Montepulciano is Pienza, named after Pope Pius II (b. here in 1405), who adorned the town with splendid buildings, mainly designed by Bernardo Rossellino, the leading Florentine architect of the day.

Piazza Pio II, surrounded by 15th c. buildings, offers a harmonious picture of Early Renaissance architecture. On the south side of the square is the cathedral, which contains a number of fine pictures, including works by the Sienese painter Matteo di Giovanni and by Lorenzo Vecchietta, and beautiful Gothic choir-stalls. In the crypt is a font by Rossellino. The Bishop's Palace to the right, adjoins the Cathedral Museum (with a cope which once belonged to Pius II). Opposite the cathedral, to the north, are the Palazzo Comunale (Town Hall) and the Palazzo Ammannati. To the left of the cathedral is the Palazzo Piccolomini, from the roof-garden of which there are magnificent views. In front of the palace is a fountain of 1462.

Situation
14 km/9 miles west

*Piazza Pio II

Chiusi

South-east of Montepulciano, above the Chiana valley, lies the little walled town of Chiusi, the former Chamars or Clevsin, one of the twelve towns of the Etruscan League and a bitter opponent of Rome about 500 B.C. During the Middle Ages the population was devastated by malaria.

Situation
23 km/14 miles south-east of Montepulciano

279

*Museo Nazionale Etrusco	In the Piazza del Duomo is the Museo Etrusco, with a rich collection of material from the Etruscan tombs of the area, including funeral urns, bronze and clay masks and pitchers.
	The cathedral (6th c., rebuilt in the 12th c.), opposite the museum, is built almost entirely with stone from Roman buildings (18 antique columns). A walk round the town affords attractive views.
*Etruscan tombs	Scattered around the outskirts of the town are about 400 notable Etruscan tombs. Some of them are accessible to the public; information from the Etruscan National Museum.
	On the road to the Lago di Chiusi can be found the early 5th c. B.C. Tomba della Scimmia (called "Tomb of the Ape" after a detail of the wall paintings which depicts scenes of funeral ceremonies).

Naples/Nápoli L9

	Region: Campania Province: Nápoli (NA) Altitude: 10 m/33 ft Population: 1,207,000
Situation	The south Italian port town of Naples, principal town of the region of Campania and of the province of Nápoli, lies on the north side of the Bay of Naples, on the Tyrrhenian Sea, extending along the lower slopes of attractive hills.
General information	The old town with its narrow streets and stepped lanes and its tall balconied houses is fringed on the west and north by extensive villa

View across the Gulf of Naples towards Vesuvius

suburbs and on the east by an industrial zone. In recent years much of the city has been redeveloped with new buildings and realigned streets, particularly in the area around the harbour, the Rione Santa Lucia.

Naples possesses many historical monuments going back almost 3000 years, particularly the treasures, to be seen in the National Museum, garnered from the cities engulfed by Vesuvius; the port of Naples is of major importance for southern Italy.

In November 1980 there was severe damage from earthquakes.

Naples was originally a Greek foundation. As early as the 8th c. B.C. the site was occupied by the Rhodian settlement of Parthenope, near which settlers from Kyme (Latin Cumae), itself a colony established by Ionians from Euboea, founded the "old town", Palaiopolis, in the 7th c. In the 5th c. the "new town", Neapolis, was founded, mainly by incomers from Chalcis on Euboea. In 326 B.C. the three settlements became allies of Rome and were amalgamated. Although favoured by Rome for its faithfulness to the alliance, Neapolis preserved its independence and its distinctive Greek characteristics until late in the Imperial period. The town became a favourite residence of the Roman magnates, and Virgil composed some of his finest poetry here.
During the period of the great migration, in 543, the town fell into the hands of the Goths, but returned to Byzantine rule in 553 and thereafter succeeded in asserting its independence until conquered by the Normans in 1139 and incorporated by Roger II in his kingdom of Sicily. Roger's grandson Frederick II of Hohenstaufen founded the university in 1224. In the reign of Charles of Anjou (1266–85) Naples became capital of the kingdom. In 1442 Alfonso I of Aragon reunited the kingdoms of Sicily and Naples. From 1503 to 1707 Naples was the residence of Spanish viceroys. Following the War of the Spanish Succession the territory passed in 1713 to the Habsburgs, and after the War of the Austrian Succession (1734) to the Bourbons, with whom it remained until its incorporation in the new united Italy in 1860.

History

Southern part of the old town

The city's busiest traffic intersection is the Piazza Trieste e Trento, on the east side of which stands the Teatro San Carlo (1737), one of the largest theatres in Europe (2900 seats). Immediately north is the Galleria Umberto, a shopping arcade built in 1887–90.

Teatro San Carlo

Adjoining the Piazza Trieste e Trento on the south is the large Piazza del Plesbiscito, occupied on the west side by the church of San Francesco di Paola (1817–46), an imitation of the Pantheon in Rome.

San Francesco di Paola

Along the east side of the Piazza del Plesbiscito is the Palazzo Reale, the former Royal Palace, begun in 1600 by Dominico Fontana and restored in 1837–41. On the façade (169 m/185 yd) are eight marble statues of the various kings who ruled Naples. The palace contains a grand staircase of white marble (1651), a theatre, seventeen richly appointed state apartments and the valuable Biblioteca Nazionale (1,500,000 volumes, 12,000 manuscripts, 5000 incunabula).

Palazzo Reale

Behind the palace to the north-east, on the south side of the Piazza del Municipio, is the five-towered Castel Nuovo, also known as the Maschio Angioino, once the residence of kings and viceroys of Naples. Originally built by Charles I of Anjou in 1279–82, it was enlarged by Alfonso I of Aragon and has recently been restored. The entrance is formed by a splendid Early Renaissance triumphal arch, with rich

*Castel Nuovo

281

Naples: San Francesco di Paola

sculptured decoration, erected between 1453 and 1467 in honour of the entry of Alfonso I of Aragon. In the courtyard is the Gothic church of Santa Barbara (or Cappella Palatina), and to the left of this the large Baron's Hall.

Town Hall

In the centre of the Piazza del Municipio, which is laid out in gardens, stands an equestrian statue of Victor Emmanuel II (1897). On the west side of the square is the fine Town Hall (1819–25), originally built to house government departmens.

San Giacomo degli Spagnoli

Adjoining the Town Hall the church of San Giacomo degli Spagnoli (1540) has behind the high altar, the sumptuous tomb of Viceroy Don Pedro de Toledo, founder of the church.

Harbour

To the east of the palace and the Castel Nuovo extends the Harbour, divided into separate docks and basins by a series of piers and break-waters, which is always a bustle of activity. Extending east from the Piazza del Municipio is the Molo Angioino, on which is the Marine Station. To the west of this is the Eliporto (Heliport), from which there are regular helicopter services to Capri, Ischia, Capodichino Airport (7 km/4½ miles north), etc. Farther south, from the quay on the Calata di Beverello, boats sail to Ponza, Capri and Ischia.

Santa Lucia

To the west of the Piazza del Plesbiscito, on the slopes of Pizzofalcone and extending down to the sea, lies the district of Santa Lucia. South of

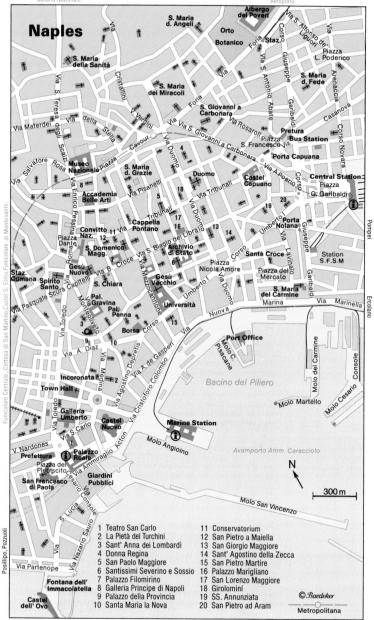

Naples

Capua
Galleria Nazionale

Benevento
Aeroporto

S. Maria
d. Angeli

Orto
Botanico

Albergo
dei Poveri

Staz.

Via S. Alfonso de' Ligori

Corso

Via S. Antonio Abate

Via S. Alfonso de' Liguori

Piazza
L. Poderico

S. Maria
d. Fede

Arenaccia

Casanova

S. Maria
della Sanità

Cristallini

Via della Stella

S. Maria
dei Miracoli

V. Vergini

S. Giovanni a
Carbonara

Via Rosaroll

Garibaldi

Piazza

Pretura

Bus Station

Via Materdei

Via S. Teresa degli Scalzi

Rosa

Enrico Pessina

Via Salvatore

Foria

Foria

Via S. Giovanni a Carbonara

S. Francesco Via

Porta Capuana

Corso Novara

Via A. Poerio

Museo
Nazionale

Piazza
Cavour

S. Maria
d. Grazie

Via Pisanelli

Duomo

Castel
Capuano

Central Station
Piazza
G. Garibaldi

Accademia
Belle Arti

Via Tribunali

Via Duomo

Via Tribunali

Convitto
Naz.

Cappella
Pontano

Via Constantinopoli

San Giovanni

Archivio
di Stato

Umberto I

Porta
Nolana

Piazza
Dante

S. Domenico
Magg.

Via S. Biagio dei Librai

Piazza
Nicola Amore

Santa Croce

Station
S.F.S.M.

Gesù
Nuovo

Via B. Croce

Gesù
Vecchio

Corso

Via Duomo

Piazza del
Mercato

Garibaldi

Staz.
Cumana

Spirito
Santo

Via Pasquale Scura

Via Toledo

Capitelli

S. Chiara

Via Mezzocannone

Università

Umberto I

S. Maria
del Carmine

Marina

Via Marinella

Pal.
Gravina

Pal.
Penna

Via Monteoliveto

Borsa

Corso

Nuova

Via

Port Office

Molo del Carmine

Ercolano

Via A. Diaz

Via Medina

Incoronata

Town Hall

Via Agostino Depretis

Via A. de Gasperi

Via Cristoforo Colombo

Bacino del Piliero

Molo C. Pisacane

Molo Martello

Molo Cesario

Molo del Carmine

Console

Galleria
Umberto

Via S. Carlo

Castel
Nuovo

Via Acton

Marine Station

Molo Angioino

Avamporto Amm. Caracciolo

V. Nardones

Prefettura

Palazzo
Reale

Piazza del
Plebiscito

San Francesco
di Paola

Giardini
Pubblici

Via Cesario Console

Via Ammiraglio Acton

N

300 m

Via Toledo

Via Nazario Sauro

Via S. Lucia

Via Partenope

Fontana dell'
Immacolatella

Castel
dell' Ovo

Molo San Vincenzo

Funicolare Centrale, Certosa di San Martino,Castel S. Elmo,Funicolare di Montesanto

Posillipo, Pozzuoli

Pompei

1 Teatro San Carlo	11 Conservatorium
2 La Pietà del Turchini	12 San Pietro a Maiella
3 Sant' Anna dei Lombardi	13 San Giorgio Maggiore
4 Donna Regina	14 Sant' Agostino della Zecca
5 San Paolo Maggiore	15 San Pietro Martire
6 Santissimi Severino e Sossio	16 Palazzo Marigliano
7 Palazzo Filomirino	17 San Lorenzo Maggiore
8 Galleria Principe di Napoli	18 Girolomini
9 Palazzo della Provincia	19 SS. Annunziata
10 Santa Maria la Nova	20 San Pietro ad Aram

© Baedeker

Metropolitana

the wide Via Santa Lucia this is an area of modern streets laid out on a regular plan, but to the north of that street it is a picturesque huddle of narrow stepped lanes in which the traditional Neapolitan way of life can be observed at any time of the day but particularly in the evening.

From the south-east corner of the Piazza del Plesbiscito a succession of streets runs round the east and south sides of the Santa Lucia district – first Via Cesario Console, which passes the Giardini Pubblici; then Via Nazario Sauro and Via Partenope, in which there are several large luxury hotels; and finally, beyond the Piazza della Vittoria, Via Caracciolo, which affords magnificent views of the Bay of Naples.

Castel dell' Ovo — From Via Partenope a causeway and a bridge lead to a little rocky islet on which stands the Castell dell' Ovo, begun in the 12th c., completed by Frederick II and rebuilt in the 17th c. On the causeway is the Porto di Santa Lucia.

*Villa Comunale

Aquarium — Between Via Caracciolo and the fine Riviera di Chiaia to the north extends the Villa Comunale, a park laid out in 1780, almost 1.5 km/ 1 mile long, which is the city's most popular promenade. Half-way along we find the Zoological Station, an important biological research institution founded by a German scientist, Anton Dorn, in 1870. In the central block is an Aquarium with 31 tanks which give an excellent survey of the fauna of the Bay of Naples.

Villa Pignatelli — North-west of the Aquarium, in a park just north of the Riviera di Chiaia, is the Villa Pignatelli, once the residence of Prince Diego Aragona Pignatelli Cortes, with a richly appointed interior in the styles of the 18th and 19th centuries.

Via Toledo

From the Piazza Trieste e Trento (also called Via Toledo after Don Pedro de Toledo who built it), the city's principal traffic artery and a scene of constant bustle and activity, runs north for a distance of 2 km/1¼ miles, rising gently uphill. It is crossed by numerous streets and lanes, many of those on the left being stepped lanes climbing up to the Corso Vittorio Emanuele (4 km/2½ miles long: beautiful views). The streets on the right, descending to the harbour and the Marine Station, are the centre of the city's business and commercial life. At the end of Via Roma, the continuation of Via Toledo, is the spacious Piazza Dante.

Via Medina and Via Monteoliveto

Santa Maria la Nova — From the Piazza del Municipio the Via Medina runs past the 14th c. church of the Incoronata. Near the end of Via Medina, on the left, is the 32-storey Grattacielo della Cattolica (1958), and a little way farther north the Piazza Matteotti, with the Post and Telegraph Office (by Vaccaro, 1936), one of the finest achievements of modern Italian architecture. In a little square just east of this building stands the church of Santa Maria la Nova (16th c.; beautiful interior), with two Renaissance cloisters of the monastery to which it belonged.

Via Monteoliveto — The line of Via Medina is continued north-west by Via Monteoliveto. At the end of this street is the fine Palazzo Gravina (1513–1549), which houses the Academy of Architecture. The street runs into the Piazza Monteoliveto, with the church of Monteoliveto or Sant'Anna dei Lombardi, begun in 1411 and later continued in Early Renaissance style; it contains eight good terracottas (15th–16th c.) and beautiful 16th c. choir-stalls.

Castle Nuovo

Piazza Gesù, with the Column of Maria

From the Piazza Monteoliveto the Calata Trinità Maggiore leads to the Piazza Gesù Nuovo, with a gilded statue of the Virgin (1748). On the north side of the square is the Jesuit church of Gesù Nuovo (1584), and to the south-east the church of Santa Chiara (founded 1310), which contains the tomb (1343–45) of Robert the Wise (1309–43) and other fine Gothic tombs belonging to members of the house of Anjou. The Nuns' Choir, behind the high altar, was used by the Poor Clares until 1925. In the adjoining Franciscan monastery is a beautiful cloister (Chiostro delle Clarisse) decorated with Capodimonte majolica.

Gesù Nuovo

Santa Chiara

Piazza San Domenico Maggiore

To the east of the Gesù Nuovo, in Piazza San Domenico Maggiore, is the church of San Domenico Maggiore (*c.* 1300), which in spite of later alteration is still one of the most interesting churches in Naples, with much Early Renaissance work. In the Cappellone Crocifisso are a 13th c. "crucifixion" and a 15th c. "Burial of Christ". The sacristy contains 45 sarcophagi belonging to members of the house of Anjou.

San Domenico
Maggiore

The Capella Sansevero (museum), a little way east, was built in 1590 as the burial chapel of the Sangro family and elaborately embellished in Baroque style in the 18th c.; it contains some fine sculpture, including a "Christ in a winding-sheet" by Sammartino (1753).

*Capella
Sansevero

From Piazza San Domenico Maggiore the Via San Biagio dei Librai runs east: 300 m/330 yd along this street, on the left, is Via San Gregorio Armeno, in which stands the little church of San Gregorio Armeno (1580), one of the richest Baroque churches in Naples, with a cloister.

San Gregorio
Armeno

Via Biagio continues north-east and leads into Via del Duomo. Along this street to the right is the Palazzo Cuomo, a fine Early Renaissance

Palazzo Cuomo
Museum

285

building (1464–90) which now houses the Museo Filangieri, with arms, majolica, porcelain, enamel-work and pictures. On the opposite side of the street, a little farther north-east, is the church of San Giorgio Maggiore, founded in the 5th c. and rebuilt in the 17th c.

*Cathedral

400 m/440 yd north, on the right-hand side of Via del Duomo, stands the cathedral, dedicated to St Januarius (San Gennaro), patron saint of Naples. Originally built between 1294 and 1323 in French Gothic style, it was considerably restored and altered after an earthquake in 1456. In the centre of the front, which dates from 1877 to 1905, is an older doorway (1407). In the south aisle is the sumptuously appointed chapel of St Januarius (1608-37), on the principal altar of which is a silver bust containing the skull of St Januarius, bishop of Beneventum, who was martyred in 305, in the time of Diocletian. In the tabernacle are two vessels containing the saint's blood, which is believed to have the power of liquefaction. The liquefaction, which, according to the legend, occurred for the first time when the saint's remains were transferred to Naples in the time of Constantine is said to take place twice a year on several successive days celebrated as special festivals (particularly on the first Saturday in May in the church of Santa Chiara and on 19 September in the cathedral). The saint's tomb can be seen in the richly decorated Confessio (1497–1506) under the high altar.

Archbishop's Palace To the left of the cathedral stands the Archbishop's Palace, and to the north of this, in Largo Donnaregina, is the Baroque church of Santa Maria Donnaregina (1649; no admission). Adjoining this church on the north is the older Gothic church of the same name (entrance at Vico Donnaregina 25), restored 1928–34, with the tomb of Queen Mary of Hungary (d. 1323) and fine frescoes by Giotto's contemporary Pietro Cavallini and his school (c. 1308) in the elevated nuns' choir.

Girolamini, San Paolo Maggiore West of the cathedral, in Via dei Tribunale, are two fine Baroque churches – the church of the Girolamini (Hieronymites) or of San Filippo Neri (1592–1619), with a collection of pictures, and San Paolo Maggiore (1590–1603), built on the ruins of a temple of the early Empire (remains on the façade).

San Lorenzo Maggiore To the south of San Paolo Maggiore, in Via San Gregorio Armeno, is the restored Gothic church of San Lorenzo Maggiore (1266–1324), with the fine tomb of Caterina d'Austria (d. 1323), and other tombs and frescoes. The adjoining Franciscan monastery, in which Petrarch stayed in 1345, has a notable cloister and a chapter-house decorated with frescoes.

Castel Capuano The Castel Capuano, usually known as the Vicaria, at the east end of Via dei Tribunali was a Hohenstaufen and later an Angevin stronghold which has been occupied since 1540 by law courts.

Santa Caterina a Formiello Opposite the north-east corner of the Castello is the domed church of Santa Caterina a Formiello (1519–93) and farther east the Porta Capuana, a beautiful Renaissance gateway (1485; further work 1535).

San Giovanni a Carbonara 500 m/550 yd north-west of the Castel Capuano, in Strada Carbonara, the former church of San Giovanni a Carbonara (begun 1343, enlarged in the 15th c., recently restored) contains the Gothic tomb of King Ladislaus (d. 1414).

South-east of Naples

Central Station A short distance south-east of the Porta Capuana in the spacious Piazza Garibaldi is the Central Station, built in 1960-64 some 250 m/275 yd east of the old station.

Santa Maria del Carmine From here the Corso Garibaldi runs south to Piazza G. Pepe, to the right of which stands the church of Santa Maria del Carmine, containing the tomb of Conradin of Hohenstaufen, Frederick II's grandson, who was beheaded at the age of sixteen. Above the tomb is a statue of Conradin from a design by Thorwaldsen (1847).

North-west of Santa Maria del Carmine, in the Piazza del Mercato, is the church of Santa Croce al Mercato, on the spot on which Conradin was executed on 29 October 1268 on the orders of Charles I of Anjou. Inside the church, to the left of the entrance, a commemorative porphyry column can be seen.

Santa Croce al
Mercato

From Piazza Garibaldi the broad Corso Umberto I runs south-west to the University, with its massive main building (1908) facing the street and behind it the former Jesuit college (1605) which was the only university building from 1777 to 1908. To the east is the church of Santi Severino e Sossio (1494; rebuilt 1731 onwards).

University

Corso Umberto I runs into the Piazza Giovanni Bovio, with the new Exchange and an old Fountain of Neptune.

Piazza Giovanni
Bovio

**Museo Archeologico Nazionale

From Piazza Dante the Via Enrico Pessina, the continuation of Via Roma, leads to the Museo Archeologico Nazionale (National Museum), with one of the world's finest collections of antiquities. The building, originally erected in 1585 as a barracks and from 1616 the home of the university, was converted in 1790 to house the royal collections. It contains the art treasures of the kings of Naples, the Farnese collections from Rome and Parma, the collections from the palaces of Portici and Capodimonte and material from Pompeii, Herculaneum and Cumae.

The ground floor is devoted mainly to the collection of sculpture in marble. Items of particular importance are the figures of Harmodius and Aristogeiton, a marble copy of a bronze group by Critius and Nesiotes (477 B.C.) which stood in the Agora in Athens; the so-called Hera Farnese, the head of a statue of Artemis in the earlier severe style; Orpheus and Eurydice with Hermes, a copy of a famous relief from the time of Phidias; and Pallas Athene, a copy of an original from the time of Phidias.

Ground floor
**Collection of
sculpture in marble

In the Galleria del Toro Farnese are the Farnese Hercules, a colossal statue 3.17 m/3½ ft high (after a 4th c. original) found in the Baths of Caracalla in Rome, and the Farnese Bull, the largest marble group which has come down to us from antiquity, a copy of a Rhodian work by Apollonius and Tauriscus (3rd–2nd c. B.C.).

On the mezzanine floor is the collection of ancient mosaics, mainly from Pompeii. Among the most notable items is the famous Alexander's Battle, a mosaic 6.20 m/6¾ yd long (copied from an important painting of the 4th c. B.C.) which was found in Pompeii in 1831. It shows Alexander, with his horsemen, charging the Persian king Darius at the battle of Issus (333 B.C.) and transfixing a Persian general who has been thrown from his horse, while Darius in his chariot prepares for flight.

Mezzanine floor
*Mosaics

On the first floor, in the central Salone dell'Atlante, is the Farnese Atlas. Here, too, is the collection of bronze sculpture, mostly from Herculaneum (recognisable by the dark patina) but also from Pompeii (with green oxidation). Particulary notable are "Apollo playing a lyre" (a 5th c. original from the Peloponnese, found in the Casa del Citarista in Pompeii), a "Dancing Faun" from the Casa del Fauno in Pompeii and the so-called "Narcissus", actually the youthful Dionysus, a masterpiece of the school of Praxiteles.

First Floor
**Bronze sculpture

Also on the first floor are the collection of ancient wall paintings, mainly from Herculaneum, Pompeii and Stabiae, and the small bronzes

**Wall paintings

287

(household utensils, etc.), together with terracottas and a large model of Pompeii (1879) on the scale of 1:1100.

The famous collection of erotic art from Pompeii can be seen by appointment only for the purposes of study.

*Collection of ancient vases

On the second floor is the collection of ancient vases, one of the largest of its kind. This collection is not open to the public but can be seen by appointment only for study purposes.

Corso Amedeo di Savoia

Santa Maria della Sanità

From the National Museum Via Santa Teresa degli Scalzi and the Corso Amedeo di Savoia run north, slightly uphill, to the park of Capodimonte, 2 km/1¼ miles away. In 750 m/820 yd it comes to the Ponte della Senità, a viaduct (lift) which carries the road over the low-lying Sanità district. Below, to the right, is the large domed church of Santa Maria della Sanità (1602–13), with the Catacombs of San Gaudioso (5th c.).

*Catacombs of San Gennaro

The Corso Amedeo di Savoia ends at a roundabout, the Tondo di Capodimonte, on the west side of which is the entrance to the 2nd c. Catacombs of San Gennaro. Like the Roman catacombs, these consist of a maze of passages and tomb chambers, but are more ambitious architecturally and have finer paintings than their Roman counterparts. The church of San Gennaro extra Moenia dates from the 5th c. (restored).

Madre del Buon Consiglio

From the Tondo di Capodimonte the Via Capodimonte, to the left, leads in 200 m/220 yd to the imposing pilgrimage church (on the left) of the Madre del Buon Consiglio (1920–60).

*Capodimonte Park

Palazzo Reale Museo di Capodimonte

Beyond this the road curves up to the Porta Grande, the main entrance to the magnificent Capodimonte Park. In the park is the Palazzo Reale di Capodimonte (1738–1838), commanding fine views. With over a hundred rooms, the palace houses the Capodimonte Museum (Galleria dell'Ottocento), with 19th c. pictures, arms and armour, porcelain, furniture, ivories and bronzes.

**Galleria Nazionale

Also in the palace is the National Gallery (Galleria Nazionale), one of the finest collections in Italy, with more than 500 pictures, including works by Titian (portraits of members of ruling families from the Farnese collection), Mantegna, Caravaggio, El Greco, Bellini and Neapolitan artists of the 17th and 18th c.

Vomero

Villa Floridiana Museum

To the west of the old town, on a plateau above the Corso Vittorio Emanuele, the district of Vomero, built from 1885 onwards, can be reached by a number of streets and three funiculars. In the southern part of this district is the Villa Floridiana public park, with the Museo Nazionale della Ceramica Duca di Martina, which contains enamels, ivories, pottery and porcelain from many different countries.

Castel Sant'Elmo

On the eastern edge of the Vomero plateau rises the Castel Sant'Elmo (224 m/739 ft), built in 1329 and extended in the 16th c., with massive walls and underground passages hewn from the rock; it is now used for exhibitions and general events.

*Carthusian monastery Museum

To the east of the castle is the former Carthusian monastery of San Martino (1325; rebuilt in the 17th c.), with the Museo Nazionale di San Martino. Notable features are the church, richly decorated with marble

Park of Capodimonte

and pictures of the 17th and 18th c., the sacristy, the treasury, the Chiostro dei Procuratori and the main cloisters, with 60 columns of white marble. The museum contains porcelain, cribs, including the Presepe di Cuciniello, a state coach of Charles III's reign (18th c.) and relics of the history of Naples and southern Italy in the 18th and 19th c. From the room known as the Belvedere there are superb views of Naples, its bay and Vesuvius extending to the Apennines.

*Camaldoli

The best view of Naples and its beautiful surroundings is to be had from the Camaldulensian monastery of Camaldoli, north-west of the city on the highest point in the Phlegraean Fields (458 m/1511 ft). The monastery was founded in 1585. The prospect from the terrace on a clear day is one of the finest in Italy.

Situation
11 km/7 miles
north-west

The same view can be enjoyed from the Belvedere della Pagliarella, 500 m/550 yd south, reached in 15 minutes by a footpath through the scrub.

Belvedere della
Pagliarella

*Posillipo

South-west of Naples is Posillipo, a ridge of hills 6 km/4 miles long, covered with villas and gardens, between the Bay of Naples and the Bay of Pozzuoli, with magnificent views. The name comes from a villa called Pausilypon ("Sans-Souci") which belonged to the notorious epicure Vedius Pollio and later to Augustus.

Situation
12 km/7 miles
south-west

From Via Caracciolo, which ends in Mergellina, the Via di Posillipo runs south-west above the sea. Climbing slightly, it comes in 4 km/2½ miles,

Parco della
Rimembranze

after passing the end of Via Boccaccio, to the Parco della Rimembranze (153 m/835 ft), lying at the south-west end of the ridge almost vertically above the sea and the rocky volcanic island of Nisida. From the road encircling the park there are beautiful views.

Mergellina

Via Boccaccio runs uphill into Via Manzoni, from which Via Petrarca continues gently downhill, affording extensive views, to Via Orazio. On the upper part of this road to the left is the pilgrimage church of Sant'Antonio, from which there is a famous view of Naples. Beyond this the road descends to the suburb of Mergellina, with a picturesque harbour, Porto Sannazzaro (hydrofoil services to Capri and Ischia). A little way north, at the exits of two tunnels through the hill of Posillipo, are the Piazza Sannazzaro and the Piazza di Piedigrotta, where stands the church of Santa Maria di Piedigrotta (13th c.), with a Renaissance cloister (famous traditional fiesta from September 5th–13th: principal celebrations on September 7th). To the west of the church, immediately beyond the railway underpass, is the entrance (on the left) to the Parco Virgiliano, in which are the tomb of the poet Giacomo Leopardi (1798–1837) and a Roman structure (actually the columbarium of an unknown family) known as the Tomb of Virgil (70–19 B.C.), who had a villa on Posillipo and desired to be buried there.

Fuorigrotta

From the entrance to the park the Galleria delle Quattro Giornate leads west to the suburb of Fuorigrotta, with huge blocks of apartments, a stadium (1959) seating 100,000 spectators, the new buildings of the Technical University (1965) and the Mostra d'Oltremare complex, a large exhibition centre, with two theatres, a swimming pool, an illuminated fountain, a zoo and a large amusement park, Edenlandia.

Pozzuoli

Situation
27 km/17 miles west

West of Naples, over the Posillipo, is Pozzuoli (28 m/92 ft; pop. 71,000), a port situated on the slopes of a tufa ridge projecting into the sea, on the edge of the area of volcanic hills known as the Phlegraean Fields. Founded in the 6th c. B.C. by Greeks from Samos, it passed in the hands of the Romans in 318 B.C. and as Puteoli developed into the principal Italian port for trade with Egypt and the East. In the old town, which is situated on a peninsula, is the cathedral of San Procolo (destroyed by fire in 1964; not open to the public), which was built on the site of a temple of the 3rd–2nd c. B.C. and has ancient columns. It contains the tomb of the composer Pergolesi (1710–36).

*Serapeum

500 m/550 yd north, on the sea, is the so-called Serapeum, an ancient market (macellum), which preserves some columns of its colonnade. South-west of the Serapeum are baths. In the harbour to the north-west remains of a temple with 14 columns and a sculptor's workshop were discovered on the sea-bed. Above the old town, on the left of the road to Naples, is the Roman Amphitheatre (149 m/164 yd long, 116 m/127 yd across; seating for 40,000). Particularly impressive are the underground passages which housed the machinery and the wild beasts' dens. The arena (72 m/79 yd long, 42 m/46 yd across) could be filled with water for naval battles.

Solfatara

1.5 km/1 mile east, near the road from Naples, is the entrance to the Solfatara, a semi-extinct volcano (only recorded eruption 1198). This is a circular area enclosed by tufa hills, with numerous fissures which emit steam and sulphurous gases. The ground sounds hollow. The temperature of the largest fumarole is 162 °C/324 °F, of the smaller ones around 100 °C/212 °F. The volume of vapour is considerably increased if a piece of burning paper or a torch is held at the mouth of one of the vents.

Solfatara, a semi-extinct volcano

6 km/4 miles west of Pozzuoli is Baia (pop. 6000), prettily situated on the west side of the Bay of Pozzuoli. As Baiae this was the most fashionable watering-place of Imperial Rome, and impressive palaces dating from this period have been excavated. At the near end of the town, amid vineyards to the right of the road, is the so-called Temple of Mercury, a large circular building with a vaulted roof open in the centre, adjoining which are the Baths of Mercury. Farther on, to the right, are the Baths of Sosandra, with the semicircular Theatre of the Nymphs and a statue of Sosandra. Immediately west are the Baths of Venus, opposite the so-called Temple of Venus.

Baia

2 km/1¼ miles south-east of Baia along the west side of the Bay of Pozzuoli (on the left the 16th c. Castello di Baia) we come to Bacoli (pop. 25,000). On a tongue of land 500 m/550 yd east is a two-storey Roman structure known as the Cento Camerelle, the upper storey of which was a cistern.

Bacoli

500 m/550 yd south of Bacoli, above the Mare Morte, is the Piscina Mirabilis, an excellently preserved Roman reservoir 70 m/77 yd long by 25.5 m/28 yd wide, with a vaulted roof borne on 48 massive pillars.

Piscina Mirabilis

From the nearby village of Miseno it is a half hour's climb to the top of Monte Miseno (167 m/551 ft), a curiously shaped crater rising out of the sea, described by Virgil as the tomb of Aeneas's trumpeter Misenus, from which there is one of the finest views of the Bay of Naples and Gaeta.

Miseno

There are also very fine views from Capo Miseno (79 m/261 ft), half an hour south. Near here was Lucullus's villa, in which the Emperor Tiberius died.

Capo Miseno

*Cumae

Situation	35 km/22 miles west of Naples are the remains of Cumae (Italian Cuma, Greek Kyme), the oldest Greek settlement in Italy, founded in the 9th or 8th c. B.C. and destroyed by the Saracens in the 9th c. A.D. The site has been excavated since 1926. Beyond a short tunnel, to the right, is the so-called Roman Crypt, a tunnel of Augustan date, 180 m/197 yd long, which runs under the acropolis to the sea. Opposite this, to the left, is the entrance of the Cave of the Sibyl (Antro della Sibilla), described by Virgil (Aeneid VI, 43 ff.) as having a hundred entrances and a hundred issues, "from which resound as many voices, the oracles of the prophetess". This is a passage hewn from the rock, 131 m/143 yd long, 2.5 m/2¾ yd wide and 5 m/17 ft high, with numerous side passages opening on to the sea which provide light and air. At the far end is the actual cave of the oracle, a square chamber with three vaulted recesses. From the Cave of the Sibyl a ramp leads up to the acropolis. The road leads past a lookout terrace to the remains of the Temple of Apollo and beyond this, on the summit of the hill, the ruins of a Temple of Jupiter which was used as a church in early Christian times. From the top of the hill there are magnificent views of the sea, extending as far as Gaeta and the Isole Ponziane, and of the Phlegraean Fields to the east.
	On the south side of the excavated area is the Amphitheatre (129 m/141 yd long, 104 m/114 yd across, 21 rows of seats).
	To the south-east is the Lago del Fusaro, linked with the sea by two canals, a shallow lake (8 m/26 ft deep) which is used for oyster-culture.

**From Naples to Amalfi and Salerno (about 97 km/60 miles)

	One excursion which no visitor to Naples should miss is the beautiful drive on S.S. 18 to Amalfi and Salerno (the motorway is shorter but less attractive).
Portici	10 km/6 miles east of Naples is Portici (26 m/86 ft; pop. 83,000), with a former royal palace which now houses the Faculty of Agriculture of Naples University.
Herculaneum	1 km/¾ mile: main entrance to the excavations of Herculaneum (see entry).
Torre del Greco	3 km/2 miles: Torre del Greco (51 m/168 ft; pop. 105,000), which has in the course of its history been repeatedly covered with lava or destroyed by earthquakes.
Torre Annunziata	8 km/5 miles: Torre Annunziata (14 m/46 ft; pop. 60,000), with a villa painted in Pompeian style, a relic of the Roman town of Oplontis. This is the starting point for the ascent to Vesuvius.
Castellammare di Stabia	9 km/5½ miles: Castellammare di Stabia (5 m/17 ft; pop. 73,000), a port built at the foot and on the lower slopes of an outlier of Monte Sant'Angelo, occupying the site of the Roman Stabiae, which was destroyed together with Pompeii in A.D. 79 (recent excavations; museum). The town is a favourite resort of the Neapolitans on account of its mineral springs, impregnated with sulphur and carbonic acid gas. In the Piazza del Municipio is the 16th c. cathedral. In the south-west of the town are the harbour, with a long breakwater, and the spa establishments, with a ruined castle (13th c.) on the hill above. In the Scanzano district, above the cathedral to the east, are the new Baths.
Monte Faito	Above Castellammare to the south-east (½ hour) is the beautiful park of the Villa Quisisana ("Here you recover your health"); the house is at the south-east end of the park. From here there is an attractive drive (12 km/7 miles; also cableway) up Monte Faito (1131 m/3732 ft; view), to the south.

Positano

Beyond Castellammare the Amalfi road runs close to the coast again, affording magnificent views of the Bay of Naples, Vesuvius and the steep rock coast of the Sorrento peninsula.

15 km/9 miles: Meta (111 m/366 ft; pop. 7000). The road then goes over a pass (310 m/1023 ft) in the Monti Lattari to reach the south side of the Sorrento peninsula, looking on to the Bay of Salerno. The following stretch of road as far as Salerno, blasted out of the rocky coast high above the sea, is one of the most beautiful roads in the world, its charm enhanced by the many little towns and villages in a rather Oriental style of architecture which cling to the precipitous slopes. Out to sea, as the road reaches the coast, can be seen the little "Isles of the Sirens", usually known as Li Galli.

Meta

13 km/8 miles: Positano (30 m/99 ft; pop. 3000), a very picturesque little town extending up the steep rocky slopes above the sea, with square flat-roofed houses reminiscent of the Saracen period. From here the road continues along the wild and rugged coast, passing several old watch-towers on the coast below.

Positano

15 km/9 miles: Amalfi (see entry).

Amalfi

Beyond Amalfi the road skirts the Capo d'Amalfi and along a stretch which is almost entirely blasted out of the cliffs or carried over gorges on viaducts, affording splendid views.

4 km/2½ miles: Minori, once the arsenal of Amalfi has a Roman villa (1st c. A.D.) with well-preserved wall paintings.

Minori

1 km/¾ mile: Maiori (15 m/50 ft; pop. 6000), a popular resort at the mouth of the Tramonti valley. On the coast near the town are a sulphur spring and a number of stalactitic caves, including the Grotta Pandona, which resembles the Blue Grotto on Capri.

Maiori

10 km/6 miles: Cetara (15 m/50 ft), a fishing village picturesquely situated in a deep ravine which was the first settlement established by the Saracens.

Cetara

293

Salerno   8 km/5 miles: Salerno (see entry).

From Naples to Nola and Montevergine (about 55 km/34 miles)

Nola
There is also a very attractive trip (28 km/17 miles east) from Naples to Nola (34 m/112 ft; pop. 32,000), where St Paulinus (354–431), a native of Bordeaux and an accomplished poet, is said to have invented the church-bell (hence the Italian word for a bell, campana, Nola being in Campania); his feast, the Festa dei Gigli ("Feast of Lilies"), is celebrated with great pomp on the last Sunday in June. In the Piazza del Duomo is a bronze statue of Augustus, who died here in A.D. 14. The cathedral, built over the remains of an ancient temple and rebuilt in 1870 after a fire, has a fine crypt. In the Piazza Giordano Bruno is a monument to the philosopher Giordano Bruno, born in Nola in 1548, who was burned at the stake in 1600 in Rome as a heretic.

Montevergine
20 km/12 miles east of Nola on the road to Avellino is a side road leading north (5 km/3 miles) to the pilgrimage centre of Montevergine (1270 m/4191 ft; cableway from Mercogliano). In the church of the monastery founded by St William of Vercelli in 1119 on the ruins of a Temple of Cybele are a number of fine tombs and, in the south aisle, a chapel with a figure of the Virgin venerated as miraculous; the head of the figure is Byzantine. Pilgrimages take place at Easter and on September 7th–8th.

It is a 45 minutes' climb from the monastery to the top of Montevergine (1493 m/4927 ft), crowned by a large cross, from which there are magnificent views of the Bay of Naples and Salerno and the mountains of the interior.

Novara   E4

Region: Piemonte
Province: Novara (NO)
Altitude: 159 m/525 ft
Population: 102,000

Situation
The provincial capital of Novara lies in the Piedmontese plain between the rivers Sesia (to the west) and Ticino (to the east). The distance between Novara and the more easterly situated city of Milan is some 40 km/25 miles.
Novara is an industrial town with a varied range of industry and a large map-making institute (De Agostini).

Sights

Cathedral
The town is surrounded by a ring of attractive boulevards on the line of the old fortifications. In the centre of the town, in the arcaded Via Fratelli Rosselli, stands the cathedral, built between 1865 and 1869 in place of an earlier church. The relief on the main altar is by Thorwaldsen.
It has an attractive cloister, entered from the south aisle. There is an important museum, the Museo Lapidario and to the west of the cathedral, opposite the imposing entrance court is a 5th c. baptistery, with 10th c. frescoes.

Corso Italia
North of the cathedral, reached by way of the beautiful courtyard of the Broletto (Municipal Museum and Art Gallery), is the Corso Italia, one of the town's two main traffic arteries (the other being the Corso Cavour).

A little way north of the Broletto, at the end of Via Gaudenzio Ferrari, the church of San Gaudenzio (by Pellegrino Tibaldi, 1577) has a prominent dome (1875–78).

West of the cathedral is the large Piazza Martiri della Livertà, with the Teatro Coccia and the Palazzo del Mercato (1840). On the south side is the rebuilt Castello Sforzesco.

Varallo Sesia

There is a very attractive drive (north-west) up the Sesia valley to Varallo Sesia (450 m/1485 ft; pop. 8000), charmingly situated in the Pre-Alps at the mouth of the narrow valley of the Mastallone, the birthplace of the painter Gaudenzio Ferrari (c. 1480–1546). The collegiate church of San Gaudenzio is picturesquely situated on a crag and another fine church, the church of Santa Maria delle Grazie, has frescoes by Gaudenzio Ferrari (1507–13).

Situation
56 km/35 miles
north-west

At Santa Maria begins the ascent, with Stations of the Cross, to the Sacro Monte (608 m/2006 ft). On the summit of the hill are 44 chapels with painted terracotta groups and frescoes depicting scenes from the scriptural story; in the 38th chapel is a Crucifixion by Gaudenzio Ferrari.

*Sacro Monte

36 km/22 miles beyond Varallo, beautifully situated at the head of the Sesia valley, is Alagna Valsesia, from which a cableway (20 minutes) runs up via Zaroltu (1825 m/6023 ft) and the Bocchetta delle Pisse (2406 m/7940 ft) to the Punta Indren (3260 m/10,758 ft), a southern outlier of Monte Rosa.

Alagna Valsesia

Lake Orta

North of Novara is Lake Orta, the Roman Lacus Cucius (area 18 sq. km/sq. miles, greatest depth 143 m/472 ft), the southern end of which is particularly beautiful.

Situation
45 km/28 miles north

In a picturesque setting at the foot of the Monte d'Orta or Sacro Monte di San Francesco (401 m/1323 ft; 20 pilgrimage chapels; view of Monte Rosa) is the little town of Orta San Giulio (293 m/967 ft; pop. 1000). In the main square is the Town Hall (1592); from the west end of the square there is a beautiful view of the Isola San Giulio, with a church traditionally said to have been founded by St Julius in 390 (rebuilt in the 11th and 12th c.). There is a pleasant drive up Monte Mottarone (1491 m/4920 ft), from which there are panoramic views.

Orta San Giulio

Vercelli

South of Novara is the old town of Vercelli (131 m/432 ft; pop. 53,000), the Roman Vercellae; it is the see of an archbishop, the centre of the largest rice-growing area in Europe and has many fine old churches. In the north of the town, near the station, stands the cathedral, re-modelled in Baroque style, with the exception of the tower, from the 16th c. onwards; the cathedral library contains valuable manuscripts. A short distance south-west is the imposing four-towered church of Sant'Andrea (1219–24), one of Italy's first buildings in Gothic style. The adjoining Cistercian abbey has a beautiful cloister. In the southern part of the town is the Dominican church of San Cristoforo, with frescoes by Gaudenzio Ferrari. The Museo Borgogna has fine work of Renaissance painters from Vercelli and its surrounding, as well as pictures by other Italian painters.

Situation
23 km/14 miles south
of Novara

South of Vercelli, on the road to Casale, were the Campi Raudii, where the Roman consul Marius defeated the Cimbri in 101 b.c.

From Novara to Vigevano (about 55 km/34 miles)

Magenta	31 km/19 miles east of Novara is Magenta (138 m/455 ft; pop. 24,000), scene of the famous battle on June 4th 1859 in which the French and Piedmontese defeated the Austrians, who thereupon withdrew from Lombardy (church of San Martino, built in 1903 to commemorate the victory; charnel-house).
Abbiategrasso	9 km/5½ miles south of Magenta in Abbiategrasso (120 m/396 ft; pop. 27,000) stands the fine parish church of San Maria Nuova (façade by Bramante, 1497).
Vigevano Piazza Ducale	12 km/7 miles south-west of Abbiategrasso is Vigevano (116 m/383 ft; pop. 66,000). In the Piazza Ducale, the central square designed by Bramante, are arcades which still preserve remains of their Early Renaissance decoration. Other features of interest are the 16th c. cathedral, the Visconti castle, rebuilt by Bramante and da Vinci in 1491–1494, and the Church of San Pietro Martire with a fine campanile.

Orvieto I7

Region: Umbria
Province: Terni (TR)
Altitude: 325 m/1073 ft
Population: 23,000

Situation	The Umbrian town of Orvieto lies some 100 km/60 miles north of Rome. The town was built on a tufa crag which rears up out of the Paglia valley. The white wine of Orvieto is renowned.
History	Founded by the Etruscans, the town was known in late antiquity as Urbibentum or Urbs Vetus, and later became a stronghold of the Guelf party, where the Popes frequently sought refuge.

**Cathedral

	The Cathedral (begun before 1285), in the south-east of the town, in the Piazza del Duomo, one of the most splendid examples of Italian Gothic architecture, was built in alternating courses of black basalt and greyish-yellow limestone and decorated by the finest artists of the day. It was founded in 1290 in honour of the "miracle of Bolsena" and consecrated in 1309. The façade, begun in 1310 but not completed until the 16th c., is decorated with scenes from the Old and New Testaments by Sienese artists (14th c.) and mosaics of overwhelming richness (originally 14th c., mostly restored in the 19th c.) including the "coronation of the Virgin" on the tympanum. The intricately carved modern bronze doors are by Emilio Greco (1969).
**Cappella Nuova	In the richly decorated interior is the Cappella Nuova or Cappella della Madonna di San Brizio, with frescoes (Apocalyptic visions), begun by Fra Angelico da Fiesole in 1447 but mainly painted by Luca Signorelli from 1499 onwards, which are among the supreme achievements of 15th c. painting.
*Reliquary	Behind the altar of the Cappella del Corporale is a reliquary (1338) containing the bloodstained chalice-cloth of the "miracle of Bolsena", which is displayed only on Easter Day and Corpus Christi.
Palazzo Soliano (Museum)	To the right of the cathedral is the Palazzo Soliano (1297–1304), with the Museo dell'Opera del Duomo containing pictures and sculpture from the cathedral; also worth seeing is the interesting archaeological section of the museum.
Palazzo Faina	Facing the cathedral is the Palazzo Faina which houses the Municipal Museum, with a collection of Etruscan and Greek vases.

Orvieto: Façade of the Cathedral and . . .   *. . . Interior*

Corso Cavour

From the cathedral the Via del Duomo runs north-west into the Corso Cavour, the main street of the town, which traverses it from east to west. At the junction of the two streets rises the Torre del Moro, a quadrangular tower over 40 m/132 ft high.

Torre del Moro

A short distance north of the Torre del Moro is the Piazza del Capitano del Popolo, with the 11th c. Palazzo del Popolo, built in volcanic tufa stone; in front of the crenellated façade is a flight of steps.

*Palazzo del Popolo

At the west end of Corso Cavour is the busy Piazza della Repubblica, with the church of Sant'Andrea (12-sided 11th c. tower) and the massive Palazzo Comunale (12th c.; façade rebuilt in 16th c.).

Palazzo Comunale

*Pozzo di San Patrizio

At the east end of the town, to the north of the Fortezza (now public gardens), can be seen the Pozzo di San Patrizio (1527–37 by Sangallo the Elder), a well 61 m/67 yd deep with two separate spiral staircases winding round the shaft, one for the descent and the other for the ascent of the donkeys which brought up water from the well.

Etruscan buildings and necropolis

Nearby the Pozzo di San Patrizio are the remains of the Tempio Etrusco. Below the north side of the town, to the left of the road to the station, is an interesting Etruscan necropolis (Tombe Etrusche del Crocifisso del Tufo), with tombs mostly dating from the 5th c. B.C.

Another Etruscan necropolis can be found to the south of the town (Tombe Etrusche di Cannicella).

Ostia I8

Region: Lazio
Province: Roma (ROMA)
Altitude: 3 m/10 ft

Warning

Thefts from cars and attacks on visitors, in public places and in broad daylight, are a frequent occurrence in Ostia.

Situation

Ostia, the port of ancient Rome, now lying 5 km/3 miles inland from the Tyrrhenian Sea and close to Fiumicino Airport, is the largest excavation site in Italy after Pompeii.

History

The excavated remains of Ostia give a vivid picture of life in the port which supplied Rome. Ancient Ostia was founded about the 4th c. B.C. in an area of salt-pans at the mouth (ostia) of the Tiber. From about 300 B.C. it was the principal Roman naval base, and under the Empire developed into a considerable town of 70,000-80,000 inhabitants and was Rome's largest suburb and commercial port, through which the city's supplies of corn were brought in. After the fall of the Roman

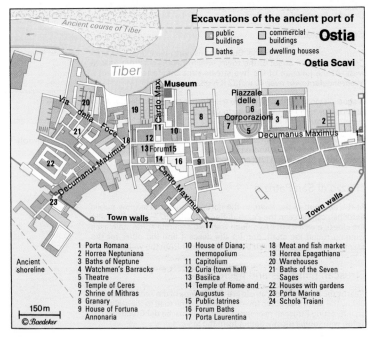

Excavations of the ancient port of **Ostia**

- public buildings
- baths
- commercial buildings
- dwelling houses

Ostia Scavi

1 Porta Romana
2 Horrea Neptuniana
3 Baths of Neptune
4 Watchmen's Barracks
5 Theatre
6 Temple of Ceres
7 Shrine of Mithras
8 Granary
9 House of Fortuna Annonaria
10 House of Diana; thermopolium
11 Capitolium
12 Curia (town hall)
13 Basilica
14 Temple of Rome and Augustus
15 Public latrines
16 Forum Baths
17 Porta Laurentina
18 Meat and fish market
19 Horrea Epagathiana
20 Warehouses
21 Baths of the Seven Sages
22 Houses with gardens
23 Porta Marina
24 Schola Traiani

Ancient shoreline

150 m

© Baedeker

Empire Ostia fell a victim to decay and the ravages of malaria. The harbour silted up, and in 1558 the Tiber changed its course.

The excavated remains date mainly from the 2nd–4th c. A.D., i.e. the period following the destruction of Pompeii. In contrast to Pompeii with its single-storey houses occupied by separate families Ostia's swarming population was housed in blocks of apartments (insulae) several storeys high, with numerous windows opening on to the street and on to the interior garden and often with loggias and balconies facing the street – typical examples of the architecture of Imperial Rome.

Recent excavations have brought to light a 4th c. Christian basilica measuring 43 × 16 m/47 × 18 yd, similar in style to the basilicas erected in Rome in the reign of Constantine.

*Excavation area Ostia Scavi

Just beyond the main entrance of the excavation area of Ostia Scavi (closed Mondays), along the ancient Via Ostiensis and in the parallel street to the south, the Via delle Tombe (even more impressive), are rows of tombs, both individual tombs, sometimes of considerable size, and columbaria with niches for large numbers of urns. The Via Ostiensis leads to the remains of the Porta Romana, the most important of the town's three gates.

Tombs

The Decumanus Maximus, the main street of ancient Ostia, more than 1 km/¾ mile long starts here. Beyond the gate, on the left, is the Piazzale della Vittoria, named after the statue of Minerva Victoria (1st c. A.D.) which was found here.

Decumanus Maximus

Further along, at the corner of Via dei Vigili (on right), are the Baths of Neptune, with heating arrangements at the north-east corner (good general view from a terrace on the first floor). At the end of Via dei Vigili, on the left, are the Watchmen's Barracks (2nd c. A.D.), with an imposing central courtyard.

Baths of Neptune

Continuing along the Decumanus past the Baths, we come to the Theatre, originally built in the time of Augustus and enlarged under Septimius Severus, which was adapted in 1927 to accommodate theatrical performances in the summer. From the highest tier of seating there is a good view of the excavations, particularly of the Piazzale delle Corporazioni immediately north of the theatre, with the columns of the Temple of Ceres. Along the east side of this square are the offices (scholae) of the various shipping corporations trading with overseas ports, mainly in Africa.

Theatre

To the west of the theatre is the House of Marcus Apuleius Marcellus (2nd–3rd c. A.D.), with a peristyle and atrium of Pompeian type. Adjoining it on the north is a shrine of Mithras.

Farther along the Decumanus, on the right, are four small temples built on an older substructure, with a large granary (Grandi Horrea) to the west. Beyond this, also on the right-hand side of the Decumanus, is a well-preserved Thermopolium, a bar with a stone counter containing basins for cooling the drinks and tiers of shelves for drinking vessels.

Temples

Beyond the Thermopolium, to the right, the imposing Capitolium (2nd c. A.D.) was the religious centre of the town. Standing on a high brick base, this was the only building of ancient Ostia which remained above ground throughout the Middle Ages.

Capitolium

To the south of the Capitolium is the Forum, in the centre of the town at the intersection of the Decumanus with the Cardo Maximus, the principal transverse street. On the south side of the Forum are the remains of the Temple of Roma and Augustus (1st c. A.D.), with a statue of the victorious Roma. To the west, beyond a basilica, is a rotunda (3rd c.

Forum

Ostia: the Capitol

A.D.) in the style of the Pantheon. South-east of the Forum are large 2nd c. Baths.

Museo Ostiense

At the north end of the Cardo Maximus is the interesting Museo Ostiense (access road), with a rich collection of excavated material.

At the south-east end of the Cardo Maximus is the triangular Campo della Magna Mater, with a temple of the 2nd–3rd c. A.D. A short distance south-east is the well-preserved Porta Laurentina and 150 m/164 yd north the Domus della Fortuna Annonaria (3rd–4th c. A.D.).

On the right of the Decumanus, west of the Capitolium, is a bazaar, a courtyard surrounded by eighteen shops. To the north of this lay the Small Market.

100 m/110 yd west of the Capitolium is the ancient west gate, and close by, towards the Tiber, are the Horrea Epagathiana, privately owned warehouses with a handsome gateway and a two-storey arcaded courtyard.

Beyond the west gate is an area excavated between 1938 and 1942. Notable features here are the House of Serapis (2nd c. A.D.), with upper storeys, in Via della Foce, off the Decumanus on the right; the Baths of the Seven Sages (large circular mosaic), the Terme della Trinacria (mosaics) and the House of the Charioteer.

The Decumanus Maximus ends some 300 m/330 yd south-west of the west gate at the Porta Marina (car park).

Beyond this excavation has brought to light remains of the harbour.

Ostia Antica

To the east of the excavations, on the line of the ancient Via Ostiensis, is the modern town of Ostia Antica (pop. 5000), dominated by a castle built in 1483–86 to protect the harbour, a fine example of medieval Italian military architecture (Museo della Rocca). Adjacent to the castle is the 15th c. church of Santa Aurea.

Lido di Ostia

South-west of Ostia Antica, on the Tyrrhenian Sea, the seaside resort of Lido di Ostia has a beach 7 km/4 miles long.
From here a road runs south-east past the Parco di Castel Fusano to the resort of Lido di Castel Fusano, 4 km/2½ miles from Lido di Ostia, at the end of the expressway from Rome, the Via Cristoforo Colombo.

Situation
4 km/2½ miles
south-west
Lido di Castel
Fusano

Padua/Padova

H4

Region: Veneto
Province: Padova (PD)
Altitude: 12 m/40 ft
Population: 231,000

The provincial capital of Padua (Padova) lies 30 km/19 miles west of Venice on the edge of the Euganean Hills.

Situation

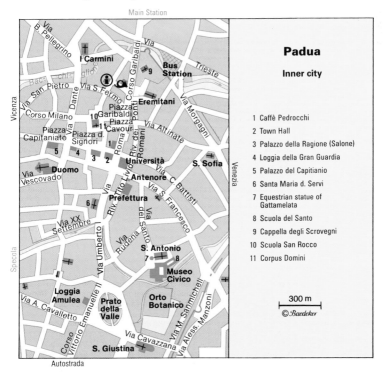

Padua

Inner city

1 Caffè Pedrocchi
2 Town Hall
3 Palazzo della Ragione (Salone)
4 Loggia della Gran Guardia
5 Palazzo del Capitianio
6 Santa Maria d. Servi
7 Equestrian statue of Gattamelata
8 Scuola del Santo
9 Cappella degli Scrovegni
10 Scuola San Rocco
11 Corpus Domini

300 m
© Baedeker

The older part of the town has a medieval aspect with its narrow arcaded streets, ancient bridges over the many arms of the River Bacchiglione and the Byzantine domes of its churches.

History and art

Under the early Empire the Roman Patavium was one of the wealthiest cities in Italy. It was destroyed by the Huns in 452, but thereafter enjoyed a further period of prosperity. In 1164 it became the first town in northern Italy to free itself from Hohenstaufen rule. During the subsequent conflicts it usually supported the Guelfs. In 1318 it passed into the hands of the house of Carrara, and in 1405 was annexed by Venice.

The Roman historian Livy lived in Padua and died there in A.D. 7. In the early 13th c. the eloquent preacher St Antony (b. in Lisbon 1195, d. 1231 at Arcella, 2.5 km/1½ miles north of Padua) lived and worked in Padua. The town's importance during the medieval period and at the Renaissance rested mainly on its university, founded in 1222 and extended by Frederick II in 1238, which became the first centre of humanism and also exerted a great attraction on artists.

During the 14th c. the finest works of art produced in Padua were by incomers like Giotto, Giovanni Pisano and Altichiero; and the great flowering of art in the 15th c. was due to Florentine artists, among them Donatello, Paolo Uccello and Andrea del Castagno, who influenced sculptors as well as the great painter Andrea Mantegna (1431–1506).

Centre

In the centre of the old town is the Piazza Cavour, from which the busy Via III Febbraio runs south. On the right is the neo-classical Caffè Pedrocchi (rebuilt after the Second World War), which when it was first opened in 1831 was the largest café in Europe. It played an important part in the history of the Risorgimento, and is still the resort of professors and students of the university.

Palazzo Municipale

Beyond this, farther south, stands the Palazzo Municipale (Town Hall), with a façade of 1930 and an older building to the rear (16th c.).

University

Opposite the Town Hall, on the east side of Via III Febbraio, is the University, built in the 16th c. In the colonnaded courtyard (1552) and inside the building are numerous names and coats of arms of distinguished graduates. Beside the Great Hall are the chairs of Galileo and other famous professors, and the Anatomy Theatre (1594), the oldest of its kind.

* Salone

From the university two streets run west, leading respectively to the Piazza delle Frutta and the Piazza delle Erbe. Between the two squares we find the Salone or Palazzo della Ragione, built 1218–19 as a law court, now an exhibition and conference hall (entrance from the Piazza delle Erbe, on the right). The huge hall, rebuilt in 1430, contains a large wooden horse (c. 1466), a copy of Gattamelata's horse in Donatello's famous statue, and astrological frescoes (15th c. restored) on the walls.

Piazza dei Signori

Loggia del Consigli

Farther west is the Piazza dei Signori, in which can be seen the Loggia del Consigli or Loggia della Gran Guardia, an elegant Early Renaissance building with an open loggia below and a closed upper storey (1496–1523).

Palazzo del Capitanio

On the west side of the square is the Palazzo del Capitanio, formerly the seat of the Venetian governor, with a fine clock-tower and remains of a Late Gothic loggia which belonged to the earlier Carrara palace.

Cathedral

To the west of the Piazza dei Signori stands the cathedral, a High Renaissance building (1552–77) with an unfinished façade. To the right of the cathedral the elegant brick-built Baptistery (13th c.) has interesting frescoes by Giusto de' Menabuoi (*c.* 1375).

**Church of Sant'Antonio

South-west of the university, beyond the wide modern streets (Riviera Vittorio Tito and Riviera dei Ponti Romani) built over an arm of the Bacchiglione, is the Prefecture. In front of this is a medieval sarcophagus (1233), popularly called the Tomb of Antenor, the mythical founder of Padua. To the east is the Via del Santo, which runs south to the Piazza del Santo, with the church of Sant'Antonio (Basilica del Santo), known as "il Santo" for short, containing the Tomb of St Antony of Padua, a shrine visited by countless pilgrims. The massive structure (13th–14th c.), a pillared basilica which shows a fantastic mingling of Romanesque, Gothic and Byzantine features, is highly picturesque, with its two slender towers, the conical dome over the crossing and seven other round domes (heightened in 1424).

Prefecture

The interior contains interesting works of art. In the north aisle is the Cappella di Sant'Antonio (1500–46), with nine 16th c. high reliefs (scenes from the life of St Antony, by Jacopo Sansovino, Antonio and Tullio Lombardi and others); within the altar, hung with numerous ex-votos, are the saint's remains. The high altar, originally by Donatello (1443–50), was subsequently removed but restored in 1895 with the original sculpture (angel musicians, entombment and bronze figures by Donatello). On the left of the altar is a magnificent bronze candelabrum by Briosco (1507–15). Beyond the ambulatory in the Cappella del Tesoro or Cappella delle Reliquie (1690) are fine examples of goldsmith's work.

Padua: Basilica of St Anthony's Cathedral

303

Equestrian statue of Gattamelata

On the south side of the church are four beautiful cloisters (13th–16th c.), the first of which in particular contains many old gravestones.

**Equestrian statue of Gattamelata

To the side of the church stands the equestrian statue of Gattamelata. Donatello, the talented sculptor of the Early Renaissance, who worked in Padua from 1441 to 1453, created the bronze statue between 1447 and 1453 in honour of Erasmo da Narni. The latter was commander-in-chief of the Venetian army (against Milan) and his diplomatic skill earned him the name of "Gattamelata" (spotted cat).

Scuola di Sant'Antonio

On the south side of the Piazza del Santo is the Scuola di Sant'Antonio, on the first floor of which are seventeen frescoes (mostly repainted) depicting the saint's miracles. In the adjoining Oratorio San Giorgio are frescoes by Altichieri and Avanzi.

Botanic Garden

South of the Scuola di Sant'Antonio lies the Botanic Garden, one of the oldest in Europe.

Basilica di Santa Giustina

A short distance from the Botanic Garden in the centre of a spacious square, the Prato della Valle, is an oval planted with trees which contains 82 statues of distinguished citizens of Padua and students of the university. In the south-east corner stands the imposing church of Santa Giustina (1518–87), in High Renaissance style. Behind the high altar is a fine painting by Paolo Veronese ("Martyrdom of St Justina", *c.* 1575); there are fine carved stalls (*c.* 1560) in the choir.

Piazza Garibaldi

Just north of Piazza Cavour is the busy Piazza Garibaldi, from which Via Emanuele Filiberto, runs west to the Piazza dell'Insurrezione, now the city's busiest traffic intersection; this was laid out after the Second World War and is surrounded by tall modern buildings. To the south are the church of Santa Lucia and the Scuola di San Rocco (frescoes).

Piazza dell'Insurrezione

North-east of Piazza Garibaldi is the former Augustinian church of the Eremitani (13th c., restored after war damage), with remains of frescoes by Mantegna in the Cappella Ovetari.

Chiesa degli Eremitani

Immediately north of the church is the chapel of the Madonna dell' Arena, built in 1303–05 as the chapel of a palace which was demolished around 1820; the chapel is also known as the Cappella degli Scrovegni, and contains Giotto's splendid frescoes (scenes from the life of the Virgin and the life of Christ; 1303–06), which are his earliest, largest and best preserved work. Particularly fine are the "Kiss of Judas" and the "Lamentation" in the third row, depicting the Passion with great dramatic force. On the altar is a "Madonna with Two Angels", a fine statue by Giovanni Pisano. Between the two churches is the Museo Civico. The art gallery has painting by Giotto, Bellini, Titian, Veronese and Tintoretto.

Cappella degli Scrovegni

Museo Civico

Albano Terme

A rewarding trip can be made south-west through the Euganean Hills (Colli Euganei), a volcanic range rising abruptly out of the plain and reaching a height of 603 m/1990 ft in Monte Venta.

Situation
10 km/6 miles
south-west

There are numerous hot springs and a number of popular spas in the hills, among them the world-famous thermal resort of Albano Terme (14 m/46 ft; pop. 17,000), the Roman Aquae Patavinae or Fons Aponi, where hot radioactive springs (87 °C/189 °F) deposit mud of volcanic origin, which, when pulverised and mixed into a paste with hot water, is known as "fango" and is used in the treatment of gout and rheumatism.

4 km/2½ miles west of Albano Terme is the Abbazia di Praglia (alt. 21 m/69 ft), a Benedictine abbey founded in 1080 and restored in the 15th–16th c., with a Renaissance church.

*Abbazia di Praglia

Montegrotto Terme

Another popular spa with hot springs is Montegrotto Terme (10 m/33 ft), where the remains of Roman baths and a theatre have been brought to light.

Situation
14 km/9 miles
south-west

Slightly farther south, on the A 13, is Battaglia Terme, another spa in the surroundings of Padua.

Battaglia Terme

Este

South-west of Padua, under Monte Calaone (415 m/1370 ft), is the little town of Este (15 m/50 ft; pop. 18,000), the Roman Ateste, which was held from c. 1050 to 1275 by the princely family of Este. The Museo Nazionale Ateastino, in the former Palazzo del Castello or Palazzo Mocenigo (16th c.), has rich prehistoric and Roman collections. Adjacent is the 14th c. Castello Carrarese, surrounded, particularly on the east side, by massive walls. Also of interest is the 18th c. Cathedral of Santa Tecla, which has a picture of the saint by Tiepolo in the choir.

Situation
30 km/19 miles
south-west

Villa Nazionale, near Stra between Padua and Venice

Montagnana	15 km/9 miles farther west is Montagnana (16 m/53 ft; pop. 10,000), with medieval town walls and 24 battlemented towers, best seen from the ring road which makes a circuit of the town. Outside the Porta Padova, on the east side of the town, is the Villa Pisani (by Palladio, 1560). In the town centre are the Gothic Romanesque cathedral (15th c.) and the Palazzo Pretorio (16th c.), now the Town Hall.
Arquà Petrarca	About 8 km/5 miles north-east of Montagnana is the medieval village of Arquà Petrarca (80 m/264 ft) where Francesco Petrarca (Petrarch) (1304–74) died. His tomb (1380) and the 14th c. house in which he lived are open to the public.

Padua to Venice (30 km/19 miles)

Brenta canal Stra	There is a very attractive excursion from Padua along the canalised River Brenta (boat services in summer). The road first reaches Stra (8 m/26 ft), a favourite resort of the Venetians in summer. At the far end of the village, in a park to the left of the road between the Brenta canal and its tributary the Veraro, stands the 18th c. Villa Pisani or Villa Nazionale, with a splendid ballroom containing a large ceiling painting by Tiepolo (1762).
Mira	The road then continues east alongside the navigable Brenta canal (Naviglio di Brenta), past a series of country houses and villas surrounded by parks. Beyond Stra, at the straggling village of Mira (6 m/20 ft), the road crosses a broad lateral canal, the Taglio Nuovissimo di Brenta, and in another 15 km/9 miles reaches the Piazzale Roma in Venice (see entry).

Paestum

Region: Campania
Province: Salerno (SA)
Altitude: 18 m/59 ft

The site of Paestum lies in southern Campania, in a plain nearby the
Gulf of Salerno, a bay on the Tyrrhenian Sea.
With its ruined temples and its cemeteries, this site possesses the finest
remains of Greek architecture on the mainland of Italy.

Situation

Paestum was founded by Greeks from Sybaris under the name of
Poseidonia about 600 B.C. In the 4th c. B.C. it passed into the hands of the
Lucanians, and in 273 B.C. became a Roman colony.
In the time of Augustus it already had a bad name for the malaria-
ridden marshland which surrounded it, and after the devastation of the
region by the Saracens in the 9th c. its inhabitants abandoned the town,
taking with them a relic of St Matthew which had according to tradition
been preserved in Paestum since the 4th c., and founded a new settlement on the neighbouring hills at Capaccio, of which Paestum with its
few modern houses is now a part.
The deserted town was despoiled of its columns and sculpture by the
Norman leader Robert Guiscard, and thereafter was forgotten until the
18th c., when there was a revival of interest in classical Greek art.

History

Town walls

The site of the ancient city is enclosed by a magnificent circuit of town
walls 4.75 km/3 miles long, with four gates and a number of towers (a
walk round the walls is recommended for the fine views of the site and
the sea).

**Museum

In the centre of the area, on the east side of the state road, is the
Museum, with prehistoric material, painted pottery and fine metopes
from the Temple of Hera on the Sele, north of Paestum, and the archaic
Treasury, including Greek statues and pictures.

Immediately south of the museum the state road cuts across the Amphitheatre of the Roman period, the rounded end of which can still be
distinguished. Some 300 m/330 yd farther south, on the right, is the
entrance to the site, near the south side of the ancient city.

Amphitheatre

*Site (Zona Archeologica)

Opposite the entrance is the magnificent Temple of Hera (misnamed
Temple of Neptune), a consummate example of the mature, strictly
disciplined architecture of the 5th c. B.C., reflecting the Greek ideal of
harmony and proportion. The stone is a porous limestone to which the
passage of time has given a beautiful yellow tone. At the east end of the
temple the tip of an earlier oval structure emerges from the ground.
10 m/11 yd east are the remains of the sacrificial altar associated with
the temple.

**Temple of Hera

To the south of the Temple of Hera can be seen the misnamed Basilica,
the oldest temple on the site, dated by the marked swelling of the

*Basilica

Paestum: Temple of Ceres

columns and the form of the capitals to the second half of the 6th c. B.C. As with the Temple of Hera, there are remains of an earlier oval temple at the east end and, 27 m/29 yd farther east, a sacrificial altar 21 m/23 yd wide.

Via Sacra

Just beyond the west end of the basilica is a section of the ancient Via Sacra which ran across the city from north to south.

Forum

200 m/220 yd north of the Temple of Hera is the Forum (150 m/165 yd long, 57 m/63 yd across), which was surrounded by a colonnade of late Doric columns.

North of the Forum are the massive substructures of the Tempio Italico (273 B.C.), with one re-erected column.

*Temple of Ceres

Still farther north the so-called Temple of Ceres has traces of stucco and painting on the gable, which shows Ionic influences.

**Cemeteries

**Tomb paintings

Outside the town walls three large cemeteries, with tomb paintings of the highest quality, have been discovered since 1968.

On the south side are tombs of the 5th c. B.C., the heyday of Magna Graecia, with frescoes in the style of the classical vase-painters ("Tomb of the Diver").

To the north are 70 tombs dating from the 4th c. (the period of Lucanian predominance) painted in vivid colours, with scenes from everyday life which throw fresh light on the discovery of colour, of light and shade and of spatial representation in Western art.

On the west side a cemetery was found, covering an area of 25,000 sq. m/29,900 sq. yd with thousands of 3rd c. tombs painted in a style which demonstrates that even during the Roman period southern Italy still belonged to the Greek (Hellenistic) cultural sphere.

Altogether more than 500 tomb paintings have been discovered so far.

Palermo

Region: Sicilia
Province: Palermo (PA)
Altitude: 19 m/63 ft
Population: 715,000

Palermo, capital of the region of Sicilia and principal port of the island, lies in a bay on the north coast of Sicily. It is bounded on the south and west by the artificially irrigated plain known as the Conca d'Oro ("Golden Shell"), with a wide arc of imposing mountains forming the background.

Situation

Although Palermo now has the aspect of an entirely modern city, it preserves a distinctive character, thanks to its Norman buildings with their rather Oriental style of architecture and the Baroque architecture it has inherited from the period of Spanish rule. The old town with its narrow and twisting side streets is still the scene of a vigorous popular life. Its numerous gardens and palm-shaded promenades give it a particular charm.

Palermo, founded by the Phoenicians and known to the Greeks as Panormos, became the principal Carthaginian base in Sicily until its capture by the Romans in 254 B.C. In A.D. 553 the Byzantine general Belisarius recovered it from the Ostrogoths, and thereafter it remained in Byzantine hands until its capture by the Saracens in 830. The Saracens were followed in 1072 by the Normans, who were in turn succeeded in 1194 by the Hohenstaufens and in 1266 by the house of Anjou, whose brief period of rule was ended by the popular rising known as the Sicilian Vespers in 1282. Palermo then came under Arago-

History

Palermo: Panorama of the town

nese and Spanish rule, passed to the Bourbons in the 18th c. and was finally liberated by Garibaldi on May 27th 1860.

*Quattro Canti

San Giuseppe dei
Teatini

The busiest traffic intersection in the old town is the square, laid out in 1609, known as the Quattro Canti ("Four Corners") or Piazza Vigliena, at the crossing of the Via Vittorio Emanuele, which runs accross the city from north-east to south-west for a distance of 2 km/1¼ miles, and the Via Maqueda, which runs from the station to the newer parts of the city, offering views of the long rows of uniform buildings, all set against a background of great scenic beauty. At the southern corner of the Quattro Canti is the church of San Giuseppe dei Teatine (1612–45), a massive pillared basilica with a sumptuous Baroque interior. Adjoining it on the south is the University.

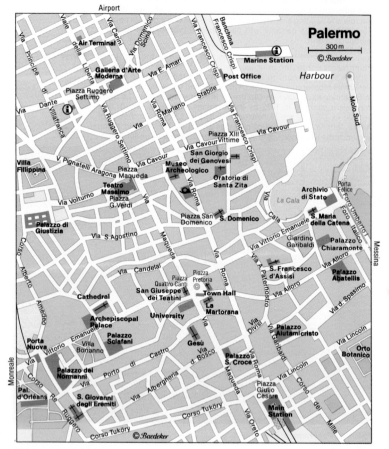

© Baedeker

Beyond this to the south stands the imposing church of the Gesù (1564–1633), also in Baroque style.

˟Cathedral

From the Quattro Canti Via Vittorio Emanuele runs south-west to the Piazza della Cattedrale. On the north-west side of this square, which is surrounded by a stone balustrade erected in 1761, with sixteen large statues of saints, stands the cathedral, originally Romanesque but frequently enlarged, with a beautiful south front (1300–59) and a dome finished in the 18th c.

In the south aisle are six royal tombs – the majestic porphyry sarcophagi, surmounted by temple-like canopies, of the Emperor Frederick II (d. 1250: on the left), his father Henry VI (d. 1197: on the right), Roger II (d. 1154: behind, on the left), his daughter the Empress Constance (behind on the right), William, son of Frederick II of Aragon (in niche on the left) and Constance of Aragon, wife of the Emperor Frederick II (by the wall, to the right). In the chapel to the right of the choir a silver sarcophagus contains the remains of St Rosalia, the city's patron saint. The sacristy, at the end of the south aisle, houses the rich Cathedral Treasury; the crypt is also of interest.

Royal tombs

Immediately south-west of the cathedral is the Archbishop's Palace (Palazzo Arcivescovile, 15th c.), with the Diocesan Museum (entrance in courtyard to the right).

Diocesan Museum

Palazzo dei Normanni

On the opposite side of the Via Vittorio Emanuele is the Piazza della Vittoria, with the palm-shaded park of the Villa Bonanno (remains of

Palermo Cathedral

Piazza Pretoria

Roman houses). The west side of the park is occupied by the Palazzo dei Normanni, the former royal palace, a fortress-like building originally dating from the Saracen period which was remodelled by the Norman kings. The last gateway on the left gives access to the palace courtyard (Renaissance arcades).

**Cappella Palatina

On the first floor is the famous Cappella Palatina (on the right), dedicated to St Peter, which was built by Roger II in 1132–40. This is surely the most beautiful palace chapel in the world with its splendid mosaic decoration and its mingling of Western and Oriental elements, including the ceiling painted in Oriental style. The glass mosaics on a gold ground which cover the walls depict scenes from the Old Testament, the life of Christ and the lives of the apostles Peter and Paul.

Near the chapel rises the Torre di Santa Ninfa, with a 15 m/50 ft high room on the ground floor which was probably the strong-room of the Norman kings.

On the second floor is an observatory, from the roof of which there is a fine view of Palermo. There are also good views from the balconies of various rooms in the palace (conducted tour). Particularly interesting is King Roger's room, with mosaics (c. 1170; hunting scenes).

Porta Nuova

Just beyond the Palazzo dei Normanni (on north) the Via Vittorio Emanuele is spanned by the Porta Nuova (1535), the upper storey of which (accessible from the palace) affords another magnificent view.

Palazzo Sclafani

At the south-eastern corner of the Piazza della Vittoria is the Palazzo Sclafani (1330) and at the south-western corner a monument to Philip V (1856).

San Giovanni degli Eremiti

Just south of the Palazzo dei Normanni is Palermo's most unusual ruined church, San Giovanni degli Eremiti (1132), a building of decidedly Oriental aspect with its five tall red domes. Adjoining the church are the remains of a small mosque. On its north side is a picturesque cloister, with tropical plants.

Villa d'Aumale

West of the church, in the Piazza dell'Indipendenza, the Villa d'Aumale or Villa d'Orléans, now the offices of the autonomous region of Sicily, has a beautiful park.

Piazza Pretoria

Palazzo del Municipio

On the east side of San Giuseppe dei Teatini is the Piazza Pretoria, with a Florentine fountain (1555–75) in the centre. On the south side of the square stands the Palazzo del Municipio (Town Hall). At the east corner is the side entrance to the church of Santa Caterina (Baroque interior), with its main front on Piazza Bellini. In this square also, a flight of steps leads up to the little church of Santo Cataldo (1161), in Byzantine style, with a dome.

*La Martorana

On its east side is the fine church of La Martorana (1143), also known as Santa Maria dell'Ammiraglio after its founder Georgios Antiochenos, grand admiral of the Norman king Roger I, with excellent Byzantine mosaics and fine painting in the vaulting.

Harbour district

Santa Maria della Catena

The eastern section of the Via Vittorio Emanuele cuts across the busy Via Roma (200 m/220 yd east of the Quattro Canti), a modern street driven through the old town from north to south, and comes to the church of Santa Maria della Catena (c. 1500; beautiful portico), on the left. It then runs into the Piazza Santo Spirito, closed on the seaward side by the ruins of the Porta Felice.

Porta Felice
Piazza Marina

West of Santa Maria della Catena lies the picturesque boating harbour, La Cala, and to the south is the Piazza Marina, almost entirely occupied by the tropical Giardino Garibaldi. The Palazzo Chiaramonte, usually known as Lo Steri, on the east side of this square, was built between 1307 and 1380 and later became the residence of the viceroy.

To the south-east, in Via Alloro, is the Palazzo Abatellis (1495), with a crenellated tower and a Gothic doorway. The palace now houses the Galleria Regionale della Sicilia, which gives a comprehensive view of Sicilian painting from the Middle Ages to modern times. Particularly notable is a magnificent wall painting, the "Triumph of Death", by an unknown 15th c. master (in Room II).

* Galleria Regionale della Sicilia

Along the seafront to the east and south-east of the Porta Felice extends the Foro Umberto I, a broad boulevard which affords magnificent views of the Bay of Palermo and is a popular resort of the citizens on summer evenings. At the southern end of the Foro Umberto I is the beautiful Villa Giulia park, also known as La Flora (laid out in 1777). On the west side of this the Botanic Garden has a magnificent variety of plants including date and coconut palms, banana trees and fine stands of bamboos and papyrus.

* Foro Umberto I

Piazza Giuseppe Verdi

From the Quattro Canti Via Maqueda runs north-west to the busy Piazza Giuseppe Verdi, lying between the old and the new town, with the Teatro Massimo (1875–97), one of the largest theatres in Italy (3200 seats).

* Teatro Massimo

From the Piazza Verdi Via Ruggero Settimo continues through the new town to Piazza Ruggero Settimo, with monuments to Sicilian patriots. On the north-east side of the square is the Politeama Garibaldi, is the Galleria d'Arte Moderna E. Restivo, with works by Sicilian artists.

Galleria d'Arte Moderna E. Restivo

From the Teatro Massimo Via della Bara runs east to the Piazza dell'Olivella, in which are the Olivella church (1598) and the Archaeological Museum (Museo Archeologico Nazionale), one of Italy's finest museums, housed in a former monastery of the Compagnia di San Filippo Neri. In addition to prehistoric material and an Etruscan collection the museum contains many important classical antiquities, among them the famous metopes from Selinunte (*c.* 550–450 B.C.), 56 waterspouts in the form of lions' heads from Himera (5th c. B.C.) and fine Greek bronzes, including Heracles and the Cerynaean hind, a fountain group from Pompeii excavated in 1805, and a large ram from Syracuse.

* Museo Archeologico Nazionale

Piazza San Domenico

From the east side of the Archaeological Museum Via Roma runs south past the Head Post Office (on right) to the Piazza San Domenico, in which is a 30 m/99 ft high marble column bearing a statue of the Virgin (1726). On the east side of the square stands the church of San Domenico (14th c., rebuilt 1636–40). It contains a number of good pictures and many monuments to prominent Sicilians. In the chapel to the right of the choir is a charming relief of the "Virgin with Angels" by Antonio Gagini. Adjoining the church is a picturesque cloister (14th and 16th c.). Behind San Domenico, in Via Bambinai, the Oratorio della Compagnia

San Domenico

del Rosario di San Domenico (entrance at No. 16, on the right), has stucco decoration by Giacomo Serpotta (1656–1732). On the high altar is the "Madonna del Rosario" (1624–25), by Van Dyck.

Santa Zita

To the north of the Oratorio in the church of Santa Zita, founded in 1369, can be seen a triptych (cona; 1517) by Antonio Gagini. Immediately behind the church, in Via Valverde, is the Oratorio della Compagnia del Rosario di Santa Zita, with stucco-work by Serpotta.

San Giorgio dei Genovesi

North-east of Santa Zita is the church of San Giorgio dei Genovesi (1591). From here Via Francesco Crispi runs north to the busy harbour.

Sights to the west

Convento dei Cappuccini

1.5 km/1 mile west of the Porta Nuova, on the edge of the town, is the Convento dei Cappuccini (1621), with underground passages which contain mummies and skeletons of ecclesiastics or well-to-do citizens in the clothes they wore during life (and which are sometimes renewed by the descendants). No further burials of this kind have been permitted since 1881.

Palazzo della Zisa

500 m/550 yd north of the convent is a former Norman palace, the Palazzo della Zisa, a plain building based on Arab models, which was erected by William I and his son William II between 1154 and 1166. On the ground floor is a square garden room with a fountain decorated with Byzantine mosaics and high stalactitic vaulting.

Santa Maria di Gesù

Situation
4 km/2½ miles south
**Views

From the former Minorite house of Santa Maria di Gesù, on the lower slopes of Monte Grifone (832 m/2746 ft) there is perhaps the finest view of Palermo and the Conca d'Oro, particularly in the morning light.

San Martino delle Scale

Situation
13 km/8 miles
south-west

South-west of Palermo is the former Benedictine monastery of San Martino delle Scale. The present buildings date from 1770–86; the church was erected in 1590.

Spianata della Sacra Grotta

Situation
13 km/8 miles north

There is a rewarding trip to the Spianata della Sacra Grotta, a cave converted into a church in 1625. According to the legend St Rosalia, daughter of Duke Sinibaldo and niece of King William II, withdrew to this remote hermitage, at the age of only fourteen.

*Monte Pellegrino

From here a steep path ascends south-east (½ hour) to the summit of Monte Pellegrino (606 m/2000 ft; two television towers), from which there are panoramic views.

From the Spianata della Sacra Grotta a good road descends, with many bends and fine views, to Mondello (8 km/5 miles; see below).

Tour around Monte Pellegrino (about 30 km/19 miles)

La Favorita

There is also a very attractive tour around Monte Pellegrino. The road runs north past the former royal country house of La Favorita (park,

orangery), near which is the little Palazzina Cinese, with the interesting
Museo Etnografico Siciliano Pitrè (folk traditions).

From here the route continues along the foot of Monte Pellegrino on   Mondello
the southern slopes of Monte Gallo (527 m/1739 ft), to Mondello, a
seaside resort (good sandy beach) lying on the Bay of Mondello between Monte Gallo and Monte Pellegrino. From Mondello the return
route runs along the coast, around the Punta di Priola, past the Cimitero
Monumentale (or Cimitero dei Rotoli), Palermo's largest cemetery, and
through the coastal suburbs of Arenella and Acquasanta to Palermo.

Piana degli Albanesi   K12

Another excursion, through country of particular scenic beauty, is to   Situation 24 km/15
Piana degli Albanesi, formerly called Piana dei Greci. The little town   miles south
was founded by Albanian settlers in 1488, and the people still preserve
their distinctive dialect and the Eastern rite of the Catholic Church. The
town is the seat of a bishop whose diocese extends to all the Albanians
in Italy. Picturesque Albanian costumes are worn on feast-days.

Island of Ustica

There is an attractive trip by boat (several times weekly) or hydrofoil   Situation
(several times daily) to the volcanic island of Ustica (area 9 sq. km/3½   67 km/42 miles north
sq. miles; pop. 1200). The highest point on the island is the Punta
Maggiore (244 m/805 ft), a remnant of the old crater rim. The island is
attracting increasing numbers of visitors with its beautiful scenery.
On its eastern tip is the only settlement, Ustica (49 m/162 ft; hotels),
with the harbour. To the south accessible only by boat, are a number of
caves – the Grotta Azzurra, the particularly beautiful Grotta dell'Acqua
and the Grotta Pastizza.

Monreale

See Sicily.

Parma   G5

Region: Emilia-Romagna
Province: Parma (PR)
Altitude: 52 m/172 ft
Population: 176,000

Parma, the former capital of the duchy of Parma, now a provincial   Situation
capital and seat of an university, lies at the foot of the Apennines in the
North Italian plain on the banks of the River Parma, a tributary of the Po.

In spite of its long history, the town, situated on the old Roman main
road, the Via Aemilia, is a city of modern aspect, with straight streets on
a regular plan. In the crowded housing areas, destroyed during the
Second World War, fine new squares have been laid out.

Parma became a Roman colony in 183 B.C. During the Middle Ages it   History
became a place of some consequence through its woollen mills and its
university. The town, always on the Guelf side, belonged to Milan from

Parma

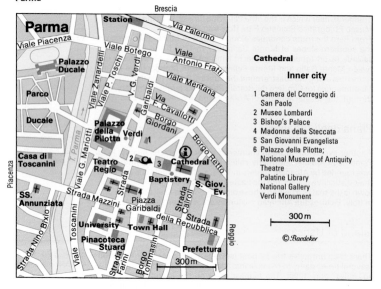

1341 to 1512, when it was annexed to the States of the Church. In 1545 Pope Paul III granted the duchies of Parma and Piacenza to his natural son Pier Luigi Farnese. When the Farnese male line died out in 1731 the duchies passed to a collateral line of the Bourbons. They came under French rule in 1806, and in 1816 were granted to Napoleon's wife Marie Louise for life, reverting to the Bourbons on her death. After the expulsion of the Bourbons in 1860 the territory was incorporated in the new kingdom of Italy.

The painter Antonio Allegri, known as Correggio (1489–1534), the great master of chiaroscuro, lived and worked in Parma.

Piazza Garibaldi

Palaces

The central feature of the town is the Piazza Garibaldi in which stands the Palazzo del Governatore, with a façade dating from 1760 and an astronomical clock. Nearby is the Palazzo del Municipio (Town Hall; 1627–73).

University

The university, south-west of the Piazza Garibaldi, has various natural history collections.

Pinacoteca Stuard

Opposite, to the south-east, is the Pinacoteca Stuard, the finest private collection in Parma.

Piazza del Duomo

*Baptistery

From Piazza Garibaldi the busy Strada Cavour runs north. On the right the short Strada al Duomo leads to the Piazza del Duomo. Immediately on the left of this square is the Bishop's Palace, on the right the Baptistery, a massive octagonal marble building begun in Romanesque style by Benedetto Antelami in 1196–1216 (the doorways, with reliefs of scriptural subjects, are his work) and completed in Gothic style in 1260; it contains 13th c. high reliefs and frescoes.

On the east side of the square is the cathedral, a Romanesque pillared basilica dating from the 12th c., whose wide façade forms an impressive group with the adjoining campanile (63 m/208 ft high) of 1284–94. In the dome is a huge fresco of the "Assumption of the Virgin" by Correggio (1526–30). In the south transept is a relief by Benedetto Antelami of the "Descent from the Cross" (1178), originally on a pulpit. In the crypt are two fine Roman mosaics.

*Cathedral

Campanile

Behind the cathedral stands the convent church of San Giovanni Evangelista, a Renaissance building (1510) with a Baroque façade of 1607 and a slender tower of 1614. It contains fine frescoes by Correggio (in the dome; 1521–23) and his pupil Parmigianino.

San Giovanni Evangelista

Beside the convent is the Storica Farmacia di San Giovanni Evangelista, an old chemist's shop, with a Renaissance interior and ceramic containers (16th–18th c.).

Palazzo della Pilotta

From the Piazza del Duomo the Strada al Duomo and Strada Pisacane lead west to the Piazzale Marconi, which was much enlarged after the Second World War. On the west side of this square is the Palazzo della Pilotta (Pilotta palace), a huge brick building begun in 1583 but left unfinished, which has a fine courtyard.

In the Palazzo are the National Museum (Museo Archeologico Nazionale) and – in the Palazzo Farnese of the Pilotta palace – the Biblioteca Palatina (closed Sundays), the Bodoni Museum (printing) and a Picture Gallery (Galleria Nazionale), with important works by Correggio

Museums

Parma: Campanile and Baptistery   *Palazzo della Pilotta*

317

	("Madonna del San Girolamo" and "Madonna della Scodella"), Parmigianino, Fra Angelico, Giulio Romano, Cima da Conegliano, Tiepolo, Canaletto, Carracci, El Greco including a drawing (study of a head) by Leonardo da Vinci.
Teatro Farnese	On the same floor is the Teatro Farnese, built entirely in wood by Aleotti, a pupil of Palladio, in 1618–28; it was then the largest theatre in the world (4500 seats).
Museo Glauco Lombardi	On the east side of the Piazza della Pace is the Museo Glauco Lombardi, housed in the Palazzo di Riserva, which contains an art collection with works of the 18th–19th c.
Camera di San Paolo	A short distance east of the Piazzale Marconi, in a former Benedictine nunnery, is the Camera di San Paolo (St Paul's room), with well-preserved frescoes by the young Correggio (1518–19: Diana; the Goddess of Love, with the famous "putti del Correggio").
Teatro Regio	South of the Piazzale Marconi, on the right-hand side of Strada Garibaldi, is the Teatro Regio (Royal Theatre; 1821–29), one of Italy's finest theatres.
Madonna della Steccata	Opposite the Teatro Regio is the fine domed church of the Madonna della Steccata (1521–39), modelled on St Peter's in Rome (Greek-cross plan). Inside there are fine frescoes on the triumphal arch and on the dome.

Museo d'Arte Cinese

In the south of the town, near the citadel, is the interesting Museo d'Arte Cinese (Chinese art), with a Museum of Ethnology.

Oltre Torrente district

Santissima Annunziata	From Piazza Garibaldi Strada Mazzini runs west over the Ponte di Mezzo (fragments of the old Roman bridge, rebuilt, in underpass) spanning the River Parma into the Oltre Torrente district or Parma Vecchio, the oldest part of the town. At the near end of Strada Massimo d'Azeglio, on the left, is the church of the Santissima Annunziata, a Baroque building (1566) with an unusual ground-plan and a boldly designed dome (1626–32).
Santa Croce	At the end of the street, also on the left, the Romanesque church of Santa Croce contains good 17th c. frescoes.
House of Toscanini	A short distance north of the church at Borgo Rodolfo Tanzi 13 is the birthplace of the conductor Arturo Toscanini (1867–1957).
Parco Ducale	Farther north, extending to the banks of the Parma, is the large Parco Ducale, in the north-east corner of which is the Palazzo Ducale (1564), now a military academy.

Torrechiara

| Situation
18 km/11 miles south | There is a fine trip to the Apennine village of Torrechiara, which has a 15th c. castle magnificently situated above the valley of the Parma (Camera d'Oro, with beautiful painted wall tiles and frescoes by Benedetto Bembo). |

Canossa

| Situation
35 km/22 miles
south-east | South-east of Parma is the ruined castle of Canossa (576 m/1901 ft), to which the Emperor Henry IV came in 1077 to seek absolution from Pope Gregory VII (small museum). From here there are fine views. |

Brescello

North-east of Parma, on the banks of the River Po, is Brescello, the town in which the stories of Don Camillo and Peppone (by Giovanni Guareschi, 1908–1968; starring Fernandel and Gino Cervi) were filmed. In the main square is a statue of Hercules dating from the Renaissance period.

Situation
20 km/12 miles
north-east

Sabbioneta

G4

North-east of Parma is the interesting little town of Sabbioneta (18 m/59 ft), which Vespasiano Gonzaga (1531–91) made the very model of a small princely residence of the Renaissance period (fortifications, Palazzo Ducale, Palazzo del Giardino, Chiesa dell'Incoronata; theatre in which performances are given in summer).

Situation
30 km/19 miles
north-east

Pavia

F4

Region: Lombardia
Province: Pavia (PV)
Altitude: 77 m/231 ft
Population: 86,000

The old Lombard town of Pavia, now a provincial capital, lies on the River Ticino near its junction with the Po, in the western part of the north Italian plain. It is linked with Milan by a shipping canal, the Naviglio di Pavia.

Situation

With its old brick buildings it has preserved much of its medieval aspect and is notable particularly for its beautiful churches in Lombard Romanesque style. Of its once numerous towers, the fortified residences of noble families, few now remain, but it still has remains of the ramparts and bastions of the Spanish period.
Pavia is the seat of a university.

Pavia, the Roman Ticinum, was a favourite residence of Theodoric the Great, and after the fall of Ravenna became for a short time the Ostrogothic capital. From 572 to 774 it was capital of the Lombard kingdom. From the 7th c. the town was known as Papia. During the Middle Ages many kings of Italy were crowned in the church of San Michele, as were the emperors Henry II and Frederick Barbarossa. The town remained for the most part faithful to the emperor, until it was handed over to the Visconti family by Charles IV in 1359. Francis I of France was defeated and taken prisoner at Pavia in 1525.

History

University

In the centre of the town, in the Strada Nuova, Pavia's main street, is the university, founded in 1361 on the basis of an earlier law school established in the 11th c. The present building was begun in the 14th–15th c. and enlarged in the 18th c. In the five courtyards are monuments and memorials to famous professors and students; in the second courtyard are a statue of Volta (1878) and reliefs from the tombs of professors. The library, founded about 1770, contains some 370,000 volumes. Beyond the first courtyard there is a picturesque view of three old brick towers, formerly belonging to noble families.

Pavia

Santa Maria del Carmine
    To the west of the university stands the huge church of Santa Maria del Carmine, an early Gothic brick structure surrounded by chapels.

Palazzo Malaspina
    A short distance north of the church, in Piazza Petrarca, stands the Palazzo Malaspina.

Piazza della Vittoria

Broletto
    South-west of the university is the Piazza della Vittoria, in which is the 12th c. Broletto, the old Town Hall.

*Cathedral
    Farther south-west stands the cathedral, a building in Early Renaissance style on a centralised plan, begun by Cristoforo Rocchi in 1488 and continued with the collaboration of Amadeo and Bramante, with a dome over the crossing added in 1884–85 and a façade of 1898.

Torre Civica
    The 78 m/257 ft high brick-built tower Torre Civica (11th c.), originally the clock-tower of an older church, collapsed on the morning of March 17th 1989 and buried four people.

Between the cathedral and the Ticino

San Teodoro
    From the cathedral we go south along Via dei Liguri and then turn right into Via Pietro Maffi to reach the Romanesque church of San Teodoro (12th c.), which has frescoes including a view of Pavia (1522), immediately left, and a fine crypt (12th c.).

*San Michele
    550 m/550 yd east of San Teodoro, on the far side of the Strada Nuova, is the old coronation church of San Michele (1155), in Lombard Romanesque style, with a beautiful façade (rich ornaments and figural reliefs in a series of bands, surmounted by a gabled gallery) and fine interior.

Pavia: Castello Visconteo

At the south end of the Strada Nuova, on the banks of the Ticino, is the
Piazzale Ponte Ticino, from which the Ponte Coperto (built 1354, re-
stored after war damage) leads into the suburban district of Borgo
Ticino.

Ponte Coperto

*San Pietro in Ciel d' Oro

In the north of the town is the old convent church of San Pietro in Ciel d'
Oro (1132; restored 1875–99), in Lombard Romanesque style. In the
choir is the splendid marble tomb (1362) of St Augustine (354–430).

*Castello Visconteo

A short distance east, on the north-east side of the town stands the
Castello Visconteo (1360–65), a square building with a spacious courtyard; it houses the Municipal Museum (archaeological finds, sculpture)
and the Picture Gallery (Pinacoteca Malaspina) with some 500 paintings, including works by Bellini, Crivelli and Correggio.

Museum

**Certosa di Pavia

North of the town, on the road to Milan, is the Certosa di Pavia, the most
famous Carthusian house after the Grande Chartreuse near Grenoble,
founded by Gian Galeazzo Visconti in 1396, suppressed in 1784, but
reoccupied between 1843 and 1881 and again since 1968. A tour of the
monastery needs the permission of the Soprintendenza ai Monumenti
di Milano. At the entrance is a good restaurant.

Situation
10 km/6 miles north

Certosa di Pavia: Marble façade of the convent church

On the west side of the outer courtyard the old Pharmacy now produces a liqueur (tasting room). To the south is the Foresteria, built about 1625 to accommodate distinguished visitors (museum, with pictures, etc.).

Church

Building of the church, on the east side of the courtyard, was started in 1396 in Gothic style and continued by Guiniforte Solari (d. 1481) from 1453 onwards. The famous marble façade, a masterpiece of north Italian Early Renaissance architecture, was begun in 1491 to the design of Giovanni Antonio Amadeo (1447–1522) and carried on by Benedetto Briosco in 1500–07; the upper part, however, was left unfinished about 1550. The plinth is adorned with medallions of Roman emperors. Above the windows are niches with numerous statues.

The nave, flanked by aisles, is still entirely Gothic in character, but the transepts, choir and dome show Renaissance features. The altarpieces and decoration of the side chapels are mainly 17th c.; the splendid choir screen dates from around 1600. Outstanding among the many works of art in the church are the marble recumbent figures of Lodovico Sforza, il Moro (d. 1508) and his wife Beatrice d'Este (d. 1496) by Cristoforo Solari (in north transept); the richly decorated altar (1568) and stalls (1486–98) designed by Bergognone in the choir; a Renaissance fountain (1490) in the lavatorium; to the right of the choir the magnificent tomb of Gian Galeazzo Visconti (d. 1402), begun in 1494 by Gian Cristoforo Romano and Benedetto Briosco but not completed until 1562 (by Galeazzo Alessi and others). In the New Sacristy an "Assumption" by Andrea Solario, and in the Old Sacristy; an ivory polyptychon with scenes from the Old and New Testaments.

Cloisters

An elegant Early Renaissance doorway (1466) leads from the south aisle into the Front Cloister (Chiostro Piccolo), with marble colonnades and charming terracotta decoration (1462–72). From the west side there is a fine view of the nave and south transept of the church.
Around the Great Cloister, to the rear, are 24 small apartments for monks.

Perugia

Region: Umbria
Province: Perugia (PG)
Altitude: 493 m/1627 ft
Population: 144,000

Situation

Perugia, capital of its province and of the region of Umbria, lies on a hill between the Trasimenian Sea and the Tiber valley.
The town is worth visiting not only for the beauty of its setting but also for its fine old buildings. It is the see of an archbishop and a university town, with a University for Foreigners.

History

The ancient Perusia, one of the twelve cities of the Etruscan federation, came under Roman rule in 310 B.C., and in the middle of the 3rd c. A.D. was raised to the status of a military colony under the name of Augusta Perusia. Considerable sections of the Etruscan walls, which extended for 2800 m/3063 yd round the town, have been preserved. In 547 Perusia was captured by the Ostrogothic king Totila. In the 14th and 15th c. it was the most powerful city in Umbria. From 1534 until the unification of Italy in 1860 it belonged to the States of the Church.

Art

Perugia is renowned as the principal centre of the Umbrian school of painting, the leading members of which, Pietro Vannucci, called Peru-

Perugia: View across the roofs of the capital of Umbria

gino (1446–1523), and Bernardino Betti, called Pinturicchio (1455–1513), both worked here. The young Raphael worked in Perugino's studio until 1504.

The town centre is closed to cars.   Tip

*Piazza IV Novembre

The main square of Perugia is the picturesque Piazza IV Novembre, in   *Fontana Maggiore
the centre of which is the Fontana Maggiore (1277–80), one of the most
beautiful fountains of the period, with reliefs by Nicola and Giovanni
Pisano. On the west side of the square is the Archbishop's Palace with
the Museum of Natural History, and beyond it the vaulting of the
so-called Maestà delle Volte, a relic of the Palazzo del Podestà which
was burned down in 1534.
From the Piazza IV Novembre the medieval Via delle Volte runs to the
Piazza Fortebraccio.

On the north side of the Piazza IV Novembre stands the cathedral of San   *San Lorenzo
Lorenzo, a 15th c. Gothic hall-church, with an unfinished façade. On the
steps leading up to the entrance, to the left, is a bronze statue of Pope
Julius III (1555). Inside there are fine choir-stalls (1486–91) and a banner
depicting a view of Perugia.
The Museo Capitolare to the left of the cathedral houses sculpture,   Museo Capitolare
valuable missals and pictures, including a "Madonna Enthroned" by
Signorelli.

East of the cathedral the church of San Severo contains a fresco by   San Severo
Raphael (1505), the Trinity.

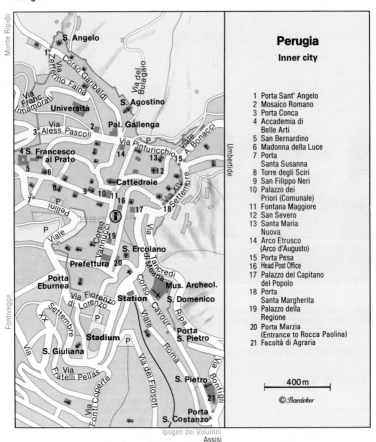

Perugia

Inner city

1 Porta Sant' Angelo
2 Mosaico Romano
3 Porta Conca
4 Accademia di
  Belle Arti
5 San Bernardino
6 Madonna della Luce
7 Porta
  Santa Susanna
8 Torre degli Sciri
9 San Filippo Neri
10 Palazzo dei
   Priori (Comunale)
11 Fontana Maggiore
12 San Severo
13 Santa Maria
   Nuova
14 Arco Etrusco
   (Arco d'Augusto)
15 Porta Pesa
16 Head Post Office
17 Palazzo del Capitano
   del Popolo
18 Porta
   Santa Margherita
19 Palazzo della
   Regione
20 Porta Marzia
   (Entrance to Rocca Paolina)
21 Facoltà di Agraria

400 m

© Baedeker

*Palazzo dei Priori

*Galleria Nazionale dell'Umbria

On the south side of the cathedral is the Palazzo dei Priori, also known as the Palazzo Comunale (Town Hall), a massive building in Italian Gothic style (1293 and 1333), with its main front on the Corso Vannucci. On the side facing the Piazza IV Novembre are a griffin (the heraldic emblem of Perugia), a 14th c. bronze lion, and chains, all of which commemorate a victory over the Sienese in 1358. On the first floor of the palace, which is entered through the richly decorated main door-way in the Corso, is the splendid Sala dei Notari, on the second floor the Municipal Library (150,000 volumes), and on the third floor the Galleria Nazionale dell'Umbria with works by Perugino and Pinturicchio, Bene-detto Bonfiglio (d. 1496), Bartolomeo Caporali (d. about 1509), Fiorenzo di Lorenzo (d. 1525), Fra Angelico, Piero della Francesca and other artists. The Sala del Collegio della Mercanzia is also worth a visit.

Loggia of the Cathedral

Palazzo dei Priori

Only a few yards from the Palazzo dei Priori is the Collegio del Cambio, the old Exchange, the audience chamber of which is decorated with frescoes by Perugino.

*Collegio del Cambio

South-east of the Piazza IV Novembre is the Piazza Matteotti, built on massive substructures, some of which date from the Etruscan period. On the east side of the square are the Palazzo del Capitano del Popolo (1472–81) and the Old University (1453–83).

Palazzo del Capitano del Popolo

*Arco d'Augusto

A short distance north of the cathedral the Arco d'Augusto, one of the Etruscan town gates, bears an inscription. "Augusta Perusia", dating from the Roman period.

In Piazza Fortebraccio, outside the gate, the Palazzo Gallenga Stuart (18th c.) now houses the University for Foreigners (language courses and introductory courses to Italian history, art and literature).

Palazzo Gallenga Stuart

From Piazza Fortebraccio the Corso Garibaldi runs north-west, passing the church of Sant'Agostino, to the Porta Sant'Angelo. To the north of this gate is the church of Sant'Angelo, a round church (5th–6th c.) of great architectural interest, with sixteen ancient columns in the nave.

Sant'Angelo

*Oratorio di San Bernardino

From the Corso Vannucci Via dei Priori, entered through an archway under the Palazzo Comunale, runs west past the medieval Torre degli Sciri and the little Renaissance church of the Madonna della Luce to the Piazza di San Francesco, in which, straight ahead, is the Oratorio di San

Bernardino, with a magnificent façade of coloured marble and terra-cotta (by Agostino di Duccio, 1457–61).

Piazza Italia

Prefecture

Corso Vanucci, the town's main street, leads south from the Town Hall to the Piazza Italia, in which stands the Prefecture, built on the site of the Papal citadel, demolished in 1860. From the terrace on the south side there are magnificent views of the Umbrian plain, with Assisi, Spello, Foligno and Trevi, and of the Tiber valley.

Porta Marzia

From the Piazza Italia Via Marzia leads south-east past the substructures of the former citadel to the Porta Marzia, at the beginning of the lower town, a remnant of one of the Etruscan town gates.

Rocca Paolina

Here is the entrance to what is left of the old 16th c. fortress, the Rocca Paolina (escalator to the lower town). Beyond this in Viale dell'Indipendenza, is the little Gothic church of Sant'Ercolano (1297–1326).

San Domenico

Continue along Corso Cavour to the church of San Domenico, a brick structure begun in 1305 and altered in 1621–34, with a huge Gothic window and the tomb of Pope Benedict XI (1304).

Museo Archeologico Nazionale dell'Umbria

In the adjoining monastery is the Museo Archeologico Nazionale dell'Umbria, with Roman and Etruscan antiquities, including the Cippus Perusianus, one of the longest known Etruscan inscriptions.

Porta San Pietro

Corso Cavour ends at the finely decorated Porta San Pietro, the inner gate of which dates from the 14th c. and the outer gate from the 15th c.

*San Pietro

Outside the gate, in Borgo XX Giugno (on the left), we find the fine church of San Pietro, an early Christian structure rebuilt in the 12th c., containing eighteen ancient columns, beautiful choir-stalls (1535) and many pictures of the early Umbrian school and of the 17th c.

To the south-west of the church, extending to the Porta San Constanzo, lies the Giardino del Frontone (views).

*Tomb of the Volumnii

Situation
10 km/6 miles east

East of Perugia, 1 km/¾ mile before Ponte San Giovanni (189 m/624 ft), is a modern building which houses the entrance to the underground Tomb of the Volumnii (Ipogeo dei Volumni), one of the finest tombs in Etruria, dating from the 2nd c. B.C. It imitates the plan of an ancient house, with nine chambers grouped round a central space, which contain urns with extraordinarily expressive carvings.

Pesaro

Region: Marche
Province: Pesaro e Urbino (PS)
Altitude: 11 m/36 ft
Population: 91,000

Situation

Pesaro, capital of the province of Pesaro e Urbino and a very popular seaside resort, lies at the mouth of the River Foglia, on the north-west Adriatic coast between Rimini and Ancona.

In the 16th and 17th c. Pesaro was the residence of the Della Rovere family, dukes of Urbino, and a centre of art and literature, famous for its majolica factories. The composer Gioacchino Rossini (1792–1868) was born here.

General

Sights

The life of the town centres on the Piazza del Popolo, in which are the Town Hall and the Palazzo Ducale (begun about 1461 for the Sforzas, completed in the 16th c. for the Della Rovere). A little way south-east is the Santuario della Madonna delle Grazie, known as San Francesco, with a beautiful Gothic doorway. Farther along are the spacious Piazza Matteotti and the adjoining Giardino Cialdini, a public park, with a 15th c. fortress, the Rocca Constanza, now used as a prison. In Via Rossini, which runs from the Piazza del Popolo to the seafront, is Rossini's birthplace (Casa di Rossini, No. 34, on the right), containing a number of pictures and caricatures. From here it is only a short distance to the 13th c. cathedral.

Palazzo Ducale

To the west of the cathedral, in the Palazzo Toschi-Mosca, are the Musei Civici, with a notable collection of pictures (works by Bellini, "Coronation of the Virgin", and Marco Zoppo) and an outstanding collection of majolica, the finest in Italy.

Musei Civici

Piacenza

F4

Region: Emilia-Romagna
Province: Piacenza (PC)
Altitude: 61 m/201 ft
Population: 109,000

The provincial capital of Piacenza lies in the north Italian plain near the right bank of the Po, some 50 km/31 miles south-east of Milan.
The town has a well-preserved circuit of mid-16th c. walls 6.5 km/4 miles long.

Situation

Piacenza was founded by the Romans in 219 B.C., under the name of Colonia Placentia, to defend the Po crossing against the Gauls. During the Middle Ages it was a member of the Lombard League, and thereafter belonged to the Viscontis, the Sforzas and (from 1521) the States of the Church. From 1545 onwards the Farnese duchy of Piacenza together with the duchy of Parma formed an independent principality, which was incorporated in the Kingdom of Italy in 1859.

History

Piazza dei Cavalli

The life of Piacenza centres on the picturesque Piazza dei Cavalli, named after the prancing Baroque equestrian statues of dukes Alessandro and Ranuccio Farnese (1587–92, 1592–1622), by the Tuscan sculptor Francesco Mocchi (1612–29).
On the south-west side of the square is the Palazzo del Comune, called "il Gotico" (Town Hall), built from 1280 onwards, the model for many other Italian town halls. On the ground floor is an arcade with five pointed arches; above this a large hall with round-arched windows richly decorated with terracotta; the attic is crowned with battlements. Opposite stands the neo-classical Palazzo del Governatore (1781), now the chamber of trade.

*Palazzo del Comune

Palazzo del Governatore

Piacenza: Palazzo del Comune

On the south-east side of the square, set a little way back, is the large brick Gothic church of San Francesco (1278).

*Cathedral

From the Piazza dei Cavalli Via XX Settembre (closed to cars) leads south-east to the cathedral, begun in 1122 in Lombard Romanesque style and completed in the mid 13th c. under Gothic influence, with three beautiful doorways. The dome is decorated with frescoes (prophets and sibyls) by Guercino. The crypt has 108 columns.

San Savino

A short way east of the cathedral is the church of San Savino (1107), with early ribbed vaulting. The choir and crypt have mosaic pavements (12th c.).

Sant'Antonio

South-west of the Piazza del Duomo, at the end of Via Chiapponi, is the church of Sant'Antonio (11th–12th c., with much later alteration), the former cathedral, with a large Gothic porch of 1350.

Galleria d'Arte Moderna

300 m/330 yd farther south-west is the Galleria d'Arte Moderna Ricci Oddi, with a collection of pictures by Italian masters of the 19th c.

Palazzo Farnese

Museo Civico

From the Piazza dei Cavalli the busy Corso Cavour, Piacenza's main street, runs north-east to the massive Palazzo Farnese, begun in 1558, continued in 1564 by Vignola and finished in 1602. The restored building houses the Municipal Museum (Museo Civico), with an archaeological section containing Etruscan, Roman and medieval sculpture.

San Sisto

To the north-west, near the northern edge of the town, is the church of San Sisto (1499–1511), in Early Renaissance style, with a Baroque façade and a fine Ionic colonnade. It was for this church that Raphael painted the "Sistine Madonna" (c. 1515), which was sold to Dresden in 1754 and replaced by a copy (c. 1725).

Madonna di Campagna

Near the north-western edge of the town is the church of the Madonna di Campagna, an Early Renaissance church on a centralised plan (by Alessio Taramello, 1522–28) containing frescoes by Pordenone (1528–31).

Collegio Alberoni

South-east of Piacenza, on the road to Parma, the Collegio Alberoni has an interesting picture gallery, library (100,000 volumes) and observatory.

Situation
3 km/2 miles
south-east

Castell'Arquato   F5

Castell'Arquato is a town with a number of medieval features. Particularly notable are the Palazzo Pretorio, the collegiate church and the remains of the castle.

Situation
25 km/16 miles
south-east

Piedmont/Piemonte   C-E4/5

Region: Piemonte
Provinces: Torino (TO), Alessandria (AL), Asti (AT), Cuneo (CU),
Novara (NO) and Vercelli (VC)
Area: 25,399 sq. km/9804 sq. miles
Population: 4,411,900

Piedmont, in northern Italy, occupies the upper Po basin and the adjoining pre-Alpine moraine and hill region, bounded on the south, west and north by the mighty mountain arc of the Apennines and the Alps, which here reach their highest points in Mont Blanc, Monte Rosa, the Gran Paradiso and the Matterhorn.
The region takes in six provinces with Turin as its capital.

Situation

The geographical diversity of the region is reflected in different economic patterns. The upland area round Turin, Ivrea and Biella, with good communications and adequate energy supplies (hydro-electric power from the mountains, natural gas in the Po plain, oil from Genoa), is one of the most progressive industrial areas in Italy. The main elements in a very varied range of industries are metal-working, the manufacture of machinery and cars, the textile industry which developed out of the famous silk-manufacturing industry of earlier days, leather goods and foodstuffs.
Agriculture is still predominant on the fertile alluvial soil of the Po valley, where fruit-growing, arable farming (wheat, maize, rice, fodder crops) and cattle-rearing achieve high yields through the application of modern methods. Vine-growing is important, particularly in the Monferrato. White truffles – the finest and most expensive form of this delicacy – are found in the Alba area.
In the hill regions tourism has developed rapidly in recent years,

Economy

supplementing the traditional pastoral farming and the relatively unproductive mining (lead, zinc, copper, coal).

History

Originally occupied by a number of different peoples, Piedmont ("foot of the mountain") was Romanised in the time of Augustus. After the fall of the Roman Empire it was held successively by the Lombards (Langobardi) and the Franks. It was devastated by the Magyars in 899 (massacre of Vercelli) and later by the Saracens. Thereafter it split up into a patchwork of counties, duchies and marquisates, the most important of which in the 10th c. were Ivrea and Turin, joined by Saluzzo and Monferrato in the 12th c. In the 11th c. most of the present-day Piedmont passed to the house of Savoy (French Piémont) as a result of a dynastic marriage; and the territory became in the 13th c. the county, and in 1416 the duchy, of Piedmont. Thereafter it was disputed between the Habsburgs and France, owing its importance and the vicissitudes of its subsequent history largely to its control of the western Alpine passes (the Great and Little St Bernard). In 1720 Piedmont acquired Sardinia in exchange for Sicily, and as the kingdom of Sardinia played a leading part in the unification of Italy. In 1861 Victor Emmanuel II (1849–78), son of the last king of Sardinia, became king of Italy, with Turin, the old Piedmontese capital, as capital of the new kingdom until 1865.

Features of interest

The most attractive tourist areas in Piedmont are to be found in the mountains – the Graian, Cottian and Ligurian Alps – and around Lake Maggiore (see entry), all of them of great scenic beauty.

Casale Monferrato

The principal towns of interest to visitors are Turin, Novara and Asti (see entries), but there are many others. In eastern Piedmont, between Vercelli and Alessandria, is the old town of Casale Monferrato (116 m/383 ft; pop. 41,000), from the 14th to the early 18th c. the residence of the marquises and later dukes of Monferrato. In the centre of the town is the imposing Town Hall (1778), and to the north of this the Romanesque cathedral of Sant'Evasio, with a beautiful porch (12th c.) and a number of fine works by Lombard sculptors in the interior. Between the cathedral and the bridge over the Po stands the church of San Domenico, with remains of frescoes and a fine cloister. To the west, near the river, is the old Castello (15th–16th c.).

Cuneo

In southern Piedmont is another interesting town, Cuneo (535 m/1766 ft; pop. 56,000), beautifully situated on a wedge-shaped plateau above the junction of the rivers Gesso and Stura di Demonte. In the centre of the town is a large arcaded square, the Piazza D. Galimberti, lying on the town's main traffic artery, formed by Via Roma and Corso Nizza in the newer south-western part of the town. The cathedral, in Via Roma, has a neo-classical façade. Farther north, in Piazza Virginio, are the Loggia dei Mercanti (14th c., restored) and the former Franciscan church (now a warehouse), in Late Romanesque transitional style (1227) with a Gothic tower (1399) and a doorway of 1481. Nearby is the church of Santa Croce, on an elliptical ground-plan (1715). The Municipal Museum (Museo Civico) contains numerous prehistoric and Roman finds. From the promenades on the line of the old fortifications there are fine views of the Alps.

Mondovi

27 km/17 miles east of Cuneo is Mondovi (pop. 22,000), which had a university from 1560 to 1719. From the industrial lower town, Mondovi-

Breo (395 m/1304 ft), a road and a funicular lead to the upper town, Mondovi-Piazza (550 m/1815 ft), with an 18th c. cathedral (sumptuous interior) and the fine Baroque church of the Gesù, also 18th c. From the Belvedere (571 m/1884 ft), with a 14th c. Gothic tower, one can enjoy impressive Alpine views.

13 km/8 miles south of Mondovi is the winter sports area of Frabosa Soprana (800–2382 m/2640–7861 ft; cableways).

Frabosa Soprana

6 km/4 miles south-east of Mondovi is the Santuario di Vicoforte (512 m/1690 ft), a magnificent pilgrimage church (1596–1733; façade and towers 19th c.). 1 km/¾ mile away is a small spa (sulphur and chalybeate springs).

Santuario di Vicoforte

Saluzzo

The old town of Saluzzo (342 m/1129 ft; pop. 17,000), 35 km/22 miles north of Cuneo, on an outlier of Monte Viso, was from the 12th to the 16th c. the chief place in the county of Saluzzo. In the lower town is the cathedral of San Chiaffredo (1491–1501), with a large crucifix (1500) in the choir. In the upper town (395 m/1304 ft) are the Palazzo del Comune (1462); the Casa Cavassa, a Renaissance mansion which now houses the Municipal Museum, and the church of San Giovanni, in French Gothic style, containing many works of sculpture of the Lombard school and the tomb of Lodovico II (d. 1504). From the old Castello Via Griselda leads to the Belvedere, a terrace from which there are splendid views of the Alps.

4 km/2½ miles south is the village of Manta (464 m/1531 ft), with a castle containing fine 15th c. frescoes.

Manta

Pisa

Region: Toscana
Province: Pisa (PI)
Altitude: 4 m/13 ft
Population: 103,000

Pisa, capital of the province of the same name, and the see of an archbishop, lies in the northern part of the Tuscanian coast astride the Arno – 10 km/6 miles from the Tyrrhenian Sea, which has retreated as a result of the deposition of soil by the river.

Situation

Pisa, the Roman Pisae, originally an Etruscan trading station, became a Roman colony in 180 B.C.. From the 11th c. onwards it developed into one of the leading maritime and commercial powers in the Mediterranean, rivalling Genoa and Venice. It took the lead in the struggle against Islam, defeating the Muslims in Sardinia, Sicily and Tunis and playing a prominent part in the Crusades. The town celebrated its victories by the erection of splendid buildings.
The building of its cathedral in the 11th c. marked a new epoch in Tuscan art and architecture. Pisa also took a leading place in sculpture, with Nicola Pisano (c. 1220–after 1278), the great forerunner of the Renaissance; and Nicola's son Giovanni (1265–1314), his pupil Arnolfo di Cambio (d. about 1302) and Giovanni's pupil Andrea Pisano (1273–1348) formed links with the art of Florence.
The fall of the Hohenstaufens was a heavy blow for the town, which

History and art

supported the Ghibelline cause. In the long-continued conflict with Genoa the Pisan fleet suffered a decisive defeat off the island of Meloria in 1284. Internal partisan struggles led to the occupation of the town by the Florentines in 1406; and Pisa finally lost its earlier importance at the end of the 17th c. when Livorno became the leading port in Tuscany.

Pisa is the birthplace of the brilliant mathematician and scientist Galileo Galilei (1564–1642).

****Campo dei Miracoli (Piazza del Duomo)**

In the north-west of the town, enclosed on two sides by the old battle-mented town walls, is the Piazza del Duomo or Campo dei Miracoli, with the cathedral, the Leaning Tower, the Baptistery and the Campo Santo – a harmoniously composed group of buildings of unrivalled beauty.

***Cathedral**

The cathedral, a Romanesque basilica of white marble with transepts and an elliptical dome over the crossing, was built after a Pisan naval victory over the Saracens at Palermo (1064–1118) and restored in 1597–1604 after a fire. The most magnificent part is the façade (12th c.), the upper part of which has four pillared galleries. The bronze doors of the main entrance (usually closed) date from the end of the 16th c., the door of the south transept (Porta di San Ranieri), decorated with reliefs from scriptural history, from 1180.

Inside the cathedral there are ancient columns on both sides of the nave. The nave has a richly gilded Renaissance coffered ceiling.

Pisa: Campo dei Miracoli

BAPTISTERY	CATHEDRAL	C Apse
1. Font	A Pulpit	D Sagrestia dei Cappellani
2. Pulpit	B Dome	E Porta di San Ranieri

The pulpit (by Giovanni Pisano, 1302–11) is decorated with nine vigorous reliefs (New Testament scenes, Last Judgment).

The beautiful bronze lamp (1587) is said to have given Galileo the idea of the pendulum as it swung to and fro.

In the south transept is the splendid Cappella di San Ranieri, with the sarcophagus of the town's patron. To the left is the tomb of the Emperor Henry VII, by Tino da Camaino (1315).

The choir contains fine Renaissance choir-stalls and pictures by Andrea del Sarto and Sodoma. In the apse are fine mosaics, one of which represents the "Head of John the Evangelist" by Cimabue (1302).

The Treasury is kept in the Sacristy (Sagrestia dei Cappellani).

*Pulpit

*Baptistery

At the west end of the cathedral is the almost entirely marble-clad Baptistery, a circular structure built between 1153 and 1278, originally Romanesque but with 14th c. Gothic additions. In the interior, under the conical dome, are a marble font by Guido Bigarelli and the famous pulpit by Nicola Pisano (1260).

**Leaning Tower (Torre Pendente)

Near the east end of the cathedral stands the celebrated Leaning Tower (Torre Pendente), a campanile built between 1173 and 1350, with a series of several superimposed pillared galleries. The tower, which was built on alluvial land, leans to the south-east and is at present 5°30' off the vertical; at present the north side of the tower is 56.5 m/186½ ft high while the south side measures only 54.25 m/179 ft. When the foundations were found to be sinking during the construction of the tower the upper section, from the 3rd and 5th floor upwards, was given a tilt towards the north. Galileo, born in Pisa, made use of the inclination of the tower in his experiments on the law of gravity.

Note: Because of the threatening increase in its inclination the tower has been closed to the public since 1990. Safety measures (including steel ropes) were undertaken in 1992

333

Campo Santo

* Views

From the platform (294 steps) there are magnificent views of the whole town. (The Tower is currently closed to the public.)

* Campo Santo

Along the north side of the Piazza del Duomo is the Campo Santo, the most famous cemetery of its kind, a colonnaded quadrangle (126 m/138 yd long by 52 m/57 yd across) in Tuscan Gothic style, built by Giovanni di Simone in 1278–83 and completed in 1463. Earth for the cemetery had been brought from Jerusalem in 1203.

* Frescoes

The cemetery, in the form of a cloister, is surrounded by arcades and has tall round-arched windows filled with beautiful tracery overlooking the central courtyard. The world-famous frescoes on the walls (notably by Benozzo Gozzoli) were mostly destroyed by melted lead from the roof during a fire caused by Allied bombing on July 27th 1944, but some have been restored and are displayed in the cloister and in two adjoining rooms. Some of the Etruscan, Roman and medieval sculpture disposed round the cloister is of high artistic value. The pavement is composed of gravestones.

Museums

* Museo delle Sinopie

On the south side of the Piazza del Duomo stands the Museo delle Sinopie, with sketches (sinopie) for the frescoes of the Campo Santo.

* Museo dell'Opera del Duomo

East of the Piazza del Duomo is the Cathedral Museum (Museo dell'Opera del Duomo), with art of the buildings situated in the Piazza and the valuable treasury including embroideries, tombs, silver church objects, sculpture and pictures.

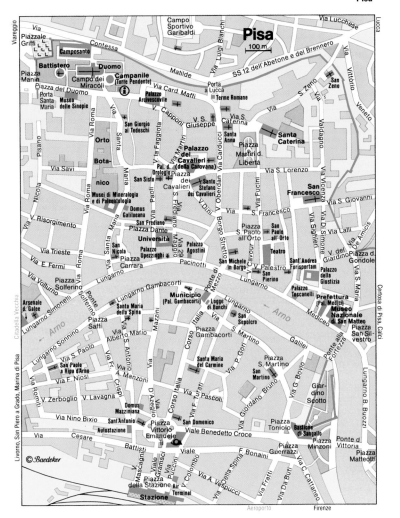

Piazza dei Cavalieri

In the Piazza dei Cavalieri in the centre of the old town are the church of
Santo Stefano dei Cavalieri (1565–96), the Palazzo dei Cavalierie and a
marble statue of Grand Duke Cosimo I (1596).
North-east is the tree-shaded Piazza Martiri della Libertà, at the north-
east corner of which stands the church of Santa Caterina (begun 1251),
with a façade in Pisan Gothic style.

Santa Caterina

| San Francesco | A little way to the south-east the Gothic convent church of San Francesco (13th c.) has a fine campanile and 14th c. frescoes. |

Lungarno Mediceo

Palazzo dei Medici	Along each bank of the Arno extends a busy riverside street (Lungarno), under various names. In the Lungarno Mediceo, on the right bank, stands the 13th c. Palazzo dei Medici, now the Prefecture.
*Museo Nazionale di San Matte	Immediately east of this is the church of San Matteo, with the former Benedictine nunnery of San Matteo, now housing the Museo Nazionale. Its collection mainly contains Pisan sculpture and pictures of the Tuscan school of the 12th to 15th c.
San Michele in Borgo	At the west end of the Lungarno Mediceo is the Piazza Garibaldi, from which runs the Borgo Stretto, a busy street flanked by arcades. At the near end of this street, on the right, stands the church of San Michele in Borgo, with a beautiful façade in Pisan Gothic style (14th c.).
University	In Lungarno Pacinotti is the Gothic Palazzo Agostini (15th c.), built in brick. A short distance north-west is the university (1493), with an Early Renaissance courtyard.
Domus Galilaeana	North-west of the university, on the south side of the Botanical Garden, is the Domus Galilaeana (house of Galileo), a memorial to the Pisa-born scientist and mathematician Galileo Galilei (library and study).

Sights on the left bank of the Arno

San Paolo a Ripa d'Arno	On the left bank of the Arno, at the west end of the Lungarno Sonnino, is the church of San Paolo a Ripa d'Arno, a basilica built about 1200 with a very fine façade.
*Santa Maria della Spina	500 m/550 yd east stands the church of Santa Maria della Spina, in French Gothic style, built in 1230 and enlarged in 1323, an elegant little church with external sculpture by pupils of Giovanni Pisano. Inside there are statues by Tommaso Pisano. The church owes it name to the fact that the interior contains a thorn (spina) of Christ's crown of thorns which was brought by the Pisans from the Holy Land.
Palazzo Gambacorti	Still farther east, at the Ponte di Mezzo, are the Gothic Palazzo Gambacorti (now Town Hall) and the Logge di Banchi (1605).
	A little way east of the Town Hall is the octagonal church of San Sepolcro (12th c.).

*San Piero a Grado

| Situation 5 km/3 miles south-west | According to legend on his way to Rome the Apostle Peter landed at this place which was then situated on the coast. It is said that he is the founder of the Ecclesia ad gradus (church on the steps). |
| | The three-aisled basilica probably dating from the 11th c., was erected over the remains of a previous building, which were discovered during excavations. Inside there are 14th c. frescoes: the lower part has portraits of popes, the centre part scenes from the life of Petri and the upper part the "heavenly" Jerusalem. |

*Certosa di Pisa

| Situation 14 km/9 miles east | East of Pisa is the Certosa di Pisa, a Carthusian house founded in 1366 and rebuilt in Baroque style in the 17th and 18th c. Interesting features |

are the two cloisters (15th and 16th c.) and the pure Baroque style of the church.

Pistoia

Region: Toscana
Province: Pistoia (P)
Altitude: 65 m/215 ft
Population: 92,000

The provincial capital of Pistoia lies at the north-west end of Tuscany on the southern slopes of the Apennines, some 28 km/17 miles north-west of Florence.

Situation

Pistoia was the Roman Pistoria. During the Middle Ages it was the scene of bitter conflicts between Ghibellines and Guelfs, and in 1295 it came under Florentine rule – a subjection confirmed in 1530. The town's surviving medieval buildings demonstrate the vigorous spirit of enterprise of even the smaller Tuscan towns. In the older churches the influence of the Pisan style, widely diffused in the 12th c., is still predominant, but from the 14th c. the artists working here came almost exclusively from Florence.

History and art

*Cathedral

In the centre of the rectangular area occupied by the old town is the Piazza del Duomo, on the south side of which stands the cathedral of Santi Zeno e Jacopo, a 12th–13th c. Romanesque building. The campanile was originally a fortified tower (1200), to which three orders of columns, Pisan-style, were later added. In the porch, added in 1311, is a terracotta medallion of the Madonna with Angels by Andrea della Robbia (1505). Inside, to the left of the entrance, is the fine tomb of Cardinal Niccolò Forteguerri (d. 1473), designed by Andrea Verrocchio and in the Cappella del Sacramento, to the left of the choir, is a Madonna by Lorenzo di Credi (1485). To the right of the choir in the Cappella di San Iacopo can be seen a rich silver altar (13th–14th c., with over 600 small figures, depicting scenes from the Old and New Testaments.

Adjoining the north aisle of the cathedral is the old Palazzo del Vescovi (Bishop's Palace; 14th c.) which houses the Diocesan Museum containing pictures and goldsmiths' and silversmiths' work.

Museo Diocesano

The Gothic Baptistery (14th c.) opposite the cathedral has an external pulpit and a fine Early Renaissance wooden door. On the font are richly decorated panels from the old pulpit (1199).

*Baptistery

Adjoining the baptistery is the 14th c. Palazzo del Podestà or Palazzo Pretorio, with a picturesque arcaded courtyard; in the arcades and on the façade are the coats of arms of podestàs of the past, sent from Florence.

Palazzo del Podestà

On the north side of the Piazza del Duomo stands the Gothic Palazzo del Comune (1294–1385), also with a beautiful courtyard. The Museo Civico on the top floor contains pictures, sculpture and material recovered by excavation.

Palazzo del Comune
Museo Civico

North-east of the Palazzo del Comune stands the 12th c. church of San Bartolomeo in Pantano, a pillared basilica in Tuscan Romanesque style, with a fine interior including a pulpit (1250) with eight reliefs from the life of Christ.

San Bartolomeo in Pantano

Pistoia: Façade of the Cathedral

Ospedale del Ceppo

In the nearby Piazza dello Spedale, to the north-west of the town, is the Ospedale del Ceppo (13th or 14th c.). In the porch is a frieze of terracotta reliefs, coloured and glazed by Giovanni della Robbia and his pupils (1514–25).

*Sant'Andrea

West of the hospital stands the church of Sant'Andrea, a 12th c. pillared basilica in Pisan style. The pulpit, one of Giovanni Pisano's principal works, is supported by seven porphyry columns (two of them standing on lions). The wooden crucifix is also by Giovanni Pisano.

San Francesco

A short distance west of Sant'Andrea, in the spacious Piazza San Francesco d'Assisi, the church of San Francesco, a Gothic convent church begun in 1294, has frescoes in the chapter-house modelled on Giotto's frescoes at Assisi (14th c.; restored in 1930). In the main choir chapel are 14th c. wall paintings, depicting scenes from the life of St Francis.

*Madonna dell'Umiltà

From San Francesco we go south on Via Bozzi and Via Curtatone e Montanara and then turn right along Via della Madonna to reach the church of the Madonna dell'Umiltà (1494–1522), with a beautiful porch and an octagonal dome added by Vasari in 1561 on the model of the dome of Florence Cathedral.

Sights south of Pistoia

*San Giovanni Fuorcivitas

To the east of the Piazza Gavinana, the town's busiest traffic intersection, is the church of San Giovanni Fuorcivitas (1160–70), in Tuscan

Romanesque style. It contains a pulpit (*c.* 1270) by Fra Guglielmo da Pisa and a terractotta group (the "Visitation") by Lucca della Robbia (*c.* 1445).

From the church Via Cavallotti leads south to the convent church of San Domenico (1380), with remains of 14th c. frescoes and fine monuments.

San Domenico

A little way east, in the broad Corso Silvano Fedi, is the church of San Paolo (*c.* 1302), with a fine Pisan-style façade.

San Paolo

Pompeii/Pompei   L9

Region: Campania
Province: Napoli (NA)
Altitude: 16 m/53 ft
Population: 23,000

The ruined city of Pompeii lies 20 km/12 miles south-east of Naples at the foot of Vesuvius, near the Gulf of Naples.

Situation

It is the finest example of a Roman town and its way of life, presented to modern eyes by excavation.

To the east of the ancient site is the newer settlement, known until 1929 as Valle di Pompei, with a conspicuous domed church, Santa Maria del Rosario, which is visited by countless pilgrims (particularly on May 8th and on the first Sunday in October).

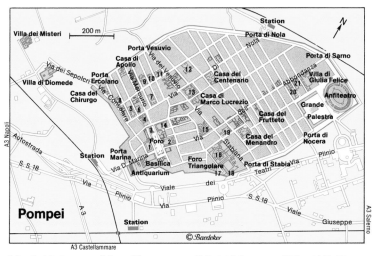

1 Temple of Apollo	7 House of Faun	13 Central Baths	19 Casa del Citarista
2 Building of Eumachia	8 House of Sallust	14 Macellum	20 House of Marcus Loreius
3 Temple of Jupiter	9 House of Labyrinth	15 Stabian Baths	Tiburtinus
4 Forum Baths	10 House of Vettii	16 Large Theatre	21 House of Venus
5 House of Pansa	11 House of Gilded Cupids	17 Doric Temple	
6 House of Tragic Poet	12 House of Silver Wedding	18 Gladiators' Barracks	

Pompeii/Pompei

Pompeii, probably founded by the Oscans, an Italic people, became Roman after the Samnite wars (290 B.C.), and by the 1st c. A.D. was a prosperous provincial capital with a population estimated at 20,000. In A.D. 63 much of the town was destroyed by a severe earthquake, and rebuilding had not been completed when an eruption of Vesuvius in A.D 79 covered the whole town, as well as Herculaneum and Stabiae, with a layer of ash and pumice-stone 6–7 m/6½–7½ yd thick – though a proportion of the population were able to escape in time. The town was now abandoned, after some at least of the survivors had recovered objects of value from the loose covering of ash.

Since the 18th c. something like three-fifths of the total area of the town (the walls of which had a perimeter of 3100 m/3391 yd) have been recovered by large-scale excavation, carried out systematically from 1860 onwards. Although the buildings are in a ruinous state and it is only in the more recently excavated areas (since 1911) that the internal arrangements and domestic equipment have, as far as possible, been left as they were found. Visitors to Pompeii get a more immediate and more vivid impression of ancient life – in luxurious mansions and more modest houses, in the markets and the streets, in baths, theatres and temples – than on any other ancient site; and much of what they see will strike them as astonishingly modern.

In November 1980 a severe earthquake caused considerable damage.

Division of the site

In modern times the site has been divided into several regions (I-IX) separated by the principal streets. The blocks (insulae) within the regions are, like them, numbered with Roman numerals (in the plan with Arabic numerals); individual houses have Arabic numerals.

The streets are paved with polygonal slabs of lava, with raised pavements on either side. At intersections and at other places along the streets are stepping-stones designed to help pedestrians to cross. Deep ruts in the paving bear witness to heavy traffic. At many street corners are fountains for public use. The inscriptions on the outside walls of houses, in the manner of modern posters, mostly relate to municipal elections.

Roman house

The Roman house was entered from the street by a narrow passage (fauces, ostium), often flanked by shops and workshops (tabernae), leading into a large court or atrium with a roof which sloped inwards. In the centre of the roof was a square opening (compluvium), below which, sunk into the ground, was a basin for catching rain-water (impluvium). On each side, and sometimes in front, were bedrooms (cubiculae); on each side too were alae, open spaces originally designed for the statues of ancestors. The fourth side of the atrium was entirely occupied by a large open apartment, the tablinum. Beyond the front portion of the house, in which visitors were received, lay the private apartments used by the family; these were built round a garden-like courtyard, known as the peristylium from the columns which enclosed it. Beyond this there was sometimes a garden (viridarium). Opening off the peristylium were the triclinium (dining-room) and sitting-room (oecus). The position of the kitchen (culina) and cellars varied. Many houses also had an upper floor with balconies.

It is interesting to compare the Pompeian single-storey house occupied by one family with the blocks of apartments built round a large central courtyard which became general under the Empire and are found at Ostia but not at Pompeii.

Pompeii: Ancient street

**Tour of the site

The main entrance to the site (open daily) is near the Pompeii–Villa dei Misteri railway station. 300 m/330 yd from the entrance is the Porta Marina, the ancient gate at the south-west corner of the town.

Immediately beyond the gate, on the right, is the Antiquarium, containing excavated material from Pompeii dating from the pre-Samnite period to Roman times. Particularly impressive are the casts of human bodies and of a dog found buried under the ashes.

Beyond the Antiquarium, also on the right, is the Basilica, used as a market and a law-court. To the left is the Temple of Apollo, surrounded by 48 Ionic columns. Beyond these two buildings is the Forum, the principal square of the Roman town, which was enclosed by colonnades. At the north end of the forum is the Temple of Jupiter, on a base 3 m/10 ft high. At the north-east corner is the Macellum, a hall for the sale of foodstuff. Down the east side are the Shrine of the Lares, the Temple of Vespasian (probably dedicated originally to Augustus) and the Building of Eumachia, probably a hall for the sale of wool. On the south side of the forum is the Curia, the meeting-place of the town council, flanked by three other rooms.

Beyond the forum the Via dell'Abbondanza, one of the principal streets of the ancient town, continues east, to the right of the Building of Eumachia, towards the new excavations. The second street on the right (Via dei Teatri) leads to the tree-shaded Triangular Forum, intended mainly for theatre-goers, which is entered through a fine arcade. On the south side of this little square are the remains of a Greek temple; facing this, to the east, are barracks for gladiators.

Adjoining the northern half of the Triangular Forum, built into the sloping ground, is the Large Theatre (Teatro Grande), which could seat

Main entrance

Antiquarium

*Forum

Triangular forum

*Large Theatre

341

some 5000 spectators and is now used for "Son et lumière" shows in summer. From the top row there are fine views.

*Little Theatre

Adjoining this the better preserved Little Theatre (Teatro Piccolo), the earliest example of a roofed Roman theatre (c. 75 B.C.); with seating for 1500, was used mainly for musical performances.

Temples

On the east side of the Little Theatre is the Via Stabiana, which runs north-west. Immediately on the left is the little Tempio di Giove Meilichio. To the west of this, in the Via del Tempio d'Iside, the Temple of Isis has an inscription scratched on its walls by the French novelist Stendhal (Henri Beyle) during a visit in 1817.

Beyond this, on the east side of the Via Stabiana, is the Casa del Citarista, one of the largest houses in Pompeii. Just beyond this the Via Stabiana joins the Via dell'Abbondanza.

Nuovi Scavi

100 m/110 yd along the Via dell'Abbondanza to the right is the beginning of the New Excavations (Nuovi Scavi), in which wall paintings and furniture have been left in place and in many cases the upper storey with its balconies and loggias has been preserved by the insertion of girders. In this area there are many election "posters" and other casual inscriptions painted on the walls, with the help of which the former director of excavations, Della Corte, was able to compile a "directory" containing 550 names. This part of the town dates from Pompeii's final period and was mostly occupied by tradesmen. Among the establishments to be seen here are an ironmonger's shop; beyond this to the right a fuller's and dyer's workshop (Fullonica di Stefano), with two restored pressing machines; and beyond this, to the south, the House with the Cryptoporticus, with a magnificent painted frieze (in a passage leading to the cellar) depicting 20 episodes from the "Iliad" and other Homeric poems.

*House of Menander

Still farther south is the large and well-preserved House of Menander which belonged to a wealthy merchant; it was named after a likeness of the Greek comic playwright Menander in a niche in the magnificent peristylium. Adjoining this is the charming little House of the Lovers. Farther along the Via dell'Abbondanza, on the left, is the Thermopolium, a tavern fully equipped with drinking vessels, a kettle, a stove and a lamp, with the last customer's money still on the counter. Beyond this, on the left, is the interesting House of Trebius Valens, the front wall of which is covered with inscriptions; and beyond this again, on the right, is the rich House of Marcus Loreius Tiburtinus, with a restored double door and an interesting interior.

*Painting of Venus

Farther east, to the south of the Via della Abbondanza, are the most recent excavations (1951–59). Of particular interest in this area are the House of Venus (Casa della Venere), with a fine painting of Venus; the House of the Orchard (Casa del Frutteto); and the Villa di Giulia Felice.

Necropolis

Farther south, outside the Porta di Nocera, we come to a necropolis (cemetery), such as lay outside the walls of all ancient towns.

Palaestra

South of the House of Marcus Loreius Tiburtinus is the Palaestra, with colonnades round three sides (each 140 m/154 yd long) and a swimming pool in the centre.

Amphitheatre

Immediately east of this is the massive Amphitheatre (136 m/149 yd long, 104 m/114 yd across, seating for 12,000 spectators), the oldest surviving Roman amphitheatre (80 B.C.).

Stabian Baths

At the corner of the Via dell'Abbondanza and the Via Stabiana are the Stabian Baths (Terme Stabiana), the largest and best-preserved baths in Pompeii (entrance from Via dell'Abbondanza). The entrance leads into the colonnaded palaestra, with a swimming pool on the left; on the right are the male and female baths, separated by the stoves for heating the water. Each establishment has a circular cold bath (frigidarium), a changing room (apodyterium) with racks for clothing, a warm bath (tepidarium) and a hot (Turkish) bath (caldarium) heated by air-ducts in the floor and walls.

Immediately north of the baths is the House of Siricus (entrance from Vicolo del Lupanare); next door is a bakery. On the threshold is the inscription "Salve lucrum" ("Long live profit!"); fine paintings in the interior. Farther along the Via Stabiana, on the right, is the House of Marcus Lucretius, also with well-preserved paintings.

In another 100 m/110 yd the Via Stabiana crosses the Via di Nola, one of the principal streets of the town, and 100 m/110 yd farther on again comes to an intersection at which the Vicolo delle Nozze d'Argento (on the right) leads to the House of the Silver Wedding (fine atrium and peristylium) and the Vicolo di Mercurio (on the left) leads past the House of the Vettii to the House of Sallust.

Houses

Farther along the Via Stabiana, also called the Via del Vesuvio in its northern section, is the elegant House of the Gilded Cupids (Casa degli Amorini dorati), with a garden which still preserves its original marble decoration. The Via Stabiana ends at the Porta del Vesuvio; from the hill outside the gate there is a fine view.

House of the Gilded Cupids

The very interesting House of the Vettii in the Vicolo di Mercurio has well-preserved ornamental paintings and fine frescoes in the triclinium. The peristylium (partly rebuilt) still has its original marble decoration and has been replanted. The kitchen still contains its cooking utensils.

South-west of the House of the Vettii is the House of the Labyrinth (Casa del Labirinto), with two atria.

House of the Vettii

Wall paintings in Pompeii

343

*House of the Faun	Opposite this, to the south, is the House of the Faun (Casa del Fauno; entrance from the Via di Nola), the most palatial mansion in Pompeii, taking up a whole insula (80 × 35 m/88 × 38 yd). By the impluvium is a copy of the statuette of a faun which was discovered here. The famous mosaic of "Alexander's Battle" was found in the room with red columns.
*Forum Baths	In the Via delle Terme, the westerly continuation of the Via di Nola (the western part of which is also called the Via di Fortuna), are the Forum Baths (Terme del Foro), smaller and more modest than the Stabian Baths but also occupying a whole insula. On the south side of the baths is a modern bar.
House of the Tragic Poet	To the north of the Baths is the elegant and richly appointed House of the Tragic Poet (Casa del Poeta tragico), on the threshold of which is a mosaic of a chained dog with the inscription "Cave canem" ("Beware of the dog").
House of Pansa	Adjoining the House of the Tragic Poet on the west is the House of Pansa (98 × 38 m/107 × 42 yd), one of the largest and most regularly planned houses in Pompeii.
House of Sallust	On the north side of the House of the Tragic Poet is a fuller's workshop, to the left of which are the House of the Large Fountain and the House of the Small Fountain, with the beautiful fountains after which they are named. From the latter house the Vicolo di Mercurio runs west to the House of Sallust, where can be seen good paintings. From here Via Consolare runs north-west to the Porta Ercolano, which probably dates from the Augustan period.

*Street of Tombs

	Outside the gate lies a suburban district of which only the main street has been excavated. This Street of Tombs is, from the scenic point of view, the most attractive part of Pompeii. Lined with imposing monuments to distinguished citizens, it ranks with the Via Appia outside Rome as the most impressive surviving example of the Roman practice of erecting tombs along public roads.
*Villa of Diomedes	At the north-west end of the street is the large Villa of Diomedes, with an extensive garden enclosed by a portico 33 m/36 yd long each way. In the centre of the garden is a basin and six columns which belonged to a pavilion. In an underground passage (cryptoporticus) were found the bodies of 18 women and children. Near the garden door (now walled up) was the body of a man, presumably the owner of the house, with a key in his hand and a slave beside him carrying money and valuables.
*Villa of the Mysteries	200 m/220 yd north-west of the Villa of Diomedes, outside the main excavation area, is the magnificent Villa of the Mysteries (Villa dei Misteri; reached from the main entrance to the excavations on a road which runs past the station (500 m/550 yd) and continues for another 700 m/770 yd), with the finest surviving ancient wall paintings, preserved in all the brilliance of their original colouring. The most remarkable of these is a frieze 17 m/19 yd long in the large triclinium with almost life-size figures, dating from the pre-Augustan period (probably based on models of the 3rd c. B.C.), which depicts scenes from the Dionysiac mysteries.

Pontine Islands/Arcipelago Pontino   I/K9

Region: Latium/Lazio
Province: Latina (LT)
Population: 4000

Boat services from Formia to Ponza and Ventotene; from Anzio to   Boat services
Ponza and from Naples via Ventotene to Ponza; hydrofoils from Anzio,
Formia and Terracina.

The Pontine Islands (Italian Arcipelago Pontino) lie off the coast of   Situation
southern Latium; they form the boundary of the Gulf of Gaeta (Golfo di
Gaeta) and the Tyrrhenian Sea. They are of volcanic origin and are
frequently shaken by minor earth tremors.
The inhabitants live mainly from vine-growing and fishing; in recent
years there has also been a developing tourist trade.

The islands

The north-western group of islands consists of the almost uninhabited   Ponza
islands of Palmarola and Zannone (known to the Romans as Palmaria
and Sinonia) and Gavi and the well-cultivated main island of Ponza, a
crater ridge 7.5 km/4¾ miles long, rising to a height of 284 m/937 ft at
the southern end in Monte della Guardia, and fringed by picturesque
coves and cliffs. Below the hill is a bay forming a
sheltered harbour, with the villages of Ponza (hotels) and Santa Maria.
The south-eastern group consists of the islands of Ventotene, part of a
former crater (3 km/2 miles long by 1 km/½ mile across), with a village of
the same name, and Santo Stefano, a granite island with a former
prison.

Portofino   F5

Region: Liguria
Province: Genova (GE)
Altitude: 3 m/10 ft
Population: 800

Portofino, some 30 km/19 miles south-east of Genova, is picturesquely   Situation
situated in a narrow cove at the south-eastern tip of the promontory of
the same name.
The village owes its popularity with visitors to its beautiful setting, its   *Holiday resort
agreeable climate and its luxuriant Mediterranean vegetation.

*Village of Portofino

The houses of the former fishing village line the bay, and the slopes are
covered with pines and olive trees. To the south, above the harbour, is
the church of San Giorgio, from which there is a beautiful view of
Portofino. There are even more extensive views from the platform
beside the Fortezza di San Giorgio, to the east, extending north-west to
Capo Mele and the Maritime Alps.

*Portofino promontory

There is a very attractive boat trip (1½ hours) under the precipitous   San Fruttuoso
south side of the promontory to San Fruttuoso, a former abbey which

Portofino: A picturesque part of the harbour

appears in the records as early as 984, with an early Gothic church and a cloister, picturesquely situated in a small rocky cove. Offshore, 17 m/56 ft below sea-level, is a bronze figure of Christ, the so-called Christo degli Abissi, 2.5 m/8¼ ft high (1954) on a concrete base weighing 80 tons.

From San Fruttuoso there is a pleasant walk (2 hours), steep in the first section, to the Semàforo Vecchio (610 m/2013 ft), the highest point on the Portofino promontory, which thrusts out squarely into the sea for 4–5 km/2½–3 miles, affording views which extend in clear weather as far as Corsica. From here it is half an hour's walk to the Portofino Vetta (450 m/1485 ft), the view from which is famous. To the north-west can be seen the coastline from Camogli to Genoa and beyond this Capo Berta, above which, best seen in the morning light, are the snow-covered Cottian Alps; to the south-east are Rapallo, Chiavari and Sestri Levante, the islands off Portovenere and the Apuan Alps. Here too is the aerial tower, 117 m/386 ft high, of the Genoa television transmitter.

Camogli

On the west side of the Portofino promontory the picturesquely situated little port of Camogli has a beautiful parish church and the ruined Castello Dragone.

Prato   H6

Region: Toscana
Province: Firenze (FI)
Altitude: 61 m/201 ft
Population: 162,000

Situation

The Tuscan town of Prato lies on the River Bisenzio, about half-way between Florence and Pistoia. The centre is surrounded by town walls.

On account of its important woollen industry, already known in the Middle Ages, Prato is also known as the "Italian Manchester".

The town centre is closed to cars.

Tip

*Cathedral

In the Piazza del Duomo, in the northern part of the town, stands the cathedral, begun in the 12th c. in Tuscan Romanesque style and re-modelled in Gothic style in 1317–20, with a Lombard tower (13th–14th c.).

On the façade (1385–1457) is a pulpit by Donatello and Michelozzo, with reliefs of dancing children (1434–38; originals replaced by copies). Above the main entrance is a terracotta relief by Andrea della Robbia of the Madonna with SS. Stephen and Lawrence (1489).

*Pulpit

The interior is decorated with green-white marble as in Pisan examples. The Cappella del Sacro Cingolo ("Holy Belt") has interesting wall paintings by Agnolo Gaddi (scenes from the life of the Virgin, particularly the Assumption of the Virgin Mary and the role the belt plays in it). In the choir are frescoes by Filippo Lippi (St John the Baptist and St Stephen). In the nave is a rich marble pulpit with reliefs by Mino da Fiesole and Antonio Rossellino (1473).

To the left of the cathedral is the Museo dell'Opera del Duomo (Cathedral Museum), containing altarpieces and the shrine of the Holy Belt, including the original reliefs (dancing children) from the outer pulpit of the cathedral.

Cathedral Museum

Town centre

From the Piazza del Duomo Via Mazzoni runs south to the Piazza del Comune in the centre of the town. At the south-west corner of the square stands the Palazzo Pretorio (13th–14th c.) which houses the Galleria Comunale, with pictures by Florentine masters of the 14th and 15th c., including Filippo Lippi.

Palazzo Pretorio
(Galleria Comunale)

Opposite the Palazzo Pretorio is the Palazzo Comunale which was restored in the 19th c.

Palazzo Comunale

The Palazzo, south of the Piazza del Comune, was the residence of the merchant and banker Francesco di Marco Datini (1330–1410). After Datini's death the façade was decorated with frescoes, depicting scenes from his life. There are only a few sinopes left.

Palazzo Datini

In the west of the town centre, in Piazza San Domenico, is the church of San Domenico (1283–1322) with an unfinished façade. Particularly notable is the richly decorated portal of the south transept. Inside there is a large painted crucifix (c. 1400).

San Domenico

Through the 15th c. cloister we reach the Museo di Pittura Murale (Wall Painting Museum), with frescoes, sinopes (13–17th c.) including documents showing fresco techniques and several restoration methods.

Museo di Pittura
Murale

From the Piazza del Comune, Via Ricasoli runs south to the Piazza San Francesco on the left side of which is the 13th c. church of San Francesco. In the beautiful cloister to the right of the church we find the entrance to the chapter-house, which has fine wall paintings of the school of Giotto (Gerini, 14th c.).

San Francesco

In the adjoining square to the east, on the left, is the church of Santa Maria delle Carceri, a good example of a church on a Greek cross plan

*Santa Maria delle
Carceri

347

Prato: External pulpit . . .

. . . and interior of the cathedral

with a dome. It contains a fine high altar by Sangallo (1515) and terracotta medallions of the Evangelists by Andrea della Robbia.

Castello dell'Imperatore

To the south of Santa Maria delle Carceri the Castello dell'Imperatore, a crenellated castle built in the reign of the Emperor Frederick II (1237–48), has two 10th c. towers.

*Centro per l'Arte Contemporanea Luigi Pecci

In 1988 the Centro per l'Arte Contemporanea Luigi Pecci (Museum of Contemporary Art) was opened in Prato. The museum, on the plan of a rectangular "U", is in the south of the old town, in Via della Repubblica (corner of Via delle Fonti di Mezzana). The building was financed by the Associazione Luigi Pecci which was founded by the industrialist Enrico Pecci who died in 1988. The house, with an adjoining research centre, is to be a forum for painting, sculpture, design, video and other forms of creative expression. At the opening of the "U" is an arena with steps for seating. The arena, in the form of a Greek amphitheatre, accommodates 600 to 800 persons.

Prócida/Isola di Prócida

K/L9

Region: Campania
Province: Napoli (NA)
Altitude: 0–91 m/0–300 ft
Population: 10,000

Situation

The island of Procida lies on the west side of the Bay of Naples between Capo Miseno and the island of Ischia.

The island, with a length of 3.5 km/2 miles and an area of 3.75 sq. km/1¼ sq. miles is of volcanic origin. It is formed of two adjoining craters, the southern rims of which have been invaded and eroded by the sea, leaving two bays on the south-east coast of the island. The Bay of Chiaiolella to the south-west may have been formed by another smaller crater, while a fourth gave rise to the neighbouring islet of Vivara.

History

Island of Prócida

On the north side of the island, extending inland from the coast onto a hill, is the little town of Prócida (32 m/106 ft), whose gleaming white houses have something of an oriental air. Particularly picturesque are the fishing harbour with its numerous boats and the district of Corricella. On a precipitous crag above the town towers a massive castle (part of it now a prison), commanding extensive views of the neighbouring islands and peninsulas.
From the town a narrow road runs 3 km/2 miles south to Chiaiolella Bay, with a fine bathing beach. Higher up to the east is the old church of Santa Margherita.

Town of Prócida

Offshore to the west is the little islet of Vivara (109 m/360 ft), which is connected to Prócida by a bridge. Olive trees grow well and there are wild rabbits. It is the intention to lay out a nature park on Vivara.

Vivara

Rapallo

F5

Region: Liguria
Province: Genova (GE)
Altitude: 2 m/7 ft
Population: 30,000

The little port town of Rapallo, a popular resort both in summer and in winter, lies on the Riviera di Levante, tucked away in the Bay of Rapallo or Golfo Tigullio, some 25 km/16 miles south-east of Genoa.

Situation

Sights

The houses in the town are built along the bay. A number of streets run parallel to this bay, others run uphill. The town's busiest square is the Piazza Cavour, in which are the old parish church with a façade of 1857, and a leaning tower of 1753. To the south-west, near the mouth of the little River Boate, is the small Giardino Pubblico, from which there is a charming view of Sestri Levante. 1 km/¾ mile south of Piazza Cavour, on the road to Santa Margherita, is the Kursaal.
On the south-east side of the fishing harbour, beyond the mouth of the Torrente San Francesco, is a medieval Castello, now an exhibition centre.

Madonna di Montallegro

North of Rapallo is the pilgrimage church of the Madonna di Montallegro, high up on the hillside (612 m/202 ft; also reached by cableway, 10 minutes). From the top there are far-ranging views of the Gulf of Rapallo.

Situation
11 km/7 miles

Portofino

From Rapallo there is a magnificent coast road, the S.S. 227, running south to the picturesquely situated Portofino.

Situation
8 km/5 miles south

Region: Emilia-Romagna
Province: Ravenna (RA)
Altitude: 3 m/10 ft
Population: 137,000

Situation

Ravenna, a provincial capital and the see of an archbishop, lies in the south-east corner of the North Italian plain, here traversed by numerous drainage canals. Originally a seaport, it is now connected with the sea by a canal 10 km/6 miles long linking it with Porto Corsini.

With its important early medieval buildings, Ravenna is one of the most interesting towns in Italy, and visitors get a vivid impression of early medieval art.

Economy

Ravenna has a large oil refinery, and other major elements in its economy are natural gas extraction and vine-growing.

History

In the time of the Etruscans and Romans Ravenna was a lagoon town like Venice. Augustus made the port of Portus Classis, 5 km/3 miles

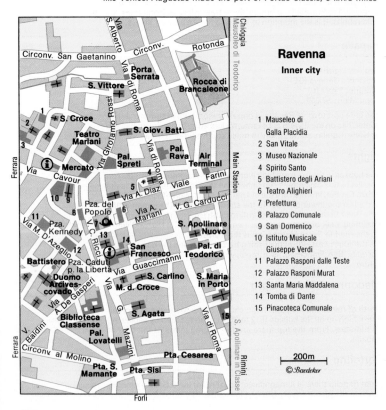

Ravenna

Inner city

1 Mauseleo di
   Galla Placidia
2 San Vitale
3 Museo Nazionale
4 Spirito Santo
5 Battistero degli Ariani
6 Teatro Alighieri
7 Prefettura
8 Palazzo Comunale
9 San Domenico
10 Istituto Musicale
   Giuseppe Verdi
11 Palazzo Rasponi dalle Teste
12 Palazzo Rasponi Murat
13 Santa Maria Maddalena
14 Tomba di Dante
15 Pinacoteca Comunale

200m

© Baedeker

from the town, the base of the Roman Adriatic fleet. Ravenna's heyday began, however, when the Western Roman Emperor Honorius moved his court from Milan to the natural fortress of Ravenna, protected by the surrounding marches, in 402. While the rest of Italy was being devastated during the great migrations, an active programme of building was carried out here under Honorius and his sister Galla Placidia (Regent 425–450), and the art of mosaic-working flourished. After the fall of the Western Roman Empire the Herulian Odoacer was proclaimed king by the Germanic mercenary troops and ruled the whole of Italy from Ravenna (476–493). After his murder the Ostrogothic king Theodoric the Great, who had been brought up in Constantinople (493–526), brought further splendour to the town, building several churches for the Arian Church, to which the Ostrogoths belonged, as well as a royal palace. In 539, under Justinian (527–565), the Byzantine general Belisarius drove out the Ostrogoths. Thereafter Ravenna became the seat of a Byzantine governor (Exarch), and, favoured by the emperor, enjoyed a third period of prosperity, which introduced Byzantine art to the West. In 751, however, the Lombards put an end to the Exarchate. From 1297 to 1441 Ravenna was ruled by the Ghibelline Polenta family, for a period thereafter belonged to the Venetians and from 1509 to 1859 was incorporated in the States of the Church.

Piazza del Popolo

In the centre of the town is the Piazza del Popolo, with the Palazzo Comunale (Town Hall, 1681). In front of the Town Hall are two granite columns erected by the Venetians in 1483. In the square stands the Palazzo Veneziano, a portico of eight granite columns, with Theodoric's monogram on four of the capitals.

Palazzo Comunale

A short distance south-west of the Piazza del Popolo is the Cathedral of Sant' Orso, built 1734–43 on the site of the oldest church in Ravenna, founded by St Ursus (d. 396); the campanile (10th c.) dates from this earlier church. In the nave, on the right, the 6th c. pulpit was reconstructed from the separate marble slabs, decorated with animal figures, of which it was originally composed. In the second chapel on the right and in the south transept are Early Christian marble sarcophagi.

Cathedral

Immediately north of the cathedral is the Baptistery of the Orthodox or Neoniana, an octagonal 5th c. brick structure. The mosaics in the dome (some of which have been restored) are among the oldest in Ravenna. The font is 16th c. but the parapet is ancient.

* Baptistery of the Orthodox

Behind the cathedral, to the south-east, stands the Archbishop's Palace (Arcivescovado), on the first floor of which, on the left, is the Museo Arcivescovile (Archbishop's Museum), with the so-called throne of Archbishop Maximilian, actually 6th c. Egyptian work, with ivory reliefs.

Archbishop's Palace (Museum)

Farther east of the Palazzo is the modern Piazza dei Caduti per la Libertà, from which several streets lead off. To the east of the square is the Franciscan church of San Francesco, founded in the 5th c., with a Romanesque tower (10th c.).

San Francesco

To the north of the church can be seen Dante's Tomb (Tomba di Dante). The exterior is neo-classical (1780); in the interior is a sarcophagus containing the remains of the poet, who died in exile in Ravenna in 1321 at the age of 56.

Dante's tomb

** San Vitale

500 m/550 yd north-west of the Piazza del Popolo is the church of San Vitale, an externally unadorned octagonal structure on a centralised

* Mosaics

Ravenna

Ravenna: Dante's tomb

Mosaic in San Vitale

San Vitale

plan (diameter 35 m/38 yd) with an octagonal dome, begun in 526 during the reign of Theodoric and consecrated in 547. The interior, which has been freed from later additions with the exception of the Baroque frescoes in the dome, is divided by eight piers into a central space and a surrounding ambulatory. The principal interest lies in its mosaics in Byzantine style. The 6th c. mosaics in the choir apse (below, left and right) depict Justinian and his wife Theodora, who are accompanied by their suite (next to the emperor is Archbishop Maximilian); above is Christ on a sphere flanked by St Vitalis (on the left) and St Ecclesius (on the right). The altar is of translucent alabaster.

Beyond San Vitale is the mausoleum of Galla Placidia (c. 440), in the form of a Latin cross, with a barrel-vaulted roof and a dome over the crossing. The interior is decorated with beautiful mosaics (5th c.) on a dark blue ground – a cross, the symbols of the Evangelists, figures of the Apostles, above the door Christ as the Good Shepherd. To the rear and in the two lateral arms of the cross are marble sarcophagi, said to be those of Galla Placidia, her second husband Constantius III (d. 421) and her son Valentinian III (d. 455).

*Mausoleum of Galla Placidia

To the west, adjoining San Vitale, is the interesting Museo Nazionale, with inscriptions, sculpture, carved ivories and other valuable objects.

Museo Nazionale

*Sant'Apollinare Nuovo

In the busy Via di Roma, on the east side of the town, is the church of Sant'Apollinare Nuovo, a basilica built by Theodoric after 500 as an Arian cathedral and converted into a Roman Catholic church in 560. The porch and the apse date from the 16th and 18th c. The interior of the church contains 24 marble columns from Constantinople. The walls of the nave have interesting 6th c. mosaics: on the left-hand wall the Roman port of Classis, with ships; on the right-hand wall the town of Ravenna, with its churches and Theodoric's palace, and saints in Byzantine costumes; above the friezes prophets; and above the windows interesting compositions from the New Testament – on the left the sayings and miracles of Christ (who is shown beardless), on the right scenes from the Passion (with a bearded Christ).
A little way south of Sant'Apollinare, at the corner of Via Alberoni, are remains of the so-called Palace of Theodoric (richly articulated façade, with a central projection).

*Mosaics

Farther south stands the large Renaissance church of Santa Maria in Porto (16th c.; façade 1784). The adjoining Logetta Lombardesco and the Renaissance cloister house the Pinacoteca Comunale (Picture Gallery).
North-east of Sant'Apollinare, in the area around the station, which suffered heavy damage during the Second World War and has been completely redeveloped since then, is the church of San Giovanni Evangelista (fine campanile), founded by Galla Placidia in 424 and rebuilt in its original form after severe war damage.
A short distance west (entered from Via Paolo Costa) are the Basilica of the Santo Spirito, built in the reign of Theodoric, and the former Baptistery of the Arians (later Santa Maria in Cosmedin), with 6th c. mosaics (Baptism of Christ), heavily restored, in the dome.

Santa Maria in Porto Pinacoteca

San Giovanni Evangelista

Baptistery of the Arians

*Tomb of Theodoric

750 m/825 yd east of the Porta Serrata (at the north end of the Via di Roma) is the Tomb of Theodoric, built about 520, probably on the order

of Theodoric himself. This is a monumental two-storey rotunda built in square blocks of Istrian limestone and roofed with a single huge block 11 m/12 yd in diameter. The tomb is reminiscent of Syrian rather than Roman models. The ornamentation shows clear Germanic influence. The lower floor is a barrel-vaulted chamber in the form of a Greek cross, on the upper floor is an antique porphyry sarcophagus.

**Sant'Apollinare in Classe

Situation
5 km/3 miles south

South of Ravenna, on the road to Rimini, stands the fine church of Sant'Apollinare in Classe, the only preserved building of the town of Classis, with a porch and a round campanile. The church, begun about 535 on a site just outside the ancient port of Classis, was consecrated in 549; it was restored in 1779 and freed from encroaching buildings in 1904. The spacious interior contains 24 Byzantine marble columns. On the walls are medallions with portraits of bishops and archbishops of Ravenna (18th c.). In the aisles are marble sarcophagi of archbishops of the 5th–8th c. The 12th c. crypt has an ancient bronze window-grating. The mosaics in the apse and on the triumphal arch date from the 6th–7th c. (restored). In the apse is a Christ as the Good Shepherd, below the church's patron with followers (shown as sheep); above the triumphal arch Christ as the pantocrater, surrounded by sheep symbolising the twelve Apostles.
Near the church are excavations (Zona Archeologica di Classe).

5 km/3 miles south-east of Sant'Appolinare are the remains of the Pineta di Classe, a once famous pinewood which has been much reduced by felling and fire. A short way to the west is "Mirabilandia", opened in 1992, the largest leisure park in Italy, with over 30 attractions.

Tomb of Theodoric

Sant'Apollinare in Classe

Marina di Ravenna

North-east of Ravenna, on the Adriatic coast, is the seaside resort of Marina di Ravenna.
Beyond the Canale Candiano (ferry) is Porto Corsini, the port of Ravenna.

Situation
11 km/7 miles
north-east

Reggio di Calabria   M11

Region: Calabria
Province: Reggio di Calabria (RC)
Altitude: 31 m/102 ft
Population: 177,000

Reggio di Calabria (to distinguish it from Reggio nell'Emilia), "Reggio Calabria" for short, lies in the south-west of Italy, on the east side of the Strait of Messina.

Situation

The old port, the Greek Rhegion (founded in 743 B.C.) or Roman Rhegium, is the principal town of Calabria, the capital of the province and the see of an archbishop.
It was destroyed by an earthquake in 1783, and again suffered heavy damage in 1908. Thereafter it was rebuilt and recovered all its former economic importance. Reggio is the world's principal centre for the production of oil of bergamot.

Importance

Town centre

The town's centre is the Piazza Italia, near the sea, in which are the Prefecture, the Palazzo Provinciale, and the Town Hall.

Piazza Italia

Along the south-east side of the square runs the Corso Garibaldi, the busy main street of the town, 2 km/1¼ miles long. Along this street to the south-west is the Piazza del Duomo, with the imposing cathedral, in Romanesque-Byzantine style, rebuilt in 1908.
Farther south-west are the gardens of the Villa Comunale.

Cathedral

From the 15th c. Castello Aragonese to the north-east of the cathedral there are magnificent views.
There are also fine views from Via Reggio Campi, 500 m/550 yd farther east.

Castello Aragonese

*National Museum

From the Piazza Italia the Corso Garibaldi runs north-east past the Tempio della Vittoria, a war memorial (1933), to the National Museum, with prehistoric, medieval and modern sculpture and early Italic and Greek archaeological material, including the "Heroes of Riace", two bronze statues (5th c. B.C.) which were found in the sea in 1972 near the town of Riace.

From the National Museum the Viale Genoese Zerbi runs north, passing close to a large bathing station, and crosses the Torrente Annunziata to reach the harbour (ferry services to Messina).

Harbour

Running south-west from the National Museum the Lungomare Giacomo Matteotti, a beautiful seafront promenade some 3 km/2 miles

*Lungomare
Giacomo Matteotti

long, affords fine views of the coast of Sicily. In the southern section of the seaside promenade can be seen remains of Greek town walls and Roman baths of which the mosaic pavement is partly preserved.

Reggio di Calabria to Aspromonte (about 43 km/27 miles)

Gambarie di Aspromonte	An interesting trip can be made to the Aspromonte, which in ancient times was counted as part of the Sila range. The best point of approach is Gambarie di Aspromonte (1310 m/4323 ft), a holiday resort (also popular with winter sport enthusiasts) 24 km/15 miles north-east of Reggio (chair-lift to the Puntone di Scirocco, 1660 m/5478 ft, to the south-east).
Montalto	From Gambarie di Aspromonte 3.5 km/2¼ miles south on S.S. 183, then 15 km/9¼ miles east on a moderately good mountain road through pine and beech forests, to Montalto (Monte Cocuzza, 1955 m/6452 ft), the highest point in the Aspromonte. On the summit is a statue of Christ: magnificent views of the sea and of Calabria and Sicily.

Reggio nell'Emilia   G5

Region: Emilia-Romagna
Province: Reggio nell'Emilia (RE)
Altitude: 58 m/191 ft
Population: 130,000

Situation	The provincial capital of Reggio nell'Emilia lies on the Via Emilia near the southern edge of the north Italian plain.
	The town was known in Roman times as Regium Lepidi; the poet Lodovico Ariosto was born here in 1474 (d. 1533).
Tip	The town centre is closed to cars.

Sights

	In the centre is the Piazza Cesare Battisti, with the 13th c. crenellated Palazzo del Capitano del Popolo. The square lies on the line of the ancient Via Aemilia, which traverses the town under the name of Via Emilia a San Pietro (to the east) and Via Emilia a Santo Stefano (to the west).
Cathedral	A little way south is the large Piazza Prampolini on the east side of which stands the cathedral (13th c., rebuilt in 15th–16th c.). Behind the unfinished Renaissance façade is the original Romanesque structure, with remains of frescoes and sculpture (on the façade and in the interior) by Prospero Spani (d. 1584), a pupil of Michelangelo's and Bartolomeo Spani, both natives of Reggio.
San Prospero	To the south-east of the cathedral stands the 16th c. church of San Prospero, on the site of an earlier Romanesque building. On the façade (rebuilt 1748) are six marble lions from the original building. The church has frescoes by Camillo Procaccini (1585–89). Adjoining the church is a fine octagonal campanile.
Musei Civici	To the north of Piazza Cesare Battisti in the Piazza Cavour is the large Municipal Theatre. Near the square can be found the Municipal

Museum (Musei Civici), with an 18th c. natural history collection, a paleo-ethnological collection, works of art of several periods and a picture collecton. A palace to the west of the Piazza Cesare Battisti houses the Galleria Parmeggiani, with folk costumes, goldsmith's work and sculpture.

In the western part of the town, in the broad Corso Garibaldi, is the church of the Madonna della Ghiaira, a Baroque church built 1597–1619, on a Greek cross plan with a dome over the crossing. The interior, notable for the beauty of its proportions, has charming stucco decoration and frescoes.

*Madonna della Ghiaira

Reggio nell'Emilia to Castelnovo ne' Monti (about 30 km/19 miles)

South-west of Reggio nell'Emilia is Felina (664 m/2191 ft), where a road branches off on the left to the little town of Carpineti (7 km/4½ miles; 562 m/1855 ft), with a castle in which the quarrelsome monk Hildebrand, later Pope Gregory VII (1073–85), once found refuge.
7 km/4½ miles south-west, beyond Felina, is Castelnovo ne' Monti (700 m/2310 ft), a small town on the north-west slopes of the conspicuous rocky peak of the Pietra di Bismantova (1047 m/3455 ft), from the top of which there are magnificent views of the Apennines. A road (5 km/3 miles) ascends the hill; then it is 15 minutes' walk to the top.

Rimini   I5

Region: Emilia-Romagna
Province: Forli (FO)
Altitude: 7 m/23 ft
Population: 130,000

Rimini lies on the Adriatic in the south-east corner of the North Italian plain, at the meeting-place of two important ancient roads, the Via Aemilia and the Via Flaminia, some 150 km/93 miles south of Venice. It is one of the most favoured seaside resorts and has a beach 20 km/12 miles long ("Riviera del Sole").

Situation

The ancient Ariminum became a Roman colony in 268 B.C., commanding the road into northern Italy. In the 13th c. it fell into the hands of the Malatesta family, and in 1528 was incorported in the States of the Church.

History

Old town

In the centre of the old town is the Piazza Cavour, in which are the Palazzo Comunale (Town Hall, 1562), the Palazzo dell'Arengo (begun 1204), in Romanesque and Gothic style. Worth visiting is the Museo delle Arti Primitive, with pre-Columbian art of Oceania (visit by appointment only).

Museo delle Arti Primitive

From Piazza Cavour the broad Corso di Augusto runs north-west to the Ponte di Tiberio, a Roman bridge completed in A.D. 20, during the reign of Tiberius.

Ponte di Tiberio

South-east of Piazza Cavour stands the Tempio Malatestiano, a 13th c. Gothic structure remodelled in Early Renaissance style in 1447–60. The façade was designed by Leon Battista Alberti, who drew his inspiration

Tempio Malatestiano

* Arco d'Augusto

from the Arch of Augustus, and it was the first structure to be based on ancient models at the very beginning of the Renaissance. The interior is finely decorated with frescoes by Piero della Francesca, depicting Sigismondo Malatesta kneeling before St Sigismondo. There is also a painted cross attributed to Giotto.

At the south-east end of the Corso di Augusto rises the Arch of Augustus (Arco d'Augusto), a triumphal arch built in 27 B.C. (the oldest one known) to commemorate the construction of the Via Flaminia. In the former Jesuit College (Via L. Tonini) is housed the Municipal Museum.

Seaside resort

To the north-east of the old town, beyond the railway, extends the resort of Rimini, with numerous villas, hotels and pensioni. A promenade with varying names (Lungomare C. Tintori, Lungomare A. Murri and Lungomare G. Di Vittoria) runs along the sea.

Delfinario

In the harbour can be found the dolphinarium (Delfinario), with a large basin for dolphin shows and an interesting sea aquarium.

Italia in Miniatura

To the north-west are the outlying districts of Rivabella, Viserba, Viserbella and Torre Pedrera, all favourite bathing resorts.

Near Viserba the miniature village "Italia in Miniatura" is worth visiting. There are more than 200 attractions, miniature imitations, among which mountains, lakes, castles and famous squares (e.g. the Campo dei Miracoli of Pisa).

3 km/2 miles south-east, on the road to Riccione, is Miramare, also a bathing resort, with a large airport.

Fiabilandia

Between Rimini and Riccione is another attraction, the amusement park "Fiabilandia", with a great choice (Show Boat, King Kong, Fort Apache, water games, Baby Park, railway, theatre, etc.).

Seaside resorts south of Rimini

Riccione

8 km/5 miles south-east of Rimini is Riccione (12 m/40 ft; pop. 32,000), one of Italy's most popular holiday resorts, with thermal springs.

Misano Adriatico

The small spa and seaside resort of Misano Adriatico is situated about 3 km/2 miles south-east of Riccione.

Cattolica

Another 4 km/2½ miles down the coast is Cattolica (10 m/33 ft; pop. 16,000), a seaside resort since the mid 19th c., particularly in favour with German visitors. There are many villas, boulevards and fine shops. The beach, 2 km/1¼ miles long, has good facilities for visitors. The town offers a rich choice for active holidays: sailing, wind-surfing, water-skiing, crazy golf, tennis, riding, bowling, etc. There are concerts and other events.

Gradara

On a hill 8 km/5 miles south of Cattolica the little town of Gradara (142 m/469 ft) has a completely preserved circuit of walls and towers and a very interesting castle.

Seaside resorts north of Rimini

Cesenatico

20 km/12 miles north-west of Rimini is Cesenatico (4 m/13 ft; 20,000), an old fishing village. The little town is traversed by a harbour canal, part of which is now a floating maritime museum, the Museo della Marineria, consisting of old fishing boats with painted sails.

Shipping Museum of Cesenatico

8 km/5 miles north-west of Cesenatico is Cervia (3 m/10 ft; 25,000), one
of the most elegant seaside resorts in Romagna, the northern part of
the Emilia-Romagna. The town has a broad beach of fine sand.
Beyond the canal harbour is the suburb of Milano Marittima, beautifully situated on the edge of a pinewood, with an excellent beach and
thermal (Fango) baths.

Cervia

Milano Marittima

*San Leo   I6

Leave Rimini on S.S. 258, which runs up the broad valley of the Marec-
chia and in 16 km/10 miles passes below the little town of Verucchio
(333 m/1099 ft; pop. 6000), with a Malatesta castle (magnificent views),
lying off the road to the left. In another 3 km/2 miles a road goes off on
the left to San Marino (frontier in 500 m/550 yd), from which it is
possible to return, making an attractive round trip.
The main road continues up the valley to (4 km/2½ miles) the little
village of Villa Nuova, where a road branches off up a side valley,
climbs steeply and comes in another 9 km/5½ miles to San Leo (583
m/1924 ft; pop. 3000), situated on a conical hill, with a massive castle
(picture gallery), a Romanesque cathedral and a 9th c. parish church.

Situation
32 km/20 miles
south-west

Riviera   D–F5/6

Region: Liguria
Provinces: Genova (GE), Imperia (IM), La Spezia (SP) and Savona (SV)

The Riviera ("coast") is the narrow coastal strip which extends along
the Mediterranean from Marseilles to La Spezia. The Italian Riviera,

General information

between Ventimiglia and La Spezia, is one of the most beautiful scenic stretches in Italy, with precipitous cliffs, forested hills, old-world little port towns and ruined watch-towers standing above the brilliant blue sea. The hills shelter it from the rough north winds, and with its southern exposure it benefits to the full from the power of the sun and the warmth of the sea. Mild winters and warm summers promote the growth of luxuriant southern vegetation. During winter and spring many visitors seek relaxation in the resorts, to which even larger numbers come in summer for sea-bathing.

Riviera di Levante

The Italian Riviera is divided by the Gulf of Genoa into two parts. To the east is the Riviera di Levante (from Genoa to La Spezia) with a mild but somewhat variable climate and large areas of forest, the south-eastern part of which, beyond Sestri Levante, still preserves its original character. The towns and villages have narrow streets and tall houses huddled on the narrow coastal plains, and side valleys. In this section there are relatively few luxury hotels outside the main centres.

Riviera di Ponente

To the west of the Gulf of Genoa is the Riviera di Ponente (From Genoa to Ventimiglia), with a more equable climate than the Riviera di Levante. The coastal plain is wider, accommodating many large resorts with numerous first-class hotels and (for the most part) excellent beaches.

Riviera dei Fiori

The western part of the Riviera di Ponente, between Alassio and the French frontier, is known as the Riviera dei Fiori on account of its large-scale flower-growing industry.

*Along the Riviera di Ponente (about 165 km/102 miles)

The road runs west from the station, past the Old Harbour, and comes to:

Cornigliano Ligure

6 km/3¾ miles: Cornigliano Ligure (10 m/33 ft), a busy suburb of Genoa, with a new industrial area extending some 800 m/880 yd into the sea on reclaimed land. Beyond the town a good road goes off on the left to Genoa's Cristoforo Colombo Airport. To the right, on a high conical hill, is the church of the Madonna del Gazzo (421 m/1389 ft).

Pegli

5 km/3 miles: Pegli (6 m/20 ft), a popular resort for holidays and week-ends throughout the year, with beautiful parks and villas. Near the station is the Villa Durazzo-Pallavicini (1837), with an archaeological museum (Museo Civico di Archeologica Ligure) and a park extending up the hillside, with various water features, grottoes, an underground lake and a medieval-style castle. In the Villa Doria, also near the station, is the Genoa Naval and Maritime Museum, with mementoes of Columbus.

Voltri

5 km/3 miles: Voltri (5 m/17 ft), Genoa's last industrial suburb, with the attractive large park of the Villa Galliera. At the upper end of the park is the pilgrimage church of the Madonna delle Grazie (fine views).

Beyond Voltri the road leaves the extensive built-up area of Genoa.

Arenzano

7 km/4½ miles: Arenzano (6 m/20 ft), a charmingly situated resort (good beach) with an old castle and a beautiful park around the Villa La Torre. The road then runs inland past a promontory covered with woodland and macchia and returns to the coast.

Varazze

12 km/7½ miles: Varazze (5 m/17 ft; pop. 15,000), a summer and winter resort, prettily situated amidst orange-groves, with a beach 2 km/1¼ miles long.

Celle Ligure

4 km/2½ miles: Celle Ligure (44 m/145 ft), an attractive resort above which is a fine old pinewood.

Albisola Marina

4 km/2½ miles: Albisola Marina (19 m/63 ft), a popular resort with a beach of fine sand. 1 km/¾ mile north is the little town of Albisola

The Italian Riviera: Beach at Celle Ligure

Superiore, with the Villa Gavotti, formerly called the Villa delle Rovere, in which Pope Julius II (1503–13) was born.

Beyond Albisola Marina the road comes in another 3 km/2 miles to the town of Savona (10 m/33 ft; pop. 75,000), a provincial capital situated on the River Letimbro, with an important harbour (export of cars) and a variety of industry (large steel rolling-mill). On the harbour quay stands the Torre Pancaldo, named after the navigator of that name. In Via Paleocapa is the church of San Giovanni Battista (16th and 18th c.), with a fine painting (at the end of the north aisle) by Samuel van Hoogstraeten (1627–78), a pupil of Rembrandt. A little way south the Pinacoteca Civica houses pictures, sculpture and majolica. Close by is the cathedral (1604; façade 1886).

Savona

6 km/4 miles: Vado Ligure (12 m/40 ft; pop. 9000), an industrial town at the junction of the old Roman Via Aurelia with the beginning of the Via Iulia Augusta. The S.S. 1 (Via Aurelia) skirts Capo Vado (lighthouse; fine view back towards Savona), an attractive stretch of road which for part of the way has been hewn out of the rock. Beyond the cape the rocky islet of Bergeggi, crowned by a Roman tower, can be seen on the left.

Vado Ligure

7 km/4½ miles: Spotorno (10 m/33 ft), a bathing resort with a beautiful beach. Beyond the town there is a fine view, ahead, of Capo Noli.

Spotorno

3 km/2 miles: Noli (4 m/13 ft), a charmingly situated little fishing town and seaside resort with a picturesque old town, remains of town walls, old towers, a castle and the late Romanesque church of San Paragorio (12th c.). From here there is a pleasant walk (1 hour) to Capo Noli (276 m/911 ft), with a signal station and the church of Santa Margherita (view).

Noli

Beyond Noli the road goes through a tunnel (114 m/376 ft long) under Capo Noli and continues along the high overhanging cliffs of the Malpasso to (9 km/5½ miles) Finale Ligure (3 m/10 ft; pop. 14,000), a prettily

Finale Ligure

Finale Ligure

situated resort, with the Castelfranco (1342) above the town and the fine Baroque church of San Giovanni Battista. Near the station is an early Christian Capuchin church. 2 km/1½ miles north-west is the walled village of Finalborgo, with a beautiful Romanesque-Baroque parish church. In the monastery of St Catherina (15th c.) is an archaeological museum containing material discovered locally. Still farther north-west in Perti is Castel Gavone with a fine keep. In the vicinity are limestone caves. Beyond Finale the road cuts across the Caprazoppa promontory.

Pietra Ligure

In 6 km/3¾ miles we reach Pietra Ligure (3 m/10 ft), a resort (sandy beach) with an interesting church and a ruined castle on an isolated crag. On the hillside are the buildings of the Pietranuova sanatorium (sun and sea-air cures).

Loana

4 km/2½ miles: Loana (4 m/13 ft; pop. 13,000), a popular resort with a former Doria palace (1578), now the Town Hall. On the hillside is the former monastery of Monte Carmello. About 6 km/3¾ miles farther is the Grotta di Toirano (tour with guide, 1½ hours). In the forecourt is the Museo Prehistorico (prehistoric history).

Beyond Loana there is an attractive view, to the right, of the Ligurian Alps, with Monte Carmo (1389 m/4584 ft).

Albenga

10 km/6 miles: Albenga (5 m/17 ft; pop. 22,000), with a picturesque old town centre, town walls and many towers which belonged to noble families. Other features of interest are the Romanesque cathedral (11–14th c.; lower part of façade 5th c.) with three Romanesque-Gothic naves; the small early Romanesque church of Santa Maria in Fontibus (13th c.); the Museo Ingauno e Battistero (5th c. baptistery, Liguria's most important early Christian work) and a Roman shipping museum. Near the Via Aurelia is the Ponte Lungo, a medieval bridge 147 m/161 yd long over the former course of the River Centa. Beyond Albenga the

rocky islet of Gallinara (90 m/297 ft), with the ruins of a 6th c. Benedictine abbey, can be seen.

7 km/4½ miles: Alassio (5 m/17 ft; pop. 14,000), a large and very popular   Alassio
resort with a beach of fine sand more than 3 km/2 miles long. On the
seafront promenade stands an old watch-tower.

3 km/2 miles: Laigueglia (11 m/36 ft), a closely built little town with a   Laigueglia
beautiful 18th c. parish church and a good beach.

The road continues along the precipitous coast, high above the sea.

3 km/2 miles: Capo Mele (lighthouse), with a fine view of Alassio to the   Capo Mele
rear. Then on through Marina di Andora and round Capo Cervo.

7 km/4½ miles: Cervo (66 m/218 ft), a picturesquely situated hillside   Cervo
village. The road then passes through the resort of San Bartolomeo al
Mare (26 m/86 ft).

3 km/2 miles: Diano Marina (4 m/13 ft). 2 km/1¼ mile north-west is the   Diano Marina
walled village of Diano Castello (135 m/446 ft).

Beyond Diano Marina the road winds its way gently uphill to Capo
Berta, from which there is a magnificent view to the rear, extending as
far as Capo Mele.

6 km/3¾ miles: Imperia (10 m/33 ft; pop. 42,000), a provincial capital,   Imperia
comprising the districts of Oneglia (to east) and Porto Maurizio (to
west), separated by the broad stony bed of the River Impero. Porto
Maurizio is picturesquely situated on the slopes of a promontory; it has
an imposing domed church (1781).

18 km/11 miles: Arma di Taggia (10 m/33 ft), a resort with a beautiful   Arma di Taggia
beach, situated at the mouth of the River Argentina, or Fiumara di
Taggia. 3 km/2 miles up the valley is the picturesque little town of
Taggia (39 m/129 ft), with old patrician houses. In the church of the
Dominican convent are pictures of the early Ligurian school.

8 km/5 miles: San Remo.   San Remo

6 km/3¾ miles: Ospedaletti (30 m/99 ft), a popular resort, with an   Ospedaletti
attractive Casino and a beautiful palm-shaded avenue, the Corso
Regina Margherita.

Beyond Ospedaletti the road continues along the steep and rocky
coast, through beautiful scenery. To the left by the shore, is a fine park
(private property). At the mouth of the Val del Sasso, are the Vallone
Gardens, laid out by a German gardener named Ludwig Winter (d.
1912), also private property and not open to the public.

6 km/3¾ miles: Bordighera.   Bordighera

Farther on, shortly before Ventimiglia, is the entrance (on the right) to   Albintimilium
the remains of the Roman town of Albintimilium, with a theatre (2nd c.
A.D.).

5 km/3 miles: Ventimiglia (9 m/30 ft; pop. 27,000), the frontier town,   Ventimiglia
situated at the mouth of the River Roia, with an important flower
market. In the new town, to the east of the river, are the Town Hall and
the palm-shaded Giardino Pubblico; in the picturesque walled old
town, on the hill west of the river, are the Romanesque cathedral, with
an adjoining baptistery, and the 11th c. church of San Michele (columns
with Roman inscriptions). From the Piazzale del Capo, a little way south
of the cathedral, there are magnificent views, extending westwards as
far as Cap Ferrat.

From Ventimiglia there is a rewarding trip to the Giardino Hanbury with
a variety of rare plants (about 6 km/3¾ miles west in Mortola Inferiore),
laid out by the Englishman Thomas Hanbury.

Another kilometre (¾ mile) farther west, near the French frontier, are
the Balzi Rossi, caves hewn from rock, which were inhabited in prehistoric times (skeletons, etc. in the museum near the Barma Grande).

From Ventimiglia an attractive excursion can be made up the beautiful

Nervia valley to the little town of Dolceaqua (50 m/165 ft), picturesquely situated on a hillside, with an old bridge 10 m/33 ft high, borne on pointed arches, and a ruined castle which was the ancestral home of the Doria family of Genoa. 4 km/2½ miles farther on is the village of Isolabona (ruined castle), and 2 km/1¼ miles beyond this in a side valley is the hill village of Apricale, clinging picturesquely to a steep hillside. From here it is another 8 km/5 miles to Baiardo (900 m/2970 ft).

Inland from the Riviera Ponente, with its crowds of summer visitors, are many quiet little villages well off the beaten tourist track which are well worth visiting not only for the beauty of their setting, on hilltops or precipitous slopes, but also for the picture they give of typical Italian hill settlements. Characteristic examples of such villages can be seen on the road from San Remo via Ceriana to Baiardo (25 km/16 miles) or on the road from Ventimiglia via Dolceaqua to Apricale (13 km/8 miles). It is also possible to take in these places on the way from San Remo to Ventimiglia (additional distance 29 km/18 miles).

*Along the Riviera di Levante (about 115 km/71 miles)

Leave Genoa by way of Corso G. Marconi; then east along Corso Italia.

Sturla — 5 km/3 miles: Sturla (18 m/59 ft), a suburb of Genoa, with bathing facilities (views of the Apennines with scattered villas). To the left is the entrance to the large Giannina Gaslini Children's Hospital, built by the Italian "oil king" Count Gerolamo Gaslini in memory of his daughter who died at an early age.

Quinto al Mare — 3 km/2 miles: Quinto al Mare (20 m/66 ft), another Genoa suburb, surrounded by orange-groves and palms, with fine villas.

Nervi — 2 km/1¼ miles: Nervi (27 m/89 ft), the oldest winter resort (rocky beach) on the Riviera di Levante, in a sheltered situation amid olive-, orange-

Sestri Levante

and lemon-groves, with a seafront promenade 1.8 km/1 mile long hewn from the rock. On the east side of the Viale delle Palme lies the Parco Municipale, with many exotic plants and the Galleria d'Arte Moderna (closed Mondays). To the east, in a beautiful park in Sant'Ilario Basso, is the Museo Luxoro (closed on Mondays), with applied art, pictures and furniture.

11 miles beyond Nervi is Recco (5 m/17 ft; pop. 11,000), from which there is an attractive detour to Uscio (361 m/1191 ft), 11 km/7 miles north. From Uscio it is possible to return to Genoa-Apparizione on a beautiful panoramic road (20 km/12 miles). | Recco

4 km/2½ miles: Ruta (290 m/957 ft), a straggling villa suburb on the saddle between the coastal hills and the Portofino promontory, projecting squarely into the sea from some 4–5 km/2½–3 miles, with scenery which is among the finest on the Riviera. | Ruta

7 km/4½ miles: Rapallo. | Rapallo

6 km/3¾ miles: Zoagli (30 m/99 ft), with many villas on the slopes of the hillside, panoramic road to Sant'Ambrogio (3 km/2 miles). | Zoagli

6 km/33 /4 miles: Chiavari (3 m/10 ft; pop. 30,000), a seaside resort situated in a fertile plain at the mouth of the Entella. Near the station, at the end of a beautiful avenue of palms, stands the cathedral (1613; pillared portico added 1841). About 5 km/3 miles north-east of Chiavara is the Basilica dei Fieschi, a fine 13th c. Gothic church. | Chiavari

2 km/1¼ miles: Lavagna (5 m/17 ft; pop. 13,000), a resort with a large yacht harbour (1976). | Lavagna

Beyond Lavagna the road runs close to the shore.

6 km/3¾ miles: Sestri Levante (4 m/13 ft; pop. 20,000), a seaside and winter resort in a picturesque setting on the saddle of the Isola promontory (70 m/231 ft), between two small bays. From the beautiful seafront promenade in the flat bay to the west there are extensive views of the Gulf of Rapallo, also called Golfo Tigullio. From the square beside the harbour, at the south end of the bay, there is a road to the tip of the promontory, which is crowned by the Castelli Gualino, imitations of medieval castles. There is also a pleasant walk (1 hour) south-east to the Telegrafo, a signal station on the southern spur of the pine-clad Monte Castello (265 m/875 ft; views). | Sestri Levante

Beyond Sestri Levante the Via Aurelia runs inland bypassing a stretch of rocky coast more than 60 km/37 miles long, some of the places on which – such as the picturesque fishing villages of the Cinqueterre – can be reached only by the railway, running through tunnels for much of its course.

18 km/11 miles: Passo del Bracco (615 m/2030 ft). On an isolated crag by the roadside is the small aerial of the Savona television station (view). | Passo del Bracco

2 km/1¼ miles: La Baracca (589 m/1944 ft). | La Baracca

From La Baracca a scenic road (S.S. 332) winds its way down (15 km/9 miles south), mostly through pine forests, to the little town, frequented by visitors both in summer and in winter, of Levanto (11 m/36 ft), with remains of its medieval town walls and castle. From here the view by morning light can sometimes extend as far as Monte Viso (210 km/130 miles west). | Levanto

35 km/22 miles: Passo della Foce (241 m/795 ft), with views of the bay of La Spezia and the Apulian Alps. | Passo della Foce

6 km/3¾ miles: La Spezia. | La Spezia

Rome/Roma 18

Region: Lazio. Province: Roma (ROMA)
Altitude: 11–139 m/36–459 ft. Population: 2,827,000

The details of Rome in this guide is purposefully brief, as there is a comprehensive Baedeker city guide to the capital.

Note

There are restrictions on the use of cars in Rome, both in particular areas of the city and at various times of day. Parts of the city are closed for cars.

Cars

Rome is the capital of the Republic of Italy, the region of Latium and the province of Rome, as well as Italy's largest city. It lies in latitude 41°52' north and longitude 12°30' east, some 20 km/12 miles from the Tyrrhenian Sea in the middle of the hilly Campagna di Roma, on the River Tiber (Tevere), the third longest river in Italy (after the Po and the Adige). The city itself covers an area some 9 km/5½ miles in diameter; the commune of Rome has an area of more than 1500 sq. km/579 sq. miles.

Situation

Rome is an important centre of air, rail and road communication, a major financial and commercial city (port at Civitavecchia, 75 km/47 miles north-west) and an international centre of fashion and the film industry (Cinecittà). The city's industries, established mainly to the east and south, consist of engineering, printing and publishing, chemicals, the manufacture of telephones, textiles and foodstuffs.

Economy

The city's numerous cultural institutions enjoy an international reputation. Among the many educational and research establishments run by the Italian state, the Roman Catholic Church and a number of foreign countries are the two state universities, the Papal Universitas Gregoriana, the Accademia Nazionale dei Lincei, the Accademia di Santa Cecilia (music), large libraries and collections of archives including the National Library, the University Library, the FAO Library and the Vatican Library; and a variety of learned societies and foreign cultural and research institutes. Rome is also the headquarters of the Food, Agriculture and Forestry (FAO) Organisation of the United Nations.

Cultural institutions

The Tiber flows through the city from north to south, with three fairly sharp bends; it is spanned by some 25 bridges. On the left bank are the famous seven hills of Rome – the Capitoline (50 m/165 ft), Quirinal (52 m/172 ft), Viminal (56 m/185 ft), Esquiline (53 m/175 ft), Palatine (51 m/168 ft), Aventine (46 m/152 ft) and Caelian (50 m/165 ft). The ancient city was built on these hills.
Between the hills and the river is a level area, the ancient Campus Martius, which was until recent times the main urban area. The Pincian (50 m/165 ft) to the north of the Quirinal, the Vatican (60 m/198 ft) and the Janiculum (84 m/277 ft) on the right bank of the river, were for long outside the city, but from the time of Augustus there was a densely populated suburb on the right bank, Trans Tiberim (now Trastevere). Imperial Rome was enclosed by the Aurelian Walls.
Rome's atmosphere is polluted by vehicle emissions, etc.; many buildings in the inner city are in danger of becoming sacrificed to the pollution. Since the beginning of the eighties the authorities have been endeavouring to halt this decay by restorative measures.

Topography

The Aurelian Walls (Mura Aureliane), a circuit of massive brick walls 19 km/12 miles long, with gates and towers, were built by the Emperor Aurelian in A.D. 272–278, after a period of some 500 years during which

Aurelian Walls

◀ *Rome: View from St Peter's*

367

no enemy had approached the city. Long stretches of the walls are still preserved, though frequently restored since the 5th c.; it is possible to walk along some sections. It is only in modern times that Rome has extended beyond the Aurelian Walls.

The principal gates are the Porta del Popolo, the Porta Pinciana, the Porta Salaria and the Porta Pia on the north; the Porta San Lorenzo and the Porta Maggiore on the east; the Porta San Giovanni, the Porta San Sebastiano and the Porta San Paolo on the south; and the Porta San Pancrazio on the west.

Historical significance

Already known in ancient times as the Eternal City (Roma aeterna), Rome was for a millennium and a half the cultural centre of Europe and the scene of great historical events. It was the first city of world stature, capital of the Roman Empire, and thereafter the home of the Popes with their world-wide spiritual authority. In the heyday of the Roman Empire, at the beginning of the 2nd c. A.D., the city had a population of over a million. Rome was the birthplace of the Roman Catholic Church, one of the most powerful single religious communities in the history of the world, and it was here that about A.D. 1200 Innocent III established a secular Papal state which subsisted until 1870 and was succeeded in 1929 by the new sovereign state of the Vatican City. Present-day Rome is a creation of its long past, and its attraction and interest to visitors are enhanced by an awareness of that past.

After the devastation suffered by Rome during the period of the great migrations and its vicissitudes in subsequent centuries, the population in the 14th c. was barely 20,000 and at the beginning of the 16th c. only 55,000. In 1832 it was 148,000 and in 1870 at the end of Papal rule it was 221,000. By 1921 it had risen to 660,000. After the First World War, and still more after the Second World War, the population began to grow on a massive scale, bringing it to its present figure of nearly 3 million.

History and art

Ancient city

The ancient city was traditionally founded on April 21st 753 B.C.; but there must have been a Latin settlement of some consequence before then on this convenient site near the mouth of the Tiber. The oldest part of the town consisted of the Palatine and Quirinal hills and between them the Forum at the foot of the Capitol.

After the destruction of the town by the Gauls (c. 387 B.C.) the development began which was to make Rome capital of the Empire – a development reflected in its architecture. Important temples and secular buildings were built; in 312 the first aqueduct and the first paved road, the Via Appia, were constructed, and the characteristic Roman technique of building vaulted structures of rubble bound with mortar was evolved. The city developed still farther in the time of Augustus (27 B.C.–A.D. 14), who "found Rome of brick and left it of marble" and extended the built-up area on to the Campus Martius, and again after the great fire in the time of Nero (54–68) which destroyed most of Rome. The zenith of its development was reached in the 2nd c. A.D.

Medieval Rome

The development of medieval Rome was shaped by Christianity, which came to Rome in the mid 1st c. and thereafter, in spite of successive persecutions, particularly during the 3rd c. and in 303 during the reign of Diocletion (the final wave of persecution), demonstrated its ability to withstand the declining authority of paganism. In 313 Constantine the Great granted freedom of religious exercise. The old religion received a final blow in 408, when the Emperor Honorius decreed the confiscation of all its property. The old temples were destroyed and their columns and other materials used in the building of Christian churches (basilicas); later whole temples were converted for use as churches. The number of churches increased rapidly. There were 25 parish churches (titoli) and five patriarchal churches. The patriarchal churches – of which the Pope himself was priest and to which all the faithful belonged – were San Giovanni in Laterano, San Pietro in Vaticano, San Paolo fuori le Mura, San Lorenzo fuori le Mura and Sant Maria Maggiore. In addition to these five churches there were two others which enjoyed particular veneration, Santa Croce in Gerusalemme and San Sebastiano, above the catacombs on the Via Appia. These were the Seven Churches of Rome, visited by pilgrims from all over the Western world down to the present day.

In political terms, however, Rome's importance declined. Constantine's decision in 330 to transfer the Imperial residence to Byzantium and Milan reduced Rome to the status of a provincial town. The Campagna reverted to wasteland, and malaria spread inland from the coastal regions. The stormy years of the great migrations, in particular the sack of Rome by Alaric's Goths and again in 455 by Gaiseric's Vandals, brought a further decline. Only the tradition of the great battles and victories of the Christian faith, which were indissolubly linked with Rome, preserved the city from extinction.

The conversion of ancient Rome into Christian Rome made the Papacy the supreme spiritual power in the West. Particularly powerful representatives of Papal authority were popes Leo the Great (440–61) and Gregory the Great (590–604). The secular power of the popes and their authority over Rome began to develop in the 8th c., when the foundations of the States of the Church were laid by the grant of territory to the Pope by the Lombard king Luitprand (727) and the Frankish king Pipin (755). On Christmas Day 800 Leo III (795–816) crowned Charlemagne Emperor and thus re-established the secular empire which was to preserve for a millennium at least the name of the old Roman Empire. In subsequent centuries Rome was ravaged by enemy attacks, the struggle between the Empire and the Papacy and strife between the great noble families. It suffered a further blow with the exile of the popes to Avignon (1309–77), during which Cola di Rienzo tried to establish a republic on the ancient Roman model (1347). The population now fell to barely 20,000.

The Renaissance, breathing fresh life into learning and art throughout Italy, established itself at the Papal court and brought a new flowering to Rome. Tuscan architects, sculptors and painters had already been summoned to Rome in considerable numbers during the 15th c., but it was in the following century that the great Renaissance popes Julius II (1503–13) and Leo X (1513–21) made the city the real centre of the High Renaissance. From here Bramante (1444–1514), Michelangelo (1474–1564) and Raphael (1483–1520) set the artistic pattern of the whole 16th c. (Cinquecento). Leonardo da Vinci (1452–1519) also worked in Rome in 1513–15. Among noted architects of this period were Baldassare Peruzzi (1481–1536) and Antonio da Sangallo the Younger (1483-1546).

Renaissance

After the occupation and sacking of Rome by Charles V's forces in 1527 ("Sacco di Roma"), which drove away almost all the city's artists, recovery was slow. In 1546 Michelangelo built the Palazzo Farnese, the plan of which was to have enormous influence on the palaces of the Baroque period. The reign of Pope Sixtus V (1585–90), for whom Domenico Fontana designed a whole series of fine buildings, saw the beginning of the vigorous and powerful Baroque style of the 17th c. The architects of this period – in particular the Neapolitan Lorenzo Bernini (1598–1680), his like-minded contemporary Francesco Borromini

(1599–1667), Carlo Maderna (1556–1629) and Carlo Rainaldi (1611–91) – created the magnificent churches and palaces, with their impressive command of space and picturesque effect, which still largely determine the architectural character of the older parts of Rome. In the field of painting Caravaggio (*c.* 1573–1610), the most gifted artist of the Early Baroque, was the leader of the naturalistic school; the chief representatives of the opposite trend, the "Eclectics" of Bologna, were Annibale Carracci (1560–1609) and his pupils Guido Reni (1575–1642), Domenichino (1581–1641) and Guercino (1591–1666). In the following century Antonio Canova (1757–1822) produced the first works of monumental sculpture in neo-classical style.

18th and 19th centuries

In the 18th and 19th centuries the economic importance and artistic achievement of Rome both declined. Nevertheless the city continued to attract increasing numbers of artists and connoisseurs from many lands in quest of the classical art of antiquity, particularly after the publication of Johann Joachim Winckelmann's history of Greek art, written in Rome about 1760. A revival of the city's life and art came only with its incorporation in the new kingdom of Italy in 1870, which gave Rome the status of a national capital and royal residence. This was the period of the "Third Rome" ("Terza Roma"). New and imposing public buildings were erected, usually aiming at a kind of ancient Roman monumentality (Banca d'Italia, Ministry of Finance, Palace of Justice, National Monument) but employing overcharged Renaissance and Baroque forms. It was only in the 20th c. that this style gave place to simpler and more straight forward structures.

20th century

The 20th century created the "Fourth Rome" ("Quarta Roma"). A development plan initiated in 1931 provided for the opening up of overcrowded slum areas, the disengagement and restoration of ancient building (the Theatre of Marcellus, Trajan's Market and Trajan's Column, the Imperial Fora and the Arch of Constantine, the Mausoleum of Augustus, Castle Sant'Angelo, etc.), the construction of large new avenues (Via dei Fori Imperiali, Corso del Rinascimento, Via Regina Elena, the Via della Conciliazione between the Ponte Sant'Angelo and St Peter's Square, etc.) and the creation of public parks and gardens and well-planned modern suburbs. Notable among recent developments are the University City, the Air Ministry building, the Via del Mare to Lido di Ostia, the new ring road, the EUR exhibition area, the Termini Station and the new underground railway system (Metropolitana). In 1960 Rome was host to the 17th Olympic Games, for which the Olympic Village, a number of major sporting facilities and new link roads (including the Strada Olimpia from the EUR to the Foro Italico) were constructed. In consequence of chronic financial difficulties the 1965 development plan has been only very partially carried out, and many buildings are still awaiting the urgent renovation they require.

In March 1957 the treaties establishing the European Economic Community and the European Coal and Steel Community (the Rome treaties) were signed in Rome. In 1968 economic leaders and experts from more than 30 countries formed the "Club of Rome". Archbishop Karol Woityla from Krakau was crowned Pope (John Paul II) in 1978; he was severely wounded in an assassination attempt in 1981.

Piazza Venezia

The busiest traffic intersection in Rome is the Piazza Venezia, at the south end of the Via del Corso.

Palazzo Venezia

On the west side of the square is the Palazzo Venezia, originally a fortress-like building erected about 1455, from 1564 the Venetian and from 1797 the Austro-Hungarian embassy to the Vatican, from 1926 to 1943 Mussolini's official residence and now a museum. It has a fine arcade (unfinished) in the inner courtyard. In the east wing the Museo di Palazzo Venezia, houses tapestries, pictures, busts, applied art, printing, porcelain and glass of various centuries.

Museo di Palazzo Venezia

*National Monument to Victor Emmanuel II

On the south side of the Piazza Venezia stands the huge National Monument to Victor Emmanuel II, in white Brescia marble, begun in 1885 to the design of Count Giuseppe Sacconi as a symbol of the newly united Italy and inaugurated in 1911. This is the largest and most magnificent monument in Italy, 135 × 130 m/148 × 143 yd and 70 m/231 ft high. At the top of several flights of steps is the Altare della Patria, the Tomb of the Unknown Soldier, and above this are an equestrian statue of Victor Emmanuel II in gilded bronze, 12 m/40 ft high, and a massive colonnade (far-reaching view from the top).

Altare della Patria

In the eastern part of the monument are the Museo Centrale del Risorgimento and the Museo Sacrario delle Bandiere della Marina Militare (Flag Museum).

Museums

Capitol

Behind the National Monument, to the south, rises the Capitol (Italian Campidoglio or Monte Capitolino), the smallest but historically the

Santa Maria in Aracoeli

National Monument to Victor Emmanuel II

371

most important of Rome's hills. On the north side of the hill (50 m/165 ft), approached by a long flight of steps, is the church of Santa Maria in Aracoeli ("on the Altar of Heaven"), on the site of the Capitoline Temple of Juno. It contains 22 ancient columns and has a gilded 16th c. ceiling; in the north aisle is a carved wooden image of the Infant Christ (the "Santo Bambino"), which is the subject of particular veneration at Christmas.

Museo Capitolino | The Capitoline Museum (Museo Capitolino), adjoining the church on the south, contains the municipal collection of ancient sculpture. Particularly notable items are the "Dying Gaul" (in the Sala del Galata Morente on the upper floor), a copy of a Greek bronze statue, and (in a side room of the Galleria) the Capitoline Venus, a variant of the Cnidian Aphrodite of Praxiteles.

Piazza del Campidoglio

The Capitoline Museum forms the north side of the Piazza del Campidoglio, which is approached from the west by a staircase of shallow steps designed by Michelangelo, and by the winding Via delle Tre Pile. The square itself, also designed by Michelangelo and constructed from 1547 onwards, is one of the most finely conceived of Renaissance squares. Here from 1538 until 1981 stood the equestrian statue of the Emperor Marcus Aurelius; restoration of the statue was completed in 1990. Discussions are under way as to whether the original should be exhibited in a museum and a copy set up in the Capitol square, or whether the original should be replaced in the square and provided with an environmentally protective coating.

Palazzo dei Senatori | On the south-east side of the square is the Palazzo dei Senatori, the official residence of the Mayor and the City Council of Rome, with a façade of 1598.

Palazzo dei Conservatori | On the south-west side of the Capitol square, partly built on the substructures (of dressed tufa blocks) of the Temple of Jupiter, is the Palazzo dei Conservatori (1568), originally the seat of the city council, which houses a collection of major importance. Notable items are the "Boy with a Thorn" ("Il Spinario", 1st c. B.C.), in the Sala dei Trionfi di Mario, and the "Capitoline She-Wolf", an Etruscan work of the 5th c. B.C. (in the adjoining Sala della Lupa). On the 2nd floor the Pinacoteca Capitolina has a fine collection of pictures, including works by Titian, Tintoretto, Velázquez and Rubens.

Museo Nuovo | The adjoining Palazzo Caffarelli houses the Museo Nuovo, with Greek sculpture of the 5th c. B.C., sarcophagi, urns, etc.

Tarpeian Rock | At the south-west corner of the Palazzo dei Conservatori is the Tarpeian Rock (Rupe Tarpea), from which in Roman times condemned prisoners were hurled to their death.

Ancient Rome

**Forum Romanum

From the Via del Campidoglio, between the Palazzo dei Conservatori and the Palazzo Senatorio, there is a magnificent view of the remains of the Forum Romanum (Foro Romano) and the massive brick walls of the

The Forum Romanum ▶

Palatine, crowned by pines and holm-oaks, with the Arch of Titus and the Colosseum to the rear.
In due course the whole of this area is to be turned into an "archaeological park".

The area of low ground, south-east of the Capitol, between the Palatine and the Esquiline, was drained in the 6th c. B.C. by the construction of the Cloaca Maxima, with its outlet into the Tiber, and thereafter was occupied by markets and other trading activities and became the meeting-place of popular assemblies and courts of law. Caesar set in train a large-scale extension of the Forum, and his plans were carried through by Augustus. Under Augustus and his successors the old buildings of the Republican period were restored and rebuilt and the Forum was embellished with splendid new buildings, triumphal arches, columns and statues, resplendent in rare marbles and gilded bronze.

The destruction of the Forum began in the 6th c. Columns and other architectural elements were torn out of the ancient buildings and used in the construction of churches or other new buildings, and the marble that still remained was burned to produce lime. The systematic clearance of the Forum and Palatine began only in 1871.

The Palazzo Senatorio is built over the remains of the Tabularium, constructed in 78 B.C. to house the State archives of Rome (tabula = document) in the form of an open hall facing on to the Forum.

Temple of Vespasian

Below the Tabularium, separated from the rest of the Forum excavations by the modern Via del Foro, are the remains of three ancient shrines – the Portico of the Twelve Gods, dating from the last days of the pagan faith (restored as late as A.D. 367); the Temple of Vespasian (A.D. 81), of which three columns survive; and the Temple of Concordia, originally built in 366 B.C. and splendidly restored by Tiberius.

*Temple of Faustina

Beyond the Via del Foro is the enclosed area containing the main part of the Forum (entrance from the Via dei Fori Imperiali, on the north side). Immediately left of the entrance is the Temple of Faustina (A.D. 141), of which the portico and part of the cella survive; it is now the church of San Lorenzo in Miranda. To the right of the entrance are the remains of the Basilica Aemilia, a portico built in 179 B.C. to provide additional accommodation for traders.

*Temple of Castor and Pollux

Opposite this, on the far side of the Sacra Via, the oldest street in Rome, which climbed up to the Capitol as the Clivus Capitolinus, stands the Basilica Iulia originally built by Julius Caesar in 46 B.C. and to the east of this the Temple of Castor and Pollux with three fine Corinthian columns of Greek marble dating from the Augustan period which are one of the most characteristic landmarks of Rome. North-west of the Basilica Iulia are the eight granite columns of the portico of the Temple of Saturn, which contained the city treasury (Aerarium publicum), and the imposing marble Arch of Septimius Severus.

*Arch of Septimius Severus

The marble triumphal Arch of Septimius Severus (23 m/76 ft high, 25 m/27 yd wide), was erected in A.D. 203 in honour of the victories over the Parthians won by the emperor and his sons Caracalla and Geta.

Rostra

To the left of the Arch of Septimius Severus are the Rostra, the orators' tribune erected in the time of Augustus and named after the ships' prows (rostra) which stood here and bounded the Forum proper, paved with limestone slabs. In front of the Rostra, on a high brick pedestal, we find the Column of Phocas, commemorating the emperor of that name, a centurion who had himself crowned emperor in Constantinople about 600. To the right of the Rostra, under a protective roof, is the Lapis

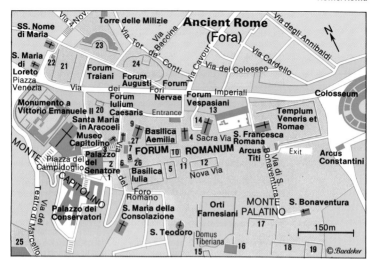

1 Portico of the Twelve Gods
  (Porticus Deorum Consentium)
2 Temple of Vespasian
  (Templum Vespasiani)
3 Temple of Concordia
  (Templum Concordiae)
4 Temple of Faustina
  (Templum Divae Faustinae
  et Divi Antonini)
5 Temple of Castor and Pollux
  (Templum Dioscurorum)
6 Temple of Saturn
  (Templum Saturni)
7 Arch of Septimus Severus
  (Arcus Septimii Severi)
8 Rostra (orator's platform)
9 Curia Julia
  (Church of Sant'Andriano)

10 Temple of Caesar
   (Templum Divi Julii)
11 Temple of Vesta
   (Aedes Vestae)
12 House of Vestal Virgins
   (Atrium Vestae)
13 Basilica of Maxentius
   or of Constantine
   (Basilica Maxentii/Constantini)
14 Church of Santi Cosma e
   Damiano
15 Temple of Cybele
   (Domus Cybelae)
16 House of Livia
   (Domus Liviae)
17 Palace of Flavians
   (Domus Flaviorum)

18 Palace of Augustus
   (Domus Augustiana)
19 Stadium (Hippodromus)
20 Temple of Venus Genetrix
   (Templum Veneris
   Genetricis)
21 Basilica Ulpia
22 Trajan's Column
   (Columna Traini)
23 Trajan's Market
   (Mercati Traiani)
24 Temple of Mars Ultor
   (Templum Martis Ultoris)
25 Theatre of Marcellus
   (Theatrum Marcelli)
26 Column of Phocas
27 Lapis Niger

Niger, a piece of black marble on a square pillar bearing a mutilated
inscription in an early form of Latin (4th c. B.C.?), which was believed in
Cicero's time to be the tomb of Romulus.

Beyond it, to the north, is the Curia Iulia or Senate House, originally   Curia Iulia
built by Julius Caesar and restored about A.D. 303. In this are temporarily displayed two marble slabs, the Anaglypha Traiani, with fine
reliefs.

At the north-east corner of the Temple of Castor and Pollux is the   Temple of Vesta
substructure of the Temple of Caesar, erected by Augustus in 29 B.C. on
the spot on which Caesar's body was burned in 44 B.C. after his murder.
To the south of this can be seen one of the most sacred shrines of
ancient Rome, the Temple of Vesta, dedicated to the virgin goddess of
the domestic hearth. Beyond it is the Atrium Vestae, the house of the
vestal virgins, with a rectangular courtyard containing three cisterns
for storing rain-water (since the vestal virgins were forbidden to use
water from the ordinary piped supply).

To the east of this are the three massive arches of the Basilica of Maxentius (access from the Via dei Fori Imperiali; see below), with the church of Santi Cosma e Damiano to the left.

*Arch of Titus

Adjoining the Basilica of Maxentius to the south-east is the site of the Temple of Venus and Rome, erected by the Emperor Hadrian in A.D. 135, which is now occupied by the church of Santa Francesca Romana. A little way south stands the Arch of Titus (Arco di Tito), erected to commemorate the capture of Jerusalem (A.D. 70), with fine reliefs under the arch (triumphal procession with Jewish prisoners, the table with the show-bread, the seven-branched candlestick).

Palatine Hill

Above the south side of the Forum rises the Palatine Hill (Monte Palatino, 51 m/168 ft), the site of the earliest settlement ("Roma Quadrata"). In late antiquity visitors to the Palatine were shown the hut occupied by Romulus and the cave of the she-wolf which suckled Romulus and Remus. Augustus, who was born on the Palatine, built on the hill the great imperial palace, the Palatium, which gave its name to all later palaces; successive emperors enlarged and embellished the structures on the hill. From the 4th c. the Palatine decayed along with the rest of Rome, and by the 10th c. the ruins of the Imperial palaces gave place to gardens, convents and defensive towers. Systematic excavation began in 1871.

Orti Farnesiani

Under the Farnese Gardens (Orti Farnesiani), which occupy the highest part of the Palatine, to the north-west, are the remains of the Palace of Tiberius. The terraces on the north-west side afford magnificent views of the Forum, the Colosseum, the Capitol and the city from the Lateran to the Ianiculum. At the other end of the gardens a flight of steps leads down to the brick substructures of the Temple of Cybele (191 B.C.) and the House of Livia (mother of Tiberius and later wife of Augustus), which contains wall paintings.

Palace of the
Flavians

To the east of the Farnese Gardens is the site of the Palace of the Flavians, which dates from the time of Domitian, the greatest builder on the Palatine (c. A.D. 92), with the throne room in which the emperor gave audiences, the basilica in which he dispensed justice and (beyond a square garden) a large dining-room. To the south are the substructures of the Palace of Augustus and the so-called Stadium, a garden in the shape of a racecourse.

From the north-east corner of the Stadium steps lead up to the ruins of the Palace of Severus and the Belvedere, a terrace affording magnificent views. From here can be seen the whole area of the Circus Maximus, Rome's "largest circus", with seating for 185,000 spectators. Along its south side runs the Via del Circo Massimo.

*Via dei Fori Imperiali

From the Piazza Venezia the Via dei Fori Imperiali, flanked by gardens, runs past the Imperial Fora to the Colosseum. The massive growth of the city in late Republican and Imperial times made it necessary to erect new buildings to house markets and courts, and the first of a series of new forums was built by Julius Caesar. He was followed by Augustus and his successors Trajan, Nero and Vespasian, each of whom created a new forum in an area previously occupied by a maze of narrow streets and embellished it with a temple as the central feature, colonnades, law courts and a profusion of monuments and works of art. From 1925 onwards the remains were systematically cleared (good views from outside).

At the near end of the Via dei Fori Imperiali, on the right, is the Foro di Cesare (Caesar's Forum), with its colonnade and the high substructure of the Temple of Venus Genetrix (the mythical mother of the Iulians), completed only in A.D. 113 by Trajan, of which three columns have survived.

Caesar's Forum

To the north is the Foro di Traiano (Trajan's Forum; entrance from Trajan's Market), built A.D. 107–118, the largest and most magnificent of the Imperial Fora, made up of four elements – the unexcavated Forum proper, in front of the massive semicircle of Trajan's Market, the partly excavated Basilica Ulpia, an unexcavated temple and two libraries of which nothing is now left. Here too stands the 27 m/89 ft high Trajan's Column (Colonna Traiana), which originally held, concealed in the base, a golden urn containing the emperor's ashes. Around the column runs a spiral band of carvings 200 m/219 yd long with scenes from Trajan's Dacian Wars (A.D. 101–106). The column, formerly crowned by a statue of Trajan, now bears a figure of the Apostle Peter set up in 1587. On the north-east side of Trajan's Forum is Trajan's Market (Mercati Traianei; excavated 1926–30), a two-storeyed semicircular structure in brick, 60 m/66 yd long. Between this and an inner semicircle faced with marble lay a paved street flanked by shops, and above this, to the rear, rose a range of multi-storeyed buildings.

*Trajan's Forum

*Trajan's Column

*Trajan's Market

Immediately south-east of Trajan's Forum is the Foro di Augusto (Forum of Augustus), with the Temple of Mars Ultor (Avenging Mars), built by Augustus in fulfilment of a vow made at the battle of Philippi (42 B.C.) in which he defeated the army of Caesar's murderers.

Forum of Augustus

Farther south-east is the Foro di Nerva (Nerva's Forum), which preserves two fine Corinthian columns and a section of the entablature on its south-east side. Adjoining Nerva's Forum is the unexcavated Forum Vespasiani (Vespasian's Forum), which had a Temple of Peace erected after the destruction of Jerusalem. Here too, on the south side of the Via dei Fori Imperiali, is the entrance to the church of Santi Cosma e Damiano, founded in the 6th c. on a site in the Forum Romanum. On the triumphal arch in the upper church and in the apse are 6th c. mosaics which are perhaps the finest in Rome. In a room to the right of the entrance is a gigantic Neapolitan crib, an 18th c. work.

Nerva's Forum

Farther along the Via dei Fori Imperiali, on the right, we come to the entrance to the massive Basilica of Maxentius, which was enlarged by his conqueror Constantine and is therefore also known as the Basilica of Constantine. Its massive barrel vaulting served as a model for many later architects. In July and August concerts are given in the basilica. At the south-east corner of the basilica of Maxentius, built partly on the site of the Temple of Venus and Rome, is the church of Santa Francesca Romana (patron saint of motorists), originally built in the 10th c. but subsequently much altered, with a handsome Baroque façade (1615) and a richly appointed interior.

*Basilica of Maxentius

Santa Francesca Romana

**Colosseum

Near the south-east end of the Via dei Fori Imperiali and the Forum Romanum stands the Colosseum or Flavian Amphitheatre, one of the world's most celebrated buildings.

With its monumental proportions and severely disciplined structure the Colosseum has long been the symbol of the greatness of Rome. Originally built by Vespasian (A.D. 72 onwards) with three storeys, it

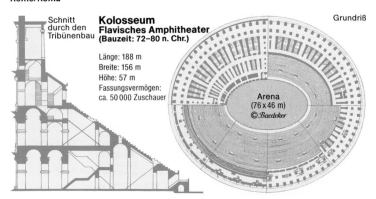

Schnitt durch den Tribünenbau

Kolosseum
Flavisches Amphitheater
(Bauzeit: 72–80 n. Chr.)

Länge: 188 m
Breite: 156 m
Höhe: 57 m
Fassungsvermögen:
ca. 50 000 Zuschauer

Grundriß

Arena
(76 × 46 m)
© Baedeker

was heightened to four storeys by Titus and inaugurated in A.D. 80 with gladitorial contests and other shows lasting 100 days and involving 1000 gladiators and 5000 animals. It is elliptical in plan, measuring 188 × 156 m/206 × 171 yd sand standing 48.5 m/160 ft high. The exterior is constructed of travertine blocks; the interior also incorporates tufa and brick. The north-east part still preserves its original four storeys, the three lower storeys being in the form of arcades, the pillars of which have semi-columns of the Doric, Ionic and Corinthian orders, while the solid wall of the fourth storey has windows set between Corinthian pilasters.

There are four main entrances, each with a triple opening; those at the

View of the Colosseum

ends were reserved for the emperor, while those on the sides were used for the processional entry of the gladiators and other participants. The spectators (some 40,000–50,000) entered through the lower arcades, which were numbered, and found their way to their seats by the appropriate staircases. The seats in the lowest row (podium) were occupied by the emperor, senators and vestal virgins. The arena, measuring 85 × 55 m/93 × 60 yd, had extensive substructures accommodating hoists and other stage machinery, cages for wild beasts, etc. The bloody gladitorial contests were abolished by the Emperor Honorius in A.D. 404; the fights with wild beasts continued until the time of the Gothic ruler Theodoric the Great.

During the Middle Ages some sections of the walls collapsed during earthquakes, and further damage was caused by the use of parts of the structure by Roman nobles as fortresses and by its later use as a quarry of building materials. Finally Pope Benedict XIV (1740–58) consecrated the remains to the Passion of Christ, in commemoration of the blood of the martyrs which had flowed in the Colosseum, and set up a bronze cross (re-erected in 1926). Restoration work on the Colosseum was started in 1992 and will last for several years.

South-west of the Colosseum stands the Arch of Constantine, a triumphal arch of white marble with a triple opening, erected by the Senate to commemorate Constantine's victory over Maxentius in the battle of the Milvian Bridge (A.D. 312). Rome's best preserved triumphal arch incorporates architectural elements and sculpture (now exposed to damage from air pollution) from earlier monuments.

*Arch of Constantine

Via di San Gregorio

From the Arch of Constantine an imposing avenue, the Via di San Gregorio (the ancient Via Triumphalis), runs south between the Caelian Hill and the Palatine. 350 m/385 yd along this street a side street branches off on the left to the church of Santi Giovanni e Paolo (originally founded c. 400 but several times rebuilt), with very early frescoes.

Santi Giovanni e Paolo

Farther along Via di San Gregorio, also on the left, is the church of San Gregorio Magno, founded by Pope Gregory I in 575 in his family palace and completely rebuilt in the 17th and 18th c.

San Gregorio Magno

Via di San Gregorio joins the Piazza di Porta Capena, at the east end of the Circus Maximus. On the south side of the square stands the Axum Obelisk (3rd–4th c.), brought here from Ethiopia in 1937.

Piazza di Porta Capena

Beyond the obelisk, extending along Viale Aventino rises the massive FAO Building, erected in 1948 to house the Food and Agriculture Organisation, with the Lubin Memorial Library. In the south-west wing is part of the Ministry of Posts.

FAO Building

*Terme di Caracalla

From the east corner of the FAO Building the Viale Guido Baccelli runs through the Parco di Porta Capena, which contains some ancient remains, to the Baths of Caracalla (Terme di Caracalla; Latin Thermae Antonianae; during the summer performances of opera), a gigantic bathing establishment (330 m/361 yd square, with an area of 109,000 sq. m/13,364 sq. yd) built by Caracalla in A.D. 216. The baths proper, in the centre of the courtyard, include a hot bath (caldarium), a pool for cold dips (frigidarium), etc. In spite of the loss of their rich marble decoration and their columns, and the collapse of the roof, the Baths still display the architectural skill of their builders and give some impression of public baths during the Imperial period.

Sepolcro degli
Scipioni

From Piazza di Porta Capena the Via delle Terme di Caracalla runs south-east to the Piazzale Numa Pompilio and then south into the Via Cristoforo Colombo, a fine modern highway built for the 1960 Olympic Games. Alternatively it is possible to bear south-east along Via di Porta San Sebastiano to the Tomb of the Scipios (Sepolcro degli Scipioni), built in 312 B.C. (still preserving the original sarcophagi).

Close by is the Columbarium of Pomponius Hylas or of the Freedmen of Ocatavia (Nero's wife), a subterranean tomb with good stucco decoration and painting.

Arco di Druso

Via di Porta San Sebastiano ends at the so-called Arch of Drusus (Arco di Druso; probably in fact dating from the time of Trajan). Immediately beyond it, in the Aurelian Walls, is the crenellated Porta San Sebastiano, the ancient Porta Appia, from which the Via Appia Antica runs south to the Catacombs.

Lateran

The Lateran Palace was for many centuries the residence of the popes; adjoining it is the Lateran Basilica. Via di San Giovanni in Laterano runs south-east from the Colosseum to the Lateran district.

*San Clemente

In Via di San Giovanni in Laterano, built over an ancient temple of Mithras, is the church of San Clemente (1108), a good example of an early Christian basilica. The nave is flanked by aisles, but there is no transept; fine marble choir screens, flanked by two ambos; in front of the main entrance is an atrium, with a fountain for ablutions; there are wall paintings (8th–11th c.) in the old lower church.

Santo Stefano
Rotondo

The Lateran can be also reached from the Colosseum by going south along Via Claudia and from there north-east through the Via di Santo Stefano Rotondo. To the south of this street, on the Caelian, stands the church of Santo Stefano Rotondo (460–480), a round church, also built over a temple of Mithras, with 56 columns in the interior and an open timber roof structure. Excavations under the church brought to light remains of a barracks (Castra Peregrinorum) for soldiers passing through and a mithraeum of the 3rd c. A.D., with frescoes and sculptures.

Obelisk

Via di San Giovanni joins the Piazza di San Giovanni in Laterano, in the centre of which rises a red granite Egyptian obelisk (15th c. B.C.), set up here in 1588; it is the largest of its kind, standing 32 m/106 ft high, not counting the base.

*Baptistery

In the south-west corner of the square is the Baptistery of San Giovanni in Fonte, the oldest baptistery in Rome (432–440) and the model for all later buildings of the same kind.

*San Giovanni in Laterano

On the south side of the square stands the church of San Giovanni in Laterano, built by Constantine the Great in a palace belonging to the Laterani, one of the five patriarchal churches of Rome, "mother and head of all churches". It was much altered between the 10th and 15th c., and its present Baroque form including the two bell-towers dates from

Plan

**San Giovanni
in Fonte**

San Giovanni
in Laterano

Palazzo Lateranense

© *Baedeker*

N

50 m

1 Bronze doors (Roman)
2 Holy Door
3 Statue of Constantine the
   Great
4 Frescoes by Giotto (Boniface VIII)
5 Orsini Chapel
6 Torlonia Chapel
7 Massimo Chapel
8 St John's Chapel
9 Papal altar
10 Tomb of Pope Martin V (crypt)
11 Baroque organ
12 Side door

13 Monument of Pope Leo XIII.
   Entrance to Portico of Leo XIII
14 Choir chapel
15 Sacristies
16 Chapterhouse
17 St Hilary's Chapel.
   Entrance to cloister
18 Chapel of St Francis of Assisi
   (monument of 1927)
19 Santorio Chapel
20 Chapel of Assumption
21 Corsini Chapel
22 Baptistery

the mid 16th c.; the massive Late Baroque façade, with its conspicuous attic storey and its crown of statues, dates from 1735; the new choir was added in 1885. Of the five doorways the central one has ancient bronze doors from the Curia Iulia.

The present interior, with five aisles, was designed by Francesco Borromini (16th–17th c.); the magnificent timber ceiling in the nave is by Daniele da Volterra (1564–72); the richly inlaid pavement is 15th c.
The ancient columns in the nave were joined in pairs by Borromini to form piers; the large statues of the Apostles in niches were added after 1700.

Interior

Four steps lead up into the transept, in the centre of which is the Altare Papale, at which only the Pope or his representative can celebrate Mass. The tabernacle dates from 1369. Among the relics preserved here are the heads of the Apostles Peter and Paul.
The choir is richly decorated with marble. In the apse are mosaics (much restored) dating from 1290.
In the south aisle, to the rear of the first pier of the nave, is a fresco (Pope Boniface VIII proclaiming the first jubilee year, 1300) attributed to Giotto but much restored.
There are numerous monuments in the church.

Altare Papale

A door beside the last chapel in the north aisle leads into the early 13th c. Cloister (Chiostro), which has numerous twisted colonnettes with mosaic decoration.

Cloister

Lateran Palace

Adjoining the north side of the Lateran Church is the Lateran Palace, built in 1586 on the site of an earlier palace, occupied by the popes from the time of Constantine onwards, which was burned down in 1308. At present it is occupied by the Vicariate of the city of Rome.

Scala Santa
Opposite the Lateran Palace to the north-east, in a 16th c. building, is the Scala Santa, a flight of 28 marble steps (now covered with wood for protection) which is believed to be the staircase ascended by Christ in Pilate's palace in Jerusalem and which the faithful climb only on their knees. At the top, beyond a grille, is the chapel known as the Sancta Sanctorum, with 13th c. mosaics.

Porta San Giovanni
Close by, on the south side of Piazza di Porta San Giovanni, stands the 16th c. Porta San Giovanni, from which the Via Appia Nuova runs south-east.

Santa Croce in Gerusalemme

From Piazza di Porta San Giovanni the Viale Carlo Felice runs east to the church of Santa Croce in Gerusalemme, one of the seven pilgrimage churches of Rome (rebuilt 1743), which may have been founded by St Helena.

Museum of Musical Instruments
To the north of the church the Museum of Musical Instruments (Museo Nazionale degli Strumenti Musicali) houses a collection dating from ancient times to 1800.

Porta Maggiore
Farther north towers the massive Porta Maggiore, originally an arch carrying the Acqua Claudia (Aqueduct of Claudius) over the Roman road, later a gate in the Aurelian Walls.

Termini Station District

Domus Aurea di Nerone
North-east of the Colosseum, in the Parco Traiano on the Esquiline Hill, are the remains of Nero's Golden House or Domus Aurea di Nerone, a palace complex with numerous magnificent State apartments, planned with a lavish disregard for expense but which was left unfinished. Trajan later used it as the substructure of his Baths. The palace contains much fine painting, which Raphael took as his model for the Loggias in the Vatican.

Museo Nazionale d'Arte Orientale
Some 500 m/550 yd north-east of Nero's Golden House is the Museo Nazionale d'Arte Orientale, which contains fine art from Asia.

*San Pietro in Vincoli

Figure of Moses
North of the Parco Traiano stands the church of San Pietro in Vincoli, an aisled basilica with 20 ancient columns, originally built in 442 to house the chains (vincula) of St Peter and completely rebuilt and enlarged in the 15th c. In the south transept is the powerful figure of Moses by Michelangelo (1513–16), created for the unfinished tomb of Pope Julius II, a symbol of strength controlled by super-human will-power. The second altar in the north aisle has 7th c. mosaic decoration; adjoining it is the tomb of Cardinal Nicolaus Cusanus (d. 1464). A shrine under the high altar, with bronze doors (1477), contains the chains of St Peter, which are displayed annually on August 1st.

*Santa Maria Maggiore

A little way north of San Pietro in Vincoli is Via Cavour, which branches off the Via dei Fori Imperiali and runs north-east to the Piazza dell'Esquilino. On the south-east side of this square is the imposing church of Santa Maria Maggiore, one of Rome's five patriarchal churches and the largest of its 80 or so churches dedicated to the Virgin. Founded in the 5th c., it was rebuilt in the 16th and 17th c.; the main front with its loggia dates from 1743. The tower (1377) is the highest in Rome (75 m/248 ft). From the porch (13th c. mosaics), with its five doorways, four entrances lead into the church; the fifth, the Porta Santa (to the left), is opened only in Holy Years.

The aisled interior is splendidly decorated. The pavement of the nave dates from the 12th c., the magnificent ceiling, richly gilded with the first gold brought from America, from 1493 to 1498. Above the architrave, borne on 40 Ionic columns, as well as on the triumphal arch, are 5th c. mosaics. In the apse are mosaics by J. Torriti (1295). | Interior

In the south transept the magnificent Sistine Chapel, or Chapel of the Holy Sacrament, has a domed roof; the chapel was built in 1585 in the reign of Sixtus V. In the north aisle is the Borghese Chapel (1611), also domed, with an image of the Virgin, believed to be miraculous, on the high altar.

300 m/330 yd north-west of Santa Maria Maggiore stands the church of Santa Pudenziana, with a 12th c. tower, which legend claims to be the oldest church in Rome. The apse contains mosaics (Christ with Apostles, 401–417) which are among the finest in Rome. | Santa Pudenziana

Just south of Santa Maria Maggiore, concealed among buildings, is the church of Santa Prassede, built in 822 in honour of St Praxedis and several times restored, most recently in 1869. It has a beautiful interior, with fine 9th c. mosaics on the triumphal arch, in the apse and in the chapel of San Zeno (south aisle). | Santa Prassede

Termini Station

At the north-east end of Via Cavour we come to the large Piazza dei Cinquecento. On the south-east side of this square is the Termini Station (Stazione Centrale Roma–Termini), completed in 1950, an imposing structure of distinctive design, making much use of glass and steel, which was a landmark in the development of modern railway architecture. In the concourse is the entrance to the Metropolitana line (partly underground, partly above ground). The Metropolitana Line A runs from the Stazione Termini to Via Ottaviano (near the Vatican) or by way of Cinecittà to Via Anagnina; the Metropolitana Line B runs by way of the Porta di San Paolo to the EUR district (Via Laurentina). | Piazza dei Cinquecento

Terme di Diocleziano

The north side of the Piazza dei Cinquecento and the area to the north are occupied by the Baths of Diocletian (Terme di Diocleziano), built A.D. 298–305, which were no less magnificent than the Baths of Caracalla and measure 350 m/385 yd each way. Michelangelo was commissioned by Pope Pius IV to convert the Baths into a Carthusian monastery, and transformed the large vaulted tepidarium (warm bath) into the church of Santa Maria degli Angeli (1563–66). Since 1885 the monastic buildings have housed the Baths Museum. The great semicircle described by the outer wall now forms the Piazza della Repubblica, with a fountain. In a rotunda at the west end is the round church of San Bernardo, consecrated 1600. | Piazza della Repubblica

Courtyard in the Baths of Diocletian

*Museo Nazionale
Romano o delle
Terme

The Museo Nazionale Romano o delle Terme (Roman National
Museum or Baths Museum), founded 1886, contains material discovered on state property in and around Rome and has developed into
the most important collection of antiquities in Rome, except for the
museums of the Vatican (at present closed).

The old rooms around the south transept of Santa Maria degli Angeli,
the actual rooms of the Baths, contain the largest collection in Italy of
Roman sarcophagi and mosaics. Particularly notable items in the new
rooms are the "Niobe Wounded", a Greek original of the 5th c. B.C.; the
"Maiden of Anzio", an original work of the early Hellenistic period; the
headless and armless "Venus of Cyrene" (4th c. B.C.); a "Kneeling
Youth" (ephebe) from Subiaco (3rd c. B.C.); a bronze "Defeated Pugi-
list" (3rd c. B.C.); and a copy of Myron's "Discobolus" (5th c. B.C.). In the
Small Cloister (Piccolo Chiostro), behind glass walls, is the Ludovisi
Collection (temporarily closed). Notable items here are the so-called
Ludovisi Throne (5th c. B.C.); the "Galatian and his Wife", a Roman
copy of the Galatian who, when threatened by enemies, killed his wife
and himself, "Ares Resting" (Ares Ludovisi), the Ludovisi Juno and the
Head of a sleeping Fury, the so-called Ludovisi Medusa.

The Large Cloister (Grande Chiostro), completed in 1565, with a fountain in the centre, contains marble sculpture, architectural elements,
sarcophagi, mosaics and inscriptions.

On the first floor of the Museum can be seen a collection of mosaics,
stucco work and frescoes, including wall paintings from the Villa of
Livia in Prima Porta.

Via XX Settembre

A little way north of the Museo delle Terme is the Via XX Settembre commemorating 20 September 1870, when Italian troops marched into Rome after the withdrawal of the French. In this street which leads to the north-eastern districts of the city, to the north of San Bernardo, is the church of Santa Maria della Vittoria, a sumptuous Baroque church designed by Carlo Aderna (1608–20), which contains (fourth chapel on left) one of the great masterpieces of High Baroque style, Bernini's "Ecstasy of Teresa" (1647).

Santa Maria della Vittoria

Opposite the church is the imposing Acqua Felice Fountain (by Domenico Fontana, 1585–87), with marble sculpture. Farther along, on the right, the Ministry of Finance (1870–77) can be seen.

Acqua Felice Fountain

Via XX Settembre ends at the Porta Pia in the old town walls (designed by Michelangelo, 1561–65).
Immediately outside the Porta Pia, on the right-hand side of Via Nomentana, which continues the line of Via XX Settembre to the north-east, is the Ministry of Public Works.

Porta Pia

San Lorenzo and Città Universitaria

North-east of the Stazione Termini stands the Basilica San Lorenzo fuori le Mura, one of the five patriarchal churches of Rome, originally founded by Constantine the Great. It was entirely remodelled in the 6th and again in the 13th c., partly destroyed during the Second World War, but restored after the war. The floor of the nave and choir dates from the 12th–13th c., the baldacchino over the high altar from 1148. The triumphal arch has 6th c. mosaics. Adjoining the church is a picturesque Romanesque cloister.
Beside the church is a large cemetery, the Campo Verano.

San Lorenzo fuori le Mura

To the west of Piazza San Lorenzo is the University City (Città Universitaria), a large complex of buildings set amid gardens established here in the 1930s, with the Biblioteca Alessandrina, the University Library.

University City

Farther south, in the Castro Pretorio, is the National Library (Biblioteca Nazionale Centrale Vittorio Emanuele II), built 1971–75. This contains some 3 million volumes, 1883 incunabula, 6169 manuscripts and 30,000 autographs, and consists of a long ten-storey book-stack, an office block, a low building housing the catalogue and reading rooms, and a low conference building.

National Library

Villa Torlonia

One kilometre (¾ mile) farther on, also on right, lies the beautiful park of the Villa Torlonia, a good example of Romantic landscape gardening. Under the ground are Jewish catacombs. In the park is the early 19th c. Palazzo Torlonia, Mussolini's residence from 1925 to 1944, the cellars of which (no admission) contain one of Italy's largest private collections of antiquities, with over 600 works of art.

Palazzo Torlonia

Another 2 km (1¼ miles) out is the church of Sant'Agnese fuori le Mura, founded by Constantine the Great to house the tomb of St Agnes and rebuilt in the 7th and 15th c. and again in 1856. The apse contains mosaics dating from the 7th c. Under the church are catacombs, some still in their original state (before A.D. 300).
Adjoining Sant'Agnese is the round church of Santa Costanza, built as a mausoleum for Constantine's daughter, with fine 4th c. mosaics.

Sant'Agnese fuori le Mura

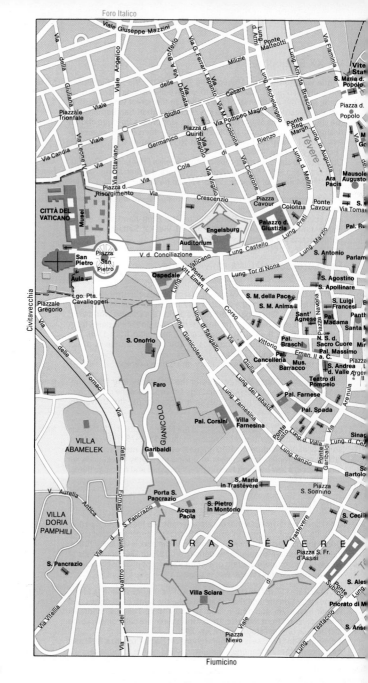

Roma

500 m

VILLA BORGHESE
VILLA ALBANI
Galleria Borghese

Galoppatoio
Villa Medici
Porta Pinciana
Piazza Fiume
Porta Pia
Piazza di S.Croce
Ministeri

Via Nomentana

Trinità dei Monti
S. Isidoro
Piazza di Spagna
Pal. Spagna

S. Maria Concezione
Min. delle Finanze
Terme di Diocleziano
Piazza d. Indipendenza

Pal. Barberini
Piazza Barberini
S. Maria d. Angeli
Piazza d. Repubblica

Fontana di Trevi
Quirinale
QUIRINALE
Min. di Difesa
S. Carlo 4 Font.
S. Andrea Quirin.
San Vitale
Teatro d. Opera
Piazza d. Cinquecento
Termini Station

Univ. Gregoriana
S. Croce
Ignazio
SS. Apostoli
Pal. Rospigliosi
Pal. Colonna
Pal. Espos.
Banca d'Italia
Min. d' Interno
Piazza d. Esquilino
S. Maria Maggiore
Piazza S. M. Maggiore

Pal. Sciara
Pal. Doria
Piazza Venezia
Monumento Vitt. Eman.
Foro Traiano
IV Nov.
S. Prassede
Via Merulana
Piazza Vitt. Eman.

Mus. Capitol.
S. M. Aracoeli
Campidoglio
Pal. dei Conservatori
Teatro di Marcello
Foro Romano
dei Fori Imperiali
S. Pietro in Vincoli
Museo d'Arte Orientale
ESQUILINO

Templo di Vesta
S. M. Cosmedin
PALATINO
Domus Aurea
OPPIO
Colosseo
Arco di Constantino
Piazza d. Colosseo
San Giovanni in Laterano
San Antonio di Padovo

Circo
Massimo
Tempio di Claudio
SS. Giov. e Paolo
S. Gregorio Magno
S. Stefano Rotondo
S. Giovanni in Laterano

Sabina
AVENTINO
Piazza di Pta. Capena
CELIO
Min. Turismo

F. A. O.
Min. Poste
Parco di Porta Carpena
Piazza Metronia

Piazza Albania
© Baedeker
Terme di Caracalla

E. U. R.
Ostia, Lido di Ostia
Via Appia
Metropolitana

Depretis
Biblioteca Nazionale

Tivoli, Frosinone, Frascati, Albano

387

Quartiere Monte Sacro

From Sant'Agnese Via Nomentana continues north-east to the Quartiere Monte Sacro, a large suburban area which has grown up since the last war on and around Mons Sacer.

To the south-west on Monte Antenne Campeggio an Islamic culture centre and mosque are being built.

Quirinal and Villa Borghese

Palazzo Colonna (Picture Gallery)

From the north side of the Piazza Venezia it is a short distance east along Via Cesare Battisti to the elongated Piazza Santi Apostoli, with the Palazzo Colonna, begun about 1417 by Pope Martin V (Colonna) and much altered in the 17th and 18th c. The richly decorated rooms on the first floor contain a collection of pictures, the Galleria Colonna (entrance in Via della Pilotta).

Santi Apostoli

On the north side of the Palazzo Colonna is the church of the Santi Apostoli (1702), with a porch dating from 1475. At the end of the north aisle is the tomb of Pope Clement XIV (by Canova, 1789).

Universitas Gregoriana

North-east of the church, in Piazza Pilotta, stands the Universitas Gregoriana or Pontifical University, founded in 1553; the present buildings date from 1930.

Torre delle Milizie

From the Palazzo Colonna Via IV Novembre runs south to the medieval Torre delle Milizie or Torre di Nerone and the Via Magnanapoli. By the Torre delle Milizie is the entrance to Trajan's Market and Forum.

Via Nazionale

From the Torre delle Milizie Via Nazionale, one of Rome's main traffic arteries, runs north-east, past the Banca d'Italia (on the right), the

Villa Borghese

Palazzo Rospigliosi (1603: ceiling paintings by Guido Reni) and the Palazzo delle Esposizioni (1880–83), to the Piazza della Repubblica. Beside the Palazzo delle Esposizioni (on the left) is the mouth of the tunnel (348 m/381 yd long) driven under the Quirinal in 1902, providing a link with the Piazza di Spagna.

Quirinal

From the Via Magnanapoli Via XXIV Maggio runs past the church of San Silvestro al Quirinale (1524: on the left) and the west wing of the Palazzo Rospigliosi to the Piazza del Quirinale, on the Quirinal Hill.

Piazza del Quirinale

In the centre of the square are the two famous marble statues of the "Horse-Tamers" (Dioscuri), fine examples of the classical style of sculpture of the Imperial period, based on Greek models of the 5th c. B.C.

*Horse-Tamers

On the east side of the Piazza del Quirinale are the Palazzo della Consulta (built 1732–34: no admission), with a beautiful staircase, and the Palazzo del Quirinale, an imposing palace built on the summit of the Quirinal Hill. Begun in 1574 as a summer residence for the Pope, it was enlarged and altered in later centuries. From 1870 to 1946 it was a royal palace, and it is now the official residence of the President of Italy, although he does not in fact live here. It is set in a beautiful park.

Palazzo del Quirinale

To the east of the Quirinal Palace stands the church of Sant'Andrea al Quirinale (by Bernini, 1658–70), one of the most harmonious creations of Roman Baroque architecture, on an oval ground-plan.

*Sant'Andrea al Quirinale

Still farther east, at the junction of Via del Quirinale with Via Quattro Fontane, are the Quattro Fontane (Four Fountains). To the right is the little church of San Carlo alle Quattro Fontane or San Carlino, a Baroque building by Borromini.

Quattro Fontane

Palazzo Barberini

In the northern part of Via Quattro Fontane, on the right, is the Palazzo Barberini, an imposing Baroque structure begun in 1626 by Carlo Maderna and completed in 1633 by Borromini and Bernini. It now houses the Galleria Nazionale d'Arte Antica, with works by Italian and foreign artists of the 13th–16th c., including Hans Holbein the Younger's "Portrait of Henry VIII", El Greco's "Baptism of Christ" and "Nativity", and Raphael's "La Fornarina". In the principal room is a fine ceiling painting depicting the "Triumph of the Barberini Family" by Pietro da Corona, a masterpiece of Baroque monumental painting (1633–39). 17th and 18th c. pictures from the Palazzo Corsini are also of interest.

Galleria Nazionale d'Arte Antica

Adjoining to the north-west in the centre of the busy, elongated Piazza Barberini can be seen the beautiful Fontana del Tritone (by Bernini, 1640), with a figure of a triton blowing a conch.

*Fontana del Tritone

Via Vittorio Veneto

From the north end of the Piazza Barberini the famous Via Vittorio Veneto (Via Veneto for short), a wide tree-lined avenue, climbs in an S-shaped curve to the Porta Pinciana, a distance of almost one kilometre ($\frac{3}{4}$ mile).

Santa Maria della Concezione
* Mortuary Chapels

A little way along the lower part, on the right, underneath the Capuchin church of Santa Maria della Concezione (1626) are five mortuary chapels, the walls of which are covered with the bones of more than 4000 Capuchins. Beyond this are various large buildings occupied by government offices and banks.

The upper section of the street, beyond the intersection with Via Ludovisi and Via Boncompagni is the territory of the "dolce vita", the rendezvous of the famous and fashionable from Rome and all over the world, with elegant luxury shops, hotels and cafés, the best known of which is the Café de Paris.

Villa Borghese

Beyond the Porta Pinciana is the beautiful park of the Villa Borghese, laid out by Cardinal Scipio Borghese in the 17th c., which was purchased by the State in 1902 and thrown open to the public under the name of Villa Umberto I. At the south end of the park is a large underground car park. Scattered about in the grounds, planted with chestnut trees, holm-oaks and beautiful umbrella pines, are a variety of ornamental buildings, fountains and monuments. In the southern section of the park is a galoppatoio (race-track).

Casino Borghese
Museo e Galleria

To the east is the Casino Borghese, built about 1615 and richly decorated with marble and frescoes at the end of the 18th c. Notable features in the interior are a figure of Pauline Borghese, Napoleon's sister, as Venus (1807), a masterpiece by Canova, and several youthful works by Bernini, including "David with his Sling" and "Apollo and Daphne". On the upper floor of the Casino the Galleria Borghese, one of Rome's finest picture galleries, has masterpieces by Raphael ("Entombment"), Titian ("Sacred and Profane Love"), Caravaggio ("David", "Madonna dei Palafrenieri"), Correggio ("Danaë"), works by painters of the Roman Baroque school, as well as by Rubens, Lucas Cranach, Domenichino and Andrea del Sarto.

Zoo

In the northern part of the park of the Villa Borghese is a Zoo, established by Karl Hagenbeck in 1911.

* Galleria Nazionale d'Arte Moderna

To the west of this, in Viale delle Belle Arti, the Galleria Nazionale d'Arte Moderna contains the largest collection of modern art in Italy, covering the period from the beginning of the 19th c. to the present day, with Italian neo-classical artists and Neo-Impressionists, other European Impressionists and Expressionists, contemporary painting and sculpture.

* Villa Giulia
Museo Nazionale Etrusco

Nearby is the Villa Giulia, built for Pope Julius III by Vignola (1550–55), with beautiful stucco-work and painting by Taddeo Zuccaro. The villa now houses the large State collection of Etruscan antiquities from the province of Rome, outstanding among which are the Cista Ficoroni (3rd c. B.C.), a cylindrical toilet casket with finely engraved scenes from the story of the Argonauts, the Apollo of Veii, a painted terracotta statue dating from about 500 B.C., and a terracotta sarcophagus from Cerveteri with the reclining figures of a man and his wife (6th c. B.C.).

Piazza di Spagna

Column of the Immacolata

From the Piazza Barberini the busy Via del Tritone runs west to join the Via del Corso. Going along this street and in 200 m/220 yd turning right

The Spanish Steps ▶

along Via Due Macelli, we come to the Piazza di Spagna, under the south side of the Pincio. It is named after the large Palazzo di Spagna, which has been the residence of the Spanish Embassy to the Holy See since the 17th c. In front of the palace rises the Column of the Immacolata, erected to commemorate the proclamation of the dogma of the Immaculate Conception by Pope Pius IX in 1854.

La Barcaccia

On the south side of the square is the Palazzo di Propaganda Fide, a centre and college for the propagation of the Roman Catholic faith (missionary archives). In the centre of the square is La Barcaccia, a low fountain in the shape of a boat (by Bernini, 1629).

*Spanish Steps
Santissima Trinità
dei Monti

From here the famous Spanish Steps (Scalinata della Trinità dei Monti), a magnificent Baroque staircase, with 137 steps, alternating with ramps, designed by Francesco de Sanctis (1723–26), usually gay with flowers, climb up to the twin-towered French church of the Santissima Trinità dei Monti, founded in 1495, on the Pincio. A little way north of the church is the 16th c. Villa Medici, which came into the hands of the Medici family in the 17th c. and has been occupied since 1803 by the French Academy of Art.

Shopping streets

To the west and north-west of the Piazza di Spagna are a number of busy streets, including Via dei Condotti, Via del Babuino and Via Margutta, with elegant shops and boutiques.

Pincio

Farther north, above the east side of the Piazza del Popolo, is the Pincio, a beautiful park laid out in 1809–14 on the hill of that name (50 m/165 ft), the most northerly of Rome's hills, with numerous busts and monuments commemorating famous Italians and a monumental piece of sculpture, 11 m/36 ft high, by Giacomo Manzù (1975). From the terrace on the west side of the park there is a famous prospect of Rome, with an impressive view of St Peter's. At the end of the park is a bridge linking it with the Villa Borghese park.

Via del Corso and side streets

The Via del Corso, which runs north-west from the Piazza Venezia to the Piazza del Popolo, flanked by numerous Baroque palaces, has long been Rome's principal street (1.5 km/1 mile long but only 12 m/13 yd wide).

*Galleria Doria
Pamphili

The first building on the left-hand side is the 17th c. Palazzo Bonaparte, and just beyond this another 17th c. mansion, the Palazzo Doria, has a handsome pillared courtyard. On the first floor of the latter is the Galleria Doria Pamphili, which contains Velázquez's famous portrait of Pope Innocent X (Pamphili), a masterpiece notable equally for its sharp delineation of character and its brilliance of colour (1650). The gallery has also fine works by Raphael, Titian, Tintoretto, Correggio, Caravaggio ("Rest on the Flight into Egypt") and Claude Lorrain.

Collegio Romano

Beyond the Palazzo Doria a short street, Via Lata, on the left, runs from the Corso, leading to the Palazzo Sciarra, into the Piazza del Collegio Romano, on the right-hand side of which we come to the Collegio Romano (by Bartolomeo Ammannati and Giuseppe Valeriani, 1583–85), a Jesuit college until 1870 and now a State school.

In a small square to the west of the Collegio Romano stands the church of Santa Maria sopra Minerva, built before 800 on the site of Domitian's temple of Minerva and rebuilt in 1280. It is Rome's only medieval church in the Gothic style. In front of the high altar, to the left, is Michelangelo's statue of the Risen Christ with the Cross (1521). The altar itself contains the relics of St Catherine of Siena (1347–80). The Cappella Caraffa, in the south transept, has frescoes by Filippino Lippi (1489). There are numerous fine monuments; to the left of the choir is the tombstone of the Dominican Fra Giovanni Angelico (1387–1455).

Santa Maria sopra
Minerva

**Pantheon

North-west of Santa Maria sopra Minerva, in the Piazza della Rotonda, the centre of the old town, is the Pantheon, the best preserved building of ancient Rome.

The Pantheon was built in 27 B.C. by Marcus Vipsanius Agrippa, Augustus's friend and general, and several times rebuilt or restored, notably by Hadrian in 120–126. After the extinction of paganism the Eastern Emperor Phocas presented it to Pope Boniface IV, who consecrated it in 609 as the church of Santa Maria ad Martyres, popularly called Santa Maria Rotonda. The portico has sixteen ancient granite columns 12.5 m/41 ft high, and the entrance still preserves its two massive ancient bronze-clad doors. The huge dome of the rotunda, lit only by a round aperture 9 m/10 yd in diameter (the "Eye"), ranks as the supreme achievement of Roman interior architecture. The overwhelming effect of the building depends on the consummate harmony of its proportions no less than on its huge dimensions: its height (43.2 m/143 ft) is the same as its diameter, and the hemisphere of the dome is the same height as its vertical walls. The figures of the gods which once stood in

The Pantheon in the Piazza della Rotonda

the seven principal niches and the rest of the valuable furnishings of the Pantheon have been removed to other places in the course of the centuries. In the second niche on the right is the tomb of King Victor Emmanuel II (d. 1878); opposite this is the tomb of Umberto I (assassinated 1900); and to the right is the tomb of Raphael (1483–1520).

Sant' Ignazio

From the Pantheon Via del Seminario runs east, past the Ministry of Posts, to the Baroque church of Sant' Ignazio (by O. Grassi, 1626–50), built on the model of the Gesù in honour of the founder of the Jesuit order, Ignatius of Loyola (1491–1556), who was canonised in 1622. It has a famous ceiling painting by Andrea Pozzo, a masterpiece of perspective, best seen from the middle of the nave.

Exchange

Facing Sant' Ignazio, to the north, is the Exchange. The north front, on Piazza di Pietra, has eleven Corinthian columns, 12.9 m/43 ft high, probably from a temple built in honour of the Emperor Hadrian (A.D. 76–138).

Piazza Colonna

*Column of Marcus Aurelius

To the east of Sant' Ignazio, on the east side of the Via del Corso, is the 17th c. Palazzo Sciarra-Colonna. A little way north, off the west side of the Corso, the busy Piazza Colonna was named after the Column of Marcus Aurelius (Colonna di Marco Aurelio: 29.5 m/97 ft high) which stands in the centre of the square. Like Trajan's column, it is covered with reliefs (originally painted) depicting Marcus Aurelius's campaigns against the Marcomanni and other Germanic tribes. The column is topped by a bronze statue of the Apostle Paul which was erected by Pope Sixtus V.

Galleria Colonna

On the east side of the Piazza Colonna (and of the Corso) is the Galleria Colonna, with a Y-shaped arcade. The Palazzo Wedekind, on the west side of the square, has a portico of sixteen Ionic columns from the Etruscan city of Veii (Veio). On the north side is the Palazzo Chigi (begun 1562, completed by Carlo Maderna), which now houses the Italian Cabinet offices.

Piazza di Montecitorio Obelisk

Adjoining the Piazza Colonna on the west is the Piazza di Montecitorio, on an eminence formed by an accumulation of rubble. In the centre of this square rises a 26 m/86 ft high Egyptian obelisk (6th c. B.C.). The north side of the square is occupied by the Italian Parliament Building, also known as the Palazzo Montecitorio. Originally built by Bernini in 1650 for the Ludovisi family, it was converted for the use of the Papal courts in 1694 by Carlo Fontana and again altered in 1871 to house the new Italian Parliament.

*Fontana di Trevi

Some 250 m/275 yd east of the Piazza Colonna is the popular Fontana di Trevi, built against the south end of the Palazzo Poli. The most monumental of Rome's Baroque fountains, it was the work of Niccolo Salvi, based on designs by Bernini (1735–62). In the central niche is a figure of Neptune, flanked by figures of Health and Fertility; in front is a large basin, some 20 m/22 yd across. It is an old custom when leaving Rome to throw a coin backwards over your head into the basin in order to ensure that you will return. At the moment the Fontana di Trevi is being restored and therefore is surrounded by a glass screen.
Facing the Trevi Fountain, to the south-east, is the church of Santi Vincenzo ed Anastasio, with a Baroque façade of 1650.

Palazzo Ruspoli
San Carlo al Corso

350 m/385 yd north of the Piazza Colonna, on the left-hand side of the Via del Corso, is the Palazzo Ruspoli (begun 1556), with a fine staircase

of about 1650. Beyond this, to the right, there is a charming glimpse along Via Condotti to the Spanish Steps. Farther north again, on the left, stands the church of San Carlo al Corso, a fine Baroque structure (17th c.).

Mausoleo di Augusto

A little way north-west of San Carlo is the Mausoleum of Augustus (Mausoleo di Augusto), a monumental rotunda, 89 m/98 yd in diameter at the base and originally 44 m/145 ft high, built by Augustus in 28 B.C. as a burial place for himself and his family, which also contained the remains of some of his successors down to Nerva (A.D. 96–98). From the 11th c. it served several purposes, but in 1936 it was restored to its original condition.

Between the Mausoleum and the Tiber, in a glass hall in Via di Ripetta, is the Ara Pacis Augustae, an altar dedicated to the goddess of peace, re-erected here in 1938. Built on the Campus Martius in 13–9 B.C., after Augustus's return from Spain and Gaul, it is decorated with fine plant ornaments, including acanthus, ivy and laurel, and noble carved friezes depicting a Roman procession.

*Ara Pacis Augustae

At Via del Corso 17 is the Goethe Museum, with pictures, manuscripts, books, etc., in a house where Goethe lived during his stay in Rome (1786–88).

Goethe Museum

Piazza del Popolo

The Via del Corso runs into the oval Piazza del Popolo, laid out in its present form in 1816–20. On the north side stands the Porta del Popolo (1565 and 1655), the old north gate of Rome.

Porta del Popolo

Mausoleum of Augustus

Obelisk — In the centre of the square, at the point of intersection of three streets from the south, the Via di Pipetta, Via del Corso and Via del Babuino, rises an Egyptian obelisk (24 m/79 ft high; including base and cross 36 m/119 ft) erected by Pope Sixtus V in 1589.

Churches — On the south side of the square are two domed churches, Santa Maria in Monte Santo to the east and Santa Maria dei Miracoli to the west, both begun by Rainaldi in 1662 and completed by Bernini and Carlo Fontana in 1675 and 1679 respectively.

*Santa Maria del Popolo — Adjoining the Porta del Popolo is the church of Santa Maria del Popolo, built in 1472–77, with a new choir by Bramante (1505–9) and a Baroque interior (remodelled in 1655). It contains numerous works of art, in particular 15th c. monuments. In the chapel to the left of the choir are two magnificent pictures by Caravaggio ("Conversion of Paul", "Crucifixion of Peter"). In the Augustinian convent which formerly stood here Luther stayed during his visit to Rome in 1510–11.

On the east side of the church of Santa Maria del Popolo is an entrance to the Pincio park.

Beyond the Porta del Popolo, in Piazzale Flaminio to the right, is an entrance to the Villa Borghese park.

From the Piazza Venezia to the Tiber

*Gesù church — From the Piazza Venezia it is a short distance west along Via del Plebiscito to the Piazza del Gesù, where stands the Gesù (il Gesù), the principal church of the Jesuit order and one of the richest and most sumptuous churches in Rome, the model for all the other splendid Jesuit churches and a magnificent example of Baroque architecture. It has a wide, high nave, with the aisles converted into chaples. In the north transept is the splendid Altar of St Ignatius (1696–1700), under which is a gilded bronze sarcophagus containing the remains of St Ignatius of Loyola (1491–1556).

Corso Vittorio Emanuele II

Largo di Torre Argentina — From the far side of the Piazza del Gesù the busy Corso Vittorio Emanuele II, driven through the medieval town from 1870 onwards to provide a link between the Piazza Venezia and the Vatican City, continues west. A short distance along this street, on the left, is the Largo di Torre Argentina. In this low-lying square, in front of the Teatro Argentina, are the remains (excavated 1927–30) of four temples (Templi di età repubblicana: 3rd c. B.C.), which – unlike those in the Forum – have preserved much of their original form.

*Fontana delle Tartarughe — A short distance south of the Largo di Torre Argentina, in the little Piazza Mattei, is the Tortoise Fountain (Fontana delle Tartarughe), a charming bronze group by Taddeo Landini (1585).

Sant'Andrea della Valle — Farther along the Corso Vittorio Emanuele II, beyond the Largo di Torre Argentina, stands the domed church of Sant'Andrea della Valle, begun by F. Grimaldi and G. della Porta in 1591, completed by Carlo Maderna in 1625, with a richly decorated façade of 1665 and a sumptuous interior. Particularly notable are the fine frescoes by Domenichino (1624–28) in the pendentives under the dome and on the vaulting of the apse.

Palazzo Massimo alle Colonne — Farther along the Corso, on the right, is the Palazzo Massimo alle Colonne, one of the finest Renaissance buildings in Rome (by Baldassare Peruzzi, 1532–36), with a curved façade adapted to a bend in the old street and a picturesque double courtyard.

Beyond this, on the left of the Piazza di San Pantaleo, we find the Piccola Farnesina (1523), a Renaissance palace which houses the Museo Barracco, with a fine collection of ancient sculpture, including Greek, Assyrian, Egyptian and Etruscan tombstones.

Museo Barracco

On the opposite side, in the Palazzo Braschi (1972), is the interesting Museo di Roma, illustrating the history of Rome in recent centuries, with three railway coaches which belonged to Pope Pius IX, two State carriages, etc. On the top floor can be seen pictures by modern Roman artists; special exhibitions are held from time to time.

Museo di Roma

*Piazza Navona

North of the Palazzo Braschi we come to an elongated square, the busy Piazza Navona (pedestrians only), the most characteristic of Rome's 17th c. squares. Its shape (240 × 65 m/264 × 71 yd) reflects the fact that it occupies the site of the Stadium of Domitian, as its official name of Circo Agonale (Greek agon = contest, fight) also indicates. It is embellished with three fountains, the one at the north end erected in 1878, the other two by Bernini c. 1650; the finest is the centre one, with magnificent vigorous figures representing the rivers Danube, Ganges, Nile and Plate and an ancient obelisk.

*Fountains

Opposite, on the west side of the square, is the church of Sant'Agnese in Agonale (by Borromini and Rainaldi, 1652–73), an imposing Baroque church on a centralised plan, with a sumptuous interior.

Sant'Agnese in Agonale

North-west of the Piazza Navona is the church of Santa Maria dell'Anima (1500–14), old church of the German-speaking Catholics, with a beautiful interior (entered only through a rear courtyard).

Santa Maria dell'Anima

Fontana dei Fiumi on the Piazza Navona

Santa Maria della Pace | Immediately north-west of this the church of Santa Maria della Pace, built in 1480, has a beautiful semicircular porch added in 1657. Above the first chapel on the right are figures of Sibyls painted by Raphael (1514), and in the octagonal dome are other fine 16th c. frescoes. The cloister is by Bramante (1504).

Palazzo Madama | To the east of Piazza Navona, in the Corso del Rinascimento, stands the Palazzo Madama (1642), the seat of the Italian Senate since 1871.

San Luigi dei Francesi | On its north side is the French national church, San Luigi dei Francesi (consecrated 1589). In the fifth chapel can be seen three notable pictures by Caravaggio depicting scenes from the life of St Matthew.

Sant'Agostino | In a little square just north of San Luigi the church of Sant'Agostino (by Giacomo da Pietrasanta, 1469–83), one of the first domed churches to be built in Rome, has a notable interior; on the third pillar on the left is a fresco by Raphael of the prophet Isaiah (1512), in the first chapel on the left Caravaggio's "Madonna dei Pellegrini" (1605).

Piazza della Cancelleria

*Palazzo della Cancelleria | Just beyond the Piazza di San Pantaleo, on the left of the Corso Vittorio Emanuele II, in the elongated Piazza della Cancelleria, is the Palazzo della Cancelleria, the Papal Chancery, one of the noblest Renaissance buildings in Rome (1486–1511), in a style suggesting Florentine influence; particularly notable is the fine arcaded courtyard.

*Palazzo Farnese | From the Piazza della Cancelleria a street runs south by way of the Campo dei Fiori to the Piazza Farnese, in which are two fountains with ancient basins. On the south-west side of the square we come to the Palazzo Farnese, one of the most typical of Rome's old palaces, now occupied by the French embassy. Built for Cardinal Alexander Farnese, later Pope Paul III, it was begun in 1514 by Antonio da Sangallo the Younger and continued from 1546 onwards by Michelangelo. On the vaulting of the principal room on the first floor are mythological paintings by Annibale Carracci and others (1597–1604).

Palazzo Spada | South-east of the Palazzo Farnese is the Palazzo Spada (c. 1540), the seat of the Italian Council of State. At the end of the second courtyard is a colonnade by Borromini which achieves an effect of depth by a skilful and typically Baroque use of perspective. On the first floor (entrance in

Galleria Spada | the inner courtyard), is the Galleria Spada, a picture gallery notable particularly for works of the 17th c. Bologna School (Guercino, Reni, etc.).

Chiesa Nuova

*Oratorio dei Filippini | Farther along the Corso Vittorio Emanuele II, on the right beyond the Palazzo della Cancelleria, stands the Chiesa Nuova or Santa Maria in Vallicella, built between 1575 and 1605 for the Oratorian order founded by St Philip Neri in 1575. To the left of the church is the Oratorio dei Filippini, with a curved façade, one of Borromini's finest buildings (1637–50); it is now used for concerts and lectures. The name of the order and the word "oratorio" are both derived from the spiritual exercises and musical performances instituted by St Philip Neri in oratories.

Ponte Vittorio Emanuele | The Corso Vittorio Emanuele II ends at the Tiber bridge, the Ponte Vittorio Emanuele (1911).

Sights in the south-west

To get from the Piazza Venezia to the Avertine, we go south, passing the National Monument, through Via del Teatro di Marcello. On the left there is a flight of steps which leads up to Santa Maria in Aracoeli and the Campidoglio.

Beyond this, on the right, is the Theatre of Marcellus (Teatro di Marcello), built by Augustus in 17–13 B.C. and named after his nephew Marcellus, who had died young in 23 B.C. The curved outer wall of the auditorium, which could seat an audience of 13,000–14,000, originally had three storeys, but the top storey was destroyed during the Middle Ages, when the theatre was converted into a fortress and residence for the Orsini family. In front of the theatre, to the right, stand three re-erected columns from a temple of Apollo.

Theatre of Marcellus

Farther along the street, on the right, is the church of San Nicola in Carcere, with fragments of three ancient temples.

San Nicola in Carcere

Piazza Bocca della Verità

Via del Teatro di Marcello joins the spacious Piazza Bocca della Verità, at the east end of the Ponte Palatino. On the north side of the square is the well-preserved so-called Temple of Fortuna Virilis or Tempio di Portuno, a tufa building in the Ionic style (1st c. B.C.).
To the south of this is another smaller circular temple which has been known since medieval times as the Temple of Vesta, with nineteen (formerly twenty) Corinthian columns.

* Temple of Fortuna Virilis

At the east end of the Piazza Bocca della Verità rises the so-called Ianus Quadrifons ("four-sided Janus") or Arco di Giano, a triumphal arch with four façades which probably dates from the time of Constantine. Here too is the ancient church of San Giorgio in Velabro, which contains sixteen ancient columns. Adjoining the church is the richly decorated Arco degli Argentari or Arch of the Money-Changers (A.D. 204).

* Ianus Quadrifons

San Giorgio in Velabro

On the south side of the Piazza Bocca della Verità we find the church of Santa Maria in Cosmedin, originally built at some time before the 6th c. on the foundations of a temple of Hercules and of a market hall (to which the marble columns on the entrance wall belonged), and rebuilt in the 11th–12th c. In the porch is the Bocca della Verità ("Mouth of Truth"), an antique marble disc with the mask of a Triton, into whose mouth according to medieval belief, the Romans used to insert their right hand when taking an oath. The church has a fine interior (aisled), with ancient columns and a 12th c. mosaic pavement.

Santa Maria in Cosmedin

On the north side of the Ponte Palatino, in the middle of the Tiber, is a pier belonging to the old Pons Aemilius, originally built in 181 B.C. but frequently damaged and finally abandoned after its destruction by flood-water in 1598; hence its Italian name of Ponte Rotto, the "Broken Bridge". On the south side of the Ponte Palatino, in a niche in the embankment wall, can be seen (provided the water level is not too high) the threefold arch at the mouth of the ancient Cloaca Maxima, the drain, which continued in use until the 20th c.

Pons Aemilius

Aventine

Immediately south of the Piazza Bocca della Verità is the Aventine (Monte Aventino, 46 m/152 ft), on which the plebeians lived in the earliest days of Rome. Later the hill was occupied by convents and vineyards, and it is only in quite recent times that it has been more intensively built up and has developed into a pleasant residential area.

*Santa Sabina | On the west side of the Aventine, in Via di Santa Sabina, which runs parallel with the Tiber above the Lungotevere Ayentino on the embankment, is the church of Santa Sabina, originally built between 423 and 435 and subsequently much altered. This was the place of origin of the Dominican order (1215), and since its restoration in 1914–19 and 1936–38 it presents an excellent example of an Early Christian basilica. The cypress-wood door of the principal entrance is decorated with fine 5th c. reliefs, including (above, left) one of the earliest known representations of the Crucifixion. The fine interior has 24 ancient marble columns. In the nave is the schola cantorum (choir), rebuilt during the last restoration. The cloister dates from the 13th century.

Sant'Alassio | South-west of Santa Sabina the church of Sant'Alassio, which is referred to in the 7th c. with a dedication to St Boniface, was completely rebuilt in the 13th and 18th centuries.

Priorato di Malta | Farther south-west, in a little square, is the entrance to the Villa del Priorato di Malta, residence of the Grand Master of the order of the Knights of Malta, founded in 1070. The round aperture above the keyhole of the park gate affords a famous view of the dome of St Peter's, glimpsed at the end of the main avenue. There is also a beautiful view from the gardens (admission only by special arrangement). In the church of Santa Maria Aventina, reached from the gardens, are the tombs of knights of the order.

Sant'Anselmo | Immediately south of the priory is the International Benedictine Seminary, with the church of Sant'Anselmo (consecrated 1900).

Porta San Paolo

Pyramid of Cestius | From here Via di Porta Lavernale and its continuation lead south into the broad Via della Marmorata, at the south end of which, in the Aurelian Walls, is the Porta San Paolo, the ancient Porta Ostiensis. To the right of the gate rises the Pyramid of Cestius, 37 m/122 ft high, a brick structure faced with marble blocks, built about 12 B.C. as the tomb of Gaius Cestius, a member of the priestly college of the Epulones.

Protestant Cemetery | Immediately south-west, beyond the pyramid but still inside the Aurelian Walls, lies the Protestant Cemetery, or more precisely the Cimiterio degli Stranieri Acattolici (entrance on the north side), the cemetery for British, Germans, Scandinavians, Americans and orthodox Russians, in which Keats is buried.

Monte Testaccio | To the west of the cemetery is Monte Testaccio, an isolated mound rising to a height of 35 m/116 ft above the Tiber and about 850 m/930 yd in circumference, composed entirely of fragments of the large earthenware jars in which wine and olives were shipped to Rome and discharged at a nearby quay on the banks of the Tiber. The hill is honey-combed with cellars, some of them connected with taverns.

San Saba | Some 500 m/550 yd north-east of the Porta San Paolo is the church of San Saba (12th–15th c.).

*San Paolo fuori le Mura

2 km/1¼ miles south of the Porta San Paolo, on the Via Ostiense, the road to Ostia and Lido di Ostia, stands the church of San Paolo fuori le Mura, one of Rome's five patriarchal churches, founded by Constantine

San Paolo fuori le Mura

the Great in 324 over the tomb of the Apostle Paul, rebuilt in 386 as an aisled basilica, destroyed by fire in 1823 with the exception of the choir and thereafter rebuilt on the original plan (1854), with the support of many Christian nations. The bronze door of the main entrance is by A. Maraini (1930–31).

The interior is imposing (120 m/132 yd long, 60 m/66 yd wide, 23 m/76 ft high). There are double aisles on each side, separated by 80 granite columns. The church has a rich coffered stucco ceiling, partly gilded, with sumptuous marble decoration. Above the columns are portraits of all the popes from Peter to Paul VI. There is beautiful mosaic (440–61, restored) on the triumphal arch and in the apse. The destroyed 13th c. mosaic from the apse was replaced in the 19th c. by a copy. Above the high altar is a Gothic tabernacle (1285) and to the right a fine paschal candlestick (c. 1180). In the south aisle, near the entrance, is a bronze door ("sacred door") of 1070, damaged in the fire but later restored.

Interior

On the south side of the church is a cloister, built between 1204 and 1241 by members of the Vassaletti family, famous mosaic artists. It belonged to a Benedictine monastery and with the varying forms of its columns and the colourful pattern of the stones, it ranks as one of the most beautiful cloisters in Rome.

*Cloister

Trastevere, Janiculum and Castel Sant'Angelo

To the rear of the Theatre of Marcellus is the Ponte Fabricio, the oldest of Rome's present-day bridges, built in 62 B.C., by which one reaches Tiber Island (Isola Tiberina), with the church of San Bartolomeo, perhaps occupying the site of a temple of Aesculapius.

Isola Tiberina

District of Trastevere

From Tiber Island the Ponte Cestio leads into the densely populated district of Trastevere, on the right bank of the Tiber. In the time of Augustus it was a suburb of Rome (Regio Transtiberina), with numerous villas; later, when the Aurelian Walls were built, it was incorporated in the city proper. Later still it became the haunt of freed slaves and prostitutes. In the 19th and 20th c. it was a working-class district with a vigorous and down-to-earth character of its own; then from about 1970 a programme of slum clearance and redevelopment was begun, unfit houses being pulled down and replaced. It is now noted for its many little restaurants, but visitors should be on their guard against pick-pockets and beggars, particularly after dark.

Santa Cecilia in Trastevere

Some 300 m/330 yd south of the Ponte Cestio is the church of Santa Cecilia in Trastevere, which is supposed to occupy the site of a house in which the patron saint of music (martyred c. 230) lived. The church, founded before 500 but much rebuilt and restored in later centuries, is preceded by a spacious court and has a 12th c. campanile. On the high altar is a beautiful tabernacle of 1283; the apse has 9th c. mosaics. In the crypt can be seen the saint's sepulchral chapel, well restored.

Porta Portese

Some 500 m/550 yd from the church of Santa Cecilia, near the Ponte Sublicio, is the Porta Portese, where a flea-market is held on Sunday mornings.

Santa Maria in Trastevere

500 m/550 yd north-west of Santa Cecilia stands the church of Santa Maria in Trastevere, one of the oldest churches in Rome, founded in the 3rd c. and rebuilt in the 12th c., with a porch added in 1702. It has a picturesque interior, with 22 ancient columns, a richly decorated ceiling (1617) and fine 12th and 13th c. mosaics.

Folk Museum

Close by the church, in Piazza Sant' Egidio, is a Folk Museum (Museo de Folclore e dei Poeti Romaneschi).

*Villa Farnesina

500 m/550 yd north of Santa Maria in Trastevere, on the banks of the Tiber beyond the Porta Settimiana, we come to the Villa Farnesina, a Renaissance palace surrounded by gardens which was built by B. Peruzzi in 1509–11 for the Pope's banker Agostino Chigi and decorated with frescoes by Raphael and other artists – scenes from the story of Amor and Psyche (1515–18) designed by Raphael and executed by his pupils, and Galates borne over the sea in a shell, by Raphael himself (1514). From 1580 to 1731 the villa belonged to the Farnese family; it is now State-owned, and also houses the Gabinetto Nazionale delle Stampe (prints and engravings; admission only by special arrangement).

Palazzo Corsini

Immediately west, opposite the villa is the Palazzo Corsini, occupied from 1668 to 1689 by Queen Christina of Sweden (daughter of Gustavus Adolphus, who became a Catholic) and rebuilt in 1729–32 for Cardinal Neri Corsini, with pillared courtyards and a beautiful view of the gardens. It now houses the Accademia Nazionale dei Lincèi, which has a large library. The 17th and 18th c. pictures, belonging to the Galleria Nazionale d'Arte Antica and formerly housed here, are now in the Palazzo Barberini.

Janiculum

San Pietro in Montorio

From the south side of the Porta Settimiana the Via Garibaldi runs south-west and then winds its way up the long ridge of the Janiculum

(Monte Gianicolo), with extensive views. At the foot of the ascent is the church of San Pietro in Montorio, a Renaissance church (15th c.) founded on the spot on which, according to a medieval legend, the Apostle Peter was crucified; it has a fine interior. In the adjoining cloister is the Tempietto, a small round pillared temple by Bramante (1502). From the square in front of the church a magnificent view can be enjoyed.

Via Garibaldi then continues uphill to the Fontana Paolo, an elaborate fountain built for Pope Paul V in 1612 by Giovanni Fontana and Carlo Maderna as the terminal point of the restored Aqua Traiana (aqueduct), and ends at the Porta San Pancrazio, on the summit of the Janiculum (84 m/277 ft).

Fontana Paolo

To the west is the entrance to the Villa Doria Pamphili, a large park laid out by Algardi after 1644 for Prince Camillo Pamphili; it is now municipal property and open to the public.

Villa Doria Pamphili

Some 500 m/550 yd south of the Porta San Pancrazio is the Villa Sciarra, a public park with a luxuriant growth of southern vegetation and a lookout pavilion.

Villa Sciarra

*Passeggiata del Gianicolo

To the north of the Fontana Paolo is a gate which marks the south entrance to the Passeggiata del Gianicolo, a broad avenue which runs along the ridge of the Janiculum through an attractive park. In the Piazzale Garibaldi is an equestrian statue (by Gallori, 1895) of Giuseppe Garibaldi (1807–82). Beyond this, on the left, is a monument (1912) to his first wife Anita Garibaldi. Nearby is a cannon, usually fired at noon. Farther on, to the right, stands a marble beacon (Italian "faro"; erected 1911) which at night flashes its green, white and red lights over Rome. The views of Rome and the Campagna from the Passeggiata del Gianicolo, which are particularly fine towards sunset, have an extraordinary variety and beauty.

At the northern end of the Janiculum is the church of Sant' Onofrio (begun 1439), with 15th–16th c. frescoes; view. In the adjoining convent is the small Museo Tassiano, with relics and mementoes of the poet Torquato Tasso (1544–95) who died here.

Sant' Onofrio

At the end of the Corso Vittorio Emanuele II the Ponte Vittorio Emanuele crosses to the right bank of the Tiber a little way downstream from the Castel Sant'Angelo. Just above it the imposing Ponte Sant'Angelo makes straight for the Castel Sant'Angelo. This bridge, for long the only road access to the Vatican, was originally built in A.D. 136 by the Emperor Hadrian and called the Pons Aelius after his family name. The ten colossal figures of angels which now adorn it were designed by Bernini, executed by various sculptors and set up on the bridge in 1668.

Ponte Sant'Angelo

*Castel Sant'Angelo

At the end of the Ponte Sant'Angelo, rising above the right bank of the Tiber, is the Castel Sant'Angelo or Mausoleo di Adriano, built by Hadrian in A.D. 130 as a mausoleum for himself and his successors and completed by Antoninus Pius in 139. The rotunda, built on a square substructure, originally faced with marble contains the tomb chambers

Castel Sant'Angelo, the mausoleum of Emperor Hadrian

(open to the public) in which the Roman emperors down to Caracalla (d. A.D. 217) were buried. From the 6th c. onwards it was used by the rulers of Rome as a fortress, and in 1379 passed into the hands of the popes. During the Middle Ages it was transformed into a defensive bridgehead, with outer works and a covered passage leading to the Vatican.

Museum   Between 1870 and 1901 the building was used as a barracks and a prison; thereafter it was restored and fitted out as a museum, with a collection of weapons, models illustrating the history of the structure, several chapels, the treasury and the library. From the upper terrace there is a magnificent view. On the highest point is a bronze statue of the Archangel Michael (1752), recalling a vision of Pope Gregory the Great (590) to which the Castel Sant'Angelo owes its name.

To the east of the Castel Sant'Angelo is the massive Palazzo di Giustizia (Law Courts; by Calderini, 1910). Via della Conciliazione (Street of Reconciliation) leads from the Castel Sant'Angelo to the Vatican.

CITTÀ DEL VATICANO (VATICAN CITY)

Stato della Città del Vaticano   Vatican City (Stato della Città del Vaticano; SCV; Santa Sede = Holy Throne) lies on the right bank of the Tiber. It was established as a substitute for the Papal States or States of the Church which had been abolished in 1870. Under the Lateran treaties of February 11th 1929 the Italian government under Mussolini recognised the sovereignty of the Pope in international relations and his jurisdiction over the territory of the Vatican City, comprising St Peter's Church, St Peter's Square, the Vatican and the Vatican gardens, with a total area of 0.44 sq. km/0.17 sq. mile, and populated by about 400 inhabitants.

The Pope ("Holy Father"), at present the Pole Karol Woityla, John Paul II, elected 1978, supreme head of the Roman Catholic Church (over 700 million adherents), has legislative, executive and judicial powers. In external affairs he is represented by the Cardinal Secretary of State, while the administration (Curia) is headed by a Governor responsible only to the Pope.

Governatorato

The Pope's bodyguard consists of the Swiss Guards who are Roman Catholic citizens of Switzerland aged between 19 and 25, unmarried (minimum height 1.78 m; period of service 2–20 years), with a present strength of 100 (4 officers, 23 non-commissioned officers, 70 halberdiers, 2 drummers and 1 chaplain).

Swiss Guards

The Vatican City has its own currency (1 Vatican lira = 1 Italian lira), postal service (issuing stamps which are valid throughout Rome), telephone and telegraph services, newspapers and journals (in particular the "Osservatore Romano"), with a circulation of 60,000–70,000), radio station (Radio Vaticana; transmissions on medium and short waves in some 35 languages), a fleet of about 100 vehicles (registration letters SCV) and its own railway station and helicopter pad.

The Vatican flag has vertical stripes of yellow and white, with two crossed keys under the Papal tiara (triple crown) on a white ground.

Vatican flag

Papal possessions outside the Vatican City include the three basilicas of San Giovanni in Laterano, San Paolo fuori le Mura and Santa Maria Maggiore, the Papal administrative offices and the Pope's summer residence at Castel Gandolfo. These places enjoy extra-territorial status and are not subject to Italian law.

The territory of Vatican City, with the exception of certain permitted areas (St Peter's, the museums, the Camposanto Teutonico, etc.) can be entered only with special permission.

**Piazza di San Pietro

Vatican City can be reached by way of the Ponte Vittorio Emanuele and the Via della Conciliazione which runs west to end in St Peter's Square (Piazza di San Pietro), a magnificent creation by Bernini (1656–67), 340 m/375 yd long, up to 240 m/265 yd wide, which enhance the effect of the most imposing church in Christendom. On either side of the oval are semicircular colonnades, formed by 284 columns and 88 pillars of the Doric order in four rows, surmounted by balustrades with 140 colossal statues of saints. In the centre of the square is an Egyptian obelisk 25.5 m/84 ft high, hewn in the reign of Caligula (A.D. 37–41) and set up here in 1586; it has stood until 1586 in a circus. On either side of the obelisk are two fine fountains 14 m/46 ft high (1613, 1675).

Obelisk

On the west side of the central oval is a forecourt, with a broad staircase. On the south side of this forecourt are the Vatican Information Office (Ufficio Informazioni Pellegrini e Turisti; bus tours of Vatican museums) and a post office (Ufficio Postale; sale of Vatican City stamps).

Forecourt

To the rear, farther south, is the large Audience Hall (Aula Paolo VI; entrance beside Palazzo del Sant'Uffizio) built by P. L. Nervi (1964–71), with seating for 6300 or standing room for up to 12,000.

Audience Hall

To the left of St Peter's Church is the Arco delle Campagne, the main entrance to the Vatican City (Swiss Guards).

Arco delle Campagne

Vatican City
Città del Vaticano

1 Information bureau
2 Head post office (telegrams)
3 Post offices
4 Arco delle Campane (entrance)
5 Portone di Bronzo (tickets for Papal audiences; Scala Regis)
6 Ufficio Scavi (tickets for tomb of St Peter and cemetery)
7 Museum of History (Treasury)
8 Logge (Loggias)
9 Stanze
10 Self-service restaurant
11 Library
12 Historical Museum (underground)
13 Camposanto Teutonico
14 Radio Vaticana (offices)
15 Palazzo di Giustizia
16 School of Mosaic Art
17 Papal Printing Ofice
18 "Osservatore Romano"

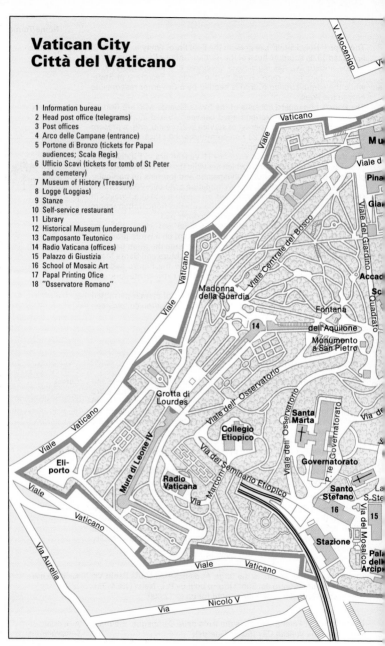

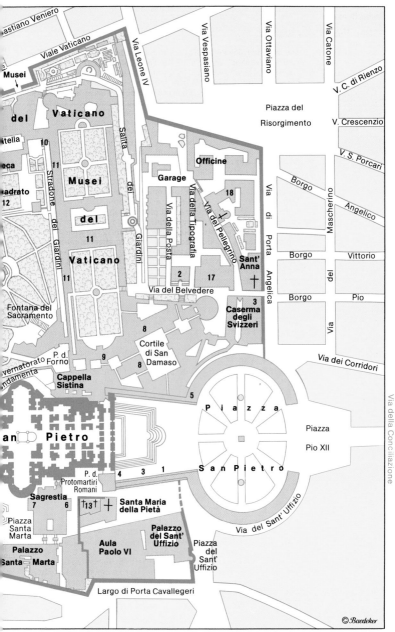

**San Pietro in Vaticano

The west side of St Peter's Square is occupied by St Peter's Church (San Pietro in Vaticano), on the site of an Early Christian basilica.

The original church was built by Constantine the Great at the request of Pope Sylvester I (314–336) over the tomb of the Apostle Peter and consecrated in 326. It was a basilica with double aisles and a pillared forecourt, later enlarged and surrounded by chapels and convents. At Christmas in the year 800 Charlemagne received the Roman imperial crown from the hands of Pope Leo III in front of the high altar, and many emperors were subsequently crowned here. In the course of time the church fell into a state of dilapidation and was replaced by the present building, begun by Bramante in 1506 in the reign of Pope Julius II. The new church was conceived by Bramante in the form of a Greek cross (i.e. with arms of equal length) with a central dome.

Dome
Façade

After his death in 1514 the work was directed by Raphael (1515–20), Antonio da Sangallo (1520–46) and other masters, and finally (1547) by Michelangelo, who designed the mighty dome, 132 m/436 ft high (1586–93). In 1605 the centralised plan favoured by Bramante and Michelangelo was replaced by a Latin-cross plan with a nave. The nave and the Baroque façade (completed 1614; 112 m/123 yd wide, 44 m/145 ft high) were the work of Carlo Maderna. The effect of the dome as conceived by Michelangelo is thus entirely lost except from a distance. From the loggia above the central doorway the Pope gives his benediction "urbi et orbi" (to the city and the world) on solemn occasions (Easter, Christmas); in addition he usually gives a benediction on Sundays at 12 noon from a window in the Papal residence (on the right).

Portico
Central doorway

The portico of St Peter's is 71 m/78 yd long, 13.5 m/14¾ yd deep and 20 m/66 ft high. The bronze doors of the large central doorway were the work of the Florentine sculptor Antonio Filarete (1433–45). The door on the left (Door of Death; 1964) has bronze reliefs by Giacomo Manzù (life of John XXIII, etc.). The door on the right (the Seven Sacraments) is by Messina (1965).

Porta Santa

To the right of this is the Porta Santa, which is opened in Holy Years (every 25 years; plenary indulgence for all pilgrims to Rome).

**Interior

The interior (appropriate dress required) is of overwhelming effect, with its huge dimensions (186 m/204 yd long, with space for a congregation of 60,000). The effect is increased as the visitor realises the beauty of the individual features and the symmetrie and harmony of the proportions. In the pavement, beginning at the central doorway, are marked the lengths of other great cathedrals: St Paul's London, 158.1 m/173 yd, Florence 149.28 m/163¼ yd, Rheims 138.69 m/151¾ yd, Milan and Cologne 134.94 m/147½ yd (Milan is actually 148 m/162 yd wide), San Petronio, Bologna, 132.54 m/145 yd, Seville and Notre Dame, Paris, 130 m/142¼ yd. The total length of St Peter's including the portico, is 211.5 m/231½ yd, its width 114.7 m/125½ yd (across the transepts 152 m/166 yd), its area 16,160 sq. m (Milan 11,700, St Paul's 7875, St Sophia in Istanbul 6890, Berlin Cathedral 6270, Cologne 6166 sq. m).

Nave

In the nave, in which the second Vatican Council met in 1962–65, is a seated figure of St Peter in bronze (4th pillar on right), probably dating from the 13th c., whose right foot has been worn smooth by the kisses of the faithful. The huge dome which soars above the Papal altar and the crypt containing the tomb of St Peter has a diameter of 42 m/46 yd and an internal height of 123.4 m/407¼ ft (external height including cross 132.5 m/437¼ ft). It is borne on four huge piers, each with a circumference of 71 m/78 yd.

St Peter's and St Peter's Square and Obelisk ▶

Swiss Vatican Guard in Historic uniform   *Pietà by Michelangelo in St Peter's*

Papal altar	Above the Papal altar is a bronze canopy or baldacchino, 29 m/96 ft high, with four richly gilded spiral columns and a fantastic superstructure (by Bernini, 1633). In front of the altar, enclosed by a balustrade with 95 sanctuary lamps which are always lit, is the confessio, a devotional area over St Peter's tomb, to which a double marble staircase leads down.
*Pietà	In the first chapel in the south aisle, protected by a glass screen, is Michelangelo's Pietà, a profoundly sensitive work created by the young Michelangelo at the age of 25 (1499, damaged by a vandal in 1972, skilfully restored 1973).
Papal tombs	Throughout the church are numerous Papal tombs, some of them of great magnificence; particularly impressive are those of Urban VIII and Paul III (both in the apse) and Innocent VIII (2nd pillar on left).
*Museo Storico-Artistico	From the north aisle we enter the Sacristy (1776–84) and the interesting Museo Storico-Artistico or Tesoro di San Pietro (Treasury of St Peter), with a cross which belonged to the Emperor Justin II (d. 578), sarcophagi of the consul Iunius Bassus (d. 359) and Pope Sixtus IV (d. 1484).
*Dome	Also in the north aisle (ticket office beyond the first chapel) is the entrance to the dome (steps or lift to roof), then easy steps to the galleries round the dome (at heights of 53 m/175 ft and 73 m/241 ft), from which there are astonishing views of the interior of the church. On the inner wall of the dome is a frieze 2 m/6½ ft high with the inscription, in blue mosaic letters on a gold ground, "Tu es Petrus et super hanc petram aedificabo ecclesiam meam et tibi dabo claves regni caelorum" ("Thou art Peter, and upon this rock I will build my church . . . And I will give into thee the keys of the kingdom of heaven": Matt. 16, 18–19). From the colonnade on the lantern of the dome (123.5 m/407½ ft above

→N

Sacre
Grotte
Vaticane

Papal altar

Transepts   Transepts

Nave

© Baedeker

St Peter's Church
San Pietro in Vaticano

|— 50 m —|

Vestibule

St Peter's Square

1 Main entrance
2 Porta Santa
3 Michelangelo's "Pietà"
4 Monument to Christina of Sweden
5 St Sebastian's Chapel
6 Monument to Margravine Mathilda of Tuscany
7 Chapel of the Sacrament
8 Gregorian Chapel
9 Altar of St Jerome
10 Statue of St Peter
11 Entrance to Vatican Sacred Grotto
12 Entrance to Dome
13 Altar to Archangel Michael
14 Altar of St Peter (restoring Tabitha to life)

15 Tomb of Pope Urban VIII
16 Cathedral Petri (by Bernini)
17 Tomb of Pope Paul III
18 Chapel of the Column
19 Altar of St Peter (healing the lame man)
20 Tomb of Pope Alexander VII
21 Altar of the Crucifixion of St Peter
22 Statue of St Andrew
23 Tomb of Pope Pius VIII
24 Clementine Chapel

25 Altar of St Gregory
26 Monument to Pope Pius VII
27 Choir Chapel
28 Tomb of Pope Innocent VIII
29 Monument to Pope Pius VII
30 Chapel of the Presentation
31 Monument to Maria Sobieska
32 Baptistery
33 Sacristy
34 Museo Storico Artistico (Treasury)
35 Canons' Sacristy

floor level) there are far-ranging views and a glimpse of the Vatican Gardens.

From the space under the dome a staircase leads down to the in-   Sacre Grotte
teresting Sacre Grotte Vaticane, lying between the floor of the present   Vaticane
church and that of the original basilica, 3.5 m/11 ft below. The 16th c.
chambers beneath the dome contain numerous monuments from the
old basilica, together with the plain stone sarcophagi of Pius XII (d.
1958), John XXIII (d. 1963), Paul VI (d. 1978) and John Paul (d. 1978). In
the older parts, under the nave, are numerous Papal tombs and Early
Christian sarcophagi.

Excavations | With a special permit it is possible to see the excavations (scavi) beneath St Peter's. Archaeologists have excavated the old cemetery on the Vatican hill, including what is supposed to be the tomb of St Peter and foundations of the old basilica of Constantine.

*Vatican Palace

To the right of St Peter's, occupying an area of some 55,000 sq. m/65,700 sq. yd stands the Vatican Palace (Palazzi Vaticani), originally built in the 6th c. but the Pope's permanent residence only since the 14th c., when it replaced the Lateran, and much enlarged and altered since then. The rooms in which the Pope lives and works are on the upper floors of the square building on the right-hand side of St Peter's Square. Among the principal features of the palace are the Stanze, the Sistine Chapel, the Logge di Raffaello, the former Garden-House or Belvedere, the Vatican Library and the Vatican collections, with major works of ancient art and valuable pictures. Altogether there are some 1400 rooms, chapels and other apartments.

Portone di Bronzo | The Portone di Bronzo (Swiss guard; access only to office which issues tickets for Papal audiences), at the end of the right-hand colonnade in St Peter's Square, is the entrance to the Papal apartments, which form only a small part of the whole palace.

Scala Regia | The corridor straight ahead leads to the Scala Regia, remodelled by Bernini in 1663–66. In spite of the limited space, which contracts towards the top, an imposing effect was achieved by the skilful arrangement of the columns and decoration.

To the right is the Scala di Pio IX (19th c.), leading to the Cortile di San Damaso.

Entrance to the State apartments | The entrance to the State apartments – i.e. to the museums, the Library, the Borgia apartments, the Stanze, the Sistine Chapel, etc. – is on the north side of the palace, 800 m/880 yd from St Peter's Square. There are regular bus services from spring until autumn to and from the Information Office, going through the Vatican Gardens; departure from upper entrance to museums. Pedestrians should go north along Via di Porta Angelica to the Piazza del Risorgimento, then west along the Vatican walls and round the bastion on Via Leone IV into Viale Vaticano.

Vatican Museums

From the entrance to the Vatican Museums (Musei Vaticani), with statues of Raphael and Michelangelo, visitors make their way up on a curving staircase or by lift to the vestibule (ticket-offices, information, sales counters, cloakroom, lavatories, etc.). The tour is for the most part a one-way route marked by coloured arrows, with video-electronic surveillance (total length 7 km/4 miles). Half-way round there is an exit at the Sistine Chapel (no admission).

**Collection of antiquities | From the vestibule we go east (left) through the Atrio dei Quattro Cancelli and up the Scala Simonetti to reach the Vatican collection of antiquities, the largest in the world, with several thousand pieces of sculpture. The origins of the collection go back to the Renaissance period (16th c.). The collection as we see it today, however, really began in the time of Clement XIV (1769–74). The main part of the collection, the Museo Pio-Clementino, is named after him and his successor Pius VI. Pius VII added the Museo Chiaramonti and the Braccio Nuovo, Gregory XVI (1831–46) the Egyptian and Etruscan museums. Most of

Vatican Museums
Musei Vaticani

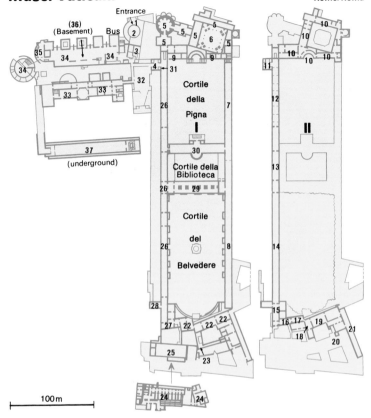

100 m

1 Lift
2 Stairs
3 Vestibule (tickets, information)
4 Atrio dei Quattro Cancelli
5 Museo Pio-Clementino
6 Cortile Ottagono
7 Museo Chiaramonti
8 Galleria Lapidaria
9 Museo Gregoriano Egizio (Egyptian Museum)
10 Museo Gregoriano Etrusco (Etruscan Museum)
11 Sala della Biga
12 Galleria dei Candelabri
13 Galleria degli Arazzi (Tapestry Gallery)

14 Galleria delle Carte Geografiche (Map Gallery)
15 Pius V's Chapel
16 Sala Sobieski
17 Sala dell'Immacolata
18 Urban VIII's Chapel
19 Stanze di Raffaello
20 Nicholas V's Chapel (Beato Angelico)
21 Logge di Raffaello (Loggias of Raphael)
22 Appartamento Borgia
23 Salette Borgia
24 Collezione d'Arte Religiosa Moderna (Museum of Modern Religious Art)

25 Sistine Chapel
26 Vatican Library
27 Museo Sacro della Biblioteca
28 Sala delle Nozze Aldobrandine
29 Salone Sistino
30 Braccio Nuovo
31 Museo Profano della Biblioteca
32 Cortile della Pinacoteca
33 Pinacoteca (Picture Gallery)
34 Museo Gregoriano Profano (Museum of Secular Art)
35 Museo Pio Cristiano
36 Museo Missionario Etnologico
37 Museo Storico (Historical Museum)

the items were found in and around Rome, and the enormous quantity of sculpture to be seen here and in the other museums in Rome gives some idea of the extraordinary wealth of art in the public buildings and private houses of ancient Rome and bears witness of the Roman interest in the culture of Greece. There are very few Greek originals, but

413

Jacob and Joseph Lunette in the Sistine Chapel

numerous copies of famous works of art, made by either Greek or Roman sculptors, as well as specially Roman works of art, have survived into modern times, often little the worse for their burial under the accumulated rubbish of the centuries. Although the restorations and retouching practised in the past may sometimes give an erroneous impression, here as nowhere else we can get a general impression of the whole range of ancient creative art.

Museo Pio-Clementino

We come first to the Museo Pio-Clementino. Particularly notable are:
In the Sala a Croce Greca the porphyry sarcophagi of St Helena and Constantia, mother and daughter of Constantine the Great (4th c. A.D.).
In the Sala Rotonda the bust of Zeus from Otricoli (4th c. B.C.).
In the Sala delle Muse the famous Belvedere Torso, a seated figure of a powerful muscled man (by Apollonius of Athens, 1st c. B.C.) and a series of portrait herms and statues of muses.
In the Sala degli Animali many figures of animals in white and coloured marble.
In the Galleria delle Statue the Apollo Sauroctonus (the Lizard-Killer), a copy of the 4th c. B.C. work.
In the Sala dei Busti busts.
In the Gabinetto delle Maschere (cabinet of masks) the famous Venus of Cnidos, an imitation of the Cnidian Aphrodite of Praxiteles.
In the courtyard of the Belvedere the famous group of Laocoön and his two sons being killed by two snakes, a masterpiece (1st c. B.C.–1st c. A.D.) by Agesandrus, Polydorus and Athenodorus of Rhodos (restored 1957–60).
In the Gabinetto dell'Apoxyomenos the Apoxyomenus, a youth scraping the oil and dust of the palaestra from his arms with a strigil, a Roman copy of the original by Lysippus (4th c. B.C.).

Michelangelo: "Creation of Adam"　　　*Laocoön group in Belvedere courtyard*

Beyond this is the Museo Chiaramonti, a corridor some 100 m/110 yd long, mostly containing Roman copies of ancient sculpture. In the adjoining Galleria Lapidaria (shut off by a grating: admission by special arrangement) are some 5000 inscriptions.

Museo Chiaramonti

Adjoining the south side of the Museo Pio-Clementino the Egyptian Museum (Museo Gregoriano Egizio) consists of ten rooms containing Egyptian sculpture, mostly found in and around Rome, including mummies, papyri, etc.

Egyptian Museum

On the floor above (reached by way of the "Staircase of the Assyrian Reliefs" from the Sala a Croce Greca) we come to the Etruscan Museum (Museo Gregoriano Etrusco), the rooms of which contain Etruscan antiquities recovered by excavation or received by gift, including sarcophagi, small items and a collection of Greek vases.

Etruscan Museum

In the west wing of the upper floor (to the right of the Assyrian Staircase) the Sala della Biga, a circular domed hall with a view of the Vatican Gardens, contains the two-horse chariot from which the room takes its name (only the body of the chariot and part of the right-hand horse are ancient) and two Discus-Throwers, one of them after an original by Myron (5th c. B.C.; head modern).

Sala della Biga

In the corridor to the south are the Galleria dei Candelabri, the Galleria degli Arazzi (tapestries of the 16th–18th c.) and the Galleria delle Carte Geografiche, with maps and views of towns painted on the walls (1580–83).
At the end of the corridor is the Chapel of Pius V (tapestries, fine decorations).

Galleria delle Carte Geografiche

In the south wing of the upper floor, above the Appartamento Borgia, are the Stanze di Raffaello, a suite of three rooms and a larger hall, the

*Stanze di Raffaello

415

private apartments of Pope Julius II, with paintings by the 25-year-old Raphael, his teacher Perugino and his pupils (1509–20). The finest paintings are: in the Stanza dell'Incendio di Borgo, the "Fire in the Borgo" (showing the façade of the original St Peter's Church); in the Stanza della Segnatura, the most famous of the rooms, named after the Papal court (the Segnatura di Grazia) which met here weekly, the "Disputa" (the glorification of the Christian faith) and "The School of Athens" (an assembly of scholars, with Plato and Aristotle in the middle); in the Stanza d'Eliodoro "Heliodorus driven out of the Temple in Jerusalem by a Heavenly Horseman" and "The Mass of Bolsena"; and in the Sala di Constantino frescoes by Giulio Romano and others, some of them based on sketches by Raphael.

Chapel of Nicholas V	From the Sala di Constantino we go diagonally across the Sala dei Palafrenieri which adjoins it on the south into the Chapel of Nicholas V, with frescoes by Fra Angelico (scenes from the lives of SS Lawrence and Stephen, 1447–50).
*Loggias	Returning across the Sala dei Palafrenieri, we enter the Loggias around the Cortile di San Damaso, the west wing of which has stucco decoration and ceiling paintings of Biblical scenes ("Raphael's Bible") by pupils of Raphael, including Giovanni da Udine (1517–19).
*Appartamento Borgia	From the Loggia we go down the staircase in the Borgia Tower to the Appartamento Borgia at the south end of the ground floor: six rooms occupied by Pope Alexander VI Borgia with brilliantly coloured wall paintings executed under the direction of Pinturicchio (1492–95). Particularly fine is the fourth room, the Sala della Via dei Santi.
Museum of Modern Religious Art	The rooms house part of the Museum of Modern Religious Art (Collezione d'Arte Religiosa Moderna, established 1973), most of which is accommodated in 55 rooms under the Sistine Chapel, including works by Barlach, Rodin, Klee, Dix, Picasso, Chagall, Dali, Moore, de Pisis, etc.
**Sistine Chapel	We now come to the Sistine Chapel (Cappella Sistina), the Papal domestic chapel, built in 1474–81 in the reign of Sixtus IV, and which is the meeting-place of the Conclave which elects a new Pope. The chapel (40.5 × 13.2 m/44¼ × 45¼ yd and over 20 m/66 ft high) owes its fame to the magnificent frescoes which cover its walls and ceiling. The paintings on the upper part of the side walls (Old Testament scenes on one side, New Testament scenes on the other) were the work of the best Florentine and Umbrian painters of the day – Perugino, Pinturicchio, Botticelli, Ghirlandaio, Roselli, Signorelli (1481–84), restored 1965–74.
*Ceiling paintings	The ceiling paintings by Michelangelo (1508–12), ranking among the most powerful master-works of world art, depict the story of the Creation, the Fall and its consequences, with the superhuman figures of seven prophets and five sibyls at the foot of the vaulting. Almost 30 years later (1534–41) Michelangelo painted the huge fresco of the last Judgment on the altar wall, with more than a hundred figures dipicted with lively vigour. (Restoration will last until 1992). There is an exit here to St Peter's (no readmission).
*Vatican Library	From the Sistine Chapel we continue north into the Vatican Library (Biblioteca Apostolica Vaticana), founded by Pope Nicholas V about 1450, which now contains some 800,000 books, 80,000 manuscripts, 10,000 incunabula and over 100,000 engravings and woodcuts.
Museo Sacro	At the south end of the library is the Museo Sacro, with material excavated in the catacombs, reliquaries, carved ivories, glass, enamelwork and textiles.
Sala delle Nozze Aldobrandine	In the Sala delle Nozze Aldobrandini are ancient paintings, including scenes from the "Odyssey" and the Aldobrandini Marriage, one of the

finest surviving ancient wall paintings, probably an Augustan copy of a Greek original of the 4th c. B.C.

From the Museo Sacro we continue through the Library's exhibition rooms (frescoes, decorative art).

We know come to the south cross-wing in which is the Salone Sistino, originally the main hall, with items of particular importance in glass cases.

*Salone Sistino

To the right is the north cross-wing, the Braccio Nuovo ("new arm"), a hall 70 m/77 yd long containing numerous statues. Notable among them are a statue of Augustus found at Prima Porta; a colossal group representing the Nile surrounded by 16 playing children (symbolising the 16 cubits which the river rises when in flood); and a Doryphorus (spear-bearer) after Polycletus.

Braccio Nuovo

From here we continue through a series of frescoed rooms belonging to the Library to the Museo Profano (ancient small sculpture, etc.), which we leave at the Atrio dei Quattro Cancelli.

Museo Profano della Biblioteca

Associated with the Library are the famous Secret Archives of the Vatican, with a school of palaeography and diplomatice.

Secret Archives of the Vatican

From the Cortile della Pinacoteca we reach the Picture Gallery (Pinacoteca Vaticana), in a building erected in 1927–32, with 15 rooms which give an excellent survey of Italian painting from the 13th to the 17th c.
Room I: Byzantine and early Italian paintings.
Room II: Giotto and his school.
Room II: Fra Filippo Lippi, Fra Angelico, Benozzo Gozzoli.
Room IV: frescoes by Melozzo da Forli (heads of Apostles), etc.
Roome V and VI: Lucas Cranach the Elder ("Pietà", Crivelli, Giotto.
Room VII: Perugino and Umbrian painters of the 15th c.
Room VIII: dedicated to Raphael: "Madonna of Foligno" (1512; in the background the town of Foligno), "Transfiguration" (1517–20, his last great work; restored 1972–76) and tapestries (arazzi) of scenes from the lives of the Apostles (woven in Brussels 1516–19 from cartoons by Raphael).
Room IX: pictures by various 16th c. masters including Leonardo da Vinci.
Room X: Titian ("Madonna in Glory"), Caravaggio, Guido Freni, Fra Bartolomeo and Veronese.
Room XI: Renaissance and Baroque masters.
Room XII: 17th c. (Baroque).
Rooms XIII and XIV: 17th and 18th c. pictures.
Room XV: portraits of popes.
Rooms XVI–XVIII: contemporary painting.

**Pinacoteca Vaticana

A new building (1970) parallel to the Pinacoteca on the north houses the former Lateran museum.

The Museo Gregoriano Profano contains Greek and Roman sculpture, either in the original or in copies, and ancient sarcophagi. In the second side room on the right is a figure of Niobe which may be an original from a group by the School of Scopas (4th c. B.C.).

*Museo Gregoriano Profano

The Museo Pio Cristiano has early Christian sarcophagi (mostly 4th–5th c.), sculpture and inscriptions.

Museo Pio Cristiano

The Museo Missionario Etnologico (on the lower floor) gives an excellent survey of the missionary activities of the Roman Catholic Church and the ethnology, prehistory and natural history of the mission lands.

Museo Missionario Etnologico

Museo Storico | From here a passage leads to the Museo Storico (historical museum, opened 1973), situated underground to the south of the Pinacoteca, which contains vehicles and relics of the military forces of the former Papal States.

Camposanto Teutonico

To the south of the Arco delle Campagne (the main visitor's entrance to Vatican City, to the left of St Peter's) is the Camposanto Teutonico, the old German cemetery. The church, originally 15th c., was restored in 1973. To the rear is the large new Audience Hall.

Giardini Vaticani

The Vatican Gardens occupy a large park of the Vatican City and include the area of St Peter's, a number of administrative buildings, churches, the Casina di Pio IV (seat of the Papal Academy of Science); they extend as far as the station and the Vatican Museums.

From the Vatican to the Foro Italico

Villa Madama | From the Piazza del Risorgimento a broad traffic artery, beginning as the Via Ottaviano, runs north to the Piazza Maresciallo Giardino, from which Via di Villa Madama continues north-west to Villa Madama, on the eastern slopes of Monte Mario. The villa was built in 1516–27 for Cardinal Giulio de' Medici from designs by Raphael. It is now a administrative building of the Italian government; fine views of the town.

Monte Mario | On Monte Mario (139 m/459 ft), the Italian zero meridian, marked by the Torre del Primo Meridiano, are a public park (view) and an observatory. On the south-east slopes are the headquarters of the Italian radio and television corporation RAI (Radiotelevisione Italiana). Higher up, to the west, is the church of the Madonna del Rosario, with a fine viewpoint.

*Foro Italico | From the Piazza Maresciallo Giardino the Lungotevere Maresciallo Cadorna runs alongside the Tiber to the Piazza De Bisis, where the Ponte Duca d'Aosta (1939) provides a link with the Via Flaminia. On the west side of the square, marked by a monolith 17 m/56 ft high, is the entrance to the Foro Italico or Campo della Farnesina, a sports centre built shortly before and after the Second World War in which the principal events in the 1960 Summer Olympic Games were held. Notable features of the centre are the Swimming Pool, the Swimming Stadium, the Stadio dei Marmi, surrounded by 60 statues of athletes in Carrara marble and the Stadio Olimpico (1953). On the north side of the complex is the Ministry of Foreign Affairs (Ministerio degli Affari Esteri). Higher up, on the slopes of the Monti della Farnesina, is the French Military Cemetery.

Ponte Milvio | East of the Foro Italico the Ponte Milvio or Ponte Molle, the Roman Pons Milvius, originally built to carry the Via Flaminia over the Tiber, was rebuilt in stone and improved in the 19th c. Only the four central arches are of Roman origin.

South of the Tiber are the Stadio Flaminio (1959), the circular Palazzetto dello Sport (1957) and the Olympic Village, built in 1960 and now occupied by government employees and their families.

Esposizione Universale di Roma (EUR)

On the southern outskirts of the city, some 7 km/4 miles from the Piazza Venezia on the road to Lido di Ostia and Anzio, straddling the Via

Cristoforo Colombo, is the extensive area (420 ha, well provided with open spaces) of the Esposizione Universale di Roma or EUR for short (Metropolitana from Termini Station). This was the site elected for a great international exhibition to be held in 1942 but cancelled because of the Second World War, and numbers of grandiose buildings were erected, most of them completed only after 1945 and now occupied by government departments, offices of various kinds and museums, including a residential area. The sports facilities in this area were provided for the 1960 Olympics.

At the north-west corner of the area, near the Magliana Metro station, is the striking Palazzo della Civiltà del Lavoro, 68 m/224 ft high. Some distance south-west is the large domed church of Santi Pietro e Paolo.

Palazzo della Civiltà del Lavoro

From the Palazzo della Civiltà the broad Viale della Civiltà del Lavoro runs east to the Palazzo dei Congressi, to the north-east of which is a large amusement park.

Palazzo dei Congressi

100 m/110 yd west of the Palazzo dei Congressi, in Piazza Marconi, we find the Museo Nazionale delle Arti e Tradizioni Popolari, with departments of folk art and folk traditions. The costume exhibits give an impression of the traditions of the various regions in Italy.

Museo Nazionale delle Arti e Tradizioni Popolari

Farther south is the Museo Preistorico ed Etnografico Luigi Pigorini, with material illustrating the prehistory of Latium and ethnographical collections from Ethiopia, Oceania, South America and other countries.

Museo Preistorico ed Etnografico Luigi Pigorini

The Palazzo delle Scienze houses the Museo dell'Alto Medioevo (Museum of the Early Medieval Period), with material of that period.

Museo dell'Alto Medioevo

Farther east again is the Museo della Civiltà Romana, an impressive collection of material illustrating the development and the greatness of the Roman Empire, as well as the architectural development in Republican and Imperial times; a particularly notable feature is the model of Rome as it was in the 4th c. A.D. (Room 37).

*Museo della Civiltà Romana

Some 500 m/550 yd north-east of the latter museum, on the spot where St Peter is supposed to have been beheaded, is the Trappist Abbazia delle Tre Fontane (Abbey of the Three Fountains), with three churches (13th and 16th c.).

Abbazia delle Tre Fontane

There are many sports facilities in the EUR: on the north side is situated the large Centro Sportivo delle Tre Fontane (several facilities); to the south on higher ground the circular Palazzo dello Sport (1960) and 750 m/825 yd west of this is the Velodromo Olimpico (1960), a cycle-racing track.

Sports facilities

8 km/5 miles south of the EUR, on S.S. 148 near Castel di Decima, a large Latin cemetery of the 9th–7th c. B.C. was discovered in 1974, containing princely graves with rich burial goods.

Latin cemetery

Fiumicino

South-west of Rome, on the coast, is the little town and resort of Fiumicino (pop. 15,000), founded only in 1825. (Take the Via Ostiense; the old road, the Via Portuense, is 4 km/2½ miles shorter, but hilly and winding.) Near the town are the excavations of the old port of Rome. Just before the town, to the right, is the large Leonardo da Vinci Airport. (There is a rail link between the airport and the city terminal.)

Situation
32 km/20 miles
south-west

Leonardo da Vinci Airport

Civitavecchia H7

Situation
75 km/47 miles
north-west

The place of the ancient port of Rome, has been taken by Civitavecchia (11 m/36 ft; pop. 49,000). The only feature of interest in the town, which was almost completely destroyed during the Second World War and was rebuilt after the war in modern style, is the fortress, begun by Bramante and Michelangelo.

*Via Appia Antica and the Catacombs

A trip along the Via Appia Antica, starting from the Porta San Sebastiano, is very rewarding. It is planned to establish an "archaeological park" here. The road, constructed in 312 B.C., originally ran from Rome via Terracina to Capua and was later extended to Benevento and Brindisi. Alongside the road can be seen the remains of the rows of tombs which lined the roads outside the city, together with the well-preserved or restored individual tombs of wealthy Romans, which combine with the huge arches of Roman aqueducts such as the Aqua Marcia and the Aqua Claudia, at varying distances from the road, to make up the particular charm of the Roman Campagna.

*Catacombs

The catacombs were originally the officially recognised burial-places of both Christians and pagans, known by the Greek name of coemeteria ("place of rest"). Until the early 9th c. the cemeteries containing the remains of martyrs were much venerated, and many relics were removed and deposited in churches. Thereafter the cemeteries were abandoned and neglected. The present name is derived from a burial-place of this kind at a spot called Catacumba, near San Sebastiano. The scientific exploration of the catacombs began at the end of the

Via Appia Antica

16th c. Recent research has shown that the catacombs were used only for burial and for Masses for the dead, not as places of refuge for persecuted Christians or for ordinary religious services. The arrangement of the catacombs is very simple – narrow passages with long recesses, hewn from the walls in several tiers, for the reception of bodies, the individual recesses being closed by tablets of marble or terracotta. The style of decoration (painting, more rarely sculpture) reflects that of the pagan art of the period. The decorative themes are mainly symbolic – the sacrificial lamb, the fish (Greek ichthys, which consists of the initial letters of the Greek phrase "Jesus Christ, Son of God, Saviour). There are also early representations of the Last Supper and the Virgin Mary. The older inscriptions give only the name of the dead person.

Some 800 m/880 yd from the Porta San Sebastiano, on the left of the road at the point where the Via Ardeatina branches off on the right, is the little church of Domine Quo Vadis, so named from the legend that Peter, fleeing from Rome to escape martyrdom, met Christ here and asked "Domine, quo vadis?" ("Master where are you going?") and received the answer "Venio iterum crucifigi" ("I come to be crucified a second time"); whereupon Peter, ashamed of his weakness, returned to Rome. In the church is a copy of Christ's footprint.

Domine Quo Vadis

1 km/⅝ mile farther on, at a clump of cypresses on the right (Via Appia Antica 110), is the entrance to the Catacombs of St Calixtus (Catacombe di San Callisto), the most interesting of these Early Christian underground burial-places which encircle Rome.
Notable features of the Catacombs of St Calixtus, which extend over a considerable area on several levels, are the Cubiculum Pontificium, containing the tombs of a number of 3rd c. popes (Urban I, Pontianus, Anterus, Fabianus, Lucius, Eutychianus); the empty tomb of St Cecilia; the tomb chamber of Pope Eusebius (309–311); and the tomb of Pope Cornelius (251–253), in what was originally the separate Cemetery of Lucina.

*Catacombs of St Calixtus

A short distance beyond the Catacombs of St Calixtus, near the point where the Via Appia Pignatelli branches off the Via Appia Antica on the left, is the Catacomb of Praetextus (martyred in the time of Diocletian), with the tomb chamber of the 2nd c. martyr Januarius. (Admission only by special arrangement.)

Catacomb of Praetextus

500 m/550 yd from the Catacombs of St Calixtus, on the right of the Via Appia Antica, is the church of San Sebastiano, one of Rome's seven pilgrimage churches, built in the 4th c. on a spot thought to have been the temporary resting-place ("Ad Catacumbas") of the bodies of the Apostles Peter and Paul. The church was rebuilt in the 17th c. with a portico of ancient columns.

Church of San Sebastiano

In the first chapel on the right is a stone with what is believed to be the footprint of Christ. On the left are St Sebastian's Chapel, the sacristy with sarcophagi, and the entrance to the impressive Catacombs of St Sebastian.
Under the centre of the church is an assembly room (triclia) for memorial services, with numerous inscriptions dating from the 3rd and 4th c. scratched on the walls. The invocations to the Apostles Peter and Paul seem to confirm the tradition that during the Valerian persecution in the year 258 the remains of the two Apostles were brought here or hereabouts from the Vatican and the Via Ostiense for safety. There are also tomb chambers on several levels dating from the 1st c., with paintings, stucco decoration and inscriptions. Behind the apse steps

Catacombs of St Sebastian

lead down to the Platonia, with the tomb of the martyr Quirinus. To the left of this is a cell with the inscription "Domus Petri" and 4th c. wall paintings.

Fosse Ardeatine

Just before San Sebastiano the Vicolo delle Sette Chiese branches off on the right. 650 m/715 yd along this are the Fosse Ardeatine, with a mausoleum, commemorating the 335 Italians who were shot here by the Germans in March 1944 in reprisal for a bomb attack.

Catacombs of Domitilla

300 m/330 yd farther on are the extensive Catacombs of Domitilla, with Early Christian inscriptions and wall paintings, and the 4th c. Basilica of St Petronilla (restored in the 19th c.).

Circus of Maxentius

Continuing along the Via Appia, we come to a large gateway on the left, near which is the Circus of Maxentius, constructed in A.D. 311, which was used for chariot races (482 m/527 yd long, 79 m/87 yd across).

*Tomb of Caecilia Metella

Just beyond this, also on the left, is the Tomb of Caecilia Metella, the best-known ruin in the Campagna, a circular structure 20 m/22 yd in diameter faced with travertine, with a marble frieze adorned with wreaths of flowers and ox-skulls. In the 13th c. it was used as a fortified tower by the Caetani family and equipped with battlements.

Beyond this point the original paving of the Via Appia is visible in several places. The road runs south-east, with beautiful views of the Alban Hills straight ahead and the arches of the Aqua Marcia and Aqua Claudia on the left. On both sides are the remains of numerous tombs, including two tumuli from which there are extensive views of the Campagna.

Villa dei Quintili

Some 2.5 km/1½ miles beyond the Tomb of Caecilia Metella, near the farm of Santa Maria Nuova, are the extensive remains of a large villa of the time of Hadrian, the Villa dei Quintili or Roma Vecchia.

Casale Rotondo

1.25 km/¾ mile farther on, at Casale Rotondo, is a large tomb of the 1st c. A.D.

From Rome to Frascati and Albano (about 35 km/22 miles)

Leave Rome by way of Porta San Giovanni and the Via Appia Nuova, and very shortly turn left into the Via Tuscolana (S.S. 215).

Cinecittà

10 km/6 miles: Cinecittà, a large complex of film studios where many Ialian films have been made.

Grottaferrata

1 km/¾ mile: road on the right (10 km/6 miles) to Grottaferrata (329 m/1086 ft; pop. 52,000), a little town in the Alban Hills, with a fortress-like monastery of Greek Basilian monks and an old church, almost entirely rebuilt in 1754; in the chapel of St Nilus in the south aisle are fine frescoes by Domenichino (1609–10).

Franscati

10 km/6 miles: Frascati (see entry).

Ponte Squarciarelli

3 km/2 miles beyond Frascati on the road to Albano one reaches the Ponte Squarciarelli, where roads go off on the right to Grottaferrata (2 km/1¼ miles), on the left to Rocca di Papa and Monte Cavo (11 km/7 miles) and straight ahead to Albano.

Marino

3 km/2 miles: Marino (355 m/1172 ft; pop. 31,000), picturesquely situated on a spur of the Alban Hills.

*Lago de Nemi
Nemi

1 km/¾ mile farther on the Via dei Laghi (17 km/11 miles), branches off on the left, runs high above the Lago Albano and comes in 9 km/5½ miles to side roads to the Lago di Nemi and the village of Nemi (521 m/1719 ft), above the Lago di Nemi (318 m/1049 ft; area 1.7 sq. km/½ sq.

mile; perimeter 5.5 km/3½ miles, greatest depth 34 m/112 ft), a crater lake surrounded by tufa cliffs 200 m/660 ft high. In the village is the Shipping Museum, with reduced scale models of the two State galleys of the Emperor Caligula which were discovered during drainage of the lake in 1928–31 and were burned by German forces in 1944.

The road continues through wooded country to Velletri. Velletri

The Lago Albano (293 m/967 ft; perimeter 10 km/6 miles; greatest *Lago Albano
depth 170 m/558 ft), above which lay the Latin federal capital of Alba Longa, destroyed at an early stage by the Romans, is of volcanic origin, and is drained by an ancient tunnel (emissario; guided visit) said to have been constructed by the Romans in the 4th c. B.C.

The road to Albano continues beyond the turn-off, running high above the west side of the Lago Albano.

3 km/2 miles: Castel Gandolfo (426 m/1405 ft; pop. 6000), the summer Castel Gandolfo
residence of the Pope, beautifully situated above the Lago Albano. In the centre of the little town is the Piazza del Plesbiscito, with the parish church of San Tommaso (by Bernini, 1661), built on a centralised plan, and the Pope's Summer Palace (by Carlo Maderna, 1629), containing the Papal observatory (established 1578; in the Vatican until 1935). Together with the adjacent Villa Barberini it was made part of the Vatican City State in 1929. In the grounds of the palace is an audience hall which can accommodate 8000 people. From Castel Gandolfo there is a funicular down to the lake.

From here Albano can be reached either on foot along the scenically attractive Galleria di Sopra, flanked by evergreen oaks (3.5 km/2¼ miles), or by car on the Galleria di Sotto, which is 1 km/¾ mile shorter but relatively featureless.

2 km/1¼ miles: Albano Laziale (384 m/1267 ft; pop. 28,000) lies on the Albano Laziale
high west side of Lago Albano. It has been the see of a bishop since 460

Castel Gandolfo, the Pope's summer residence

and is a resort much favoured by the people of Rome in summer for its beautiful setting. In the south-eastern outskirts of the town, on the right-hand side of the Via Appia, is a cube-shaped tomb of the late Republican period known (without any justification) as the Tomb of the Horatii and Curiatii. On the north-west side of the town, in the garden of a house at Via Saffi 86, are the remains of a large underground cistern known as il Cisternone, dating from the time of Septimius Severus and built for his mercenaries. Farther north-west, between the convent of San Paolo and a Capuchin convent, the remains of an amphitheatre, also dating from the reign of Septimius (3rd c. A.D.) can be seen through a gate.

From Rome over the Agro Pontino to Terracina (about 125 km/78 miles)

Pontine Marshes	Leave Rome by the Porta San Paolo or by the Porta Ardeatina and then take the Via Pontina (S.S. 148), which gives a good impression of the land reclaimed from the former Pontine Marshes. After passing through the EUR the road runs through the Roman Campagna.
Pomezia	31 km/19 miles: a road on the right (1 km/¾ mile) leads to the little town of Pomezia (89 m/194 ft; pop. 30,000), founded in 1939.
Agro Pontino	15 km/9 miles: the Via Pontina enters the Agro Pontino, an area of some 800 sq. km/309 sq. miles criss-crossed by countless canals and water channels. This low-lying area between the Monti Lepini and the sea, fringed by lines of dunes, degenerated after the abandonment of the Roman drainage system into marshland (the Pontine Marshes). From 1928 onwards the land was drained and brought into cultivation.
Latina	26 km/16 miles: Latina (21 m/69 ft; pop. 96,000) was founded in 1932 and known until the Second World War as Littoria, with concentric rings of streets round a large central square, the Piazza del Popolo; it is the provincial capital.
Sabaudia Terracina	From Latina it is 23 km/14 miles to Sabaudia (12 m/40 ft; pop. 13,000) and then 27 km/17 miles on the coast road to Terracina.

From Rome to Lido di Ostia, Anzio and Terracina (about 145 km/90 miles)

	Leave Rome by the Porta San Paolo and the Via Ostiense, and shortly before the church of San Paolo fuori le Mura bear right into S.S. 8 (the "Via del Mare", of motorway standard), which runs close to the Tiber for most of the way.
Leonardo da Vinci Airport	8 km/5 miles: road on the right (motorway standard) over the Tiber to the Leonardo da Vinci Airport.
Ostia	16 km/10 miles: road to the excavations of ancient Ostia (see entry).
Lido di Ostia	4 km/2½ miles: Lido di Ostia (see Ostia).
	The road to Anzio runs along the south-east side of Lido di Ostia, past the end of a road from Rome running through the area once occupied by an international exhibition, and then skirts the beautiful Pineta di Castel Fusano, 4 km/2½ miles long, in which the paving of the ancient Via Severiana has been brought to light. It then follows the coast, passing close to the excavations of ancient Lavinium.
Tor Vaianica	20 km/12 miles: the road reaches Tor Vaianica (3 m/10 ft), a small bathing resort.
Ardea	11 km/7 miles: road (sharp left) to Ardea (8 km/5 miles), with the Museo Manzù, devoted to the work of the famous sculptor.
Lavinio	6 km/3¾ miles: Lavinio Lido di Enea (20 m/66 ft) is a seaside resort on the territory of Anzio.

8 km/5 miles: Anzio (10 m/33 ft; pop. 28,000), a seaside resort, is situated at the end of a small promontory. It was the birthplace of the emperors Caligula and Nero. On the east side of the town is the new harbour built by Pope Innocent XII in 1698. To the west of the pier (view extending to Capo Circeo and the Pontine Islands) is Nero's harbour, now silted up, with remains of the old breakwater. There are attractive boat trips along the coast, which is littered with ancient remains. Below the lighthouse the promontory is riddled with ancient passages, the "Grotte di Nerone", which led to a large imperial villa. To the north-west is the Arco Muto, an artificial archway in the rock.

Anzio

The road to Terracina continues past villas and bathing beaches.
3 km/2 miles: Nettuno (11 m/36 ft; pop. 30,000), another seaside resort which was the scene of heavy fighting in January 1944, when American forces landed here while British forces landed in Anzio. In the northern outskirts of the town is the largest American military cemetery in Italy (7500 graves). Also in Nettuno is the tomb of Maria Goretti (1890–1902), who was canonised in 1950.

Nettuno

12 km/7 miles: a narrow side road on right goes to the Torre d'Astura, 2 km/1¼ miles south on an islet linked to the mainland by a bridge. The tower is the only remnant of a castle of the Frangipani family in which Conradin of Swabia vainly sought shelter after the battle of Tagliacozzo in 1268.

Torre d'Astura

Shortly after this the main road returns to the coast and then runs inland in a wide bend between the Lago di Fogliano on the left and the little Lage dei Monaci on the right. Beyond this it skirts the Lago di Caprolace (4 km/2½ miles long).

Lago di Fogliano
Lago di Caprolace

28 km/17 miles: a road on the left goes to Sabaudia (3 km/2 miles), along the north side of the Lago di Sabaudia, a much indented lake 7 km/4¼ miles long.

Lago di Sabaudia

Beyond the turning for Sabaudia the coast road runs between the west side of the Lago di Sabaudia and the sea.
7 km/4¼ miles: the road crosses the Emissario Romano, an ancient channel from the Lago di Sabaudia, which was used as a harbour in Roman times. Beyong this is Monte Circeo, the Roman Promontorium Circaeum, the traditional site of the palace of the Homeric enchantress Circe. The promontory is an isolated outlier of the Apennines which has been joined to the mainland by alluvial deposits (rich flora; national park).

Monte Circeo

Beyond the bridge over the Emissario, on the hillside to the right, is the massive Torre Paola, from which a footpath (sometimes closed) ascends to Circe's Cave (no entry); the walk takes half an hour.

Circe's Cave

The road continues along the north side of the promontory.
5 km/3 miles: take the road on the right (2 km/1¼ miles) to the village of San Felice (89 m/294 ft; pop. 8000), in a commanding situation on the north-east slope of Monte Circeo, with an old castle which belonged to the Caetani family (beautiful view from the tower). Above the village is a wall of polygonal cyclopean masonry known as the Cittadella Vecchia, a relic of the town of Cercei or Circei. From here a narrow and winding hill road climbs (3.5 km/2¼ miles west) to the Semáforo (448 m/1478 ft; military area), from which there are superb views south-west as far as Ischia, Capri and Vesuvius, and south to the Pontine Islands. From the Semáforo there is a rewarding climb (1 hour) to the summit of the hill (541 m/1785 ft), from which the dome of St Peter's can be seen in clear weather.

San Felice

Beyond the turn-off the main road continues, keeping close to the coast all the way.

15 km/9 miles: Terracina. The town is magnificently situated at the foot of high limestone crags, on the boundary between central and southern Italy. In the upper town which rises above the main road to the north

Terracina

stands the 12th c. cathedral of San Cesareo, incorporating a temple of Roma and Augustus, with a portico borne on eleven ancient columns and a fine campanile (view). The church has a notable interior, with remains of a mosaic pavement, a magnificent pulpit and a richly ornamented Easter candlestick, all 13th c. Cosmatesque work.

Monte Sant'Angelo

From the cathedral a strada panoramica leads (3 km/2 miles) to the summit of Monte Sant'Angelo or Monte Teodorico (228 m/752 ft), from which there are splendid views, extending in fine weather as far as Vesuvius. On a projecting spur of rock is a terrace, partly supported on arcades with the remains of an imposing temple of Jupiter Anxur (1st c. B.C.).

On the eastern outskirts of the town is the Taglio di Pisco Montano, a notable example of Roman road-building, where the rock face was cut away to lower the course of the Via Appia by some 40 m/44 yd.

Salerno   L5

Region: Campania
Province: Salerno (SA)
Altitude: 4 m/13 ft
Population: 156,000

Situation

Salerno, capital of the province of the same name, lies some 50 km/31 miles south-east of Naples at the north end of the Gulf of Salerno, where the hills of the Sorrento peninsula fall steeply down to the Tyrrhenian Sea.

Importance

The old town, rising up the slopes of the hill on the site of the ancient Salernum, still preserves many memories of its great days during the medieval period. It had the oldest medical school in Europe, which flourished from the 11th c. until it was closed down by Murat, Napoleon's brother-in-law, in 1812.

Harbour and town centre

Along the seafront to the east of the harbour, now used only by local shipping (trips to Capri, Amalfi and Positano), extends the Lungomare Trieste, a fine promenade lined by imposing modern buildings and affording extensive views. Parallel to the Lungomare Trieste is Via Roma, which with its continuation to the south-east, the Corso Giuseppe Garibaldi, is the town's principal traffic artery. At the west end of Via Roma we come to the Piazza Amendola, bounded on the east by the Palazzo di Città (Town Hall) and on the south-west by the Prefecture. Behind the Prefecture are the beautiful Public Gardens (Villa Comunale), on the west side of which is the Teatro Verdi.

*Cathedral

Half-way along Via Roma stands the Palazzo di Provincia. From here Via del Duomo runs north, crossing the picturesque Via dei Mercanti, to the cathedral of San Matteo, built about 1080 in the time of Robert Guiscard and restored in 1768 and after 1945. A flight of steps leads up to an atrium with 28 ancient columns from Paestum and fourteen ancient sarcophagi. The magnificent bronze doors were made in Constantinople in 1099.

Above the doorway is a large half-length mosaic of St Matthew, of the Norman period. In the nave are two ambos (12th c.) with rich Cosma-

Salerno on the Tyrrhenian Sea

tesque mosaic decoration, and near the right-hand one is an Easter candlestick decorated in similar style. At the end of the north aisle is the splendid tomb of Margaret of Anjou (d. 1412).

The pavement of the choir and the choir screens are decorated with mosaics. In the chapel to the right of the high altar is the tomb of Pope Gregory VII, who died in Salerno in 1085; in the apse of the chapel is a mosaic figure of the Archangel Michael (1260).

In the richly decorated crypt under the altar lie the remains of the Evangelist Matthew, brought here from Paestum.

In the Cathedral Museum is a 12th c. altar frontal, with ivory reliefs of Biblical scenes.

Cathedral Museum

Museo Provinciale in Salerno

A little way east of the cathedral, in Via San Benedetto, is the interesting Provincial Museum, with antiquities, including an over-life-size bronze head of Apollo of the 1st c. B.C. and pictures.

Castello di Arechi

From the cathedral it is a 45 minutes' walk to the old Lombard Castello di Arechi (263 m/868 ft) on the hill north-west of the town. The castle was strengthened by Robert Guiscard in the 11th c. From here there are extensive views.

San Gimignano

H6

Region: Toscana. Province: Siena (SI)
Altitude: 324 m/1069 ft. Population: 7500

The little town of San Gimignano lies on a hill, visible from afar, some 35 km/22 miles north-west of Siena and 50 km/31 miles south-west of Florence.

Situation

San Gimignano

San Gimignano is one of the most attractive little towns in Tuscany, still preserving a picturesque medieval aspect with its circuit of walls and its towers.

In the 13th and 14th c. San Gimignano was an independent city, but in 1353 it became subject to Florence. Until then it was involved in the strifes between the house of Ardinghelli (Guelf) and the house of Salvucci (Ghibelline). The rivalry lead to the erection of the towers (originally 56). The remaining thirteen towers and the walls surrounding the town give it a medieval aspect.

**Sights

Palazzo del Popolo
(Pinacoteca Civica)

The central feature of San Gimignano is the Piazza della Cisterna with a beautiful fountain surrounded by tall towers. Adjoining this square, on the north-west is another square, the Piazza del Duomo, on the south side of which is the Palazzo del Popolo, built in 1288–1323 as the Palazzo Nuovo del Podestà, with the tallest tower in the town, the Torre Grossa ("Big Tower", 54 m/178 ft high; views). The palace houses the Town Hall (Palazzo Comunale) and the Pinacoteca Civica (Municipal Museum), with a large collection of pictures; particularly notable is a large fresco, "Maestà" (Madonna Enthroned), by Lippo Memmi (1317).

*Cathedral

On the west side of the Piazza del Duomo is the cathedral, usually called the Collegiata, a Romanesque structure with three aisles, dating from the 12th c. and enlarged in 1456 by Giuliano da Maiano on the plan of a Latin cross. In the course of time the façade has been remodelled several times but it has remained without any external decoration. The inside of the façade is decorated with frescoes (1456) by Benozzo

The towers of San Gimignano

Gozzoli depicting the martyr of St Sebastian, and there are two wooden statues, the Annunciation, by Jacopo della Quercia (1421).

In the south aisle are monumental 14th c. frescoes by Barna da Siena consisting of three rows with scenes from the New Testament. At the end of the south aisle is the Cappella di Santa Fina (the town's patron saint), a Renaissance masterpiece by Giuliano and Benedetto da Maiano (1468).

On the altar is a carved altar-piece bearing a sarcophagus which contained the remains of Santa Fina until 1738. Beyond can be seen the Madonna with Child flanked by two angels.

The side arcades have fine frescoes by Domenico Ghirlandaio (1475) depicting the life and death of Santa Fina.

Facing the cathedral is the Palazzo del Podestà (13th–14th c.). The tall Torre dell' Orologio (51 m/168 ft) marks the height which privately built towers were not allowed to exceed.

Palazzo del Podestà

Adjoining the cathedral is the Museo d'Arte Sacra (Museum of Religious Art), which contains 14th–15th c. sculpture and robes.

Museo d'Arte Sacra

The same building houses the Museo Etrusco, with a small collection of Etruscan urns, vases, coins, etc.

Museo Etrusco

A little way west of the cathedral, by the town walls, is the ruined Rocca, from which there is a fine view of the town's towers and of the surrounding area.

Rocca

At the north-west end of the town stands the church of Sant'Agostino. Particularly notable in the choir chapel are the frescoes by Benozzo Gozzoli (1465), depicting in seventeen scenes the life of St Augustine (354–430), a famous Church Father.

Sant'Agostino

San Marino

I6

Repubblica di San Marino
Area: 61 sq. km/24 sq. miles
Altitude: 640 m/2112 ft
Population: 22,400 (country); 4500 (town)

San Marino, capital of the little republic of the same name (Repubblica di San Marino), lies some 23 km/14 miles south-west of Rimini on the eastern fringe of the Apennines. The territory is bounded by the Italian region of Emilia-Romagna to the north and the Marche to the south, and is one of the smallest states in Europe.

Situation

With its magnificent situation on Monte Titano (745 m/2486 ft), its three castles crowning the triple peaks of the hill and its picturesque old houses and streets, it attracts large numbers of summer visitors, particularly from the seaside resorts around Rimini.

State flag

Legend has it that San Marino was founded in A.D. 301 by St Marinus, a stone-mason from the Dalmatian town of Rab who fled here during the Diocletian persecutions. The present republic developed out of a settlement which grew up around a convent mentioned in the records in 885. It received the constitution which is still in force in 1263, was recognised by Pope Urban IV in 1631 and has since maintained its independence, from 1862, under the protection of Italy.

History

Legislative power rests with the 60 members of the Consiglio Grande e Generale, executive power with the ten deputies of the Congresso di Stato and the two Capitani reggenti, who change every six months. Old

Constitution

429

medieval costumes are worn at the ceremonial change-over on April 1st and October 1st and on San Marino's National Day September 3rd.

Città di San Marino

The old town (Centro Storico) is surrounded by town walls. On the south-west side of the town is the 15th c. Porta San Francesco or Porta del Loco. Just inside the town walls, on the right, stands the church of San Francesco (14th c.), which houses the Pinacoteca, with notable pictures by Matteo Loves and others. North-west of the church is a memorial stone commemorating Garibaldi who marched through the town.

In the centre of the old town is the Piazza della Libertà, the town's attractive main square, on the north-west side of which is the neo-Gothic Palazzo del Governo or Palazzo Pubblico (1894), with a sumptuously appointed interior, particularly notable features being the Hall of the Grand Council, the Audience Chamber and the Voting Chamber which contains a painting of St Marinus, the state's patron, by Guernico. From the roof of the palace there are magnificent views.

A little way north of the main square is the neo-classical Basilica di San Marino (1836), with a richly decorated interior; the remains of the saint are preserved in the high altar. To the right of the basilica is the chapel of San Pietro, which claims to possess the stone beds of St Marinus and his companion St Leo.

North-west of the main square is the lower station of a funicular, situated on the Strada Panoramica which encircles the town. To the right is the State Tourist Office (Ufficio di Stato per il Turismo).

Borgo Maggiore

The funicular leads to Borgo Maggiore, with three museums: the Firearms Museum, the Postal Museum, with stamps and coins and the Garibaldi Museum. Once a week there is a market in the Borgo.

Fortress on the edge of the Apennines

*Rocche

From the Basilica di San Marino a road runs south-east to the three peaks of Monte Titano with their three castles: first the 11th c. Rocca or Guaita, with coloured panels depicting the history of the castle; then the 13th c. Cesta or Fratta, on the highest peak (745 m/2459 ft), commanding extensive views, with a museum of arms and armour; and finally the 13th c. Montale, at the foot of which is a park; in the eastern part of the park can be seen the Kursaal (Palazzo dei Congressi).

San Remo/Sanremo   D6

Region: Liguria
Province: Imperia (IM)
Altitude: 11 m/36 ft
Population: 63,000

San Remo, Italy's largest and oldest winter health resort, lies on the "Riviera dei Fiori", in a bay enclosed by a semicircle of hills. From San Remo it is only about 20 km/12 miles to the Italian-French frontier.

*Situation

Thanks to its sheltered situation San Remo has a mild and equable climate in winter, and in summer it is a lively and popular resort, with a beach which is partly artificial. Here olive groves have given place to glasshouses in which carnations and roses are grown for export.

General information

Every year in February the Italian Popular Song Festival takes place here.

Festival di San Remo

Yacht harbour on the Italian Riviera

431

Old Town

On a steep hill between the short valleys of the Torrente San Francesco and Torrente di San Romolo is the Old Town (Città Vecchia or La Pigna), a huddle of narrow lanes, flights of steps and tall sombre houses, linked by arches as a protection against earthquakes.

New Town

The New Town occupies the low-lying alluvial land at the foot of the hill. Its main traffic artery is Corso Matteotti, a long street lined with shops. At its west end is the Casino Municipale, with gaming rooms, a theatre and other facilities. A short distance north-east stands the cathedral of San Siro, founded in the 13th c. Corso Matteotti is continued westward by the Corso Imperatrice, a promenade shaded by Canary palms (Phoenix canariensis) which skirts the west bay, with the beautiful Parco Marsaglia at its far end.

*Corso Imperatrice

The main traffic artery of the east bay is the Corso Garibaldi, the eastward continuation of Corso Matteotti, with the Flower Market (Mercato dei Fiori) near its west end. The Corso Trento e Trieste runs along the seashore.

Between the east and west bays lies the harbour, with the old Genoese Forte Santa Tecla (now a prison).

In San Remo there is a new underground station, part of a large-scale project to move the railway from the beach area further inland.

Monte Bignone

There is an attractive trip (45 minutes) by cableway or by road via the golf-course (18 holes) and the summer holiday resort of San Romolo (786 m/2594 ft) to the summit of Monte Bignone (1299 m/4287 ft), with far-ranging views in clear weather of the Riviera and the Maritime Alps, extending south to Corsica.

Baiardo

Situation
25 km/16 miles
north-west of San
Remo

Another rewarding excursion is to Baiardo (900 m/2970 ft), situated on a hill, with a beautiful parish church and the ruins of another church (16th c.) destroyed by an earthquake in 1887. From a nearby terrace there are magnificent views of the mountains.
From Baiardo the trip can be continued via Apricale to Ventimiglia.

Bussana Vecchia

Situation
8 km/5 miles east of
San Remo

East of San Remo is Bussana Vecchia (201 m/663 ft), a hill village, which was destroyed in 1887 by an earthquake. At present it is occupied by painters and other artists.

Sardinia/Sardegna

E/F8–11

Region: Sardegna
Provinces: Cagliari (CA), Nuoro (NU), Oristano (OR) and Sassari (SS)

Area: 24,090 sq. km/9299 sq. miles
Population: 1,628,700

Regular services (carrying cars) from Civitavecchia to Golfo Aranci, Olbia and Cagliari, from Genoa to Porto Torres, Olbia resp. Arbatax and Cagliari, from Livorno to Porto Torres, Olbia and Cagliari and from Naples to Cagliari.   Boat services

Cagliari International Airport, 4 km/2½ miles west of the town; airports for domestic services at Olbia and Alghero.   Air services

The island of Sardinia lies in the Mediterranean, to the west of the Italian mainland. It is separated from the south tip of the neighbouring French island of Corsica by the narrow Strait of Bonifacio.
The island forms the autonomous region of Sardinia, made up of the four provinces of Cagliari, Nuoro, Oristano and Sassari.   Situation

Geologically the island is a remnant of a rump mountain range composed of gneisses, granites and schists, overlaid by a band of limestone running from north to south and partly covered with recent volcanic deposits. The only plain of any size, the Campidano, lies between the Iglesiente uplands with their rich mineral resources to the south-west and the rest of the island, a hilly region with gentler slopes in the west and more rugged country in the east, rising in Gennargentu to a height of 1834 m/6052 ft and falling steeply down to the sea in the sheer cliffs on the east coast.   Geology

The summers on the island are hot and dry; the winters bring heavy rain.   Climate

Mountainous terrain near Oliena in the east of Sardinia

433

Sardinia/Sardegna

Women in Sardinian costume

Population

The population, which from the late Middle Ages until the beginning of this century was decimated by malaria, is concentrated in the coastal areas.

Agriculture

More than half the population obtain their subsistence from agriculture. Corn, vine, olives, citrus fruits, vegetables and tobacco are grown in the Campidano plain, in the coastal areas and in the fertile valleys of the numerous rivers. The upland regions are mainly devoted to pastoral farming (sheep, goats and cattle). In the coastal regions fishing (tunny, anchovies, spiny lobsters) also makes a contribution to the economy.

Fishing

Mining

Mining was already an important activity in ancient times. The main mining area is the Iglesiente, where zinc, lead, manganese and barytes are worked (now declining considerably). Around Carbonia there is opencast coal-mining. At present the Sardinian mining has entered a state of crisis which results in unemployment and migration.

Industry

Recent development has led to the establishment of various industries. The building of the new oil harbour nearby Cagliari is the base for new petro-chemical industry. Mining in the Iglesiente has created new industrial areas such as Sulcis in Portovesme. Other new developments can be seen in Tortoli and Arbatax, with paper-processing industries on the east coast and inland, at Ottana, a centre for the production of synthetic fibres.

Salt

The extraction of magnesium and cooking salt from sea-water is also an industry of some significance.

Tourism

In recent years tourism has developed into an important element of the island's economy. In addition to the established tourist areas around

Alghero and Santa Teresa a very modern holiday resort has been developed on the Costa Smeralda.

Evidence of the earliest inhabitants of Sardinia is provided by the remains of numerous prehistoric settlements, in particular the nuraghi (singular nuraghe), massive towers characteristic of the island culture of the Bronze and Iron Ages which show a striking similarity to the talayots of the Balearics. Like the talayots, they no doubt served as fortresses, watch-towers and burial-places, and can be dated to the period between 1500 and 500 B.C. History

From the 9th c. onwards Phoenicians and later Carthaginians settled on the coasts. In 238 B.C. the island was occupied by the Romans, attracted by its rich deposits of minerals. About A.D. 455 it fell into the hands of the Vandals and later became subject to Byzantium. Between the 8th and 10th c. it was frequently ravaged by Saracen raids; but these piratical activities were repressed by Pisa and Genoa following an appeal by the Pope, who rewarded them with the grant of the territory. The traditional system of rule by four giudici (judges) in the districts of Torre, Gallura, Cagliari and Arborea was, however, maintained. In 1297 Sardinia was granted by the Pope to the crown of Aragon. Under the treaty of Utrecht in 1713 it was assigned to Austria, and in 1718 was exchanged with Sicily and passed to the dukes of Savoy as the kingdom of Sardinia. In 1948 it was given the status of an autonomous region within the Republic of Italy.

Thanks to the ruggedness and remoteness of much of the island its old customs and traditions are still vigorously alive. The Sardinian language is a Romance tongue which has developed independently of mainland Italian and preserves certain archaic features. Customs and traditions
Language

Tour of the island (about 720 km/446 miles)

The first section of the tour leads from Cagliari to Sassari. Leave Cagliari on S.S. 131, which runs north-west.

20 km/12 miles: Monastir (83 m/274 ft), a village of Oriental aspect on the slopes of a volcanic hill, with rock-cut tombs. 5.5 km/3½ miles south-west at San Sperate is an open-air museum of modern sculpture. Beyond Monastir the road follows the east edge of the Campidano plain. Monastir

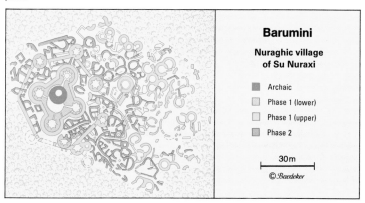

Barumini

**Nuraghic village
of Su Nuraxi**

- ▓ Archaic
- ▢ Phase 1 (lower)
- ▢ Phase 1 (upper)
- ▓ Phase 2

30m

© Baedeker

435

Sardinia/Sardegna

Sanluri

23 km/14 miles: Sanluri (135 m/446 ft; pop. 8000), with a 14th c. castle containing a small military museum.

Excursion:

Barumini
**Su Nuraxi

24 km/15 miles north-east of Sanluri is the village of Barumini, near which (1 km/¾ mile west, to the left of the road to Tuili) is the largest nuraghic village in Sardinia, Su Nuraxi, with 396 houses and a massive central structure with several towers.

Excursion:

Costa Verde

From Sanluri S.S. 197 runs west to the wooded Costa Verde, a coastal region now being developed as a popular holiday area, with new roads, hotels and sports facilities.

Sardara

9 km/5½ miles: Sardara (163 m/538 ft). By the little church of Santa Anastasia is an underground spring sanctuary of nuraghic type. 3 km/2 miles west is a small spa with thermal springs (50 and 68 °C/122 and 154 °F).

Santa Giusta

36 km/22 miles: Santa Giusta (10 m/33 ft), on the north side of a marshy lake, the Stagno di Santa Giusta, with a 12th c. church in Pisan style.

Oristano

3 km/2 miles: Oristano (9 m/30 ft; pop. 30,000), which is noted for its pottery. It still preserves a number of towers belonging to its medieval defences. Notable are the 18th c. cathedral, on the site of an earlier building of the 13th–14th c. and the Archaeological Museum, with finds from the ancient city of Tharros, which lay to the north-west of the Gulf of Oristano. Beautiful traditional costumes can often be seen here on market days.

Excursion:

San Vero Milis

An interesting trip can be made to the nature reserve of San Vero Milis,

Su Nuraxi, near Barumini, Sardinia

21 km/13 miles north-west. This is a marshy area, and numerous fla-
mingos can be seen here in September and October.

16 km/10 miles: Bauladu (29 m/96 ft), on the north edge of the Campidano plain. The road then continues up the Bobolica valley.

Bauladu

Excursion:
5 km/3 miles farther on S.S. 131 d. branches off. Running diagonally
across the island this is the quickest and shortest route from Cagliari or
Oristano to Olbia (309 km/192 miles and 182 km/113 miles respectively). In 50 km/36 miles it bypasses the provincial capital of Nuoro
(546 m/1802 ft; pop. 37,000), charmingly situated on a hillside, between
limestone hills of Alpine type to the south and the peak of Ortobene
(995 m/3284 ft; view) to the east. Beautiful local costumes are worn on
the feast of the Saviour (last Sunday in August). Nuoro was the birthplace of the writer Grazia Deledda (1893–1936; Nobel prize 1926). At the
south-east end of the town is the 19th c. neo-classical cathedral. Worth
visiting is the Civico Museo Speleo-Archeologico, where finds from
caves and prehistoric material can be seen, inculding menhirs.
1.5 km/1 mile north-east are the pilgrimage church of Nostra Signora
della Solitudine (view) and, beyond the Colle di San Onofrio (594
m/1960 ft; view), the Sardinian Museum of Costume, housed in over 20
buildings in the style of Sardinian peasants' houses. Around the town
are several nuraghi.

Nuoro

From Nuoro there is a beautiful drive south to the villages of Mamoiada
(644 m/2125 ft; costumes) and Fonni (1000 m/3300 ft; pop. 5000), the
highest village on the island. In the surrounding area are numerous
nuraghi and "fairies' houses".

Mamoiada
Fonni

Fonni is the starting point for the ascent (4 hours, with guide), of Bruncu
Spina (1829 m/6036 ft; panoramic views), the northern peak of the
Gennargentu massif, from which the southern peak, Punta la Marmora
(1834 m/6052 ft), can be climbed (¾ hour).

* Gennargentu
massif

Shortly after the turning on the road Nuoro to Olbia, we see on the left
the well-preserved nuraghe of Losa, with a number of subsidiary
structures.

Nuraghe of Losa

2 km/1¼ miles: Abbasanta (315 m/1040 ft), the largest livestock market
in Sardinia, on the southern edge of the Abbasanta plain, an area of
black basaltic rock. 10 km/6 miles south-east is the Tirso Dam, which
has impounded the water of the island's principal river to form Lago
Omodeo, 22 km/14 miles long and up to 5 km/3 miles wide.

Abbasanta

16 km/10 miles: Macomer (563 m/1858 ft; pop. 11,000), situated on a
high plateau of basalts and trachytes on the slopes of the Catena del
Marghine, with beautiful far-ranging views. In front of the church of
Macomer are three Roman milestones found in the area.
Some of the best preserved nuraghi in Sardinia can be seen in the
immediate surroundings of the town. Particularly fine is the nuraghe of
Santa Barbara (648 m/2138 ft; 45 minutes north), a conical structure on
a high square base.

Macomer

Excursion:
3 km/2 miles beyond Macomer S.S. 129 bis goes off on the left to the
village of Suni (23 km/14 miles: extensive views) and, 6 km/3¾ miles
beyond this, the little port of Bosa (10 m/33 ft; pop. 8000), with the castle
of Serravalle (1112). 16 km/10 miles south of Suni lies Cuglieri (479
m/1581 ft; pop. 5000), on the lower slopes of Monte Ferru (1050 m/3465
ft), an extinct volcano.

Bosa
Curglieri

2 km/1¼ miles: on the left of the road is the almost completely preserved nuraghe of Succoronis (Muradu).

* Nuraghe of
Succoronis

437

Sardinia/Sardegna

Nuraghe of Santu Antipe	27 km/17 miles: road on right (1 km/¾ mile south-east) to the three-storey nuraghe of Santu Antine, 16 m/53 ft high.
Bonnanaro	Excursion: 5 km/3 miles: Bonnanaro (405 m/1337 ft), where a road goes off on the left (4 km/2½ miles south-west) to the richly ornamented church of San Pietro di Sorres (Pisan period, 12th c.). Beyond Bonnanaro the road runs through the beautiful wooded uplands of Logudoro.
*Santissima Trinità di Saccargia	Excursion: 21 km/13 miles: S.S. 597, the direct road from Sassari to Olbia, goes off. 2 km/1¼ miles along this road is the former abbey church of the Santissima Trinità di Saccargia, the finest example of Pisan architecture in Sardinia, with 13th c. frescoes.
Sassari	15km/9 miles: Sassari.

For the next section of the tour from Sassari to Olbia or La Maddalena, there are alternative routes – either by the direct road on S.S. 597 (101 km/63 miles) or the more interesting S.S. 127.

Osilo	14 km/9 miles (600 m/1980 ft; pop. 6000), renowned for its beautiful costumes. From the ruined Malaspina castle and the nearby Cappella di Bonaria there are beautiful views. The road continues through the wooded Aglona district.
Castelsardo	Excursion: 39 km/24 miles: turn-off, a road through beautiful scenery, via the village of Sedini (16th c. church), picturesquely situated above gorges, to the little port town of Castelsardo (114 m/376 ft; pop. 5000), in a magnificent situation on a promontory which falls sheer down to the

The abbey church of Santissima Trinità di Saccargia

Golfo dell'Asinara. This is the principal basketwork centre in Sardinia. In the parish church is a beautiful 15th c. Madonna, a masterpiece of the Sardinian-Spanish school of painting. From the ruined castle there are fine views.

Some 4 km/2½ miles beyond the turning for Castelsardo, at Perfugas (just off S.S. 127), a fortified village of the nuraghic period and a spring sanctuary have been excavated.

26 km/16 miles: Tempio Pausania (566 m/1868 ft; pop. 13,000), formerly chief town of the district of Gallura, situated below the north face of the jagged Monti di Limbara (cork industry).

Tempio Pausania

10 km/6 miles: Calangianus (518 m/1709 ft; pop. 6000), an old town surrounded by forest, with a pretty parish church.

Calangianus

35 km/22 miles: Olbia (15 m/50 ft; pop. 33,000), formerly known as Terranova Pausania, lying at the west end of the deeply indented Gulf of Olbia. A causeway 1.5 km/1 mile long carrying the road and the railway which links the town with the little Isola Bianca, where the ships from Civitavecchia come in.

Olbia

Beside the town railway station is the 11th c. church of San Simplicio, in Pisan style, with a collection of Roman inscriptions (particularly milestones), and a sarcophagus with a decoration of garlands. From the church and from the harbour there are fine views of the bay and the massive offshore island of Tavolara (up to 555 m/1832 ft; area 6 sq. km/2¼ sq. miles).

Excursion:

To the north of Olbia, extending along the shores of a large peninsula, is the beautiful Costa Smeralda (Emerald Coast), whose beaches of fine sand are being developed as a holiday area by the construction of new roads and the provision of tourist facilities. The roads to the various resorts branch off S.S. 125, which runs north from Olbia to Palau.

*Costa Smeralda

6 km/3¾ miles: road (8 km/5 miles) to the Golfo di Marinella.

Golfo di Marinella

1 km/¾ mile: coast road via Cala di Volpe (15 km/9 miles) and Romazzino (17 km/11 miles) to Porto Cervo (30 km/19 miles), the chief place on the Costa Smeralda.

Porto Cervo

3 km/2 miles north, beyond Capo Ferro, is the bay of Liscia di Vacca, and 5 km/3 miles farther on Baia Sardinia (51 m/168 ft; pop. 4000), with numerous hotels.

Baia Sardinia

At the south end of the Costa Smeralda lies the holiday centre of Portisco.

17 km/11 miles north on S.S. 125 is Arzachena.

Arzachena

12 km/7 miles: Palau (5 m/17 ft).

Palau

From Palau there is a boat service several times daily (30 minutes) to La Maddalena (19 m/63 ft; pop. 11,000), a port on the island of the same name (157 m/518 ft; area 20 sq. km/7 sq. miles), which together with the neighbouring islands was strongly fortified until the Second World War, commanding the Strait of Bonifacio between Sardinia and Corsica.

La Maddalena

The island is traversed by a panoramic road 7 km/4¼ miles long which is carried by a swing bridge over the Passo della Moneta, a strait fully 500 m/550 yd wide, on to the neighbouring island of Caprera ("Goat Island", up to 212 m/700 ft; area 15.75 sq. km/6 sq. miles). 1.5 km/1 mile east of the bridge is a house once occupied by Garibaldi, who died here on June 2nd 1882 (collection of mementoes). In front of the house stands a monument to Garibaldi, behind it an olive-grove containing his tomb, which attracts visitors from all over Italy, particularly on the anniversary of his death.

*Caprera

The third section of the Sardinian tour, from Olbia to Cagliari, is on S.S. 125, which runs south-east past a number of salt-water lagoons. Thereafter the road continues at varying distances from the coast.

Porto Cervo, on the Costa Smeralda of Sardinia

Siniscola	57 km/35 miles: Siniscola (42 m/139 ft; pop. 9000), at the west end of a large coastal plain, renowned for its beautiful costumes. From Peniscola a panoramic road (edges not guarded) runs along the rocky ridge of Monte Albo (1127 m/3719 ft), through a region well stocked with wildlife, to Bitti (549 m/1812 ft; pop. 6000).
La Caletta	6 km/3¾ miles north-east of Siniscola is the developing resort of La Caletta.
	From Siniscola it is possible to return to Cagliari either by taking the shorter but less interesting road via Nuoro and Oristano or by continuing on the coast road.
Orosei	36 km/22 miles: Orosei (19 m/63 ft; pop. 5000), on the right bank of the River Cedrino, with a ruined castle.
Dorgali	21 km/13 miles: Dorgali (387 m/1277 ft; pop. 8000), a little town (costumes), situated on the slopes of Monte Bardia (882 m/2911 ft). Notable is the Museo Civico Archeologico.
Stalactitic caves	In the surrounding area are a number of beautiful stalactitic caves (Grotta Toddeitu, Grotta del Bue Marino and Grotta Ispinigoli) and the rock-cut tombs, the so-called domus de janas. 11 km/7 miles north-west of Dorgali is the nuraghic village of Serra Orrios.
	Excursion:
Cala Gonone	2 km/1¼ miles: side road (7 km/4¼ miles) which winds its way down to the little port of Cala Gonone (25 m/83 ft).
	Beyond Dorgali the road passes through beautiful montainous country.
Tortoli Arbatax	61 km/38 miles: Tortoli (15 m/50 ft; pop. 8000), at the beginning of an extensive plain. 5 km/3 miles east is the attractively situated little port of Arbatax (pop. 1000), formerly also known as Tortoli Marina, which ships the agricultural produce and minerals of the Ogliastra region. Nearby are picturesque red porphyry cliffs.

Porphyry cliffs near Arbatax

Excursion:
From Tortoli there is a very attractive trip, first on S.S. 198 through the Ogliastra uplands, with hills of crystalline limestone, sometimes in curiously contorted shapes, to Lanusei (595 m/1964 ft; pop. 5000), prettily situated amid vineyards, Seui (800 m/2640 ft) and the Cantoniera di Santa Lucia; then on S.S. 128 and S.S. 131 to Cagliari.

Ogliastra
Lanusei

Beyond Tortoli S.S. 125 follows a winding course through the south-eastern part of the Ogliastra region.

10 km/6 miles: Bari Sardo (50 m/166 ft), from which there is a view of the Gennargentu massif. The road continues, with many bends, through lonely hill country.

Bari Sardo

121 km/75 miles: Quartu Sant'Elena (6 m/20 ft; pop. 42,000), a thriving town, in an area which produces the famous white wine, Malvasia. On the feast of St Helena (May 21st) there is a picturesque procession of richly decked teams of oxen. The parish church has a large altarpiece, probably by Antioco Mainas (16th c.).

Quartu Sant'Elena

8 km/5 miles: Cagliari.

Cagliari

Sassari

Region: Sardegna
Province: Sassari (SS)
Altitude: 225 m/743 ft
Population: 120,000

Sassari, Sardinia's second largest town, the capital of the province of the same name, lies on a limestone plateau, in the north-west of the island, some 15 km/9 miles south of the Golfo dell'Asinara.

Situation

Sassari

Sassari is an archiepiscopal see and a university town.

Sights

The hub of the town's traffic is the palm-shaded Piazza Cavallino de Honestis, immediately south-east of which is the large Piazza d'Italia, with a monument to Victor Emmanuel II and a modern Prefecture.

Museo G. A. Sanna

From the Piazza d'Italia the tree-lined Via Roma runs south-east to the Museo G. A. Sanna, with the collections assembled by Giovanni Antonio Sanna, a member of the Italian Parliament, containing prehistoric, Punic and Roman antiquities and pictures of the 14th–19th c. by Sardinian, Italian and foreign artists.

San Nicola

North-west of the Piazza Cavallino de Honestis, reached by way of Piazza Azuni, is the Corso Vittorio Emanuele, Sassari's principal street. From this we turn left along Via del Duomo to reach the cathedral of San Nicola, with a Baroque façade and a restored interior.

East of this in Via Santa Catarina is the fine Palazzo del Duca, now the Town Hall.

Santa Maria di Betlem

To the west of the cathedral, in the spacious Piazza Santa Maria, stands the church of Santa Maria di Betlem, rebuilt in modern style but still preserving its Romanesque façade of the Pisan period. The interior has been remodelled in Gothic style.

Fonte Rosello

On the north side of the town is the pretty Fonte Rosello, with a Baroque well-house of 1605.

Porto Torres

Situation
19 km/12 miles
north-west

A pleasant drive through the coastal district of Nura leads to the little industrial town of Porto Torres (10 m/33 ft; pop. 21,000), the port of Sassari, situated in the Golfo dell'Asinara. On the east side of the town is the church of San Gavino (11th–13th c.; fortified in the 18th c.), a basilica in Pisan Romanesque style. In the interior are 22 ancient columns and six pillars, and in the crypt several Roman sarcophagi of the 3rd–4th c. To the west of the harbour a seven-arched Roman bridge spans the little Rio Turritano, and near this are the remains of a large Temple of Fortuna, popularly known as the "Palazzo Re Barbaro".

Stintino

North-west of Porto Torres we come to the fishing village of Stintino (9 m/30 ft), and 5 km/3 miles beyond this is the Punta del Falcone, the north-west tip of Sardinia. Lying off the promontory to the north are the little Isola Piana (24 m/79 ft) and the long indented Isola Asinara (up to 408 m/1346 ft high; area 52 sq. km/18 sq. miles).

Alghero

Situation
37 km/23 miles
south-west

Another very attractive trip is to the charmingly situated town and seaside resort of Alghero, whose inhabitants still speak a Catalan dialect (7 m/23 ft; pop. 38,000). Features of interest are the cathedral (1510; Spanish Gothic doorway), the church of San Francesco (cloister), the picturesque Spanish bastions and towers and many old houses.

*Grotta di Nettuno

14 km/9 miles west of Alghero (also reached by motorboat), on the west side of the precipitous Capo Caccia is a beautiful stalactitic cave, the Grotta di Nettuno.

Selinunte

Region: Sicilia
Province: Trapani (TP)
Altitude: 74 m/244 ft

The ruins of Selinunte, lie on both banks of the little river Modione (Greek Selinon) and Gorgo di Cottoni, near the south-west coast of Sicily, some 15 km/9 miles south of Castelvetrano and 70 km/45 miles north-west of Agrigento.

Situation

Selinus, the most westerly Greek colony in Sicily, was founded about 650 B.C. on a hill near the sea, and later extended on to the plateau to the north. A sacred precinct was established on the hill to the east during the 6th c. B.C. In 409 B.C. the flourishing city was conquered and destroyed by the Carthaginians, and a new fortified town built on the western hill from 407 onwards was in turn destroyed by them in 250 B.C., during the first Punic War.

History

The importance of the ancient city is attested by the extent and scale of the ruins, in particular the massive remains of eight Doric temples (6th–5th c. B.C.), which probably collapsed as a result of earthquakes between the 5th and 8th c. B.C. and were then gradually covered with blown sand. Since 1925 restoration and further excavation has been carried on steadily: two temples have been re-erected, and others are to follow.

*Sites

On the western hill are the remains of the Acropolis (450 m/495 yd long and up to 350 m/385 yd across), formerly surrounded by walls and traversed by two principal streets, one running north-south, the other east-west. In the south-east section are the remains of the small Temple A and the foundations of the very similar Temple O. Immediately north on the east-west street is the tiny Temple B, of which no columns remain erect, and to the north of this, on top of the hill, is Temple C (columns re-erected in 1925 and 1929), the oldest on the Acropolis and together with Temple E the most striking features of the site. Farther north again is the rather later Temple D.

* Acropolis

On the northern edge of the Acropolis are the excavated remains of the Greek defensive walls (restored in 407 B.C.), an excellent example of the highly developed Greek art of fortification. Beyond this point, on the Manuiza plateau to the north of the Acropolis, extends the town proper, of which only a few remains have been preserved.

Defensive walls

Following the east-west street westward from the Acropolis, we cross the River Modione, at the mouth of which the west harbour was situated, and come to the hill of Manicalunga. On the slopes of this hill, in the sacred precinct, lie the remains of the Temple of Demeter, dedicated to Demeter Malophoros (the "Fruit-Bringer"). At the north corner of the precinct is the little shrine of Zeus Meilichios ("the Forgiving").

Temple of Demeter

To the west of the Temple of Demeter is a necropolis extending for some 2 km/1¼ miles.

Necropolis

From the Acropolis a road 1.5 km/1 mile long runs east over the Gorgo di Cotone to the eastern hill, with the remains of three large temples which even in their present state of ruin are overwhelmingly impressive. To the south is Temple E, dedicated to Hera, which was re-erected in 1959, with 38 columns. To the north are Temple F and Temple G (113 m/123½ yd long), probably dedicated to Apollo, which, with the Temple of Zeus at Agrigento and the Artemision at Ephesus, ranks as the largest of all Greek temples.

* Temple E

443

Temple C in Selinunte, Sicily

Sicily

Region: Sicilia
Provinces: Agrigento (AG), Caltanissetta (CL), Catania (CT), Enna (EN), Messina (ME), Palermo (PA), Ragusa (RG), Siracusa (SR) and Trapani (TR)
Area: 25,708 sq. km/9923 sq. miles
Population: 5,051,400

Boat services	Regular services (carrying cars) from Reggio Calabria and Villa S. Giovanni to Messina, from Genoa and Livorno to Palermo, from Naples to Palermo and Catania resp. Syracuse.
Air services	Sicily's International Airport is close by Catania; airports for internal flights are near Palermo and Comiso and about 12 km/7½ miles south of Trapani.
Situation	Sicily, the largest Italian island, lies south-west of the Italian peninsula in the Mediterranean. It is an autonomous region with its capital at Palermo.
Scenery	Sicily is an almost entirely mountainous island, bearing the marks of vigorous volcanic activity. Its most notable landmark is the massive snow-covered cone of Etna (3343 m/11,032 ft), Europe's largest active volcano, which rises above the east coast, visible from afar.
Population	The main concentration of population, including most of the large towns, are on the fertile and well-watered coastal plains.
Agriculture	Sicily's productive and rapidly developing agriculture gives it a leading place among the farming regions of Italy. Intensive vegetable growing

Etna, the symbol of Sicily

(tomatoes, cucumbers, early potatoes, etc.), fruit orchards (citrus fruits, almonds, olives) and wine production, particularly at the western tip of the island around Marsala, predominate in the fertile coastal areas; the dry and hilly interior is suitable only for extensive arable cultivation (wheat alternating with beans) and some pastoral farming (sheep, goats). The traditional feudal system and the often inefficient working of the land by small tenant farmers, which is its legacy, stand in the way of the more rapid development which the potential of the land would permit.

Significant contributions to the economy are also made by the coastal fisheries (tuna, anchovies, cuttlefish, swordfish) and the extraction of salt in the Trapani area.

Fishing

Sicily has little industry. The only industrial activities of any consequence are petro-chemical (around Syracuse and Gela), the mining of potash, which has superseded the once considerable sulphur-workings, and the working of asphalt (around Ragusa) and marble. In recent years, however, there has been a significant development of industry which has helped to reduce the drift of population to the highly industrialised states of northern Europe.

Industry

Sicily's magnificent scenery and its beautiful beaches, particularly on the north and east coast, its great range of ancient remains, including the best preserved Greek temples to be found anywhere, and the very remarkable art and architecture of its Norman rulers, have long made the island one of the great Meccas of travellers and tourists. In recent times tourism has become an important factor of the economy. There are several club villages and holiday complexes on the island, among which is Città del Mare, some 40 km/25 miles west of Palermo.

Tourism

Circuit of Sicily (about 930 km/577 miles)

The first part of the circuit, from Messina to Palermo, is partly on the A 20 motorway and partly on S.S. 113 (the "Settentrionale Sicula"), following the coast of the Tyrrhenian Sea through scenery of great beauty and variety.

The road runs north-west from Messina through garden suburbs, crosses the Colle San Rizzo pass (465 m/1533 ft; motorway tunnel) in the wooded Monti Peloritani (1374 m/4534 ft) and descends to the sea.

Milazzo | 37 km/23 miles: Milazzo/Isole Eolie motorway exit. 6 km/3¾ miles north is Milazzo (30 m/100 ft; pop. 31,000), with good beaches and boat services to the Lipari Islands. The town, founded by the Greeks in 716 B.C., has a Norman castle. 7 km/4¼ miles farther north we come to the Capo di Milazzo.

Castroreale Terme | 12 km/7 miles along S.S. 113 lies the spa (sulphureous water) of Castroreale Terme.

Excursion:

Novara di Sicilia
Francavilla di Sicilia | The S.S. 185 goes off on the left 3 km/2 miles farther on and follows a winding course to the little town of Novara di Sicilia (675 m/2228 ft), 20 km/12 miles inland; then over the Portella Mandrazzi (1125 m/3713 ft) to the ridge of the Monti Peloritani; on, with a magnificent view of Etna, to Francavilla di Sicilia (675 m/2228 ft); and from here another 22 km/14 miles, passing close to the Gola dell'Alcantara, to Giardini, below Taormina.

Excursion:

Tyndaris | Farther along S.S. 113, 12 km/7 miles beyond the exit for Milazzo, a road branches off on the right, passes the monastery of the Madonna del Tindari, traverses the village of Tindari and comes in 2 km/1¼ miles to the remains of Tyndaris, the last Greek colony in Sicily, founded by

Milazzo, on the north-east coast of Sicily

Dionysius I in 396 B.C. and probably destroyed by the Saracens. Here can be seen remains of the town walls, a theatre, a Roman basilica and mosaic floors, including the notable Museum, the "Antiquarium".

29 km/18 miles beyond Milazzo/Isole Eolie on the motorway is the exit for Patti (157 m/518 ft; pop. 13,000), with large monasteries and a cathedral which occupies the site of an earlier castle and contains the tomb of Adelasia of Montferrat (d. 1118), wife of King Roger I of Sicily. 9 km/5½ miles: tunnel through the precipitous Capo Calavà, and beyond this a fine view of the fertile coastal area, with Capo d'Orlando (93 m/307 ft) reaching far out to sea.
24 km/15 miles: exit for Capo d'Orlando (12 m/40 ft; pop. 11,000), a little town which is also a seaside resort.

Patti

Capo Calavà

Capo d'Orlando

Excursion:
From Capo d'Orlando S.S. 116 runs south via Naso (497 m/1640 ft) and over the Portella dello Zoppo (1264 m/4171 ft), a pass on the ridge of the Monti Nebrodi (1847 m/6095 ft), to Randazzo (764 m/2521 ft; pop. 12,000), which, with its old houses built of dark-coloured lava blocks, still preserves much of its medieval character.
At the east end of the main street, Via Umberto I, stands the church of Santa Maria (1217–39), with columns which are hewn from black lava. From here the picturesque Via degli Archi runs west to the church of San Nicolò (originally Norman, remodelled in the 16th c., badly damaged during the Second World War), which contains a statue of St Nicholas by Antonio Gagini (1523). Beyond the church, to the northwest, is the Palazzo Finocchiaro (1509), with a fine façade. At the west end of Via Umberto I the church of San Martino, has a 14th c. campanile and a rich treasury; nearly opposite is a tower of the old ducal palace.

Randazzo

From Capo d'Orlando we continue on S.S. 113 over the fertile coastal plain, the Piana del Capo, and then through the Bosco di Caronia, the largest forest in Sicily (mainly scrub).

Excursion:
49 km/30 miles: S.S. 117 branches off and runs south via Mistretta (900 m/2970 ft; pop. 7000) and over the Portella del Contrasto (1107 m/3653 ft), a pass on the ridge of the Monti Nebrodi, to Nicosia (46 km/29 miles; alt. 720 m/2376 ft; pop. 16,000), with the 14th c. cathedral of San Nicolà, the 18th c. church of Santa Maria Maggiore (marble reredos 8 m/26 ft high by Antonio Gagini, 1512) and a castle.

Nicosia

Beyond the mentioned junction the coast road skirts the foot of the Madonie hills (Pizzo Carbonaro, 1979 m/65311 ft).
37 km/3 miles: Cefalù.
Beyond Cefalù we take the motorway.

Cefalù

15 km/9 miles: junction with the A 19 motorway to Enna and Catania. 2 km/1¼ miles south on A 19 is the Buonfornello exit, from which we continue on S.S. 113. A short distance along this, on the right, are the remains of the Greek city of Himera, founded in 648 B.C. and destroyed by the Carthaginians in 409 B.C. (Doric temple of c. 480 B.C.; temple of 6th c. B.C.; Antiquarium). The Targo Florio car race (72 km/45 miles) is held at Buonfornello annually in May.
13 km/8 miles: exit for Termini Imerese (77 m/254 ft; pop. 26,000), finely situated on a promontory. In the lower town is the spa establishment (warm radioactive saline springs, 42° C/108° F), in the upper town the cathedral and the Belvedere park. The Museo Civico contains archaeological finds of several periods.
10 km/6 miles south, on a rocky crag above the Fiume San Leonardo, perches the little town of Caccamo (521 m/1719 ft; pop. 9000), with a

Himera

Termini Imerese

Caccamo

	well-preserved 12th c. castle, containing the notable "Room of Conspiracy".
Trabia	4 km/2½ miles: exit for Trabia (pop. 6000), on the coast, with a battlemented castle.
Casteldaccia	16 km/10 miles: exit for Casteldaccia.

Excursion:

Santa Flavia	From Casteldaccia we continue on the coast road to Santa Flavia, where a road goes off on the right via Porticello and Sant'Elia to Capo Zafferano (14 km/9 miles: 225 m/743 ft; lighthouse). From this road a
Soluntum	side road (1.5 km/1 mile) winds steeply up to the remains of Soluntum (or Solus; Italian Solunto), a Phoenician settlement and later a Roman town, situated on the south-east slopes of Monte Catalfano (376 m/1241 ft). Particularly notable is the re-erected part of a peristyle belonging to a building known as the Gymnasium, the remains of a theatre and the Antiquarium. From the top of the hill there are magnificent views westward of Palermo Bay and eastward, on clear days as far as Etna.

Bagheria	3 km/2 miles beyond Trabia on the motorway take the exit for Bagheria (80 m/264 ft; pop. 42,000), notable for its numerous Baroque villas (18th c.). At the end of the Corso Butera, the town's main street, is the Villa Butera (1658; "Certosa", with wax figures in Carthusian habits). A little way east the Villa Palagonia (1715) has an extraordinary collection of grotesque sculptured figures. Still farther east stands the Villa Valguarnera (1721; view from the terrace and from the nearby hill of Montagnola).
Palermo	12 km/7 miles: exit for Palermo.

	The next part of the circuit, from Palermo to Trapani, can be done either direct on the A 29 and A 29d motorways or on the coast road (S.S. 187), passing through the little port of Castellammare del Golfo and Erice. Longer, but well worth the extra distance, is the route via S.S. 186 and S.S. 113. For this route leave Palermo by the Porta Nuova and the Corso Calatafimi.
Monreale	8 km/5 miles: Monreale (300 m/990 ft; pop. 25,000), the see of an archbishop, beautifully situated above the Conca d'Oro.
* Cathedral	On the left-hand side of the main street is the cathedral with its two towers, the finest example of Norman architecture in Sicily. 102 m/112 yd long by 40 m/44 yd wide, in the form of a basilica, it boasts a beautiful choir with interlaced pointed arches of dark grey lava which preserves the structure of a Byzantine church. The main doorway has a fine bronze door by Bonanno Pisano, with reliefs from scriptural history and inscriptions in early Italian (1186). The left-hand doorway, below a porch of 1569, has a bronze door by Barisanus of Trani (1179). In the interior are eighteen ancient columns with fine capitals, and its walls
* Mosaics	are covered with magnificent mosaics, completed in 1882, which cover an area of 6340 sq. m (the largest area of mosaics in Sicily), with scenes from the Old Testament and the life of Christ and the Apostles. In the south transept are the sarcophagi of William I and II, son and grandson of Roger II. In the south aisle is the 16th c. Cappella di San Benedetto (marble reliefs), in the north aisle the Cappella del Crocifisso (1690), with fine wood-carvings of the Passion on the side doors. It is well worthwhile making the ascent to the roof of the cathedral for the view it affords.
* Cloister	To the right of the cathedral stands the former Benedictine monastery. Of the original building nothing is left but the cloister (Chiostro di Santa Maria Nuova), the largest and finest in the Italian Romanesque style, with 216 columns. The cloister is overshadowed on the south side by a ruined wall of the original monastery.

Monreale: panorama

Mosaics in the cathedral

Cloister of the former monastery

Sicily

Partinico

21 km/13 miles beyond Monreale on S.S. 186 lies Partinico (175 m/578 ft; pop. 25,000), dominated by an ancient tower. From here we continue on S.S. 113.

Alcamo

20 km/12 miles: Alcamo (56 m/185 ft; pop. 45,000), a town founded by the Arabs. In the main street is the 17th c. cathedral, with a 14th c. campanile. Inside can be seen paintings by Borreman (1736–37) and sculpture by Antonio Gagini and his pupils. In the churches of Santa Chiara and the Badia Nuova are stucco figures by Giacomo Serpotta. There is also a 14th c. castle. Above the town rises Monte Bonifato (825 m/2723 ft; view); the climb takes two hours.

Segesta
*Temple

15 km/9 miles: road to the remains (about 3 km/2 miles west) of the ancient city of Segesta or Egesta (318 m/1049 ft), one of the oldest towns in Sicily, founded by the Elymians in pre-Greek times. It was almost incessantly at war with its Greek neighbours; later it became Carthaginian and then Roman, and was finally destroyed by the Saracens. From the end of the access road a stepped path leads up to the temple, standing in majestic solitude on a levelled ridge of hill below the west side of the ancient city. Begun in 430 B.C. but left unfinished, it is one of the best preserved temples in Sicily (61 m/67 yd long by 26 m/28½ yd across), with 36 Doric columns still supporting the entablature and gable.

From the end of the access road a track winds up to the site of the ancient city, situated 1.5 km/1 mile south-east on Monte Barbaro (415 m/1370 ft), with remains of fortifications, houses (mosaic pavements) and a theatre hewn from the rock (3rd–2nd c. B.C.).

Calatafimi

3 km/2 miles beyond the turning for Segesta is Calatafimi (350 m/1155 ft; pop. 8000), with a castle on a hill to the west of the town.

Excursion:
1 km/¾ mile: minor road (3 km/2 miles south-west) to the Ossario, a

Temple in Segesta

conspicuous monument to Garibaldi erected in 1892 to commemorate his first victory over numerically superior Bourbon forces on May 15th 1860.

1 km/¾ mile: the road forks. S.S. 113, to the right, leads to Trapani (35 km/22 miles); S.S. 188A, to the left, runs via Salemi (10 km/6 miles; 442 m/1459 ft; pop. 13,000), with a castle built in the time of Frederick II in which Garibaldi proclaimed his dictatorship of Sicily in 1860 (commemorative column), to Castelvetrano (another 26 km/16 miles).

The third part of the circuit of Sicily, from Trapani to Syracuse, is on S.S. 115.

32 km/20 miles: Marsala.

19 km/12 miles: Mazara del Vallo (8 m/26 ft; pop. 46,000), with an 11th c. cathedral (remodelled in the 17th and 20th c.) founded by Count Roger and the 17th c. Norman-style church of San Nicolò Regale.

15 km/9 miles: Campobello di Mazara (110 m/363 ft; pop. 12,000). 3 km/2 miles south-west are the ancient quarries known as the Rocche di Cusa or Cave di Campobello which supplied the building material for Selinus or Selinunte (closed 409 B.C.).

8 km/5 miles: Castelvetrano (190 m/627 ft; pop. 32,000), with the churches of San Giovanni (statue of John the Baptist by Antonio Gagini (1512) in the choir); San Domenico (stucco figures by Antonio Ferraro, 1574–80 and marble Madonna by Domenico Gagini); and the 16th c. Chiesa Madre (Renaissance doorway).

3.5 km/2¼ miles west of the town is the restored Norman church of the Santissima Trinità della Delia (12th c.), in Byzantine style on a centralised plan.

9 km/5½ miles: road on right to the ruins of Selinunte.

37 km/23 miles: Sciacca or Sciacca Terme (60 m/198 ft; pop. 38,000), with the spa and holiday centre of Sciaccamare.

At the west entrance to the town is the Porta San Salvatore. Just beyond it, to the right, stands the church of Santa Margherita (1342, remodelled in the 16th c.), the northern doorway of which is in marble (1486), and to the left the Chiesa del Carmine. North-east of the Porta San Salvatore, in Corso Vittorio Emanuele, is the Gothic Casa Steripinto, with a façade of faceted stones. Nearby is the cathedral, with a Madonna by Francesco Laurana (1467, in the fourth chapel on right). Farther east are the Giardino Comunale (view) and the Terme Selinuntine, the spa establishment (sulphur baths), on the site of the ancient baths. Higher up, on the line of the town walls, are the remains of the castle of Count Luna (1380).

Excursion:

7 km/4¼ miles: road on left into the picturesque valley of Cava d'Ispica, the rock walls of which contain numerous caves used as dwellings and tombs in the Byzantine period.

32 km/20 miles: Noto (158 m/521 ft; pop. 24,000), a small town, laid out in terraces. It was built from 1703 onwards to replace the older town, 11 km/7 miles south-east, which was destroyed by an earthquake in 1693. On the town's main street, the Corso Vittorio Emanuele, which traverses it from west to east, are three monumental squares. In the first of these, the Piazza Ercole (officially the Piazza XVI Maggio), are the Baroque church of San Domenico (18th c.) and an ancient statue of Hercules. In the second, the Piazza del Municipio, stand the cathedral, with an imposing Baroque façade, the Palazzo Ducezio (Town Hall) and the church of San Salvatore. In the third, the Piazza Immacolata, we find the church of the Immacolata (or San Francesco) and the monastery of San Salvatore. To the north is the Chiesa del Crocifisso, with a Madonna by Francesco Laurana (1471).

Sicily

Avola	9 km/5½ miles beyond Noto, on S.S. 115, is Avola (40 m/132 ft; pop. 31,000). The road then crosses the River Cassibile, the ancient Kakyparis, where Demosthenes and his 6000 Athenians were compelled to surrender to the Syracusans in 413 B.C. Upstream, in the rock faces of the Cave Grande, is a Siculan necropolis.
Syracuse	23 km/14 miles: Syracuse.

The last part of the circuit of Sicily, from Syracuse to Messina, is on S.S. 114 (the "Orientale Sicula"; from Catania also the A 18 motorway), running close to the sea for most of the way.

Lentini	14 km/9 miles from Syracuse the road forks. Straight ahead is the old and more interesting road via Lentini (53 m/175 ft; pop. 31,000); to the right the new road, S.S. 114, is 8 km/5 miles shorter and much faster.
Augusta	S.S. 114 passes large oil refineries and comes in 7 km/4¼ miles to the turning for Augusta, the principal Italian naval base in Sicily (14 m/46 ft; pop. 40,000).
Catania	63 km/39 miles: Catania.
Aci Castello	9 km/5½ miles beyond Catania on S.S. 114 lies the little town of Aci Castello, dominated by a picturesque ruined castle on a high crag (15 m/50 ft; pop. 15,000).
Scogli de'Ciclopi	Just beyond the town can be seen the seven Scogli de' Ciclopi (Cyclops' Islands) or Faraglioni, traditionally the rocks which the blinded Cyclops hurled after Odysseus' ship ("Odyssey"). On the largest of the islands, the Isola d'Aci, is a marine biological station.
Acireale	7 km/4¼ miles: Acireale (Sicilian Iaci; 161 m/531 ft; pop. 50,000). On the near side of the town to the right of the road, are the Terme di Santa Venera (warm radioactive water containing iodine, sulphur and salt). Here begins the town's main street, the Corso Vittorio Emanuele, with the church of San Sebastiano (Baroque façade) on the right, beyond

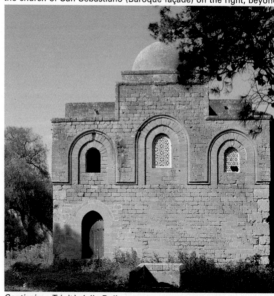

Santissima Trinità della Delia

this, in the Piazza del Duomo, are the cathedral, the Town Hall and the church of Santi Pietro e Paolo. From the municipal park at the north end of the town there are fine views.

18 km/11 miles: Mascali, a little town which formerly lay farther west but was destroyed by lava in 1928 and rebuilt on its present site.

Mascali

15 km/9 miles: Taormina.

Taormina

48 km/30 miles: Messina.

Messina

Excursion:

From the Porta San Salvatore a road runs 7.5 km/4½ miles north-east to the limestone hill of Monte San Calogero (388 m/1280 ft), with the Santuario San Calogero on its summit (monastery; view). Below the monastery are caves with vapour baths (Le Stufe: temperature 34–40° C/93–104° F).

Monte San Calogero

Excursion:

20 km/12 miles north-east of Sciacca is the little town of Caltabellotta (839 m/2802 ft; pop. 5500), dominated by its castle, which has a cathedral dating from the Norman period.

Caltabellotta

Excursion:

23 km/14 miles farther along S.S. 115 a road goes off on the right to the remains (6 km/3¾ miles south-west on Capo Bianco) of the ancient city of Eraclea Minoa, destroyed in the 1st c. B.C. Notable features are a theatre (3rd c. B.C.) and the remains of the town walls.

Eraclea Minoa

41 km/25 miles: Porto Empedocle, the port of Agrigento.

Porto Empedocle

6 km/3¾ miles: road on left to Agrigento, running between the temples of Zeus and Hera and then winding its way up to the town.

Agrigento

32 km/20 miles: Palma di Montechiaro (165 m/545 ft; pop. 22,000), with a fine Baroque church. On the hill beyond it, to the right, is the 14th c. Castello di Montechiaro (286 m/944 ft).

Palma di Montechiaro

20 km/12 miles: Licata (12 m/40 ft; pop. 42,000), beautifully situated on the sloping hillside at the mouth of the river Salso, an expanding port which is the principal commercial town on the south coast of Sicily (export of sulphur). The Museo Civico contains numerous archaeological finds, particularly from graves. Farther up, to the west, is the 16th c. Castel San Angelo (restored).

Licata

11 km/7 mile: on the coast, to the right, is the 15th c. Castello di Falconara (restored).

Falconara

22 km/14 miles: Gela (45 m/149 ft; pop. 77,000), a port which was formerly called Terranova di Sicilia (oil refineries), also frequented as a seaside resort.

Gela

To the west of the town are the extensive cemeteries of the ancient city, founded by Dorian settlers in 689 B.C., and the Zona Archeologica di Capo Soprano, with the imposing remains of Greek defensive walls of the 5th–4th c. B.C. (200 m/220 yd long, built of regular stone blocks in the lower part and sun-dried bricks in the upper part, the earliest known use of such bricks) and Greek baths of the 4th c. B.C. At the east end of the town is the Museo Regionale Archeologico; adjoining are the most recent excavations (houses and shops of the 4th c. B.C.). South of the museum, on the Molino e Vento (Windmill) hill, the Acropolis, is the municipal park, with the remains of two Doric temples (6th and 5th c. B.C.).

33 km/20 miles beyond Gela on S.S. 115 is Vittoria (168 m/554 ft; pop. 53,000), the principal centre of the Sicilian wine trade. In the main square are the neo-classical Teatro Vittorio Emanuele and the church of the Madonna delle Grazie (18th c.).

Vittoria

8 km/5 miles: Comiso (209 m/690 ft; pop. 29,000), with two 18th c. domed churches, the Chiesa Madre and the Chiesa della Santissima

Comiso

Annunziata, a 14th c. castle and a beautiful Fountain of Diana in the Piazza Municipio.

Ragusa 17 km/11 miles: Ragusa (562 m/1855 ft; pop. 67,000), a provincial capital, picturesquely situated above the gorge of the River Irminio, with a Baroque cathedral (18th c.) and the splendid Baroque church of San Giorgio (18th c.) in the old part of the town, Ibla, to the east (steep winding streets). The Museo Archeologico Ibleo contains finds of the surroundings of Ragusa.

From the bypass to the south of the town there are fine views. Around the town are deposits of bituminous limestone, large asphalt pits. In recent years oil has been worked here.

Modica 15 km/9 miles beyond Ragusa, on S.S. 115, is Modica (296 m/977 ft; pop. 50,000), a flourishing town rising up the slopes on both sides of the Modica valley. In the lower town, at the top of a flight of steps, is the church of San Pietro (18th c.); the massive church of San Giorgio (18th c.) stands in the upper town.

Siena H6

Region: Toscana
Province: Siena (SI)
Altitude: 322 m/1063 ft
Population: 64,000

Situation The provincial capital of Siena lies 70 km/43 miles east of Florence in the Tuscan hills. From this area comes the brown pigment known as burnt sienna.

**Architecture The town has a university, as well as a language school for foreigners, and is the see of an archbishop. It is one of the great art centres, with a profusion of fine architecture and numerous churches and palaces.

Tip The town centre is closed to cars, but access to the hotels is permitted.

History In Roman times Saena Iulia was a place of no importance, but under the Franks it became the residence of a count. After the death of Countess Matilda of Tuscany in 1115 the town asserted its independence. Thereafter it was governed by the Ghibelline nobility, and this brought it into sharp conflict with Florence, a stronghold of the Guelfs. The two towns were constantly at war. After the fall of the Hohenstaufens (1270) Charles of Anjou succeeded in establishing his influence in Siena and incorporated it in the Guelf federation of Tuscan towns. In 1348 the town was ravaged by the plague. After a period of internal strife Siena was governed by tyrants, among them Pandolfo Petrucci (1487 onwards). In 1555 Siena was occupied by the Spaniards, and in 1559 it was ceded to Duke Cosimo I of Tuscany.

Art The heyday of Sienese art was in the 13th and 14th c. The cathedral and many of the palaces are magnificent examples of Gothic architecture. The availability of good brickmaking clay in the area favoured the use of brick in building. The delicate, graceful Sienese painting of the 13th and 14th c. (Duccio, Simone Martini, Ambrogio and Pietro Lorenzetti) surpassed the early painting of Florence. Jacopo della Quercia (1374–1438) was one of the founders of Renaissance sculpture, and his influence can still be detected in the work of Michelangelo.

**Piazza del Campo

In the centre of Siena a spacious semicircular area, the Piazza del Campo extends in front of the massive Town Hall, the uniform architec-

Siena: Piazza del Campo with the Palazzo Pubblico

ture making it one of the finest squares in Italy. The "Palio delle Contrade" is held on July 2nd and August 16th. The Palio is a picturesque procession in medieval costumes and a horse-race; the price for the winners being a banner (Latin pallium) bearing the image of the Madonna.

On the north side of the square stands a copy of the marble fountain, the Fonte Gaia, a masterpiece by Jacopo della Quercia, the original of which can be seen in the Museo Civico.

Fonte Gaia

Along the south side of the Campo extends the Palazzo Pubblico, a huge Gothic building of travertine and brick (1297–1310); the top floor of the lower side wing was added in 1680. At its side is the Torre del Mangia, built 1338–48 (102 m/337 ft high; 412 steps), from the top of which there are fine views. Below this is the Cappella di Piazza, a loggia built after the great plague of 1348, with a Renaissance upper storey added in 1468.

Palazzo Pubblico

The interior of the Palazzo Pubblico is notable for the numerous frescoes of the Sienese school which reflect the views and attitudes of the proud citizens of Siena in the 14th and 15th c.; particularly interesting is the painting by Ambrogio Lorenzetti in the Sala della Pace, "Good and Bad Government" (1337–43), with a contemporary view of the city.

On the first and second floors the Museo Civico houses drawings, paintings and other documents of the history of the town.

Museo Civico

On the third floor is a loggia in which the original sculpture from the Fonte Gaia has been assembled.

Buildings in the vicinity of the Croce del Travaglio

From the north-west side of the Campo, steps lead up to the Loggia della Mercanzia (1428–44), the old commercial tribunal, near the so-

Loggia della Mercanzia

455

called Croce del Travaglio ("Cross of Work"). There the three principal streets of the town meet: to the north the Banchi di Sopra, to the east the Banchi di Sotto and to the south-west the Via di Città.

Palazzo Chigi-Saracini

In Via di Città stands the Palazzo Chigi-Saracini (14th c.), now occupied by the Accademia Musicale Chigiana (Music Academy; concerts). The building also contains pictures by Botticelli, Pinturicchio, Sodoma and Spinello Aretina (visit by appointment).

*Palazzo Piccolomini

In Banchi di Sotto is the University and opposite it, on the right, the Palazzo Piccolomini, one of the finest Early Renaissance palaces in Siena, built for Nanni Piccolomini, father of Pope Pius II after 1469 and now the repository of the extensive State Archives.

Logge del Papa

Situated in the nearby Piazza Piccolomini, the elegant Logge del Papa was built for Pius II in 1462.

*Baptistery of San Giovanni

From Via di Città the Via dei Pellegrini runs west past the Palazzo del Magnificio (1508), on the left, to the little Piazza San Giovanni, on the south-west side of which is the choir of the cathedral, which occupies the highest point in the town. Beneath the cathedral is the Baptistery of San Giovanni, with a beautiful but unfinished Gothic façade of 1382. The interior contains a fine font by Jacopo della Quercia (1427–30), with bronze reliefs by Donatello and other artists.

Palazzo Arcivescovile

From the Piazza San Giovanni we go to the Archbishop's Palace (Palazzo Arcivescovile), which contains the famous "Madonna del Latte" ("Nursing Madonna"), a panel ascribed to Ambrogio Lorenzetti.

Cathedral and Piazza del Campo

Siena Cathedral
Santa Maria Assunta

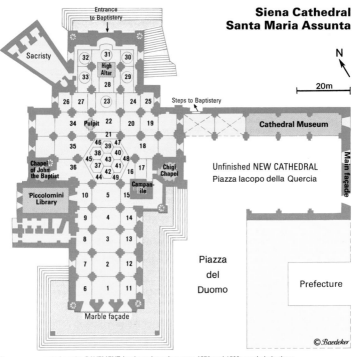

Scenes represented on the PAVEMENT (various dates between 1372 and 1562: partly imitations
and copies – originals in Cathedral Museum)

1 Hermes Trismegistus
2 Coats of arms of Siena (centre), Pisa, Lucca, Florence, Arezzo, Orvieto, Rome, Perugia, Viterbo, Massa, Grosseto, Volterra and Pistoia
3 Imperial Altar
4 Fortune
5 Wheel of Fortune; for philosophers
6–15 Sibyls
16 Seven Ages of Man

17 Faith, Hope, Charity, Religion
18 Jephthah defeats the Ammonites
19 Death of Absalom
20 Emperor Sigismund
21 Moses draws water from the rock
22 Dance round the Golden Calf
23 David and Goliath
24 Moses
25 Samson defeats the Philistines

26, 27 Joshua
28 Abraham's Sacrifice
29 Wisdom
30 Moderation
31 Compassion
32 Justice
33 Strength
34 Judith and Holofernes
35 Massacre of the Innocents
36 Fall of Herod
37–49 Ahab and Elijah

**Cathedral

From the Archbishop's Palace it is only a few steps to the Piazza del
Duomo, which lies on the highest point of the town. Here stands the
cathedral of Santa Maria Assunta. It was begun in the mid 12th c., and
by 1264 it had been completed as far as the dome; then about 1317 the
choir was extended eastwards over the baptistery. In 1339 the citizens
of Siena resolved to carry out a large-scale rebuilding which would
have made the cathedral the largest and finest in Italy; but this project
was abandoned as a result of structural defects and the great plague in

Siena

	1348. The present cathedral has a total length of 89 m/97 yd and a width of 24 m/26½ yd (across the transepts 54 m/59½ yd).
*Façade	The façade, in red, black and white marble, was not completed until 1380; the rich sculptural decoration consists largely of reproductions dating from 1869, and the mosaics were added in 1877. The campanile dates from the late 13th c.
Interior	The interior, with its regularly alternating courses of black and white marble, at first produces a rather strange effect.
* *Pavement	A unique feature is the marble pavement, with its beautiful graffito figures and scenes, mostly from the Old Testament, carried out to designs of famous artists. (Some of them are copies; originals in the Cathedral Museum).
	Along the cornice in the nave are numerous terracotta busts of Popes (15th c.).
	In the north aisle is a masterpiece of decorative sculpture, the entrance wall of the Cathedral Library by Marrina, a fine sculptor of the Sienese High Renaissance.
Cappella di San Giovanni Battista	In the north transept, decorated with frescoes by Pinturicchio, the Cappella di San Giovanni Battista has a beautiful doorway by this artist and a bronze statue of John the Baptist by Donatello (1457).
*Pulpit	A particularly notable feature is the white marble pulpit, with fine reliefs of New Testament scenes by Nicola Pisano (1266–68).
*Piccolomini Library	From the north aisle we enter the famous Cathedral Library (Libreria Piccolomini), one of the finest and best preserved creations of the Early Renaissance. It was built in 1492 for Cardinal Francesco Piccolomini (later Pope Pius III) in honour of his kinsman Aeneas Sylvius Piccolomini (Pope Pius II, 1458–64) and decorated by Pinturicchio and his pupils with brilantly coloured frescoes depicting scenes from the life of Aeneas Sylvius (1502–09).
Cathedral Museum	Opposite the south-east side of the cathedral, three long buildings belonging to the New Cathedral, house the Cathedral Museum (Museo dell'Opera Metropolitana), with material illustrating the constructional history of the cathedral, pictures by Sienese masters, including Duccio di Buonisegna's "Maestà", a picture of a Madonna enthroned with angels and saints painted in 1308–11 for the high altar of the cathedral, the "Birth of the Virgin", a wooden "Crucifixion" and embroidered vestments (14th–18th c.).
Santa Maria della Scala	Opposite the façade of the cathedral are the church and hospital of Santa Maria della Scala (13th–14th c.), with frescoes depicting the work of the hospital in the 15th c.

*Pinacoteca Nazionale

Palazzo Buonsignori	From the Piazza del Duomo the Via del Capitano runs south-east past the Prefecture, the former Palazzo Reale (on the left), and the Palazzo del Capitano del Popolo (on the right) to the little Piazza di Postierla, from which Via di San Pietro leads to the Palazzo Buonsignori, a 14th c. brick building now housing the Pinacoteca Nazionale, with an important and representative collection of works of the Sienese school from the 12th to the 16th c. Represented in the gallery are works by Guido da Siena, Duccio di Buonisegna, Ambrogio Lorenzetti, Pietro Lorenzetti, Giovanni de Paolo, Pinturicchio and the Lombard artist Giovanni Antonio Bazzi, surnamed Il Sodoma.
Sant'Agostino	Via San Pietro ends in the Prato Sant'Agostino, in which is the church of Sant'Agostino.

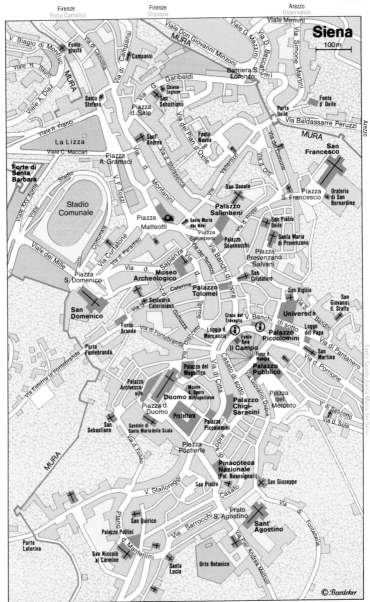

Siena

Sights in the north-east

Palaces

In Via Banchi di Sopra, going north from the Loggia di Mercanzia, stands the Early Gothic Palazzo Tolomei (on the left). Beyond this, in Piazza Salimbeni, are the battlemented Palazzo Salimbeni and, on the south side, the Palazzo Spannocchi, a fine Early Renaissance building by the Florentine Giuliano da Maiano (begun 1470).

San Francesco

To the east, on the edge of the town, is the church of San Francesco (1326–1475), founded by the Franciscans, with a façade of 1913. In the north transept is a fine fresco by Pietro Lorenzetti ("Crucifixion"; *c.* 1330).

Oratorio di San
Bernardino

Adjoining the church of San Francesco is an Oratory built in the 15th c. on the spot where the Franciscan St Bernard of Siena used to preach. The upper floor of the little church has particularly fine frescoes by Sodoma and Early Renaissance ceiling decoration.

Museo Archeologico

North-west of the Palazzo Tolomei is situated the Museo Archeologico Nazionale (National Archaeological Museum). The collections consist of finds, mainly from the surroundings of the town, particularly of the Etruscan period, including urns, bronze work and a remarkable variety of coins.

San Domenico

On the west side of the town is the fortress-like church of San Domenico, a rough brick structure in the Gothic style (1226–1465) with a crenellated campanile. In the north-west wall of the nave is the entrance to the domed chapel containing the oldest picture of St Catherine of Siena (1347–1380), a fresco painted by Andrea Vanni (*c.* 1400).

Fonte Branda

Below the hill of San Domenico the Fonte Branda, a fountain which is mentioned in the records as early as 1081, has a colonnade of three arches built over it in 1246.

Santuario Cateriniano

A little way east of the fountain, in Via Santa Caterina, is the Sanctuary of St Catherine. St Catherine of Siena (1347–80), the daughter of a dyer named Benincasa, prevailed on Pope Gregory XI to return from Avignon to Rome in 1377. The best known of her visions was her "mystic marriage" to the Infant Christ, a favourite theme with painters. The fine Renaissance doorway has the Latin inscription "Sponsae Kristi Catherinae Domus" ("House of Catherine, Bride of Christ").

Forte di Santa Barbara

From San Domenico we can go either north-west along the Viale dei Mille, past the Stadium, or north round the Stadium to a beautiful park, the Passeggio della Lizza, with a monument to Garibaldi (1896). At the west end of the park is the entrance to the Forte di Santa Barbara, a fortress built by Duke Cosimo I in 1560, which is now used for open-air performances. In the cellar of the first bastion (on the left) is the Enoteca Italica, a permanent wine exhibition.

Fontegiusta

A short distance north of the Lizza park is the little church of Fontegiusta (1484), with a high altar by Marrina, one of the finest examples of High Renaissance work of its kind (1519).

Santa Maria dei Servi

In the south-east of the old town is the church of Santa Maria dei Servi (13th–15th c.), with a fine campanile. The interior contains several pictures by artists of the Sienese school, including the famous fresco "Child Murder at Bethlehem" (c. 1330) by Pietro Lorenzetti.
A little way south is the Porta Romana in the town wall, a massive town gate of 1327.

Porta Romana

Colle di Val d'Elsa

North-west of Siena on S.S. 2 is Colle di Val d'Elsa (pop. 16,000), situated above the River Elsa. The little town consists of an industrial lower town, Colle Basso (137 m/452 ft), and the old upper town or Colle Alta (223 m/736 ft), with medieval palaces and a 17th c. cathedral.

Situation
23 km/14 miles
north-west of Siena

From Colle di Val d'Elsa it is possible either to drive to Volterra, 27 km/17 miles west, or to go north to Poggibonsi and then west to the interesting town of San Gimignano (20 km/12 miles); see entry.

*Monte Oliveto Maggiore

Another very interesting excursion is to the large monastery of Monte Oliveto Maggiore (273 m/901 ft). One of the most renowned monasteries of the Olivetans (a branch of the Benedictines), it was founded in 1313 by Bernardo Tolomei. A visit to the monastery is most rewarding. In the cloister are fine frescoes with scenes from the life of St Benedict by Luca Signorelli (1497–98) and Sodoma (1505).

Situation
35 km/22 miles
south-east of Siena

Abbazia di San Galgano

South-west of Siena is the abbey of San Galgano (Abbazia di San Galgano), the ruins of which are an excellent example of Cistercian Gothic in Italy. The ruins of the church, built in 1224 to 1288, have an overwhelming effect.

Situation
33 km/20 miles
south-west of Siena

Sorrento

L9

Region: Campania
Province: Napoli (NA)
Altitude: 50 m/165 ft
Population: 17,000

The little town of Sorrento (in the local dialect Surriento), the ancient Surrentum, is situated amid lemon and orange-groves on the south side of the Bay of Naples, on the edge of tufa cliffs 50 m/165 ft high rising precipitously from the sea.
Sorrento is the see of an archbishop.

*Situation

*Sights

The two harbours, Marina Grande and Marina Piccolo, extend along the steep coast. From the Villa Comunale, a terrace above the Marina

Sorrento: panorama, with the yacht harbour

Grande, there are far-ranging views of the Gulf of Naples. Sorrento's main street is the Corso Italia. In Piazza Tasso, near the town's centre, stands a marble statue of the poet Torquato Tasso (1544–95), who was born in Sorrento. From here a road runs down to the Marina Piccolo, where the boats come in.

Museo Correale

In the new part of Sorrento the Museo Correale, founded in 1924, contains a death mask of Torquato Tasso and some special editions of his works, pictures, interarsia work, furniture and porcelain, including the so-called "basis of Sorrento", reliefs from Augustan times and the remains of a medieval choir screen.

Piano di Sorrento

To the east of Sorrento extends the fertile Piano di Sorrento, in Roman times a favourite residence of the great and the wealthy and still a popular holiday resort which attracts visitors from far and wide.

*From Sorrento to Positano

Massa Lubrense

From Sorrento the road runs south-west to the little town of Massa Lubrense or Massalubrense (120 m/396 ft; pop. 11,000), with the Castello di Santa Maria (224 m/409 ft) rearing above it.

Punta della Campanella

From here it is a 2 hours' walk to the Punta della Campanella, at the farthest tip of the peninsula of Sorrento opposite the island of Capri.

Sant'Agata

Beyond Massa Lubrense the road skirts Monte San Nicola and comes in another 5 km/3 miles to Sant'Agata sui due Golfi (391 m/1290 ft), a pleasant little summer resort below the Deserto. On a hill 1 km/¾ mile north-west is the Deserto (455 m/1502 ft), a former monastery which is now an orphanage. From the roof there are fine views of the bays of Naples and Salerno.

From Sant'Agata it is another 13 km/8 miles on a beautiful road (the stretch to Colli San Pietro being known as the "Nastro Azurro" or the "Blue Ribbon") which passes close to the conspicuous chapel of Sant'Angelo (462 m/1525 ft; view), to the left of the road, before coming to Positano.

Positano

La Spezia

F5

Region: Liguria
Province: La Spezia (SP)
Altitude: 3 m/10 ft
Population: 113,000

The provincial capital of La Spezia lies between Genoa and Pisa on the wide Golfo della Spezia, one of the largest and safest natural harbours in the Mediterranean, extending 9 km/5½ miles into the coast and 7 km/4½ miles wide. It is some 70 km/43 miles north-west to Genoa and about 45 km/28 miles south-east to Pisa.

Situation

Sights

The main street of La Spezia is the Corso Cavour, where, at No. 251, are the Biblioteca Civica (some 80,000 volumes), the Musei Civici (local history, natural history) and the Museo Archeologico Lunense (Roman antiquities and finds from Luni).

Museums

The Corso Cavour runs south-east into Via D. Chiodo, which is lined with orange trees, and near which is the Giardino Pubblico, with fine palms and yuccas. From here Viale Mazzini and Viale Italia run north-east, separated by a line of palms and flanked on the seaward side by the Passeggiata Morin, from which there are beautiful views of the bay and the Apuan Alps with the shimmering white spoil heaps of Carrara.

Via Chiodo leads north-east to the Piazza G. Verdi, with modern office blocks, and beyond this the Piazza Italia, in which stands the new Town Hall. On a terrace above the square rises the new cathedral (1976).

Cathedral

North-west of Piazza Verdi, running along the hillside, is Via XXVII Marzo, with the 14th c. Castello San Giorgio.

At the south-west end of Via Chiodo is the Piazza Chiodo and farther on, beyond a canal, the main entrance to the Naval Arsenal, the basic features of which were outlined by Napoleon. The interesting Shipping Museum at the entrance contains models illustrating the history of seafaring from the origins to the present day and also charts and navigation apparatus.

Shipping Museum

Passo della Foce

There is a very attractive drive around the north side of the town on the Giro della Foce, which follows the slopes of Monte Castellazzo (285 m/941 ft) to the Passo della Foce (241 m/795 ft), with views of the Gulf of Spezia and the Apuan Alps.

Coast road

Riomaggiore	The coast road is also very beautiful. 11 km/7 miles west we come to Riomaggiore, the first village in the Cinqueterre (see p. 145). 10 km/6
Portovénere	miles south on the west side of the gulf is Portovénere (10 m/33 ft; pop. 5000), an old-world little port picturesquely situated on the Bocchette, the narrow strait, only 150 m/165 yd wide, between the Costa dell'Olivo promontory and the island of Palmaria. From the little church of San Pietro (1277) at the southern tip of the promontory there are charming views of the precipitous cliffs of the Cinqueterre to the north-west and the bay of Lerici to the east. Above the church are a Genoese castle and the parish church of San Lorenzo.

Lérici

Situation 11 km/7 miles south-west	South-west of La Spezia lies the little port of Lérici (10 m/33 ft; pop. 14,000), which in the Middle Ages, together with Portovénere, was the principal port on the Gulf of Spezia. Beside the church of San Rocco is an unusual Romanesque campanile. On a projecting tongue of land
Tellaro	stands a well-preserved 13th c. castle, now a museum. From Lérici there is a pleasant drive, passing a number of pretty coves and the fishing village of Fiascherino, to the picturesquely situated village of Tellaro (4 km/2½ miles south-east).

Sarzana   F/G5

Situation 16 km/10 miles east of La Spezia	East of La Spezia is Sarzana (21 m/69 ft; pop. 20,000), founded in 1202 as the successor to the ancient Etruscan city of Luni (of which sparse remains can be seen 7 km/4½ miles south-east). The town has remains

Portevénere

of its 15th c. walls, the Cittadella, and a white marble cathedral in Italian Gothic style (13th c.; completed in 1474), containing a painted crucifix from Luni (by Guillelmus, 1138), the earliest dated panel painting in Italy. To the north of the town stands the picturesque castle of Sarzanello (121 m/399 ft; view).

Spoleto

Region: Umbria
Province: Perugia (PG)
Altitude: 305–453 m/1007–1495 ft
Population: 38,000

Spoleto is situated in the Central Italian region of Umbria above the left bank of the River Tessino, which here emerges from a narrow valley in the Umbrian Apennines into the plain of Umbria. Spoleto is the see of an archbishop.

Situation and importance

Piazza del Duomo

In the long Piazza del Duomo on the east side of the town, stands the cathedral of Santa Maria Assunta, raised to cathedral status in 1067, destroyed by Emperor Frederick I (Barbarossa) in 1155 and restored immediately afterwards. It has a stone pulpit on each side of the porch (1491). The upper part of the façade is dominated by a large mosaic by Solsterus (1207). The interior was remodelled in 1634–44, probably by Bernini. The choir contains damaged frescoes ("Annunciation",

*Cathedral

Spoleto: Cathedral and Rocca

"Nativity", "Death of the Virgin" and, in the semi-dome,"Coronation of the Virgin") by Fra Filippo Lippi (1467–69), completed after his death by Fra Diamante (1470). In the south transept (on the left) is the tomb of Filippo Lippi (1412–69).

Museo Civico

On the north-west side of the Piazza del Duomo, in the former Palazzo della Signoria (14th c.), the Museo Civico houses prehistoric and ancient material.

Palazzo Comunale
Picture Gallery

The Palazzo Comunale (Town Hall; entrance on south side), approached by a flight of steps at the south end of the Piazza del Duomo, contains an interesting picture gallery on the first floor; the exhibits include frescoes by Lo Spagna.

Santa Eufemia

To the north of the Town Hall, in the courtyard of the Archbishop's Palace, stands the Romanesque church of Santa Eufemia (12th c.), with a fine altar and a 15th c. triptych.

Arco di Druso

West of the Town Hall we find the spacious Piazza del Mercato, below which, to the south, is the Arch of Drusus (Arco di Druso), erected in 24 A.D. to commemorate a victory over the Germans. Near the Arch of Drusus is the church of San Ansano, built on the site of a Roman temple.

Teatro Romano

South-west of the Arch of Drusus, near Piazza della Libertà, are the remains of a Roman theatre (Teatro Romano).

Rocca

On the east side of the Town Hall lies the tree-shaded Piazza Campello. From here Via della Rocca runs to the Rocca, built in the 14th c. as the residence of the Papal governor and now a prison. The castle has two fine courtyards surrounded by a rectangular wall with towers.

Porta Rocca

Below the Rocca Via del Ponte leads to the Porta Rocca, outside which are remains of the old town walls (on the left).

* Ponte delle Torri

Continuing past these above the deep ravine of the Tessino, we come to the imposing Ponte delle Torri, an aqueduct and viaduct (pedestrians only) linking the town with Monte Luco (804 m/2653 ft). Built of freestone, with ten arches (230 m/250 yd long, 81 m/267 ft high), it was constructed in the 14th c., probably on the foundations of an earlier Roman aqueduct.

Sights in the north

San Gregorio
Maggiore

In the large Piazza Garibaldi in the northern part of the town the Romanesque church of San Gregorio Maggiore, consecrated in 1146, has a 16th c. porch and an interesting interior with old frescoes.

Roman Bridge

From Piazza Garibaldi the Porta Garibaldi leads into the Piazza della Vittoria (gardens). Immediately east of the gate are the remains of a Roman Bridge, the Ponte Sanguinario (24 m/26 yd long, 10 m/33 ft high), to which visitors can descend.

San Salvatore

From the Porta Garibaldi we cross the Tessino and 100 m/110 yd beyond the bridge turn right along the river and then left up the hill to reach the church of San Salvatore (also known as il Crocifisso), on a

terrace in the Camposanto, which was originally built at the end of the
4th c. within the remains of a Roman temple.
A short distance south is the 13th c. church of San Ponziano. San Ponziano

San Pietro

From the east end of the Ponte delle Torri a road follows the edge of the
Tessino ravine (1 km/¾ mile) to the church of San Pietro (388 m/1280 ft),
founded in the 5th c. and rebuilt in the 14th c., with 11–12th c. reliefs on
the façade (the four upper scenes are later).

Monteluco

Another road from the east end of the Ponte delle Torri winds its way up   Situation
the wooded hillside to Monteluco (804 m/2653 ft), from which there are   8 km/5 miles
magnificent views. Below the summit is a Franciscan friary.   south-east

From Spoleto to Ascoli Piceno (about 125 km/78 miles)

From Spoleto there is an attractive drive to Ascoli Piceno. The road   Norcia
passes through beautiful upland country, much of it forest-covered and
comes in 49 km/30 miles to Norcia (604 m/1993 ft; pop. 5000), the
Roman Nursia a little walled town below the west side of the Monti
Sibillini which was the birthplace of St Benedict and his sister Scholastica. In the main square are the Town Hall, the 14th c. church of San
Benedetto, built over the remains of the house in which St Benedict was
born, and the Prefecture, in a castellated 16th c. building, the Castellina
(beautiful courtyard).
The road continues east from Norcia, climbs up to the crest of the ridge,
coming in 19 km/12 miles to the Forca Canapine (1543 m/5092 ft), a pass
on the boundary between Umbria and the Marche, with magnificent
views of the Gran Sasso d'Italia to the south-east and the Monti Sibillini
to the north-east.
It then descends with many bends, into the beautiful valley of the   Arquata del Tronto
Tronto and comes in 20 km/12 miles to Arquata del Tronto (777 m/2564
ft), with a 13th c. castle. This is the starting point for the ascent (4½
hours, with guide) of Monte Vettore (2476 m/8171 ft), the highest peak
in the Monti Sibillini which are snow-covered until well into the summer (winter sports). It is possible also to drive to the Forca della Presta
(1540 m/5082 ft), 13.5 km/8½ miles north-west (first part of road dust-
free), climb to the Rifugio Zilioli (2215 m/7310 ft; 3½ hours) and continue from there to the summit (1 hour).
The road continues down the Tronto valley, which at times narrows   Acquasanta Terme
into a gorge, and comes in another 13 km/8 miles to Acquasanta Terme
(411 m/1356 ft), a spa which was already frequented in Roman times (ad
Aquas), with warm sulphur springs.
12 km/7 miles beyond Acquasanta we join the road from Macerata and   Ascoli Piceno
follow it for another 8 km/5 miles down the valley to Ascoli Piceno.

Subiaco   K8

Region: Lazio
Province: Roma (ROMA)
Altitude: 408 m/1346 ft
Population: 9000

Sulmona

Situation

The little town of Subiaco, 70 km/43 miles east of Rome, is situated on a hill above the Aniene valley, dominated by an 11th c. castle.

History and importance

The Roman Sublaquem grew up on the site of a large villa belonging to Nero, who narrowly escaped being struck by lightning while dining here. The main features of interest in the town, which still preserves its medieval aspect, are the famous Benedictine monasteries.

Monastery of Santa Scolastica

2 km/1¼ miles south-east of the town centre on the road to Ienne, situated above the River Aniene (on the right), is the large monastery of Santa Scolastica, with a fine campanile from 1052, founded by St Benedict about 510 and later named after his sister. In 1052 a second monastery was built here, and later rebuilt in Gothic style and in 1235 a third, with a Romanesque cloister with mosaic decoration. The present buildings are modern. The church of Santa Scolastica, founded in 975, was completely remodelled in the 18th c. In 1464 two German printers, Arnold Pannartz and Konrad Schweinheim, stayed in the monastery and produced what are probably the earliest Italian printed books.

*Monastery of San Benedetto

1.5 km/1 mile farther east, above the road to Ienne (on the left), is the monastery of San Benedetto or Sacro Speco (640 m/2112 ft), built against a sheer cliff in a magnificent lonely mountain setting. Both the upper and the lower church are decorated with frescoes. The lower church has 13th c. frescoes in Roman style while the frescoes of the upper church dating from the 14th–15th c. are in Sienese and Umbrian style. The chapel adjoining the upper church contains a unique early picture of St Francis, who, according to legend, while he was staying in the monastery about 1223 transformed the thorns grown by St Benedict into the roses which still flourish in the monastery garden. In the cave in which St Benedict lived as a hermit until he moved to Montecassino in 529 is a statue of the saint by a pupil of Bernini.

Vallepietra

Situation
21 km/13 miles east

The road continues down the Aniene valley beyond the monastery of San Benedetto to (9 km/5½ miles) the beautifully situated little town of Ienne (834 m/2752 ft). 12 km/7 miles from here along the Simbrivio valley lies the village of Vallepietra (825 m/2723 ft), in a cirque on the south-east side of Monte Autore.

Monte Autore

From Vallepietra it is a climb of 1½–2 hours to the Santuario della Santissima Trinità (12th c. frescoes; festival on Sunday after Whitsun), situated at an altitude of 1337 m/4412 ft below a vertical rock face 300 m/990 ft high. From here it is another 2½–3 hours' climb (with guide) to the summit of Monte Autore (1853 m/6115 ft), the second highest peak in the wooded Monte Simbruini (2156 m/7115 ft); magnificent panoramic views from the top.

Sulmona

Region: Abruzzo
Province: L'Aquila (AQ)
Altitude: 403 m/1330 ft
Population: 24,000

Sulmona lies in a fertile valley between the Gran Sasso massif to the
north and the Maiella group, with the Morrone hills in the foreground,
to the east. It was the Roman Sulmo, birthplace of Ovid, who was much
attached to his "cool home country, abounding in water".
Sulmona is the see of an archbishop.

Situation

Sights

At the north end of the town stands the cathedral of San Panfilo, with a
Romanesque crypt and a Gothic doorway. From here Viale Roosevelt
and the Corso Ovidio, Sulmona's principal street lead to the 15th c.
Palazzo Santa Maria Annunziata, which has a Gothic doorway and
Renaissance elements. The church, founded in 1320 was rebuilt in 1710
after earthquake damage. The palace houses the Museo Civico which
contains a 15th c. wooden tabernacle painted by Giovanni da Sulmona.
Farther along the Corso Ovidio is a Romanesque doorway, all that
remains of the church of San Francesco della Scarpa, destroyed by an
earthquake. Opposite is a beautiful Renaissance fountain (1474), fed by
an aqueduct constructed in 1256.

From Sulmona to Pescara

There are alternative routes from Sulmona to Pescara: either down the
Pescara valley via Popoli (pop. 5000; castle of the counts of Cantelmi),
with a detour to the abbey of San Clemente a Casauria, founded by the
Emperor Ludwig II in 871 (12th c. church; museum); or along the lower
slopes of the Maiella group (Monte Amaro, 2795 m/9224 ft) via Campo

Situation
76 km/47 miles and
83 km/51 miles
respectively north-
east

Sulmona: Piazza Garibaldi

di Giove (1064 m/3511 ft; from here ascent of Monte Amaro, 10–12 hours) and Caramanico Terme (sulphur springs; ascent to Monte Amaro, 6–9 hours) and thereafter down into the Pescara valley.

From Sulmona to Villetta Barrea

Situation
60 km/37 miles south

There is a very fine drive from Sulmona through the wild Sagittario gorge and the rocky gateway of La Foce to Scanno (1050 m/3465 ft; pop. 3000), a delightfully situated hill village (traditional costumes), and from there past the Fonti di Pantano and down the Sangro valley to Velletta Barrea, a village at the west end of the Lago di Barrea, an artificial lake 5 km/3 miles long (entrance to Abruzzi National Park).

Syracuse/Siracusa   M12

Region: Sicilia
Province: Siracusa (SR)
Altitude: 17 m/56 ft
Population: 118,000

Situation

Syracuse, capital of its province, is situated partly on an island off the east coast of Sicily, separated by a narrow channel from the Sicilian mainland, on which are the modern town and the principal remains of the ancient city. The bay of Porto Grande, which cuts deep inland to the south of the town, is perhaps Italy's largest and best natural harbour.

**Holiday resort

The town's situation, its beautiful surroundings and the monuments and relics of its splendid past make Syracuse one of the most fascinating places in Sicily.

History

Syracuse (Greek Syrakusa, Latin Syracusae) was founded on the island of Ortygia in the second half of the 8th c. B.C. by settlers from Corinth, and rapidly rose to prosperity. From the 5th c. onwards it was ruled mostly by tyrants, the first of whom were Gelo (485–478) and Hiero (478–467). Some of Greece's greatest poets, including Aeschylus and Pindar, lived at Hiero's court. In 415 B.C. Syracuse was drawn into the conflict between Athens and Sparta, but an Athenian expedition against the city (415) ended in the total annihilation of the Athenian army and fleet in 413. During the struggle with Carthage, Syracuse rose during the reigns of Dionysius I (406–357) and his successors to become the most powerful Greek city, with a perimeter, according to Strabo, of 180 stadia (33 km/20 miles) and a population of half a million. Among the eminent men who lived in Syracuse during this period was the mathematician and physicist Archimedes.

After the first Punic War, in which Syracuse was allied with Rome, the city went over to the Carthaginian side. Thereupon it was besieged and captured by the Romans (212 B.C.). Thereafter Syracuse shared the destinies of the rest of Sicily but never recovered its earlier importance.

Syracuse is the see of an archbishop.

Old town

The old town, with its narrow winding streets and its old houses and palaces – many of them with attractive balconies – lies on an island.

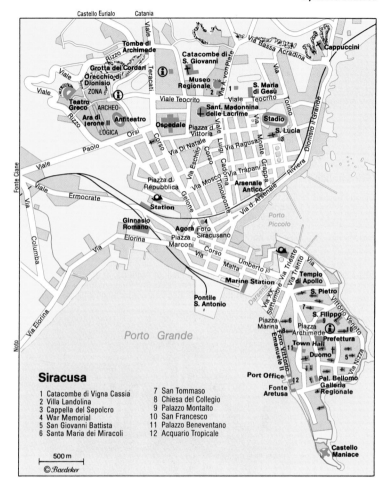

Siracusa

1 Catacombe di Vigna Cassia
2 Villa Landolina
3 Cappella del Sepolcro
4 War Memorial
5 San Giovanni Battista
6 Santa Maria dei Miracoli
7 San Tommaso
8 Chiesa del Collegio
9 Palazzo Montalto
10 San Francesco
11 Palazzo Beneventano
12 Acquario Tropicale

500 m

© Baedeker

Piazza Archimede

The town's centre is the Piazza Archimede, which is surrounded by old palaces. On the west side of the square is the Banca d'Italia, with a 15th c. courtyard, and a little way north-east the Palazzo Montalto (1397), with magnificent Gothic windows.

From here Via Dione runs north to the Temple of Apollo (6th c. B.C.), which was also dedicated to Artemis (the Roman Diana). The oldest Doric temple in Sicily, it was excavated in 1933 and has recently been partly re-erected.

Temple of Apollo

471

Piazza del Duomo

*Cathedral

South-west of Piazza Archimede is the elongated Piazza del Duomo, with the Palazzo del Senato (Town Hall, 17th c.) and next to it the cathedral, built in the 7th c. on the site of a temple of Athena of the 5th c. B.C., enlarged in the 17th c. and provided with a fine Baroque façade between 1728 and 1757. Notable features in the interior are a Romanesque font (13th c.) and a picture by Antonello da Messina.

Fonte Arethusa

From the south end of the Piazza del Duomo Via Picherale continues south to the semicircular basin of the Fountain of Arethusa (Fonte Arethusa) with its papyrus plants. The legend of the nymph Arethusa, pursued by the river god Alpheus from Olympia to here, reflects the idea that the Peloponnesian river Alpheus continues flowing under the sea and emerged at this point.

*Foro Italico

Acquario Tropicale

To the north of the Fountain extends the Foro Italico, a fine seafront promenade with view of the harbour and of Etna. At the south end of the Foro, in a small park, is the entrance to the Acquario Tropicale, with rare fishes from tropical seas.

Porta Marina

At the north end of the Foro are the Porta Marina, with Hispano-Mauresque ornaments (15th c.), and the church of Santa Maria dei Miracoli (1501).

Palazzo Bellomo
Galleria Regionale

A little way east of the Fountain of Arethusa, at the south end of Via Roma, which runs down from Piazza Archimede, is the Palazzo Bellomo (15th c.), with the Galleria Regionale, which contains medieval and

Syracuse: Baroque façade of the cathedral

472

Renaissance collections, and a picture gallery with the famous "Propagation" by Antonello Da Messina (1474).

The Castello Maniace, a Hohenstaufen stronghold built about 1239 at the southern tip of the island, has a fine gateway; there is a good view from the south bastion.

Castello Maniace

New town

At the north end of the island, west of the Temple of Apollo, is the Piazza Pancali, from which there is a bridge over the canal (Darsena) to the new town on the mainland, with the railway station (Stazione Centrale) and the impressive remains of the ancient city. The Corso Umberto I, the main street of the modern town, runs west from the bridge to the large Foro Siracusano on which remains of the ancient agora can be seen. To the west are the remains of the Ginnasio Romano (Gymnasium), once surrounded by colonnades.

Foro Siracusano

*Parco Archeologico della Neapoli

1 km/¾ mile north-west of the Foro Siracusano, to the left of the Corso Gelone (the Catania road, S.S. 114), is the Parco Archeologico della Neapoli (admission fee), with the Amphitheatre (probably 3rd c.; 140 m/154 yd long, 119 m/140 yd across), in the part of the Roman town known as Neapolis. 100 m/110 yd west of this is the Altar of Hierro II (Ara di Ierone II), a gigantic altar 198 m/216 yd long by 22.5 m/24½ yd broad which originally rose in two tiers to a height of 10.5 m/34½ ft. Here probably was performed the annual sacrifice of 450 oxen.

Amphitheatre
Altar of Hierro II

Opposite the altar is the entrance to the Latomia del Paradiso, an ancient quarry 30–40 m/98–144 ft deep, now covered with a luxuriant growth of vegetation, which was used, like other latomie, as a prison for offenders who were condemned to stone-breaking and also for confinement of prisoners of war.

*Latomia del
Paradiso

Keeping left immediately inside the entrance archway along the garden wall, we come to the so-called Ear of Dionysius, an S-shaped cave hewn from the rock, 65 m/213 ft deep, 23 m/76 ft in height and 5–11 m/5½–12 yd wide, contracting towards the top, in which sound is considerably amplified without any recurring echo. It has born its present name since the 16th c., reflecting the belief that the tyrant Dionysius was thus able to overhear even the whispered remarks of state prisoners confined in the quarry. Farther to the right, under the west wall of the quarry, is the Grotta del Cordari, named after the ropemakers who carried on their trade there.

*Ear of Dionysius

Immediately east is the Latomia di Santa Venera, with a particularly lush growth of vegetation.

Latomia di Santa
Venera

From the Latomia di Santa Venera a stony path leads to the Necropoli Grotticelli, a necropolis with Greek (5th–4th c.), Hellenistic, Roman and Byzantine tombs.

Necropoli Grotticelli

Immediately west of the Latomia del Paradiso is the Greek Theatre (Teatro Greco, 5th c. B.C.), with a semicircular auditorium hewn from the rock, the largest in the Greek world (diameter 138.5 m/151½ yd. Two tunnels under the auditorium give access to the orchestra (diameter 24 m/26 yd). In this theatre Aeschylus (d. 456 B.C.) directed the performance of his "Persian" (c. 472 B.C.), and it is still used for the performance of classical plays (in spring, in alternate, even-numbered years). From the top of the theatre there is a magnificent view at sunset of the town, the harbour and the sea.

**Greek Theatre

In the rock face above the theatre is the so-called Nymphaeum, a cave which was the terminal point of an ancient aqueduct.

Nymphaeum

473

Latomia del Paradiso, an ancient quarry

The cave known as the "Ear of Dionysus"

Streets of Tombs	From the left-hand side the Streets of Tombs (Via dei Sepolcri), hewn from the rock, runs up in a curve for some 150 m/165 yd with numerous cavities and tomb chambers of the late Roman period.

Catacombs

San Giovanni alle Catacombe	500 m/550 yd north-east of the Amphitheatre, to the right of the Catania road (S.S. 114), stands the little church of San Giovanni alle Catacombe, the western part of the early medieval cathedral, of which nothing is left but the west front of the present church, with a conspicuous round window, and the 15th c. porch.
*Catacombs	From the church a flight of steps leads down to the cruciform Crypt of St Marcian (4th c., with remains of frescoes) and the adjoining Catacombs (Catacombe di San Giovanni), which are among the most imposing known, far larger than the catacombs of Rome.
*Latomia dei Cappuccini	From the catacombs, going north-east along Via Augusto von Platen, with the entrance to the Catacombs of Vigna Cassia, and then 500 m/550 yd east along Via Bassa Acradina, past the Old Cemetery, we come to a Capuchin monastery and beside it the Latomia dei Cappuccini, one of the ancient quarries, in which the 7000 Athenian prisoners taken in 414 B.C. were probably confined.

**Museo Regionale

A little way south-east of San Giovanni alle Catacombe is the Villa Landolina. In the garden of the villa stands the Museo Regionale, one of the most important archaeological museums in Italy, with a large collection of antiquities, mostly of Sicilian origin, ranging in date from prehistoric to early Christian times. Particularly notable items are the sarcophagus of Valerius and Adelfia (4th c. A.D.) from the catacombs of San Giovanni, with carvings of scenes from the Old and New Testaments, and the Landolina Venus (Venus Anadyomene), with a dolphin by her side, a copy (2nd c. A.D.) of a fine Hellenistic work.

*Fort of Euryelos

North-west of the Foro Siracusano, at the west end of the outlying district of ancient Syracuse, Epipolae, on higher ground, is the Fort of Euryelos (Castello Eurialo), built between 402 and 397 B.C. at the meeting of the north and south edges of the plateau, one of the best preserved works of fortification (view).

Situation
8 km/5 miles
north-west

Fountain of Cyane

A pleasant outing from Syracuse is a boat trip (3–4 hours there and back) from the harbour up the little River Ciane (on a hill to the left two columns of the Olympieion, a temple of Zeus of the 6th c. B.C., between tall stands of papyrus, to the Fountain of Cyane (Fonte Ciane or Testa della Pisma), the "azure spring" into which the nymph of that name was metamorphosed for opposing Pluto when he was abducting Proserpina.

Fort Euryelos, near Syracuse

Fonte Ciana, "cornflower-blue" spring

475

From Syracuse to the Necropoli Pantalica (aout 70 km/43 miles)

Palazzolo Acreide

33 km/20 miles west is the interesting town of Palazzolo Acreide, the ancient Akrai (Latin Paceolum, Arabic el-Akrat), which was founded by settlers from Syracuse in 664 B.C. On the nearby hill of Acremonte, the site of the ancient city, is a Cinta Archeologica containing the remains of the late Greek theatre (seating for 600), to the west of this the Bouleuterion (Council Chamber), to the south-east latomie (gorges) containing Greek and early Christian tombs, and two tomb chambers known as the Templi Ferali (funerary temples).

Reliefs of the Santoni

From here it is a 15 minutes' walk to the valley of Contrada dei Santi-celli, near the large Cemetery of Acrocoro della Torre, to the reliefs (mutilated in the 19th c.) of the so-called Santoni, crudely carved cult images in niches in the rock. Most of them represent a seated goddess, presumably Cybele, with Hermes beside her. On the far side of the valley is Monte Pineta, with many small tomb chambers.

*Necropoli di Pantalica

34 km/21 miles north-east of Palazzolo Acreide via Ferla is the Necropoli di Pantalica, the cemetery of the Siculan town (13th–8th c. B.C.) on the hill to the north with thousands of tomb chambers hewn from the rock faces in the Anapo valley. During the Middle Ages the tombs were used as dwellings. Jewellery and ornaments found in the tombs are displayed in the Museo Nazionale in Syracuse.

Taormina   M12

Region: Sicilia
Province: Messina (ME)
Altitude: 204 m/673 ft
Population: 10,000

Situation
**Scenery

The little town of Taormina, the ancient Tauromenium, enjoys a magnificent situation on a terrace high above the Ionian Sea on the east coast of Sicily. A ruined castle on a rocky crag and the little hill town of Castelmola tower above it. Taormina is one of the most beautiful places in the whole of Sicily.

A hilly road leads from the coast to the town of Taormina; the nearest beaches, at Mazzarò and Isola Bella, are of only moderate quality; the sandy beaches at San Alessio Siculo (14 km/9 miles north) and Santa Teresa (20 km/12 miles north) are to be preferred.

Piazza Vittorio Emanuele

Porta Messina

The centre of the northern part of the town is the Piazza Vittorio Emanuele. The scenic road which winds its way up to Taormina from the coast, Via L. Pirandello, terminates at the Porta Messina, to the north of the square. A little way north-east the church of San Pancrazio, occupies the cella of a Greek temple. In the Piazza Vittorio Emanuele stand the Gothic Palazzo Corvaia (15th c., with a fine façade) and the little church of Santa Caterina. Near the church of Santa Caterina are the remains of a Roman odeon, built in Imperial times. In the vicinity of the Piazza Vittorio Emanuele is a congress centre, the Palazzo del Congressi.

*Teatro Greco

From the Piazza Vittorio Emanuele the Via del Teatro Greco runs south-east of the Greek Theatre, which was reconstructed in Roman style in

Taormina: Greek theatre

the 2nd c. A.D. With a diameter at the top of 109 m/358 ft, it is the largest theatre in Sicily after the one in Syracuse. It is renowned for its excellent acoustics (performances of classical plays). The view from the top of the theatre of the precipitous east coast of Sicily, with the gigantic cone of Etna, snow-covered for most of the year, and of the Calabrian coast is one of the most breathtaking in Italy.

Sights in the south-west

From the Piazza Vittorio Emanuele the town's main street, Corso Umberto, flanked by fine old houses, runs south-west to the Piazza IX Aprile (view) with the church of San Giuseppe and the deconsecrated church of Sant'Agostino.

Piazza IX Aprile

It then passes the Palazzo Ciampoli (on the right), and joins the Piazza del Duomo, where stands a beautiful 12th c. fountain. In the small cathedral (13th–16th c.) are a number of fine altarpieces and, to the right of the high altar, a 15th c. Madonna.

Cathedral

On the hillside north of the Piazza del Duomo are the ruins of the Gothic Badia Vecchia (14th c.). To the south, on the edge of the terrace, a finely situated Dominican monastery is now the Hotel San Domenico Palace (fine cloister); from the tower of the church (destroyed in 1943) there is a beautiful view.

San Domenico

To the west of the Piazza del Duomo, beyond the Porta Catania or Porta del Tocco, is the Palazzo Duca di Santo Stefano (1330), its vaulting supported on a massive granite column. The palace contains modern sculpture.

Palazzo Duca di Santo Stefano

477

Bird's-eye view of the coast at Taormina

Villa Comunale

Below the former Dominican monastery, Via Roma (fine views) runs east to the municipal gardens (Villa Comunale), in a commanding situation, from which Via Bagnoli Croce continues to the Belvedere (magnificent views). From here we can return on Via Luigi Pirandello, passing below the Greek Theatre, to the Porta Messina.

Castello di Taormina

From the west end of the town near the Badia Vecchia, a road winds steeply uphill, with sharp bends, to the chapel of the Madonna della Rocca (2 km/1¼ miles), from which it is a few minutes' climb to the Castello di Taormina on Monte Tauro (398 m/1313 ft).

Castelmola

Even more attractive is the further stretch of road (3 km/2 miles) to the village of Castelmola (529 m/1746 ft), perched on a precipitous crag, which commands panoramic views from its various lookout terraces, but particularly from its highest point near the ruined castle.

From Castelmola it is a 2 to 3 hours' climb to Monte Venere (884 m/2917 ft), from the top of which there are magnificent views.

**Etna

A very rewarding excursion from Taormina is the ascent of Etna (see entry), or the circuit of the mountain by rail.

Taranto   O9

Region: Puglia. Province: Taranto (TA)
Altitude: 15 m/50 ft. Population: 245,000

Taranto, the capital of the Apulian province and the see of an arch-bishop, lies on the Mare Grande, the northern bay of the Gulf of Taranto, on the south coast of Italy.

The old town is built on a low rocky island between the Mare Grande and the Mare Piccolo, which runs deep inland on the north-east side of the town. From here a bridge leads to the Borgo, an industrial suburb (large steelworks) to the north-west, which in turn is linked by a swing bridge with the new town, situated on a peninsula, to the south of the old town.

The port is also a considerable industrial and commercial town, which ranks with La Spezia as one of Italy's two principal naval bases. Taranto is renowned for its honey and fruit. Fishing and the culture of oysters and shellfish also make a contribution to the town's economy.

The town (Greek Taras, Latin Tarentum) was founded by Spartan set-tlers in 708 B.C., and by the 4th c. B.C. was the most powerful city in Magna Graecia. In the time of Augustus it still had a predominantly Greek population, but thereafter it was Romanised. In A.D. 494 it was occupied by the Ostrogoths, and in 540 came under Byzantine rule. Taranto was destroyed by the Saracens in 927 but was rebuilt, and in 1063 was incorporated by Robert Guiscard in the Norman kingdom of southern Italy. Thereafter Taranto shared the destinies of the kingdom of Naples.

History

Old Town (Città Vecchia)

In the centre of the Old Town (Città Vecchia), a rectangle of narrow lanes traversed by four parallel longitudinal streets, stands the cathedral of San Cataldo (originally built in the 11th c.; rebuilt in the 18th c., with the exception of the dome and campanile), on the site of the ancient acropolis. The dome shows Byzantine influences. The interior contains columns with ancient and early medieval capitals. To the right of the choir is the richly decorated Baroque chapel of San Cataldo, with the tomb of the town's patron saint. The crypt has Byzantine frescoes.

Cathedral

At the south-east corner of the old town stands the Castello Aragonese (15th–16th c.).

Castello Aragonese

New Town (Città Nuova)

From the old town the Ponte Girevole leads over the Canale Navigabile, one of the few places in the Mediterranean where the ebb and flow of the tide can be observed, into the New Town (Città Nuova), with its wide parallel streets. 100 m/110 yd beyond the bridge is the palm-shaded square known as Villa Garibaldi, on the east side stands the imposing Palazzo degli Uffici (1896).

On the north side of the square the National Museum (Museo Nazi-onale), one of the most important museums in southern Italy, houses prehistoric antiquities, a collection of vases (fine decoration, including scenes from mythology), old jewellery and a collection of coins.

* National Museum

To the south, on the Mare Grande, is an avenue of palms, the Lungo-mare Vittorio Emanuele III, with the modern premises of the Prefecture and the Head Post Office.

Lungomare Vittorio Emanuele III

To the north of the National Museum, on the Mare Piccolo, the Institute of Oceanography (Istituto Talassografico; visitors admitted) has the municipal park, the Villa Comunale Peripato, on its east side.

Institute of Oceanography

Taranto: the Castello in the Old Town

Tarquinia

Region: Lazio
Province: Viterbo (VT)
Altitude: 133 m/439 ft
Population: 13,000

Situation

The town of Tarquinia, founded in the early medieval period on the territory of ancient Tarquinii, occupies a commanding situation on a limestone plateau above the River Marta, 5 km/3 miles from the Tyrrhenian Sea and some 20 km/12 miles north of Civitavecchia.

Sights

Palazzo Vitelleschi
*Museo Nazionale
Tarquiniense

The main square of Tarquinia is the Piazza Cavour, at the west end of the town. In this square a magnificent palace, part of it in Gothic style and part of it Romanesque, with a beautiful pillared courtyard, the Palazzo Vitelleschi (1436–39), now houses the Museo Nazionale Tarquiniense, an important collection of Etruscan antiquities of the 6th–2nd c. B.C. The collection includes sarcophagi, vases, jewellery, glass, carved ivories, coins, fragments of large decorative reliefs and also pictures of the 15th and 16th c.

Cathedral

Nearby is the modernised cathedral with 16th c. frescoes by Antonio da Viterbo in the chancel.
The picturesque quarters in the north of the town with their churches, towers and old houses, built around the Palazzo dei Priori, and the church of San Pancrazio, have preserved medieval features.

Tarquinia: the Etruscan "Tomba dei Leopardi"

At the north-west tip of the town, near the remains of the Castello, the church of Santa Maria di Castello (1121–1208) has a three-naved basilica and is both externally and internally embellished with Cosmatesque decoration.

Santa Maria di Castello

On higher ground in the east of the town stands the fine Romanesque and Gothic church of San Francesco (13th c.).

San Francesco

**Etruscan necropolis

On a stony hill 3 km/2 miles east of Tarquinia are the meagre remains of ancient Tarquinii, the most notable of the twelve cities of the Etruscan federation. The town, originally surrounded by a wall 8 km/5 miles long, was devastated by the Saracens in the 13th c. and razed to the ground in 1307 by the inhabitants of the neighbouring town of Corneto. Around the old town, particularly on the hill of Monterozzi (157 m/518 ft) to the south, extends the necropolis (discovered in 1823), one of the best preserved of Etruscan cemeteries. A tour of the tombs takes anything from 1½ to 5 hours. The splendid painted decoration of the tombs (hewn from rock) gives a picture of the culture, art and religion of the Etruscans.

Tarquinii

Tuscania

There is an interesting trip north-eastwards from Tarquinia on the Viterbo road to the little town of Tuscania (166 m/548 ft; pop. 8000) which is still surrounded by medieval walls and towers. The ancient Tuscana, it was known until 1911 as Toscanella. A severe earthquake of

Situation
25 km/16 miles
north-east of
Tarquinia

481

Terni

February 6th 1971 destroyed the old town and damaged the churches outside the town. The houses have been rebuilt or restored, and the town has regained its former appearance.

*San Pietro

To the east of the town, on the Viterbo road, is the Romanesque church of San Pietro (8th–12th c.), with a richly decorated façade, a fine interior and an ancient crypt.

Santa Maria Maggiore

Nearby, in the valley, the fine church of Santa Maria Maggiore (1050–1206), has an old pulpit and a fresco of the Last Judgment (14th c.) on the wall of the choir.

*Museo Nazionale Etrusco

North of Tuscania is the 15th c. church of Santa Maria del Riposo. The adjoining monastery houses the Museo Nazionale Etrusco (Etruscan National Museum).

During the last years several Etruscan necropolises have been discovered in the surroundings of Tuscania.

Capalbio

Situation
30 km/19 miles north of Tarquinia

From 1979 to 1987 the French artist Niki de Saint Phalle built the "Park of the Tarot" near the village of Capalbio. The 22 huge concrete sculptures depict the symbols of the tarot cards.

Terni

Region: Umbria
Province: Terni (TR)
Altitude: 130 m/429 ft
Population: 113,000

Situation and importance

Terni, the capital of the Umbrian province of the same name, lies in the fertile valley of the Nera some 100 km/62 miles north of Rome.
Terni is a rising industrial town which since its rebuilding after severe destruction in the Second World War has a predominantly modern aspect.

Sights

Cathedral

In the centre of the town, in the Piazza della Repubblica, stands the Town Hall. To the south-west, in the Piazza del Duomo, is the cathedral (13th–17th c.), with a crypt of the 10th c. A short distance south of the cathedral are the outer walls of an amphitheatre (1st c. A.D.). Beyond the cathedral and the amphitheatre extends the municipal park, from where there is an attractive view of the Nera valley.

Palazzo Carrara Archaeological collection

North-east of the Piazza della Repubblica is the Palazzo Carrara, which houses the archaeological department of the Municipal Museum (Musei Civici), and the Municipal Library.

Palazzo Manassei Picture gallery

The nearby Palazzo Manassei contains the Picture Gallery (Pinacoteca), with pictures by Benozzo Gozzoli (Wedding of St Catherine, 15th c.), Niccolò Alunno, Giovanni Spagna, Domenico Alfani, Francesco Melanzio, Arrigo Fiammingo, Gerolamo Troppa and other artists.

San Salvatore

In the south of the town is the church of San Salvatore, the town's oldest building, probably erected in early Christian times (5th c.) on the site of a Roman building. The church is a rotunda with a cylindrical dome, a vestibule and the Manassei Chapel, which is decorated with frescoes by an Umbrian painter (14th c.).

In the north of the town the interesting church of San Francesco has notable frescoes (*c.* 1400) in the Cappella Paradisi (on the right of the choir), with scenes from the "Divine Comedy". The bell-tower (1445) was desgined by Angelo de Orvieta.

San Francesco

*Cascate delle Marmore

East of Terni beyond the industrial suburb of Papigno, to the right of the Ferentillo road (S.S. 209), are the Cascate delle Marmore, the falls formed by the River Velino at its confluence with the Nera. The falls were created by a Roman consul in 271 B.C. to prevent further marshiness of the area (coloured illuminations between May and August). The falls plunge down vertically in three leaps, a total drop of 165 m/545 ft. The best view is from the Cascate tram stop. From here it is possible to cross the Nera on a natural bridge and climb up on a steep path and flights of steps to a series of lookout terraces, joining the road from Terni to Rieti after some 45 minutes' walk.

Situation
6 km/3¾ miles east
of Terni

Lago di Piediluco

There is also a very attractive drive to the beautiful Lago di Piediluco (368 m/1214 ft; area 165 hectares), on the north side of which is the charmingly situated village of Piediluco (377 m/1244 ft), towered over by a ruined castle.

Situation
14 km/9 miles east of
Terni

Cascata delle Marmore, near Terni

Narni

Situation 13 km/8 miles south-west of Terni	South-west of Terni, commandingly situated on a high crag on the left bank of the Nera, which here forces its way out of the Terni basin through a narrow ravine, is the little medieval town of Narni (240 m/792 ft; pop. 21,000). In the centre of the town stands the cathedral, which is mainly 11th c., with a porch of 1497 and a fine interior. In the nearby Piazza Priora are the beautiful Loggia dei Priori (14th c.) and the Palazzo del Podestà which now houses the municipal offices. Below the town, on the line of the ancient Via Flaminia, are the ruins of the so-called Bridge of Augustus.

Tivoli   I8

	Region: Lazio Province: Roma (ROMA) Altitude: 235 m/776 ft Population: 52,000
Situation and history	The town of Tivoli, the ancient Tibur, lies 30 km/19 miles east of Rome in the Sabine Hills, magnificently situated on a limestone ridge extending south from Monte Gennaro (1271 m/4194 ft; cableway), above the ravine carved by the River Aniene. In Roman Imperial times it was a favourite resort of the great Roman nobles, including Maecenas and the Emperor Augustus himself.

*Villa d'Este

At the Porta Santa Croce, the south-west entrance to the town, is the spacious Largo Garibaldi. A short way north of this, in the little Piazza Trento, is the entrance to the Villa d'Este (son et lumière shows in summer), one of the classic creations of the Renaissance period, designed by Pirro Ligorio for Cardinal Ippolito d'Este (1549). It was owned by Archduke Francis Ferdinand of Austria-Este, who was assassinated at Sarajevo in 1914. From the villa and from the beautiful gardens, laid out in terraces with magnificent fountains and cascades and what are said to be the tallest cypresses in Italy, there are attractive views of the Roman Campagna.

Cathedral

In the north of the town stands the cathedral of San Lorenzo, originally Romanesque but rebuilt in 1635. In the side chapels are the remarkable group "Descent from the Cross" (13th c.) and a triptych depicting the Saviour between the Virgin and St John (12th c.).

*Temple of Vesta

Going east from the cathedral along Via San Valerio to the Piazza Rivarola and turning left along the Via della Sibilla, we come to the Temple of Vesta (Tempio di Vesta), a circular structure with Corinthian columns (2nd c. B.C.) which stands on a crag in the grounds of a hotel. Close by is the so-called Temple of Sibyl (Tempio di Sibilla) and also the exit from the park of the Villa Gregoriana.

*Villa Gregoriana

*Waterfalls	To the east of Piazza Rivarola the Ponte Gregoriana spans the gorge of the Aniene, and beyond the bridge is the main entrance to the park of

Tivoli

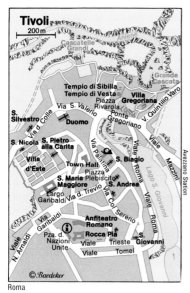

Roma

Tivoli: Fountains at the Villa d'Este

the Villa Gregoriana. The waters of this river are diverted through the Traforo Gregoriano, a double tunnel (270 m/297 yd and 300 m/330 yd long) driven through the west side of Monte Catillo in 1826–35 to prevent the floods which had repeatedly devastated the town. The water emerging from the tunnel forms magnificent waterfalls with a total drop of 160 m/528 ft (volume reduced at night to supply a power station). At the end of the tunnels is the Grande Cascata (108 m/356 ft), of which there are fine views from the upper and middle terraces. Also in the park are the Sirens' Grotto and, at the end of a gallery, the Grotto of Neptune, through which the main channel of the Aniene formerly flowed. From the entrance to the gallery a path zigzags up to the exit near the two temples.

*Via delle Cascatelle

From the entrance to the Villa Gregoriana the Via Quintilio Varo runs around the outside of the park and then along the right bank of the Aniene, past an arch in honour of the Virgin erected in 1955, to the Via delle Cascatelle, which affords beautiful views of the waterfalls and the town, particularly from the Belvedere lookout terrace and the church of Sant'Antonio.

**Villa of Hadrian

South-west of Tivoli, to the right of the Via Tiburtina, is the Villa of Hadrian (Villa Adriana), a magnificent complex of buildings and gardens covering an area of 0.75 sq. km/⅓ sq. mile. It dates from the later years of the widely travelled emperor (d. A.D. 138), who sought to

Situation
6 km/3¾ miles
south-west

485

Lake theatre at the Villa Adriana

reproduce here some of the great buildings of Greece and Egypt. Near the houses temples, a library and a museum were erected. Many of the works of art to be seen in the museums of Rome came from here. The chief charm of the villa lies in its scenic beauty. There is a model of the whole complex in a building at the car park.

Todi

Region: Umbria
Province: Perugia (PG)
Altitude: 410 m/1353 ft
Population: 17,000

Situation

Todi, the ancient Umbrian city of Tuder, lies in the south of the central Italian region of Umbria, some 40 km/25 miles south of Perugia. The town occupies a triangular site still partly surrounded by its rings of Etruscan, Roman and medieval walls, on a ridge above the Tiber valley.

Sights

*Piazza del Popolo
Cathedral

In the centre of the town is the Piazza del Popolo surrounded by medieval palaces. On the north side of the square, approached by a flight of steps, stands the Late Romanesque cathedral (12th–16th c.), with beautiful choir-stalls of 1530.

On the south side of the square is the Palazzo dei Priori or Palazzo del Podestà (13th–14th c.), with an eagle (1339), the arms of Todi, on its façade. On the east side of the square are the 13th c. Palazzo del Popolo and Palazzo del Capitano, linked by a later flight of steps. Both palaces

Todi: Cathedral

Santa Maria della Consolazione

have picture collections and house the Municipal Museum, with Etruscan and Roman material.

South of the Piazza del Popolo, in the Piazza della Repubblica, is the fine Gothic church, the Tempio di San Fortunato (13th–14th c.), approached by a flight of steps with a landing half way up. The façade (unfinished) has a beautiful central doorway (c. 1320). In the fourth chapel on the right is a fresco of the Madonna by Masolino da Panicale (1432) and there are also some beautiful choir-stalls. In the crypt (on the left) is the tomb of the monk Jacopone da Todi (1230–1306), supposed author of the solemn Passion hymn "Stabat Mater dolorosa".
To the east of the church lies the picturesque oldest part of the town, above which, to the west, are the ruins of the old Rocca, from where there are fine views.

Tempio di San Fortunato

On a terrace outside the town walls is the pilgrimage church of Santa Maria della Consolazione, a domed church notable for its nobility and beauty, one of the finest creations of Renaissance architecture by Cola di Matteuccio da Caprarola, started in 1508 and completed in 1607.

*Santa Maria della Consolazione

Trani

Region: Puglia
Province: Bari (BA)
Altitude: 7 m/23 ft
Population: 46,000

The little port of Trani, the ancient Turenum, lies on the Adriatic coast between Bari (30 km/19 miles south-east) and Barletta (10 km/6 miles north-west). Trani is the see of an archbishop.

Situation

Sights

[*]Cathedral	To the north-west of the harbour, by the sea, stands the cathedral (1150–1250), one of the finest Romanesque churches in Apulia, which shows Norman influences. It has a Romanesque west doorway (13th c. carvings) and beautiful bronze doors (c. 1180) by the bronze founder Barisano da Trani. The 32 sections are decorated with figures of Christ, the Virgin, Apostles and Saints. The campanile (reconstructed) is almost detached from the nave.

The impressive interior of the cathedral, the only example of an Apulian church with double columns, was restored to its original Romanesque form in 1952–55. From the side aisles there is access to the Crypt of St Nicholas the Pilgrim (d. 1094), begun about 1100 and decorated with fine capitals. The lower church, the Chiesa dei Santa Maria della Scala (7th c.), a rectangular space with an ambulatory, contains the Crypt of St Leucius (c. 670) under the transept. St Leucius was the first bishop of Brindisi (7th c.).

Hohenstaufen Castello — To the west of the cathedral is the Castello (1233–49) of Frederick II.

Church of Ognissanti — On the west side of the harbour we find the Gothic Palace of Simone Caccetta (15th c.) and a little way south of this the church of Ognissanti, with a deep porch, which was formerly a Templars' hospice; above the doorway are Romanesque carvings of the Annunciation and the Tree of Life.

Municipal gardens — East of the harbour, by the Baroque church of San Domenico, are the municipal gardens (Villa Comunale), with three Roman milestones from the Via Traiana which ran from Benevento by way of Canosa, Ruvo, Bari and Egnazia to Brindisi. From the west end of the gardens a view of the harbour and the cathedral can be enjoyed.

Trani: the harbour and the cathedral

Molfetta

In Molfetta (pop. 65,000), near the harbour, stands the Duomo Vecchio (7th–8th c.), a Romanesque building, which is considered to be the most important example of a domed church in Apulia.

Situation
15 km/9 miles
south-east

Ruvo di Puglia

South-east of Trani is Ruvo di Puglia (260 m/858 ft; pop. 25,000), with a Norman cathedral (12th–13th c.), which has a fine doorway. The Palazzo latta contains a fine collection of vases (6th–3rd c. B.C.) found here.

Situation
22 km/14 miles
south-east of Trani

Trapani

I11

Region: Sicilia
Province: Trapani (TP)
Altitude: 3 m/10 ft
Population: 73,000

Trapani, capital of the province of the same name, lies on a sickle-shaped peninsula on the north-west coast of Sicily.

Situation

In antiquity it was named Drepanon (= sickle) and was the port of the ancient city of Eryx, lying inland to the north-east. It is still a port of some consequence, shipping salt, wine and tunny meat.

Importance

Sights

The main street is the Corso Vittorio Emanuele; in its eastern half are the 17th c. cathedral of San Lorenzo and the Chiesa del Collegio (1636), which was elaborately adorned with marble and stucco in the 18th c. At the east end of the Corso is the Old Town Hall (17th c.: now the registry office), with a magnificent Baroque façade. To the south-east the former church of Sant'Agostino, with a beautiful rose window, once belonged to the Templars; it is now a concert and lecture hall. Farther east is the church of Santa Maria di Gesù (15th c.).

From the Old Town Hall the Via Torrearsa runs south to the harbour, skirted by an attractive seafront promenade. At the north end of the peninsula, on a spit of land, stands the Torre di Ligny, which houses a museum (prehistoric material). In the north-east of Trapani extend the Villa Margherita public gardens, opposite which is the busy Piazza Vittorio Emanuele.

Santuario dell'Annunziata

From the Piazza Vittorio Emanuele the wide Via Fardella runs east into the Borgo Annunziata quarter. In this district is the Santuario dell'Annunziata (1315–1332; most of it restored in 1760), with a 14th c. Madonna (in the Cappella della Madonna di Trapani), richly decked with jewellery and other votive gifts, which is venerated as miraculous (candle procession on August 16th).

The old monastic buildings, with a beautiful cloister, house the Museo Regionale with pictures, including one by Titian depicting St Francis of

Museo Regionale
Pepoli

489

Assisi with stigmata, sculpture, decorative art (coral carvings), prehistoric and classical antiquities.

Erice

Situation
15 km/9 miles
north-east of Trapani

There is a rewarding drive (north-east) on a road with numerous steep bends (also accessible by cableway) to Erice (751 m/2478 ft; pop. 27,000), magnificently situated on an isolated hill. Known until 1934 as Monte San Giuliano, this was the ancient Eryx, much venerated in antiquity, particularly by seamen, as the hill of Venus Erycina. The Elymians built a walled town here, of which a few traces remain. The Chiesa Matrice at the Porta Trapani, the west entrance to the town, was restored in 1865 and only the west porch (15th c.) and campanile (1312) are old. In the third chapel on the right stands a beautiful statue of the Madonna by Francesco Laurana (1469). In Piazza Umberto I stands the Town Hall (library, museum). At the east end of the town are the municipal gardens, with a number of medieval towers, and the Castello di Venere (12th–13th c.), built on the site of a temple of Venus (inside remains of the Tempio di Venere), from which there are magnificent views. To the south-west Trapani and the Isole Egadi can be seen and occasionally, Cap Bon (175 km/109 miles) on the African coast. To the south the view frequently extends to the island of Pantelleria and to the east sometimes as far as the summit of Etna, 210 km/130 miles away.

Isole Egadi

A pleasant trip from Trapani is by boat (daily) or hydrofoil (several times daily) to the Isole Egadi, situated off the Sicilian coast, the main tunny-fishing area.

Castle tower in Erice, near Trapani

The coast near Erice

The boats call at the islands of Favignana (314 m/1036 ft; area 19.75 sq. km/7½ sq. miles), the largest island of the archipelago, Levanzo (278 m/917 ft; 7 sq. km/2¾ sq. miles) and Marettimo (686 m/2264 ft; 12.25 sq. km/4¾ sq. miles).

*Gibellina   I12

A new village has been built on the site of Gibellina which was de-   Situation
stroyed by an earthquake in 1968.   55 km/35 miles south
The buildings were erected from plans drawn by well known Italian   of Trapani
architects. Numerous sculptures, some created by foreign artists adorn
the houses.

Tremiti Islands/Isole Tremiti   M7

Region: Puglia
Province: Foggia (FG)
Area: 3.06 sq. km/1 sq. mile
Population: 350

Regular services from Manfredonia or Rodi Garganico, Termoli and   Boat services
Ortona to San Nicole, from there to San Domino as required.

The Tremiti Islands (Italian Isole Tremiti) lie some 20 km/12 miles north   Situation and
of the Monte Gargano promontory in the Adriatic.   scenery
The beautiful rocky limestone archipelago has preserved its traditional
character unspoiled. The precipitous coasts with their numerous inlets
and sea caves offer ideal conditions for scuba diving.

The islands

The most westerly and scenically most attractive of the three major   Isola San Domino
islands is San Domino (up to 16 m/53 ft; area 2 sq. km/1¾ sq. mile), an
island with large areas of pine-forest which was used as a place of exile
until 1943 and is now becoming an increasingly popular tourist resort.
The largest place on the island, San Domino, lies above the east coast.
There are a number of interesting caves accessible only from the sea,
such as the Grotta delle Viole and the Grotta del Bue Marino, both with
a beautiful play of light.

North-east of San Domino is the smaller island of San Nicola (up to 75   Isola San Nicola
m/248 ft; area 0.5 sq. km/⅕ sq. mile), on which is the little walled village
of San Nicola, capital of the archipelago, with a castle (rebuilt in the
15th c.), the church of Santa Maria (1045), situated on a hill, and the
remains of a 9th c. abbey with a beautiful Renaissance doorway and
parts of a Romanesque mosaic pavement (11th–12th c.).

To the north, between San Domino and San Nicola, are the island of Il   Il Cretaccio
Cretaccio and a number of isolated stacks.

The most northerly of the three larger islands is the almost uninhabited   Isola Caprara
island of Caprara or Capraia (up to 53 m/175 ft; area 0.5 sq. km/1/5 sq.
mile).

Trento   H3

Region: Trentino–Alto Adige. Province: Trento (TN)
Altitude: 193 m/637 ft. Population: 100,000

Trento

Situation

Trento, capital of the province of the same name and of the region of Trentino–Alto Adige, lies on the left bank of the Adige in a valley enclosed by high limestone hills.
It is the see of an archbishop.

The town forms part of the southern part of the territory of Tirol which was transferred from Austria to Italy in 1919. With its numerous towers and palaces, many of them with painted façades, it is a town of distinctly Italian character.

History

The town (the Roman Tridentum) was a place of some importance from an early period by virtue of its commanding situation at the junction of the trading route from Venice up the Val Sugana with the road over the Brenner, and was strongly fortified. From 1027 to 1803 it was the residence of a prince-bishop directly subject to the emperor. From 1545 to 1563 it was the meeting-place of the Council of Trent, which laid down the pattern of the Counter-Reformation.

Between 1814 and 1918 it belonged to Austria, and after the peace treaty of Saint-Germain to Italy. In 1948 (the "Gruber-De Gaspari-Agreement") the province of Trento was combined with the province of Bolzano (which included the German-speaking Alto Adige or South Tirol) to form the autonomous region of Trentino–Alto Adige.

Sights

* Cathedral

In the centre of the town is the Piazza del Duomo, which has a beautiful Neptune Fountain (1768). The cathedral (11th–12th c.), on the south side of the square, was remodelled internally at the beginning of the

Trento: panorama

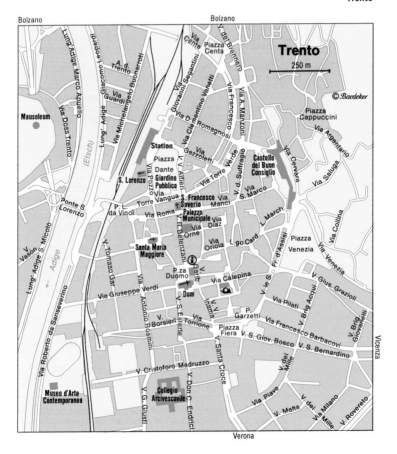

13th c. as a pillared basilica in Lombard Romanesque style; the central dome was entirely renewed in 1887–89. The Council of Trent met in the church from 1545 to 1563. The interior has 13th–14th c. frescoes and numerous bishops' tombs (mostly 14th and 15th c.). Under the cathedral are the remains of an early Christian church (6th c.), with a fine mosaic floor.

On the east side of the square is the Palazzo Pretorio, with the Torre Grande (Clock-Tower). The palace houses the Diocesan Museum, with a notable treasury and 16th c. Flemish tapestries.

Diocesan Museum

In the choir of the Renaissance church of Santa Maria Maggiore (1520–23) north-west of the cathedral are a beautiful organ gallery (1534) and a picture of 1563 with likenesses of the members of the Council of Trent, which sometimes met here.

Santa Maria Maggiore

Trento

Palazzo Municipale

From the Piazza del Duomo the wide Via Belenzani runs north. This, the finest street in the town, has a series of fine palaces with remains of painting on the façades. Near the north end of the street, on the right, is the 16th c. Palazzo Municipale, with the 15th c. Casa Geremia opposite.

Giardino Pubblico

Via Belenzani joins the main street of the town, Via Manci, which has also a number of fine palaces, as well as the beautiful Baroque church of San Fancesco Saverio. Farther north in front of the station is the Giardino Pubblico, with a monument to Dante (1896) 17.6 m/58 ft high, and a monument to Alois Negrelli (1799–1858), an early advocate of the Suez Canal. On the west side of the gardens stands the 12th c. church of San Lorenzo (restored).

Castello del Buonconsiglio (Museums)

On the north-east side of the town is the Castello del Buonconsiglio, former residence of the prince-bishop, from 1811 to 1918 a barracks and since then a museum. The 13th c. Castelvecchio, built around the oldest part, the massive round tower, was remodelled in Venetian Gothic style from 1475 onwards. The Magno Palazzo, a magnificent Renaissance building with arcaded courtyards and frescoes by Romanino and Dosso Dossi was built in 1528–35, and a linking wing added in 1686. The Castello houses the Museo Provinciale d'Arte; among its exhibits are pictures of the months in the Torre dell'Aquila by an unknown 15th c. painter, sculptures, period furniture, archaeological and ethonological collections. The building also houses the Museo del Risorgimento, with relics of the struggle for the liberation of Italy, including mementoes of the "irredentists" (supporters of the reunion of the Trentino with Italy) Cesare Battisti, Chiesa and Filzi, who were executed by the Austrians for treason in 1916.

Mausoleum of Cesare Battisti

On the Doss Trento (307 m/1013 ft) on the right bank of the Adige, is the conspicuous mausoleum of Cesare Battisti (1875–1916), from which there are fine views of Trento and the Adige valley.

From Trento to Monte Bondone

For an attractive drive to Monte Bondone leave Trento on the Riva road, going north-west, and in 3 km/2 miles turn left into a road which winds its way south-west via the village of Sardagna (571 m/1884 ft, also reached by cableway from the banks of the Adige) and Candriai (1025 m/3383 ft), to the hotel settlement of Vaneze (1300 m/4290 ft), beautifully situated on the slopes of Monte Bondone and popular both as a summer and winter sports resort.

The highest peak in the range, Palon (2098 m/6923 ft), can be climbed in 2 hours, or can be reached by means of two chair-lifts (via Vason, 1650 m/5445 ft).

There are other chair-lifts on the north side of Monte Bondone (e.g. Montesel, 1739 m/5739 ft).

From Trento to Paganella

Another rewarding drive is from Trento to Paganella. The road goes first to Fai della Paganella, about 18 km/11 miles north-west (1030 m/

3399 ft), then there is a twin chair-lift from Santel to Paganella (2125 m/7013 ft), with magnificent views, particularly of the nearby Brenta group.

Rovereto

H4

South of Trento is Rovereto (204 m/6763 ft; pop. 33,000). In the centre of the town is the Piazza Rosmini, and a little way north of this the fine Renaissance palace now occupied by the Savings Bank, with an arcaded courtyard (restored in its original style 1902–5). Nearby is the Museo Civico, with a geological collection. In the Castello (14th–15th c.), on higher ground, is a War Museum, with a collection of First World War mementoes. To the south of the old town stands a conspicuous circular building, the Sacrario di Castel Dante (306 m/1010 ft; view), in which more than 20,000 dead of the First World War are buried. Above it is a gigantic bell (22.6 tons), cast in 1965 to commemorate the dead of all nations, which is rung every evening at 8.30 or 9.30 p.m.

Situation
25 km/16 miles south of Trento

Treviso

I4

Region: Veneto
Province: Treviso (TV)
Altitude: 15 m/50 ft
Population: 85,000

Treviso, capital of the province of the same name, lies in the Veneto plain, some 20 km/12 miles north of Venice.

Situation

The ancient town of Treviso was the Roman Tarvisium, later the seat of a Lombard duchy, and in the late Middle Ages a colony of German "Venetian" merchants.

General information

It is an old-world town of narrow streets, many of them lined with arcades, and it is still surrounded by well-preserved 15th c. walls and a circuit of canals or moats.

Town walls

Sights

In the centre of the town is the picturesque Piazza dei Signori, with the Palazzo dei Trecento (after 1217), once the seat of the Great Council of the town, and the Palazzo del Podestà or Palazzo della Prefettura, with the tall Torre del Comune.

From the Piazza dei Signori Via Calmaggiore, the main street of the town, flanked by fine 15th and 16th c. houses, runs north-west to the Piazza del Duomo. The cathedral of San Pietro, with five domes, was built in the 15th and 16th c. on the site of an earlier Romanesque church, with a crypt dating from the 11th and 12th c.); the porch was added in 1836. The interior contains pictures by Titian ("Annunciation", 1517) and Paris Bordone, and fine frescoes by Pordenone (1519–20). The Cappella del Sacramento is decorated with fine sculptures by Pietro and Tullio Lombardo and L. Bregno.
To the left of the cathedral stands the Romanesque Baptistery (11th–12th c.), with 13th c. frescoes and a fine font.

*Cathedral

From the cathedral Via Canova and Via Cavour lead north-west to the Museo Civico, with an archaeological collection and an excellent pic-

Museo Civico

ture gallery, which contains frescoes by Tommaso da Modena and pictures by Bellini, Lotto, Pisanello, Titian and many other artists.

San Nicolò

In Via San Nicolò, at the south-west corner of the old town, the Dominican church of San Nicolò, a spacious Gothic church built in brick (13th–14th c.), has round piers and an unusual vaulted timber roof (restored). In the interior are a "Madonna Enthroned" by Fra Marco Pensaben and Savoldo (1521; on the high altar) and the tomb of Senator Agostino Oningo (d. 1490) by Pietro and Tullio Lombardi.
In the chapterhouse of the former Dominican monastery are frescoes by Tommaso da Modena (1352).

Porta San Tommaso

At the north-east corner of Treviso is the fine Porta San Tommaso (1518). The northern rampart walk which begins here affords beautiful views of the Alps.

Trieste   K4

Region: Friuli-Venezia Giulia
Province: Trieste (TS)
Altitude: 54 m/178 ft
Population: 239,000

Situation

The port of Trieste, capital of the region of Friuli-Venezia Giulia, lies on the Gulf of Trieste, framed by the precipitous slopes of a limestone plateau, in the north-east corner of the Adriatic.

Importance

Trieste is an important port in the Adriatic. With a greatly increased capacity since its reconstruction after war damage, it has gained considerably in importance compared with the pre-war period as a transhipment point for goods from Central Europe and the Danube region (particularly Austria). For some years Trieste has had to hold its own against the Yugoslavian ports.
An annual Trade Fair is held in Trieste.

History

Trieste, the Roman Tergeste, was held by Austria from 1382 until 1919. It was made a free port by the Emperor Charles VI in 1719, and from the end of the 18th c., after the construction of an artificial harbour, it captured the trade with the Near East which had been dominated by Venice for more than 500 years. As the last harbour of any size left to Austria Trieste developed into the leading commercial town in the Adriatic, particularly after the construction of the Semmering railway line (1854) and the new port installations to the north of the town (1867–83). After the First World War the town, mainly inhabited by Italians, was assigned to Italy and thus lost its hinterland; but the consequent decline in trade was made good by the large-scale development of industry. Under the Allied treaty with Italy in 1947 the territory immediately bordering on Trieste, with a predominantly Slav population, was ceded to Yugoslavia and the town itself (in Serbo-Croat Trst) together with part of the Istrian peninsula became a free state under the United Nations, divided into two zones. On the basis of a later treaty between Italy and Yugoslavia (5 October 1954) Zone A (area 223 sq. km/; pop. 296,000) and the town of Trieste were returned to Italian administration (and finally incorporated in Italy in 1963), while Zone B (area 516 sq. km/; pop. 67,000) was assigned to Yugoslavia; the frontier was formally defined in a treaty of November 10th 1975.

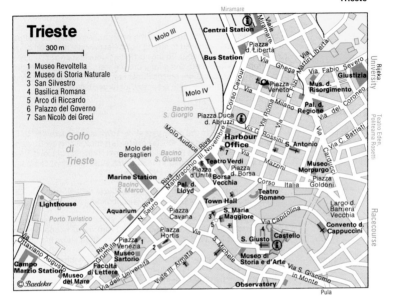

Trigste

300 m

1 Museo Revoltella
2 Museo di Storia Naturale
3 San Silvestro
4 Basilica Romana
5 Arco di Riccardo
6 Palazzo del Governo
7 San Nicolò dei Greci

Miramare

Molo III

Central Station

Bus Station

Piazza
d. Libertà

Via Ghega

Via Martiri Libertà

Via Fabio Severo

Giustizia

Molo IV

Corso Cavour

Via

Piazza
Veneto

Mus. d.
Risorgimento

Via del Coroneo

Bacino
S. Giorgio

Piazza Duca
d. Abruzzi

Via G.

Via Roma

Via Milano

Pal. d.
Regione

Golfo
di
Trieste

Molo dei
Bersaglieri

Bacino
S. Giusto

Molo Audace Riva III Novembre

Harbour
Office

Via

Rossini

S. Antonio

Via C. Battisti

Mandracchio Riva

Teatro Verdi

Mazzini

Museo
Morpurgo

Piazza
Goldoni

Marine Station

Bacino
S. Marco

Riva N. Sauro

Pal. d.
Lloyd

Piazza
d'Unità

Borsa

Piazza
d. Borsa

Corso

Italia

Lighthouse

Porto Turistico

Aquarium

Piazza
Cavana

Town Hall

Vecchia

Teatro
Romano

Largo d.
Barriera
Vecchia

Via Ottaviano Augusto

Riva Grumula

Piazza
Hortis

Via

3

S. Maria
Maggiore

Via Capitolina

Convento d.
Cappuccini

Campo
Marzio Station

© Baedeker

Museo
Sartorio

Facoltà
di Lettere

Museo
del Mare

Piazza
Venezia

2

1

Viale III Armata

S. Michele

5

S. Giusto

4

Museo di
Storia e d'Arte

Castello

Via S. Giacomo
in Monte

Observatory

Pula

Rijeka
University

Teatro Eden,
Politeama Rossetti

Racecourse

Canal Grande

497

Harbour

On the west side of the town lies the harbour, which has no natural anchorage and is exposed to strong north-east winds (the bora) blowing down from the plateau. To the north the Punta Franco Vecchio (Old Free Port) has four piers and a long breakwater. To the south, beyond the Campo Marzio station, are the Punta Franco Nuovo (New Free Port) and the industrial zone, with a number of large shipyards.

Town centre

Piazza dell'Unità d'Italia

The largest square in the older part of the town is the Piazza dell'Unità d'Italia, on the Old Harbour. On its north side is the Palazzo del Governo (1904), on the south side the massive palazzo (1882–83) of Lloyd Triestino, a shipping line founded in 1836 as the Austrian Lloyd company, and on the east side the Town Hall (1876).

Old Exchange

A little way north-east of the Town Hall, in Piazza della Borsa, is the Old Exchange (Borsa Vecchia), a neo-classical building of 1806.

Teatro Verdi
Molo Audace

North-east of the Piazza dell'Unità d'Italia, along the quay, stands the Teatro Verdi, with the Theatre Museum. From the pier opposite the theatre, on the left, the Molo Audace, there are good views of the town and the harbour.

Canale Grande

Farther along the quay, on the right, is the Greek church of San Nicolò dei Greci, and farther north again is the Canale Grande (1756), the harbour formerly used by sailing ships.

Corso Italia

From the Old Exchange the Corso Italia, the town's principal traffic artery, lined with modern buildings, runs east to the busy Piazza Gol-

Panorama of Trieste

doni, which is linked with the industrial suburbs to the south by a tunnel 347 m/380 yd long under the castle hill and another tunnel 1000 m/1094 yd long.

South-east of the Town Hall is the broad Via del Teatro Romano, at the east end of which towers the Grattacielo ("Skyscraper"). To the right of this is the Roman Theatre (Teatro Romano; 2nd c. A.D.), which was excavated in 1938. Some of the fine marble statues from the stage of the theatre are now in the Museum of History and Art.

Teatro Romano

Castle hill

To the south-west of the Roman Theatre is the castle hill. Half-way up the hill, on the right, is the small Protestant church of San Silvestro (11th c.), and opposite it, on the left, the Jesuit church of Santa Maria Maggiore (1627–82), with a Baroque interior.

Churches

Close by stands the so-called Arco di Riccardo, a gateway which probably dates from the 1st c. B.C.

Arco di Riccardo

From the Arco di Ricardo it is only a few steps to the Museo di Storia e d'Arte, in Via Cattedrale 15, which contains antiquities of varying provenance and a number of pictures, including 274 drawings by Giovanni Battista Tiepolo.

Museo di Storia e d'Arte

In the Orto Lapidario is the tomb (c. 1830) of the German classical scholar Johann Joachim Winckelmann (1717–68), who was murdered in Trieste.

Orto Lapidario

At the end of Via Cattedrale stands the cathedral of San Giusto, on the site of an Augustan temple. It was formed in the 14th c. by the joining up of two churches (6th–11th c.) and a baptistery: to the right San Giusto and to the left Santa Maria, their lateral aisles combined to make the central aisle or nave of the cathedral. Fragments of Roman work can be seen in the doorway and campanile (enlarged in 1337). In the lateral apses are fine mosaics (7th and 12th c.).
To the left of the cathedral is a column of 1560. Beyond it are the remains of a Roman forum (2nd c.), the so-called Tempio Capitolino (1st c.) and an Italian war memorial of 1934.

*Cattedrale di San Giusto

On top of the castle hill the Castello (15th–17th c.) contains the interesting Castle Museum, with medieval weapons, furniture, tapestries, etc. From the Castello and from the Parco delle Rimembranza on the north side of the castle hill there are fine views of the town and the sea.

*Castle, Museum

Piazza Venezia

On the pier to the south of the Piazza dell'Unità d'Italia is the Marine Station, and farther along the quay the Pescheria (Fish Market), with an interesting Aquarium.
Beyond this lies the Piazza Venezia.
At the corner of the square is the Museo Civio Revoltella, with good modern pictures by Italian artists and some sculpture.
Beyond the Museo Civico Revoltella is the Piazza A. Hortis. On the south-east side of the square are the Museum of Natural History (Museo di Storia Naturale) and the Municipal Library.
Nearby is the Museo Sartorio, which contains ceramics, majolica, porcelain and pictures, typical equipment of Trieste's villas at the end of the 19th century.

Marine Station
Fish Market
Aquarium

Museo Civico Revoltella
Museo di Storia Naturale

Museo Sartorio

Trieste

Museo del Mare | To the south of the harbour the Museum of the Sea (Museo del Mare) has numerous ship models of all times, particularly sailing ships.

Sights in the north

Sant'Antonio | At the end of the canal (Canale Grande) we come to the neo-clasical church of Sant'Antonio (1849), Trieste's largest church. To the right of this is the Serbian Orthodox church of San Spiridione.

Piazza Oberdan
Museo Civico del
Risorgimento | A short distance to the east of Sant'Antonio the Via G. Carducci runs north-west from near the castle hill to the Piazza Oberdan, the main square of the newer part of the town. In this square is the Museo Civico del Risorgimento.

From the Piazza Oberdan we can go north by tram to the Piazza Scorcola, with the lower station of an electric funicular to Villa Opicina.

From the Piazza Oberdan the Via Fabio Severo leads past the massive Palazzo di Giustizia to the university, built in 1939–50.

Villa Opicina

Situation
9 km/5½ miles
north-east | Reached by road from Piazza Oberdan or by funicular from Piazza Scorcola is the villa suburb of Villa Opicina (348 m/1148 ft). From the obelisk at Villa Opicina there are magnificent views of Trieste and the sea. A footpath runs north-west from the obelisk to the viewpoints of Villa Opicina (397 m/1310 ft) and Vedetta d'Italia (365 m/1205 ft), from which there are extensive prospects in all directions.

Grotta Gigante | 3 km/2 miles north of Villa Opicina is the Grotta Gigante, a stalactitic cave with a huge chamber 280 m/306 yd long and 107 m/353 ft high; at the entrance is a museum.

From Trieste to Montefalcone (about 20 km/12 miles)

Victory Beacon | 2.5 km/1½ miles north-west of Trieste, above Barcola (5 m/17 ft) rises the 68 m/224 ft-high Victory Beacon, erected in 1927, from which there are beautiful views (open throughout the day).

*Castello di
Miramare | 3.5 km/2¼ miles farther north-west, on a crag above the sea, stands the Castello di Miramare, built in 1855–60 for Archduke Maximilian of Austria, later briefly emperor of Mexico. Now owned by the State, it houses a historical museum (closed Mondays). From the terrace and the park (bronze statue of Maximilian) there are magnificent views of the sea, here protected as a nature reserve, the Parco Marino di Miramare, with the interesting flora and fauna of the northern Adriatic.

Duino | 7 km/4½ miles along the coast of the Gulf of Trieste is the little port and seaside resort of Duino, where Rainer Maria Rilke (1875–1926) wrote his "Duino Elegies". The Castel Nuovo (destroyed 1916, rebuilt 1929 onwards: no admission) and the picturesque ruins of the Castel Vecchio are magnificently situated on a projecting crag (fine views). Near the castle is the International Centre of Theoretical Physics.

San Giovanni al
Timavo | Beyond Duino the village of San Giovanni al Timavo (4 m/13 ft) has a 15th c. Gothic church, San Giovanni in Tuba, containing the remains of a mosaic pavement belonging to an earlier basilica of the 5th–6th c. At San Giovanni the River Timavo, with an abundant flow of water, emerges after an underground course of 40 km/25 miles from the caves of Skocjan in Yugoslavia, and soon afterwards flows into the sea.

Monfalcone | 7 km/4½ miles from Duino is Monfalcone (6 m/20 ft; pop. 30,000), a port and industrial town in the foothills of the karstic plateau. Continuing on

S.S. 305 we come to the military cemetery of Redipuglia, finely situated on the slopes of Monte Sei Busi (118 m/389 ft), with the graves of 100,000 men who fell in the First World War.

Turin/Torino

Region: Piemonte
Province: Torino (TO)
Altitude: 230 m/759 ft
Population: 1,035,000

Turin, capital of the north Italian region of Piedmont and the province of the same name, lies on the left bank of the Po in a fertile plain, at the confluence of the Rivers Dora Riparia and Po.

Situation

The regularity of the city's layout is an inheritance from Roman times; its present aspect was largely shaped by the architects of the Baroque period, chief among whom were Guarino Guarini (1624–83) of Modena and the Sicilian Filippo Juvarra (1678–1736). Many of the long straight streets of Turin are lined with arcades. In recent times many modern buildings have been erected, including some tower blocks.

Features of the town

The city's varied range of industry includes a number of large firms, among them the Fiat and Lancia car plants, factories manufacturing engines and rolling-stock, an electricity corporation, plants producing man-made fibres (Snia, Viscosa), woollen and cotton mills, etc. Turin is also renowned for its vermouths (Martini & Rossi, Cinzano), its chocolate and the sweets called caramelle.

Economy

Taurasia, capital of a Celto-Ligurian tribe, the Taurini, became a Roman colony in the time of Augustus under the name of Augusta Taurinorum. In the Frankish period it was the seat of a marquis, but the town did not really begin to develop until it passed in 1418 to the main branch of the counts of Savoy. During the War of the Spanish Succession it was besieged by the French but was relieved in 1706 by Prince Eugene of Savoy and Prince Leopold of Anhalt-Dessau. In 1720 it became capital of the Kingdom of Sardinia and Piedmont, and after the French occupation (1798–1814) became the centre of the Italian striving towards unity. From 1861 to 1865 it was capital of the Kingdom of Italy. The house of Savoy kept its royal status until 1945.

History

Piazza Castello

The central feature of the older part of the town is the Piazza Castello, in the middle of which stands the massive Palazzo Madama. The core of the structure is a 13th c. castle built on the remains of the Roman east gate which was enlarged in the 15th c. and embellished by Filippo Juvarra in 1718 with the handsome west front, a fine example of Piedmontese Baroque architecture, and the magnificent double staircase.

* Palazzo Madama

The palace now houses the Museo Civico d'Arte Antica (ground floor and second floor), with a valuable collection of sculpture in stone and wood, stained glass; pictures and applied art (Duc de Berry's Book of Hours, with Dutch miniatures of c. 1400). On the first floor are the state apartments, richly appointed in 18th c. style.

Museo Civico d'Arte Antica

On the north side of the Piazza Castello is the courtyard of the Royal Palace, to the left of which can be seen the Baroque church of San Lorenzo (1668–80) by Guarini, with an unusual and boldly designed

San Lorenzo
Palazzo Reale

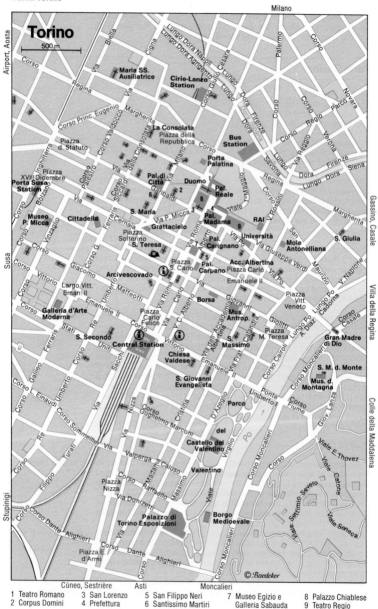

Milano

Torino

500 m

Airport, Aosta

Corso

Maria SS.
Ausiliatrice

Cirie-Lanzo
Station

Corso Princ. Eugenio

Margherita

La Consolata

Piazza della
Repubblica

Piazza
d. Statuto

Bus
Station

Porta
Palatina

Piazza
XVIII Dicembre

Pal. di
Città

Duomo

**Porta Susa
Station**

2

Pal.
Reale

S. Maria

8

3

4

**Museo
P. Micca**

Cittadella

Grattacielo

Pal.
Madama

9

RAI

Universitá

S. Giulia

S. Teresa

5

Pal.
Carignano

Mole
Antonelliana

Piazza
Solferino

Arcivescovado

Piazza
S. Carlo

Pal.
Carpano

Acc. Albertina
Piazza Carlo

Largo Vitt.
Eman. II

Emanuele II

Piazza
Vitt.
Veneto

Borsa

**Galleria d'Arte
Moderna**

S. Secondo

Piazza
Carlo
Felice

Mus.
Antrop.

Gran Madre
di Dio

Central Station

S.
Massimo

Piazza
M. Teresa

S. M. d. Monte

Chiesa
Valdese

Mus. d.
Montagna

S. Giovanni
Evangelista

Parco

del

Castello del
Valentino

Valentino

Piazza
Nizza

Palazzo di
Torino Esposizioni

Borgo
Medioevale

Piazza E.
d'Armi

© Baedeker

Gassino, Casale

Villa della Regina

Colle della Maddalena

Stupinigi

Cúneo, Sestrière   Asti   Moncalieri

1 Teatro Romano	3 San Lorenzo	5 San Filippo Neri	7 Museo Egizio e	8 Palazzo Chiablese
2 Corpus Domini	4 Prefettura	6 Santissimo Martiri	Galleria Sabauda	9 Teatro Regio

A 1907 "Itala" in the Motor Museum

an example of early industrial architecture. There are plans to change it into an office and shopping centre, with a museum, etc. A kilometre farther south, in the suburb of Mirafiori, is the new Fiat plant (1939).

In the Colli Torinesi

10 km/6 miles north-east of Turin, reached on a road which follows the Po to the suburb of Sassi (218 m/719 ft) and then winds its way up to the top of the hill (or rack railway from Sassi, 16 minutes), is the Basilica di Superga (672 m/2218 ft), on the second highest hill in the Colli Torinesi. This large and conspicuous church, built on a centralised plan with a dome 75 m/248 ft high flanked by 60 m/198 ft high towers, the master-piece of the great Baroque architect Juvarra, was erected in 1717–31 to commemorate Prince Eugene's victory in 1706 and served as the mau-soleum of the royal house of Savoy from 1730 to 1849 (tombs in crypt). From the terrace in front of the church, in clear weather, there is a prospect of the Alps; from the forecourt there is a view of Turin.

Another attractive excursion (10 km/6 miles) is to the Colle della Mad-dalena (715 m/2360 ft), the highest of the Colli Torinesi, crowned by the Faro della Vittoria, a beacon in the form of a bronze statue (by E. Rubino, 1928) of the goddess of victory carrying a torch, 18.5 m/61 ft high on an 8 m/9 yd base; from the top there are fine panoramic views.

*Basilica di Superga

Faro della Vittoria

From Turin via Sestriere to Montgenèvre (about 115 km/71 miles)

Turin is a good base for some magnificent drives into the mountains. Particularly fine is the road to Sestriere and the Montgenèvre pass. Leave Turin by way of the Fiat works at Mirafiori.

Stupinigi | 11 km/7 miles: Stupinigi (244 m/805 ft), a magnificent Baroque castle (by Filippo Juvarra, 1729–33), set in a large park which now houses the Museo d'Arte e dell'Ammobigliamento (closed Mondays and Fridays).

Pinerolo | 27 km/17 miles: Pinerolo (376 m/1241 ft; pop. 36,000), a beautifully situated town with an 11th c. cathedral. In the church of San Maurizio is a burial vault of the house of Savoy. Beyond this stands the church of the Madonna delle Grazie, from which there is a fine view of Monviso (3841 m/12,675 ft).

Torre Pellice | From Pinerolo a detour (15 km/9 miles south-west) can be made to the little town of Torre Pellice (516 m/1703 ft), a popular summer resort prettily situated in the Pellice valley, a stronghold of the Waldensians, Protestants who fled from France during the Albigensian wars (1209–29) and sought refuge in the Piedmontese valleys on the east side of the Cottian Alps, where they were able to maintain themselves in spite of frequent persecution. There are now some 25,000 Waldensians, most of them still French-speaking, in the Pellice valley and the lower Chisone valley.

Beyond Pinerolo the road to Montgenèvre ascends the Chisone valley, towards the main chain of the Cottian Alps.

Perosa Argentina | 18 km/11 miles: Perosa Argentina (614 m/2026 ft; pop. 5000), a little industrial town mainly populated by Waldensians. The road then traverses a gorge and before reaching Fenestrelle passes the large Agnelli Sanatorium, on a hill to the right (1700 m/5610 ft; road, 6.5 km/4 miles, and cableway).

Fenestrelle | 16 km/10 miles: Fenestrelle (1154 m/3808 ft), a village with imposing fortifications extending up to the 18th c. fort of San Carlo, linked by 4000 steps.

Sestriere | 22 km/14 miles: Sestriere (2033 m/6709 ft), on the saddle between the Chisone valley and the valley of the Dora Riparia. This is one of Europe's largest winter sports resorts, also popular in summer. Cableways to Monte Fraitève (2690 m/8877 ft) to the north-west, Monte Sises (2658 m/8771 ft; upper station 2597 m/8570 ft) to the south-east, Monte Banchetta (2552 m/8421 ft) to the east; chair-lift, many ski-lifts.

Beyond Sestriere the road descends into the valley of the Dora Riparia.

Cesana Torinese | 11 km/7 miles: Cesana Torinese (1354 m/4468 ft), where it joins the road from Turin via Susa. Chair-lift to Sagna Longa (2002 m/6607 ft) and Colle Bercia (Monti della Luna, 2203 m/7270 ft). Beyond Cesana the road continues to climb.

Claviere | 6 km/3¾ miles: Claviere or Clavières (1760 m/5808 ft), a resort much favoured by winter sports enthusiasts; chair-lift to La Cloche (1960 m/6468 ft).

Soon after Claviere the road comes to the French frontier.

Col de Montgenèvre | 2 km/1¼ miles: Col de Montgenèvre (1854 m/6118 ft; winter sports, chair-lifts to 2600 m/8580 ft), formerly an important Alpine pass providing the shortest route between the Po valley and southern France, used by Julius Caesar and in the Middle Ages by the Emperor Barbarossa among many others.

Turin via Susa to the Montgenèvre pass (about 95 km/59 miles)

Rivoli | Leave Turin on S.S. 25, going west. In 13 km/8 miles the road comes to Rivoli (390 m/1287 ft; pop. 5000), an old-world town situated between morainic hills, once a favourite residence of the house of Savoy, with a Baroque palace (by Juvarra, 1712), of which only a third was completed (419 m/1383 ft).

Beyond Rivoli the road enters the Cottian Alps and ascends the Val di Susa, the valley of the Dora Riparia. At the mouth of the valley, on a hill to the left, is the Sacra di San Michele abbey (11th–13th c.: alt. 962 m/3175 ft).

40 km/25 miles: Susa (503 m/1660 ft; pop. 7000), an old town, beauti-   Susa
fully situated between high mountains, which controlled the Montgenèvre and Mont Cenis roads. On the west side of the picturesque old
town, on the right bank of the Dora, rises a marble triumphal arch (13.5
m/44½ ft high) erected in 8 B.C. in honour of the Emperor Augustus by
the prefect Cottius, after whom the Cottian Alps are named. North-east
of the arch stands the cathedral of San Giusto (11th–13th c.), with a
beautiful campanile.

At Susa the road forks: Montgenèvre to the left, Mont Cenis straight
ahead.

The road to Mont Cenis (S.S. 25), constructed by Napoleon in 1803–10,
runs uphill, with numerous curves and sharp bends.

10 km/6 miles: Molaretto (Italian customs).

9 km/5½ miles: Passo del Paradiso, which since 1947 has marked the   Passo del Paradiso
French-Italian frontier.

4 km/2½ miles: to the left the Lac du Mont Cenis, in a beautiful setting
(1913 m/6313 ft).

4 km/2½ miles: Mont Cenis pass (Col du Mont Cenis, 2084 m/6877 ft), on   Mont Cenis pass
the old French-Italian frontier.

Beyond Susa the Montgenèvre road (S.S. 24) passes through a gorge
formed by the Dora Riparia.

12 km/7 miles: Exiles (on left), a picturesque village dominated by a   Exiles
massive fortress (17th c.); fine views.

The defensive fortress of Exiles

509

Oulx Sauze d'Oulx	11 km/7 miles: Oulx (1100 m/3630 ft), 5 km/3 miles east of which is the winter sports resort of Sauze d'Oulx (1510 m/4983 ft; chair-lifts, including to Sportinia (2170 m/7161 ft), to the south.
Bardonecchia	14 km/9 miles north-west of Sauze d'Oulx is the village of Bardonecchia, a popular resort both in summer and winter (1312 m/4330 ft; pop. 3000). It lies near the entrance to the Galleria del Fréjus, the first Alpine tunnel (1861–70), leading to the French town of Modane (Mont Cenis rail tunnel, 13.6 km/8½ miles long; road tunnel 12.3 km/7½ miles long). From Bardonecchia there are a number of chair-lifts, including one via Granges Hyppolites (1520 m/5016 ft: change lifts) up Colomion (2054 m/6778 ft).
Cesana Torinese	11 km/7 miles: Cesana Torinese, where the road from Turin via Sestriere comes in.
Montgenèvre pass	8 km/5 miles: Montgenèvre pass (1854 m/6118 ft).

Turin to the Santuario d'Oropa (about 100 km/62 miles)

Biella	86 km/53 miles north-east of Turin, beautifully situated in the foothills of the Alps on the River Cervo, is the industrial town of Biella (420 m/1386 ft; pop. 52,000). In the lower town are the cathedral (originally built 1402, rebuilt 1772, façade 1825), and adjoining an early Romanesque baptistery (9th–11th c.) and the Town Hall. In the south-west part of the lower town stands the beautiful Renaissance church of San Sebastiano (1604; façade 1882). To the west, above the lower town (funicular), is the picturesque upper town or Piazzo, from which there are fine views.
Santuario della Madonna d'Oropa	From Biella an interesting excursion on S.S. 144 (13 km/8 miles), goes north, with beautiful views, past the little spa of Oropa Bagni (1060 m/3498 ft) to the magnificent Santuario della Madonna d'Oropa (1180 m/3894 ft), the most popular place of pilgrimage in Piedmont, said to have been founded by St Eusebius in 369. From here a cableway runs up to the Rifugio Mucrone (1820 m/6006 ft), near the Lago di Mucrone, and then to Monte Mucrone (2335 m/7706 ft; cableway, station 2189 m/7224 ft). From the Rifugio Mucrone there is another cableway up Monte Camino (2391 m/7890 ft; mountain hut); from which there are superb views, including Monte Rosa and the Matterhorn.

Through the Monferrato (about 155 km/96 miles)

	There is an attractive drive through the Monferrato uplands, famous for their wine.
Alba	The road comes to Alba (34 km/21 miles; alt. 172 m/568 ft; pop. 31,000), which has a Gothic cathedral (beautiful choir-stalls of 1512), fine churches and medieval towers. It then continues through the vine-growing Langhe region, where the much sought-after white truffles are harvested in autumn, and down the valley of the Bormida, on the edge of the Ligurian Apennines, to Savona, on the Riviera dei Fiori.

Turin via Acqui Terme to Genoa (about 185 km/115 miles)

	Another interesting drive leads from Turin via Acqui Terme to Genoa. Leave on S.S. 29 (the Alessandria road), which runs through Poirino (249 m/822 ft).
Asti	56 km/35 miles: Asti.
Piano d'Isola	9 km/5½ miles: Piano d'Isola (130 m/429 ft). The road now leaves the Tanaro valley and traverses a densely populated upland region (vine-growing).

20 km/12 miles: Nizza Monferrato (138 m/455 ft; pop. 10,000), a little vine-growing town on the River Belbo. The road runs over a hill and enters the wide valley of the Bormida.

Nizza Monferrato

19 km/12 miles: Acqui Terme (164 m/541 ft; pop. 22,000), a spa and centre of the wine trade on the left bank of the Bormida, with a cathedral consecrated in 1067, and the church of San Pietro (c. 1015). The mineral springs, containing salt and sulphur, are recommended for the treatment of rheumatic conditions. The hottest spring (La Bollente, 75° C/167° F) is in the Nuove Terme, in the town. From here the Corso Bagni leads over the river (beyond the bridge, on the right, remains of an ancient aqueduct) and past a large thermal swimming pool (6500 sq. m) to the Antiche Terme.
Beyond Acqui the road continues for a short distance along the Bormida valley and then climbs into the Ligurian Apennines, goes over a hill and descends into the Orba valley.

Acqui Terme

24 km/15 miles: Ovada (186 m/614 ft), at the junction of the Stura and the Orba.

Ovada

17 km/11 miles: Campo Ligure (342 m/1129 ft; pop. 4000), a picturesquely situated little town and summer resort with a tower which belonged to a 13th c. castle. There is an interesting museum with local filigree work.

Campo Ligure

8 km/5 miles: Passo del Turchino (532 m/1756 ft: short tunnel), from which the road runs down into the pleasant valley of the Leiro.

Passo del Turchino

28 km/17 miles: Genoa.

Genoa

Tuscany/Toscana   G/H5–7

Region: Toscana
Provinces: Firenze (FI), Arezzo (AR), Grosseto (GR), Livorno (LI), Lucca (LU), Massa-Carrara (MS), Pisa (PI), Pistoia (PT), Siena (SI)
Area: 22,992 sq. km/8875 sq. miles
Population: 3,580,600

Tuscany is a Central Italian region. It extends from the ridge of the Tuscan or Etruscan Apennines over the Tuscan uplands, with their gently rounded hills and their clumps of slender cypresses, to the Maremma along the Tyrrhenian coast, and beyond this to Elba and a number of smaller islands off the Tuscan coast.
The capital of Tuscany is Florence.

Situation
* *Scenery

Most of the inhabitants of Tuscany live in the catchment areas of the industrial conurbations in the Arno valley, between Florence and Livorno and from there north along the coast to Carrara. In this area are concentrated a multiplicity of enterprises, mostly of small and medium size, covering an extraordinary range of crafts and industries. The major industries are the working of minerals (iron, lignite, mercury) and marble, but other important activities are engineering, shipbuilding, pharmaceuticals, glass and crystal manufacture, textiles and various forms of applied and decorative art.

Economy

In the upland areas the predominant activity is agriculture, together with the various industries concerned with the processing of its produce. A leading place among these is taken by the wine-making industry. Tuscany is the home of the famous dry dark red wine, Chianti, which is found here in excellent quality. Corn and olives are also grown in large quantities, and in the Arno valley and along the coast there is much market gardening and flower-growing.

Wine-making industry

Tuscany/Toscana

A vineyard in the Arno valley, Tuscany

Tourism

A major contribution to the economy is also made by the tourist trade, particularly in the great art centres of Florence, Siena and Pisa, the numerous spas (Montecatini Terme, Bagni di Lucca, etc.) and the resorts on the coast.

History

The present territory of Tuscany coincides broadly with that of ancient Etruria, occupied by the numerous city states of the Etruscans which flourished between the 9th and 5th c. B.C., forming a kind of federation (the league of twelve towns), which varied in membership and nature from time to time, and extending their power and influence into Campania and the Po valley. Since the surviving documents in the Etruscan language are confined to inscriptions of a funerary or votive nature or relating to the ownership of property, they tell us little about the advanced culture of the Etruscans, the origins of which are still obscure. Much more informative are the objects recovered from their tombs, which usually imitate the form of houses, and their sculpture and tomb painting, predominantly depicting scenes from everyday life, which bear witness to a high standard of art and craftsmanship, particularly of the goldsmiths.

Necropolises

The Etruscan cities usually occupied strong defensive positions, preferably on isolated rocky plateaux with good views of the surrounding area. Outside the cities lay the extensive necropolises. As the massive circular tombs of this period show, the Etruscans were familiar with the principle of the false dome and the barrel vault. They were a seafaring people who carried on an active trade with the other peoples of the Mediterranean but were also – if Greek accounts are to be believed – much given to piracy.

The power of the Etruscans began to decline in the 5th c., and by the beginning of the 4th c. the decline was irremediable. More and more of their territory fell into the hands of the Romans, and by about 300 B.C. the whole of Etruria was under Roman control.

After the fall of Rome Tuscany was successively ruled by the Ostrogoths, the Byzantines, the Lombards and the Franks, and in the 11th c. it became part of the county of Tuscia. In the 13th c. Florence, now steadily increasing in strength, succeeded in establishing its dominance over the rival cities in the region, particularly Siena and Pisa, and after the defeat of these two towns in the 15th c. asserted its position as the intellectual and political centre of the Duchy of Tuscany, which became a Grand Duchy under Cosimo I Medici.

In later centuries the region suffered from the effects of the War of the Spanish Succession, from epidemics of plague and from crippling taxation. Under the Treaty of Vienna in 1735 Tuscany passed to Francis Stephen of Lorraine, husband of the Empress Maria Theresa. On 1 October 1800, as the kingdom of Etruria, it was assigned to Duke Luigi of Parma, but in 1807 it was incorporated in the French Empire and ruled by Napoleon's sister Elisa Bachiocchi, who took the title of duchess of Tuscany. Her successor Ferdinand II and his son Leopold II of Austria came into violent conflict with nationalist and anti-Austrian forces in the country, and in 1859 Leopold, finding himself without any support, abdicated under protest. In 1860, following a referendum, Tuscany was formally annexed by the kingdom of Sardinia and Piedmont, the nucleus of the later united kingdom of Italy.

Every visitor to Tuscany will of course want to visit the great art cities of Florence, Pisa and Siena.

**Art centres

There is also much of interest to see along the Via Aurelia, which runs south from Pisa via Livorno to Grosseto, now keeping close to the coast, now a little way inland.

Via Aurelia

Populonia

On the way down it is well worth making a detour from the rather featureless port and industrial town of Piombino (19 m/63 ft; pop. 40,000) to the village of Populonia (179 m/591 ft), situated high above the sea on the north side of a promontory, formerly an island, 14 km/9 miles north of Piombino. This was the Etruscan port of Pupluna, with remains of its circuit of walls and an interesting Etruscan necropolis on the coast below the village. The Etruscan Museum (Museo Etrusco) contains numerous finds from the necropolis.

Grosseto

The provincial capital of Grosseto (12 m/40 ft; pop. 70,000) is the economic centre of the strip of coastal territory known as the Maremma. The town was founded in the Middle Ages round a small castle which was erected to protect the Via Aurelia, the old Roman road from Pisa to Rome. The main square of the town, which is still surrounded by a wall with six bastions, is the Piazza Dante, on the north side of which stand the Town Hall and the cathedral (begun 1294; façade restored 1840–45). In the north transept of the cathedral is an "Assumption" by Matteo di Giovanni (15th c.). A little way north of the cathedral is the interesting Museo d'Arte Sacra e d'Arte della Maremma which contains prehistoric finds, particularly from the Etruscan and Roman period. The museum also has a collection of sacral art.

6 km/3¾ miles north-east of Grosseto we come to the sulphur springs of Bagno Roselle (25 m/83 ft). Nearby are the remains of Rusellae (184 m/

*Rusellae

Piazza Dante in Grosseto

607 ft), one of the twelve principal cities of the Etruscan federation, with sections of its circuit of walls still standing, a number of Etruscan houses and a Roman amphitheatre.

*Vetulonia

Some 20 km/12 miles north-west of Grosseto, on higher ground, is Vetulonia (344 m/1135 ft), now part of the community of Castiglione della Pescaia. Under the name of Vatluna it belonged to the Etruscan federation. To the north-east and the west of the former town are Etruscan necropolises. The principal part of the finds of the tombs can be seen in the museums of Grosseto and Florence.

Abbadia San Salvatore

About 60 km/37 miles south-east of Siena is the old town of Abbadia San Salvatore (812 m/2680 ft; pop. 8000). The Abbazia di San Salvatore (Abbey of the Saviour), to which the little old town owes its name, is one of the oldest abbeys in Tuscany, of which only the church is left. The notable crypt contains columns with partly richly decorated capitals.

*Monte Amiata

There is an attractive road from Abbadia San Salvatore (14 km/9 miles) to the top of Monte Amiata (1738 m/5735 ft), an extinct and craterless volcano. From the summit, with a mountain hut and an iron cross 22 m/73 ft high, there are magnificent views.
The drive round Monte Amiata from Abbadia San Salvatore (65 km/40 miles) is also very rewarding.

Udine

Region: Friuli–Venezia Giulia
Province: Udine (UD)
Altitude: 110 m/363 ft
Population: 100,000

Udine, capital of the province of the same name, lies at the east end of the north Italian plain in the flood-plain of the River Tagliamento. The town is about 40 km/25 miles from the Adriatic coast and about 20 km/12 miles from the frontier of the former Yugoslavia.
The town is the see of an archbishop.

Situation

Udine, the Roman Utina, was from 1238 to 1752 the residence of the Patriarchs of Aquileia (south of Udine on the Adriatic coast), to whom the Emperor Otto II had granted the castle in 983. The town came under Venetian control in 1420.

History

Piazza della Libertà

The town contains many old noble palaces, some of them with rather faded painting on their façades. The principal square, at the foot of the castle hill, is the Piazza della Libertà, in which stands the Palazzo del Comune (Loggia del Lionello), in the style of the Doge's Palace in Venice (1457, restored 1876).

Palazzo del Comune

Opposite the Palazzo del Comune is the Porticato di San Giovanni or Loggia di San Giovanni (1533), a triumphal arch surrounded by arches on slender columns, the entrance of St John's chapel, now a war

Porticato di San Giovanni

Udine: Porticato di San Giovanni

515

memorial. Inside there is a victory column by Raimondo d'Aronco. The adjoining clock-tower resembles the one in Venice.

On the south side of the Piazza della Libertà is a tall column bearing the lion of St Mark, and on the north side a statue of the Goddess of Peace, commemorating the peace of Campoformio (1797) between France and Austria, in which Venice came under Austrian control.

Castello

Museums

On the castle hill, north of the Piazza della Libertà, is the 16th c. Castello, which suffered severe damage from an earthquake in 1976, but has since been restored. In the Hall of Honour, in the centre of the main building, the members of the parliament of Friuli once met. The Castello now houses the Museo Civico and the Galleria d'Arte Antica. The Art Museum contains pictures and sculpture of the 15th c. up to modern times, including pictures by Carpaccio, Giovanni Battista Tiepolo, Bicci di Lorenzo, Ghirlandaio, Caravaggio and Canova.

From the Watch Tower of the castle there are fine views of the Alps.

Cathedral

A short distance south-east of the Piazza della Libertà, in the Piazza del Duomo, stands the cathedral, a Gothic structure of 1236, remodelled in the 18th c. It has a hexagonal campanile. Above the main doorway is a lunette, the reliefs of which depict the crucifixion of Christ. The interior is decorated with stucco and frescoes by Giovanni Battista Tiepolo.

Oratorio della Purità

Behind the cathedral is the little Oratorio della Purità, with frescoes by Giovanni Battista Tiepolo and his son Giovanni Domenico Tiepolo.

Archbishop's Palace

North of the cathedral is the Archbishop's Palace, with notable frescoes by Giovanni Battista Tiepolo (1726–1730) and Giovanni da Udine (1487–1584).

Tempio Ossario dei Caduti

In the west of the town, the newer part, is the Piazzale XXVI Luglio. In its centre is a sculpture of 1969, a memorial to the resistance fighters who fought fascism in the Second World War. In the same square stands the Tempio Ossario dei Caduti d'Italia, a domed structure of 1931 and a mausoleum for 22,000 Italians who died in the First World War.

Umbria H/IG/7

Region: Umbria
Provinces: Perugia (PG) and Terni (TR)
Area: 8456 sq. km/3265 sq. miles
Population: 815,000

Situation

The Central Italian region of Umbria extends on both sides of the Tiber, whose wide valley is flanked by the foothills of the Apennines. Umbria is bounded on the west by Tuscany, on the east by the Marche and on the south by Latium.

The political region of Umbria, with its capital Perugia, takes in the two provinces of Perugia and Terni.

Economy

The spacious countryside of Umbria, with its easily accessible hills and its fertile lowlands, has been from time immemorial a prosperous farming region (corn, olives, wine, sugar-beet, tobacco, market gardening; sheep). Umbria is one of the regions where truffles can be found.

View of the Umbrian town of Orvieto

Only around the towns of Terni, Narni and Foligno, where power is supplied by large hydro-electric stations, has there been any considerable development of industry (chemicals, metal-working); textile manufacture and the production of craft articles have also become established in the Perugia and Spoleto areas.
An important contribution to the economy is also made by the tourist trade.

In ancient times this was the homeland of the Umbrians, and there was also some Etruscan settlement in the region. In 295 B.C. it came under Roman control, and in the reign of Augustus was combined with Etruria to form the sixth region (Regio VI) of the Empire. After the fall of Rome and the subsequent Gothic wars it became part of the Lombard duchy of Spoleto and of the States of the Church. During the Middle Ages, rent by bitter conflicts between the various towns – which enjoyed a large measure of independence – and the ruling families, the region fell into a decline, until the Church succeeded in establishing its authority in the 16th c.
In 1860, after a plebiscite, Umbria and its capital Perugia became part of the united kingdom of Italy.

History

Umbria has a number of towns which stand high among Italy's tourist attractions, in particular Perugia, Assisi and Orvieto.

Features of interest

Lake Trasimene

To the west of Perugia is Lake Trasimene (Lago Trasimeno; Latin Lacus Trasimenus). The lake, lying at an altitude of 259 m/855 ft, is the largest in the Italian peninsula (area 128 sq. km/, circumference c. 50 km/31 miles; greatest depth 7 m/8 yd) and is well-stocked with fish. Fed almost solely by rain-water, it is subject to considerable variation of level.

Lake Trasimene is famous as the scene of the second Punic War, a battle between Carthaginians and Romans, in which Hannibal defeated the Roman consul Gaius Flaminius in 217 B.C.

On a promontory on the north side of the lake is the ancient little town of Passignano sul Trasimento (289 m/954 ft), with an old castle; on another promontory rising above the west side of the lake is Castiglione del Lago (304 m/1003ft), with the ducal castle of the Cornia family.

Urbino I6

Region: Marche
Province: Pesaro e Urbino (PS)
Altitude: 485 m/1601 ft
Population: 16,000

Situation
The town of Urbino lies on a steep-sided hill in the north of the Central Italian region of Marche, some 35 km/22 miles west of Pesaro and about 70 km/43 miles south of Rimini.
Urbino is the see of an archbishop.

History
Urbino was the Roman Urvinum Metaurense. In 1213 it came into the hands of the Montefeltro family, which acquired the ducal title in the 15th c. The court of Duke Federico di Montefeltro (1444–82), a discrimating patron of art and learning, was recognised to be the most splendid of its day. From 1508 to 1631 the duchy was held by the Della Rovere family; thereafter it was incorporated in the States of the Church.

Art
In the 15th c. the painters Paolo Uccello, Piero della Francesca, Melozzo da Forli and Giovanni Santi (Raphael's father) worked in Urbino. The great architect Bramante (1444–1514) was born near the town, and probably worked for Luciano de Laurana. Raphael (1483–1520) and the Baroque painter Federigo Barocci (c. 1537–1612) were natives of Urbino.

Cathedral

In the centre of the town is the Piazza della Repubblica, the market square. From here Via Vittorio Veneto leads up to the Piazza Duca Federico, on the north side of which stands the cathedral, rebuilt in 1801 after the destruction of an earlier church by an earthquake in 1789. It contains a number of fine paintings, including in particular works by Federigo Barocci. In the third chapel in the crypt (entered from outside the church, under the arcades to the left) is a marble figure of the dead Christ by Giovanni Bandini.

Cathedral Museum
To the right of the cathedral is the Museo del Duomo "Albani", which contains 14th c. frescoes, ceramics, sacral objects and chasubles, 14th–17th c. pictures and a bronze paschal candelabra.

*Palazzo Ducale

The Palazzo Ducale, opposite the cathedral, built by the Dalmatian architect Luciano da Laurana from 1465 onwards, is the most perfectly

Urbino: Palazzo Ducale

preserved example of an Italian princely residence of the period. Notable features are the colonnaded courtyard (*c.* 1470) and the staircase. The magnificent state apartments on the first and second floors now house the Galleria Nazionale delle Marche (National Gallery of the Marche), a rich picture gallery, with Raphael's "Mute" and pictures by Paolo Uccello ("Miracle of the Communion"), Piero della Francesca, Titian, Barocci, Gentileschi and Simone de Magistris. There are also tapestries and sculpture.

*Galleria Nazionale delle Marche

Opposite the Ducal Palace can be seen the church of San Domenico (14th–5th c.), with a fine doorway by Maso di Bartolomeo (1449–54). A little way south is the university founded in 1671, with a coat of arms above the doorway.

San Domenico

Piazza della Repubblica

From the Piazza della Repubblica Via Raffaello climbs up towards the north-west. At the near end, on the right, is the church of San Francesco (14th c.), with a porch and a fine campanile. On the left (No. 57) is Raphael's Birthplace (Casa Natale di Raffaello; plaque and museum); Raphael lived here until the age of fourteen.

Raphael's birthplace

Via Raffaello meets the spacious, park-like Piazzale Roma, with a Monument to Raphael (1897).
From the adjoining bastion, Pian del Monte, there are excellent views, extending as far as San Marino.

Monument to Raphael

South-west of the Piazza della Repubblica, at the end of the short Via Barocci, the Oratorio di San Giuseppe has a life-size Nativity group by Federico Brandano.

Oratorio di San Giuseppe

Nearby in the Oratorio di San Giovanni are paintings by Lorenzo and Jacopo Salimbeni (1416).

*Furlo Gorge

Situation
20 km/12 miles
south-east of Urbino

There is a rewarding drive to the Furlo Gorge (Gola del Furlo), enclosed by sheer rock faces. At the narrowest point is the Galleria Romana del Furlo or Forulus (177 m/584 ft), a tunnel 37 m/40 yd long carrying the Via Flaminia through the rock. It bears an inscription recording that it was cut by the Emperor Vespasian in A.D. 76. Adjoining is the older Galleria Piccola del Furlo 8 m/9 yd long (3rd c. B.C.).

Varese   E4

Region: Lombardia
Province: Varese (VA)
Altitude: 383 m/1264 ft
Population: 88,000

Situation

The provincial capital of Varese is attractively situated on hills along the southern edge of the Alps near the Lago di Varese, with the Campo dei Fiori looming above it. The town, a centre of shoe manufacture, lies some 20 km/12 miles west of Como and some 50 km/31 miles north-west of the Lombardian city of Milan.

Sights

The hub of the town's traffic is the Piazza Monte Grappa, with monumental modern buildings and a tower. From here the main street of Varese, the arcaded Corso Matteotti, leads to the Piazza del Podestà. A little way east stands the church of San Vittore, built in its present form to the design of Pellegrino Tibaldi (1580–1615), with a neo-classical façade (1795) and a campanile (1617–1773) 72 m/238 ft high. Behind it is a baptistery (1185–87).

Palazzo Ducale

A short distance west of Piazza Monte Grappa, on the left-hand side of Via Luigi Sacco, the Palazzo Ducale or Palazzo Estense, built for Duke Francesco III of Este in 1766–73 and used as a summer residence until 1780, is now the Town Hall.

Municipal Museums

Behind the palace is the Giardino Pubblico (formerly the palace grounds), beautifully laid out in traditional Italian style. In the southern part of the gardens is the Villa Mirabello, in which are the Municipal Museums. Of particular interest are the Museo del Risorgimento, with records of Garibaldi and the movement for a united Italy, and the fine Museo Archeologico, with prehistoric and Roman antiquities, including material from pile dwellings on the Lago di Varese and from Roman tombs.

Colle dei Campigli

1.5 km/1 mile west of the Palazzo Ducale is the Colle dei Campigli (453 m/1495 ft), on which are the Kursaal and the Grand Hotel Palace. From the top there are magnificent views of the Lago di Varese and the western Alps, with Monte Rosa.

Lago di Varese

Villa Cagnola

A little way west of the town we come to the Lago di Varese. Near the east end of the lake, above the village of Gazzada, is the Villa Cagnola,

Sacro Monte, with Varese in the distance

bequeathed to the Vatican by Count Cagnola, with valuable furniture and tapestries. From the large park there are magnificent views of the lake and the Alps.

Sacro Monte

The road runs north-west to Sant'Ambrogio Olona and from there up the Sacro Monte (880 m/2904 ft), on the summit of which is a pilgrimage chapel (view).

Situation
8 km/5 miles west

Campo dei Fiori

Another rewarding trip is to take the road which runs up from Sant' Ambrogio Olona to the Campo dei Fiori (1032 m/3406 ft; far-ranging views).
Continue on foot (20 minutes) to the summit of Monte Tre Croci (1083 m/3574 ft), from where there is a famous view embracing six lakes, the Lombard plain and part of the chain of the Alps.

Situation
10 km/6 miles
north-west

Fort of Sibrium

South of Varese, in the forest near the village of Castelseprio, are the remains of the Lombard fort of Sibrium, with a restored castle. In the adjoining church of Santa Maria Foris Portas (7th or 8th c.) frescoes dating from the 7th resp. 8th–9th c. were exposed in 1944.

Castiglione Olona

Situation
10 km/6 miles south
of Varese

A little way west of S.S. 233 (the Milan road), is the old-world village of Castiglione Olona (307 m/1013 ft). In the Gothic collegiate church are fine frescoes by Tuscan masters, among them a Virgin Mary by Masolino da Panicale, a pupil of Giotto. The frescoes in the baptistery (1435) depict scenes from the life of John the Baptist, also by Masolino. Inside the notable Chiesa di Villa (1430–41) is the tomb of Count Guido Castiglioni.

Venetia/Veneto   H/I3–5

Region: Veneto
Provinces: Venezia (VE), Belluno (BL), Padova (PD), Rovigo (RO), Trevisio (TV), Verona (VR) and Vicenza (VI)
Area: 18,364 sq. km/7088 sq. miles
Population: 4,366,200

Situation

The region of Venetia, the territory of the old Republic of Venice, lies in the north-east of the North Italian plain, extending northward from the lower course of the Po to the Venetian Alps and bounded on the west by Lake Garda and the River Mincio, on the east by the Adriatic coast, a strip of former marshland now occupied by numerous lagoons.

The area is now divided into three administrative regions: in the east Friuli–Venezia Giulia (see Friuli); in the north Trentino–Alto Adige (see Alto Adige); and between these two, extending towards the Po and the Adriatic, the region of Veneto (formerly Venezia Euganea), the heartland of the old territory of Venetia.

Economy

The region of Veneto is notable for its scenic variety and economic diversity. The population is concentrated mainly in the larger cities of the Po plain, which has a highly developed agriculture (grain, particularly maize and rice, vines, fruit, vegetables, cattle-farming), with the associated processing industries (canning, manufacture of foodstuffs). Large companies have settled here as there is much general industrial development (textiles, building materials, metalworking, chemicals, petro-chemicals, shipbuilding), promoted by an abundant supply of power (hydro-electric schemes in the Alps, natural gas in the Po plain). The region is also famous for its applied and decorative art, in particular the glass-blowing and lace-making of the Venice area.

Tip

The holiday and tourist trade is an additional source of income. Lake Garda and the area around Cortina d'Ampezzo in the Dolomites attract visitors from far and wide with the beauty of their scenery, and the old cities of Venice, Padua, Verona and Vicenza are among the highlights of any tour of Italy.

Belluno

In northern Venetia, on the River Piave, is the provincial capital of Belluno (389 m/1265 ft; pop. 36,000). The cathedral, built from 1517 onwards and restored in 1873, has two beautiful altarpieces in the south aisle; from the campanile, 68 m/223 ft high, there are fine views. Also in this square are the Palazzo dei Rettori (1496), a fine Early Renaissance building which now houses the Prefecture, and the Gothic church of Santo Stefano (1468), with an adjoining cloister. The Museo Civico, with pictures and bronzes, is worth visiting.

12 km/7 miles south-east is a winter sports area on the Nevegal (chair-lift to Rifugio Cadore, 1600 m/5280 ft; Alpine garden).

Nevegal

There is an attractive road from Belluno (30 km/19 miles north-west) through the magnificent gorge on the River Cordevole known as the Canal d'Agordo (15 km/9 miles long) to the little town of Agordo (611 m/2021 ft; pop. 4000), ringed by high mountains, a popular walking and climbing centre. In the main square is the picturesque Palazzo Crotta di Manzoni (17th–18th c.).

Agordo

From Agordo it is another 18 km/11 miles north to the south end of the Lago D'Alleghe (966 m/3188 ft), a lake 2 km/1¼ miles long formed by a landslide in 1771.

Lago D'Alleghe

On the east side of the lake lies the village of Alleghe (979 m/3231 ft), a popular summer resort and climbing centre. From here there is a pleasant walk on a bridle-path which goes east (3 hours) to the sombre Lago Coldai (2146 m/7082 ft); then another 20 minutes over the Coldai pass (2190 m/7227 ft) to the Rifugio Coldai (2150 m/7095 ft), magnificently situated on the northern slopes of the massive Monte Civetta (3218 m/10,619 ft), which can be climbed from here in 6 hours (guide necessary).

Alleghe
Monte Civetta

3 km/2 miles north-west is the village of Caprile (1023 m/3376 ft), from which an excursion can be made up the Pettorina valley to the villages of Rocca Piétore (3 km/2 miles; 1143 m/3772 ft) and Sottoguda (7 km/4½ miles; 1252 m/4132 ft). From here it is possible in summer to continue for another 7 km/4½ miles on the old road through the gorge of Serrai di Sottoguda to the Malga Ciapela (1428 m/4712 ft; cableway via the Forcella Serauta 2270 m/7491 ft to the Punta di Rocca 3270 m/10,791 ft) and the Pian di Lobbia (1841 m/6075 ft); then 2 km/1¼ miles to the Fedaia pass (2047 m/6756 ft) and another 3 km/2 miles along the Lago di Fedaia to the Rifugio Marmolada; chair-lift to Marmolada glacier and road to Canazei.

Caprile
Fedaia pass

18 km/11 miles north-east of Belluno, at the mouth of the Zoldo valley, is the little town of Longarone (468 m/1544 ft), which was destroyed on 9 October 1963, together with four neighbouring villages, by a flood wave 100 m/330 ft high when a landslide on Monte Toc caused the Lago di Vajont to overflow. Some 2000 people, including 1700 in Longarone, lost their lives in the disaster; the town is being rebuilt on the slopes to the west.

Longarone

From Longarone a road climbs up (sharp bends, tunnels), passing through the wild Vajont gorge (4 km/2½ miles long; galleries through rock), to the Lago di Vajont, a reservoir formed by a dam 265 m/765 ft high, now largely drained, and then over the Passo di Sant'Osvaldo (827 m/2729 ft) to the summer resort of Cimolais (652 m/2152 ft).

Vajont gorge

25 km/16 miles north-east of Longarone up the Piave valley, which becomes steadily narrower, is Pieve di Cadore (878 m/2897 ft), chief town of the upper Piave region and a popular health and winter sports resort, beautifully situated high above the River Piave, here dammed to form a lake 8 km/5 miles long. In the main square is a monument to Titian, who was born here; his birthplace (museum) is in a little square with a fountain. The parish church has a Madonna with Saints by Titian.

Cimolais
Pieve di Cadore

Bassano del Grappa

In the west of the region of Veneto, some 40 km/25 miles north of Padova, lies Bassano del Grappa (122 m/403 ft; pop. 39,000) where an old wooden bridge leads over the River Brenta. The town is noted as the home of the Da Ponte family, the most important member of which was Jacopo da Ponto, called Bassano. The Museo Civico and the cathedral contain works by this painter.

Bassano del Grappa in Venetia

Rovigo

In the south of the Veneto region, on the Naviglio Adigetto, lies the provincial capital of Rovigo (7 m/23 ft; pop. 53,000). In the centre of the town in the elongated Piazza Vittorio Emanuele are a tall column bearing the lion of St Mark, the Palazzo del Municipio or Loggia dei Notai (Town Hall, with tower) and the Pinacoteca dei Concordi (picture gallery, with paintings of the Venetian school). To the west is the cathedral (17th c.; restored) and to the north of this two towers and the remains of the old castle.

Portogruaro

At the east end of the region of Venetia is Portogruaro (5 m/16 ft; pop. 25,000), with fine old arcaded houses, a Gothic Town Hall (14th–16th c.) and a Romanesque, leaning tower (the campanile of the cathedral). The Museo Nazionale Concordiese contains Roman and Early Christian remains from Concordia Sagittaria, the Roman military station of Concordia, 2 km/1¼ miles downstream, which preserves a Roman bridge and an early medieval baptistery.

Pordenone

28 km/16 miles north-west of Portogruaro, in the Friuli–Venezia Giulia region, is the old provincial capital of Pordenone (24 m/79 ft; pop. 51,000), birthplace of the painter Giovanni de Sacchis, known as Pordenone (1484–1539). There are pictures by this artist in the Late Gothic cathedral (15th c.) and in the Municipal Museum. The Town Hall was built between 1291 and 1365.

Venice/Venezia

Region: Veneto
Province: Venezia (VE)
Altitude: 1 m/3 ft
Population: 331,000

The description of Venice in this guide book is only in broad detail, as   Note
there is a comprehensive City Guide to Venice in the Baedeker series.

Venice, capital of the Veneto region and the province of Venezia, lies at   Situation
the very head of the Adriatic, 4 km/2½ miles from the mainland (rail and
road causeway) in the Laguna Veneta, a salt-water lagoon 55 km/34   Lagoon
miles long and up to 12 km/7½ miles wide which is separated from the
Adriatic by a series of narrow spits of land (lidi). There are more than 30
larger and smaller islands in the lagoon.

The town is built on 118 small islands and traversed by something like   **Architecture
100 canals (canale, rio), which are spanned by almost 400 bridges,
mostly stone-built. Its 15,000 houses, built on piles, form a close-
packed huddle of narrow streets and lanes (calle, salizzada, etc.), often
no more than 1.5 m/5 ft wide, filled with bustling activity. There is only
one piazza; smaller squares are called campo or campiello. The quays
or embankments are called riva or fondamenta.

In the inner city boats play an important part in public transportation   City traffic
(see Piazzale Roma-landing-stage).

In the past Venice's industry was confined to craft products (particularly   Industry
glass and lace), boatbuilding, etc., but there has been a considerable
development of large-scale industry since the First World War in the
suburban district of Mestre. The port is one of Italy's largest, with an
annual turnover of some 24 million tons. The industrial port is Porto di
Maghera, Mestre; the Bacino della Stazione Marittima, south-west of
the Piazzale Roma, also handles freight traffic.

In ancient times the Venice area was occupied by an Illyrian tribe, the   History
Veneti, who formed a defensive alliance with Rome in the 3rd c. B.C. and
rapidly became Romanised. In A.D. 451, the inhabitants of the coastal
region fled to the safety of the islands in the lagoon, and in 697 they
joined to form a naval confederation under a doge (from Latin dux,
"leader"). In 811 Rivus Altus (Rialto) – i.e. present-day Venice – became
the seat of government. In 829 the remains of the Evangelist Mark were
brought to Venice from Alexandria, and thereafter Mark became the
patron saint of the Venetian republic, which took his name and used his
lion as its emblem. The young state prospered as the main channel and
entrepôt for trade between Western Europe and the East, occupied the
east coast of the Adriatic, conquered Constantinople in 1204 and established itself on the coasts of Greece and Asia Minor. The so-called
"Hundred Years War" with Genoa was decided by the Venetian naval
victory off Chioggia in 1380, and in the 15th c. the republic reached the
peak of its power, controlling the whole of the eastern Mediterranean
and extending its conquests on the Italian mainland as far as Verona,
Bergamo and Brescia ("terra ferma"). In the 15th and 16th c. Venice
achieved its finest cultural flowering.
Towards the end of the 15th c., however, the advance of the Turks and
the discovery of America and the new sea routes to India brought the
beginnings of decline. In the 16th c. the Venetian possessions on the
mainland of Italy involved the republic in the conflicts between Austria

Venezia

300 m

Canale delle Navi

Fondamenta dei Riformati
S. Alvise
Fond. Madonna dell'Orto
Madonna dell'Orto
Fondamenta Cappuccine
Fondamenta della Sensa
Fondamenta Ormesini
Sacca della Misericordia
Fondamenta di Cannaregio
Canale di Cannaregio
CANNAREGIO
Fondamenta Misericordia
Abbazia d. Mis.
Fondamenta della
Chiesa dei Gesuiti
Fondamenta Nuove
Rio Terrà S. Leonardo
Rio Terrà Maddalena
Pal. Labia
S. Marcuola
Pal. Correr
S. Caterina
Calle Racchetta
Calle Lunga Caterina
Pal. Zeno
S. Geremia
Canal Grande
Pal. Vendramin-Calergi
S. Sofia
S. Lazzaro dei Mendicanti
Gli Scalzi
Ponte Scalzi
Central Station
Ferrovia di Spagna
S. CROCE
Strada Nuova
SS. Apostoli
Piazzale Roma
S. Giacomo dell'Orio
S. Stae
Cà d'Oro
Cà da Mosto
SS. Giov. e Paolo
San Simeone Piccolo
Ruga Bella
S. Cassiano
Pescheria
S. Maria dei Miracoli
Teatro Malibran
Cpo d'Lana
Canal
Calle della Lacca
Scuola di San Giovanni Evangelista
6
7
Salizz. S. Giov. Grisostomo
Barbaria delle Tole
I Tolentini
C. Vida
Pal. Corner-Mocenigo
S. Aponal
S. POLO
8
Mercerie
Aprile
S. Lio
CASTELLO
S. Rocco
Sal. S. Pantalon
Fond. Minotto
S. Polo
Pal. Bernardo
10
S. Silvestro
Salizzada
S. Lio
S. M. Formosa
I Frari
Pal. Disani-Moretta
11
Pal. Manin
Calle Bande
Pinacoteca Querini-Stampalia
Calle P. Crosera
9
Canal Grande
Mercerie S. Zulian
S. Giovanni Nuovo
S. Pantalon
12
Teatro Rossini
Pal. Balbi
Pal. Garzoni
Cd. Fuseri
S. Marco
Scuola di San Giorgio degli Schiavoni
Cà Foscari
13
S. Angelo
18
Piazza San Marco
20
Pal. Ducale
Cd. Rezzonico
14
Pal. Grassi
17
Teatro La Fenice
19
I Carmini
15
S. MARCO
Riva degli Schiavoni
S. Barnabè
Campo Francesco Morosini
16
Treves Bonfili
Canale di San Marco
Pal. Loredan
Pal. Pisani
Ponte dell'Accademia
Pref. Cà Grande
Pal. Contarini-Fasan
Pal. Giustinian
Ognissanti
25
S. Trovaso
DORSO
24
Pal. Contarini del Zaffo
23
22
21
Dogana di Mare
Chiesa Gesuati
S. Agnese
S. Maria d. Salute
Zattere
DURO
Zattere
S. Giorgio Maggiore
Spirito Santo
Isola di S. Giorgio Maggiore
Fondamenta S. Biagio
Fondamenta S. Eufemia
S. Eufemia
Fondamenta al
Ponte Piccolo
Fondamenta S. Giacomo
Fondamenta della Croce
Fondamenta delle Zitelle
Le Zitelle
Fondamenta S. Giovanni
Teatro Verde
Grazia
G I U D E C C A
Chiesa del Redentore
Canale della Giudecca
La Laguna
Canale della Giudecca

Marine Station
San Sebastiano

© Baedeker

and Spain on the one hand and France on the other, and the struggle against the Turks ended in 1718 with the loss of all Venice's possessions in the East. In 1797 the French put an end to the city's independence, and under the treaty of Campoformia in that year it was assigned provisionally to Austria. In 1815 it formally became part of Austria, and remained so until it joined the new Kingdom of Italy in 1866.

Venice occupies a special place in the history of art through its relations with the Greek Empire of the East. St Mark's Church is Byzantine in style, as are its earliest mosaics. Gothic, which reached Venice only in the 14th c., took on a different aspect here from the rest of Italy, displaying a lively fantasy and a wealth of decoration and colour. The Early Renaissance style came in the second half of the 15th c., producing buildings which cannot compare with those of Tuscany in harmony of proportions, since the façades seek above all to achieve a picturesque effect. Some of the Venetian churches, in particular Santi Giovanni e Paolo and the Frari church, are notable for their numerous fine tomb monuments. The leading architects of the period were Mauro Coducci, Antonio Rizzo and Pietro Lombardi, who were also sculptors, together with the Florentine Jacopa Sansovino, who brought the High Renaissance to Venice, and Andrea Palladio, whose influence was felt even by such vigorous exponents of the Baroque style as Vincenzo Scamozzi (1552–1616) and Baldassare Longhena (1604–82).

Art

The sculptors working in Venice included Alessandro Leopardi (d. 1522) and, slightly later, Alessandro Vittoria (1525–1608). Among 15th c. painters were Vivarini and Jacopo Bellini (Mantegna's father-in-law), both from Murano, and Carlo Crivelli, a native of Venice. Jacopo's son Giovanni Bellini (c. 1430–1516), with his skill in composition and his love of colour, was the precursor of the great period of Venetian painting. Among his contemporaries were his elder brother Gentile Bellini (c. 1429–1507), Vittorio Carpaccio (c. 1455 to after 1523) and Cima da Congliano (c. 1459–1518). His greatest pupils were Girogione (c. 1477–1510, born in Castelfranco), Palma il Vecchio from Bergamo (c. 1480–1528) and the greatest of them all, Titian (Tiziano Vecellio, c. 1490–1576, born in Pieve di Cadore), who lavished his skill and vigorous imagination equally on representations of the Renaissance delight in life and on highly charged religious scenes, and enjoyed high favour as a portrait painter with the Italian princes as well as with Charles V and Philip II of Spain. The contemporaries of these three great masters included such artists as Sebastiano del Piombo, Lorenzo Lotto, Bonifazio dei Pitati, Pordenone and Paris Bordone.

The tradition was carried on by a younger generation which included Paolo Veronese (Caliari, 1528–88, born in Verona), the Bassano family and Palma il Giovane. A fresh lead was given by Jacopo Tintoretto (Robusti, 1518–94), whose works, combining vigorous light and colour with the expression of profound spiritual emotion, mark the high point of Venetian Baroque painting.

In the 18th c. the two Canalettos (Antonio Canal and his pupil Bernardo Bellotto) and the talented Francesco Guardi (1712–93) excelled in the painting of townscapes, Pietro Longhi (1702–85) in the depiction of contemporary manners. The last great Venetian painter, heir to a

Venice: Ponte di Rialto

brilliant tradition of 300 years, was the decorative painter Giovanni Battista Tiepolo (1696–1770), notable for the glowing colour and spatial effect of his wall and ceiling paintings.

Piazzale Roma

At the end of the causeway from Mestre, on the mainland, is the Piazzale Roma, with a large parking area and multi-storey garage.

A short distance north of the Piazzale Roma, on the Canale di Santa Chiara, is the landing-stage for the city boat services.
From the landing-stage there are motor-boats (motoscafi) to St Mark's Square. The trip along the Grand Canal takes 25 minutes, the more direct route by the Rio Nuovo 10 minutes.
There are also motor-launches (vaporetti) which ply along the Grand Canal to St Mark's Square (30 minutes), taking another 15 minutes to reach the Lido or San Giorgio Maggiore.
The famous gondolas (gondole) take about an hour to reach St Mark's Square.
Opposite, on the north side of the Canale di Santa Chiara, is the modern Stazione Santa Lucia (main station). In the street running from the station, the Lista di Spagna, are most of the hotels in the western part of the city.

Landing-stage (City boat services)

Stazione di Santa Lucia

✱✱Grand Canal

The Grand Canal (Canal Grande: 3.8 km/2⅓ miles long, with an average breadth of 70 m/77 yd and depth of 5 m/16 ft), Venice's principal traffic

◀ *Campanile di San Marco, the symbol of Venice*

529

Ca' d'Oro

artery, starts from the station and traverses the city from north-west to south-east in a reversed S-curve; it gives an overwhelming impression of the wealth and splendour of Venice in its heyday with a continuous succession of great palaces of the princely Venetian merchants. Every style of architecture from the 12th to the early 18th c. is represented along the Grand Canal. Particularly charming is the Venetian Gothic style with its fantastic arcades; and the Early Renaissance buildings are scarcely less splendid. The posts (pali) in front of the steps leading into the palaces, painted in their owner's heraldic colours, serve to protect the gondolas lying at their moorings.

**Piazza San Marco

From the Riva degli Schiavoni we cross the Piazzetta and walk past the Doge's Palace into St Mark's Square (Piazza di San Marco, or the "Piazza" for short), the hub of the city's life and one of the world's finest squares, giving striking evidence of Venice's past greatness and still serving as a setting for great occasions (concerts, etc.). The square, 175 m/192 yd long and between 56 and 82 m/61 and 90 yd wide, is paved with slabs of trachyte and marble and lined on three sides by tall arcades housing shops and cafés. The square is particularly beautiful on bright moonlit nights. The innumerable pigeons (colombi, piccioni) are regularly fed.

Procuratie

On the north and south sides of the square are the Procuratie, formerly the administrative offices of the procurators, the highest officials of the Republic.

Procuratie Vecchie

The Procuratie Vecchie on the north side were built from 1514 onwards, and are a fine example of Venetian Early Renaissance. The façade is decorated with arcades on the ground and top floor.

Piazzetta di San Marco, with St Mark's Church

Mosaics in St Mark's Church

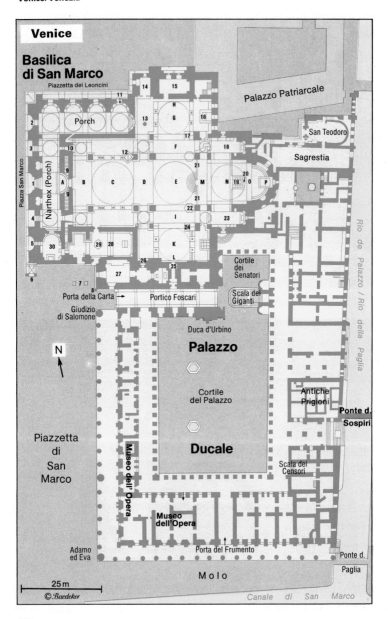

Venice

Basilica di San Marco

Piazzetta dei Leoncini

Palazzo Patriarcale

San Teodoro

Sagrestia

Piazza San Marco

Narthex (Porch)

Porch

Cortile dei Senatori

Scala dei Giganti

Porta della Carta

Portico Foscari

Giudizio di Salomone

N

Duca d'Urbino

Palazzo

Cortile del Palazzo

Antiche Prigioni

Ponte d. Sospiri

Piazzetta di San Marco

Museo dell' Opera

Ducale

Scala dei Censori

Museo dell'Opera

Porta del Frumento

Adamo ed Eva

Ponte d.

Paglia

Rio de Palazzo / Rio della Paglia

M o l o

25 m

© Baedeker

Canale di San Marco

Legend to plan of St Mark's Basilica.

1 Main portal	17 Altare di San Pietro	**MOSAICS**
2–5 Portal recesses	18 Cappella di San Pietro	A Arch of Paradise
6 Pietra del Bando	19 High Altar	B Arch of the Apocalypse
7 Pilastri Acritani	20 Pala d'Oro	C Scenes of Pentecost
8 Sculpture of the Tetrarchs	21 Iconostasis	D Scenes from the Passion
9 Stairs up to the Museo	22 Reliquary	E The Ascension
Marciano	23 Cappella di San Clemente	F St Michael with sword
10 Porta di San Pietro	24 Altare di San Giacomo	G St John
11 Porta dei Fiori	25 Passage to the Doges'	H Mary's family tree
12 Capitello del Crocifisso	Palace	I The Washing of the Feet,
(Capital of the Cross)	26 Entrance to the Treasury	Temptation in the Wilderness
13 Romanesque stoup with	27 Tesoro (Treasury), with	K St Leonard
angels (12th c.)	goldsmiths' work, etc.	L Four miracles of Jesus
14 Cappella della Madonna dei	28 Battistero (Baptistery)	M St Peter, The Resurrection,
Mascoli	29 Font dating from 1546	etc.
15 Cappella di Sant'Isidoro	30 Cappella Zen, named	N Choir mosaics
16 Cappella della Madonna	after Cardinal G. B. Zen	O Lamb of God
Nicopeia	(d. 1501)	P Christ in Majesty, with Saints

The Procuratie Nuove on the south side were begun in 1584 by Vincenzo Scamozzi and used from the time of Napoleon I as a royal palace. The former residence of the procurators now houses the archaeological museum (Museo Archeologico). Its entrance is at the Libreria Marciana (Piazzetta No. 17). The museum provides a unique comparision of the ancient archaeological finds with the art of the Renaissance. Here the observer will notice the influence of ancient art on the artists of the Renaissance.

Procuratie Nuove, Museo Archeologico

Along the west end of the square is the Ala Napoleonica, a linking wing added in 1810 on Napoleon's request, which houses the Museo Correr, with an excellent collection illustrating the history and culture of Venice, including pictures by old masters.

Ala Napoleonica, *Museo Correr

At the south-east corner of St Mark's Square rises the Campanile of St Mark (Campanile di San Marko), a 96.8 m/319½ ft high bell-tower rebuilt in 1905–12 after the collapse of the original campanile in 1902; from the top (lift) there are fine views. The Loggetta on the east side of the campanile (by Jacopo Sansovino, 1540) was originally the meeting-place of the Venetian nobles.

**Campanile of St Mark

Almost opposite the campanile, at the east end of the Procuratie Vecchie, is the Clock-Tower (Torre dell'Orologio, 1496–99); on the platform are two bronze moors (1497) which strike the bell every hour.
At the foot of the clock-tower an arched gateway leads into the Merceria (shopping street).

Clock-Tower

**Basilica di San Marco

St Mark's Church (Basilica di San Marco), dedicated to the Evangelist Mark, whose remains are in the high altar, was begun in 829, rebuilt after a fire in 976 and remodelled in the 11th c. in Byzantine style with an Oriental lavishness of decoration. 76.5 m/83 yd long by 51.75 m/56½ yd wide, it has the form of a Greek cross, with five domes. Externally and internally it is adorned with ancient marble columns, mostly from the East. Until 1981 there stood above the main doorway four bronze horses from Constantinople, 1.6 m/5¼ ft high, the only surviving example of the four-horse team of an ancient quadriga. They have been replaced by copies and the originals are in the Museo di San Marco. Two of the original horses are in Roman style (4th c.), the remaining two are in Greek style (4th–3rd c. B.C.).

Construction and exterior

Interior **Mosaics	The interior of St Mark's is notable for the beauty of its lines and the picturesque and constantly changing vistas which it affords. The vaulting is decorated with mosaics, most of them dating back to 1160–1200, depicting scenes from the lives of the Virgin and Christ (Passion and Ascension).
**Pala d'Oro	On the high altar the Pala d'Oro is a masterpiece of enamel work set with jewels, originally an altar frontal made in Constantinople (best side to rear). Its completion took about five centuries.
*Treasury	In the south transept the valuable Treasury (Tresoro) filled with precious objects the Venetians brought back from Constantinople after its conquest in 1204.
Cappella Zen	In the Cappella Zen can be seen the fine tomb of Cardinal Giambattista Zen (d. 1501).
Museo di San Marco	From the gallery (entrance at main doorway, on the left) there is access to the outer gallery and the bronze horses. Adjoining the gallery the Museo di San Marco, the Church Museum, houses 15th c. tapestries, Byzantine sculpture (12th c.) and pictures.

*Piazzetta di San Marco

On the south-east side of St Mark's Square, extending to the Canale di San Marco, is the Piazzetta di San Marco. Near the water's edge, on the Molo, where the gondoliers wait for custom, are two granite columns from Syria or Constantinople, erected here in 1180, topped by a figure of St Theodore (copy, original in Palazzo Ducale), Venice's earlier patron saint, and the winged lion of St Mark.

Libreria Marciana (Library)	On the west side of the square is the Library (Libreria Marciana), Jacopo Sansovino's finest work (1536–53). The building houses the celebrated Library of St Mark (Biblioteca Nazionale Marziana; tour by appointment). The ceiling painting in the vestibule is by Titian (1560), and part of the ceiling of the Hall of Honour was painted by Veronese; the walls have portraits of philosophers, including works by Tintoretto. The rooms contain manuscripts, illuminated books, etc. The original Library of St Mark is now housed in the former Mint (Zecca; 1536), which is connected to the exhibition rooms.
Museo Diocesano	In the Castello quarter to the north, in the Renaissance Palazzo Ducale, is the Diocesan Museum (Museo Diocesano). The treasures of the museum include liturgical vessels and silver work.

**Doge's Palace

The east side of the Piazzetta is occupied by the Doge's Palace (Palazzo Ducale), said to have been the residence of the Doges since about 814. The oldest part of the present building is the 71 m/78 yd long south wing on the Molo (1309–40); the 75 m/82 yd long west wing facing on to the Piazzetta was added in 1424–38.

The main feature of the building is the upper part of the battlemented façade, decorated with coloured marble in a lozenge pattern.

*Loggia	Around the ground floor runs a beautiful arcade with free-standing columns, and above this is the Loggia, with elegant pointed arches and quatrefoil decoration in Venetian Gothic style. Large windows and a Gothic balcony on each side give relief to the marble block above this. The Gothic Porta delle Carta leads into the magnificent Cortile dei Senatori, a courtyard which shows a picturesque mingling of late Gothic and Early Renaissance styles.
Interior	The interior of the palace is reached from the courtyard by way of the Scala dei Giganti and the Scala d'Oro, which lead to the upper floors,

with the State Apartments, redecorated after damage by fire in 1574 and 1577. Notable features of these rooms – magnificent examples of the Late Renaissance and Baroque periods – are the richly decorated and gilded ceilings and the numerous pictures (by Titian, Paolo Veronese, Tintoretto and other artists) glorifying Venice and its doges in historical scenes and allegories.

The Museo dell'Opera on the ground floor of the Doge's Palace houses original items of the decoration of the palace which had to be replaced by copies.

Museo dell'Opera

On the second floor the Sala del Maggior Consiglio (54 m/59 yd long, 25 m/27 yd wide, 15.5 m/51¼ ft high) has scenes from the history of Venice on its walls. On the frieze are 76 portraits of doges ranging in date from 804 to 1559, and on the entrance wall is Tintoretto's "Paradise", the largest oil painting in the world (24.65 m/81 ft long by 7.45 m/24½ ft high). From the balcony of the Sala there are magnificent views of the lagoon, the islands of San Giorgio Maggiore and Giudecca, and the Lido.

Sala del Maggior Consiglio

In the east wing are the Doge's Private Apartments (Appartamento Ducale), which escaped damage in the fire.

Doge's Private Apartments

On the third floor are the large Sala del Senato, the meeting-place of the Senate, with pictures by Tintoretto, Palma il Giovane and other artists, and the Sala d'Armi, the armoury of the Republic, with a fine collection of weapons.

Sala del Senato

From the first floor of the palace visitors can enter the Prigioni, dark and dismal cellars with which are associated a torture chamber and place of execution.

Prigioni

From the Doge's Palace the Molo runs east to the Ponte della Paglia ("Straw Bridge"), from which there is a good view, to the left, of the Bridge of Sighs (Ponte dei Sospiri), built about 1595 to link the palace with the Prigioni (erected 1571–97), its name recalling the sighs of the criminals led over the bridge to the place of execution.

Ponte della Paglia
*Bridge of Sighs

*Riva degli Schiavoni

From the Ponte della Paglia we go straight ahead and come to the Riva degli Schiavoni, a busy and lively promenade 500 m/550 yd long with several landing-stages for boats serving the city and the lagoon (including services to the Lido), and fine views of the passenger vessels in the harbour.

Beyond the second bridge the Sottoportico San Zaccaria, on left, leads to the nearby church of San Zaccaria (15th c.), which contains (to the left, on the second altar) a "Madonna Enthroned" by Giovanni Bellini (1505).

San Zaccaria

North-east of San Zaccaria is the Scuola di San Giorgio degli Schiavoni, the house of the brotherhood of the Dalmatian merchants, the "Schiavoni". In the beginning of the 16th c. Vittore Carpaccio decorated it with cycles of pictures, which today are among the greatest art treasures of the city.

Scuola di San Giorgio degli Schiavoni

On the continuation of the Riva degli Schiavoni are the Giardini Pubblici (landing-stage for motor-launches), a beautiful municipal park with the Paradiso café-restaurant and the galleries used for the Biennale d'Arte,

Giardini Pubblici

the international art exhibition held every other year from June to September.

In the surroundings of the Merceria

The narrow Merceria (Marzaria), which leaves the north-east corner of St Mark's Square, by the Clock-Tower, and runs north-west under various names (Merceria San Zuliàn, etc.) is the city's principal shopping street, providing a direct link between St Mark's Square and the Rialto Bridge (500 m/550 yd).

Near the north end of the shopping street is San Salvatore, the finest High Renaissance church in Venice (by Giorgio Spavento and Tullio Lombardi, 1506–34), with a Baroque façade added in 1704.

San Salvatore

From Merceria San Zuliàn, beyond the church of San Giuliano (San Zuliàn), Calle della Guerra and Calle delle Bande lead to the church of Santa Maria Formosa, which contains in the second chapel to the right of high altar a "St Barbara" by Palma Vecchio.

Santa Maria Formosa

A little way south of the church is the Palazzo Stampalia, with a collection of pictures by Venetian artists of the 14th–18th c., including works by Donato Veneziano, Palma the Younger, Giovanni Bellini, Lorenzo di Credi, Palma the Elder, Pietro Longhi, Alessandro Longhi and Tiepolo.

Palazzo Querini-Stampalia, Pinacoteca

From Santa Maria Formosa we go along Calle Lunga and turn into the street on left (Calle Cicogna) to reach the Campo Santi Giovanni e Paolo, with the church of the same name and the famous statue of Bartolomeo Colleoni (Monumento di Colleoni), a mercenary leader working for Venice (d. 1475), the finest equestrian statue of the Italian Renaissance, modelled by the Florentine sculptor Andrea del Verrochio in 1481–88 and cast by Alessandro Leopardi in 1496. The statue depicts the ideal of a proud and mighty condottiere.

**Statue of Colleoni

The former Dominican church of Santi Giovanni e Paolo (San Zanipolo), a Gothic brick-built structure (1246–30) is the burial-place of many doges, and contains numerous handsome monuments (the finest being that of Doge Andrea Vendramin, on the north side of the choir).
To the left of the church stands the Scuola di San Marco (now a hospital), with a richly decorated Renaissance façade (1485–95).

Santi Giovanni e Paolo

A little way west the church of Santa Maria dei Miracoli, an elegant Early Renaissance building by Pietro and Tullio Lombardi (1481–89), is entirely clad in marble both externally and internally. The church is dedicated to a miraculous picture of the Virgin.

*Santa Maria dei Miracoli

Sights in the south-west

From the south-west corner of St Mark's Square we go along a busy shopping street, the Salizzada San Moisè, with the Baroque church of the same name, and its continuation Calle Larga XXII Marzo, passing the Baroque church of Santa Maria Zobenigo, to reach the large Campo Francesco Morosini.

Campo Francesco Morosini

On our way to the square we pass (to the east) the Teatro La Fenice (1790–1792), the largest theatre in Venice (1500 seats).

*Teatro La Fenice

To the south of the Campo Francesco Morosini the Palazzo Pisani a Santo Stefano (now the Conservatoire) is a good example of a wealthy merchant's mansion of the Baroque period.

Palazzo Pisani

◀ *Gondola regatta on the Canal Grande*

**Galleria dell'Accademia

To the south-west of the Palazzo Pisani is the Ponte dell'Accademia, which leads to the Accademia di Belle Arti, in premises once occupied by the brotherhood and convent of Santa Maria della Carità. The academy's picture gallery contains more than 800 pictures, mainly by Venetian artists and including some works of the highest quality, which give an excellent survey of the achievement of the Venetian schools.

Among the outstanding works in the collection are the brilliantly coloured pictures of Venetian life by Gentile Bellini (in Room XX) and Vittore Carpaccio (including nine scenes from the legend of St Ursula in Room XXI); beautiful religious paintings by Giovanni Bellini (particularly in Rooms IV and V); and masterpieces by Giorgione (including "The Storm", the finest work in the collection, Room V); Titian ("Presentation of the Virgin", Room XXIV; "Lamentation", his last picture, completed by Palma il Giovane, Room X); Paris Bordone ("Presentation of the Ring", Room VI); Jacopo Tintoretto (particularly the large pictures from the Scuola di San Marco in Room X and other works in Rooms VI and XI) and Paolo Veronese ("Jesus in the House of Levi", 12.3 × 5.7 m/ 40 × 19 ft, one of the artist's finest works, Room X).
The collection also includes notable pictures by Mantegna ("St George", Room IV), Cima de Conegliano, Pietro Longhi, Francesco Guardi, Sebastiano Ricci, Palma Vecchio, Piero della Francesca, Lotto, Tiepolo, Antonia Canaletto, Alvise, Bartolomeo and Antonio Vivarini.

I Frari

From the Accademia landing-stage we can take the motor-launch north to the next landing place, San Tomà. A short distance north-west is the former Franciscan church of I Frari or Santa Maria Gloriosa dei Frari, a brick-built Gothic basilica (1338) with a tall campanile, the largest and most beautiful church in Venice after St Mark's. Like Santi Giovanni e Paolo, it is the burial-place of many famous Venetians. On the high altar is Titian's "Assumption", the finest work of his early period (1516–18). In the north aisle, beside the tomb of Bishop Jacopo Pesaro, is Titian's "Madonna of the House of Pesaro" (1519–26).
The adjoining monastery houses the State Archives of Venice, one of the finest collections of the kind in the world.

*Scuola di San Rocco	From the Franciscan church it is only a few steps to the Scuola di San Rocco (1524–60), an impressive structure built in white marble. The school is famous for its large wall and ceiling paintings by Tintoretto (16th c.), depicting scenes from the New Testament.
San Rocco	Opposite, on the north, the church of San Rocco has a façade of 1771 and some fine pictures by Tintoretto.
Scuola di San Giovanni Evangelista	From here we cross the Campo San Stin to reach the Scuola di San Giovanni Evangelista, with an outer courtyard in the style of Pietro Lombardo (1481) and a staircase by Moro Coducci (d. 1504).

Isola della Giudecca

Il Redentore	On the long island of Giudecca, lying to the south of the main part of the city and separated from it by the Canale della Giudecca (300 m/330 yd wide), is the conspicuous church of the Redentore, formerly belonging to the Franciscans. Built in 1577–92, by Palladio; after his death it was completed by his pupils. It has two slender round towers to the rear of the central dome and a harmoniously proportioned interior. On the

high altar are marble reliefs by Giuseppe Mazza and bronze statues by Girolamo Campagna.

Isola di San Giorgio Maggiore

East of La Giudecca lies the little island of San Giorgio Maggiore, with the prominent monastic church of the same name, a domed structure begun by Palladio in 1565 and completed in 1610. It has fine Baroque choir-stalls and contains several pictures by Tintoretto. From the 60 m/198 ft high campanile (entrance from choir) there is the finest view in Venice.

The former monastic buildings (beautiful staircase by Longhena, two cloisters) have been occupied since 1951 by the Fondazione Giorgio Cini, which is concerned with the promotion of research on the cultural history of Venice. There is also an international art and culture centre with 30 rooms, a theatre and an open-air theatre.

Fondazione Giorgio Cini

Lido di Venezia

From the Riva degli Schiavoni it is a 15 minutes' trip by motor-launch to the Lido, the northern part of the spit of land known as the Malamocco which borders the east side of the lagoon. The Lido was once Italy's most famous seaside resort, with numerous hotels, pensions and summer villas.

From the Santa Maria Elisabetta landing-stage the Gran Viale Santa Maria Elisabetta runs across the spit to the Hôtel des Bains. South of the hotel is the Lungomare G. Marconi, a large square in which are the Casino Municipale and the Palazzo del Cinema (1937–52), the scene of the Biennale film festival. On the Lido there are also numerous sporting facilities (golf-course, tennis courts, riding).

From the Lido there is a motor-boat service (and also a car ferry) to the Punta Sabbioni, from which a road runs 20 km/12 miles north to the large resort of Lido di Iesolo (2 m/7 ft; pop. 6000). With its beautiful broad beach Lido di Iesolo ranks with Rimini, Riccione and the Venice Lido as one of the most popular resorts on the Adriatic.

*Lido di Iesolo

Murano

From the Fondamente Nuovo, the seaside promenade on the north side of Venice there is a motor-launch service (landing-stage near the church of the Gesuiti: 10 minutes), passing the cemetery island of San Michele, to the little town of Murano (pop. 8000), on the island of the same name, which has been the main centre of the Venetian glass industry since the end of the 13th c. A few minutes from the Colonna landing-stage is the church of San Pietro Martire (15th c., restored 1511), which has a beautiful Madonna by Giovanni Bellini (1488) in the south aisle. Beyond this, on the far side of the main canal, stands the cathedral of Santi Maria e Donata (12th c.), with fine columns of Greek marble, a mosaic pavement and a Byzantine mosaic in the apse. Near the cathedral is the Town Hall, with the Museo dell'Arte Vetraria (products of the local glass-making industry, which had its heyday in the 15th and 16th c.). Now each glass-blowing workshop has a shop where Murano glass can be bought.

*Glass industry

Santi Maria e Donato on the island of Merano

*Torcello

Situation 8 km/5 miles north-east of Venice	Another very attractive boat trip is to the picturesque little fishing town of Burano (pop. 5500), centre of the Venetian lace-making industry, and the island of Torcello, with the ancient little town of the same name. Torcello has a beautiful cathedral (Santa Maria Assunta, 7th–11th c.), with fine mosaics (13th–15th c.) and a campanile, from the top of which there are far-ranging views. Near the octagonal church of Santa Fosca (11th c.) the 14th c. Palazzo dei Consigli houses the Museo dell'Estuario, with pictures, sculptures and objects d'art of several centuries.

*Chioggia

Situation 45 km/28 miles south of Venice	Near the south end of the Venice lagoon (on S.S. 309, the Strada Romea, from Marghera) lies the interesting island town of Chioggia (2 m/7 ft; pop. 50,000), formerly the centre of Venetian salt production, destroyed by the Genoese in 1379 and now a large fishing port. With its narrow streets of old houses, picturesque in decay, its canals and its bustling life and activity, it is a popular resort of artists. In the main street the Corso del Popolo, are the cathedral (rebuilt by Longhena), with a 64 m/211 ft high campanile (14th c.), and the little Gothic church of San Martino (1392).
Sottomarina	A bridge 800 m/880 yd long leads from the old town of Chioggia to Sottomarina (2 m/7 ft), a popular bathing resort.
Albarella	20 km/12 miles south-east of Sottomarina is the lagoon island of Albarella, a tourist resort with many facilities, including a tennis and riding centre, a golf course with 18 holes, and a yacht harbour.

Verona

Region: Veneto
Province: Verona (VR)
Altitude: 59 m/195 ft
Population: 259,000

Verona, capital of the province of the same name, lies at the point where the River Adige emerges from the Alps into the north Italian plain. The main part of the town is situated below the Alpine foothills of the Altipiano dei Lessini on a peninsula enclosed on two sides by the rapidly flowing Adige and linked with the districts on the left bank by ten bridges.
Verona, a city rich in art and architecture, lies about 80 km/50 miles from Venice and the Adriatic.

Situation

It is also a considerable commercial centre, handling the produce (particularly fruit and vegetables) of the province's fertile irrigated soil.

Verona, which still preserved the name of the prehistoric settlement on this site, became a Roman colony in 89 B.C. and thereafter developed into a town of considerable importance, as the remains of the amphitheatre and other buildings testify. In the 6th c. the Ostrogothic king Theodoric (d. 626) made it one of his royal residences, together with Pavia and Ravenna. During the Frankish period Charlemagne's son Pepin reigned here as king of Italy, and later the Saxon and Hohenstaufen emperors found the town, situated at the end of the road over the Brenner, a convenient base from which to control Italy. From the middle of the 13th c. Verona was ruled by the Ghibelline family of Della Scala (the Scaligers), but in 1387 they were expelled by the Viscontis. In 1405 the town passed into the hands of Venice.
During the Austrian period (1814–66) Verona became a fortress town, forming with Peschiera, Mantova and Legnago the famous defensive "quadrilaterial". In 1866 it was incorporated in the united Kingdom of Italy.

History

Verona is notable for its fine Romanesque churches (11th c.), but is was also a considerable artistic centre in the Renaissance period, particularly in the field of architecture. Its leading architects were the Dominican monk Fra Giocondo (c. 1433–1515) and Michele Sammichele (1484–1559). Sammichele sought to embellish his works of fortifications by the use of classical architectural forms, erected numerous splendid buildings and built the bastioned town walls (1530 onwards).

Art

*Piazza delle Erbe

The central feature of the old town is the elongated Piazza delle Erbe, one of the most picturesque squares in Italy, on the site of the Roman forum (now a fruit and vegetable market). In the centre of the square is the Berlina (16th c.), a canopy borne on four columns, formerly used for the election of the Signori and the Podestà. To the north of it is the Market Fountain (1368), with the "Madonna Verona", an ancient marble statue (restored). At the north end of the square the Marble Column bears the lion of St Mark, the emblem of Venetian authority. At the north-east corner stands the Casa Mazzanti, originally built by the Scaligers; like many houses in the town, it is adorned with Renaissance frescoes. On the north side of the square is the Baroque Palazzzo Maffei (1668), and to the left of this the Torre del Gardello (1370). The Casa dei Mercanti at the corner of Via Pellicciai was rebuilt in 1878 in its original

Verona

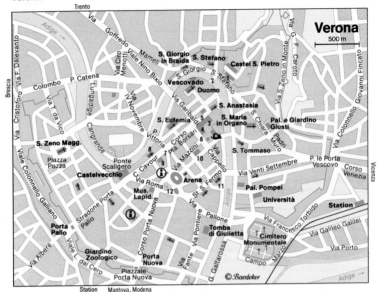

1 Teatro Romano/Museo Archeologico
2 Ponte Pietra
3 Arche Scaligere
4 Palazzo della Ragione

5 Loggia del Consiglio
6 Piazza delle Erbe
7 Porta dei Borsari
8 San Lorenzo

9 Palazzo Bevilacqua
10 Santa Maria della Scala
11 San Fermo Maggiore
12 Town Hall

form (1301). Opposite rises the 84 m/277 ft high Torre del Comune (lift to the top; fine view).

*Piazza dei Signori

Palazzo della Ragione

The short street to the left of the Torre del Comune runs east into the Piazza dei Signori (a name recalling the rule of the Scaligers), surrounded by palaces. In the centre is a monument to Dante (1865). The Palazzo della Ragione (Town Hall), on the south side of the square, was begun in 1193 but much altered in later centuries; the main front is Renaissance (1524). In the courtyard are a Gothic grand staircase (1446–50) and the entrance to the Torre del Comune.
Also in the square are a battlemented tower and the Palazzo dei Tribunali, formerly the Palazzo del Capitano with a Renaissance doorway by Michele Sammichele, converted in 1530–31 from a Scaliger Palace. On the east side of the square we find the Palazzo del Governo (Prefecture), originally another Scaliger palace, rebuilt in the 16th c. (doorway by Sammichele, 1532).

*Loggia del Consiglio

On the north side of the Piazza dei Signori stands the Loggia del Consiglio, one of the finest Early Renaissance buildings in Italy (by Fra Giocondo, 1486–93), crowned by statues of famous citizens of Verona in antiquity.

*Tombs of the Scaligers

The passage between the Prefecture and the Tribunal leads to the church of Santa Maria Antica (12th c.), with a Romanesque campanile. Adjoining it are the imposing Gothic Tombs of the Scaligers (Arche Scaligere), with the ladder (scala) which was the heraldic emblem of

Verona: Piazza delle Erbe

the family frequently recurring in the elaborate wrought-iron railings. Above the church door are the sarcophagus and a copy of an equestrian statue of Cangrande della Scala (d. 1329); to the left are seen the mural monument of Giovanni (d. 1359) and the sarcophagus of Mastino I (d. 1277). Within the railings, under a canopy, are the sarcophagi and equestrian statues of Mastino II (d. 1351) and Cansignorio (d. 1375).

To the north of the tombs, at the end of the Corso Sant'Anastasia, on the Adige, is the Dominican church of Sant'Anastasia, a brick-built Gothic structure (1290–1323, 1422–81) with a magnificent interior (richly decorated altars of the 15th–18th c.)

Sant'Anastasia

From here it is a short distance north-west to the cathedral, a 12th c. Romanesque basilica with a 15th c. Gothic nave. Adjoining it is a campanile on a Romanesque base, designed by Sammichele but not completed until 1927. On the beautiful main doorway of the cathedral are figures of Charlemagne's two paladins Roland and Oliver (c. 1139–53). Within the church, on the first altar on the left, is an "Assumption" by Titian (1525), at the end of the south aisle the Gothic tomb of St Agatha (1353).

Cathedral

To the left of the cathedral is a Romanesque cloister (1123), with an Early Christian mosaic pavement on a lower level.

From the cathedral we continue towards the river and cross the Ponte Garibaldi to the left bank.

Ponte Garibaldi

Corso Porta Borsari and Corso Cavour

On to the right bank of the Adige, we go upstream along the Lungadige Panvinio (views) and then turn left past the church of Sant'Eufemia into the Corso Porta Borsari, which begins at the Piazza delle Erbe. At its

Porta dei Borsari

west end is the Porta dei Borsari, one of the Roman city gates (1st c. A.D.; restored in 265).

Castelvecchio
(Museums)

Farther west the Corso Cavour, once the main street of Verona, is flanked by fine old palaces. On the left (No. 19) is the imposing Palazzo Bevilacqua (by Sammichele, 1530), with the Romanesque church of San Lorenzo (c. 1110) opposite. At the end of the Corso Cavour, on the banks of the Adige, stands the Castelvecchio, built by the Scaligers in 1354–55; from the platform of the main tower (completed 1375) there are extensive views. The castle now houses the Civico Museo d'Arte, which contains Veronese sculpture, applied art and an excellent picture gallery with works of the 15th–16th c. Veronese school.

Ponte Scaligero

Below the castle the Adige is spanned by the fine Ponte Scaligero (14th c.; restored 1949–51 after wartime destruction).

Piazza Brà

To the south of Corso Cavour and linked with it by a number of streets is the spacious Piazza Brà (from Latin pratum, "meadow"). On the north side of the square, near the end of Via Mazzini, is the Palazzo Malfatti, by Sammichele. Opposite it stands an equestrian statue of Victor Emmanuel II (1883).

**Amphitheatre
(Arena)

The Roman Amphitheatre (Arena), one of the largest of its kind, on the east side of the square, was built in the reign of Diocletian (c. A.D. 290). Of the outer wall only four arches on the north side have survived. With its 43 rows of seating it can accommodate some 22,000 spectators; from the top rows there are fine views. The overall length of the structure was 152 m/176 yd, its height 32 m/16 ft. In July and August a famous operatic festival is held in the Arena.

Palazzo Municipale

On the south side of the Piazza Brà is the Palazzo Municipale or Town Hall (1836–38, semicircular extension built after 1945). To the right the long building of the Gran Guardi was the old guard-house (1614), and adjoining this the Portoni della Brà, an old gateway and tower. Beyond this are the Museo Lapidario Maffeiano (Lapidarium) and the Teatro Filarmonico (opera).

*San Fermo
Maggiore

From the Piazza delle Erbe Via Cappello, with the so-called Casa di Giuletta (Gothic, 13th c. – Juliet's House with her balcony), and its continuation Via Leoni (on left, the Roman Porta del Leoni) runs southeast to the church of San Fermo Maggiore, with a Romanesque lower church (11th–12th c.) and a Gothic upper church (13th–14th c.), its façade beautifully decorated with marble. It contains a number of notable monuments and pictures by Pisanello and others.

Immediately beyond the church is the Ponte delle Navi.

Tomba di Giuletta

In the Campo di Fiera, near the Adige in the southern part of the town, visitors are shown, in a cloister built in 1899, a medieval trough which purports to be the coffin of Juliet Capulet (Tomba di Giuletta), Shakespeare's heroine.

Corso di Porta Nuova

Porta Nuova

Passing through the Portoni della Brà, we follow the wide Corso di Porta Nuova to the Porta Nuova (by Sammichele), beyond which is the principal railway station, the Stazione di Porta Nuova.

Porta Palio

From the Porta Nuova we follow the tree-lined avenue inside the old walls, past the zoo and come to the magnificent Porta Palio (by Sammichele, 16th c.).

From here we go east along the wide Stradone di Porta Palio and then turn left into Via Aurelio Saffi to reach the former Franciscan church of San Bernardino (15th c.), with a large arcaded courtyard (gravestones, remains of frescoes). The Cappella Pellegrini (begun by Sammichele before 1554) has fine Renaissance decoration.

San Bernardino

**San Zeno Maggiore

To the north of San Bernardino is the large Basilica of San Zeno Maggiore (11th–12th c.), perhaps the finest Romanesque building in northern Italy, with a beautiful main front flanked by a slender Romanesque campanile (1045–1178) and the battlemented defensive tower (14th c.) of a former Benedictine abbey. The doorway has Romanesque reliefs with Biblical and other scenes. The interior boasts an unusual timber roof (14th c.) and beautiful Romanesque capitals, and in the aisles are frescoes of the 13th–15th c. In the choir can be seen a marble figure, ascribed to the 14th c., of St Zeno, bishop of Verona (d. 380), whose reliquary is in the crypt. On the high altar is a "Madonna with Saints" by Mantegna (1456–59) and on the north side of the church an elegant Romanesque cloister.

Sights on the left bank of the Adige

Beyond the Ponte delle Navi, going north-east through the Interrato dell'Acqua Morta and then turning right into Via Carducci, we come to the Palazzo Giusti (1580) and the Giardino Giusti, with beautiful old cypresses (delightful views from the terrace).

Giardino Giusti

Farther north is the church of Santa Maria in Organo, originally founded in the Lombard period and rebuilt in Renaissance style in 1481,

Santa Maria in Organo

Basilica of San Zeno

Bridge over the Adige with Castel Vecchio

with an unfinished façade designed by Sammichele (1592). The choir has fine stalls by Fra Giovanni da Verona (1519).

Roman Theatre

Beyond the Roman bridge, the Ponte della Pietra, on the hillside, below the commandingly situated Castel San Pietro, is the Roman Theatre (Teatro Romano), with remains of the stage wall; built in the reign of Augustus, it was excavated between 1904 and 1939.

Archaeological Museum

Near the theatre in the former Convento di San Girolamo, the Archaeological Museum (Museo Archeologico) contains prehistoric and Roman material.

Santo Stefano

A little way north of the Roman theatre stands the Romanesque church of Santo Stefano, a very ancient building (originally 5th-8th c.) with two ambulatories round the choir (8th c. capitals); the choir itself contains an episcopal throne of 1008. The façade bears interesting inscriptions.

* San Giorgio in Braida

Farther west the 16th c. church of San Giorgio in Braida has a beautiful dome by Sammichele. The altarpieces are by masters of the Veronese and Brescian schools. On the high altar is "The Martyrdom of St George" by Veronese. In the fourth chapel (on the left) is a notable Madonna by Girolamo dai Libri.

Madonna di Lourdes

To the north of the town stands the pilgrimage church of the Madonna di Lourdes (1964).

Villafranca di Verona   G4

Situation
16 km/10 miles
south-west

South-west of Verona, on the River Tione, is Villafranca di Verona (54 m/178 ft; pop. 25,000), with a ruined castle, part of the "Serraglio", the frontier fortifications of Verona, which extend to Valeggio, 9 km/5½ miles west. In 1859 an armistice agreement was made in Villafranca between France and Austria.

In Valeggio is the well-tended park of Sigurtà.

Verona to Giazza (45 km/28 miles)

Another attractive excursion from Verona (north) is to the beautiful uplands of Monti Lessini and Giazza (758 m/2501 ft), the only one of the "Tredici Comuni" (Thirteen Communes) inhabited by the descendants of settlers from Bavaria and Tirol, and where German is still spoken.

*Soave

East of Verona is the little medieval town of Soave (40 m/132 ft; pop. 6000), renowned for its white wine, with battlemented town walls and towers and fine palaces.

Situation
15 km/9 miles east of Verona

Vesuvius/Vesuvio

Region: Campania
Province: Napoli (NA)

Rearing abruptly out of the plain some 15 km/9 miles south-east of Naples on the shores of the bay of Naples, Vesuvius has been since the 17th c. the only volcano on the European mainland which is still intermittently active.

Situation

The height of Vesuvius varies from time to time, since every eruption of any violence alters the shape of the summit: at present it is 1281 m/4227 ft high. The crater now has a circumference of 1400 m/1532 yd, a maximum diameter of 600 m/656 yd and a depth of 216 m/236 yd; before the last major eruption in 1944 the circumference was 3400 m/3720 yd.

North-east of the main crater, and separated from it by the deep valley known as the Atrio del Cavallo, is Monte Somma (1132 m/3736 ft), a relic of the caldera of an older volcano which had a diameter of 4 km/2½ miles.

Vesuvius first emerged in the Quaternary in the form of an island. In antiquity it was regarded as extinct until the violent eruption on August 24th in the year A.D. 79 which destroyed Pompeii, Herculaneum, Stabiae and a number of smaller places.
Between that date and 1139 there were 15 eruptions, after which the volcano appeared to be quiescent, and woodland and scrub spread right up to the rim of the crater. In 1631, however, it came back to life with a fearsome eruption. The last eruption was on March 10th 1944, when the funicular from Ercolano (then known as Resina) up the mountain was destroyed. Since then Vesuvius – as is normally the case for a few years after a major eruption – has remained inactive apart from a number of fumaroles.
The ash cone and the more recent lava flows are almost devoid of vegetation, but the older weathered lavas form a fertile soil for the growth of oaks and chestnuts at medium heights and of fruit and vines (Lacrima Christi wine) below 500 m/1640 ft.

Eruptions

Vesuvius from Naples harbour

The crater of Vesuvius

**Ascent of Vesuvius

For the ascent of Vesuvius, leave the Naples-Salerno motorway at the Ercolano exit and take the Strada del Vesuvio, which winds its way uphill between lava flows. In 7 km/4½ miles it comes to the Albergo Eremo, where a short side road goes off to the Observatory, founded in 1845, with a museum.

In another 3 km/2 miles the road forks. To the left is a road running up the north side of Vesuvius to the Colle Margherita (3 km/2 miles), from which it is a 20 minutes' climb on foot to the rim of the crater. The road continues straight ahead and in 1.5 km/1 mile comes to the lower station of a chair-lift (753 m/2485 ft) which goes up to the upper station (1158 m/3821 ft); at present the chair-lift is not in operation. At the top there is a fascinating one-hour walk around the crater and magnificent views.

Another road (toll payable) runs from Torre Annunziata, a village to the south-west of the volcano. The route first leads north-east for 2 km/1¼ miles to Boscotrecase, then 10 km/6 miles north-west, past the Nuova Casa Bianca restaurant and up the south-east slopes of Vesuvius with numerous bends. Some time ago the area around the crater was designated a protected area.

Viareggio   G6

Region: Toscana
Province: Lucca (LU)
Altitude: 2 m/7 ft
Population: 58,000

The seaside resort of Viareggio lies on the Gulf of Genoa, some 55 km/34 miles south-east of La Spezia and about 25 km/16 miles west of Lucca.

Situation

Sights

Thanks to its long sandy beach Viareggio is one of the most important resorts on the west coast of Italy. The town has a rectangular network of streets. There is much tourist traffic in the area which extends along the through road up to the beach.

In the northern part of the town is the large Pineta del Ponente, a park with tall umbrella pines. Farther south the Burlamacca-canal extends to the yachting harbour.

There is a pleasant walk along the pier which extends several hundred metres into the sea. Beyond the canal begins the Riviera di Levante.

Pineta del Ponente

Viareggio is renowned for its carnival. Thousands of masked revellers accompanied by decorated vehicles join the colourful parade on the wide seafront promenade.

*Carnival

Torre del Lago Puccini

East of Viareggio, near the Lago Massaciuccoli, is the town of Torre del Lago Puccini (2 m/7 ft). The composer Giacomo Puccini (1858–1924) lived here in the Villa Puccini, and he and his wife (d. 1930) are buried in the park. The villa is open to the public. In the open-air theatre near Torre del Lago Puccini performances of Puccini operas are given in summer.

Situation
6 km/3¾ miles south

Carnival in Viareggio

Vicenza

Region: Veneto
Province: Vicenza (VI)
Altitude: 39 m/129 ft
Population: 110,000

Situation

The provincial capital of Vicenza lies north-west of Padua on the edge of the fertile Po plain on both sides of the River Bacchiglione.

Art

The old town, still partly enclosed by its walls, is renowned for its numerous palaces of the 15th–18th c., most notably those built by the Vicenza-born Andrea Palladio (1508–80), the last great master of the High Renaissance, whose grand style, based on his study of ancient architecture, provided a model for the whole of the Western world. His principal successors were Vincenzo Scamozzi (1552–1616) and Ottone Calderari (1730–1803). The leading painter of the 15th c. Vicenza school was Bartolomeo Montagna (*c.* 1450–1523), a native of Orzinuovi, whose works can be seen in the picture gallery of the Museo Civico and in several churches in the town.

*Piazza dei Signori

In the heart of the old town is the Piazza dei Signori, with two columns dating from the Venetian period and the slender Torre di Piazza, 82 m/271 ft, built in 1174 for defensive purposes.

Loggia del Capitano

At the north-west corner of the square the Loggia del Capitano (now part of the Town Hall), was formerly the residence of the Venetian governor; it was begun by Palladio in 1571 but only half finished.

Vicenza: Basilica Palladiana

To the right is the Palazzo del Monte di Pietà, flanking the Baroque façade of the church of San Vincenzo (1617).

✳✳ Basilica Palladiana

On the south-east side of the square stands the Basilica Palladiana (1549–1614), Palladio's masterpiece, with open colonnades of two storeys (lower part Doric and upper part Ionic), a very impressive combination. The basilica was not built as a church but as a meeting-place for the Grand Council. On the first floor is a hall 52 m/172 ft long with a wooden vaulted roof. In front of the west end of the basilica is a marble statue of Palladio (1859). The basilica houses the Museo Palladiano, with models, designs and other work by Palladio.

Museo Palladiano

Cathedral

From the Basilica Palladiana Via Garibaldi runs south-west to the Piazza del Duomo, on the north-side of which stands the cathedral, a Gothic structure with a façade of white and red marble (15th c.) and a fine interior. Under the cathedral are the foundations of three earlier churches. On the south-west side of the Piazza del Duomo the Bishop's Palace has a neo-classical façade of 1819. In the courtyard, on the right, is an elegant Early Renaissance Hall by Bernardino da Milano (1494).

Corso Andrea Palladio

A little way north-west of the Piazza dei Signori is the main street of Vicenza, the Corso Andrea Palladio, lined with palaces. Half-way along

Palazzo del Comune

this street we find the fine Palazzo del Comune (formerly Palazzo Tris-sino, by Vincenzo Scamozzi, 1592–1662) and 100 m/110 yd north-east of this the Gothic Palazzo Da Schio, known as the Cà d'Oro.

Santo Stefano
A little way north is the Baroque church of Santo Stefano (by Guarini, early 18th c.), which has a "Madonna Enthroned" by Palma il Vecchio in the north transept.

Santa Corona
From here Via Santo Stefano runs north-east to the Gothic church of Santa Corona (13th c.), which has a "Baptism of Christ" by Giovanni Bellini (*c.* 1501; fifth altar on left). On the third altar, on the right, is an "Adoration of the Kings".

Museo Civico
At the north-east end of the Corso Andrea Palladio, in the Palazzo Ciericati, one of Palladio's finest buildings, is the Museo Civico. On the ground floor are archaeological collections, on the first floor a picture gallery containing major works by painters of the Vicenza school (Bartolomeo Montagna, Giovanni Buonconsiglio, etc.), Venetian masters (Carpaccio, Veronese, Tintoretto, Tiepolo) and others.

*Teatro Olimpico
Opposite the museum is the Teatro Olimpico (damaged by an earth-quake shock in 1976), which was begun by Palladio in 1580 and com-pleted by Vincenzo Scamozzi in 1584. Built of wood and stucco, this is a Renaissance adaption of the ancient type of theatre. The auditorium, with seating for 1000, rises in semi-oval tiers; the magnificent stage wall offers vistas through three openings of streets contrived to secure the effect of perspective.

San Lorenzo
From the middle section of the Corso Andrea Palladio the Via Fogazzaro (at No. 16, on the right, the Palazzo Valmarana) runs north-west to the church of San Lorenzo, a brick-built Romanesque and Gothic structure (1280–1344) with a slender campanile and a beautiful main doorway; fine interior with a fresco by Bartolomeo Mantagna (Beheading of St Paul, *c.* 1500).

Porta Castello
At the south-west end of the Corso Andrea Palladio are a number of fine palaces, including the Palazzo Bonin (No. 13, on the north side) and the Palazzo Zileri Dal Verme (No. 36, on the south side).
The Corso ends in the Piazza Castello, in which is the Porta Castello. To the left, on the shorter side of the square, the unfinished Palazzo Porto-Breganze, was probably designed by Palladio and built by Vin-cenzo Scamozzi about 1600.

Chiesa dei Santi Felice e Fortunato

In the south-west of Vicenza stands the Chiesa dei Santi Felice e Fortu-nato, which was rebuilt in the 10th–12th c. in its present form, with notable floor mosaics (4th–5th c.) from an earlier building. The church has a 12th c. leaning tower (campanile).

Basilica di Monte Berico

Situation
2 km/1¼ miles south
From the Villa Roi, on the southern outskirts of the town, the Portici di Monte Berico (1746), a series of arcades, lead up to the Basilica di Monte Berico. This pilgrimage church was built by the Bologna archi-tect C. Borella in 1668; it has a centralised plan modelled on the Rotonda (see below). In the chapel to the right of the high altar is a "Lamentation" by Bartolomeo Montagna (1500), in the refectory a large picture by Bartolomeo Montagna ("Banquet of St Gregory Magnus").
From the square in front of the church there are magnificent views of the city and the Pre-Alps, including Monte Pasubio and Monte Grappa.

Basilica di Monte Berico *La Rotonda*

*La Rotonda

At the bend in the Portici a road runs east, and 2 minutes along this a footpath goes off on the right and leads past the Villa Valmarana (with mythological frescoes by Giovanni Battista, 1757) to reach in 10 minutes the famous Rotonda, a square structure crowned by a dome which was begun by Palladio about 1550 and completed by Scamozzi in 1606. (The Villa Valmarana and the Rotonda can also be reached by road from the Strada della Riviera Berica, which skirts the east side of Monte Berico.

Situation
2 km/1¼ miles
south-east of
Vicenza

Viterbo

17

Region: Lazio
Province: Viterbo (VT)
Altitude: 293–354 m/967–1168 ft
Population: 59,000

The provincial capital of Viterbo is situated at the foot of the Monti Cimini, some 80 km/50 miles north-west of Rome.
Noted in the past as the "city of beautiful women and beautiful fountains", it still preserves its old Lombard walls, fine historic buildings and picturesque old-world nooks and crannies. It suffered much damage during the last war, but this has now been repaired.

Situation

The town was presented to the Pope by Pepin the Short in the 8th c. At the end of the 11th c. it became a free city, but in 1396 was again incorporated in the States of the Church.

History

Sights

Palazzo Comunale	The central feature of the town is the Piazza del Plebiscito, on the west side of which stands the Palazzo Comunale (begun 1247; porch 15th c.). In the courtyard, from which there is an attractive view of the western part of the town, is an elegant 17th c. fountain.
Piazza della Morte	From the Piazza del Plebiscito Via di San Lorenzo runs south to the little Piazza del Gesù, with the church of San Silvestro, and the Piazza della Morte, which has another charming fountain, the Fontana a Fuso.
*San Lorenzo	Continuing west past the 15th c. Palazzo Farnese (on right), we come to the Piazza San Lorenzo, with the fine Cathedral of San Lorenzo, a Romanesque basilica with a Gothic campanile; the façade was renewed in 1570.
*Palazzo Papale	To the right of the cathedral stands the Palazzo Papale (1266), with a Gothic loggia, which has been the Bishop's Palace since the 15th c. In its huge hall various conclaves met for the election of a pope in the 13th c.
*San Pellegrino	South-east of the Piazza della Morte lies the picturesque San Pellegrino quarter, which has preserved many medieval houses, particularly in the Piazza San Pellegrino, with the Case degli Alessandri.

Piazza Fontana Grande

*Fontana Grande	From the Piazza del Plesbiscito the busy Via Cavour runs south-east to the Piazza Fontana Grande, with the town's largest fountain, the Fontana Grande, completed in 1279.
San Sisto	From the square Via Garibaldi continues east to the Porta Romana (1653). To the left of the gate is the church of San Sisto, a Lombard building of the 9th c. with a fine apse which was increased in height in the 12th c.

Santa Maria della Verità

Museo Civico	Going north from the Porta Romana outside the town walls, we come to the former monastic church of Santa Maria della Verità (12th c.; restored after 1945), with a beautiful cloister. The Cappella Mazzatosta is decorated with fine frescoes by Lorenzo da Viterbo. The monastic buildings now house the Museo Civico, with Etruscan sarcophagi, archaeological finds, medieval pictures, etc.

Sights in the north

Santa Rosa	In the north-east of Viterbo, inside the town walls, is the church of Santa Rosa (rebuilt from 1840 onwards), with the mummified body of St Rosa (d. 1261). Every year on September 3rd, the eve of her feast-day, the saint's statue is borne on a 30 m/100 ft high tower from the Porta Romana to the church – a ceremony first introduced in 1664.
San Francesco	North-west of Santa Rosa, in the Piazza San Francesco, the Gothic church of San Francesco contains the tombs of Pope Clement IV (d. 1268) in the north aisle (on the right) and of Pope Hadrian V (d. 1276) in the south aisle (on the left).
Rocca (Museum)	Adjoining the Piazza San Francesco on the west is the Piazza della Rocca, with a fountain which is ascribed to Vignola and the remains of the Rocca (1457), which suffered severe destruction during the Second World War. It now houses the Museo Archeologico Nazionale.

In the Park of Monsters, near Bomarzo

Still farther west, outside the Porta Fiorentina (1768), lies the beautiful Giardino Pubblico.

La Quercia

3 km/2 miles north-east of Viterbo, in the suburb of La Quercia, is the pilgrimage church of the Madonna della Quercia (1470–1525), a fine Renaissance building with an interesting interior. In the adjoining Dominican monastery are two beautiful cloisters with fountains of 1508 and 1633.

Bagnaia

On the road coming from Viterbo and running eastward is the village of Bagnaia (441 m/1455 ft), with the Villa Lante, once the summer residence of the ducal family of that name. In the park are beautiful fountains.

Situation
5 km/3 miles east

Ferento

North of Viterbo is Ferento, originally an Etruscan settlement, the inhabitants of which formed an alliance with the Romans in the 3rd c. B.C. (Ferentum). Here can be seen the restored remains of a Roman theatre (1st c. A.D.), now used for theatrical performances.

Situation
9 km/5½ miles north

Bagni di Viterbo

Situation
5 km/3 miles west

West of Viterbo we come to the little spa establishment of Bagni di Viterbo (258 m/851 ft).

1 km/¾ mile north-east of Bagni di Viterbo, on a flat-topped hill of travertine with a fine view of Viterbo and the Monti Cimini, is the sulphur spring known as the Bullicame (298 m/983 ft), a pool of clear blue water surrounded by a low wall, constantly effervescing with bubbles of gas. The water of the spring, which is mentioned by Dante ("Inferno", XIV, 79), is still used for medicinal bathing.

Bomarzo

Situation
23 km/14 miles
north-east

One trip which will appeal to children as well as to adults is to the little town of Bomarzo (263 m/868 ft), picturesquely situated on a high crag above the Tiber valley north-east of Viterbo. In the town is a palace of the Orsini family (16th c.), now the Town Hall. From the terrace in front of the church there is a superb view of the Tiber valley.

*Parco dei Mostri

Outside the town, on the slopes of the hill, is the Parco dei Mostri ("Park of Monsters"), a beautiful terraced park with a whole series of monstrous and grotesque beasts, hewn from the rock in the 16th c. by Turkish prisoners of war.

Volterra   G6

Region: Toscana
Province: Pisa (PI)
Altitude: 555 m/1832 ft
Population: 14,000

Situation

Volterra lies on a hill in the Tuscan uplands, about 50 km/31 miles off the Maremma coast, and 65 km/40 miles south-east of Pisa.

Alabaster

The town is noted for its alabaster industry, which provides employment for about a third of the population; many articles on sale.

History

Volterra was one of the twelve cities of the Etruscan confederation, under the name of Velathri. In the 3rd c. B.C. it became the Roman municipium of Volaterrae. A free city during the medieval period, it passed under Florentine control in 1361.

*Piazza dei Priori

Palazzo dei Priori

The central feature of the town is the Piazza dei Priori, surrounded by medieval palaces. On the west side of the square the fine Palazzo dei Priori (1208–54), now the Town Hall, has Renaissance coats of arms and two lions on the façade. On the first floor is the frescoed Sala del Consiglio.

Palazzo Pretorio

Opposite the Town Hall is the Palazzo Pretorio (13th c.), with the Torre del Podestà integrated in the building.

*Cathedral

Behind the Town Hall, to the west, stands the cathedral, consecrated in 1120 and enlarged in Pisan style in 1254, with a fine interior, including a fresco ("The Three Kings") by Gozzoli.

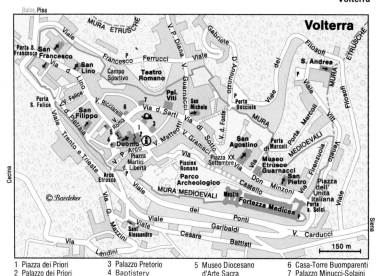

1 Piazza dei Priori   3 Palazzo Pretorio   5 Museo Diocesano   6 Casa-Torre Buomparenti
2 Palazzo dei Priori   4 Baptistery   d'Arte Sacra   7 Palazzo Minucci-Solaini

Opposite it is the Baptistery of San Giovanni, an octagonal structure on a centralised plan (1283), with a font by A. Sansovino (1502).

Baptistery

From the cathedral it is only a few steps to the Museo d'Arte Sacra (Diocesan Museum), with sacral requisites, valuable chasubles, etc.

Museo Diocesano
d'Arte Sacra

A little way south, in the circuit of Etruscan town walls, is the Arco Etrusco or Porta dell'Arco, a town-gate with supports of the 4th–3rd c. B.C., from the top there are extensive views.

Arco Etrusco

Palazzo Minucci-Solaini

Near the Piazza dei Priori stands the Palazzo Minucci-Solaini, which houses the Pinacoteca (picture collection), with works by Ghirlandaio, Signorelli and other painters. The same palace contains the Municipal Museum (Museo Civico).

Pinacoteca e Museo
Civico

West of the museum, at the crossing of Via Roma and Via Ricciarelli, is the Casa-Torre Buonparenti, a 13th c. residential tower.

Casa-Torre
Buonparenti

*Museo Etrusco Guarnacci

In the eastern part of the old town, at Via Minzoni 15, the Museo Etrusco Guarnacci houses a rich assemblage of Etruscan material from the town and surrounding area. Particularly notable is its collection of over 600 ash-urns, mostly of alabaster, dating from the Etruscan period (6th–1st c. B.C.), with curiously foreshortened figures of the dead persons on the lids.

South-east of the museum is the Citadel (Fortezza Medicea, now a prison), a massive Renaissance structure. It consists of the Rocca Vecchia (the old castle; 14th c.) to the east and the Rocca Nuova (the new

Citadel

Volterra

Volterra: Façade of the cathedral

Arco Etrusco

castle; 15th c.) to the west. The round tower in the middle of the new castle is called "Maschio" ("Little Man") and the tower of the old castle is known as the "Femmina" ("Little Woman").

Parco Archeologico

At the west end of the Citadel extends the Archaeological Park. In 1926 the remains of an ancient acropolis with the foundations of two temples (2nd c. B.C.) and a cistern have been excavated here.

Sights in the north

Mura Etrusche

Leaving the Piazza dei Priori on Via Ricciarelli, we continue past the church of San Lino and San Francesco to the Porta San Francesco; a little north are the remains of the Etruscan town walls (Mura Etrusche).

Teatro Romano

From the Porta San Francesco we follow the Via Volterrana and in 100 m/110 yd turn right into Viale Francesco Ferrucci, which runs along the north side of the town walls to the Roman Theatre (Teatro Romano) dating from the 1st c. A.D., which has been excavated from 1951 onwards.

Close by, in Via del Mandorlo, can be found a large alabaster works (exhibition hall; visits possible).

*Balze

Situation
north-west

Very impressive is the Balze, north-west of the town, an inhospitable area, almost devoid of vegetation, formed by landslides and erosion, which engulfed the Etruscan necropolises, a section of the ancient walls and the medieval church.

San Girolamo

North-east of the town stands the monastic church of San Girolamo, notable for its pictures and its terracotta altarpieces by Giovanni della Robbia.

Situation
1 km/¾ mile north-east

Massa Marittima

Take the road which runs 10 km/6 miles south-west to Saline di Volterra, noted for its salt-works, which supply the whole of Tuscany, then south over the bare uplands of the Colline Metallifere (Poggio di Montieri, 1051 m/3468 ft) and via the little town of Pomarance (25 km/16 miles; 367 m/1211 ft; pop. 8000) to Larderello (10 km/6 miles; 390 m/1287 ft), lying off the main road on the slopes of Monte Cerboli (691 m/2280 ft). The volcanic water vapour which issues from the ground in jets (soffioni) deposits the boric acid and other chemicals which it contains in underground reservoirs (lagoni) and supplies the motive power for the turbines of an electric power station. The columns of steam can be seen from a long distance away.

Situation
85 km/53 miles south
Larderello

From Larderello the road continues past ancient mines (copper pyrites and argentiferous galena) and comes in 34 km/21 miles to Massa Marittima (380 m/1254 ft; pop. 10,000), one of the principal towns in the Maremma. The main square of the town is the fine Piazza Garibaldi, with the principal public buildings. The Cathedral of San Cerbone (11th–13th c.), a Romanesque-Gothic structure in Pisan style, has a notable font by Giroldo da Como (1267) and in the crypt the reliquary of San Cerbone by Goro di Gregorio da Siena (1324). In the Romanesque Palazzo Comunale (13th c.) is a five-part altarpiece by Ambrogio Lorenzetti (c. 1330). The Palazzo Pretorio (13th c.) houses the Museo Archeologico, with numerous finds of Etruscan tombs. Other features of interest are the Pinacoteca ("Maestà" by Lorenzetti) and the massive ruins of the 14th c. Fortezza dei Senesi in the "Città Nuova".

Massa Marittima

Practical Information from A to Z

Accommodation

See Hotels, Youth Hostels, Camping and Caravanning.

Air Travel

Italy is linked with the international network of air services by a number of airports. The most important international airport is the Leonardo da Vinci Airport at Rome/Fiumicino.

Airports

The national airline, Alitalia, flies both international and domestic routes. It has desks at all Italian and the principal foreign airports.

Alitalia

The Italian company Alisarda flies services to Sardinia.

Alisarda

For children under 2 years of age accompanied by an adult and not occupying a seat there is a reduction of 90% on the adult fare; for children between 2 and 12 the reduction is 50%; for young people between 12 and 22 it is 30%. There are also reductions for adults at weekends.

Concessions

Alitalia
Via Bissolati 13, I-00187 Roma
tel. (06) 54 56

Airline addresses
in Rome

British Airways
Via Bissolati 54, I-00187 Roma
tel. (06) 47 99 91

Canadian Airlines
Via Barberini 3, I-00187 Roma
tel. (06) 46 35 14

TWA
Via Barberini 59, I-00187 Roma
tel. (06) 4 72 11

Banks

See Currency

Bus Services

Bus services play a major part in public transport, particularly in the more thinly populated upland regions. They are run by the Italian State Railways and by a number of private companies.

◀ *San Remo: yacht harbour*

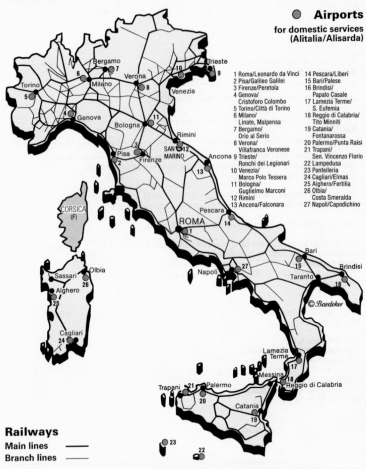

● **Airports**
for domestic services
(Alitalia/Alisarda)

1 Roma/Leonardo da Vinci
2 Pisa/Galileo Galilei
3 Firenze/Peretola
4 Genova/
  Cristoforo Colombo
5 Torino/Città di Torino
6 Milano/
  Linate, Malpensa
7 Bergamo/
  Orio al Serio
8 Verona/
  Villafranca Veronese
9 Trieste/
  Ronchi dei Legionari
10 Venezia/
  Marco Polo Tessera
11 Bologna/
  Guglielmo Marconi
12 Rimini
13 Ancona/Falconara

14 Pescara/Liberi
15 Bari/Palese
16 Brindisi/
  Papalo Casale
17 Lamezia Terme/
  S. Eufemia
18 Reggio di Calabria/
  Tito Minniti
19 Catania/
  Fontanarossa
20 Palermo/Punta Raisi
21 Trapani/
  Sen. Vincenzo Florio
22 Lampedusa
23 Pantelleria
24 Cagliari/Elmas
25 Alghero/Fertilia
26 Olbia/
  Costa Smeralda
27 Napoli/Capodichino

Railways

Main lines ——
Branch lines ——

Information about bus services can be obtained from ENIT offices (see Information) and from Italian State Railways (see Railways).

Business Hours

Shops	Mon.–Sat. 8.30/9 a.m.–1 p.m. and 3.30/4–7.30 or 8.30 p.m. Some food shops open as early as 8 a.m. Closed on Sundays and on a weekly half day.
Banks	Mon.–Fri. 8.30 a.m.–1.30 p.m. and 3–4 p.m.
Petrol stations	Petrol stations are usually closed at lunch-time, from 12.30 to 3.30 p.m. They remain open until 7.30 p.m. (7 p.m. in winter).

In summer Mon.–Fri. 8.30 a.m.–1 p.m. and 4–8 p.m.; in winter Mon.–Fri. 8.30 a.m.–1 p.m. and 4–7.30 p.m.

Mon.–Fri. 8.25 a.m.–1.50 p.m., Sat. 8.25–noon. Post offices at airports and telegram counters at head post offices are open 24 hours a day.

Most restaurants are open from 12 noon to 3 p.m. and from 5 p.m. to midnight (in winter from 7.30 to 10 p.m.). As a rule they are closed on one day a week.

Museums are usually open on weekdays from 9 a.m. to 2 p.m. and on Sundays from 9 a.m. to 1 p.m., and sometimes also from 5 to 8 p.m.; as a rule they are closed on Mondays. Open-air museums are open from 9 a.m. to sunset.
There are, however, many local variations in opening hours.

The larger churches are usually open until 12 noon and from 4 or 5 p.m. until dusk; some major churches are open throughout the day.
Visitors can also see the interiors of churches during services. They should, however, try to be as inobtrusive as possible and avoid disturbing the worshippers.

Camping and Caravanning

Italy has large numbers of good camping sites, most of them in the Alto Adige, in the Aosta valley, on the North Italian lakes and on the coasts of the Adriatic, Tyrrhenian and Ligurian Seas. During the main holiday season it is advisable to reserve a place in advance if you plan to stay for some time at a particular site.
"Wild" camping on public land is not permitted (except for a one-night stand by a trailer or motor caravan). Permission to camp on private property should be obtained from the owner.

Visitors intending to camp on the island of Elba should make reservations in good time, both for the return crossing on the ferry and for a camping site. This also applies to Sardinia. Many camping sites on Sicily are of a high standard but most – as on Sardinia – can only be reached along field-tracks.

Lists of camping sites can be obtained from ENIT offices (see Information) or from the Italian camping organisation:
Federazione Italiana del Campeggio e del Caravanning
Via Vittorio Emanuele 11
I-50041 Calenzano/Firenze
tel. (055) 88 23 91

Car Rental

The international car rental firms have offices at airports and in the larger towns and resorts in Italy, and there are numerous small local firms. Tariffs are relatively high, and it is likely to be much cheaper to arrange for the hire of a car before leaving home through one of the well known international companies. The car can usually be picked up at one place (the airport or town of arrival) and left at another.

Consulates

See Embassies and Consulates

Currency

The unit of currency (which circulates also in the Vatican City and San Marino) is the Italian *lira* (plural *lire).*

There are banknotes for 1000, 2000, 5000, 10,000, 50,000 and 100,000 lire and coins in denominations of 5, 10, 20, 50, 100, 200 and 500 lire.

Exchange rates (subject to variation)	£1 sterling = 2200 lire $1 (US) = 1175 lire	1000 lire = £0.45 1000 lire = $0.85

Lira nuova

The Italian Parliament has been discussing currency reform for years. The proposal under consideration is to introduce a "new lira" *(lira nuova)* which will be worth 1000 old lire. If and when the necessary legislation will be introduced remains uncertain. If the change does take place the old lira will remain in circulation along with the new one for at least two years.

Currency regulations

There are no restrictions on the import of lire and foreign currency into Italy; but since there may sometimes be a strict control on the export of currency it is advisable to declare any large amount on the appropriate form (Modulo V2), obtainable at the frontier when entering the country. The export of foreign currency without declaration on entry is permitted only up to the equivalent of 5,000,000 lire per person; no more than 1,000,000 lire of Italian currency may be taken out.

Eurocheques

Eurocheques can be drawn in Italy and San Marino to a maximum figure of 300,000 lire.
Loss of Eurocheques or Eurocheque card should be reported at once by telephone to the bank which issued them.

Credit cards

Most international credit cards, in particular Visa cards, are accepted by banks, the larger hotels and better restaurants, car rental firms and many shops.

Changing money

Banks are open Monday-Friday from 8.30 a.m. to 1.30 p.m. and from 3 to 4 p.m.

Postcheques

Postcheques of the British Girobank can be cashed at post offices up to the equivalent of £120 per cheque.

Customs Regulations

Entry to Italy

Personal effects are admitted without formality. Video recorders, citizen's band radios and car phones must be declared on entry.
The import of sheath knives and large multipurpose knives is prohibited. Information on taking in sporting guns, etc., can be obtained from Italian consulates.
Spare cans of petrol may not be taken into Italy.

Currency

On the import of Italian and foreign currency, see Currency (above).

Customs allowances in European Community countries

Since January 1st 1993 all EC nationals have been permitted to import into another EC country reasonable amounts of alcoholic drinks, tobacco, perfume, etc., *provided they have been purchased tax paid in an EC country, are for personal use and are not intended for resale.*

Information concerning allowances for non-EC nationals can be obtained from Customs and Excise offices.

"Duty-free" goods are still available at major airports, on aircraft and ferries; the allowances for passengers over 17 years of age are as previously viz: 1 litre of spirits, 2 litres of alcoholic drinks under 38.8% proof or 2 litres of fortified wine, plus 3 litres of still table wine; 200 cigarettes or 100 cigarillos or 50 cigars or 300 g of tobacco; 50 g of perfume and 250 cc of toilet-water.

Persons over 15 years of age may also bring into Italy other goods and gifts up to a total value of 930,000 lire

Young people below 17 years of age may not bring in wines, or spirits.

Goods purchased in Italy may be exported without liability to tax up to a value of 500 US dollars. For the export of works of art and antiquities a licence must be obtained from the Ministero dei Beni Culturali ed Ambientali (whose address can be obtained from the local tourist information office). | Leaving Italy

The duty-free allowances for British subjects are as for entry into Italy. In addition they are allowed £32 worth of other duty-free purchases or £250 worth where the goods have been bought in an ordinary shop. | Return to Britain

U.S. citizens can take in 200 cigarettes, 100 cigars and one litre of alcohol, plus $400 worth of other purchases (with a 10% tax on the next $1000 worth). | Return to the U.S.A.

Canadian citizens can take in 200 cigarettes, 50 cigars and 40 ounces of alcohol, plus $150 worth of other purchases ($300 worth if they have been abroad for a week or more). | Return to Canada

Electricity

Electricity supplies in Italy are normally 220 volts AC.
An adaptor is required for British and American-type plugs.

Embassies and Consulates

Embassy: | United Kingdom
Via XX Settembre 80A
I-00187 Roma (Rome)
tel. (06) 4 75 54 41, 4 75 55 51

Consulates:
Via San Lucifero 87
I-09100 Cagliari
tel. (070) 66 27 55

Palazzo Castelbarco
Lungarno Corsini 2
I-50123 Firenze (Florence)
tel. (055) 21 25 94, 28 41 33, 28 74 49

Via XII Ottobre 2/132
I-16121 Genova (Genoa)
tel. (010) 56 48 33

Via San Paolo 7
I-20121 Milano (Milan)
tel. (02) 8 69 34 42

Via Francesco Crispi 122
I-80122 Napoli (Naples)
tel. (081) 66 35 11

Corso Massimo d'Azeglio
I-10126 Torino (Turin)
tel. (011) 68 78 32, 68 39 21

Via delle Ville 16
I-34100 Trieste
tel. (040) 76 47 52

Accademia 1051, Dorsoduro
P.O. Box 679
I-30100 Venezia (Venice)
tel. (041) 5 22 72 07, 5 22 74 08

USA

Embassy:
Via Vittorio Veneto 119A
I-00187 Roma (Rome)
tel. (06) 4 67 41

Consulates:
Lungarno Amerigo Vespucci 38
I-50100 Firenze (Florence)
tel. (055) 2 39 82 76

Banca d'America e d'Italia Building
Piazza Portello 6
I-16124 Genova (Genoa)
tel. (010) 28 27 41

Via Principe Amedeo 2/10
I-20121 Milano (Milan)
tel. (02) 65 28 41

Piazza della Repubblica
I-80122 Napoli (Naples)
tel. (081) 7 61 43 03

Via Vaccarini 1
I-90143 Palermo
tel. (091) 30 25 90

Via Pomba 23
I-10123 Torino (Turin)
tel. (011) 51 74 37

Canada

Embassy (Consular Section):
Via Zara 30
I-00198 Roma (Rome)
tel. (06) 4 40 29 91

Consulate:
Via Vittor Pisani 19
I-20124 Milano (Milan)
tel. (02) 6 69 74 51

Emergencies

It is advisable always to carry a few 100 and 200 lire coins and telephone tokens (*gettoni*, obtainable from newspaper kiosks, tobacconists and bars with pay phones) so as to be able to telephone in case of emergency.

N.B.

For fire, police and ambulance services (Pronto Soccorso) dial 113 (throughout Italy).

Fire, police, ambulance

For the ACI (Automobile Club Italiano) breakdown service dial 116 (throughout Italy).
If help cannot be obtained locally drivers covered by the Automobile Association emergency service can telephone the AA Continental Emergency Centre in Boulogne (tel. 00 33 21 87 21 21) or, by arrangement with the Dutch motoring club ANWB, ANWB's English-speaking emergency service at Mendrisio on the Swiss-Italian border (tel. 00 41 91 46 88 61).

Breakdown service

Events

San Remo: Italian Festival of Popular Songs	February
Rome: Festa de la Candelora (Candlemas: processions)	February 2nd
Viareggio, San Remo, Pisa, Turin and some towns on Riviera: colourful parades and celebrations Venice: Venetian Carnival	Carnival
Verona: Gnocco (Festival of Bacchus)	Friday before Shrovetide
Many places: San Giuseppe (St Joseph's day)	March 19th
Rome: Festa de la Primavera (Spring Festival)	March/April
San Marino: Installation of Regents	April 1st
Many places, particularly Rome and Florence: Blessing of palms, with processions	Palm Sunday
Many places, particularly Rome: Mercoledi Santo (Lamentations, Miserere)	Wednesday before Easter
Many places, particularly Rome and Florence: Washing of the Feet (Rome: in the Basilica of San Giovanni in Laterano, with papal mass)	Maundy Thursday
Many places, particularly Rome and Florence: Adoration of the Cross (Rome: Way of the Cross, with the Pope)	Good Friday
Many places, particularly Rome and Florence: Lighting of the Sacred Fire	Easter Saturday
Rome: Papal blessing "urbi et orbi"	Easter Day

Events

	Florence: Scoppio del Carro ("Burning of the Cart" between the Cathedral and the Baptistery)
May 1st	Florence: Gioco del Calcio (historical ball-game) Cagliari (Sardinia): Sagra di Sant'Efisio (procession, with local costumes)
May	Florence: Maggio Musicale Fiorentino (musical festival)
First Saturday in May	Naples: San Gennaro (feast of St Januarius)
May 8th	Bari (Apulia): Sagra di San Nicola (feast of St Nicholas; procession of fishing boats)
Second Sunday in May	Camogli (Liguria): Sagra del Pesce (fishermen's festival)
May 15th	Gubbio (Umbria): Corsa dei Ceri (race with wax figures of saints)
Second half of May	Rome: Antiques Show in Via dei Coronari
Last Sunday in May	Gubbio (Umbria): Palio (shooting with crossbows)
End of May	Taormina (Sicily): Costume festival and parade of floats
Ascension	Florence: Festa del Grillo (Festival of the Cricket in the Parco delle Cascine) Sassari (Sardinia): Cavalcata Sarda (Sardinian Cavalcade, with fine local costumes)
Corpus Christi	Many places, particularly Orvieto (Umbria): processions
June–September	Venice: Biennale d'Arte (art show, held in alternate, even-numbered years)
First Sunday in June	Pisa (Tuscany): Gioco del Ponte (Bridge Festival; historical regatta)
Mid June to mid July	Many places: Ascension processions Spoleto (Umbria): Festival dei Due Mondi (Two Worlds Festival: an international festival of music, dance and drama)
June 23rd–24th	Rome: Vigilia di San Giovanni Battista (St John's Eve; fireworks)
June 29th	Rome: Santi Pietro e Paolo (feast of SS Peter and Paul)
July	Genoa–Nervi: International Ballet Festival in park of Villa Gropallo
July 2nd	Siena (Tuscany): Palio delle Contrade (horse race in traditional costumes round the Piazza del Campo)
July 15th	Rome: Festa de' Noiantri (popular festival in Trastevere; fireworks, roast sucking pigs eaten in streets)
July 16th	Naples: festival of Santa Maria del Carmine
Third Sunday in July	Venice: Festa del Redentore (Feast of the Redeemer; fireworks; on following day procession over bridge of boats from St Mark's to the church of the Redentore)
July–August	Verona: Festival of Opera in the Arena (Roman amphitheatre)
Beginning of August	Assisi (Umbria): Perdono (Forgiveness) Festival

Venice: International Film Festival (in Palazzo del Cinema on the Lido)	August–September
Ascoli Piceno (Marches): Quintana (parade and tournament)	First Sunday in August
Sassari (Sardinia): Processione dei Candelieri (candle-lit procession)	August 14th
Many places: Assunta (Assumption; processions, fireworks)	August 15th
Siena (Tuscany): Palio delle Contrade (horse race in traditional costumes round the Piazza del Campo)	August 16th
Stresa (Piedmont): Settimane Musicale (musical festival, lasting four weeks)	August–September
Arezzo (Tuscany): Giostra del Saracino (jousting in traditional costumes) Venice: Regatta Storica (procession of historic vessels and gondola race on Grand Canal)	First Sunday in September
Naples: Madonna della Piedigrotta (folk song festival)	September 5th–7th
Florence: Festa delle Rificolone (lantern festival)	September 7th
Loreto (Marches): Feast of Nativity of the Virgin Recco (Liguria): Feast of Nativity of the Virgin (with firework display)	September 8th
Foligno (Umbria): Quintana (tournament, with tilting at the ring) San Sepolcro (Tuscany): Crossbow contest	Second Sunday in September
Lucca (Tuscany): Luminaria di Santa Croce (candle-lit procession)	September 13th
Ravenna: Dante Festival Asti (Piedmont): Palio (parade and horse races in traditional costumes)	Mid September
Naples: Liquefaction of St Januarius's blood	September 19th
San Marino: Installation of Regents	October 1st
Many places: Santa Cecilia (St Cecilia's day)	November 22nd
Loreto (Marches): Santa Casa (procession)	December 10th
Rome: Papal blessing "urbi et orbi"	December 25th

Various church festivals feature prominently in the annual programme, in particular church consecration festivals and patronal festivals (in almost every place of any size). In addition there are pilgrimages and performances of Passion plays in many places.

The festival of opera in Verona is particularly famous, but there are similar events in a number of other towns (e.g. in Macerata and Ravenna).

Visitors who want to include a visit to the opera or some other musical event in their holiday programme should consult the Italian State Tourist Office (ENIT: see Information) before leaving home.

Farmhouse Holidays

A farmhouse holiday offers an attractive alternative to staying in hotels. The term farmhouse covers a wide range, from a modest cottage to a

Food and Drink

country house. Details are given in a useful booklet, "Guida dell'Ospitalità Rurale".

Information

Agriturist
Corso Vittorio Emanuele 101
I-00186 Roma
tel. (06) 6 51 23 42

Food and Drink

General

Gastronomically Italy takes a high place among the countries of Europe. Its cuisine is notable both for its variety and its excellence.

Italian cuisine

Apart from the numerous pasta dishes, served in infinite variety and with a wide range of different sauces or dressings, the Italian menu includes many excellent fish dishes. Much use is made of olive oil in cooking. The famous Italian pizza was originally made of bread dough spread with tomatoes and herbs and is a simple but tasty alternative to ordinary bread; the numerous variations with cheese, salami, ham, mushrooms, artichoke hearts, etc., developed later with increasing prosperity, particularly in northern Italy and under the influence of tourism.

Drinks

The standard drinks with all meals are wine and mineral water. Beer is found everywhere, both the light Italian beer and foreign brands *(birra estera),* particularly German, Danish and Dutch.

Mealtimes

Lunch is usually served in Italian restaurants from 12 noon onwards, though in Rome and the southern parts of the country it tends to be taken considerably later. Dinner is seldom eaten before 7, and 8 o'clock is widely regarded as the "normal" time.

Italian meals

Breakfast is a meal of little consequence to the Italians. The hotels, however, have mostly adapted to northern European habits and provide bread, butter and jam – plus eggs, sausage or cheese if required – to accompany the morning cup of coffee (usually *cappuccino,* with foaming hot milk).
Lunch usually consists of several courses. Spaghetti and other forms of pasta (and in the north, rice dishes) are merely a substitute for soup – hence the term *primo,* "first course". They are often preceded by an *antipasto* (hors d'œuvre). The pasta is followed by the *secondo* (second course), a meat or fish dish, and this in turn is often followed by cheese and fruit or a sweet of some kind. Lunch always ends with a cup of *espresso* (strong black coffee), which some connoisseurs prefer *corretto* – "corrected" by the addition of grappa (Italian brandy) or cognac. The evening meal is usually also a substantial one.

Reading an Italian Menu (lista, carta)

The table

Table-setting *coperto;* spoon *cucchiaio;* teaspoon *cucchiaino;* knife *coltello;* fork *forchetta;* plate *piatto;* glass *bicchiere;* cup *tazza;* napkin *tovagliolo;* corkscrew *cavatappi.*

Meals

Breakfast *prima colazione;* lunch *pranzo;* dinner *cena.*

Hors d'œuvre *(antipasti):* anchovies, sardines, olives, artichokes, mushrooms, radishes, sausage, ham, eggs, salads of seafood or with mayonnaise, etc.

Brodo broth; *consommé* consommé, clear soup; *minestra* soup with pasta, vegetables, etc.; *minestrone* thick vegetable soup; *stracciatella* broth with beaten eggs; *suppa (di pesce,* etc.) (fish, etc.) soup.

Pasta or *farinacei:*
Agnelotti a kind of ravioli with meat filling; *cannelloni* large rolls of pasta; *capellini* long thread-like spaghetti; *cappeletti* "little hats", a form of ravioli with various fillings; *fettucine* egg noodles; *gnocchi* a form of ravioli; *lasagne* broad strips of pasta, often green; *maccheroni* macaroni; *panzotti* small packets of pasta with cheese and spinach filling; *pasta asciutta* the general term for all kinds of pasta; *ravioli* ravioli; *rigatoni* short macaroni; *spaghetti* spaghetti; *vermicelli* vermicelli (thread-like spaghetti).

Risotto risotto; *riso* rice.

Polenta boiled maize flour (solid when cold).

Uova eggs; *alla coque, al guscio* soft-boiled; *sode* hard-boiled; *al piatto, al tegame* fried; *frittata* omelette.

Pane bread; *panini* rolls; *grissini* thin sticks of rusk-like bread.

Italy has a wide range of different kinds of fish *(pesce)* and seafood *(frutti di mare):*
Acciughe anchovies; *anguilla* eel; *aragosta* lobster; *aringa* herring; *baccalà* dried cod; *calamari* cuttlefish; *carpa, carpone* carp; *cefalo* mullet; *cernia* grouper; *cozze* mussels; *datteri* clams; *dentice* dentex; *fritto misto mare* mixed fried fish; *gamberetti* shrimps; *gambero* crayfish; *gambero di mare* lobster; *gamberoni* prawns; *granchio* crab; *luccio* pike; *merluzzo* hake; *moscardino* curled octopus; *muscoli* mussels; *nasello* hake; *orata* gilthead bream; *ostriche* oysters; *pescatrice* angler fish; *pesce persico* perch; *pesce spada* swordfish; *pesce ragno* greater weever; *polpo* octopus; *razza* skate; *riccio marino* sea-urchin; *rombo* turbot; *salmone* salmon; *sarde* pilchards; *sardine* sardines; *scampi* scampi; *sogliola* sole; *sgombro* mackerel; *spigola* bass; *storione* sturgeon; *tonno* tunny; *triglia* red mullet; *trota* trout; *vongole* palourdes; *zuppa di pesce* fish soup.

Lumache snails.

Rane frogs' legs.

Carne meat.
Animals/kinds of meat:
Abbacchio spring lamb; *agnello* lamb; *bue* ox/beef; *capretto* kid; *coniglio* rabbit; *maiale* pig/pork; *manzo* bullock/beef; *montone* ram/mutton; *porchetto, porcello* sucking pig; *vitello* calf/veal; *vitellone* older calf/young beef.
Cuts of meat:
Animelle sweetbreads; *cervello* brain; *bistecca* steak; *coda* tail; *coscia* haunch, leg; *cuore* heart; *costoletta, costata* cutlet; *fegato* liver; *filetto* fillet; *lingua* tongue; *lombata* loin; *ossobuco* shin of veal; *paillard* veal fillet; *petto* breast; *piccata* sliced veal; *piede, piedino* foot; *polmone* lung; *rognoni* kidneys; *scaloppa* scallop, schnitzel; *spezzatino* veal goulash; *testa, testina* head; *trippa* tripe; *zampone* pig's trotter.

Food and Drink

Methods of cooking:
Arrosto roast; *bollito* boiled; *bolliti misti* mixed boiled meats; *cibrero* ragout; *ben cotto* well done; *ai ferri* grilled; *al girarrosto* roasted on the spit; *alla griglia* grilled; *all'inglese* underdone; *lesso* boiled; *pasticcio* pie; *polpette* rissoles, meat balls; *al sangue* rare; *stracotto, stufato, stufatino* steamed, stewed.

Sausage	*Salame* slicing sausage; *salsiccia* small sausage.
Ham	*Prosciutto* ham; *crudo* raw; *cotto* boiled; *coppa* cured shoulder of pork; *pancetta* stomach of pork.
Cold meat	*Affettato* cold meat.
Game	*Selvaggina* game: *camoscio* chamois; *capriolo* roebuck; *cervo* venison; *cinghiale* wild boar; *fagiano* pheasant; *faraona* guineafowl; *lepre* hare; *pernice, starna* partridge; *piccione* pigeon; *tordo* thrush.
Poultry	*Pollame* poultry: *anitra* duck; *gallinaccio, dindo, tacchino* turkey; *oca* goose.
Vegetables and garnishings	*Verdure, legumi* vegetables; *guarnizioni* garnishings. *Asparagi* asparagus; *barbaforte* horse-radish; *brocoli* broccoli; *carciofi* artichokes; *cardoni* cardoons; *cavolfiore* cauliflower; *cavolo* cabbage; *cavolini di Bruxelles* Brussels sprouts; *cipolle* onions; *crudezze* raw vegetable salads; *fagioli* haricot beans; *fagiolini* French beans; *fave* broad beans; *finocchio* fennel; *funghi* mushrooms; *lenticchie* lentils; *melanzana* aubergine; *patate* potatoes; *peperoni* sweet peppers; *piselli* peas; *pomodori* tomatoes; *rafano* horse-radish; *ravanelli* radishes; *sedano* celery; *spinaci* spinach; *zucchini* courgettes. *Insalata* salad.
Sauces	*Salsa al burro* butter sauce; *salsa alle noci* walnut sauce (made from ground almonds and cream); *salsa napoletana* tomato sauce; *salsa bolognese* tomato sauce with meat; *salsa verde* parsley sauce with oil, egg, spices and capers; *maionese* mayonnaise; *pesto alla genovese* green basil sauce with pine nuts, parmesan cheese and garlic.
Condiments	*Aceto* vinegar; *aglio* garlic; *burro* butter; *mostarda* candied fruit in mustard sauce; *olio* oil; *pepe* pepper; *sale* salt; *senape* mustard; *sugo* gravy, juice.
Desserts	*Dessert, dolce* dessert. *Bavarese* a mousse of cream and egg; *budino* pudding, mousse; *cassata* sponge cake or ice-cream with candied fruits; *frittata* omelette; *gelato* ice; *macedonia* fruit salad; *panettone* cake with dried fruit; *torta* flan, tart; *zabaglione* egg-flip with marsala.
Fruit	*Frutta* fruit. *Anguria, cocomero* water-melon; *arancia* orange; *ciliege* cherries; *fichi* figs; *fragole* strawberries; *frutta secca* dried fruit; *lamponi* raspberries; *limone* lemon; *mandorle* almonds; *mela* apple; *melone* melon; *nespola* medlar; *noci* walnuts; *pera* pear; *pesca* peach; *pistacchi* pistachios; *pompelmo* grapefruit; *popone* melon; *prugna* plum; *uva* grapes; *uva seccha, passa* raisins.
Cheese	*Formaggio* cheese. Bel Paese (soft); Brancolino (goat's-milk); Gorgonzola (blue-veined); Mozzarella (moist curd cheese); Parmigiano (parmesan); Provolone (mellow, soft, sometimes smoked); Pecomo (ewe's-milk); Ricotta (soft,

unsalted); Romano (ewe's-milk); Stracchino (with mould but without blue veins).

Table wine *(vino da pasto)* is served in carafes.   Table wine
Nero, rosso red; *bianco* white; *secco* dry; *asciutto* very dry; *abboccato, amabile* slightly sweet; *dolce, pastoso* sweet; *vino del paese* local wine; *un litro* a litre; *mezzo litro* half a litre; *un quarto* a quarter litre; *un bicchiere* a glass.
Older wines and wines of high quality are served in the normal way in corked and labelled bottles.

Other popular drinks *(bevande)* are *birra* beer, *acqua minerale* mineral   Beer, soft drinks
water, *aranciata* orangeade, *limonata* lemonade, *succo (di ...)* fruit juice
and *spremuta (di ...)* freshly pressed fruit juice.

Wine

The Wine-Growing Regions and Wines of Italy

1 Piedmont, Aosta valley, Liguria.
Barbera d'Asti: ruby-red, dry. Barbera d'Alba: ruby-red, dry. Barbera del Monferrato: deep red. dry to slightly sweet, semi-sparkling. Nebbiolo d'Alba: deep ruby-red, dry or slightly sweet, sparkling. Moscato d'Asti (various kinds): straw-coloured to golden yellow, sweet. Barolo: garnet-red, dry, full and fragrant. Gattinara: garnet-red, dry. Carema: garnet-red, soft, velvety and full-bodied. Barbaresco: garnet-red, dry

2 Lombardy.
Moscato dell'Oltrepò Pavese: light yellow, aromatic. Barbera dell'Oltrepò Pavese: ruby-red, dry. Pinot dell'Oltrepò Pavese: greenish-yellow, . dry, aromatic. Riesling dell'Oltrepò Pavese: light yellow, dry. Valtellina (Veltliner): deep red, dry to very dry

3 Alto Adige, Trentino.
Santa Maddalena: ruby-red to garnet-red, full, velvety. Lagarina: deep red, full, soft, velvety. Terlaner: greenish-yellow to golden . yellow, dry, fresh. Cabernet: ruby-red, dry, full. Teroldego: light red to ruby-red, dry

4 Veneto.
Valpolicella: ruby-red to garnet-red, dry to semi-sweet, full-bodied, well rounded. Bardolino: light red, dry, well rounded. Soave: straw-coloured to greenish-yellow, dry, well rounded

5 Friuli–Venezia Giulia.
Grave del Friuli: red and white, made from different varieties of grape. Isonzo: white, several kinds made from Tokay, Malvasia, Riesling or Weissburgunder grapes; red, several kinds made from Merlot or Cabernet grapes.

6 Emilia–Romagna.
Lambrusco: ruby-red, sparkling; several kinds, dry to sweet. Albano di Romagna: straw-coloured to golden yellow, dry to semi-sweet. Sangiovese di Romagna: ruby-red, dry, well rounded

7 Tuscany.
Chianti: ruby-red to garnet-red, dry, well rounded. Vernaccia di San Gimignano: light yellow, dry, well rounded

8 Umbria, Latium.
Colli Albani: straw-coloured, dry to slightly sweet. Frascati: straw-coloured, soft, velvety, semi-sweet to sweet (several varieties). Est Est Est (Montefiascone): straw-coloured, full, slightly sweet. Orvieto: light yellow to straw-coloured, dry

9 Marche, Abruzzi.
Verdicchio dei Castelli di Iesi:. straw-coloured, dry, well rounded.

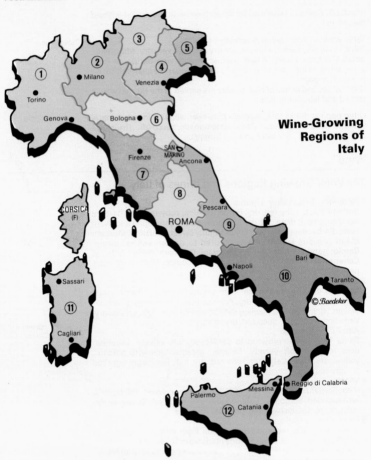

Wine-Growing Regions of Italy

© Baedeker

Montepulciano d'Abruzzo: deep ruby-red, dry, soft. Bianchello del Metauro: straw-coloured, dry, fresh

10 Campania, Apulia, Calabria, Basilicata.
Ischia: red and white, several kinds. San Severo: straw-coloured, fresh and well rounded; ruby-red, dry, full-bodied. Locorotondo: greenish-yellow to straw-coloured, dry, pleasant. Rossa Barletta: ruby-red, dry, well rounded

11 Sardinia.
Cannonau: ruby-red, dry to slightly sweet, pleasant. Monica di Sardegna: light ruby-red, dry, aromatic. Nuragus: light straw-coloured, dry

12 Sicily.
Etna: red and white, several kinds. Marsala: the famous dessert wine, amber-yellow, full-bodied, dry or sweet

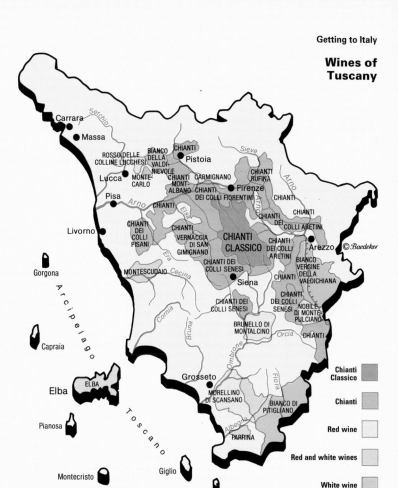

**Wines of
Tuscany**

Carrara

Massa

ROSSO DELLE
COLLINE LUCCHESI

BIANCO
DELLA
VALDI-
NIEVOLE

CHIANTI

Pistoia

Serchio

Sieve

Lucca

MONTE-
CARLO

CHIANTI CARMIGNANO
MONT-
ALBANO

CHIANTI
RUFINA

Arno

Pisa

CHIANTI
DEI COLLI FIORENTINI

Firenze

CHIANTI

Arno

CHIANTI

Elsa

CHIANTI
DEI
COLLI
PISANI

CHIANTI
VERNACCIA
DI SAN
GIMIGNANO

CHIANTI
CLASSICO

CHIANTI
DEI
COLLI
ARETINI

CHIANTI
DEI COLLI
ARETINI

Livorno

Arezzo   © Baedeker

Era

CHIANTI DEI
COLLI SENESI

BIANCO
VERGINE
DELLA
VALDICHIANA

Gorgona

MONTESCUDAIO

Cecina

Siena

CHIANTI

A r c i p e l a g o

CHIANTI DEI
COLLI SENESI

Cornia

CHIANTI
DEI COLLI
SENESI

NOBILE
DI MONTE-
PULCIANO

Capraia

Bruna

BRUNELLO DI
MONTALCINO

Orcia

CHIANTI

Elba

ELBA

Ombrone

Grosseto

T o s c a n o

MORELLINO
DI SCANSANO

Fiora

Pianosa

BIANCO DI
PITIGLIANO

Albegna

PARRINA

Montecristo

Giglio

Giannutri

	Chianti Classico
	Chianti
	Red wine
	Red and white wines
	White wine

Getting to Italy

By Car

It is a long way from Britain or northern Europe to Italy. Motorists will be well advised, therefore, to use motorways and trunk roads wherever possible. The quickest route from the Channel is via Calais, Basle and the St Gotthard tunnel, but there are many alternative routes via France or Germany and Switzerland. The road journey can be shortened by using the car sleeper services which operate in summer from Boulogne, Brussels and Paris to Milan.

Motorways are free in Holland, Belgium and Germany, but are subject to tolls in France and Italy. Drivers using the Swiss motorways must pay a flat-rate tax and display a vignette on the windscreen. The vignette can be bought from motoring organisations in the UK or at the Swiss frontier.

Italian motorway tolls are reduced for foreign visitors who have bought petrol coupons (see Petrol).

By Bus

In addition to numerous package tours by coach from Britain to Italy there are various regular bus services. Euroways run services from London to Aosta, Bologna, Brindisi, Florence, Genoa, Milan, Rome, Turin and Venice, and National Express Eurolines have services from London to Aosta, Bologna, Florence, Milan, Rome, Turin and Venice.

Information

Eurolines UK Ltd
52 Grosvenor Gardens
London SW1
tel. (071) 730 8235

National Express Eurolines
Victoria Coach Station
London SW1
tel. (071) 730 0202

By Rail

British Rail can issue tickets from main stations in Britain to main stations in Italy, covering the Channel crossing and sleeping cars (first class, second class or couchettes) from the continental port. Advance booking is advisable.

Information

European Rail Travel Centre
P.O. Box 303
Victoria Station
London SW1V 1JY

By Air

There are regular direct flights from London to Bologna, Genoa, Milan, Naples, Pisa, Rome, Turin and Venice; from Manchester to Milan and Rome; and from Birmingham and Glasgow to Milan. There are connections from Milan and Rome to other Italian airports as well as numerous charter flights from Britain, particularly during the main holiday season.

Hotels (A Selection)

The hotels in the higher categories in large towns and holiday centres offer the usual international standards of comfort and amenity, but in remoter areas the accommodation available will often be of a more modest standard. In the larger towns and in spas and seaside resorts there are numerous *pensioni* (pensions, guesthouses).

Categories

Italian hotels *(alberghi,* singular *albergo)* are officially classified in five categories: categoria di lusso, di prima, di seconda, di terza and di quarta categoria (luxury and I, II, III and IV). The range is from the 5-star luxury hotel to the one-star hotel of more modest pretensions.

In this guide the luxury hotels are indicated by the letter L and a red star before the name. The categories of other hotels are shown by the Roman figures I, II, III and IV. In terms of stars the equivalence is as follows:

*****	L
****	I
***	II
**	III
*	IV

For most hotels the number of beds is indicated (e.g. 40 b.); for some the number of rooms is given (e.g. 20 r.). SP indicates that the hotel has a swimming pool.

Hotel tariffs vary considerably according to season, and are substantially higher in large towns and popular holiday areas than in the rest of the country. Tariffs are also affected by changes in the purchasing power of the lira. **Tariffs**

Visitors should keep their hotel bills. Proof of payment for accommodation and meals in Italian hotels and restaurants must be produced on demand to a police officer checking on tax evasion, and failure to do so may entail a fine.

Lists of hotels in particular towns or areas can be obtained, before leaving home, from the Italian State Tourist Office (ENIT: see Information) or, in Italy, from local tourist information offices.

*Grand Hotel Orologio, Viale delle Terme 66, L, 330 b.; Bristol Buja, Via Montirone 2, I, 244 b.; La Résidence, Via Monte Ceva 8, I, 177 b.; Leonardo da Vinci, in Monteortone, I, 105 r.; Michelangelo, in Monteortone, I, 111 r.; Mioni Pezzato, Via Marzia 34, I, 272 b.; President, Via Montirone 31, I, 186 b.; Savoia, Via Pietro d'Abano 49, I, 180 r.; Trieste e Victoria, Via Pietro d'Abano, I, 154 b.; Ariston Molino, Via Augure 5, II, 271 b.; Alexander, Via Martiri d'Ungheria 24, II, 221 r.; Centrale, Via Jappelli 37, II, 136 r.; Metropole, Via Valerio Flacco 99, II, 145 r.; Ritz, Via Montirone 19, II, 221 b.; Terme Astoria, Piazza Cristoforo Colombo 1, 93 r.; Terme Columbia, Via Augure 15, II, 151 b.; Terme Internazionale, Viale Mazzini 5, II, 200 b.; Universal, Via Valerio Flacco 28, II, 115 r.; Terme Italia, Viale Mazzini 7, III, 132 r.; Terme Verdi, Via Flavia Busonera 200, III, 90 r.; all with private bathing facilities. **Abano Terme**

Giardino, Via I Maggio 63, II, 77 b.; Adriana, Via Serdini 76, III, 39 r.; Roma, Via Matteotti 32, III, 20 r. **Abbadia San Salvatore**

Baia Verde, in Cannizzaro, I, 254 b., SP; Catania Sheraton, in Cannizzaro, I, 340 b., SP; I Faraglioni, Lungomare, I, 125 b.; I Malavoglia, Via Provinciale, II, 63 r. **Aci Castello**

Aloha d'Oro, II, 162 b., SP; La Perla Ionica, in Capomulini, II, 1000 b., SP; Maugeri, Piazza Garibaldi, II, 68 b.; Santa Tecla Palace, in Santa Tecla, II, 605 b., SP. **Acireale**

Italia, III, 327 b. **Acquasanta Terme**

Ariston, Piazza Matteotti, II, 36 r.; Mignon, Via Monteverde 34, III, 25 r.; Pineta, Passeggiata dei Colli, III, 100 r. **Acqui Terme**

Jolly dei Templi, Parco Angeli, Villaggio Mosè, on S.S. 115, I, 292 b., SP; Villa Athena, Via dei Templi, I, 56 b., SP; Akrabello, Parco Angeli, II, 247 b., SP; Della Valle, Via dei Templi, II, 164 b.; Tre Torri, on S.S. 115, II, 118 r., SP; Belvedere, Via San Vito 20, III, 63 b. **Agrigento**

Hotels

Alassio

Grand Hotel Diana, Via Garibaldi 110, 127 b., SP; Europa e Concordia, Piazza Partigiani 1, I, 103 b.; Méditerranée, Via Roma 63, I, 141 b.; Spiaggia, Via Roma 78, I, 83 r.; Columbia, Passeggiata Cadorna 12, II, 29 r.; Firenze, Corso Dante 35, II, 24 r.; Lido, Via IV Novembre 9, 52 r.; New West End, Via Roma 42, II, 105 b.; Nuovo Suisse, Via Mazzini 119, II, 49 r.; Majestic, Via Leonardo da Vinci 300, II, 77 r.; Rosa, Via Conti 10, III, 45 r.

Albenga

Sole e Mare, II, 52 b.; Marisa, Via Pisa 28, III, 16 b.

Alberobello

*Dei Trulli, L, 54 b.; Astoria, I, 89 b.; Colle del Sole, Via Indipendenza 61, II, 18 r.; Sovrano, Viale Alcide de Gasperi 35, II, 18 r.

Albisola Marina

Corallo, Via Repetto 116, II, 44 b.; Villa Chiara e Garden, Viale Faraggiana 5, II, 48 b.; Villa Verde, Via Gentile 16, II, 52 b.

Alghero

Villa Las Tronas, Lungomare Valencia 1, I, 56 b., SP; Calabona, Località Calabona, II, 226 b., SP; Carlos V, Lungomare Valencia, II, 220 b., SP; Continental, Via Kennedy 66, II, 63 b.; Il Gabbiano, Via Garibaldi 97, II, 93 b.; Mediterraneo, Via Kennedy 67, II, 81 b.; Coral, Via Kennedy 64, III, 76 b.; Eliton, Via Garibaldi, III, 24 b.

Alicudi

See Lipari Islands

Amalfi

*Il Saraceno, L, 112 b., SP; *Santa Caterina (with annexes), Via Statale Amalfitana, L, 131 b., SP; Cappuccini Convento, I, 71 b., SP; Grand Hôtel Excelsior, 4 km/2½ miles SW on Agerola road, I, 163 b., SP; Luna e Torre Saracena, I, 74 b., SP; Aurora, II, 61 b.; Bellevue, II, 45 b.; Dei Cavalieri, II, 95 b.; La Bussola, II, 120 b.; Marina Riviera, II, 32 b.; Miramalfi, II, 83 b., SP; Residence, II, 46 b.

Ancona

Grand Hôtel Palace, Lungomare Vanvitelli 24, I, 68 b.; Grand Hôtel Passetto, Via Thaon de Revel 1, I, 76 b.; Jolly Miramare, Rupi di Via XXIX Settembre 14, I, 130 b.; Emilia, Collina di Portonovo, II, 64 b., SP; Fortuna, Piazza Rosselli 15, II, 99 b.; Grand Hôtel Roma e Pace, Via Leopardi 1, II, 114 b.; Il Fortino Napoleonico, Portonovo, II, 60 b.; Motel Agip, 6 km/4 miles W in Palombina Nuova, II, 102 b.; Sporting, Via Flaminia 220D, II, 187 b.

Anzio

Dei Cesari (with annexes), Via Mantova 3, II, 144 b., SP; Casa Lieta, II, 67 b.; Golfo, II, 92 b.; Lido Garda, Piazza Caboto 8, II, 58 b.; La Bussola, III, 80 b.; La Tavernetta, III, 30 b.

Aosta

Europe, Piazza Narbonne 8, I, 132 b.; Valle d'Aosta, Corso Ivrea 146, I, 208 b.; Ambassador, Via Duca degli Abruzzi 2, II, 41 r.; Rayon de Soleil, Località Saraillon 16, II, 78 b.; Résidence Mont Blanc, Viale G. S. Bernardo 2, II, 143 b.; Roma, Via Torino 7, II, 57 b.; Turin, Via Torino 14, II, 84 b.; Au Coin Vert, Corso Ivrea 112, III, 61 b.; Cecchin, Via Ponte Romano 27, III, 18 b.; Gran Paradiso, Via Binel 12, III, 57 b.

Aquileia

Aquila Nera, IV, 35 b.

Arbatax

Cala Moresca, Località Cala Moresca, II, 550 b., SP; La Bitta, Località Porto Frailis, II, 26 b.; Villaggio Saraceno, Località San Gemiliano, II, 186 b.; Villaggio Telis, Località Porto Frailis, II, 506 b., SP.

Arenzano

Grand Hôtel Arenzano, Lungomare, I, 109 b., SP; Miramare, Lungomare, II, 77 b.; Ena, Via Matteotti 12, II, 41 b.; Europa, Viale Mina, III, 13 b.

Arezzo

Continentale, Piazza Guido Monaco 7, II, 137 b.; Etrusco, Via Fleming 39, II, 160 b.; Europa, Via Spinello 45, II, 81 b.; Minerva, Via Fiorentina 4,

II, 216 b.; Astoria, Via Guido Monaco 54, III, 50 b.; Cecco, Corso Italia 215, III, 83 b.; Truciolini, Via Pacinotti 6, III, 46 b.

Marche, Viale Kennedy 34, I, 62 b.; Gioli, Viale de Gasperi 14, II, 81 b.; **Ascoli Piceno** Pennile, Via G. Spalvieri, II, 56 b.; Piceno, Via Minnuccia 10, III, 49 b.

Fontebella, Via Fontebella 25, I, 66 b.; Subasio, Via Frate Elia 2, I, 116 b.; **Assisi** Dei Priori, Corso Mazzini 15, II, 48 b.; Giotto, Via Fontebella 41, II, 124 b.; Hermitage, Via del Pozzo 1, II, 35 b.; San Francesco, Via San Francesco 48, II, 78 b.; Umbra, Vicolo degli Archi 6, II, 48 b.; Windsor Savoia, Viale Marconi 1, II, 68 b.; Roma, Piazza Santa Chiara, III, 45 b.

Aleramo, Via E. Filiberto 13, I, 70 b.; Hasta Hotel, Località Valle Bene- **Asti** detta 23, I, 50 b.; Palio, Via Cavour 106, I, 50 b.; Salera, Via Mons. Marello 19, I, 96 b.; Lis, Via Fratelli Rosselli 10, II, 58 b.; Mini Motel, Località Valterza, II, 12 b.; Rainero, Via Cavour 85, II, 64 b.

Nuova Italia, II, 110 b.; Principe, Via Corradini, II, 90 b.; Bianchi, II, 74 b.; **Avezzano** Motel Belvedere, on S.S. 5, II, 70 b.

Alberghi Termali, Via del Paretaio 1, II, 19 b.; Silvania, Località Lugliano, **Bagni di Lucca** II, 16 b.; Bernabo, Via delle Terme, III, 10 b.; La Frantoia, Via Tovani 26, III, 19 b.

Riky Grand Hôtel, I, 148 b.; Asplenia, II, 46 b.; Betulla, II, 75 b.; Des **Bardonecchia** Geneys–Splendid, II, 105 b.; Bucaneve, III, 28 b.; Tabor, III, 40 b.

Ambasciatori, Via Omodeo 51, I, 331 b., SP; Grand Hôtel Leon d'Oro, **Bari** Piazza Moro 4, I, 190 b.; Jolly, Via G. Petroni 15, I, 322 b.; Palace, Via Lombardi 13, I, 204 r.; Villa Romanazzi Carducci, Via Capruzzi 326, I, 193 b., SP; Astoria, Via G. Bozzi 59, II, 204 b.; Boston, Via Piccinni 155, II, 72 r.; Grand Hôtel & d'Oriente, Corso Cavour 32, II, 282 b.; Grand Hôtel Moderno, Via Crisanzio 60, II, 78 b.; Plaza, Piazza L. di Savoia 15, II, 40 r.; Sette Mari, Via Verdi 60, II, 56 r.; Victor, Via Nicolai 71, II, 146 b; Windsor Residence, Parall. M. Amoruso, II, 277 b., SP.

Artù, Piazza Castello 67, II, 32 r.; Helios Residence, II, 144 b.; Royal, Via **Barletta** Leontina de Nittis 13, II, 42 b.; Vittoria, II, 53 b.; Centrale, II, 38 b.

*Grand Hôtel Villa Serbelloni, L, 152 b., SP; Ambassador Metropole, II, **Bellagio** 86 b.; Belvedere, II, 90 b., SP; Du Lac, II, 86 b.; Excelsior Splendide, II, 93 b., SP; Florence, II, 70 b.; Fiorini, II, 28 b.; Silvio, III, 38 b.

Astor, Piazza dei Martiri 26/e, II, 44 b.; Dolomiti, Via Carrera 46, II, 32 r.; **Belluno** Villa Carpenada, Via Mier 158, II, 28 r.

President, Via Perasso 1, I, 113 b.; Italiano, Viale Principe di Napoli 137, **Benevento** II, 120 b.; La Cittadella, Contrada Piano Cappelle, II, 70 b.

Cristallo Palace, Via B. Ambiveri 35, I, 166 b., SP; Excelsior San Marco, **Bergamo** Piazza della Repubblica 6, I, 230 b.; Arli, Largo Porta Nuova 12, II, 81 b.; Cappello d'Oro e del Moro, Viale Giovanni XXIII 12, II, 196 b.; Città dei Mille, Via Autostrada 3, II, 66 b.; Commercio, Via T. Tasso, II, 56 b.; Il Gourmet, Via S. Vigilio 1, II, 19 b.; Piemontese, Piazzale G. Marconi 11, II, 94 b.

*Baglioni, Via dell'Indipendenza 8, L, 237 b.; *Royal Hotel Carlton, Via **Bologna** Montebello 8, L, 460 b.; Al Cappello Rosso, Via Fusari 9, I, 50 b.; Corona d'Oro, Via Oberdan 12, I, 62 b.; Crest, Piazza della Costituzione, I, 268 b., SP; Elite, Via A. Saffi 36, I, 156 b.; Garden, Via Lame 109/2, I, 142 b.;

Hotels

Internazionale, Via dell'Indipendenza 60, I, 206 b.; Jolly Hôtel de la Gare, Piazza XX Settembre 2, I, 252 b.; Milano Excelsior, Viale Pietramellara 51, I, 123 b.; Pullman Bologna, Viale Pietramellara 59, I, 440 b.; Alexander, Viale Pietramellara 47, II, 210 b.; Astoria, Via Fratelli Rosselli 14, II, 60 b.; City, Via Magenta 8/10, II, 100 b.; Cristallo, Via San Giuseppe 5, II, 72 b.; Dei Commercianti, Via Pignattari 11, II, 52 b.; Donatello, Via dell'Indipendenza 65, II, 60 b.; Europa, Via C. Boldrini 4, II, 114 b.; Maggiore, Via Emilia Ponente 62/3, II, 88 b.; Motel Agip, Via M. E. Lepido 203/14, II, 126 b.; Nettuno, Via Galliera 65, II, 54 b.; Palace, Via Montegrappa 9/2, II, 181 b.; Re Enzo, Via S. Croce 26, II, 95 b.; Roma, Via d'Azeglio 9, II, 121 b.; San Donato, Via Zamboni 16, II, 93 b.; San Felice, Via Riva Reno 2, II, 50 b.; Orologio, Via IV Novembre 10, III, 54 b.

Bolsena

Columbus Hotel del Lago, Via del Lago, II, 82 b.; Moderno, Via Roma 2, III, 65 b.; Le Naiadi, Via Guadetto 1, III, 28 b.

Bolzano

Alpi, Via Alto Adige 35, I, 180 b.; Grifone/Greif, Piazza Walther 7, I, 210 b.; Luna/Mondschein, Via Piave 15, I, 130 b.; Park Hotel Laurin, Via Laurino 4, I, 190 b., SP; Asterix, Piazza Mazzini 35, II, 52 b.; Chrys, Via della Mendola 100, II, 57 b.; Bagni di Zolfo/Schwefelbad, Via San Maurizio 93, II, 60 b.; Città/Stadthotel, Piazza Walther 21, II, 167 b.; Scala/Stiegl, Via Brennero 11, II, 100 b.; Cappello di Ferro/Eisenhut, Via Bottai 21, III, 58 b.; Metropol, Via Rosmini 14, III, 64 b. – In Gries: Reichrieglerhof, Via Miramonti 9, II, 38 b., SP.

Bordighera

Grand Hôtel Cap Ampelio, Via Virgilio 5, I, 160 b., SP; Grand Hôtel del Mare, Portico della Punta 34, I, 209 b., SP; Parigi, Lungomare Argentina 18, I, 71 b.; Astoria, Via T. Tasso 2, II, 42 b.; Britannique et Jolie, Via Regina Margherita 35, II, 90 b.; Centro, Piazza Eroi Libertà 10, II, 56 b.; Excelsior, Via Gen. Biamonti 30, II, 76 b.; Florida, Via Vittorio Emanuele 310, II, 140 b.; Mar Ligure, Via Aurelia Ponente 22, II, 66 b.

Bormio

Baita dei Pini, I, 46 r.; Nazionale, I, 48 r.; Palace, I, 83 r.; Alù, II, 30 r.; Astoria, II, 44 r.; Larice Bianco, II, 45 r.; Rezia, II, 45 r.; San Lorenzo, II, 38 r.

Boscotrecase

Principe, III, 28 b.; Vesuvio, III, 33 b.

Brescia

*Vittoria, Via delle Dieci Giornate 20, L. 103 b.; Ai Ronchi Motor Hotel, Viale Bornata 22, I, 75 b.; Ambasciatori, Via Crocifissa di Rosa 90/92, I, 102 b.; Ca' Nöa, Via Triumplina 10, I, 58 b.; Continental, Via Martiri della Libertà 267, Roncadelle, I, 102 b.; Igea, Viale della Stazione 15, I, 96 b.; Master, Via Apollonio 72, I, 106 b.; President, on S.S. 235, Roncadelle, I, 74 b.; Alabarda, Via Labirinto 6, II, 41 b.

Bressanone

Dominik, Via Terzo di Sotto 13, I, 45 b., SP; Elefante (with annexe), Via Rio Bianco 4, I, 43 r., SP; Al Sole, Via Erhard 8, II, 40 b.; Corona d'Oro/Goldene Krone, Via Fienili 4, II, 62 b.; Jarolim, Piazza Stazione 1, II, 65 b., SP; Albero Verde/Grüner Baum, Via Stufles 11, II, 125 b., SP; Mirabel, Via Otto von Guggenberg 4A, III, 30 b.; Senoner, Lungo Rienza 22, II, 41 b.; Temlhof, Via Elvas 76, II, 100 b., SP.

Brindisi

Corso, Corso Roma 87, I, 68 b.; Internazionale, Lungomare Regina Margherita 26, I, 139 b.; Majestic, Corso Umberto I 151, I, 111 b.; Mediterraneo, Viale Liguria 70, I, 113 b.; La Rosetta, I, 83 b.; Regina, Via Cavour 5, I, 64 b.; Barsotti, Via Cavour 1, II, 82 b.; L'Approdo, Via del Mare, II, 37 b.; Torino, Largo Palumbo 6, II, 25 b.

Cadenabbia

Bellevue, I, 240 b.; Britannia Excelsior, II, 293 b.; Riviera, III, 25 b.; Rodrigo, III, 24 b.

Regina Margherita, Viale Regina Margherita 44, I, 202 b.; Al Solemar, **Cagliari**
Viale Diaz 146, II, 85 b.; Italia, Via Sardegna 31, II, 175 b.; Mediterraneo,
Viale Diaz 147, II, 284 b.; Moderno, Via Roma 159, II, 142 b.; Motel Agip,
Circonvallazione Pirri, II, 111 b.; Panorama, Viale Diaz 231, II, 227 b., SP;
Sardegna, Via Lunigiana 50/52, II, 152 b.

Roxy, Piazza Savoia 7, I, 70 b.; Skanderbeg, Via Novelli, I, 68 r.; Kappa, **Campobasso**
Via Sant'Antonio dei Lazzari 21, II, 41 r.

La Tartaruga, in San Gregorio, 2 km/1¼ miles on Messina road, II, 70 b.; **Capo d'Orlando**
Il Mulino, Via Andrea Doria 46, II, 34 r.; Nettuno Villaggio, Via Marina
346, II, 56 b.; Bristol, Via Umberto 37, III, 75 r.

*Quisisana e Grand Hôtel, Via Caramelle 2, L, 260 b., SP; 'A Pazziella, **Capri**
Via Fuorlovado, I, 36 b.; Calypso, Via I. Cerio, I, 14 b.; La Palma, Via V.
Emanuele 39, I, 143 b.; La Scalinatella, Via Tragara 8, I, 57 b., SP; Luna,
Viale Matteotti 3, I, 93 b., SP; Palatium, Via Gr. Marina, I, 46 b., SP; Punta
Tragara, Via Tragara, I, 77 b., SP; Regina Cristina, Via F. Serena, I, 107 b.,
SP; Tiberio Palace, Via Croce, I, 144 b.; Gatto Bianco, Via V. Emanuele,
II, 76 b.; La Certosella, Via Tragara, II, 30 b., SP; La Pineta, Via Tragara, II,
99 b., SP. – In Anacapri: Caesar Augustus, Via G. Orlandi, II, 90 b.;
Europa Palace, Via A. Munthe, I, 189 b., SP.

Michelangelo, Corso Fratelli Rosselli 3, II, 56 b.; Da Roberto, Via Apuana **Carrara**
5, III, 21 b.

Garden, Viale Montebello 1, II, 85 b.; Milano, Via Trevigi 49, III, 48 b.; **Casale Monferrato**
Principe, Via Cavour 55, III, 49 b.

Cristallo Palace, I, 128 b., SP; La Madonnina, I, 37 b.; Manzi, I, 62 r., SP; **Casamicciola**
Elma, II, 68 r.; Stefania, II, 30 r. **Terme**

Europa, Via Roma 29, I, 114 b.; Jolly, Viale Vittorio Veneto 9, I, 147 b.; **Caserta**
Centrale, Via Roma 170, II, 41 r.; Vittoria, Via Cesare Battisti 44, III, 43 b. –
In San Nicola la Strada: Reggia Palace, Viale Carlo II, I, 160 r., SP.

Forum Palace, Via Casilina Nord, I, 104 r.; Rocca, Via Sferracavallo 105, **Cassino**
II, 35 r., SP; Alba, Via di Biasio 71, III, 26 r.; Al Boschetto, Via Ausonia 54,
III, 45 r.; Continental, Piazza de Gasperi, III, 20 r.; La Pace, Via Abruzzi 8,
III, 38 r.; Silvia Park, Via Ausonia 47, III, 80 b., SP.

Delle Terme, I, 190 b., SP; Dei Congressi, II, 132 b.; La Medusa, Via **Castellamare**
Passeggiata Archeologica 5, II, 54 r.; Miramare, II, 136 b.; Stabia, II, 109 **di Stabia**
b.; Villa Serena, II, 91 b.; Virginia, III, 86 b.

Castello, Lungomare Anglona, 15, II, 40 b.; Hotel Villaggio Pedra Ladda, **Castelsardo**
Via Zirulla, II, 243 b., SP; Riviera, Lungomare Anglona 1, II, 51 b.; Cinzia,
Via Colle di Frigiano 1, III, 38 b.

Selinus, Via Bonsignore 22, II, 68 b.; Zeus, Via V. Veneto 6, II, 77 b. **Castelvetrano**

Trasimeno, Via Roma 114, II, 30 b.; Santa Lucia, Via B. Buozzi 180, III, **Castiglione**
52 b. **del Lago**

Excelsior, Piazza Verga, I, 268 b.; Jolly, Piazza Trento 13, I, 223 b.; **Catania**
Central Palace, Via Etnea 218, II, 178 b.; Motel Agip, Via Messina 626,
4 km/2½ miles S of S.S. 114, II, 87 b.; Nettuno, Viale Ruggero di Lauria
121, II, 99 b.; Villa Dina, Via Caronda 129, III, 30 r.

Guglielmo, Via A. Tedeschi 9, I, 73 b.; Grand Hotel, Piazza Matteotti, II, **Catanzaro**
158 b.; Motel Agip, Viadotto sulla Fiumarella, II, 152 b.; Sant'Antonio,
Via Sant'Antonio 7, II, 128 b.

Hotels

Cattolica Caravelle, Via Padova 6, I, 70 b., SP; Handy-Sea, Via Santa Chiara 10, I, 69 b.; Madison, Via Don Minzoni 80, I, 90 b.; Negresco, Via del Turismo, I, 135 b., SP; Royal, Via Carducci 30, I, 112 b., SP; Savoia, Via Carducci 38, I, 81 b.; Victoria Palace, Via Carducci 24, I, 160 b.; Beaurivage, Via Carducci 82, II, 129 b.; Belsoggiorno, Via Carducci 139, II, 68 b.; Cormoran, Via Francia 2, II, 295 b.; Diplomat, Via del Turismo 9, II, 123 b.; Europa Monetti, Via Curiel 39, II, 105 b., SP; La Rosa, Via Gran Bretagna 13, II, 112 b.; Leon d'Oro, Via Santa Chiara 1, II, 143 b.; Nord Est, Via Carducci 60, II, 129 b.; Renzo, Lungomare Rasi-Spinelle 44, II, 63 b.; Luxor, Via Carducci 32, III, 90 b.; Ninfea, Via Carducci 117, III, 88 b.

Cefalù Baia del Capitano, Località Mazzaforno, II, 64 b., SP; Carlton Riviera, Località Capo Plaia, II, 281 b., SP; Kalura, Località Caldura, II, 117 b., SP; Le Calette, Località Caldura, II, 100 b., SP; Le Sabbie d'Oro, Località S. Lucia, II, 420 b., SP; Santa Lucia, Località S. Lucia, II, 94 b., SP; Tourist, Via Lungomare, II, 90 b., SP.

Celle Ligure Riviera, Via Colla 55, I, 104 b.; Felice, Via Mulino a Vento 26, II, 17 r.; San Michele, Via Monte Tabor 26, II, 104 b.; Ancora, Via de Amicis 3, III, 18 r.

Cernobbio *Villa d'Este, L, 320 b., SP; Asnigo, I, 65 b.; Regina Olga Reine du Lac, I, 155 b., SP; Miralago, II, 56 b.

Cerveteri El Paso, III, 39 b.

Cervia Grand Hotel Cervia, Lungomare Grazia Deledda 9, I, 68 b.; Beau Rivage, Lungomare Grazia Deledda 116, II, 40 r.; Bristol, Lungomare d'Annunzio 22, II, 51 r.; Buenos Aires, Lungomare Grazia Deledda 130, II, 94 b.; K2 Cervia, Viale dei Mille 98, II, 66 b.; Nettuno, Lungomare d'Annunzio 34, II, 77 b., SP; Strand, Lungomare Grazia Deledda 104, II, 33 r.

Cesenatico Britannia, Viale Carducci 129, I, 82 r., SP; Esplanade, Viale Carducci 120, I, 96 b.; Internazionale, Viale Ferrara 7, I, 97 b., SP; Des Bains, Viale dei Mille 52, II, 57 b.; Grand Hotel, Piazza A. Costa 1, II, 176 b., SP; Miramare, Viale Carducci 2, II, 57 b.; Roxy, Viale Carducci 193, II, 76 b., SP; San Pietro, Viale Carducci 194, II, 139 b., SP; Sporting, Viale Carducci 191, II, 82 b.; Torino, Viale Carducci 55, II, 87 b., SP; Atlantica, Viale Bologna 28, III, 42 b.; Byron, Viale dei Mille 108, III, 46 b.; Genny, Piazza A. Costa 3, III, 117 b.

Chiavari Giardini, Via Vinelli 9, I, 62 b.; Monterosa, Via Marinetti 6, II, 126 b.; Torino, Corso Colombo 151, II, 25 r.; Mignon, Via Salietti 7, III, 32 r.; Moderno, Piazza N. S. dell'Orto, III, 73 b.

Chieti Diangio, Via Solferino 20, II, 80 b.; Grande Albergo Abruzzo, Via Asinio Herio 26, II, 111 b.; Sole, Via dei Domenicani 1, II, 75 b.

Chioggia Grande Italia, Piazza Vigo 1, II, 114 b.

Cinqueterre See Monterosso or Riomaggiore.

Città di Castello Europa, Via V. E. Orlando, II, 91 b.; Garden, Via Aldo Bologni, II, 113 b.; Tiferno, Piazza Sanzio 13, II, 64 b.

Cividale del Friuli Roma, Piazza Picco, III, 100 b.; Al Castello, IV, 20 b.

Civitavecchia Sunbay Park Hotel, I, 118 b., SP; Mediterraneo Suisse, II, 119 b.; Miramare, III, 42 b.; Traghetto, III, 60 b.

Como Barchetta, Piazza Cavour 1, I, 137 b.; Como, Via Mentana 28, I, 140 b.; Firenze, Piazza Volta, I, 50 b.; Metropole e Suisse, Piazza Cavour 19, I,

127 b.; Villa Flori, Via Provinciale per Cernobbio 12, I, 85 b.; Continental, Via Innocenzo XI 15, II, 114 b.; Park Hotel, Viale Rosselli 20, II, 77 b.; Plinius, Via Garibaldi 33, II, 50 b.; Engadina, Viale Rosselli 22, III, 39 b.; Tre Re, Via Boldoni 20, III, 54 b.

*Miramonti Majestic, Località Pezziè, 103, L, 242 b., SP; Cristallo, Via **Cortina d'Ampezzo** Menardi 42, I, 162 b., SP; Grand Hôtel Savoia, Via Roma 62, I, 284 b., SP; Cortina, Corso Italia 94, II, 96 b.; De la Poste, Piazza Roma 14, II, 160 b.; Europa, Corso Italia 207, II, 104 b.; Parc Hotel Victoria, Corso Italia 1, II, 90 b.; Splendid Hotel Venezia, Corso Italia 209, II, 184 b.; Concordia Parc Hotel, Corso Italia 28, III, 120 b.; Corona, Via Cesare Battisti 15, III, 94 b.; Franceschi, Via Cesare Battisti 86, III, 88 b.; Menardi, Via Majon 112, III, 96 b.; Motel Agip, Via Roma 70, III, 84 b.; Nord, Via La Verra, III, 68 b.; Pontechiesa, Via Marangoni 3, III, 70 b.; Trieste, Via Majon 28, 56 b.

Miravalle, Località Torreone, II, 13 b.; Oasi, Località Le Contesse, II, 69 **Cortona** b.; Portole, Località Portole, II, 38 b.; Sabrina, Via Roma 37, II, 14 b.; San Luca, Piazza Garibaldi 2, II, 106 b.; San Michele, Via Guelfa 15, II, 69 b.; Nuovo Centrale, Località Camucia, III, 38 b.

Centrale, Via dei Tigrai, II, 83 b.; Imperiale, Viale Trieste 50, II, 99 b.; **Cosenza** Alexander, Via Monte San Michele, III, 81 b.

*Cala di Volpe, Località Cala di Volpe, L, 236 b., SP; *Pitrizza, Località **Costa Smeralda** Liscia di Vacca, L, 56 b., SP; *Romazzino, Località Porto Cervo, L, 184 b., SP; Cervo, Località Porto Cervo, I, 189 b., SP; Cervo Tennis Club, Località Porto Cervo, I, 32 b., SP; Le Ginestre, Località Golfo Pevero, I, 126 b., SP; Balocco, Località Porto Cervo, II, 56 b., SP; Capriccioli, Località Capriccioli, II, 55 b.; Liscia di Vacca, Località Liscia di Vacca, II, 82 b., SP; Luci di la Muntagna, Località Porto Cervo, II, 139 b.; Nibaru, Località Cala di Volpe, II, 89 b., SP.

Les Jumeaux, I, 90 b.; Palace Bron, I, I, 50 b.; Pavillon, Strada Regionale **Courmayeur** 60, I, 72 b., SP; Royal, Via Roma 83, I, 181 b., SP; Centrale, Via Mario Puchoz 7, II, 54 b.; Courmayeur, Via Roma 158, II, 47 b.; Cresta et Duc, Via Circonvallazione 7, II, 72 b.; Del Viale, Viale Monte Bianco 74, II, 41 b.; Majestic Parigi, Strada Regionale 36, II, 80 b.; Edelweiss, III, 53 b.; Svizzero, Superstrada Traforo del Monte Bianco, III, 55 b.

Continental, Piazza Libertà 27, I, 114 b.; Motel Agip, Cremona Nord, on **Cremona** S.S. 45, I, 151 b.; Astoria, Via Bordigallo 19, II, 57 b.; Duomo, Via Gonfalonieri 13, II, 34 b.; Este, Viale Po 131, II, 44 b.; Impero, Piazza della Pace 23, II, 57 b.; San Giorgio, Via Dante 20, II, 76 b.

Carossa, Lungomare, I, 182 r., SP; Solaria, Via per Capo Colonna, II, 346 **Crotone** b., SP; Bologna et de la Ville, Via M. Nicoletta, II, 128 b.; Capitol, Piazza Umberto I, II, 114 b.; Costa Tiziana, Località Costa Tiziana, II, 220 b., SP; Italia, Piazza Vittoria, III, 37 b.

Principe, Via Cavour 1, II, 67 b.; Royal Superga, Via Pascal 3, II, 50 b.; **Cuneo** Ligure, Via Savigliano 11, III, 26 r.; Smeraldo, Corso Nizza 27, III, 31 b.; Torrismondi, Via Coppino 33, III, 36 r.

Grand Hotel Boario e delle Terme, I, 139 b., SP; Rizzi, I, 76 b.; Bossi, II, 76 **Darfo Boario Terme** b.; Brescia, II, 80 b.; Excelsior, II, 110 b.; Mina, II, 39 b.; Trieste, II, 40 b.

City, Via Nazario Sauro 29, I, 56 b.; Lido International, I, 26 b., SP; **Desenzano** Miralago, Viale Dal Molin 27, I, 44 b.; Park Hotel, Lungolago Cesare **del Garda** Battisti 19, I, 124 b.; Residence Oliveto, I, 84 b., SP; Sole e Fiori, I, 78 b.; Tripoli, I, 42 b.; Villa Rosa, I, 74 b.; Benaco, Viale Cavour 30, II, 41 b., SP;

Hotels

Europa, II, 61 b.; Piccola Vela, Viale Dal Molin 20, II, 62 b.; SP; San Francesco, II, 38 b.; Astoria, III, 60 b.; Flora, III, 18 b.; Villa Erme, III, 29 b.

Diano Marina
Diana Majestic, Via degli Oleandri 15, I, 160 b., SP; Bellevue-Méditerranée, Viale Gen. Ardoino 2, I, 139 b., SP; Caravelle, Via Sausette 24, II, 96 b., SP; Gabriella, Via dei Gerani 9, II, 97 b.; Golfo e Palme, Via Torino 12, II, 77 b.; Palace, Via Torino 2, II, 86 b.; Tiziano, Via Sant'Elmo, II, 48 r.; Metropol, Via Divina Provvidenza 2, III, 39 r.

Enna
Grande Albergo Sicilia, Piazza Colaianni 7, II, 102 b.

Faenza
Vittoria, Corso Garibaldi 23, II, 78 b.; Al Moro, Piazza Martiri della Libertà 40, III, 25 r.; Cavallino, Via Emilia Levante 32, III, 60 b.; Torricelli, Piazzale Cesare Battisti 7, III, 25 b.

Fano
Elisabeth Due, Piazzale Amendola 2, I, 32 r.; Grand Hotel Elisabeth, Viale Carducci 12, I, 37 r.; Augustus, Via Puccini 2, II, 24 r.; Continental, Viale Adriatico 148, II, 52 r.; Excelsior, Via Simonetti 21, II, 30 r.; Corallo, Via Leonardo da Vinci 3, III, 22 r.

Ferrara
Astra, Viale Cavour 55, I, 122 b.; De la Ville, Piazzale Stazione 11, I, 135 b.; Ripagrande, Via Ripagrande 21, I, 80 b.; Carlton, Via Garibaldi 93, II, 108 b.; Europa, Corso Giovecca 49, II, 59 b.; Ferrara, Piazza Repubblica 4, II, 98 b.; Touring, Viale Cavour 11, II, 54 b.; Santo Stefano, Via S. Stefano 21, III, 40 b.

Filicudi
See Lipari Islands.

Finale Ligure
Moroni, Viale delle Palme 20, I, 193 b.; Park Hotel Castello, Via Caviglia 26, I, 34 b.; Residenza Punta Est, Via Aurelia 1, I, 71 b., SP; Astoria, Via Calvisio 92, II, 112 b.; Colibri, Via Colombo 57, II, 77 b.; Miramare, Via San Pietro 9, II, 63 b.; Internazionale, Via Concezione 3, III, 32 r.

Fiuggi
Imperiale, Via Prenestina 29, I, 148 b.; Silva Hotel Splendid, Corso Nuova Italia 40, I, 221 b., SP; Vallombrosa e Majestic, Via Vecchia Fiuggi 209, I, 146 b., SP; Villa Igea, Corso Nuova Italia 32, I, 108 b., SP; Alfieri, Viale Fonte Anticolana 49, II, 40 r.; Astoria, Via Prenestina 105, II, 95 b.; Casino dello Stadio e del Golf, Via 4 Giugno 19, II, 49 r.; Daniel's, Via Prenestina, II, 38 r.; Fiuggi Terme, Via Prenestina 9, II, 104 b., SP; Moderno, Via dei Villini 11, II, 48 r.; Michelangelo, Via Rettifilo 24, II, 138 b.; Mondial Park Hotel, Via Sant'Emiliano 82, II, 43 r., SP; Mirage, Via Diaz 295, III, 33 r.

Florence
*Excelsior, Piazza Ognissanti 3, L, 377 b.; *Grand Hotel, Piazza Ognissanti 1, L, 74 b.; *Grand Hotel Villa Cora, Viale Machiavelli 18, L. 97 b., SP; *Regency Umbria, Piazza d'Azeglio 3, L, 50 b.; *Savoy, Piazza della Repubblica 7, L, 184 b.; *Villa Medici, Via Il Prato 42, L, 198 b., SP.
Anglo Americano, Via Garibaldi 9, I, 219 b.; Astoria Pullman, Via del Giglio 9, I, 157 b.; Augustus e dei Congressi, Piazzetta dell'Oro 5, I, 129 b.; Crest, Viale Europa 205, I, 184 b., SP; Croce di Malta, Via della Scala 7, I, 183 b., SP; De la Ville, Piazza Antinori 1, I, 135 b.; Grand Hotel Baglioni, Piazza Unità Italiana 6, I, 359 b.; Grand Hotel Majestic, Via del Melarancio 1, I, 185 b.; Grand Hotel Minerva, Piazza Santa Maria Novella 16, I, 198 b., SP; Grand Hotel Cora, in Colli, Viale Machiavelli 18, I, 48 r., SP; Jolly Carlton, Piazza V. Veneto 4A, I, 293 b., SP; Kraft, Via Solferino 2, I, 120 b., SP; Londra, Via Jacopo da Diaccето 18/20, I, I, 178 b.; Lungarno, Borgo San Jacopo 14, I, 128 b.; Michelangelo, Via Fratelli Rosselli 2, I, 253 b.; Montebello Splendid, Via Montebello 60, I, 81 b.; Pierre, Via Lamberti 5, I, 78 b.; Plaza Hotel Lucchesi, Lungarno della Zecca Vecchia 38, I, 172 b.; Raffaello, Viale Morgagni 19, I, 276 b.; Villa la Massa, in Candeli, I, 42 r., SP.

Alexander Antonio Stoppani, Viale Guidoni 101, II, 168 b.; Atlantic Palace, Via Nazionale 12, II, 86 b.; Berchielli, Lungarno Acciaiuoli 14, II, 175 b.; Bernini Palace, Piazza San Firenze, 29, II, 142 b.; Continental, Lungarno Acciaiuoli 2, II, 105 b.; Della Signoria, Via delle Terme 1, II, 40 b.; Executive, Via Curtatone 5, II, 53 b.; Fenice Palace, Via Martelli 10, II, 114 b.; Laurus, Via Cerretani 8, II, 80 b.; Milano Terminus, Via Cerretani 10, II, 128 b.; Mirage, Via Baracca 231 int. 18, II, 159 b.; Monginevro, Via di Novoli 59, II, 220 b.; Mona Lisa, Borgo Pinti 27, II, 35 b.; Nord Florence, Via Baracca 199A, II, 139 b.; Park Palace, Piazzale Galileo 5, II, 52 b.; Principe, Lungarno Vespucci 34, II, 35 b.; Queen Palace Hotel, Via Solferino 5, II, 33 b.; Relais Certosa, Via di Colle Ramole 2, II, 33 b.; Ritz, Lungarno Zecca Vecchia 24, II, 55 b.; Rivoli, Via della Scala 33, II, 100 b.; Villa Belvedere, Via Castelli 3, II, 51 b., SP; Villa Carlotta, Via Michele di Lando 3, II, 46 b.; Villa le Rondini, Via Bolognese Vecchia 224, II, 51 b., SP; Villa Sull'Arno, Lungarno C. Colombo 1, II, 85 b., SP.

Adriatico, Via Maso Finiguerra 9, III, 222 b.; Ambasciatori, Via Alamanni 3, III, 165 b.; Aprile, Via della Scala 6, III, 48 b.; Astor, Viale Milton, 41, III, 38 b.; Auto Hotel Park, Via Valdegola 1, III, 198 b.; Balestri, Piazza Mentana 7, III, 87 b.; Capitol, Viale Amendola 34, III, 141 b.; Caravel, Via Alamanni 9, III, 103 b.; Cavour, Via del Proconsolo 3, III, 116 b.; Concorde, Viale Luigi Gori 10, III, 146 b.; David, Viale Michelangelo 1, III, 45 b.; Fleming, Viale Guidoni 87, III, 174 b.; Golf, Viale Fratelli Rosselli, III, 70 b.; Helvetia e Bristol, Via dei Pescioni 2, III, 101 b.; Mediterraneo, Lungarno del Tempio, III, 668 b.; Porta Rossa, Via Porta Rossa, III, 130 b.; Villa Liberty, Viale Michelangelo 40, III, 31 b.

Foggia — Cicolella, Viale 24 Maggio 60, I, 174 b.; Palace Sarti, Viale XXIV Maggio 48, I, 132 b.; White House, Via Monfalcone 20, I; Europa, Via Monfalcone 52, II, 129 b.; President, Viale Aviatori 80, II, 136 r.; Salice, Via Bari, 4 km/2½ miles outside town, II.

Foligno — Nuovo Poledrini, Viale Mezzetti 3, I, 42 b.; Italia, II, 50 r.; Umbria, Via Cesare Battisti 3, II, 43 b.; Posta, III, 70 b.

Fondi — Deutschland, Via Mola della Corte, III, 16 b.

Forlì — Della Città, Via Fortis 8, I, 72 b.; Air Hotel, Via Morandi 7, II, 38 b.; Masini, Corso Garibaldi, 28, II, 60 b.; Astoria, Piazza Ordelaffi, III, 51 b.; Lory, Via Lazzarini 20, III, 30 r.; Masini, Corso Garibaldi 28, III, 60 b.; Vittorino, Via Baratti 4, III, 21 r.

Frascati — Flora, II, 60 b.; Park Hotel Villa Campitelli, II, 123 b.; Villa Mercede, II, 25 b.; Bellavista, III, 44 b,

Frosinone — Henry, Via Piave 10, I, 63 b.; Cesari, on A2, II, 56 r.; Palombella, Via Maria 234, II, 34 r.

Gaeta — Aenea's Landing, Via Flacca, II, 30 b., SP; Flamingo, Corso Italia 109, II, 87 b., SP; Il Ninfeo, Via Flacca, II, 94 b.; Le Rocce, Via Flacca, II, 106 b.; Mirasole, in Serapo, II, 234 b., SP; Serapo, in Serapo, II, 249 b., SP; Summit, Via Flacca, II, 138 b.

Garda — Regina Adelaide, Via XX Settembre, I, 97 b.; Du Parc, Via Marconi 3, II, 26 r.; Flora, II, 63 r., SP; Terminus, II, 40 r.; Cortina, III, 27 r.; Marco Polo, III, 138 b.

Gardone — Fasano Grand Hotel, I, 130 b., SP; Grand Hotel, I, 303 b., SP; Villa del Sogno, I, 45 b., SP; Bellevue, II, 65 b.; Monte Baldo, II, 84 b.; Park Hotel Villa Ella, II, 87 b., SP; Villa Fiordaliso, II, 14 b.

Genoa — *Colombia, Via Balbi 40, L, 288 b.; Bristol Palace, Via 20 Settembre 35, I, 230 b.; Eliseo, Via M. Piaggio 5, I, 65 b.; Nuova Astoria, Piazza Brignole

Hotels

4, I, 125 b.; Plaza, Via Piaggio 11, I, 138 b.; Savoia Majestic, Via Arsenale di Terra 5, I, 184 b.; Aquila e Reale, Piazza Acquaverde 1, II, 161 b.; City, Via San Sebastiano 6, II, 114 b.; Crespi, Via A. Doria 10, II, 89 b.; Firenze e Zurigo, Via Gramsci 199r, II, 151 b.; Londra e Continentale, Via Arsenale di Terra 1, II, 83 b.; Metropoli, Vico Migliorini 8, II, 84 b.; Milano Terminus, Via Balbi 34, II, 60 b.; Minerva Italia, Via 25 Aprile 14, II, 82 b.; Moderno Verdi, Piazza Verdi 5, II, 85 b.; Tirreno, Via dei Mille 17, II, 69 b.; Vittoria e Orlandini, Via Balbi 33, II, 73 b.; Agnello d'Oro, Vico Monachette 6, III, 42 b.; Assarotti, Via Assarotti 22C, III, 36 b.; Brignole, Vico Corallo 13r, III, 40 b.

Gorizia Palace, Corso Italia 63, I, 126 b.; Alla Transalpina, Via Caprin 30, III, 55 r.

Grado Adria, Viale Europa Unita 18, I, 118 b.; Antica Villa Bernt, Via Colombo 5, I, 43 b.; Diana, Via Verdi 3, I, 106 b.; Savoy, Via Carducci 33, I, 132 b.; Villa Erica, Via Dante 69, I, 46 b.; Abbazia, Via Colombo 12, II, 105 b.; Adriaco, Via Pleiadi 11, II, 36 b.; Ai Pini, Via Andromeda 16, II, 60 b.; Al Bosco, La Rotta, II, 85 b.; Argentina, Viale Italia 21, II, 200 b.; Bellevue, Viale dei Moreri 49, II, 138 b.; Friuli, Riva Ugo Foscolo 14, II, 45 b.; Il Guscio, Via Venezia 2, II, 12 b.; Tiziano Palace, Riva Slataper 8, II, 94 b.; Touring, Viale Kennedy 38, II, 91 b.; Helvetica, III, 68 b.; Hungarica, III, 83 b.; Villa d'Este, III, 68 b.

Grosseto Bastiani, Piazza Gioberti 64, I, 92 b.; Lorena, Via Trieste 3, I, 95 b.; Motel Agip, Via Aurelia, II, 54 b.; Nalesso, Via Senese 35, II, 50 b.; Ombrone, Via Matteotti 69, II, 16 b.; Leon d'Oro, Via San Martino 46, III, 53 b.

Gubbio Grand Hotel Ai Cappuccini, Via Cappuccini, I, 69 b.; Bosone, Via XX Settembre 22, II, 60 b.; San Marco, Via Perugina, II, 95 b.

Herculaneum Eremo, III.

Imperia Centro, Piazza Unità Nazionale 4, II, 21 r.; Corallo, Corso Garibaldi 29, II, 42 r.; Croce di Malta, Via Scarincio 142, II, 70 b.; Salvo Kristina, Spianata Borgo Peri 8, II, 41 b.

Ischia Ponte Hermitage e Park Terme, Via Leonardo Mazzella 67, II, 170 b., SP; Miramare e Castello, II, 82 b.; Residence, II, 53 b.; Aragonese, III, 41 b., SP.

Ischia Porto Alexander, Lungomare Telese già Colombo, I, 171 b., SP; Continental Terme, Via Michele Mazzella 60, I, 355 b., SP; Excelsior, Via Emanuele Gianturco 19, I, 126 b., SP; Jolly, Via de Luca 42, I, 369 b., SP; Punta Molino, Lungomare Telese già Colombo, I, 156 b., SP; Ambasciatori, II, 86 b.; Aragona Palace Terme, Via Porto 12, II, 80 b., SP; Bristol Palace, Via Venanzio Marone 10, II, 71 b.; Felix Hotel Terme, Via de Luca 48, II, 87 b., SP; Flora, II, 124 b., SP; Oriente, II, 115 b., SP; Floridiana Terme, II, 88 b., SP; Regina Palace, II, 81 b., SP.

Isernia Europa, on S.S. 17 (Campobasso direction), II, 55 b.; La Tequila, Via San Lazzaro 85, II, 137 b., SP; Sayonara, Via G. Berti 132, II, 34 b.

Isola San Domino See Tremiti Islands.

Isole Egadi On Favignana: L'Approdo di Ulisse, in Calagrande, II, 176 b.; Egadi, Via C. Colombo 17, IV, 12 r.
On Levanzo: Paradiso, Via Calvario 133, IV, 8 r.

Laigueglia Splendid, Piazza Badarò 4, I, 86 b.; Aquilia, Via Asti 1, II, 64 b.; Beau Séjour, Piazza Cavour 8, II, 63 b.; Mediterraneo, Via Andrea Doria 18, II, 65 b.; Villa Ida, Via Roma 90, II, 65 b.; Windsor, Via XXV Aprile 7, III, 76 b.

Grand Hotel del Parco, Corso Federico II, I, 64 b.; Castello, Piazza Battaglione Alpini, II, 82 b.; Duca degli Abruzzi, Viale Duca degli Abruzzi 10, II, 152 b.; Le Cannelle, Rivera, II, 230 b.; Motel Amiternum, Bivio Sant'Antonio, II, 115 b.; Sole, Largo Silvestro dell'Aquila 4, III, 112 b.
L'Aquila

Jolly, Via XX Settembre 2, I, 188 b.; Residence Hotel G, Via del Tino 62, I, 98 b.; Astoria, Via Roma 139, II, 97 b.; Firenze e Continental, Via Paleocapa 7, II, 49 b.; Genova, Via Fratelli Rosselli 84, II, 50 b.; Mary, Via Fiume 177, II, 52 b.; Tirreno, Piazza Paita 4, II, 133 b.; Venezia, Via Paleocapa 10, II, 29 b.
La Spezia

Admiral Lido, Via dei Devoto 89, II, 22 r.; Sud Est, Via Previati 200, II, 62 r.; Tigullio, Via Matteotti 3, II, 66 b.
Lavagna

President, Via Salandra 6, I, 277 b.; Zenit, Via Adriatica, I; Delle Palme, Via Leuca 90, II, 180 b.; Grand Hotel, Via O. Quarta 28, II, 108 b.; Patria Touring, Piazzetta G. Riccardi 13, II, 92 b.; Risorgimento, Via Imperatore Augusto 19, II, 57 r.
Lecce

Don Abbondio, Piazza Era 10, II, 33 b.; Giordano, Lungo Lario Cadorna 20, II, 28 b.; Croce di Malta, Via Roma 41, III, 84 b.; Moderno, Piazza Diaz 5, III, 58 b.
Lecco

Carmes, Via Vittorio Emanuele 10, III, 34 b.
Lentini

Crystal, Località Vallesanta, 2 km/1½ miles in direction of Bracco, II, 32 b.; Dora, Via Martiri della Libertà 27, II, 36 r.; Stella d'Italia, Corso Italia 26, II, 73 b.
Levanto

Anthony, Via Padova 25, I, 120 b., SP; Aurora, Piazza Aurora 8, I, 77 r.; Byron Bellavista, Via Padova 83, I, 100 b., SP; Cavalieri, Via Mascagni 1, I, 58 r., SP; Las Vegas, Via Mascagni 2, I, 184 b., SP; Majestic Toscanelli, Via Canova 2, I, 100 b., SP; Alexander, Piazza Nember 20, II, 74 r., SP; Atlantico, Via A. Bafile, II, 69 r.; Capitol, Via Padova 85, II, 64 r., SP; Heron, Via Padova 3, II, 96 r.; Imperial Palace, Via Zara 29, II, 103 b., SP; Le Soleil, Via Treviso 3, II, 216 b., SP; Nettuno, Via A. Bafile, II, 74 r.; Ritz, Via Zanella 2, II, 80 b., SP; Tahiti, Via Dante Alighieri 44, II, 95 r.; La Bussola, Via Levantina 4, III, 47 r., SP.
Lido di Iesolo

Airport, Viale dei Romagnoli 165, I, 453 b., SP; Satellite Palace, Via delle Antille 49, I, 460 b., SP; Kursaal, Via F. d'Aragona 10, II, 58 b.; Ping Pong, II, 38 b.; Sirenetta, II, 70 b.; Belvedere, III, 98 b.
Lido di Ostia

See Lipari Islands.
Lipari

On Alicudi: Ericusa, IV, 24 b.
On Filicudi: Phenicusa, II, 69 b.
On Lipari: Carasco, Porto delle Genti, II, 163 b., SP; Giardino sul Mare, Via Maddalena 65, II, 30 r., SP; Meligunis, Via Marte, II, 33 r.; Gattopardo Park Hotel, Via Marconi, III, 99 b.
On Panarea: Cincotta, III, 19 r., SP; Lisca Bianca, III, 25 r.
On Salina: Punta Scario, in Malfa, III, 17 r.; Villa Orchidea, in Malfa, III, 18 r.
On Stromboli: La Sciara Residence, II, 122 b., SP; La Sirenetta, in Ficogrande, II, 77 b.
On Vulcano: Arcipelago, in Vulcanello, II, 157 b., SP; Eolian, in Port Ponente, II, 162 b.; Garden Vucano, in Porto Ponente, II, 60 b.; Conti, III, 60 r.
Lipari Islands

Intermonti, II, 324 b.; Parè, III, 80 b.; Sport Hotel, III, 70 b.; Bucaneve, III, 82 b.; Paradiso, III, 48 b.
Livigno

Hotels

Livorno
Palazzo, Viale Italia 195, I, 220 b.; Atleti, Via dei Pensieri 50, II, 80 b.; Boston, Piazza Mazzini 40, II, 55 b.; Excelsior, Via D. Cassuto 1, II, 105 b.; Gennarino, Viale Italia 301, II, 45 b.; Giappone, Via Grande 65, II, 98 b.; Gran Duca, Piazza Micheli 16, II, 92 b.; Touring, Via Goldoni 61, II, 59 b.

Loano
Garden Lido, Lungomare N. Sauro 9, I, 168 b., SP; Moderno, Via Carducci 3, I, 161 b.; Continental, Via Carducci 1, II, 120 b.; Mary, Via T. Minniti 6, II, 26 r.; Perelli, Corso Roma, 13, II, 41 r.; Savoia, Via N. Sauro 1, II, 27 r.

Locri
Demaco, Lungomare, II, 63 b.

Lodi
Europa, Viale Pavia 5, II, 77 b.; Anelli, Viale Vignati 7, III, 33 b.

Loreto
Bellevue e Marchigiano, II, 120 b.; Giardinetto, II, 135 b.; Casa San Gabriele, II, 127 b.; Casa San Francesco, III, 137 b.

Lucca
Napoleon, Viale Europa 1, I, 98 b.; Villa la Principessa, Massa Pisana, I, 83 b., SP; Celide, Viale Giusti 27, II, 93 b.; Universo, Piazza Puccini 1, II, 105 b.; Bernardino, Via di Tiglio 109, III, 26 b.

Macerata
Motel Agip, Via Roma 149B, I, 102 b.; Centrale, Via Armaroli 98, II, 34 b.; Della Piaggia, Via Santa Maria della Porta 18, II, 41 b.

Maiori
Regina Palace, I, 107 b., SP; Due Torri, II, 69 b.; Garden, II, 147 b.; Miramare, II, 58 b.; Panorama, II, 152 b.; Pietra di Luna, II, 160 b., SP; Panoramic Residence, III, 59 b.

Malcesine
Alpi, II, 40 r., SP; Maximilian, in Val di Sogno, II, 33 r., SP; Vega, II, 19 r.; Erika, III, 14 r.

Mantua
Rechigi, Via Calvi 30, I, 78 b., SP; San Lorenzo, Piazza Concordia 14, I, 72 b.; Apollo, Piazza Don Leoni 17, II, 61 b.; Broletto, Via Accademia 1, II, 16 r.; Dante, Via Corrado 54, II, 40 r.; Mantegna, Via Fabio Filzi 10B, 55 b.

Marina di Ravenna
Park, Viale delle Nazioni 181, I, 289 b., SP; Belvedere, Viale Lungomare 59, III, 70 b.; Bermuda, Viale della Pace 363, III, 17 r.; Internazionale, Viale delle Nazioni 163, III, 52 b.

Marsala
Cap, Via Trapani 161, II, 86 b., SP; President, Via Nino Bixio 1, II, 136 b., SP; Motel Agip, Via Mazara 14, II, 77 b.; Stella d'Italia, Via M. Rapisardi 7, II, 77 b.

Massa Lubrense
Delfino, I, 93 b., SP; Bellavista Francischiello, II, 25 r., SP; Maria, II, 30 r., SP; Villa Pina, III, 11 r.

Massa Marittima
Duca del Mare, Via Massetana, III, 30 b.; Il Girifalco, Via Massetana, III, 30 b.

Matera
De Nicola, Via Nazionale 158, II, 138 b.; Motel Park, on S.S. 99, II, 112 b., SP; President, Via Roma 13, II, 116 b., SP; Italia, Via Ridola 5, III, 67 b.

Menaggio
Grand Hotel Menaggio, I, 97 b., SP; Grand Hotel Victoria, I, 99 b., SP; Bellavista, II, 70 b.; Royal, II, 19 b.; Corona, III, 50 b.

Merano
Adria (with annexe), Via Glim 2, I, 66 b., SP; Augusta, Via Huber 2, I, 44 b.; Bavaria, Kirchsteig 15, I, 84 b.; Bellevue, Corso della Libertà 194, I, 156 b.; Castel Freiberg, Freiberg, I, 66 b.; Eurotel, Via Garibaldi 5, I, 226 b.; Grand Hotel Bristol, Via Huber 14, I, 240 b., SP; Grand Hotel Emma, Piazza Mazzini 1, I, 230 b.; Irma, Via Belvedere 17, I, 81 b., SP; Juliane.

Via dei Campi 6, I, 65 b., SP; Schloss Rundegg, Via Scena 2, I, 58 b., SP;
Mirabella, Via Garibaldi 35, I, 55 b.; Meranerhof, Via Manzoni 1, I, 105 b.,
SP; Palace, Via Cavour 2, I, 200 b., SP; Mignon (with annexe), Via
Grabmayr 3, I, 70 b., SP; Regina, Via Cavour 101, I, 137 b., SP; Riz
Stefanie, Via Cavour 12, I, 101 b., SP; Savoy, Via Rezia 1, I, 89 b.;
Sittnerhof, Via Giuseppe Verdi 58, I, 74 b., SP; Villa Eden, Via Winkel 68,
I, 68 b.; Aurora, Passeggiata Lungo Passirio 38, II, 56 b.; Europa Splen-
did, Corso della Libertà 178, II, 95 b.; Pollinger, Maria-Trost-Strasse 30,
II, 48 b., SP; Steiner, Via Laurin 60, II, 51 b.; Tappeiner, Schlehdorf-Weg
21, II, 60 b.

Jolly Hotel dello Stretto, Via Garibaldi 126, I, 150 b.; Riviera Grand   **Messina**
Hôtel, Viale della Libertà 516, I, 265 b.; Royal, Via Tommaso Cannizzaro
224, I, 83 r.; Europa, in Pistunina, 6 km/4 miles S, II, 186 b.; Excelsior, Via
Maddalena 32, II, 71 b.; Giardino delle Palme, Lido Mortelle, II; Paradis,
Via Consolare Pompea 441, II, 92 r.; Commercio, Via I Settembre 15, III.

*Excelsior Gallia, Piazza Duca d'Aosta 9, L, 413 b.; *Grand Hotel Brun,   **Milan**
Via Caldera 21, L, 660 b.; *Palace, Piazza della Repubblica 20, L, 308 b.;
*Principe di Savoia, Piazza della Repubblica 17, L, 489 b.
Duca di Milano, Piazza della Repubblica 13, I, 110 b.; Grand Hôtel et de
Milan, Via Manzoni 29, I, 158 b.; Milano Hilton, Via Galvani 12, I, 461 b.;
Pierre Milano, Via de Amicis 32, I, 93 b.; Accademia, Via Certosa 68, I, 80
b.; Ambasciatori, Galleria del Corso 3, I, 141 b.; Anderson, Piazza Luigi
di Savoia 20, I, 118 b.; Andreola, Via Scarlatti 24, I, 136 b.; Ascot, Via
Lentasio 3/5, I, 66 b.; Atlantic, Via N. Torriani 24, I, 91 b.; Auriga, Via
Pirelli 7, I, 90 b.; Berna, Via N. Torriani 18, I, 127 b.; Bristol, Via Scarlatti
32, I, 111 b.; Brunelleschi, Via Baracchini 12, I, 182 b.; Capitol, Via
Cimarosa 6, I, 169 b.; Carlton Senato, Via Senato 5, I, 121 b.; Cavalieri,
Piazza Missori 1, I, 270 b.; Cavour, Via Fatebenefratelli 21, I, 192 b.;
Concorde, Via Petrocchi 1, I, 168 b.; Crivi's, Corso Porta Vigentina 46, I,
91 b.; De la Ville, Via Hoepfli 6, I, 198 b.; Diana Majestic, Viale Piave 42, I,
151 b.; Duomo, Via San Raffaele 1, I, 244 b.; Executive, Viale Don Luigi
Sturzo 45, I, 840 b.; Galileo, Corso Europa 9, I, 131 b.; Grand Hotel Fiera
Milano, Viale Boezio 20, I, 357 b.; Ibis, Via Zarotto 8, I, 240 b.; Jolly
President, Largo Augusto 10, I, 466 b.; Jolly Touring, Via Ugo Tarchetti
2, I, 500 b.; Leonardo da Vinci, Via Senigallia 6, I, 580 b., SP; Lloyd,
Corso Porta Romana 48, I, 80 b.; Madison, Via Gasparotto 8, I, 123 b.;
Manin, Via Manin 7/9, I, 156 b.; Mediolanum, Via Mauro Macchi 1, I, 98
b.; Michelangelo, Via Scarlatti 33, I, 440 b.; Nasco, Via Spallanzani 40, I,
198 b.; Plaza, Piazza Diaz 3, I, 219 b.; Raffaello, Viale Certosa 108, I, 155
b.; Rosa, Via Pattari 5, I, 250 b.; Royal, Via Cardano 1, I, 164 b.; Rubens,
Via Rubens 21, I, 116 b.; Splendido, Via Andrea Doria 4, I, 207 b.; St
George, Viale Tunisia 9, I, 99 b.; Washington, I, 44 b.; Windsor, Via
Galileo Galilei 2, I, 181 b.
Adriatico, Via Conca del Naviglio 20, II, 126 b.; Ambrosiano, Via Santa
Sofia 9, II, 111 b.; Astoria, Viale Murillo 9, II, 120 b.; Canada, Via Lentasio
15, II, 54 b.; Casa Svizzera, Via S. Raffaele 3, II, 79 b.; Cristallo, Via
Scarlatti 22, II, 167 b.; Domus, Piazza Gerusalemme 6, II, 149 b.; Euro-
peo, Via Canonica 38, II, 55 b.; Fiera, Via Spinola 9, II, 45 b.; Flora, Via
Napo Torriani 23, II, 72 b.; Lancaster, Via Abbondio Sangiorgio 16, II, 37
b.; Lombardia, Viale Lombardia 74, II, 100 b.; Lord Internazionale, Via
Spadari 11, II, 76 b.; Manzoni, Via Santo Spirito 20, II, 77 b.; Mediterra-
neo, Via Ludovico Muratori 14, II, 141 b.; Mennini, Via Napo Torriani 14,
II, 106 b.; Monte Bianco, Via Monterosa 90, II, 66 b.; Rex, Via Marco
d'Agrate 34A, II, 104 b.; Sempione, Via Finocchiaro Aprile 11, II, 57 b.;
Wagner, Via M. Buonarroti 13, II, 93 b.
Corallo, Via Cesena 20, III, 39 b.; Emilia, Via Ponte Seveso 38, III, 62 b.;
Garden, Via Rutilia 6, III, 40 b.; MacMahon, Via MacMahon 45A, III, 45
b.; Piccolo, Via Piero della Francesca 60, III, 33 b.

Hotels

Milano Marittima *Exclusive Waldorf, VII Traversa, L, 42 b., SP; *Mare e Pineta, Viale Dante 40, L, 242 b., SP; Aurelia, Viale II Giugno 34, I, 189 b., SP; Bellevue Beach, XIX Traversa 31, I, 124 b., SP; Deanna, Viale Matteotti 131, I, 124 b., SP; Doge, Viale II Giugno 36, I, 139 b., SP; Michelangelo, Viale II Giugno 113, I, 91 b., SP; Miami, III Traversa 31, I, 150 b., SP; Rouge, III Traversa 26, I, 140 b., SP; Acapulco, VI Traversa 19, II, 82 b.; Ariston, Viale Cesare Battisti 16, II, 112 b.; Globus, Viale II Giugno 59, II, 96 b., SP; Majestic, X Traversa 23, II, 100 b.; Sahara, Anello del Pino 4, II, 96 b., SP; Savini, XVIII Traversa 14, II, 120 b.

Milazzo Eolian Inn, II, 500 b., SP; Silvanetta Palace, 2 km/1½ miles on Messina road, II, 215 b., SP; Saverly, Via Col. Magistri, II, 37 r.

Modena Canalgrande, Corso Canalgrande 6, I, 139 b.; Central Park, Viale Vittorio Veneto 10, I, 80 b.; Fini, Via Emilia Est 441, I, 124 b.; Grand Hotel Raffaello e dei Congressi, Strada Cognento 5, I, 230 b.; Palace, Via Emilia Est, 27, I, 89 b.; Donatello, Via Giardini 402, II, 136 b.; Eden, Via Emilia Ovest 666, II, 51 r.; Europa, Corso Vittorio Emanuele 52, II, 173 b.; Estense, Via Berengario 11, II, 98 b.; Roma, Via Farini 44, II, 79 b.

Modica Motel di Modica, Corso Umberto, II, 67 b.

Monreale Carrubbella Park, Via Umberto I, II, 44 b.; Il Ragno, Località Giacalone, III, 28 b.

Montecassino See Cassino.

Montecatini Terme *Bellavista Palace e Golf, Viale Fedeli 2, L, 183 b., SP; *Grand Hotel e La Pace, Via della Torretta 1A, L, 230 b., SP; Ambasciatori Grand Hotel e Cristallo, Viale IV Novembre 12, I, 126 b., SP; Cristallino, Viale Diaz 10, I, 89 b., SP; Croce di Malta, Viale IV Novembre 18, I, 189 b., SP; Du Park et Regina, Viale Diaz 8, I, 88 b., SP; Nizza e Suisse, Viale Verdi 72, I, 189 b.; Panoramic, Viale Bustichini 65, I, 142 b., SP; Plaza Locanda Maggiore, Piazza del Popolo 7, I, 179 b., SP; Tamerici e Principe, Viale IV Novembre 2, I, 274 b., SP; Tettuccio, Viale Verdi 74, I, 136 b.; Vittoria, Viale della Libertà 2A, I, 114 b.; Adua, Viale F. Cavalotti 100, II, 108 b., SP; Ariston, Viale Manzoni 30, II, 90 b.; Astoria, Viale Fedeli 1, 65 r., SP; Augustus, Viale Manzoni 19, II, 88 b.; Belvedere, Viale Fedeli 10, II, 167 b., SP; Cappelli/Croce di Savoia, Viale Bicchierai 139, II, 94 b., SP; Corallo, Viale Cavalotti 116, II, 96 b., SP; De la Ville, Viale San Francesco d'Assisi 5, II, 174 b.; Ercolini e Savi, Via San Martino 18, II, 54 b.; Francia e Quirinale, Viale IV Novembre 77, II, 187 b., SP; Imperial Garden, Viale Puccini 20, II, 138 b., SP; Lago Maggiore, Corso Matteotti 70, II, 50 b.; Manzoni, Viale Manzoni 28, II, 91 b.; Mediterraneo, Via Baragiola 1, II, 54 b.; Michelangelo, Viale Fedeli 15, II, 121 b., SP; President, Corso Matteotti 118, II, 69 b.; Salus, Viale Marconi 5, II, 60 b.; San Marco, Viale Rosselli 3, II, 106 b.; Settentrionale Esplanade, Viale Grocco 2, II, 110 b., SP; Torretta, Viale Bustichini 63, II, 90 b.; Brasile, Viale Bicchierai 53, III, 50 b.; Lido Palace, Viale IV Novembre 14, III, 90 b.

Montefiascone Altavilla, Via Alighieri 16C, III, 47 b.; Italia, Piazzale Roma 10, III, 46 b.

Montegrotto Terme *Bertha International, Largo Traiano 1, L, 200 b., SP; Augustus Terme, Viale Stazione 150, I, 180 b., SP; Des Bains, Via Mezzavia 22, I, 151 b., SP; Esplanade Tergesteo, Via Roma 54, I, 179 b., SP; Garden Terme, Viale delle Terme 7, I, 175 b., SP; Grand Hôtel Terme Caesar, Via Aureliana, I, 135 r., SP; Grand Hôtel Terme, Viale Stazione 23, I, 166 b., SP; Montecarlo, Viale Stazione 109, I, 154 b., SP; Terme Miramonti, Piazza Roma 19, I, 140 b., SP; Terme Neroniane, Via Neroniana 21/23, I, 141 b., SP; Continental, Via Neroniana 8, II, 140 b., SP; Bellavista, Via dei Colli 5, II, 77 r., SP; Cristallo, Via Roma 69, II, 119 r., SP; Delle Nazioni, Via Mezzavia, II, 100 r., SP; Eliseo, Viale Stazione 12A, II, 95 b., SP; Olympia, Viale Stazione 25, II, 151 b., SP; Petrarca, Piazza Roma 23, II, 129 r., SP; Sollievo, Viale Stazione 113, 135 r., SP; Vulcania, Viale Stazione 6, III, 78 r., SP.

Il Marzocco, Piazza Savonarola 25, III, 34 b. – On S.S. 146: Panoramic, in Boscalti (3 km/2 miles in direction of Chianciano), II, 25 r.; Tre Stelle, in Sant'Albino (5 km/3 miles in direction of Chianciano), II, 24 r. **Montepulciano**

Palme, II, 96 b.; Porta Roca, in Corone, II, 84 b.; Cinque Terre, III, 102 b.; Joli, III, 58 b. **Monterosso al Mare**

*Excelsior, Via Partenope 48, L, 252 b.; *Vesuvio, Via Partenope 45, L, 292 b.; Jolly Ambassador, Via Medina 70, I, 501 b.; Majestic, Largo Vasto a Chiaia 68, I, 213 b.; Mediterraneo, Via Nuova Ponte de Tappia 25, I, 432 b.; Oriente, Via A. Diaz 44, I, 270 b.; Parker's, Corso Vittorio Emanuele 135, I; Royal, Via Partenope 38, I, 492 b., SP; Santa Lucia, Via Partenope 46, I, 219 b.; Terminus, Piazza Garibaldi 91, I, 458 b.; Britannique, Corso Vittorio Emanuele 133, II, 168 b.; Cavour, Piazza Garibaldi 32, II, 151 b.; Domitiana, Viale Kennedy 143, II, 40 r.; Miramare, Via Nazario Sauro 24, II, 49 b.; Rex, Via Palepoli 12, II, 64 b.; San Germano, Via Domitiana, II, 189 b., SP; Serius, Viale Augusto 74, II, 128 b.; Bristol, Piazza Garibaldi 63, III, 61 b.; San Giorgio, Vico III Duchesca, III, 95 b.; Washington, Corso Umberto I 311, III. 90 b. **Naples**

Astor, Viale delle Palme 16, I, 59 b.; Esperia, Via Val Cismon 1, II, 37 b.; Nervi, Piazza Pittaluga 1, II, 61 b.; Corallo, Via Val Cismon 3, III, 13 r.; Internazionale, Piazza Pittaluga 2, III, 23 r. **Nervi**

Pineta (on road to Enna), II, 93 b. **Nicosia**

Italia, Corso Italia 23, II, 19 r.; Miramare, Corso Italia 2, II, 53 b.; Diana, Via Defferari 1, III, 50 b. **Noli**

Stella, Via G. Aurispa, III, 32 b. **Noto**

Italia, Via Solaroli 10, I, 68 b.; La Rotonda, Bordo M. d'Azeglio 43, I, 43 b.; Europa, Corso Cavallotti 38A, II, 95 b.; Maya, Via Boggiani 54, II, 176 b.; Parmigiano, Via del Cattaneo 4, II, 65 b.; Victoria, Corso della Vittoria 101, II, 72 b. **Novara**

Grazia Deledda, Via Lamarmora 175, I, 108 b.; Motel Agip, Viale Trieste, II, 102 b.; Paradiso, Via Aosta, II, 170 b.; Sandalia, Via Einaudi 14, II, 94 b.; Fratelli Sacchi, Località Monte Ortobene, II, 35 b.; Da Giovanni, Via IV Novembre, III, 20 b. **Nuoro**

President, Via Principe Umberto 9, I, 60 b.; De Plam, Via de Filippi 43, II, 117 b.; Mediterraneo, Via Montello 3, II, 119 b.; Motel Olbia, Viale Aldo Moro 40, II, 40 b.; Centrale, Corso Umberto 85, III, 35 b. **Olbia**

Mistral, Via Martiri di Belfiore, I, 92 b.; Amsicora, II, 48 b.; Ca-Ma, Via Vittorio Veneto 119, II, 90 b. **Oristano**

Aquila Bianca, Via Garibaldi 13, I, 76 b.; La Badia, Località La Badia, I, 41 b.; Maitani, Via Maitani 5, I, 72 b.; Filippeschi, Via Filippeschi 19, II, 25 b.; Grand Hotel Reale, Piazza del Popolo 25, II, 57 b.; Virgilio, Piazza Duomo 5/6, II, 20 b. **Orvieto**

Le Rocce del Capo, I, 40 b., SP; Alexandra, Corso Regina Margherita 9, II, 19 r.; Firenze, Corso Regina Margherita 97, II, 50 b.; Madison, Via **Ospedaletti**

Hotels

Aurelia Levante 1, II, 33 r.; Petit Royal, Corso Regina Margherita 92, II, 57 b.; Delle Rose, Via de' Medici 17, III, 14 r.; Le Palme, Corso Regina Margherita 92, III, 16 r.

Ostia

Airport, Viale dei Romagnoli 165, I, 453 b., SP; Satellite Palace, Via delle Antille 49, I, 460 b., SP; Kursaal, Via F. d'Aragona 10, II, 58 b.; Ping Pong, II, 38 b.; Sirenetta, II, 70 b.

Padua

Admiral (with annexe), Via Vigonovese 88, I, 38 b.; Antenore, Via Brava 14B, I, 44 b.; Brenta (with annexe), Strada San Marco 128, I, 44 b.; Executive, Corso Stati Uniti 14B, I, 199 b.; Le Padovanelle, Via Chilesotti, I, 80 b.; Milano, Via Vicenza 2, I, 92 b.; Plaza, Corso Milano 40, I, 261 b.; Sheraton Padova, Corso Argentina 5, I, 441 b.; Biri, Via Grassi 2, II, 151 b.; Corso, Corso del Popolo 2, II, 95 b.; Donatello, Via del Santo 102, II, 80 b.; Grande Italia, Corso del Popolo 81, II, 120 b.; Leon Bianco, Piazzetta Pedrocchi 12, II, 44 b.; Majestic Toscanelli, Piazzetta dell'Arco 2, II, 70 b.

Paestum

Ariston, Località Laura, II, 94 b., SP; Calypso, II, 60 b.; Le Palme, Località Laura, II, 100 b., SP; Schuhmann, II, 53 b.; Taverna dei Re, II, 34 b.; Villa Rita, III, 26 b.

Palermo

*Villa Igiea Grand Hotel, Via Belmonte 43, L, 173 b., SP; Excelsior Palace, Via Marchese Ugo 3, I, 143 b.; Grande Albergo e delle Palme, Via Roma 396, I, 282 b.; Jolly Hotel del Foro Italico, Foro Italico 22, I, 468 b., SP; Politeama Palace, Piazza Ruggero Settimo 15, I, 176 b.; President, Via Francesco Crispi 230, I, 238 b.; Astoria Palace, Via Montepellegrino, II; Centrale, Corso V. Emanuele 327, II, 176 b.; Europa, Via Agrigento 3, II, 143 b.; Mediterraneo, Via Rosolino Pilo 43, II, 185 b.; Metropol, Via Turrisi Colonna 4, II, 73 b.; Motel Agip, Viale della Regione Siciliana 2620, II, 195 b.; Ponte, Via Francesco Crispi 99, II, 270 b.; Sole, Corso V. Emanuele 291, II, 257 b.; Touring, Via M. Stabile 136, II, 28 b.; Le Terrazze, Via Roma 188, III, 31 b.; Moderno, Via Roma 276, III, 44 b.

Palinuro

King's Residence, I, 156 b., SP; Saline, I, 80 b., SP; Eden, II, 44 b., SP; Gabbiano, II, 68 b., SP; La Conchiglia, II, 44 b.; San Paolo, II, 71 b.; San Pietro, II, 49 b., SP.

Panarea

See Lipari Islands.

Parma

Palace Hotel Maria Luigia, Viale Mentana 140, I, 179 b.; Park Hotel Stendhal, Via Bodoni 3, I, 88 b.; Park Hotel Toscanini, Viale A. Toscanini 4, I, 72 b.; Brenta, Via G. B. Borghesi 12, II, 21 b.; Button, Borgo Salina 7, II, 61 b.; Daniel, Via Gramsci 16, II, 56 b.; Principe, Via Emilia Est 46, II, 57 b.; Savoy, Via XX Settembre 3, II, 30 b.; Torino, Via A. Mazza 7, II, 37 b.; Croce di Malta, Borgo Palmia 8, III, 20 b.; Moderno, Via A. Cecchi 4, III, 75 b.

Passignano sul Trasimeno

Belvedere, Via dei Mandorli, II, 38 b.; Lido, Via Roma 1, II, 100 b.; Villa Paradiso, Via Rosselli 5, II, 53 b.; Sayonara, Località San Donato, II, 25 r., SP; La Vela, Via Rinascita 2, III, 54 b.

Pavia

Ariston, Via A. Scopoli 10, II, 75 b.; Palace, Viale della Libertà 89, II, 73 b.; Rosengarten (with annexe), Piazzale Policlinico 19, II, 90 b.; Aurora, Via V. Emanuele II 25, III, 30 b.; Excelsior, Piazzale Stazione 25, III, 32 b.

Perugia

Brufani, Piazza Italia 12, I, 45 b.; Grifone, Via S. Pellico 1, I, 80 b.; Hit, Strada Trasimeno Ovest 159/10, I, 152 b.; La Rosetta, Piazza Italia 19, I, 166 b.; Perugia Plaza, Via Palermo 88, I, 195 b.; Barone, Via Tuderte 20 P,

II, 32 b.; Della Posta, Corso Vannucci 97, II, 96 b.; Fortuna, Via Bonazzi 19, II, 56 b.; Tirrenius, Via Tuderte 75, II, 72 b.; Il Postiglione, Località Collestrada, III, 35 b.; Palace Hotel Bellavista, Piazza Italia 12, III, 128 b.

Savoy, Viale della Repubblica 22, I, 92 b.; Vittoria, Piazzale della Libertà 2, I, 49 b.; Ambassador, Viale Trieste 291, II, 80 b.; Astoria, Viale Trieste 86, II, 190 b., SP; Baltic, Viale Trieste 36, II, 96 b.; Beaurivage, Viale Trieste 30, II, 92 b., SP; Caravelle, Viale Trieste 296, II, 125 b.; Clipper, Viale Marconi 53, II, 87 b.; Diplomatic, Via Parigi 2, II, 84 b., SP; Due Pavoni, Viale Fiume 79, II, 88 b.; Embassy, Viale Trieste 64, II, 130 b., SP; Excelsior, Lungomare N. Sauro, II, 132 b., SP; Flamingo, Via Parigi 8, II, 160 b., SP; Leonardo da Vinci, Viale Trieste 54, II, 80 b.; Nautilus, Viale Trieste 26, II, 85 b., SP; Nettuno, Viale Trieste 367, II,85 b., SP; Principe, Viale Trieste 180, II, 98 b.; Spiaggia, Viale Trieste 76, II, 132 b., SP; Sporting, Lungomare N. Sauro 23, II, 90 b., SP; Brig, Viale Marconi 44, III, 116 b.; Capitol, Viale Rovereto 19, III, 84 b.; Losanna, Viale Dante 39, III, 72 b. **Pesaro**

Carlton, Viale della Riviera 35, I, 101 b.; Esplanade, Piazza I Maggio, I, 278 b.; Singleton, Piazza Duca d'Aosta 4, I, 132 b.; Astoria, Via Roma 24, II, 116 b.; Maja, Viale della Riviera 201, II, 85 b.; Plaza Moderno, Piazza Sacro Cuore, II, 160 b.; Alba, Via M. Forti 14, III, 80 b.; Ambra, Via Quarto dei Mille 28–30, III, 95 b. **Pescara**

Garden, Via Stazione 18, II, 22 r.; Dolci Colli, on road to Ponti sul Mincio, III, 25 r.; San Marco, Lungolago Masseni 15, III, 30 r. **Peschiera del Garda**

Grande Albergo Roma, Via Cittadella 14, I, 171 b.; Florida, Via C. Colombo 29, II, 62 b.; Milano, Viale Risorgimento 47, II, 75 b.; Nazionale, Via Genova 37, II, 140 b.; Motel K2, Via Emilia Parmense 133, II, 82 b.; Sportivo, Via I Maggio 82, III, 34 b.; Stella, Via Cipelli 41, III, 37 b. **Piacenza**

Corsignano, Via Madonnina 9, II, 36 r. **Pienza**

Royal, Via Don Bado 129, I, 174 b.; Paco, Via Crispi 63, II, 80 b.; Sartore, Corso Italia 54, II, 140 b.; Azucena, Via della Repubblica 76, III, 53 b.; Miramare, Via Don Bado 75, III, 22 r. **Pietra Ligure**

Centrale, Piazza Verdi 2, II, 62 b.; Collodi, Via Collodi 7, III, 49 b. **Piombino**

Cavalieri, Piazza della Stazione 2, I, 142 b.; D'Azeglio, Piazza Vittorio Emanuele 18, I, 52 b.; Duomo, Via Santa Maria 94, I, 160 b.; California Park, I; Ariston, Via Cardinale Maffi 42, II, 57 b.; La Pace, Via Gramsci, Galleria B, II, 125 b.; Roma, Via Bonanno 111, II, 50 b.; Terminus e Plaza, Via Colombo 45, II, 89 b.; Bologna, Via Mazzini 57, III, 87 b.; La Torre, Via Cesare Battisti 17, III, 54 b.; Moderno, Via Corridoni 103, III, 38 b. **Pisa**

Il Convento, Via S. Quirico 33, II, 42 b., SP; Le Rose, Viale Adua 89, II, 32 b.; Leon Bianco, Via Panciatichi 2, II, 51 b.; Milano, Viale Pacinotti 10, II, 94 b.; Patria, Via F. Crispi 6, II, 52 b.; Piccolo Ritz, Via A. Vannucci 67, II, 33 b.; Appennino, Via XX Settembre 21, III, 46 b. **Pistoia**

Bristol, II, 62 b.; Del Santuario, Piazza Bartolo Longo 2/6, II, 51 r.; Del Sole, II, 97 b.; Rosario, Villa Laura, Via della Salle, 13, II, 20 r.; Delle Rose, III; Diomede, III, 39 b.; Europa, III, 28 r. **Pompeii**

In Ponza: Chiaia di Luna, I, 119 b., SP; Bellavista, II, 30 b.; Cernia, II, 84 b., SP; La Baia, II, 44 b.; La Torre dei Borboni, II, 64 b.; Casa Giulia, II, 24 b. **Pontine Islands**

Palace Hotel Moderno, Viale Martelli 1, II, 148 b.; Villa Ottoboni, Via XXX Aprile, I, 111 b.; Minerva, Piazzale XX Settembre 5, II, 62 b.; Park, Via Mazzini 43, II, 116 b. **Pordenone**

Hotels

Porto Cervo See Costa Smeralda.

Portoferraio Airone Residential Hotel, in San Giovanni, I, 206 b.; Biodola, in Biodola, I, 142 b.; Fabricia, in Magazzini, I, 120 b.; Hermitage, in Biodola, I, 220 b.; Picchiaie Residence, in Monte Orello, I, 209 b.; Villa Ottone, in Ottone, I, 124 b.; Garden, in Schiopparello, II, 99 b.; Massimo, Calata Italia 23, II, 132 b.; Nuova Padulella, Viale Einaudi, II, 76 b.; Touring, Via Roma 13, II, 53 b.

Portofino *Splendido, L, 123 b., SP; Nazionale, I, 90 b.; San Giorgio, II, 34 b.; Piccolo, III, 26 r.

Portogruaro Spessotto, III, 50 r.; Trieste, III, 20 b.

Potenza Motel Agip, on S.S. 407, II, 109 r.; Park, Superstrada Basentana, II, 171 b.; Tourist, Via Vescovado 4, II, 130 b.; Miramonti, Via Caserma Lucana, III, 15 b.

Pozzuoli Solfatara, Via Solfatara II, 31 r.; Tennis, II, 140 b.; American, III, 172 b.; Mini, III; Terme La Salute, III, 114 b.

Prato Palace, Via Piero della Francesca 71, I, 145 b., SP; President, Via Simintendi 20, I, 117 b.; Flora, Via Cairoli 31, II, 55 b.; Milano, Via Tiziano 15, II, 118 b.; Moderno, Via. C. Balbo 11, II, 36 b.; San Marco, Piazza San Marco, II, 83 b.; Villa S. Cristina, Via Poggio Secco 58, II, 39 b.; Giardino, Via Magnolfi 2, III, 37 b.

Procida Le Arcate, Via M. Scotti 16, III, 72 b.; L'Oasi, Via Elleri 18, III, 28 b.; Riviera, in Chiaiolella, III, 42 b.

Ragusa Ionio, Via Risorgimento 49, II, 69 b.; Mediterraneo, Via Roma 189, II, 174 b.; Montreal, Via San Giuseppe 19, II, 63 r.

Rapallo *Grand Hotel Bristol, Via Aurelia Orientale 369, L, 180 b., SP; Eurotel, Via Aurelia Ponente 22, I, 99 b., SP; Grande Italia e Lido, I, 73 b.; Rosa Bianca, Lungomare Vittorio Veneto 42, I, 28 b.; Astoria, Via Gramsci 4, II, 42 b.; Giulio Cesare, Corso Cristoforo Colombo 52, II, 53 b.; Miramare, Via Vittorio Veneto 27, II, 43 b.; Moderno e Reale, II, 82 b.; Bel Soggiorno, Via Gramsci 10, III, 40 b.; Riviera, III, 39 b.; Stella, Via Aurelia Ponente 10, III, 42 b.; Vittoria, Via San Filippo Neri 11, III, 57 b.

Ravenna Bisanzio, Via Salara 30, I, 60 b.; Jolly, Piazza Mameli 1, I, 114 b,; Argentario, Via di Roma 45, II, 64 b.; Astoria, Via Circ. Rotonda 26/28, II, 34 b.; Centrale Byron, Via IV Novembre 14, II, 84 b.; Romea, Via Romea Sud 1, II, 66 b.; Trieste, Via Trieste 11, II, 52 r.; Piccolo, Via Balona 59, III, 60 b.

Recco Elena, Via Garibaldi 5, III, 52 b.

Reggio di Calabria Ascioti, Via San Francesco da Paola 79, I, 52 b.; Excelsior, Via Vittorio Veneto 66, I, 172 b.; Continental, Via Florio 10, II, 59 b.; Fata Morgana, Gallico Marina, Via Lungomare, II, 64 b.; Primavera, Via Nazionale 177, II, 116 b.

Reggio nell'Emilia Grand Hotel Astoria, Viale L. Nobili 2, I, 98 b.; Posta (with annexe), Piazza C. Battisti 4, I, 85 b.; Cristallo, Viale Regina Margherita 30, II, 84 b.; Europa, Viale Olimpia 2, II, 124 b.; Park, Via G. di Ruggero 1B, II, 54 b.; San Marco, Piazzale Marconi 1, II, 84 b.; Scudo d'Italia, Via Vescovado 5, II, 60 b.

Riccione Abner's, Lungomare della Repubblica 7, I, 85 b.; Alexandra Plaza, Viale Torino 61, I, 96 b.; Atlantic, Lungomare della Libertà 15, I, 124 b., SP;

Augustus, Viale Oberdan 18, I, 71 b.; Baltic, Piazzale di Vittorio 1, I, 130 b.; Boemia, Viale Gramsci 87, I, 98 b.; Concord, Viale Rismondo 1, I, 150 b.; Corallo, Viale Gramsci 113, I, 145 b., SP; De la Ville (with annexe), Viale Spalato 5, I, 81 b., SP; Luna, Viale Ariosto 5, I, 76 b., SP; Lungomare, Lungomare della Libertà 7, I, 116 b.; Mediterraneo, Piazzale Togliatti (corner Via Ceccarini), I, 207 b., SP; Nautico, Lungomare della Libertà, 132 b., SP; President, Viale Virgilio 12, I, 36 b.; Promenade, Viale Battisti 1, I, 72 b.; Roma, Viale Milano 17, I, 54 b.; Savioli Spiaggia, Viale d'Annunzio 6, I, 207 b., SP; Vienna e Touring, Viale Milano 78, I, 145 b., SP; Anna, Viale Trento Trieste 48, II, 43 b.; Ardea, Viale Monti 77, II, 42 b., SP; Falco, Viale Gramsci 86, II, 56 b.; Maestri, Viale Gorizia 4, III, 91 b.; Margareth, Viale Mascagni 2, II, 90 b.; Darsena, Viale Galli 5, III, 31 r.; Residenz, Viale d'Annunzio 8, III, 36 r.; Select, Viale Gramsci 89, III, 35 r.

Blu, Via Salaria per l'Aquila 18, II, 25 b.; Cavour, Piazza Cavour, II, 70 b.; **Rieti**
Flash, Via Padre Ettore Salvatori, II, 20 b.; Miramonti, Piazza Oberdan 7, II, 52 b.; Quattro Stagioni, Piazza C. Battisti 14, II, 70 b.; Serena, Viale della Gioventù, II, 59 b.; Valentino, Località Vazia, II, 42 b.; Europa, Via San Rufo 49, III, 60 b.; Moderno, Via Tullio Crispolti 36, III, 20 b.

*Grand Hotel, Piazzale Indipendenza 2, L, 230 b., SP; Ambasciatori, **Rimini**
Viale Vespucci 22, I, 66 r., SP; Bellevue, Piazzale Kennedy 12, I, 116 b.; Club House, Viale Vespucci 52, I, 28 r.; Imperiale, Viale Vespucci 16, I, 120 b., SP; Park, Viale Regina Elena 6, I, 129 b., SP; Residenza Grand Hotel, Via Ramusio 1, I, 86 b.; Rosabianca, Viale Tripoli 195, I, 86 b.; Waldorf, Viale Vespucci 28, I, 105 b., SP; Abarth, Viale Mantegazza 12, II, 156 b.; Admiral, Viale Regina Elena 67, II, 136 b., SP; Aristeo, Viale Regina Elena, II, 40 r., SP; Corallo, Viale Vespucci 46, II, 128 b.; Diplomat, Viale Regina Elena 70, II, 91 b.; Junior, Viale Parisano 40, II, 57 r.; Napoleon, Piazzale C. Battisti 22, II, 85 b.; Villa Adriatica, Viale Vespucci 3, II, 114 b., SP; Villa Verde, Viale Vespucci 38, II, 35 r.; Atlas, Viale Regina Elena 74, III, 122 r.; Belvedere, Viale Regina Margherita 80, III, 57 r.; Bolognese, Via San Salvador 156, III, 38 r.

Due Gemelli, Località Campi, II, 29 b.; Villa Argentina, II, 26 b.   **Riomaggic re**

*Du Lac et du Parc, Viale Rovereto 44, L, 467 b., SP; Grand Hotel Riva, **Riva del Garda**
Piazza Garibaldi 10, I, 167 b.; Liberty, Viale Carducci 3/5, I, 134 b., SP; Lido Palace, Viale Carducci 108, I, 126 b., SP; Astoria, Viale Trento 9, II, 179 b., SP; Brione, Viale Rovereto 75, II, 105 b., SP; Bristol, Viale Rovereto 71, II, 85 b., SP; Europa, Piazza Catena 9, II, 135 b.; Garda, Viale Rovereto 71, II, 120 b.; Giardino Verdi, Piazza Giardino Verdi 4, II, 71 b.; Luise, Viale Rovereto 9, II, 117 b., SP; Oasi, Viale Rovereto 110, II, 63 b.; Gabry, Via Longa 6, III, 78 b.

Near Stazioni Termini: **Rome**
*Grand Hôtel et de Rome, Via Vittorio Emanuele Orlando 3, L, 328 b. Alabani, Via Adda 41, I, 157 r.; Anglo-Americano, Via Quattro Fontane 12, I, 165 b.; Atlantico, Via Cavour 23, I, 129 b.; Commodore, Via Torino 1, I, 100 b.; Genova, Via Cavour 33, I, 175 b.; Londra Cargill, Piazza Sallustio 18, I, 198 b.; Massimo d'Azeglio, Via Cavour 18, I, 302 b.; Mediterraneo, Via Cavour 15, I, 452 b.; Metropole, Via Principe Amedeo 3, I, 443 b.; Mondial, Via Torino 127, I, 138 b.; Napoleon, Piazza V. Emanuele 105, I, 141 b.; Palatino, Via Cavour 213, I, 380 b.; President, Via E. Filiberto 173, I, 249 b.; Quirinale, Via Nazionale 7, I, 339 b.; Royal Santina, Via Marsala 22, I, 208 b.; San Giorgio, Via G. Amendola 61, I, 340 b.; Universo, Via Principe Amedeo 5B, I, 381 b.
Aretusa, Via Gaeta 14, II, 109 b.; Archimede, Via dei Mille 19, II, 196 b.; Diana, Via Principe Amedeo 4, II, 293 b.; Esperia, Via Nazionale 22, II,

174 b.; Globus, Viale Ippocrate 119, II, 174 b.; Impero, Via Viminale 19, II, 70 b.; La Capitale e Santa Maria Maggiore, Via C. Alberto 3, II, 137 b.; Lux Messe, Via Volturno 32, II, 161 b.; Madison, Via Marsala 60, II, 184 b.; Medici, Via Flavia 96, II, 116 b.; Milani, Via Magenta 12, II, 150 b.; Nizza, Via M. d'Azeglio 16, II, 96 b.; Nord–Nuova Roma, Via G. Amendola 3, II, 250 b.; Rex, Via Torino 149, II, 95 b.; San Marco, Via Villafranca 1, II, 118 b.; San Remo, Via M. d'Azeglio 36, II, 113 b.; Siracusa, Via Marsala 50, II, 197 b.; Sorrento e Patrizia, Via Nazionale 251, II, 150 b.; Tirreno, Via S. Martino ai Monti 18, II, 77 b.; Torino, Via Principe Amedeo 8, II, 172 b.; YMCA, Piazza Indipendenza 23C, II, 193 b.

Embassy, Via A. Salandra 6, III, 62 b.; Igea, Via Principe Amedeo 97, III, 63 b.; Marconi, Via G. Amendola 97, III, 94 b.; Maxim, Via Nazionale 13, III, 51 b.; Salus, Piazza Indipendenza, III, 60 b.; Stazione, Via Gioberti 36, III, 102 b.

Bergamo, Via Gioberti 30, IV, 22 b.; Bruna, Via Marghera 13, IV, 32 b.; Gioberti, Via Gioberti 20, IV, 37 b.; Reatina, Via San Martino della Battaglia 11, IV, 36 b.

Between the Quirinal and the Villa Borghese:
*Ambasciatori Palace, Via V. Veneto 70, L, 267 b.; *Bernini Bristol, Piazza Barberini 23, L, 222 b.; *Eden, Via Ludovisi 49, L, 184 b.; *Excelsior, Via V. Veneto 125, L, 658 b.; *Hassler–Villa Medici, Piazza Trinità dei Monti 6, L. 190 b.

Boston, Via Lombardia 47, I, 221 b.; Eliseo, Via di Porta Pinciana 30, I, 97 b.; Flora, Via V. Veneto 191, I, 264 b.; Imperiale, Via V. Veneto 24, I, 155 b.; Jolly Vittorio Veneto, Corso d'Italia 1, I, 346 b.; Majestic, Via V. Veneto 50, I, 200 b.; Parco dei Principi, Via G. Frescobaldi 5, I, 366 b.; Regina Carlton, Via V. Veneto 72, I, 230 b.; Savoia, Via Ludovisi 15, I, 212 b.; Victoria, Via Campania 41, I, 60 b.

Alexandra, Via V. Veneto 18, II, 70 b.; King, Via Sistina 131, II, 122 b.

In the old town:
Cardinal, Via Giulia 62, I, 114 b.; Colonna Palace, Piazza Montecitorio 12, I, 160 b.; Delle Nazioni, Via Poli 7, I, 132 b.; Delta, Via Labicana 144, I, 269 b.; D'Inghilterra, Via Bocca di Leone 14, I, 185 b.; Forum, Via Tor de' Conti 25, I, 156 b.; Grand Hôtel de la Ville, Via Sistina 69, I, 357 b.; Marini Strand, Via del Tritone 17, I, 212 b.; Nazionale, Piazza Montecitorio 131, I, 139 b.; Plaza, Via del Corso 126, I, 311 b.; Raphael, Largo Febo 2, I, 132 b.; Valadier, Via della Fontanella 15, I, 66 b.

Adriano, Via di Pallacorda 2, II, 116 b.; Bologna, Via Santa Chiara 4A, II, 195 b.; Cesari, Via di Pietra 89A, II, 92 b.; Genio, Via G. Zanardelli 28, II, 99 b.; Lugano, Via Tritone 132, II, 53 b.; Pace–Elvezia, Via IV Novembre 104, II, 110 b.; Santa Chiara, Via Santa Chiara 21, II, 114 b.; Sole al Pantheon, Via del Pantheon 63, II, 48 b.

Arenula, Via S. Maria dei Calderai 47, III, 61 b.; Della Lunetta, Piazza del Paradiso 68, III, 58 b.; Piccolo, Via dei Chiavari 32, III, 27 b.; Sole, Via Biscione 76, III, 88 b.

In northern districts:
*Lord Byron, Via G. de Notaris 5, L, 91 b.

Aldrovandi, Via U. Aldrovandi 15, I, 212 b., SP; Beverly Hills, Largo B. Marcello 220, I, 315 b.; Borromini, Via Lisbona 7, I, 147 b.; Claridge, Viale Liegi 62, I, 166 b.; Hermitage, Via E. Vajna 12, I, 154 b.; Residence Palace, Via Archimede 69, I, 323 b.; Ritz, Via Chellini 41, I, 612 b.

Fleming, Piazza Monteleone di Spoleto 20, II, 489 b.; Rivoli, Via Taramelli 7, II, 86 b.

In eastern districts:
Porta Maggiore, Piazza Porta Maggiore 25, II, 230 b.; San Giusto, Piazza Bologna 58, II, 97 b.

In southern districts:
Sheraton Roma, Viale del Pattinaggio (EUR), I, 1174 b.
American Palace EUR, Via Laurentina 554, II, 160 b.; Dei Congressi, Viale Shakespeare 29 (EUR), II, 152 b.; EUR Motel, Via Pontina 416, II, 43 b.; Piccadilly, Via Magna Grecia 122, at Porta San Giovanni, II, 92 b.

On right bank of Tiber:
*Cavalieri Hilton, Via Cadlolo 101, L, 631 b., SP.
Atlante Star, Via Vitelleschi 34, I, 70 r.; Cicerone, Via Cicerone 55C, I, 445 b.; Ergife Palace, Via Aurelia 619, I, 1316 b.; Giulio Cesare, Via degli Scipioni 287, I, 139 b.; Holiday Inn EUR, Via della Magliana 65, I, 626 b.; Holiday Inn St Peter's, Via Aurelia Antica 415, I, 620 b., SP; Jolly Leonardo da Vinci, Via dei Gracchi 324, I, 415 b.; Midas Palace, Via Aurelia 800, I, 700 b.; Michelangelo, Via Stazione di S. Pietro 14, I, 264 b.; Princess, Via A. Ferrara 33, I, 412 b.; Visconti Palace, Via F. Cesi 37, I, 489 b.
Alicorni, Via Scossacavalli 11, II, 78 b.; Clodio, Via S. Lucia 10, II, 209 b.; Columbus, Via della Conciliazione 33, II, 190 b.; Cristoforo Colombo, Via C. Colombo 710, II, 141 b.; Fiamma, Via Gaeta 61, II, 127 b.; Imperator, Via Aurelia 619, II, 79 b.; Marc'Aurelio, Via Gregorio XI 135, II, 220 b.; Motel Agip, on S.S. 1 (Via Aurelia) km 8, II, 440 b., SP; Nova Domus, Via G. Savonarola 38, II, 149 b.; Olympic, Via Properzio 2A, II, 91 b.; Pacific, Viale Medaglie d'Oro 51, II, 120 b.; Rest, Via Aurelia 325, II, 135 b.
Beethoven, Via Forte Braschi 2, III, 96 b.; Motel Boomerang, Via Aurelia km 10.5, III, 76 b.; Nordland, Via A. Alciato 14, III, 198 b.
Domus Aurelia, Via Aurelia 218, IV, 49 b.; Foyer Phan Diem, Via Pin. Sacchetti 45, IV, 121 b.; Zurigo, Via Germanico 198, IV, 25 b.

Flora, Via Abetone 94, II, 33 r.; Leon d'Oro, Via Tacchi 2, II, 60 b.; Rialto, Via Carducci 13, II, 62 b.; Rovereto, Corso Rosmini 82, II, 87 b.	**Rovereto**
Cristallo, Viale Porta Adige 1, II, 66 b.; Corona Ferrea, Via Umberto I 21, II, 48 b.; Granatiere, Corso del Popolo 235, II, 52 b.	**Rovigo**
Jolly Hotel delle Palme, Lungomare Trieste 1, I, 140 b.; Fiorenza, Via Trento 145, II, 55 b.; Hotel K, Via D. Somma 47, II, 95 b.; Montestella, Corso V. Emanuele 156, II, 85 b.; Plaza, Piazza Ferrovia 42, II, 75 b.; Garibaldi, Via Torrione 54, III, 38 b.	**Salerno**
See Lipari Islands.	**Salina**
Centrale Bagni, Largo Roma 4, I, 158 b.; Cristallo, Via Rossini 1, I, 78 b.; Daniel, Via M. d'Azeglio 8, I, 60 b.; Excelsior, Viale Berenini, 3, I, 72 b.; Gran Albergo Bolognese e Cavour, Viale Cavour 1, I, 135 b.; Grand Hôtel et de Milan, Via Dante 1, I, 188 b., SP; Grand Hotel Porro, Viale Porro 10, I, 153 b., SP; Regina, Largo Roma 3, I, 147 b.; Roma, Viale Mascagni 10, I, 48 b.; Tiffany's, Viale Berenini 2, I, 43 b.; Brescia, Via Viale Romagnosi 1, II, 52 b.; Ritz, Via Milite Ignoto 5, II, 54 b.; Suisse, Viale Porro 5, II, 43 b.; Villa Fiorita, Via Milano 2, II, 76 b.; Europa, Viale Matteotti 45, III, 140 b.	**Salsomaggiore Terme**
Astor, Piazza Garibaldi 39, II, 42 b.; Persico, Vicolo Mercanti 10, III, 33 b.	**Saluzzo**
Bel Soggiorno, Via San Giovanni, II, 54 b.; La Cisterna, Piazza della Cisterna, II, 89 b.; Leon Bianco, Piazza della Cisterna, II, 40 b.; Pescille, Località Pescille (4 km/2½ miles in direction of Volterra), 62 b., SP; Le Renaie, Località Pancole (6 km/4 miles in direction of Certaldo), 50 b.	**San Gimignano**
Grand Hotel San Marino, Viale Antonio Onofri 31, I, 140 b.; Joli San Marino, Viale Federico d'Urbino 233, I; La Grotta, Contrada Santa	**San Marino**

Hotels

Croce, I, 42 b.; La Rocca, Salita alla Rocca, I, 28 b., SP; Titano, Contrada del Collegio 21, I, 110 b.; Excelsior, Viale J. Istriani, II, 57 b.; Panoramic, Via del Voltone, II, 71 b.

San Pellegrino Terme

Terme, I, 86 b.; Bigio, II, 96 b.; Centrale, II, 54 b.; Excelsior, II, 117 b.; Italia, II, 48 b.; La Ruspinella, II, 31 b.

San Remo

*Royal Corso Imperatrice 80, L, 270 b., SP; Astoria West End, Corso Matuzia 8, I, 225 b., SP; Des Etrangers, Corso Garibaldi 82, I, 200 b., SP; Grand Hôtel et des Anglais, Corso Imperatrice 84, I, 196 b.; Grand Hôtel de Londres, Corso Matuzia 2, I, 280 b., SP; Méditerranée, Corso Cavalotti 76, I, 125 b., SP; Miramare Continental Palace, Corso Matuzia 9, I, 97 b., SP; Nazionale, Via Matteotti 3, I, 155 b.; Nyala, Strada Solaro 134, I, 72 b.; Principe, Via Fratelli Acquasciati 96, I, 94 b., SP; Residence Imperiale, Via Grande Albergo 6, I, 210 b.; Ariston Montecarlo, Corso Mazzini 507, II, 90 b., SP; Beau Rivage, Lungomare Trento e Trieste 53, II, 55 b.; Bobby Motel, Corso Marconi 208, II, 89 b., SP; Eden Via Solaro 4, II, 96 b., SP; Nizza, Corso Nuvoloni 26, II, 30 b.; Gli Ulivi, Via Volta 123, III; Maristella, Corso Imperatrice, III.

Sant'Agata sui Due Golfi

Hermitage, Golfo di Napoli e Vesuvio, I, 112 b., SP; Iaccarino, Golfo di Napoli e Vesuvio, I, 170 b., SP; Delle Palme, II, 76 b., SP; Montana, II, 94 b.

Sassari

Grazia Deledda, Viale Dante 47, I, 206 b.; Frank, Via Diaz 20, II, 140 b.; Marini Due, Via Chironi, II, 75 b.; Motel Agip, Via C. Felice 43, II, 114 b.; Giusy, Piazza Sant'Antonio 21, III, 37 b.

Savona

Riviera Suisse, Via Paleocapa 24, I, 127 b.; Ariston, Via Giordano 11, II, 16 r.; Motel Agip, in Zinola, Via Aurelia, II, 120 b.

Sciacca

Delle Terme, Lungomare Nuove Terme, II, 72 r., SP; Garden, Via Valverde 2, II, 120 b.; Torre Macauda, on S.S. 115 (direction Agrigento), II, 504 b., SP.

Sestriere

Belvedere, I, 48 b.; Cristallo, I, 134 b.; Grand Hotel Principi di Piemonte, I, 174 b.; Grand Hotel Sestriere, I, 190 b.; Miramonti, II, 68 b.; Olimpic, II, 36 b.; Savoy Edelweiss, II, 48 b.; Sud-Ovest, II, 32 b.

Sestri Levante

*Albergo dei Castelli, Via alla Penisola, L, 82 b.; Villa Balbi, Viale Rimembranze 1, I, 182 b., SP; Due Mari, Vico del Coro 18, II, 48 b.; Helvetia, Via Cappuccini 43, II, 28 r.; Vis à Vis, Via della Chiusa 28, II, 76 b., SP; Daria, Viale Rimembranze 46, III, 23 r.; Sereno, Via Val di Canepa 96, III, 10 r.

Siena

*Park, Via Marciano 16, L, 137 b., SP; Athena, Via P. Mascagni 55, I, 210 b.; Jolly Hotel Excelsior, Piazza la Lizza 1, I, 222 b.; Certosa, Via di Certosa 82, I, 28 b., SP; Villa Patrizia, Via Fiorentina 58, I, 66 b., SP; Villa Scacciapensieri, Via di Scacciapensieri 10, I, 52 b., SP; Castagneto, Via dei Cappuccini 39, II, 21 b.; Duomo, Via Stalloreggi 38, II, 24 b.; Garden, Via Custoza 2, II, 107 b., SP; Santa Caterina, Via E. S. Piccolomini 7, II, 34 b.; Vico Alto, Via delle Regioni 26, II, 82 b.

Sirmione

*Villa Cortina, Via Grotte 12, L, 98 b., SP; Grand Hotel Terme, I, 109 b., SP; Broglia, Via Piana 36, I, 59 b., SP; Continental, Punta Staffalo 7, I, 95 b., SP; Eden, Piazza Carducci 17/18, I, 63 b.; Flaminia, Piazza Flaminia 8, I, 58 b.; Ideal, Via Catullo 23, I, 48 b.; Olivi, Via San Pietro 5, I, 107 b.; Sirmione, Piazza Castello, I, 134 b.; Azzurra, II, 30 b.; Brunella, Via Catullo 29, II, 35 b.; Du Lac, Via XXV Aprile 60, II, 65 b.; Du Parc, II, 172 b.; Florida, II, 52 b.; Fonte Boiola, Viale Marconi 7, II, 101 b.; Golf et Suisse,

Via Condominio 2, II, 62 b., SP; La Rondine, Via Benaco 24, III, 36 r.; Miramar, Via XXV Aprile 22, II, 56 b.

Ambasciatori, Via Ambasciatori, I, 198 b., SP; Aminta, Via Nastro Verde 7, I, 134 b., SP; Belair, Via Capo 29, I, 77 b., SP; Carlton, Via Correale 15, I, 131 b., SP; Cesare Augusto, Via degli Aranci 116, I, 220 b., SP; Continental, Piazza della Vittoria 4, I, 150 b., SP; De la Ville, Via Rota 15, I, 215 b., SP; Europa Palace, Via Correale 34, I, 137 b.; Flora Grand Hotel, Corso Italia 248, I; Imperial Hotel Tramontano, Via Vittorio Veneto 1, I, 195 b., SP; Michelangelo, Corso Italia 275, I, 180 b.; Parco dei Principi, Via Rota 1, I, 349 b.; President, Via Colle Parisi, I, 148 b., SP; Riviera, Via Califano 22, I, 170 b.; Royal, Via Correale 42, I, 180 b., SP; Bellevue Syrene, Via Marina Grande 1, II, 91 b.; Eden, Via Correale, II, 110 b., SP; Gran Paradiso, Via Privata Rubinacci, II, 160 b., SP; Tirrenia, Via Capo 1, II, 99 b.; Désirée, Via Capo 31 bis, III, 22 r. **Sorrento**

Ritz, Lungomare Adriatico 48, I, 150 b.; Bristol, Lungomare Adriatico 46, II, 120 b.; Mosella, Via S. Felice 3, II, 45 r.; Vittoria Palace, Lungomare Adriatico 28, II, 220 b.; Park, Lungomare Adriatico Sud, III, 82 b. **Sottomarina**

La Playa, Località Fiorelle, II, 76 b., SP; Miralago Motel, Via Flacca, II, 41 b.; Parkhotel, Località Fiorelle, II, 49 b., SP; Amyclae, Via C. Colombo 77, III, 67 b.; Aurora, Via C. Colombo III, 78 b.; La Sirenella, Via C. Colombo 25, III, 52 b.; Punta Cetarola, Località Montepiano, III, 120 b., SP. **Sperlonga**

Gattapone, Via del Ponte 6, I, 16 b.; Clarici, Piazza della Vittoria 32, II, 24 r.; Dei Duchi, Viale Matteotti 2, II, 94 b.; Motel Agip, on S.S. 3 (direction Flaminia), II, 114 b.; Nuovo Clitunno, Piazza Sordini 8, II, 60 b.; Lello Caro, Piazza Garibaldi 40, III, 68 b.; Moderno Due Mondi, Piazza della Vittoria 26, III, 36 b. **Spoleto**

Royal, Lungomare Kennedy 125, I, 178 b., SP; Tirreno, Via Aurelia 2, I, 75 b.; Aurora, Piazza Rizzo 9, II, 33 r.; La Pineta, Via Serra 22, II, 55 b.; Ligure, Piazza della Vittoria 1, II, 38 b.; Roma, Piazza Colombo 7, II, 19 r.; Zunino, Via Serra 23, II, 29 r.; Méditerranée, Via Rapallo 3, III, 35 r.; Vallega, Via XXV Aprile 12, III, 60 b. **Spotorno**

*Des Iles Borromées, Lungolago Umberto 67, L, 219 b., SP; Astoria, Lungolago Umberto 31, I, 183 b., SP; Bristol, Lungolago Umberto 73, I, 438 b., SP; La Palma, Lungolago Umberto 33, I, 240 b., SP; Milano, Piazza Imbarcadero, I, 132 b.; Regina Palace, Lungolago Umberto 27, I, 329 b., SP; Speranza du Lac, Piazza Imbarcadero, I, 141 b.; Boston, II, 62 b.; La Fontana, on S.S. to Sempione 3, II, 38 b.; Meeting, Via Bonghi 9, II, 46 b.; Moderno, Via Cavour 33, II, 72 b.; Italia e Svizzera, Piazza Imbarcadero, III, 54 b. **Stresa**

See Lipari Islands. **Stromboli**

Belvedere, III, 32 b.; Roma, III, 56 b.; Miramonti, Località Contrada Varole, IV, 26 b. **Subiaco**

Armando's, Via Montenero 16, II, 35 b.; Artu, II, 31 b.; Europa Park, on road to Badia Morronese, II, 210 b.; Salvador, Viale della Repubblica (2 km/1½ miles NW), III, 67 b. **Sulmona**

Jolly, Corso Gelone 45, I, 146 b.; Bellavista, Via Diodoro Siculo 4, II, 76 b.; Fontane Bianche, Via Mazzarò 1, II, 308 b., SP; Grand Hotel, Viale Mazzini 12, II, 79 b.; Grand Hotel Villa Politi, Via M. Politi 2, II, 164 b., SP; Motel Agip, Viale Teracati 30, II, 165 b.; Panorama, Via N. Grotticelle 33, **Syracuse**

Hotels

II, 90 b.; Park, Via Filisto 80, II, 137 b.; Relax, Via Monterosa 11, II, 83 b.; Scala Greca, Via Avola 7, III, 180 b.

Taormina

*San Domenico Palace, Piazza San Domenico 5, L, 177 b., SP; Jolly Hotel Diodoro, Via Bagnoli Croce 75, I, 202 b., SP; Excelsior Palace, Via Toselli 8, I, 166 b., SP; Méditerranée, Via Circonvallazione 61, I, 93 b., SP; Continental, Via Dionisio 1, II, 43 r.; Vello d'Oro, Via Fazzello 2, II, 57 r.; Villa Belvedere, Via Bagnoli Croce 79, II, 41 r.; Villa Paradiso, Via Roma 2, II, 33 r.; Villa Schuler, II, 22 r.

In Mazzarò: *Mazzarò Sea Palace, L, 146 b., SP; Atlantis Bay, I, 174 b., SP; Villa Sant'Andrea, I, 48 b.; Lido Méditerranée, II, 144 b.

Taranto

Delfino, Viale Virgilio 66, I, 282 b., SP; Mar Grande Park Hotel, Viale Virgilio 90, I, 155 b., SP; Palace, Viale Virgilio 10, I, 121 b.; Blue Garden, Via Ionio, 431, II, 51 b.; Bologna, Via Margherita 4, II, 68 b.; Plaza, Via D'Aquino 46, II, 186 b.; President, Via Campania 136, II, 180 b.; Imperiale, Via Pitagora 94, III, 102 b.; Miramare, Via Toma 4, III, 74 b.

Tarquinia

Tarconte, Via Tuscia 19, II, 100 b.; Aurelia, Via Aurelia 8, III, 49 b.
In Tarquinia Lido: Grand Hotel Helios, Via Porto Clementino, I, 190 b., SP; La Torraccia, Viale Mediterraneo 45, II, 36 b.; Velca Mare, Via degli Argonauti, III, 18 b.

Tempio Pausania

Delle Sorgenti, Località Fonti Rinaggiu, II, 53 b.; Petit, Piazza A. de Gasperi 9, II, 81 b.; San Carlo, Piazza Libertà 5, III, 140 b.

Teramo

Abruzzi, Viale Mazzini 18, II, 79 b.; Garden, Viale Cricioli 3, II, 52 b.; Gran Sasso, Via L. Vinciguerra 12, II, 62 b.; Michelangelo, Coste Sant'Agostino, II, 150 b.; Sporting, Via de Gasperi 41, II, 105 b.

Terni

Valentino, Via Plinio il Giovane 3, I, 117 b.; Allegretti, Strada Staino 7B, II, 70 b.; Brin, Viale Brin 148, II, 12 b.; De Paris, Viale Stazione 52, II, 99 b.; Garden, Via Bramante 4/6, II, 156 b.; Brenta II, Via Montegrappa 51, III, 28 b.

Terracina

L'Approdo Grand Hotel, Viale Circe, II, 97 b.; Grand Hotel Palace, Lungomare Matteotti 2, II, 135 b.; River, Via Mediana, II, 186 b.; Torre del Sole, Via Mediana, II, 234 b.

Tivoli

Torre Sant'Angelo, I, 78 b.; Padovano, III, 32 b.; Padovano II, III, 32 b.

Todi

*San Valentino, Frazione Fiori, L, 24 b., SP; Bramante, Via Orvietana, I, 85 b.; Di Todi, Via Tiberina, II, 43 b.; Tuder, Via Maestà dei Lombardi, II, 40 b.; Villa Luisa, Via A. Cortesi 147, II, 81 b.; Cavour, Corso Cavour 13, III, 34 b.

Torbole

Lago di Garda, I, 91 b.; Piccolo Mondo, I, 70 b., SP; Caravel, II, 114 b., SP; Lido Blu, II, 70 b.; Torbole, II, 114 b.; Villa Verde, II, 49 b.; Panorama, III, 36 b.

Torre Pellice

Gilly, Corso Lombardini 1, I, 62 b.; Du Parc, III, 56 b.

Tortoli

Victoria, Via Mons. Virgilio, II, 70 b.; Il Giardino, Viale Umberto, III, 60 b.

Toscolano-Maderno

In Maderno: Benaco, II, 60 b., SP; Maderno, II, 53 b., SP; Milano, II, 68 b.; Eden, III, 28 r. – In Toscolano: Garden, III, 37 b.; Sorriso, III, 18 r.

Trani

Royal, Via de Robertis 29, I, 75 b.; Trani, Corso Imbriani 137, I, 75 b.; Capirro, II, 23 b.; Riviera, Lungomare Colombo, II, 52 b.

Trapani

Nuovo Russo, Via Tintori 4, II, 48 b.; Cavallino Bianco, Lungomare Dante Alighieri, III, 103 b.

On Isola San Domino: Eden, I; Gabbiano, I, 36 r.; Kyrie, I, 63 r., SP; San Domino, II, 50 b.; Villa Olimpia, III. **Tremiti Islands**

Grand Hotel Trento, Via Alfieri 3, I, 153 b.; Accademia, Vicolo Colico 4, II, 80 b.; America, Via Torre Verde 50, II, 80 b.; Everest, Corso degli Alpini 14, II, 220 b.; Monaco, Via Torre d'Augusto 25, II, 100 b. **Trento**

Continental, Via Roma 16, I, 142 b.; Al Fogher, Viale della Repubblica 10, II, 67 b.; Cà del Galletto, Via Santa Bona Vecchia 30, II, 50 r.; Carlton, Largo Altinia 15, II, 141 b.; Campeol, Piazza Ancillotto 4, III, 16 r.; Giustiniani, Piazza Giustiniani 9, III, 33 b. **Treviso**

Adriatico Palace, Località Grignano, I, 174 b.; Duchi d'Aosta, Piazza Unità d'Italia 2, I, 103 b.; Jolly Cavour, Corso Cavour 7, I, 280 b.; Savoia Excelsior Palace, Riva del Mandracchio 4, I, 293 b.; Abbazia, Via della Geppa 20, II, 35 b.; Colombia, Via della Geppa 18, II, 59 b.; Continentale, Via San Nicolò 25, II, 73 b.; San Giusto, Via Belli 3, II, 56 b. **Trieste**

Alexandra, Lungodora Napoli 14, I, 80 b.; City, Via F. Juvarra 25, I, 73 b.; Concorde, Via Lagrange 47, I, 227 b.; Diplomatic, Via Cernaia 42, I; Jolly Hotel Ambasciatori, Corso V. Emanuele, 104, I, 336 b.; Jolly Hotel Ligure, Piazza Carlo Felice 85, I, 225 b.; Jolly Hotel Principi di Piemonte, Via Piero Gobetti 15, I, 206 b.; Majestic, Corso V. Emanuele 54, I, 127 b.; Royal, Corso Regina Margherita 249, I, 115 b.; Sitea, Via Carlo Alberto 35, I, 167 b.; Turin Palace, Via Sacchi 8, I, 227 b.; Villa Sassi, Via Traforo del Pino 47, I, 24 b.; Astoria, Via XX Settembre 4, II, 104 b.; Boston, Via Massena 70, II, 63 b.; Bramante, Via Genova 2, II, 59 b.; Cairo, Via La Loggia 6, II, 50 b.; Genio, Corso V. Emanuele 47B, II, 119 b.; Giotto, Via Giotto 27, II, 80 b.; Gran Mogul, Via Guarini 2, II, 72 b.; Lancaster, Corso F. Turati 8, II, 132 b.; Luxor, Corso Stati Uniti 7, II, 108 b.; President, Via A. Cecchi 67, II, 144 b.; Venezia, Via XX Settembre 70, II, 119 b.; Victoria, Via Nino Costa 4, II, 100 b.; Campo di Marte, Via XX Settembre 7, III, 97 b.; Eden, Via Donizetti 22, III, 41 b.; Italia, Via G. Barbera 6, III, 42 b. **Turin**

Ambassador Palace, Via Carducci 46, I, 153 b.; Astoria Hotel Italia, Piazza XX Settembre 24, I, 123 b.; Casa Bianca, Via Podgora 16, II, 67 b.; Continental, Viale Tricesimo 73, II, 92 b.; Cristallo, Piazza d'Annunzio 43, II, 129 b.; President, Via Duino 8, II, 134 b.; Apollo, Via Paparotti 11, III, 63 b.; Vienna, Viale Europa Unita 47, 45 b. **Udine**

Bonconte, Via delle Mura 28, I, 24 b., SP; La Meridiana, Via Cal Biancone 154A, Località Trasanni, II, 89 b., SP; Montefeltro, Via Piansevero 2, II, 95 b.; Piero della Francesca, Viale Comandino 53, II, 152 b. **Urbino**

Monte Bondone, I, 58 b.; Vaneze, III, 18 r. **Vaneze**

Cristallo, Via Cilea 4, I, 91 b.; Eden, Via Villagrande 1, I, 95 b.; El Chico, Via Aurelia 63, I, 45 r., SP; Savoy, Via Marconi 4, I, 92 b.; Torretti, Via Nazioni Unite 6, I, 79 b.; Europa, Via Garibaldi 10, II, 35 b.; Ideale, Via Santa Caterina 34, II, 38 r.; Manila, Via Villagrande 3, II, 13 r. **Varazze**

Du Lac, I, 33 b.; Royal Victoria, I, 117 b.; Milano, III, 17 b.; Olivedo, III, 38 b. **Varenna**

Palace, Via Manara 11, I, 185 b.; City, Via Medaglie d'Oro 35, I, 83 b.; Crystal, Via Speroni 10, I, 78 b.; Acquario, Via Giusti 7, II, 72 b.; Europa, Piazza Beccaria 1, II, 58 b.; Varese Lago, Via Macchi 61, II, 68 b.; Mira, Via Walder 45, III, 41 b. **Varese**

*Bauer Grünwald, Campo San Moisè 1459, L, 401 b.; *Cipriani, Isola della Giudecca 10, L, 189 b., SP; *Danieli, Riva degli Schiavoni 4196, L, **Venice**

423 b.; *Europa e Regina, Via XXII Marzo 2159, L, 358 b.; *Gritti Palace, Santa Maria del Giglio 2467, L, 163 b.

Londra Palace, Riva degli Schiavoni 4171, I, 121 b.; Carlton Executive, San Simeon Piccolo 578, I, 197 b.; Cavaletto e Doge Orseolo, Calle Cavaletto 1107, I, 133 b.; Concordia, Calle Larga San Marco 367, I, 106 b.; Gabrielli Sandwirth, Riva degli Schiavoni 4110, I, 194 b.; Luna, Calle dell'Ascensione 1243, I, 223 b.; Metropole, Riva degli Schiavoni 4149, I, 117 b.; Monaco e Grand Canal, Calle Vallaresso 1325, I, 130 b.; Principe, Lista di Spagna 146, I, 270 b.; Pullman Park, Fondamenta Condulmer 245, I, 180 b.; Saturnia e International, Via XXII Marzo 2398, I, 174 b.; Splendid Suisse, Ponte dei Baretteri 760, I, 296 b.

Accademia–Villa Maravegie, Fondamenta Bollani 1058, II, 47 b.; Ala, Santa Maria del Giglio 2494, II, 133 b.; Al Sole Palace, Fondamenta Minotto 136, II, 115 b.; American, San Vio 628, II, 53 b.; Bisanzio, Calle della Pietà 3656, II, 68 b.; Bonvecchiati, Calle Goldoni 4488, II, 149 b.; Continental, Lista di Spagna 166, 166 b.; Do Pozzi, Corte do Pozzi 2373, II, 43 b.; Flora, Calle Bergamaschi 2283A, II, 82 b.; Giorgione, SS. Apostoli 4587, II, 103 b.; La Fenice et des Artistes, Campiello Fenice 1936, II, 116 b.; Montecarlo, Calle Specchieri 463, II, 77 b.; San Marco, Calle dei Fabbri 877, II, 110 b.; Savoia e Iolanda, Riva degli Schiavoni 4187, II, 100 b.; Torino, Calle delle Ostreghe 2356, II, 30 b.; Universo e Nord, Lista di Spagna 121, II, 118 b.

Basilea, Rio Marin 817, III, 55 b.; Dolomiti, Calle Priuli 73, III, 80 b.; Gallini, Calle della Verona 3673, III, 87 b.; Nazionale, Lista di Spagna 158, III, 163 b.

On Lido: *Excelsior, Lungomare Marconi 41, L, 402 b., SP; Des Bains, Lungomare Marconi 17, I, 430 b., SP; Le Boulevard, Gran Viale S. M. Elisabetta 41, I, 80 b.; Quattro Fontane, Via Quattro Fontane 16, I, 125 b.; Villa Laguna, Via San Gallo 6, I, 64 b.; Villa Mabapa, Riviera San Nicolò 16, I, 99 b.; Belvedere, Via Cerigo 1, II, 59 b.; Biasutti Adria Urania-Nora, Via E. Dandolo 29, II, 136 b.; Buon Pesce, Riviera San Nicolò 50, II, 44 b.; Hungaria, Gran Viale S. M. Elisabetta 28, II, 180 b.; La Meridiana, Via Lepanto 45, II, 62 b.; Villa Otello, Via Lepanto 12, II, 64 b.; Villa Parco, Via Rodi 1, III, 42 b.

In Marghera: Motel Agip, Via della Fonte 28, I, 375 b.; Colombo, Via Paulucci 5, II, 66 b.; Lugano Torretta, Via Rizzardi 11, II, 118 b.; Mondial, Via Rizzardi 21, II, 103 b.; Vienna, Via Rizzardi 54, II, 95 b.; Lloyd, Via Rizzardi 32, III, 89 b.

In Mestre: Alexander, Via Forte Marghera 193, I, 99 b.; Ambasciatori, Corso del Popoli 221, I, 167 b.; Michelangelo, Via Forte Marghera 69, I, 96 b.; Ramada, Via Orlanda 4, I, 364 b.; Albatros, Viale Don Sturzo 32, II, 255 b.; Bologna e Stazione, Via Piave 214, II, 204 b.; Capitol, Via Orlanda 1, II, 160 b.; Venezia, Via Teatro Vecchio 5, II, 119 b.; Aquila Nera, Via Essicatoio 38, III, 78 b.; Aurora, Piazza G. Bruno 16, III, 62 b.; Centrale, Piazza Donatori di Sangue 15, III, 195 b.

Ventimiglia Sea Gulf, Via Marconi 13, II, 51 b.; Splendid, Via Roma 33, II, 50 b.; Calipso, Via Matteotti 8, III, 52 b.; Sole e Mare, Via Marconi 12, III, 53 b.

Verbania In Intra: Il Chiostro, I, 34 b.; Miralago, Corso Mameli 173, II, 78 b.; Villa Aurora, III, 20 b.

In Pallanza: Europalace Residence, Viale delle Magnolie 16, I, 86 b.; Majestic, Via Vittorio Veneto 32, I, 212 b.; Astor, Via Vittorio Veneto 17B, II, 92 b.; Belvedere, Piazza Imbarcadero, II, 88 b.; San Gottardo, Piazza Imbarcadero, III, 54 b.

Verona *Due Torri, Piazza Sant'Anastasia 4, L, 160 b.; Accademia, Via Scala 12, I, 184 b.; Colomba d'Oro, Via C. Cattaneo 10, I, 81 b.; Firenze, Corso

Porta Nuova 88, I, 84 b.; Grand Hotel, Corso Porta Nuova 105, I, 80 b.; Leopardi, Via Leopardi 16, I, 105 b.; Montresor, Via Gian Matteo Giberti 7, I, 145 b.; Nuovo Hotel San Pietro, Via S. Teresa 1, I, 106 b.; San Luca, Vicolo Volto San Luca 8, I, 73 b.; San Marco, Via Longhena 42, I, 69 b.; Victoria, Via Adua 6, I, 72 b.; Antica Porta Leona, Corticella Leoni 3, II, 54 b.; Europa, Via Roma 8, II, 83 b.; Milano, Vicolo Tre Marchetti 11, II, 88 b.; Touring, Via Q. Sella 5, II, 75 b.; Arena, Stradone Porta Palio 2, III, 27 b.; Elena, Via Mastino della Scala 9, III, 39 b.; Trieste, Corso Porta Nuova 57, III, 58 b.

See Boscotrecase. **Vesuvius**

Astor Hotel e Residence, Viale Carducci 54, I, 129 b., SP; De Russie e **Viareggio**
Plaza, Viale Manin 1, I, 90 b.; Excelsior, Viale Carducci 88, I, 154 b.; Grand Hôtel et Royal, Viale Carducci 44, I, 209 b.; Palace, Via F. Gioia 2, I, 120 b.; Principe di Piemonte, Piazza Puccini 1, I, 221 b.; Belmare, Viale Carducci 5, II, 76 b.; Bristol, Viale Manin 14, II, 64 b.; Eden, Via S. Martino 1, II, 66 b.; Lucas, Piazza Puccini 5, II, 34 b.; Stella d'Italia, Via U. Foscolo 57, II, 65 b.; Bonelli, Via Regia 96, III, 56 b.; Flamingo, Via Buonarroti 219, III, 54 b.

Alfa, Via dell'Oreficeria 52, I, 174 b.; Campo Marzio, Viale Roma 21, I, 54 **Vicenza**
b.; Europa, Viale S. Lazzaro (on S.S., direction Verona), I, 129 b.; Motel Agip, Via degli Scaligeri 68, I, 258 b.; City, Viale Verona 12, II, 35 b.; Continental, Viale Trissino 89, II, 95 b.; Cristina, Corso San Felice 32, II, 42 b.; Adele, Via Medici 36, III, 100 b.; Giardini, Via Giuriolo 6, III, 51 b.

Balletti Park Hotel (with annexe), Via Umbria 2A, I, 84 b., SP; Mini Palace **Viterbo**
Hotel, Via S. Maria della Grotticella 2B, I, 72 b.; Leon d'Oro, Via della Cava 36, II, 74 b.; Antico Angelo, Via Orologio Vecchio 1, III, 51 b.; Tuscia, Via Cairoli 41, III, 75 b.

San Lino, Via San Lino 26, I, 88 b.; Africa, Via Borgo Lisci 10, II, 20 b.; **Volterra**
Etruria, Via Matteotti 32, II, 40 b.; Nazionale, Via dei Marchesi II, 66 b.; Villa Nencini, Borgo S. Stefano 55, II, 27 b.

See Lipari Islands. **Vulcano**

Information

Ente Nazionale Italiano per il Turismo (ENIT) **Italian Government**
Via Marghera 2, I-00185 Roma **Travel Office**
tel. (06) 4 97 71 **(ENIT)**

Italian State Tourist Office **In United Kingdom**
1 Princes Street, London W1R 8AY
tel. (071) 408 1254

Italian Government Travel Office **In USA**
500 North Michigan Avenue, Suite 1046
Chicago IL 60611
tel. (312) 644 0990

630 Fifth Avenue, Suite 1565
New York NY 10111
tel. (212) 245 4822

360 Post Street, Suite 801
San Francisco CA 94108
tel. (415) 392 6206

Insurance

In Canada

Italian Government Travel Office
Store 56, Plaza, 1 Place Ville Marie
Montreal H3B 3M9
tel. (514) 866 7667–9

Information
within Italy

There are ENIT offices at the main frontier crossings and at Rome,
Milan and Naples airports.
Within Italy tourist information is provided by the Regional Tourist
Offices (Assessorati Regionali per il Turismo) in regional capitals, provincial tourist offices (Enti Provinciali per il Turismo, EPT), and spa
administrations and local tourist offices (Aziende Autonome di Soggiorno, Cura e Turismo, AA). In small towns information can be
obtained from the local Pro Loco organisation.

Insurance

General

Visitors are strongly advised to ensure that they have adequate holiday
insurance including loss or damage to luggage, loss of currency and
jewellery.

Health insurance

British citizens, like nationals of other European Community countries,
are entitled to obtain medical care under the Italian health services on
the same basis as Italians. Before leaving home they should apply to
their local social security office for a form E111, which certifies their
entitlement to insurance cover. If possible this should be presented to
the local health office (Unità Sanitaria Locale) before seeking
treatment.
It is nevertheless advisable, even for EC nationals, to take out some
form of short-term health insurance (available, for example, under the
AA's 5-Star Service) providing full cover and possibly avoiding bureau-
cratic delays. Nationals of non-EC countries should certainly have insurance cover.

Vehicles

Visitors travelling by car should ensure that their insurance is comprehensive and covers use of the vehicle in Italy.
See also Travel Documents.

Motoring in Italy

See also Practical Information: Safety on the Road

Roads

The Italian road system is extensive, well laid out and well maintained.
It consists of motorways, national highways (trunk roads), provincial
roads and secondary roads. See map, page 605.

Motorways

Practically all towns of any size are served by motorways (*autostrade*,
numbered and prefixed with the letter S), which are mostly toll roads.
Among the motorways of most importance to visitors are those from
Varese or Como via Milan, Genoa and Pisa to Livorno or Florence; from
Milan via Parma, Bologna and Florence to Rome, and from there to
Naples; and from Bologna to Ravenna or via Rimini, Ancona, Pescara
and Bari to Taranto. The motorway from the Brenner (Austrian–Italian
frontier) via Bolzano, Trento and Verona links up with the Milan–
Bologna motorway at Modena. There is also an important west/east
link from Milan via Verona, Padua and Venice to Trieste.

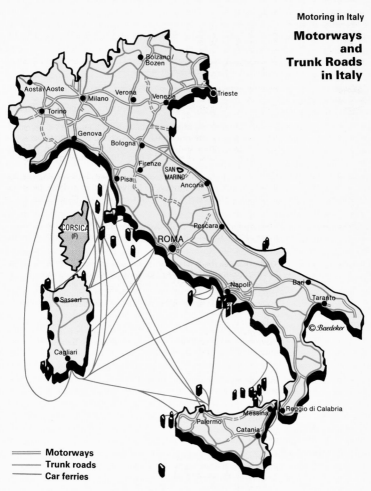

Legend	
═══	**Motorways**
──	**Trunk roads**
──	**Car ferries**

The national highways (*strade statali*, numbered and prefixed with the letters SS), most of them well built and maintained, also serve important trunk routes. Many of them have names as well as numbers (e.g. Via Aurelia, Via Emilia), and these are often more generally used than the numbers. At intervals along these roads are road maintenance depots (*case cantoniere*), conspicuous with their reddish-brown colouring.

National highways

The provincial roads (*strade provinciali, strade di grande comunicazione*), which are unnumbered, are also of good quality.

Provincial roads

Local connections are provided by the secondary roads (*strade secondarie*).

Secondary roads

Road signs and markings are in line with international standards.

Road signs

605

Motoring in Italy

Rule of the road	As in the rest of continental Europe, traffic goes on the right, with overtaking on the left.
Seat belts	All occupants of a car over the age of 14 must wear seat belts. Children under 4 must be in special children's seats.
Alcohol	Driving under the influence of alcohol is strictly prohibited.
Speed limits	The speed limit in built-up areas is 50 km p.h./31 m.p.h. for all types of vehicle. The speed limit on ordinary roads, outside built-up areas, is 90 km p.h./56 m.p.h. for cars, 80 km p.h./50 m.p.h. for cars with trailers. On motorways the speed limit for cars over 1100 cc capacity is 130 km p.h./80 m.p.h., for cars under 1100 cc 110 km p.h./68 m.p.h., for cars with trailers 100 km p.h./62 m.p.h. For motorcycles up to 99 cc capacity the speed limit on ordinary roads is 80 km p.h./50 m.p.h.; for cycles between 100 and 149 cc the limit is 90 km p.h./56 m.p.h.; for those above 149 cc the limits are the same as for cars.
Motorcycles	The lower age limit for motorcycles over 350 cc capacity is 21. Motorcycles under 150 cc are not allowed on motorways. Sidecars are not permitted.
Priority	Traffic on main roads has priority over side roads only if the main road has the priority sign (a white or yellow square, corner downwards, in a red or black and white frame); otherwise, even at roundabouts, traffic coming from the right has priority. On narrow mountain roads the ascending vehicle has priority. Vehicles on rails always have priority.
Overtaking	Drivers moving from one lane to another before and after overtaking must give warning of their intention by the use of their direction indicators. Outside built-up areas the horn must also be sounded before overtaking.
Ban on use of horn	In towns of any size the use of the horn is prohibited. The ban is indicated by a sign showing a horn with a bar through it or by the words *zona di silenzio*.
Lights	On roads or streets with good lighting only sidelights may be used. In tunnels and galleries dipped headlights must be used.
Petrol	See entry
Breakdowns	For breakdown assistance, see Emergencies. In the event of a breakdown on a motorway it is not permitted to have the car towed away by another private car; on ordinary roads, however, this is permissible.
Accidents	See Safety on the Road
Motoring organisations	See entry

Motoring Organisations

Touring Club Italiano (TCI)	Head office: Corso Italia 10 I-20122 Milano (Milan) tel. (02) 8 52 61 The TCI has branch offices in Rome, Turin and Bari.

Head office:
Via Marsala 8
I-00100 Roma (Rome)
tel. (06) 4 99 81
The ACI has offices in all provincial capitals, in major tourist centres and
at the main frontier crossing points.

Petrol

The price of petrol (*benzina*) in Italy is considerably above the European average.

Petrol coupons

Most of the filling stations supplying lead-free petrol are on the motorways. A list of stations selling lead-free petrol can be obtained from the Italian motoring organisations (see Motoring Organisations).

Lead-free petrol

It is prohibited, on safety grounds, to carry a reserve supply of petrol or to fill a can with petrol at a filling station.

Spare petrol

Post and Telephone

See Business Hours

Opening times

Post-boxes in Italy are painted red.

Post-boxes

Stamps can be bought at tobacconists (identified by a sign with the letter T over the door) as well as in post offices.

Stamps

Public telephones can be operated either with telephone tokens (*gettoni*) or with 100 lire or 200 lire coins.

Telephone

You can also telephone from post offices or from special telephone offices (SIP).

Most bars have pay phones (identified by a yellow disc over the entrance), from which local calls can be made with either telephone tokens or 100 and 200 lire coins. If the disc bears the legend *teleselezione* or *interurbana* trunk and international calls can also be dialled.

From Italy to the United Kingdom: 0044
From Italy to the United States or Canada: 001
(In calls to the United Kingdom the initial zero of the local dialling code should be omitted).

International
dialling codes

Public Holidays

January 1st (New Year's Day)
January 6th (Epiphany)
Easter Monday
April 25th (Liberation Day, 1945)
May 1st (Labour Day)
August 15th (Ferragosto; Assumption; family celebrations; the climax of the Italian holiday season)

Statutory
public holidays

November 1st (All Saints)
December 8th (Conception of the Virgin)
December 25th and 26th (Christmas)

Radio

RAI

RAI (Radiotelevisione Italiana), the Italian radio and television corporation, puts out special English-language transmissions (news, commentaries, weather) during the holiday season.
RAI also transmits urgent messages for tourists on medium and ultra-short waves. Information about the arrangements can be obtained from the Italian motoring organisations or the police.

Railways

Ferrovie Italiane
dello Stato (FS)

The Italian railway system, now 50% electrified, has a total length of some 16,000 km/10,000 miles: see map on page 562. Most of it is run by the Italian State Railways (Ferrovie Italiane dello Stato, FS), but there are also a number of privately run lines, the timetables for which are included in the published timetables of the State Railways.

Information

The State Railways have information bureaux in the larger Italian towns.

Head office

Piazza della Croce Rossa
I-00161 Roma (Rome)
tel. (06) 84 90/29 31

Offices in UK, USA
and Canada

Wasteelf Travel
121 Wilton Road, London SW1
tel. (071) 834 7066

500 North Michigan Avenue
Chicago IL 60611
tel. (312) 644 6651

666 Fifth Avenue
New York NY 10103
tel. (212) 397 2667

6033 West Century Boulevard
Suite 1090
Los Angeles CA 90045
tel. (213) 338 8620

111 Avenue Road
Toronto, Ontario M5R 3J8
tel. (416) 927 7712

2055 Peel Street
Montréal, Québec H3A 1V4
tel. (514) 845 901

International tickets

International tickets are valid for two months and allow the journey to be broken as often as desired.

Tourist tickets

The best bargain for holidaymakers is the Italian Tourist Ticket (biglietto turistico di libera circolazione), available for periods of 8, 15,

21 or 30 days, which covers unlimited travel on all State Railways lines in mainland Italy, Sicily and Sardinia. It can be purchased (only by residents outside Italy) at offices of the State Railways' travel office, CIT, and authorised travel agencies. Children between 4 and 11 are half price.

The *biglietto chilometrico,* which offers a reduction of 10% on standard rates, permits up to 3000 km/1860 miles in up to 20 trips within a two-month period. On trains for which a supplement is charged this must be paid in addition. | Kilometric tickets

Children under 4 accompanied by an adult and not occupying a seat travel free. Children between 4 and 12 pay half fare. | Reductions for children

The Inter-Rail Pass, for young people up to the age of 26, allows unlimited travel (2nd class) in Italy for a month, and also entitles the holder to substantial reductions in his own country.
Young people under 26 can also get a substantial reduction on ordinary fares in Italy. | Inter-Rail Pass

Families (at least 3 persons) can purchase a Rail Europe Family Pass which entitles them to a reduction of 30% on adults' and children's fares. The REF pass is valid for a year. | Reductions for families

Holders of a Senior Citizen's Railcard can obtain a Rail Europe Senior (RES) pass which entitles them to a 30% reduction on fares in Italy. | Reductions for senior citizens

Restaurants

As a means of checking possible tax evasion restaurants are required to give their clients a receipted bill, which the police may ask them to produce within 50 metres of the restaurant; failure to produce it may lead to a fine. | **N.B.**

Il Ciarlocco, Via Don Bosco 1; La Schiavia, Vicolo della Schiavia | **Acqui Terme**

Taverna Mosè, Contrada San Biagio, on exit road for Porto Empedocle and Caltanissetta | **Agrigento**

Albergo Columbia, Passeggiata Cadorna 12; Palma, Via Cavour 5 | **Alassio**

Minisport da Luciano, Viale Italia 35 | **Albenga**

Il Poeta Contadino, Via Indipendenza 21 | **Alberobello**

Al Tuguri, Via Maiorca 57; La Lepanto, Via Carlo Alberto 135 | **Alghero**

Il Tarì, Via Capuano 9/11; Marina Grande, Viale della Regione | **Amalfi**

Passetto, Piazza IV Novembre; La Moretta, Piazza del Plebiscito 52 | **Ancona**

Al Buongusto di Alceste, Piazza Sant'Antonio 6 | **Anzio**

Cavallo Bianco, Via E. Aubert 15; Vecchio Ristoro, Via Tourneuve 4 | **Aosta**

Al Sole, Via Sant'Anna 35 | **Arco**

Da Dria, Via Raffaello Sanzio 3 | **Arenzano**

Buca di San Francesco, Via San Francesco 1 | **Arezzo**

Restaurants

Arzachena Grazia Deledda, on road to Baia Sardinia

Ascoli Piceno Kursaal, Corso Mazzini 221

Assisi Buca di San Francesco, Via Brizi 1; Medio Evo, Via Arco dei Priori 4B; Umbra, Via degli Archi 6

Asti Gener Neuv, Lungo Tanaro 4; Il Cenacolo, Viale Pilone 59; La Greppia, Corso Alba 140; Il Cascinale Nuovo, on road to Alba

Bari La Pignata, Via Melo 9; La Serra, Via Amendola 197H; Vecchia Bari, Via Dante 47

Belluno Al Borgo, Via Anconetta 8

Bergamo Ristorante dell'Angelo, Borgo Santa Caterina 55; Taverna del Collioni, Piazza Vecchia 7; Da Vittorio, Viale Papa Giovanni XXIII 21; Lio Pellegrini, Via San Tomaso 47

Bologna Antica Osteria Romagnola, Via Rialto 13; Becco di Legno, Via Gianni Palmieri 7; Al Solito Posto, Via Turati 112; Cordon Bleu, Via A. Saffi 38; Sandro al Navile, Via del Sostegno 17; Franco Rossi, Via Goito; I Carracci, Via Manzoni 2; L'Asterico, Via Murri 168D; Notai, Via de' Pignattari 1; Papa Re li due Gambari, Piazza dell'Unità 6; Pappagallo, Piazza Mercanzia 3C; Silverio, Via Nosadella 37A; Luciano, Via Nazario Sauro 19; Battibecco, Via Battibecco 4B; Panoramica, Via San Mamolo 31

Bolzano Da Abramo, Piazza Gries 16; Rastbichler, Via Cadorna 1

Bordighera La Réserve Tastevin, Via Arziglia 20; Carletto, Via Vittorio Emanuele 339

Brescia Castello Malvezzi, Via Colle San Giuseppe 1; La Sosta, Via San Martino della Battaglia 20

Bressanone Fink, Via Portici Minori 4

Cagliari Dal Corsaro, Viale Regina Margherita 28

Capo d'Orlando La Tartaruga, Lido San Gregorio

Capri La Capannina, Viale Botteghe 12B; La Certosella, Via Tragara 13

Casale Monferrato La Torre, Via Garoglio 3

Castelsardo La Guardiola, Piazza del Bastione

Catania La Siciliana, Viale Marco Polo 52A

Cattolica Moro da Osvaldo, Via Mazzini 91

Celle Ligure Villa Alta, Via Aurelia 1A

Cesenatico Al Gallo, Via Baldini 21; La Buca, Corso Garibaldi 41

Chieti La Regina dell'Hotel Dangiò, in Tricalle district

Como Da Angela, Via Ugo Foscolo 16; Del Gesumìn, Via Cinque Giornate 44; Sant'Anna, Via Turati 1/3; Villa Maderni, Via Cardano 53

Cortina d'Ampezzo Baita Fraina, in Fraina district; El Toulà, Via Ronco 123; Il Meloncino, in Gillardon 17, on road to Pocòl; Tivoli, Via Lacedel 34

Ceresole, Via Ceresole 4	**Cremona**
La Sosta da Marcello, Via Alvaro	**Crotone**
Antica Hostaria Cavallino, Via Murachette 29; Esplanade, Via Lario 10; Pesce d'Oro da Rocco, Corso Garibaldi 7	**Desenzano del Garda**
Amici Miei, Corso Mazzini 54	**Faenza**
Corallo, Via Leonardo da Vinci 3	**Fano**
Italia, da Giovanni, Largo Castello 32	**Ferrara**
Briga, Altipiano delle Manie	**Finale Ligure**
Enoteca Pane e Vino, Via Poggio Bracciolini 48; Sabatini, Via de' Panzani 9A; Da Dante, Via delle Terme 23r; Harry's Bar, Lungarno Vespucci 22r; Gourmet, Via Il Prato 68r; Lorenzaccio, Via Rucellai 1A; Al Campidoglio, Via del Campidoglio 8r; Del Coco Lezzone, Via del Parioncino 26r; Giuseppe Alessi, Via di Mazzo 24/25r; Pepolino, Via Francesco Ferrucci 16r; Don Chisciotte, Via Cosima Ridolfi 4/6r; Piniochorri, Via Ghibellina 87; Il Verrocchio, Via La Massa, on road to Ripoli; La Capannina di Sante, Piazza Ravenna; La Vecchia Cucina, Via de Amicis 1r; Lo Strettoio, Via di Serpiolle 7; Sostanza, detto Il Troia, Via del Porcellana 25r; San Zanobi, Via San Zanobi 33r	**Florence**
La Rugantino del Nonno Galileo, Via Luigi Sturzo 23/25; La Mangiatoia, Viale Virgilio 2	**Foggia**
Villa Roncalli, Viale Roma 25	**Foligno**
Vicolo di Molò, Corso Italia 126	**Fondi**
Masaniello, Al Vecchio Leone, Piazza Commestibili 6	**Gaeta**
Villa Fiordaliso, Via Zanardello 132	**Gardone**
Da Giacomo, Corso Italia 1r; Vittorio al Mare, in Boccadasse, Belvedere Firpo 1; Il Primo Piano, Via XX Settembre 36; Le Fate, Via Ruspoli 31; Toe Drüe, Via Carlo Corsi 44r; Aladino, Via Ettore Vernazza 8; Da Genio, Piazza San Leonardo; Gran Gotto, Via Fiume 11r; Bella Napoli, Sestro Ponente, Via Giacomo Puccini 43r; Saint Cyr, Piazza Marsala 4; Detta del Bruxiaboschi, Via F. Mignone 8; Il Cucciolo, Viale Sauli 33; Zeffirino, Via XX Settembre 20	**Genoa**
Alla Fortuna, Da Nico, Via Marina 10; All'Androna, Calle Porta Piccola 4; Serena, Riva Sant'Andrea 31	**Grado**
Buca di San Lorenzo, Via Manetti 1; Eno Oliteca Ombrone, Viale G. Matteotti 71	**Grosseto**
Porta Tessenaca, Via Piccardi 21	**Gubbio**
Lanterna Blu da Tonino, Via Scarincio 32	**Imperia**
Maresca, Corso Marcelli 186	**Isernia**
Tre Marie, Via Tre Marie 3	**L'Aquila**
La Locandina, Via Sapri 10; Al Negrao, Via Genova 428; Da Caran, Via Genova 1	**La Spezia**

Restaurants

Latina	Premiata Trattoria Giggetto, Borgo Grappa Centro; Enoteca dell'Orologio, Piazza del Popolo 20; Fioretto, Via dell'Agora 91; Miro, Villa Mimi, Via Isonzo 3
Lavagna	Il Gabbiano, Via San Benedetto 26
Lecco	Al Porticciolo, Via Valsecchi 5; Les Paysans, Lungo Lario Piave 14
Lipari	Filippino, Piazza Municipio; El Pulera, Via Diana
Livorno	Il Sottomarino, Via Terrazzini 48; L'Antico Moro, Via Di Franco 59
Lucca	La Mora, Sesto di Moriano 104; Buca di Sant'Antonio, Via della Cervia 3; Canuleia, Via Canuleia 14; Solferino, on road to Viareggio; Vipore, in Pieve Santo Stefano district
Macerata	Da Secondo, Via Pescheria Vecchia 28; Floriani, Borgo Compagnoni 9, in Montanello district
Mantua	Il Cigno, Piazza d'Arco 1; San Gervasio, Via San Gervasio 13; Aquila Nigra, Vicolo Bonacolsi 4; Rigoletto, Strada Cipata 10
Marsala	Mothia, Via Ettore Infersa 13
Matera	Da Mario, Via XX Settembre 14; Cucina Casalinga, Via Lucana 48
Merano	Andrea, Via Galilei 44; Villa Mozart, Via San Marco 26
Messina	Alberto, Via Ghibellina 95; Pippo Nunnari, Via Ugo Bassi 157; Belle Epoque, Via Tommaso Cannizzaro 155; Agostino, Via Maddalena 70
Mestre	Dall'Amelia, Via Miranese 113; Tonin Geremia, Calle Legrenzi 20
Milan	Antica Trattoria della Pesa, Viale Pasubio 10; Grill Casanova, Piazza della Repubblica 20; Romani, Via Trabazio 3; Grattacielo, Via Vittor Pisani 6; Savini, Galleria Vittorio Emanuele 11; El Toulà, Piazza Paolo Ferrari 6; St Andrews, Via Sant'Andrea 23; Don Lisander, Via Manzoni 12A; Peck, Via Victor Hugo 4; Bifi Scala, Piazza della Scala; Canoviano, Via Hoepfli 6; Suntory, Via Verdi 6; Luciano, Via Ugo Foscolo 1; Alfio-Cavour, Via Senato 31; Boeucc, Piazza Belgioioso 2; Barbarossa, Via Cervia 10; L'Innominato, Via Fiori Oscuri 3; Prospero, Via Chiossetto 20; Il Punto Malatesta, Via Bianca di Savoia 19; San Vito da Nino, Via San Vito 5; Da Alfredo, Gran San Bernardo, Via Borghese 14; Gualtiero Marchesi, Via Bonvesin de la Riva 9; Giannino, Via Amatore Sciesa 8; Al Porto, Piazza Generale Cantore; Soti's, Via Pietro Calvi 2; L'Ami Berton, Via Nullo 14; Angelo, Via Goldoni; Da Aimo, Via Montecuccoli 6; Da Alfredo, Via Borghese 14; Da Berti, Via Algarotti 20; Da Gianni e Dorina, Via G. Pepi 38; I Malavoglia, Centro Commerciale Milano San Felice Sagrate; Il Montalcino, Via Valenza 17; La Pantera, Via Festa del Perdono 12; La Parete, Via Borromei 13; La Scaletta, Piazzale Stazione di Porta Genova; L'Ulmet, Via Olmetto 21; Il Battivacco, Via Bardolino 3; Da Franca Paola Lele, Viale Certosa 235; Ruzante, Corso Sempione 17; Rovello 18, Via Rovello 18; San Bernardo, Via San Bernardo 36, in Chiaravalle district
Modena	Fini, Rua Frati Minori 54; Borso d'Este, Piazza Roma 5; La Calamita, Via Hannover 63; Baia del Re, Via Vignolese 1684, in San Donnino district; Uva d'Oro, Piazza Mazzini 38
Montecatini Terme	Gourmet, Viale Amendola 6; San Francisco, Corso Roma 112

La Cucina di Sergio da Cencio, Via Fermi 11; Da Mario, Corso Terme 4	**Montegrotto Terme**
Il Gigante, Via IV Novembre 9, in Fegina district	**Monterosso al Mare**
La Sacrestia, Via Orazio 116; Rosiello a Posillipo, Via Santo Strato 10; Gra-Pa-Lù, Via Toledo 16; Da Giovanni, Via Domenico Morelli 14; Don Salvatore, Via Mergellina 5; La Cantinella, Via Cuma	**Naples**
Astor Hotel, Viale delle Palme 16; Pianeta Mare, Via Aurelia 31r	**Nervi**
Ines, Via Vignolo 1; Italia, Corso Italia 23; La Scaletta, Via Verdi 16	**Noli**
Amicizia, Tri Scalin, Via N. Sottile 25	**Novara**
Canne al Vento, Viale Repubblica 66	**Nuoro**
A Tavola da Leone e Anna, Via Bardellona 90; Gallura, Corso Umberto I 145; Il Gambero, Via Lamarmora 6	**Olbia**
Il Faro, Via Bellini 25	**Oristano**
Morino, Via Garibaldi 37/45; Cucina Tipica Monaldo, Via Angelo da Orvieto 7	**Orvieto**
El Toulà, Via Belle Parti 11; Bordin al Cacelletto, Via Corsica 4; Antico Brolo, Vicolo Cigolo 14	**Padua**
Charleston, Piazza Ungheria 30; Gourmand's, Via della Libertà 37E; Il Ristorante di Pino Ingrao, Via Torrearsa 22; Friend's Bar, Via Brunelleschi 138; L'Approdo, Ristorante Renato e Vecchia Cucina della Bandita, Via Messina Marine 28B; Chamade, Via Torrearsa 22; Trattoria Trittico, Largo Montalto 7	**Palermo**
Antica Osteria con Cucina Parma Rotta, Via Langhirano 158; Cocchi, Via Gramsci 16; Croce di Malta, Borgo Palmia 8; La Filoma, Via XXII Marzo 15; Parizzi, Via Repubblica 71; Il Cortile, Borgo Paglia 3	**Parma**
Vecchia Pavia, Via Cardinal Riboldi 2; Al Cassinino, Via Cassinino 1; Della Madonna, Via dei Liguri 28; Vecchio Mulino, in Certosa di Pavia, Via al Monumento 5	**Pavia**
Bartolo, Via Bartolo 30; Olmo, Stazione Ellera 8, in Olmo district; La Bocca Mia, Via Ulisse Rocchi 36; M. R., Via dei Priori 78	**Perugia**
Di Teresa, Viale Trieste 180; Il Castiglione, Viale Trento 148; Da Carlo al Mare, Via Trieste 265	**Pesaro**
Guerino, Viale della Riviera 4; Duilio, Via Regina Margherita 11	**Pescara**
Antica Osteria del Teatro, Via Verdi 16	**Piacenza**
Sergio, Lungarno Pacinotti 1; Dei Vecchi Macinelli, Via Volturno 49; Lo Schiaccianoci, Via Vespucci 104	**Pisa**
Il Principe, Piazza B. Longo 8	**Pompeii**
Le Casette, Via Ospedale Vecchio 6; Noncello, Viale Marconi 34	**Pordenone**
Panino, Bibio Boni, in Carpani district	**Portoferraio**
U Batty, Vico Nuovo 17; Hotel Splendido, Viale Baratta 13	**Portofino**

Restaurants

Potenza	Oraziana, Via Orazio Flacco 2
Prato	Bruno, Via Verdi 12; Il Piraña, Via Tiziano 15; Pietro, Via Balbo 9A; Il Piraña, Via Valentini 110
Ragusa	Le Gemelle, Via Sant'Anna 89
Rapallo	U. Giancu, Via San Massimo 78
Ravenna	Tre Spade, Vi G. Rasponi 37; Al Gallo, Via Maggiore 87
Reggio di Calabria	Baylik, Via Leone 1; Rodrigo, Via XXIV Maggio 25
Riva del Garda	Al Volt, Via Fiume 73; Bastione, Via Bastione 19
Rome	Relais le Jardin, Via de Notaris 5; Hostaria dell'Orso, Via Monte Brianzo 93; El Toulà, Via della Lupa 29; Ranieri, Via Mario de' Fiori 26; Quattro Colonne, Via della Posta 4; Passetto, Via Zanardelli 14; Sans Souci, Via Sicilia 20/24; Harry's Bar, Via Vittorio Veneto 150; Le Terrazze, Via Oriolo Romano 59; Alberto Ciarla, Piazza San Cosimato 40; Checchino dal 1887, Via di Monte Testaccio 30; Da Patrizio e Roberto del Pianeta Terra, Via Arco del Monte 94; Coriolano, Via Ancona 14; Cul de Sac 2, Vicolo dell'Atleta 21; Il Cardinale, Via delle Carceri 6; Il Drappo, Vicolo del Malpasso 9; La Rosetta, Via della Rosetta 9; Papa Giovanni, Via dei Sediari 4; Paris di Dario Cappellanti, Piazza San Callisto 7; Severino a Piazza Zama, Piazza Zama 5
Rovereto	Al Borgo, Via Garibaldi 13; Mozart 1789, Contrada Portici Sisler, Via Roma 18
Salò	Laurin, Viale Landi 9; Rosa dell'Hotel Duomo, Via Lungolago Zanardelli 91
Salsomaggiore Terme	Al Tartufo, Viale Marconi 30
San Remo	Au Rendez-Vous, Corso Matteotti 126; Din Don, Via Roma 47; L'Angolo di Beppe, Corso Inglesi 31; La Posada, Via al Mare 87; Sciabecco, Via Gaudio 42; Da Giannino, Lungomare Trento e Trieste 23
Sant'Agata sui Due Golfi	Don Alfonso 1890, Piazza Sant'Agata
Sassari	Piccolo Mondo, Piazza Fiume 1; Da Giamaranto, Via Alghero 69
Sestriere	Last Tango, Via Laglesia 1A
Sestri Levante	Angiolina, Viale Rimembranze 49
Siena	Bottega Nova, Strada Chantigiana 29; Le Logge, Via del Porrione 33; Il Giuggiolo, Via Massetana 32; Al Marsili, Via del Castoro 3
Sorrento	Campidoglio 'o Canonico, Piazza Tasso 5; Il Glicine, Va Sant'Antonio 2
Stresa	L'Emiliano, Corso Italia 52
Syracuse	Il Cenacolo, Via del Consiglio Reginate, Corte degli Avolio 9/10; Ionico 'a Rutta e Ciauli, Riviera Dionisio il Grande 194
Taormina	Angelo a Mare, Il Delfino, Via Nazionale Mazzarò; Il Pescatore, Via Nazionale 107
Taranto	Al Faro, Via Galeso 126

L'Erba Dolce, Via Castello 2	**Terni**
Hotel Flipòt, Corso Gramsci 17; La Civetta, Piazza Pietro Micca 4	**Torre Pellice**
P. e G., Via Spalti 1; Da Peppe, Via Spalti 50; Corso, Corso Italia 51	**Trapani**
Chiesa, Via San Marco 64; Suban 1865, Via Comici 2, in San Giovanni district; Bellavista, Via Bonomea 52; Ai Vini Tipici, da Stelio, Via Tonello 7; Alle Maschere, Via Giulia 57A; Mario, Draga Sant'Elia 22; Silvio, Via Lloyd 15; Ai Fiori, Piazza Hortis 7; Accademia, Vicolo Colico 6	**Trento**
Scala, Viale Felisseni	**Treviso**
Villa Sassi, El Toulà, Strada al Traforo del Pino 47; Del Cambio, Piazza Carignano 2; Tiffany, Piazza Solferino 16H; Vecchia Laterna, Corso Re Umberto 21; Al Gatto Nero, Corso Filippo Turati 14; Al Saffi, Via Aurelia Saffi 2; Due Lampioni da Carlo, Via Carlo Alberto 45; Montecarlo, Via San Francesco da Paola 37; Campagnolo, Corso Casale 162; C'era una Volta, Corso Vittorio Emanuele II 41; Ostu Bacu, Corso Vercelli 226	**Turin**
Lago Maggiore, Via Carrobbio 19; Marruecos, Via Dazio Vecchio 7	**Varese**
Cipriani, Giudecca 10; Antico Martini, Campo San Fantin 1983; Harry's Bar, Calle Vallaresso 1323; Do Leoni, Riva degli Schiavoni 4175; La Caravella, Calle Larga XXII Marzo 2397; Taverna la Fenice, San Marco 1938; Malamocco, Campiello del Vin 4650; Do Forni, Calle dei Specchieri 457/468; Do Leoni dell'Albergo Londra Palace, Riva degli Schiavoni 4179; La Regina di Cipro, Calle della Regina, Santa Croce; Antico Pizzo, San Polo 814; La Corte Sconta, Calle del Pestrin, Castello 3886	**Venice**
Balzi Rossi, Piazzale de Gasperi; Marco Polo, Passeggiata Felice Cavallotti; Nanni, Via Milite Ignoto 2	**Ventimiglia**
Il Desco, Via Dietro San Sebastiano 7; Dodici Apostoli, Corticella San Marco 3; Arche, Via Arche Scaligere 6; Nuovo Marconi, Via Fogge 4	**Verona**
Il Patriarco, Viale Carducci 79; Tito del Molo, Lungomolo Corrado del Greco 3; Da Pino, Via Matteotti 20; Da Romano, Via Mazzini 122; L'Oca Bianca, Via Aurelia 312; Fedi da Gianfranco, Via Verdi 111; Margherita, Piazzale Margherita; Montecatini, Via Manin 8	**Viareggio**
Tre Visi, Contrà Porti 6; Cinzia e Valerio, Piazzetta Porta Padova 65/67; Da Sergio e Ciacio al Pozzo, Via Sant'Antonio 1; Il Tinello, Corso Padova 181	**Vicenza**
Etruria, Piazza dei Priori 6/8	**Volterra**

Shopping and Souvenirs

It is still possible to find in Italy an astonishingly wide range of traditional arts and crafts. All over Italy there are good shoes, leather articles and textiles (particularly woollens), and in some places also well-designed silver jewellery. In the Alto Adige visitors will be tempted by the famous woodcarving of Val Gardena, and in northern Piedmont by the charming local pottery. Cremona is noted for the making of violins, Venice for its glass, its lace and its copper ware, Tuscany for alabaster articles, woodworking and pottery. The south of Italy produces fine iron and copper wares, corals, porcelain, pottery and terracotta, occasional furniture, textiles, embroidery and carpets.

Some visitors may like to take home Italian confections like *panettone* or candied fruit, or a bottle or two of Italian wines or spirits.

Warning

Visitors may well be offered watches, jewellery, etc., by street vendors at what appear to be very low prices. Such goods are almost invariably worthless; gold and silver assay stamps are frequently forged.

N.B.

If you buy any valuable articles or have to pay a large garage bill, etc., you should take care to keep the receipt, since you may be required to produce it to a police officer checking on tax evasion.

Recovery of VAT

Value-added taxes in Italy are high, but can be recovered by foreign visitors. If you have bought any expensive item in Italy you should present the receipted bill to a customs officer on leaving the country and ask for a certificate confirming that it has been exported. This certificate should then be sent to the shop where you bought the article, and they should then refund the VAT paid on it.

Telephone, Telegraph

See Post and Telephone

Time

Italy is on Central European Time (one hour ahead of Greenwich Mean Time, six hours ahead of New York time).
From the end of March to the end of September summer time (two hours ahead of GMT, seven hours ahead of New York time) is in force.

Tipping

In general tips should be given for particular services rendered. Although a service charge is normally included in a restaurant bill, it is customary to leave something extra. Hotel porters and ushers/usherettes in theatres and cinemas expect small tips. Taxi drivers should be tipped in the range 10–15%.

Travel Documents

Personal papers

British and USA citizens require only a passport (or the simpler British Visitor's Passport) to enter Italy. No visa is required for a stay of under 3 months. This applies also to citizens of Australia, Canada, Ireland, New Zealand and many other countries. Children under 16 must either have an individual passport or be entered in a parent's passport.

Car papers

British, US and other national driving licences are accepted in Italy, but must be accompanied by a translation, available free of charge from the AA, offices of the Automobile Club d'Italia (ACI) at the Italian frontier and within Italy, and the Italian State Tourist Office. (A translation is not officially required for the new pink licences in European Community format, but it may sometimes save trouble to have one). Motorists should also take their car registration document and (though this is not now a legal requirement for European Community citizens) a "green card" (international insurance certificate).

Foreign cars must bear an oval nationality plate.
It is a good idea to make photocopies of travel documents, since this
will simplify their replacement in case of loss.

When to Go

The best times of year for travelling in Italy are spring (from the end of
March to the middle of June) and autumn (from mid September to mid
November). At the height of summer the most popular places are the
coastal and hill resorts. In the south of the country, particularly in the
towns, it can become unbearably hot in summer. It should be remem-
bered, too, that over the Ferragosto (Assumption) holiday in mid

**Winter Sports
in Italy**

Winter sports areas of
international standing

Areas mainly frequented
by Italians

Areas frequented by
local people

© Baedeker

Wine

August many museums and other institutions in towns are closed. Towards the end of September the sirocco, a warm, moist south-east wind, can be disagreeable, particularly on the coast and in Tuscany. In winter the most popular resorts are the skiing areas in the Italian Alps.

Wine

See Food and Drink

Winter Sports

The Alps

The winter sports areas in the Italian Alps have long enjoyed an international reputation. In the Western Alps the principal area is the Aosta valley, to the south-east of the Mont Blanc massif, which can be

▼ *Dolomite Superski area*

conveniently reached from Turin. The best known resorts are Courmayeur and Breuil-Cervinia.

Another popular winter sports region lies east of Lake Como and north
of Bergamo. Livigno, on the west side of the Ortles group, attracts
many skiing enthusiasts with its dependable covering of good snow
and its advantages as a customs-free area.

Particularly well equipped with winter sports facilities and other
amenities is the area known as Dolomiti Superski, to which such old-
established resorts as Cortina d'Ampezzo and San Martino di Castrozza
belong, as well as the Alpi di Siusi, the Val Gardena, the Val di Fassa and
the Val d'Ega. The most striking peak is Marmolada (3342 m/10,965 ft),
which offers the possibility of summer skiing. A well co-ordinated
system of lifts and cableways brings the pistes within easy reach.

Perhaps the best known "round trip" (possible only if snow conditions
are right over the whole distance) is the Sella Ronda, a circuit of the
Sella massif.

The ski pass for Dolomiti Superski is valid for the whole of the Dolomites apart from Marmolada and for some adjoining areas and gives

Dolomiti Superski

access to more than 400 facilities (cableways, ski-lifts, etc.) and more than 1000 km/600 miles of pistes. It is not cheap, and does not cover bus services in the valleys.

Apennines

There are popular skiing areas, almost exclusively frequented by Italians, in the Apennines to the west of Bologna, in the Ancona area, and north and south of Pescara.

Youth Hostels

Youth hostels (*ostelli per la gioventù*) provide accommodation at very reasonable rates, particularly for younger visitors. Priority is given to young people under 30 travelling on foot. If the hostel is full the period of stay is limited to three nights. Advance booking is advisable during the main holiday season and for groups of more than five.

Hostellers are not allowed to use their own sleeping bags: the hire of a sleeping bag is included in the overnight charge.

Foreign visitors must produce a membership card of their national youth hostel association.

Information

Associazione Italiana Alberghi per la Gioventù
Via Cavour 44 (3rd floor)
I-00184 Roma (Rome)
tel. (06) 46 23 42

Index

Index

Index